Fraynham 67-28810 (May 14, 1965)

THE BLAST OF WAR

By the same author

WINDS OF CHANGE
1914–1939

THE BLAST OF WAR
1939–1945

THE BLAST
OF WAR

1939 - 1945

HAROLD MACMILLAN

*

HARPER & ROW, PUBLISHERS

New York and Evanston

Contents

Illustrations

The following are grouped in a separate section after page 114

Harold Macmillan with Winston Churchill at Casablanca
With Lord Davies in Finland
With Herbert Morrison
Lord Beaverbrook
Cartoon by George Whitelaw
General Giraud and General de Gaulle with Roosevelt and Churchill
General Charles de Gaulle
Major General George S. Patton and General Noguès
Taking the salute at Algiers, St. Joan of Arc's day, May 9, 1943
The visit of 'General Lyon', June 12, 1943
Luncheon party, June 5, 1943
Sholto Douglas, Macmillan, Walter Bedell Smith, Robert Murphy
Churchill and the war leaders in North Africa
King Victor Emmanuel and Marshal Badoglio
General Sir Harold Alexander
Andrei Vyshinsky
Marshal Tito, Churchill, Dr. Subašić
General Sir Humfrey Gale, Macmillan, General Alexander
Robert Murphy and Macmillan at Cassibile, near Syracuse
With General Alexander at Cassino
The Cairo Conference
Churchill and Archbishop Damaskinos in Athens
With General Oliver Leese in the Republic of San Marino
Peace-making in Athens, December 26, 1944
The liberation of Modena, April 23, 1945

Maps

Acknowledgements

I have once more to record my debt to a number of histories, biographies and autobiographies which I have consulted, especially those mentioned in the footnotes.

I am also grateful to Miss Anne Glyn-Jones, who has continued her research work for this volume, and to Miss Anne Macpherson and Miss Bunty Morley, who have worked with notable skill and patience on the text.

I am particularly grateful to my friend Field-Marshal Earl Alexander of Tunis for putting his collection of photographs at my disposal.

The official documents included in this book are Crown copyright and are reproduced with the permission of the Controller of Her Majesty's Stationery Office.

H.M.

Preface

In May 1938 I received a significant letter. It ran as follows:

Dear Sir,
  In case of invasion, the Cuckfield Rural District Council will need the use of extra road-vehicles as emergency ambulances. Can you lend any? . . . Types of automobiles . . . *not* asked for are 1-ton Ford lorries . . . or any milk-delivery lorries or vans. Horse-draught carriages are asked for to be a reserve in case of petrol shortage. . . . Drivers are expected to enrol as A.R.P. volunteers . . . and be trained in first aid to the wounded and gas-infected.

This cyclostyled appeal, circulated by a respected resident of our village, was received with a characteristic mixture of scepticism and alarm by my Sussex neighbours. However, Munich was soon to relieve the anxieties of Horsted Keynes.

After months and years of vacillation, in September 1939 the British Government, Parliament and people rose to a true sense of their destiny. But would it be too late? Only immense efforts could serve to fill the gaps and weaknesses of the locust years. Had we yet, in September 1939, shaken off all the old Adam? Were we a guilty generation? The First War had come to me when I was only twenty. Whatever our failings, at any rate we young men had been innocent. It was not our political mistakes or miscalculations which had been at fault. Even if we could blame the disaster of 1914 upon the political leaders of the European countries, there was little of which the British people need be ashamed. Our statesmen, whether Conservative or Liberal, had striven hard for peace. At the same time they had nourished the Navy on the grand scale. It was ready and equal to its task. If our armies were modest, they were admirably trained and well equipped; and there was no difficulty in landing the six or seven divisions we had promised to our French allies. The French were buoyant, conscious of

a fine Army with a high morale. Although in the vicissitudes of
fortune during the four years of war there were anxious periods, none
of us ever for a moment contemplated the possibility of anything that
could be called defeat. Even Lord Lansdowne's famous intervention in
1917 was not based on fear of defeat. It was a plea for the European
peoples to end their fighting and start to lick their wounds before it
was too late; before forces had been set in motion which would
undermine the supremacy of European traditions, and might end in
the liquidation of European civilisation.

But now it was bitter indeed to admit that after all the sufferings of
our youth, we had not been able to protect our successors from the
horror of another war. We few survivors of the First War seemed to
have failed in our duty and to have betrayed our fallen friends. How
strange it all was—the repetition of 1914 but without the glamour!
The First War had struck, at least in its opening phase, an Elizabethan note, with its poets, its artists, its gay youth setting out on
something like a crusade, or like knights of old, called suddenly and
unexpectedly from the routine of everyday life to the splendours of the
tourney. There was no such feeling now, only a sense of guilt. Some of
us, in the later stages of this tragic drift to disaster, had tried our best.
But the official party organisations—Conservative, Liberal and Labour
—had all shown equal folly and blindness. In the last months before
the catastrophe, the British people had begun to accept the inevitability
of the Second World War with a kind of sullen resignation. As I walked
back from the House of Commons on that afternoon, 3 September, I
thought of my son. He was now eighteen years old, and an under-
graduate at Oxford, as I had been twenty-five years before. He would
go to the war. Would he come back? I began now to think of war not
as young men think of it, with the natural buoyancy of youth, but
with the realism of middle age; not as sons think about it, with little
understanding of the long-drawn-out anxieties, and sometimes the
agony, of parents, but as a father. Once more, in addition, all the same
degrading things would happen. Certainly there was to be National
Service from the start. This would indeed avoid some of the inequali-
ties of the old days. All the same there would be a good deal of
selectiveness, exercised by one method or another, on behalf of those
who had no stomach for this fight. The rigours of the campaign would
doubtless be undergone by many young men of military age only in

the chilly corridors of the various Ministries. In the years that I fore-saw, many must die; and once again they would be the best.

'Well, you have got your war now,' said a friend to me rather bitterly. He had suffered much in the First War and was destined to suffer in the Second. He had been a convinced supporter of Chamberlain and 'appeasement'. Yes, but in what conditions were we now embarked! We were pledged to succour the Poles for whom we could do nothing by sea or by land and for whom we were soon to prove unwilling to do anything by air. We had guaranteed countries, such as Roumania, which we were quite powerless to assist. Russia, a sullen and unfriendly neutral, was still giving material assistance to Germany. With the thirty or more divisions of the Czechoslovak Army cast away, and all their great arsenals and stocks of arms and munitions transferred to Hitler's stores without a blow, Germany was secure on the east, for the defeat and partition of Poland could only be a matter of weeks. With the French Army ill equipped, both morally and technically, and the French people torn by dissension, there was little hope of serious attack across the western frontier. How different would have been the situation in 1936, before the remilitarisation of the Rhineland. These were indeed grim conditions in which to launch ourselves into so demanding an adventure.

As we trooped out of the Chamber of the House of Commons on that Sunday morning, the first day of war, there was a sense not of fear but of awe. We knew in our hearts that here was another of the great turning-points in history: 4 August 1914; 3 September 1939. What were we to endure this time? And what would be the end of it? Many of us had witnessed the troubles and disorders which the First War had brought in its train—not merely the frightful losses and suffering, but the strains and stresses on the organised life of nations. We knew, too, something of the changes—often revolutionary changes —at home and throughout the world that had followed that first convulsion. What would spring from the second? The broad outlines of the picture, then so blurred, have now become easier to discern— and perhaps to comprehend. Although much was hidden from us, we already sensed, amidst the uncertainty and darkness of those first days of war, that we were approaching the end of an epoch. Fear of the future did not then deter us or chill our hearts. Nor should it today. The Book of Life remains open, and who runs must read.

The Second World War, coming so soon after the First, was to strike an almost fatal blow at the material predominance and the moral supremacy of the nations of Western Europe and their world-wide systems of power. For this country, the inevitable decline in relative strength and authority was to be masked by the triumphs of the most splendid and memorable years in our long story.

As the years of war dragged on, the relative military strength deployed by Britain and the United States in the struggle against Germany began to alter. Even so, as Churchill was never tired of pointing out to the Americans, in all the great conflicts in the Mediterranean and even in the first stages of the liberation of France, Britain, by sea and land and air, was still an equal if not a predominant partner. Yet gallant as was the struggle of the Old Country, surrounded by her loyal Dominions, India and the colonies, the last phase of the war marked the change. Supreme military power, in its widest sense, began to pass into other hands.

Equally, on the economic side, although in the strenuous efforts and daily excitements of war their significance was somewhat obscured, similar forces were at work. Once again the great reserves of British wealth had to be sacrificed. All or nearly all our foreign investments were expended in the common effort; large sections of our foreign trade passed temporarily and perhaps permanently to neutral or American hands. Thus serious injury was done in the industrial and commercial field. In finance, the historic pre-eminence of London was once more to be menaced and perhaps finally overthrown. The gulf of bankruptcy was bridged during the war by the introduction of Lend-Lease, and immediately after the war was to be narrowed by large-scale loans. Yet the fundamental problem has remained.

The rise on one side of the world of the United States, with its immense population and productive capacity; the emergence on the other of Soviet Russia, with unexpected reserves both of resistance and strength; the self-destruction of Western and Central Europe, whose nations and peoples were for the second time to be locked in an internecine and mortal combat, and the consequent loss of much of European power and prestige in the East: all these were in the course of these years to mark out to all who had eyes to see the course of history.

Fortunately unaffected by these considerations and ignorant of these

historic forces, the British people were about to rise to the immediate
crisis. Their finest hour was now at hand. After the end of that strange
interlude which Churchill (following Chamberlain) has called 'the
Twilight War' (the Americans dubbed it, rather brutally, 'the Phoney
War'), the threat of invasion was to become a grim reality. Once
again, after more than a century, the armies were to be marshalled and
the flat-bottomed boats were to be mustered on the French coast.
Once again, our island was to face all the vast resources of a conquered
and terrorised Europe. Even the humblest could feel that they were
taking part in the making of history. As the new Armada was being
prepared against us, we seemed indeed the heirs of Queen Elizabeth
and her captains. All the great figures of the past—Drake, Raleigh,
Marlborough, Chatham, Wolfe, Pitt, Nelson, Wellington—seemed
alive again and almost standing at our side. The unity of the nation
was complete and unshakeable. We were inspired by the greatest
Englishman of all time. We had passed through the valley of humiliation. We were alone but we were not ashamed.

But what could I do? I was too old to fight. I had already tried to get
back into the Reserve Battalion of my regiment; but they did not
want officers of my age and physique. There were many younger and
fitter than me, and unless there was fighting on a prodigious scale, I
saw no hope of employment. I was too late; but my son was in time. I
could not serve; but within a few days he had abandoned Oxford, as
I had done, and joined the Army. I held no post, even in the lowest
ranks of the administration. In these opening weeks, Parliament did
not seem likely to play a great role in the drama that was unfolding.
The prospect, therefore, seemed flat and uninspiring. However, there
was plenty to do in my business and in organising ourselves to the best
of our ability to meet the commercial and financial problems that
would confront us. There was something, too, to be done at home, to
help my wife with the 'evacuees'. If the worst came to the worst, and
the invasion seemed imminent, I could perhaps drive a lorry for the
Cuckfield Rural District Council.

PART ONE

The First Years

September 1939 - December 1942

CHAPTER ONE

The First Months

THE ultimatum to Germany expired at 11 a.m. on Sunday 3 September 1939. At 11.15 Chamberlain spoke to the nation. His words summed up the personal tragedy of the last years of his life. But they were in the main an apologia, rather than a call to battle. 'You can imagine what a bitter blow it is to me that all my long struggle to win peace has failed. Yet I cannot believe that there is anything more, or anything different, that I could have done.' He ended with some impressive words. 'Now may God bless you all and may He defend the right. For it is evil things that we shall be fighting against, brute force, bad faith, injustice, oppression and persecution.' In the House, he gave the story of the last few days—Germany's aggression against Poland, and the British determination, in conjunction with France, to implement her guarantees by declaring war. 'Everything that I have worked for,' he added, 'everything that I have believed in during my public life has crashed into ruins.'

It would perhaps have been better if, at this moment of failure and disappointment, he had passed the burden into other and stronger hands. For any just appreciation of the power of Germany and the weakness of the Western Allies must have led to the conclusion that the war would be long and the issue doubtful. Only a leader whose record was clear, and only a National Government representing a united nation, could hope to face so grim a future. Moreover, in the opening phase, our impotence was bound to add to the public sense of frustration and even humiliation. Unable to take any effective action ourselves to rescue Poland, we must look to the French Army as the only available means of diversion, if not of succour. Yet so anxious were the French about their position, that not only were the French authorities unwilling to allow their Army to assault the German positions in the west, while the main German forces were engaged elsewhere, but they pleaded with us not to launch any air attacks on Germany, for fear of attracting retaliation.

Chamberlain lived during the next few months in a strange world of illusion. He was confident as to the outcome but seemed to have little grasp of reality. He trusted to the efficacy of the blockade; to German economic difficulties; to the public opinion of neutral States and the growing unpopularity of the war in Germany. He did not believe that the enemy could face a second winter.[1] In this mood, he seemed almost to welcome what he called 'the Twilight War'. But while the first act in the terrible drama was being played—the destruction and partition of Poland—the curtain was soon to rise on the next. Norway; Denmark; Holland; Belgium; France: each in turn was to be the victim of the insatiable machine which served the German bid for world power.

At home the first weeks and even months were marked by a strange contrast between the expectation of sudden and violent bombing attacks and the inactivity which in fact prevailed. Everyone had expected massive bombardments from the air. After all, had not Baldwin said that the bomber would always get through? Accordingly, provision for hospital beds was made on a prodigious scale, and extensive evacuation of women and children from the crowded cities, especially London, was carried out. Whatever the difficulties of the evacuation scheme, it certainly proved a splendid dress rehearsal for the following year, when the Blitz began in full earnest. Included among the prospective perils was the menace of gas attack. For many months no one ever went out without a gas-mask. Its actual value was somewhat doubtful, yet it gave us much moral support. In the absence of any weapons of offence or defence, the gas-mask became a kind of symbol of resistance.

Meanwhile, my wife was fully engaged with the care of our young visitors and in moving from our house into the cottage.[2] One agreeable interlude was a visit from the Queen at the end of November. This happy event was not forgotten in the harsher days that were soon to come.

Perhaps the most puzzling symptom of the Government's lack of grip was the slow pace of mobilisation, at any rate on the industrial

[1] Keith Feiling, *Life of Neville Chamberlain* (London, 1947), p. 428.
[2] A London nursery school had moved into our house in Sussex; see *Winds of Change* (New York, 1966), pp. 551-52.

and economic side. There were still very large numbers of unemployed.[3] In spite of the expected demand for labour in the war industries, there was in some areas an increase in their number. The Government seemed equally fumbling both in economic measures against Germany and in regard to the organisation of Britain's man- and machine-power. A full blockade of German exports was not instituted in the first days of the war. It was then only justified as a reprisal for the sinking of the liner *Athenia*. Rationing of commodities was not set in train, as it should have been, at the very start. Indeed, in the course of this winter, the Germans were ridiculed for the institution of a coupon system for clothing and other necessities.

Two important debates were held on economic co-ordination and on economic warfare in the course of the autumn and winter, and I spoke in both. In the first, I reminded the House that it had long been recognised that war, if it came, would be totalitarian, and we must learn what this implied:

It means that the total energy of the nation has to be organised and directed to secure the maximum results and, therefore, that every error of policy or administration, even on the remote fringes of economic activity, will be paid for by a prolongation of the struggle and the consequent sacrifice of additional lives.[4]

Planning of industry, whatever might be argued in peace-time, was clearly necessary in war. But exports had to be kept going, and it was wrong to close down enterprises until plans were ready to re-employ the labour and resources released:

Tens of thousands of men were thrown out of work in the early stages of the war, and today they are pathetically seeking something to do to enable them to get a living and to preserve their self-respect; and a feature of this new class of unemployment is that they are not insurable under the Unemployment Insurance Act.[5]

The first repercussions of war were deflationary, because the machinery for increasing war production, so long delayed, was not yet in full play.

What was happening at the Ministry of Supply? The Minister, no

[3] In January 1940 the figure was almost 1,300,000.
[4] *Hansard,* 18 October 1939.
[5] Ibid.

doubt, was doing his best, but the Ministry had begun too late. That was not the fault of my friends or myself, but 'due to the incredible obstinacy of the Government'.[6] What was the Ministry of Economic Warfare doing?

[It] has . . . done most creditable work in seeking out information regarding enemy trade on the basis of which the Admiralty enforces the blockade, but economic warfare is not confined to stopping enemy supplies. It has its creative side as well. It has to do three vital things. It has to purchase and transport the materials which we ourselves need. It has to give such facilities and support to the export trade as will enable us to build up the foreign assets by which these supplies are to be paid; and last, but not least, it has to buy from neutrals as much as possible of what the enemy wants regardless, perhaps, of price and even regardless of what we ourselves want.[7]

All these things for which I asked were to become the urgent tasks of the next Government.

In January 1940, the Minister of Economic Warfare, Ronald Cross, adopted a confident line and told us that Germany, economically, was now in the same position as she had been in after two years of the last war. I could not help observing that this might be true, but that Germany had for five years been preparing her armaments for this war, while we were only making a beginning. I continued:

She has vast reserves of many of the necessary materials for war, and I think we run a risk of making our people unwilling to understand how great are the sacrifices they will be called upon to make if we adopt too complacent a view of the sufferings and difficulties of Germany today.[8]

As regards rationing, I said:

We ought to have had rationing of almost every article from the very beginning of the war. That is no reason for us to laugh at the Germans; we should have done it ourselves.[9]

Nor did the composition of the Government command general confidence. Churchill had joined as First Lord of the Admiralty at the beginning of the war when the famous signal went out to the fleet: 'Winston is back'. But Churchill was not Minister of Defence and had

6 Ibid.
7 Ibid.
8 Ibid., 17 January 1940.
9 Ibid.

at this stage no authority beyond his own character and the power of
the Navy in any joint planning for war. Eden was back, too, and both
these appointments naturally gave satisfaction to my friends. These
men were our real leaders, and we trusted them. But, with the exception of Gwilym Lloyd-George, all the other changes made during the
remaining months of Chamberlain's administration were painfully
orthodox. While the old gang were occasionally shuffled from one post
to another, promotion was confined to the most devoted supporters of
Chamberlain through the Munich crisis. The Press began to ask why it
was that men like Amery and Duff Cooper were not given positions,
and why no chance was given to the Conservative opponents of
Munich like Robert Boothby, Richard Law, Ronald Cartland and
myself. The creation of a Ministry of Shipping was after great pressure
agreed to by the Prime Minister. But he chose as its head an amiable
and ageing politician, Sir John Gilmour, who indeed died a few
months later.

The Government was still a party Government. The Prime Minister
was the same man who, in the opinion of a growing number of people,
had presided disastrously over the events of recent years. The Liberal
and Labour parties, while giving patriotic support, had no enthusiasm
for the administration. A situation was already developing not unlike
that of 1916 when Asquith, with all his merits, had to give way to the
stronger personality of Lloyd George. But who was to play the role? In
a debate on 1 February, I ventured a prophetic note:

. . . the First Lord of the Admiralty ought . . . to be given the major
credit for having fought this battle alone for ten years. As a result he is a
figure in this country holding a position greater than that of any other Member
in the House.[10]

If on the political and administrative side the House was critical of
the Government, on the military side it was equally restless and
confused—and so was the country. On 6 September, while the most
terrible attacks were in progress by the German Luftwaffe upon Polish
towns, an official statement was made in the House of Commons that
the Germans were only bombing military objectives. This, of course,
was completely 'out of line with the facts', as the Polish Ambassador
was quick to explain to his friends in the House and as all the Press

[10] *Hansard,* 1 February 1940.

well knew. General Spears took a particularly active part in protesting against the complete abandonment of the Poles. Although it was the German attack upon them that was the occasion, if not the cause, of the war, neither we nor the French made any attempt to give them any air support. Whether this was logistically or technically possible was not known to the public; but the situation was made worse by the futility of our reply to the 'Blitzkrieg'. This took the form of dropping pamphlets all over Germany. Instead of attacking German airfields and communications, which would have taken some of the pressure off the unhappy Poles, all we did was to indulge in what became known as 'the Confetti War'. The true motive is difficult now to understand. There may have lingered in the minds of Chamberlain and his friends the notion that if we appealed to what were known as the 'good Germans', they would rise and overthrow Hitler. Since Hitler had up to now succeeded in every adventure which he had undertaken, this seemed a curious delusion.

An extraordinary example of the mentality of this period is revealed by Leo Amery's account of his proposal to the Secretary of State for Air that we should try to set fire to the Black Forest with incendiary bombs, since this area was an important reserve of timber and was packed full of stores. Kingsley Wood turned down this proposal with some warmth. Bombing should be confined to strictly military objectives and neither forests nor stores could be so described. There should not even be any question of bombing the munition works at Essen, for, after all, these were 'private property'.[11]

Nor did the French do anything to help the Poles. As we now know, the Germans were amazed at Allied inactivity in the air. Moreover, an attack by the French Army upon the Western Front might well have been successful. The German defences had by no means reached perfection, and the number of divisions which they had retained on this front was small. But the Western Allies appeared, both in the air and on the ground, to be in a state of bemusement. The British, no doubt conscious of their own weakness and the puny contribution which they could make to any Allied effort, were unwilling or unable to stimulate the French. The French Government was divided, and the French people unhappy. Many still hoped that, somehow or other, real

[11] L. S. Amery, *My Political Life*, vol. iii: *The Unforgiving Years, 1929–1940* (London, 1955), p. 330.

war might be avoided. The British Government, to do them justice, had no defeatist elements. But, basing themselves upon the memories of the First World War, they reached the conclusion that nothing could be done in the early stages of the struggle. We must perfect our blockade, strengthen our economic pressure, develop our forces, and hope for the best.

With this in mind, certain definite plans were now agreed. Fifty-five Imperial divisions, of which thirty-three were to be provided by the United Kingdom, were to be raised, and accordingly conscription from the ages of eighteen to forty-one was introduced. Shipbuilding was to be increased from 800,000 to 1½ million tons a year; land under plough was to be increased by 2 million acres. All these were sound objectives. But to reach them would need a new mental and moral approach. This was for the future.

Meanwhile, the war at sea had begun in earnest, and serious difficulties and losses were being encountered. The delay over the declaration of war caused by French hesitations had prevented our Navy from successfully bottling up the whole German fleet. Two pocket battleships were at large, and the submarines had begun the long struggle for supremacy. The liner *Athenia,* a vessel of 13,500 tons, was sunk the day following the outbreak of war. The aircraft-carrier *Courageous* was also sunk in September, and in the same month, between Iceland and the Faeroes, the *Rawalpindi* went down, after a heroic but hopeless fight with the *Scharnhorst*. In October, the *Royal Oak* was torpedoed in Scapa Flow by an enemy submarine which penetrated the defensive barrier. The German attack on shipping followed the same cruel methods as in the First World War. Indeed, it was even more ruthless, for lightships, which had been spared before, now became targets. These naval losses, unaccompanied by any corresponding successes by land or air, alarmed the public and brought criticism upon the Minister in the Cabinet who least deserved it. Churchill's friends were unhappy and silent. His enemies were more vocal.

All this time, Ministers as a whole went on bleating nonsense about attacking military objectives only and excluding from this category German arsenals. We were, of course, told that America would be impressed by our restraint. On the contrary, American opinion was shocked and openly mocked at 'the Phoney War'.

All this uncertainty and wavering by the Western Allies created the atmosphere, of which Hitler was quick to take advantage, for a renewed 'peace offensive'. Already Lloyd George had asked the Government not to reject out of hand any proposals for peace which might come from Germany. He favoured a world conference to try to settle all the issues in dispute. This intervention drew down upon the now rapidly ageing statesman—he was in his seventy-sixth year— strong and effective rebukes, both from Duff Cooper and from a much respected Labour Member, 'Dai' Grenfell. Nevertheless, peace was in the air—certainly on the Continent—and, on 6 October, Poland having been disposed of, Hitler made his offer. It was promptly met by Chamberlain with a firm and decisive rejection, in the name of the Government and people of Britain. But still peace propaganda continued, especially in France. There were weak elements in every section of French life, from the top to the bottom. Suspicion of Britain was sedulously fostered, both from the Right and from the Left. Why had we abandoned France between the wars? Where was the British Army? Why should France fight for Poland? What hope was there of victory now that Russia and Germany were in collusion? Better make peace at once, before it was too late.

Throughout the winter an uneasy truce was maintained in the political world. Chamberlain, in spite of his change of heart, had neither the experience nor the imagination to be a great War Minister. He knew little of the organisation necessary for war. One of the reasons for our failures in the Scandinavian campaign which was soon to be launched was the lack of any clear system or any firm leadership to weld the Service departments into an effective instrument. He was, moreover, seriously handicapped on personal grounds. He never achieved the mastery of the House of Commons which Baldwin acquired so easily. The Opposition were not only against him politically, but disliked him personally. This was due partly to his manner, and partly to the genuine contempt he felt for those who disagreed with him, which he was unable to conceal. Nor had he the massive intellectual power which carried Asquith at least through the first eighteen months of the First World War. The Labour Party were not prepared, as was soon to be shown, to work with him. The Liberals disliked him; and he made little attempt to reunite the divided Conservatives. For this he was to pay a heavy price in May 1940. A number of groups of private Members soon came into being, some of them in continuation of those which had been formed after Munich. The anti-Munich Conservatives dined every Wednesday under Amery's chairmanship. An all-party action group, of which Boothby and Thomas Horabin[12] were secretaries and which was led, in effect, by Clement Davies, a Liberal, met frequently. Later on, a watching committee was formed under Lord Salisbury,[13] with Paul Emrys-Evans[14] as secretary. All these groups were intent on improving and perfecting the machinery for war, governmental, industrial and military. All of them feared that Churchill would become more and more involved in the failures which they saw looming ahead. Those of us who were specially Churchill's friends knew that if there was a long war there could be no other leader. Yet such was Churchill's natural loyalty and magnanimity that he became a steadfast colleague of a Prime Minister who had for many years treated him and his appeals with contempt.

I warned my constituents of the unsatisfactory state of affairs, and of the dangers ahead. I told them[15] that I thought Germany would inevitably attack Holland and Belgium. We should have to undergo great hardships, but there was no reason why we should not win through as we had done before. But new efforts were required, more radical and more drastic, if we were to fight total war: 'We muddled through the last war, we dare not muddle through this one.' Meanwhile, hardly noticed by many of us, a new phase was about to begin. It was another of the sinister results of Hitler's compact with Stalin. Russia, secure from any German reaction, was to follow her seizure of the Baltic States by an attack on Finland.

[12] Independent Liberal (later Labour) M.P. for North Cornwall, 1939–50.
[13] 4th Marquess of Salisbury.
[14] Conservative M.P. for South Derbyshire, 1931–45.
[15] 16 October 1939.

CHAPTER TWO

The Russian Thrust

IN the twenty-two years between the Russian Revolution and the signing of the Molotov–Ribbentrop Pact, British feelings about Russia had been fluctuating and confused. The revolution of March 1917 had been hailed as an auspicious event, marking the end of the Tsarist régime, with all its crudities and cruelties. We hoped that a new era of democratic life would be opened for the great Russian people. We believed, moreover, that a fresh impetus would be given to the resistance of the Russian armies, who would now be fighting not for an obsolete Imperial system but for the ideals of a new freedom.

This mood lasted for only a few months. It was rapidly followed by disgust at the seizure of power by the Bolshevik minority in November and the subsequent disappearance or liquidation of all the liberal personalities. The 'dictatorship of the proletariat', as the new phrase went, was seen to be merely a screen for the emergence of a revolutionary junta. In the following years, however, in spite of British antipathy to the brutalities of the new régime, which were regarded as the necessary concomitants of revolution, there was considerable sympathy for the Russian people. We hoped that there would be, as in the French Revolution, a gradual development from the bloody scenes of the opening years to a more settled, stable and perhaps, ultimately, more democratic system.

After some controversy, official recognition was granted to the new Soviet Government and our relations in the intervening years, although often interrupted by such incidents as the Zinoviev letter[1] and the Arcos raid,[2] as well as by the arrest and trial of the Vickers engineers, became, in general, friendly.

[1] *Winds of Change*, p. 152.
[2] Ibid., p. 13.

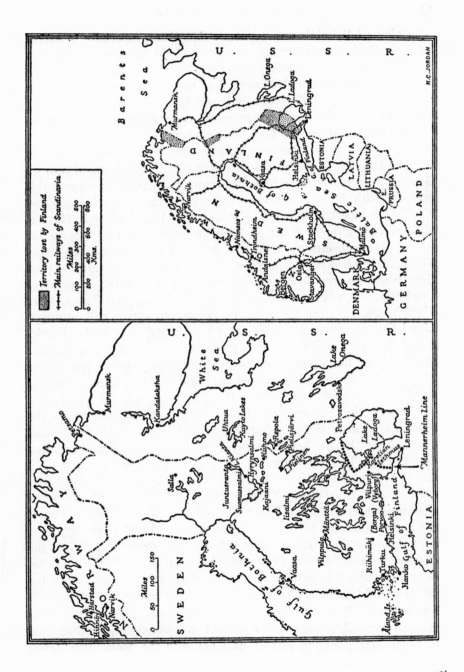

In view of Britain's own economic difficulties, especially in export markets, there were naturally persistent efforts to extend trade with Russia. These were to a minor extent successful; but Russia, under the Soviet Government, remained to most of us as great a mystery as ever. In the 1930s, as Hitler's power grew and his ambitions became patent except to those who could not or would not see, there arose a strong demand in the House of Commons that some alliance, or at least understanding, should be sought with the Soviet Government, in order to build up in the East a defensive system which would restrain German aggression. It is true that most Conservatives viewed this prospect with little enthusiasm. Unhappily, these sceptics included Neville Chamberlain, the Prime Minister, and his leading colleagues. Nevertheless, after each act of Hitlerite aggression, the pressure for some agreement increased. At one stage in the Munich crisis, the Foreign Office had itself issued a statement, more in the nature of bluff than based on any firm arrangement, that a German invasion of Czechoslovakia would be resisted by Britain, France and Russia. After Munich, the demand for a direct negotiation grew still stronger. Lloyd George returned to this subject over and over again. He declared that without Russia it was impossible for the Western Allies to stand against the strength of the new Germany. Indeed, our failure to come to terms with Russia was the cause of the mood of defeatism to which he seemed to succumb in the early months of the war.

Although the Government showed only a tepid interest in the concept of an East–West combination against Hitler, their critics on all sides of the House began to press them forward with increasing urgency. Finally, after the seizure of Prague by Hitler in March 1939, the British and French Governments took the plunge, and negotiations began in Moscow. Chamberlain's sudden and ill-considered guarantees to Poland and Roumania added to the difficulties. For, if the anti-Communist States of Eastern Europe feared Germany, their apprehensions about Russia were scarcely less compelling. When the discussions were started, in a somewhat dilatory fashion, it became clear that Poland, in particular, was altogether averse to any guarantee which would involve the movement of Russian troops into or through her territory. Roumania was equally suspicious. So the discussions dragged on; and, in the end, the Soviet Government decided that their best reinsurance was to make a pact not with the democratic States, but with Nazi Germany.

This famous agreement, negotiated by Ribbentrop and Molotov and confirmed by Hitler and Stalin, had no real basis of confidence, even between the signatories. Certainly the Russians, with their usual suspicious nature, believed that the Western Allies might not be sorry to see Russia dragged into a war with Germany from which they were excluded. If that was so, Moscow would not play the game of London or Paris. The Soviet Government also needed time to build up their Army, which had been weakened by Stalin's 'purges', and to strengthen their strategic positions. They may equally have hoped that a long and mutually destructive war confined to Germany and the Western Allies would have the result of exhausting both sets of so-called 'capitalist States'. Thus Russia—neutral, unscathed, uninvaded —would emerge stronger militarily and economically. The Russians had little confidence in the strength or duration of the unnatural marriage between Bolshevism and Hitlerism. They certainly continued to supply Germany with munitions and materials, to their own later disadvantage.[3] But the most potent reason which swayed Stalin's decision is clear. He obtained, without a blow, large strategic and territorial advantages. These were guaranteed to him by the secret clauses of the Russo-German treaty. Great as must have been his underlying anxieties about German expansion in Central and Eastern Europe, the immediate gains were irresistible.

All through its history, the land-locked Russian Empire had sought two main objectives: outlet to the warm seas and a defensive ring of territory on its western borders. The revolutionary Government pursued the same aims as its predecessors. Among the people, Napoleon's invasion in 1812 had never been forgotten and the lesson did not depend upon the régime—it was bitten deep into all Russian hearts. Peter the Great had subdued and incorporated in Russia the Baltic States—Estonia, Latvia and Lithuania. In 1918, in what was called the War of Liberation, they had freed themselves from Russian control

---

[3] Between 1 January 1940 and 22 June 1941, Germany received the following deliveries: 1.5 million tons of grain, 100,000 tons of cotton, 2 million tons of petroleum products, 1.5 million tons of timber, 140,000 tons of manganese and 26,000 tons of chromium. The last two items were of particular importance in view of the British blockade. The Russians were supposed to receive industrial equipment in return, but that the bargain was one-sided is shown by an estimated balance of 239 million Reichsmarks in the Russian favour. This sum was not claimed by the Russians at the end of the war: Alexander Werth, *Russia at War, 1941–1945* (London, 1964), pp. 113, 114, based on the authority of Professor Friedensburg of the West German Government (Deutsches Institut für Wirtschaftsforschung).

and been recognised as independent nations. The great estates had been largely, if not entirely, broken up by the land reforms then undertaken, and a strong peasant society was established. But it was the consistent aim of Soviet as well as of Imperial policy in Russia to reimpose their authority on these countries. Their wealth and population were insignificant, but their strategic position was vital. Together with Finland, they could either bar or open the way to St. Petersburg, now called Leningrad. The same reasons which induced Peter the Great to occupy them—that is, the protection of his new capital and his major western port—applied now.

The Soviet Government were not slow to exploit their advantage. In October 1939, in agreement with Hitler, Stalin took his share of eastern Poland and began to apply the usual Russian methods. The landowning classes, the capitalists and the merchants were rapidly 'liquidated', sometimes by murder, sometimes by imprisonment, sometimes by deportation. In the Baltic States, where a system of peasant proprietorship had been instituted, it was not so easy to apply the same methods. Nor could any fault be found with their foreign policy, which was scrupulously neutral. They were therefore invited for their own protection to accept the introduction of large Russian forces. Since they had no means of resistance, this occupation took place with great rapidity. The anti-Communist and patriotic elements were dealt with in the usual brutal way. Uncounted thousands disappeared by imprisonment or execution. In Churchill's grim words, 'This process was described as "Mutual Assistance Pacts" '.[4] Later in the war, after the fall of France, the Baltic States were quietly annexed.

These measures in 1939, terrible as they were, can perhaps be explained, though not excused; for the Russians knew that their pact with Germany, so cynically entered into, was too fragile a basis for their national defence. The occupation of these territories, therefore, especially that of Estonia, lying athwart the route to Leningrad, was a sign that the Soviet Government foresaw that sooner or later they might find themselves in conflict with Hitler and his armies.

But if the Baltic States were strategically important, Finland was equally vital. The Finnish people, however, had both a highly organised Army and a heroic spirit. Moreover, they had succeeded in

[4] Winston S. Churchill, *The Second World War*, vol. i: *The Gathering Storm* (London, 1948), p. 382.

steering an even course between the Right and Left of politics with a
flourishing industrial, commercial and agricultural structure. They
were thus united. They could be defeated, perhaps, but not intimidated.

The Finns, in spite of their national sympathy with the West, had
been shocked and offended by Hitler. Poised between the ambitions of
Germany and Russia and unable to rely on the Western democracies,
Finland's position was full of danger. In 1938, a Russian special
emissary, Yartsev, had held discussions with Finnish Ministers, and
had argued that the Germans would sooner or later begin a war
against Russia and that the left wing of the German front would
operate through Finland. Russia could not afford to wait. She demanded the right to aid Finland, and the joint fortification of the
Åland Islands by Russia and Finland. Against these demands the
Finns continued to assert their strict neutrality. Here was repeated the
problem already confronting Poland, Roumania and, earlier, Czechoslovakia. Neutrality was a sound and sensible policy. But would the
Finns have the power to sustain it? In a sense, the situation was not
unlike that of Belgium in relation to the Western Allies. We should
have liked a definite agreement with Belgium. But she preferred to
trust in neutrality, with fatal results. For it was the unwillingness of
the King of the Belgians, even after the war began, to allow the French
or the British to occupy forward positions or even to have staff talks,
that led to the overrunning of Belgium in a few days. We can therefore feel some sympathy with the Russian argument. Perhaps the
Finns, a very tough and obstinate people, did not give sufficient weight
to Russian apprehensions. But, like all the other countries of Eastern
Europe, they undoubtedly feared that, once they let the Russians in,
they would never get them out.

The signing of the Molotov–Ribbentrop Pact in August 1939 must
have seemed to the Finns on the whole advantageous. For if these two
Great Powers—their closest neighbours—were on good terms, peace
would be more probable. The German Government assured the Finns
that there was no provision in the treaty regarding spheres of influence
which could in any way affect Finland. This was untrue; for in the
secret Protocol, in addition to arrangements dealing with Poland and
the Baltic States, it was agreed not only that Russia should have a
sphere of influence in Finland but that parts of Petsamo should be

transferred, and the Russian border pushed westwards from Leningrad into Finland proper, so as to include the town and area of Viipuri, or Vyborg. If Russia were to annex still more territory, then Germany should have some part of western Finland to maintain the balance. In other words, the fate and perhaps ultimate partition of Finland was ruthlessly and cynically included in the pact to which Hitler and Stalin had put their names.

It was against this background that during the course of October 1939 the Russians, having obtained full control over the eastern shores of the Baltic, made a threatening approach to the Finnish Government. The latter prudently agreed to send a delegate to Moscow for discussion. But at the same time they mobilised their Army and determined to defend themselves in the last resort. They firmly rejected an alliance with Soviet Russia. The other Russian demands they were prepared to meet, including some readjustment of the Karelian frontier, in order to give Leningrad greater safety, and the leasing of Petsamo, Finland's only ice-free port in the Arctic. But they resolutely refused to lease the port of Hanko, at the entrance to the Baltic, which the Russians demanded as a naval and air base. To abandon Hanko, which commanded the Gulf of Finland and on which the life of their capital city of Helsinki depended, was to give up any real independence.

As soon as the Finnish delegates had left Moscow, the Russian Press and wireless campaign began. On 26 November, the Russians even asserted that Finnish troops had opened fire across the border and demanded that they should retire from twenty to twenty-five kilometres from the frontier. The Finns promptly denied the allegation, which is one of the almost conventional accusations preliminary to war by an aggressor, and asked for a joint inquiry. Two days later, on 28 November, the Soviet Government unilaterally denounced the ten-year non-aggression pact of 1934 and broke off diplomatic relations. Finland still continued to make conciliatory suggestions, but it was of no avail. On the 30th, the war began. The Russians attacked at several points in the long frontier. They also bombed the capital, Helsinki. With that curious heaviness of touch which is typical of totalitarian Governments, the Soviet wireless denied the bombing, and claimed that the Russian planes had flown over Helsinki for the charitable purpose of dropping bread to feed the poor. To the Finns, who had a grim humour of their own, these bombs soon became known as 'Molotov's bread-baskets'.

Opinion in the West was outraged by the brutality of Russia's action. Finland might perhaps have been wiser to have made some concessions over the Hanko base. But Russia's ambitions for territorial expansion were only too clearly known, and, in the fate of Poland and the Baltic States, only too recently demonstrated. Public opinion in the United States was deeply moved by this act of aggression against a tiny State by its giant neighbour. President Roosevelt immediately proposed mediation, which the Finns accepted and the Russians rejected. In Britain, the feeling was equally strong, partly because of the anger already caused by the Molotov-Ribbentrop Pact and partly because of our traditional sympathy for small and democratic countries. 'Aid to Finland' became a universally popular cry.

Finland, in accordance with her tradition, appealed to the League of Nations. The Soviet Government had meanwhile resorted to a singularly inept piece of 'double-talk'. They denied that the U.S.S.R. was at war with Finland, and claimed that a mutual-assistance pact had been signed on 2 December with the new Government of the 'Finnish Democratic Republic'. This was a purely fictitious body led by a Communist agitator named Otto Kuusinen. The Germans were soon to find in Norway a notorious and unhappily more successful imitator of Kuusinen by the name of Quisling. The Russians asserted that under this pact the legal Government of Finland had asked for Russian help in order to suppress the old reactionary leaders. This absurdity can, of course, have deceived no one, except perhaps some of the Russian people.

The League of Nations rejected the Kuusinen fiction, and on 14 December the Assembly declared that the Russian action was contrary to the general treaties by which Russia was bound, as well as the specific treaties between Finland and Russia. League members should therefore give all aid to Finland. Russia was in violation of the Covenant and was accordingly expelled from the League. This was almost the last dying act of the now impotent League of Nations. Perhaps it was not an unworthy end.

The war began in the last week of November. By the end of December, contrary to universal expectation, a state of something like stalemate was reached.

What had happened is now clear, although at the time misunderstood. One Russian division was successful in seizing Petsamo in the far north from a small Finnish force. Elsewhere, the Russian attacks were decisively repulsed. On the Karelian Isthmus, in spite of great superiority of numbers—the Russians deployed twelve divisions in the attack—the invaders made little progress. The Mannerheim Line, named after the great Marshal, the hero of the war of 1918–19, who was still in command of the whole Finnish Army, stood firm. Further north, the frontier was crossed in force at various points. But the Finns proved superior both in skill and determination. By a series of slow withdrawals into the forest, they would lure their enemy on towards strongly prepared positions. Then, while the frontal assault was held, the flanks and rear would be fiercely attacked. By these tactics whole Russian formations were in some cases utterly destroyed.

These events led not only to enthusiasm for the Finns and a strong pressure to afford them all possible help in spite of the many other calls upon the Allies, but also to unduly hasty deductions about the effectiveness of the Russian Army. Our military experts readily assumed that its morale had been gravely shaken, partly by the terrible purge with which Stalin had, some years before, removed all 'dangerous' elements, and partly by the alleged failure of Communism and Stalinism to inspire the devotion of their people. Nevertheless, the lull that followed this first phase of the Winter War was to prove illusory.

As a first and largely symbolic step, the British Cabinet, at the beginning of January 1940, approved the formation of a movement to organise aid to Finland, including the recruitment of a small volunteer international force. I heard of this through Leo Amery, under whose aegis a working committee was set up. Although the Government gave full support to our efforts, it was thought wiser to preserve at least the appearance of a private venture. M. Gripenberg, the Finnish Minister in London, acted as chairman. The other members, in addition to Amery, were Lord Balfour of Burleigh, Lord Phillimore, Lord Davies, General Macdonogh and myself. I accepted with alacrity the invitation to join this body. In the first place, I shared in the general admiration of the valour of the Finns. Secondly, I was distressed, after so many months of war, to find myself without any job connected with war in any form. Before I agreed to serve, I consulted Churchill. He encouraged me, and I gathered from what he said that there might be some greater advantages to Britain than the succouring of the Finns, however desirable and honourable that purpose might be. I did not, of course, know that he was already engaged on his long struggle to allow decisive measures to be taken to prevent, or at least reduce, the shipment of the precious iron-ore by German ships through Norway's territorial waters. Nor did I know that any major effort to help the Finns must involve using Narvik as a base:

If Narvik was to become a kind of Allied base to supply the Finns, it would certainly be easy to prevent the German ships loading ore at the port and sailing safely down the Leads to Germany.[5]

Gradually, after the committee was formed, an outline of these designs began to emerge.

Our members were diverse in experience and temperament. Lord Phillimore was a distinguished judge and a well-known philanthropist. Lord Balfour of Burleigh had all the enthusiasm of a crusader. General Macdonogh was prudent and practical. Lord Davies combined in his person a curious and attractive mixture of qualities. He was at the same time a very rich man and an extreme Radical. He had sat in the House of Commons for many years as Radical Member for Montgomery, and had acted as Parliamentary Private Secretary to Lloyd George. He also at one time kept two packs of foxhounds. In the inter-war years he had become a devoted exponent of the principle of collective security to be enforced by military means.

Our assistance was to include both arms and men. The Swedish Government would not allow volunteers to pass through Sweden in uniform, and they therefore had to go in plain clothes and armlets. If the war had lasted, the volunteer organisation could no doubt have been strengthened and developed on a considerable scale, largely from America. One of the keenest supporters was Kermit Roosevelt, a son of President 'Teddy' Roosevelt—a man of considerable charm and quite intrepid spirit. Eventually, the volunteers amounted to two battalions.

The problem of arms was more complicated. The United States Government gave Finland a loan of $30 million, but the American neutrality legislation did not allow this to be used for the purchase of arms from the United States. But at this early stage of the war a

[5] Churchill, *The Gathering Storm*, p. 430.

limited quantity of weapons and munitions was still obtainable from private sources. There were a number of armament pedlars around, to whom the British and French Governments could give unofficial approval. There were also some neutral Governments who might be persuaded, if sufficient discretion was observed, to part with some weapons. Nevertheless, the main source of supply must be whatever Britain and France could spare.

On 5 February, the Supreme War Council met in Paris. All through January, the Finnish lines had stood firm. It was therefore decided in principle to send in due course two British divisions and 50,000 trained volunteers from the French Army—100,000 men in all—to help the Finns. They must reach Finland by April. In order to make this operation effective, it would be necessary either to recapture Petsamo, which the Russians had already seized, or to use Narvik and other Norwegian ports. A new Finnish front might be opened up, which could play the role of Salonika in the First World War.

Our committee was given sufficient indication of these decisions to fill us with new interest and enthusiasm for our work. It was, of course, clear that the success of any such plan must depend on the assent of the Norwegian and Swedish Governments. Britain and France therefore informed Sweden that, in accordance with the League of Nations' decision, it was her duty to allow the transit of any troops coming to the help of the victims of aggression. In response to this declaration, the Swedes and the Norwegians showed both hesitation and alarm. Nor indeed could they be altogether blamed for their reserve.

It was now decided to send a delegation from our committee to Finland. To my delight, Lord Davies and I were chosen to go. Colonel Serlachius, of the Finnish Legation, was to accompany us. We left London together on 10 February 1940, five days after the decision taken in Paris. At this very time, the Russians, who had brought up better-trained troops to the Karelian Isthmus, amounting to some thirty divisions in all and supported by new reserves of heavy artillery and tanks, were about to launch a fresh offensive.

CHAPTER THREE

The Winter War

W E reached Stockholm on the morning of 12 February. The expedition began with comedy:

Lord Davies has left his teeth in the train. Great confusion, followed by much diplomatic activity. . . .

Lord Davies has lost his passport.

Later. Lord Davies's passport has turned up, but not his teeth. As a Director of the G.W.R. he is appealing to the Swedish Railway to give up his teeth, which he left in the sleeper. A search of an intense kind has been made. As the Malmö train connects with the Berlin train, it is thought that the teeth have been stolen by a Gestapo agent.[1]

Later still:

Lord Davies's teeth have been found.

About 4 p.m. we left by air for Finland. The cold was intense.

It was getting dark when we left, except for the reflected light from the snow. We flew northwards at first and then turned eastwards. The course lies past the Åland Island and afterwards turns eastwards toward Turku. . . . It was quite dark when we reached the Finnish coast.

The Gulf of Bothnia is completely frozen over. Indeed this has been some help to the Finns, as a roadway has been organised across the sea, and a continual stream of lorries and motor transport is taking supplies and goods of all kinds from Sweden, thus relieving the railways and saving a good deal of time. . . .

As we approached Turku aerodrome one or two lights became visible—like lighthouses—then when we got near, a complete circle of lights—making a kind of lighted arena—was switched on. The searchlight found the aeroplane; and the pilot made a beautiful landing in this quite small aerodrome. As he landed, all the lights were switched off, and except for one beam of light to guide him to the buildings, all was absolute darkness. . . .

---

[1] This and subsequent quotations are extracts from a diary which I kept of this trip.

We left at about 7.30 for a drive of . . . 250 kilometres or so. About two or three miles from [the airport] we passed through Turku, and in spite of the darkness we could see (by the light of the headlights) some of the destruction of that town, which had been heavily bombed by the Russians. . . .

We reached Helsinki about 1 a.m. . . .

The winter of 1939–40 proved the most severe for a hundred years. The temperature was 15 or 20 degrees below zero. I had provided myself against the bitter cold with a fine fur coat. It had belonged to my father-in-law and was lent to me by his son. I had also purchased, while in Sweden, a white 'wedge' of fur or wool, specially recommended for the Mannerheim Line. This headgear subsequently obtained a certain notoriety when I wore it as Prime Minister on my visit to Russia in 1959. Since I did not doubt that the Russian dossier on my life was pretty complete, I saw no objection to sporting this hat which dated back to the Winter War.

After the first air attacks, embassies and legations—including the British—had moved from Helsinki to a village some fifteen miles away. This diplomatic timidity had made a very bad impression, and brought the Western countries into contempt among ordinary folk. Our Military Attaché, Colonel Goodden, had remained at his post. In fact, the city did not seem to have suffered great damage, for most of the bombing had been random and from a great height. Other provincial towns, I was told, had been subjected to low bombardments, with devastating effects.

In the afternoon of 13 February, Lord Davies and I called to see Risto Ryti, the Prime Minister, who combined this office with that of Governor of the Bank of Finland. From him we heard the first news of the renewed Russian attacks with larger forces and on a much more formidable scale:

These sustained attacks have resulted in Russians obtaining some footholds in the Mannerheim Line and are causing great anxiety in official circles. The Russians have endless supplies of troops—the numbers being only governed by the difficulties of movement and supply. The Finns have, I understand, only about five divisions in the Isthmus—and perhaps one or two divisions hastily got together in reserve. In the north, they are able to hold the Russians and worry them in that difficult terrain. But in the Isthmus there is the danger that repeated Russian attacks will finally overwhelm the tired Finnish troops. . . .

M. Ryti received us very gracefully and appeared—like all Finns, it seems—

absolutely calm and unruffled. Lord Davies explained the efforts to raise volunteer forces in England, and discussed the possibility of raising troops in Ireland, Canada and especially America. I [raised] with M. Ryti the question of the time factor and the question of the usefulness of semi-trained volunteers. On the first he emphasised—very quietly but firmly—the vital urgency of the need. On the second, he shared my doubts as to the efficacy of genuine volunteers and agreed that this would not apply in the same degree to camouflaged volunteers—that is units formed and trained at home and passing into Finland as volunteers but re-forming on arrival.

On the question of military supplies, he merely said that they needed everything—more especially, of course, aeroplanes and heavy artillery.

It was clear from this talk that the situation was perilous, and this was confirmed later by Colonel Goodden. As regards help from the West, he told us that some aeroplanes were beginning to reach Finland:

Light bombers were particularly needed. If enough aeroplanes could be obtained, the Finns could attack the Russian concentrations and railway communications round Leningrad, which is now impossible owing to shortage of machines.

The Russians have allotted 1,500 planes to this front. Over 1,000 have attacked at the same time in the early raids. The Russians have fair machines but are bad fighters. They turn back when attacked or fired on. . . . In the first attacks on Helsinki, they flew very low. In the later attacks, when the anti-aircraft fire was getting pretty accurate, they flew very high and bombed at random.

The next day, 14 February, Thomas Snow, British Minister in Finland, came to dine with Lord Davies and me at our hotel. He gave us a full picture of the general position as he saw it. We were impressed by his knowledge and the objectivity of his approach:

1. The Russians have always intended the conquest of Finland and probably also intend the occupation of Norway and particularly the port of Narvik.

2. Ever since the fall of Litvinov, this has been Russian policy, if not before.

3. British policy seems to be based on fear of bringing the Germans and Russians closer together. How do we know that they have not already a complete co-operation?

4. Swedish policy is based on fear of offending Germany. Is there any certainty that Swedish help to Finland would involve Germany?

He went on to explain the action which must be taken if Finland was to be saved:

(a) They are now fighting a desperate battle on the Isthmus—what Mannerheim calls 'a Thermopylae every day'.

There is grave danger that they will be overwhelmed in the next few weeks. In that case, especially if they do not make an early enough retreat, the conquest of Finland is merely a 'mopping-up' operation, desperately contested by the Finns, but hopeless.

(b) In the present stage—until early April at least—Western European troops, whether genuine volunteers, camouflaged volunteers, or regular troops, cannot successfully operate in the climatic conditions.

(c) To help the Finns *now*, there must be an immediate supply of (say) 100 bombers, which could attack Leningrad, the railway junctions and the massing and communications of troops and/or field artillery and ammunition. The list of supplies is very disappointing.

(d) Alternatively, an attack on Petsamo and the occupation of the Murmansk railway. This would wind up the northern war, allow the Finns to shorten their line, and strengthen the Isthmus. Incidentally, this would encourage the Norwegians and Swedes to further action in support of Finland.

(e) If these measures succeeded, then a volunteer force could usefully be organised and brought here to fight in April.

The next day, we lunched at the officers' mess in the Industrie-Savoy building. I sat between the War Minister, Juho Niukkanen, and General Walden, the representative of the Field-Marshal at the War Office. Major Gripenberg, brother of the Finnish Minister in London, and several other officers were present. I was struck by the fact that many of the leading officers were industrialists engaged in the timber and paper industries. They had joined for the war and were employed in important positions. There seemed no jealousy between regulars and reservists. We were joined by Major Magill, of the Coldstream Guards, an extremely able and intelligent young man, who in peacetime was employed in the Finnish timber trade and spoke both Finnish and Swedish. He had recently arrived to act as assistant Military Attaché.

At my request, the Minister authorised General Walden to provide me with a list of the appeals for material which had been sent to London and the response to date. Later in the day Major Magill gave us a full account of his visit to the Front and his conversations with the Chief of Staff, the Director of Operations and the Field-Marshal. This appreciation he was sending back to the War Office:

In spite of repeated attacks and tactical successes by the Russians, the Mannerheim system as a whole still holds. To show the size of the Russian effort, over 300,000 projectiles were used on a two-mile front in one day. To this, Finnish guns may not reply at all, as they have orders only to use artillery when the Russian infantry are actually attacking. The Russians advance gallantly, although they bunch together and do not seem at home in wooded country. The Ukrainian machine-gunners are very good and their artillery fire is improving. The general suspicion (shared by the Field-Marshal) is that the Germans are directing the present attacks. But this is only based on the fact that they are far more intelligently conceived and better carried out than hitherto. But the Front still holds. The Chief of the Finnish Staff thinks that it will hold, subject to tactical losses, till the thaw. But it may collapse at any moment, chiefly through the physical exhaustion of the Finnish troops and the serious casualties among their officers.

During this day, from our talks both with Finns and British officials, it had become clear that a desperately anxious and critical period was approaching. If only some material could actually arrive, the Finns might survive. Could nothing be done? Lord Davies and I decided to send personal telegrams to London. I was rather doubtful of our right to interfere in this way, but the position was so serious and our friends so anxious that this was agreed. I accordingly wrote the following telegrams, which were sent in cipher by the Legation:

To Prime Minister
    Foreign Secretary

Secret.

Respectfully urge on you following considerations stop In spite of heroic resistance Finnish army and unbroken spirit of confidence Finnish Command expert military opinion here admits situation very grave stop Unless further material aid can arrive rapidly position will become critical stop Urgent need artillery all calibres and appropriate ammunition and aeroplanes both bombers and fighters stop If these made available at once believe position can be held till thaw gives short respite stop After that our volunteers or troops could operate here and preparation should be hastened on for this stop Please forgive my intrusion which only after consultation with Finnish and English opinion here.

Harold Macmillan

Rt. Hon. Winston Churchill,
Admiralty

Please ask to see my telegram Prime Minister today stop Situation here demands urgent action stop Do your best.

H.M.

Lord Davies in addition telegraphed to Lloyd George, Archibald Sinclair (the Liberal leader) and Harold Gibson. He also asked that Leo Amery should be informed of the situation.

In the afternoon of 16 February we

went with Colonel Serlachius to an exhibition of war material captured from the Russians. Types of various guns, tanks, aeroplanes, machine-guns, anti-tank guns, and uniform were being shown. Altogether 387 aeroplanes have been shot down by the Finns—17 yesterday. A large number, about 400, tanks have been destroyed. As the tanks cannot shoot quite near, the Finns have developed a method of crawling into the dead ground right up to the tanks, and either striking the machine-gun muzzles with a heavy crowbar, so as to put them out of action, or sticking a piece of wood into the caterpillar mechanism, so as to stop the tank, or throwing a tin of petrol into the tank at the back, through the air-cooling apparatus or into the exhaust. Sometimes, they bang on the top of the tank, and when one of the Russians opens, they throw in a bomb. By this means, they have put out of action these 400 tanks. Having so little artillery these are the best means open to them.

We dined that evening with the British Minister, who, in spite of the evacuation of his Legation, seemed to spend most of his time in Helsinki. The news from the Front was worse. The Russians had succeeded in breaking the Mannerheim Line at several points. Nevertheless, we decided to continue with our journey as arranged and at 8 o'clock that night we left by train for Vilppula. Our party consisted of Lord Davies and myself, accompanied by Colonel Serlachius and Major Magill.

Arriving at Vilppula early Saturday morning (17 February), we were taken by Colonel Serlachius to his home, Joenniemi, in Mänttä, a house of great beauty and considerable size. During the afternoon, Count Vitzhum, a man of German origin but now a naturalised Finn, and Colonel Serlachius's son, who had just come from Berlin, gave us their views about the Swedish position, the German-Soviet treaty, the state of Germany and other relative matters. The chief facts of interest were as follows:

On policy.

1. Germany did not intend to go to war with England. They were genuinely amazed at getting so much—to which they knew they were not entitled—at Munich. They therefore expected to get away with the [Polish] Corridor, where (in their view) they had a much better claim. They never expected Chamberlain to strain at the gnat after swallowing the camel.

2. Germany did not want to see Russia conquer Sweden and *may* have given a guarantee to Sweden that they will not allow it. (This would explain Sweden's inaction.)

3. Germany does not now want a war to the death with England. She would not attack on the Western Front or Holland and Belgium (unless Hitler had a brainstorm), but hoped that after eight months or one year of a stalemate war, England would make a reasonable peace.

4. Germany's ambitions were still Ukraine, not the British Empire. The 'free hand' in the Baltic to Russia was not intended to include conquest of Finland.

5. Germany would *not* object to Swedish help for Finland, however dangerous she might consider Anglo-French support of Finland.

On conditions in Germany.

1. No apparent shortage of petrol. Plenty of taxis in Berlin. Nevertheless they believe petrol will ultimately be short and that petrol is one of main reasons justifying Russian alliance (other than general undesirability of war on two fronts).

2. Plenty of food in Germany.

3. Ribbentrop the most unpopular man in Germany.

4. Next to Hitler, Ribbentrop the most powerful man in Germany, having superseded Goering in this respect.

Both Serlachius junior and Vitzhum naturally regard Russia as real enemy of the world and the German-British war as a foolish and fratricidal strife, from which Russia alone can benefit.

This point of view was perhaps understandable, but neither of them seemed to realise the degree of Hitler's insane desire to dominate the world.

During the day, Lord Davies had been very unwell. It was decided that he should stay in Colonel Serlachius's comfortable house and that I should go on without him. At 8 p.m., Magill and I, accompanied by Forelius, a Finnish lieutenant from Headquarters, set out for Kajaani. Forelius was normally employed in the textile trade in Lancashire, where he had married an English wife and settled down. He had returned for the war, as a reservist. He spoke excellent English and was a splendid companion and guide. The news was grim, the Marshal having issued an appeal to the troops reminiscent of Haig's famous 'back to the wall' message. The train was continually stopped by air-raid warnings and the procedure on these occasions followed a fixed routine:

All passengers . . . ordered to get out and take cover in the forest. This we did, presenting a ludicrous appearance, with one of the Company's sheets each to cover our dark overcoats. To drop off the train (a drop of several feet) into a deep snowdrift, to stumble along for twenty yards in snow up to one's waist, to climb up an embankment and over a fence of pointed stakes, and finally to sit in a forest of fir trees, wearing a fur hat, a smart London fur coat, a sheet, and carrying a dispatch case—all this represented an absurd and fatiguing manœuvre which we resolved not to repeat. After about ten minutes, the 'all clear' was given, the passengers climbed painfully back into the train, and we proceeded on our journey.

This happened at 10 a.m. and again at 11. On each occasion, when the 'all clear' was given, the Druid-like figures returned from the forest and re-embarked. We changed into another train at Iisalmi and in the evening were again bombed, although no actual damage was done. The weather was wonderful, cold—10 or 15 degrees below zero—but little wind. The air was crisp and clear. Nobody liked this weather; for the Russians could attack better, both on land and in the air. Everyone was praying for blizzards and heavy falls of snow. Finally, we arrived at Kajaani at about 7.30 p.m. on 18 February, without further incident.

Kajaani was the H.Q. of General Toompo, the commander of a front of about 200 kilometres, running from Pielisjärvi, near Lake Pielinen, in the south to north of Lake Kianta, near Juntusranta, in the north. For this task he had forces amounting to less than one division's strength. General Toompo sent Lieutenant Vihma, of his staff, to meet us and bring us to his headquarters for a meal. After supper, the General gave us an enthralling description of the course of the war in this sector. Major Magill translated. There were plenty of maps to illustrate the story.

The General explained that in his sector the Finns had been taken completely by surprise. Before hostilities began it had been difficult to obtain information, since they had no reconnaissance aeroplanes and the frontier guards of both sides were pretty efficient. They had now learned that in the spring of 1939 the Russians had built two new roads—one from Uhtua on the north side of the Kuyto Lakes and the other from Repola. The first attacks, therefore, found the Finns unprepared and outflanked their positions. In the southern of these two areas the Russian 54th Division was still maintaining itself, though much harried by the Finns. General Toompo regarded this division as well handled and efficient. In the northern area, however, the Finns had adopted a very successful technique:

[They] retired from Suomussalmi through Hyrynsalmi, allowing the Russians to advance. They then slipped in behind them and by clever guerrilla tactics succeeded in harassing their communications and finally in cutting them off. By tactics which have now become famous they succeeded in destroying the 163rd Division. The 44th, which was sent to its support, marched along the road at Suomussalmi and took up a position in the woods, just off the road, in a very amateurish manner. This division was also destroyed.

In these actions . . . at least 10,000 Russians were killed. The Finns have collected and buried, since re-occupying this terrain, about this number of corpses. . . . [The Russians] also lost an enormous quantity of tanks, guns, baggage, waggons and equipment of all kinds.

The 54th Division at Kuhmo were unable to use their tanks, since they could not bring up enough petrol:

They form themselves into a sort of 'laager', with their tanks buried up to the guns in the snow. They send out strong patrols, but these are not very good in the woods and are apt to be destroyed by the much smaller Finn forces. For instance, three battalions of about 600 men each, of picked skiers, were sent up to help the division at Kuhmo. While they were engaged in reaching their division, the Finns succeeded in engaging and destroying them all—killing practically every man. Similarly, the General told us he had just heard of the success of 6 men, as a small patrol, who met 44 Russians on patrol, shot 42 and captured 2.

In spite of these successes, however, which have necessarily involved the Finns in losses in officers and men which they can ill afford, General Toompo was under no illusions. The Russians have even less initiative than the old Russian Army, but they are incomparably better armed, and they have all the traditional Russian courage. The supply of tanks, heavy artillery, light artillery, machine-guns, automatic rifles is apparently limitless. And they have an immense supply of manpower.

The Finnish resources were ludicrously small. On the General's front he was holding 200 kilometres with something between four and five thousand men and three batteries of light artillery. Reliefs were impossible. He had no aeroplanes.

Magill, Forelius and I slept that night in an inn at Kajaani. Magill and I left at 4 a.m. next morning, 19 February, accompanied by

Lieutenant Vihma, in the General's car. Forelius stayed behind to receive any telegrams that might come in. This day provided us with a thrilling experience. Our drive covered about 160 kilometres, passing through Suomussalmi. We halted at a rough wooden signpost marking a path to the battalion headquarters of Major Kari.

Although the Finns have buried most of the corpses—an immense task—and taken away all the material of value to them from the two Russian divisions which met their doom in this area, nevertheless an immense mass of gun-carriages, waggons, carts and other impedimenta of all kinds is strewn for miles on each side of the road. It took the Finns ten days' hard work to clear the road for their own use, and all this mass of material is thrown off the road into the snow. A considerable number of corpses remain about, and in the course of the day we examined them carefully. Of course, owing to the cold, no kind of putrefaction has set in. The dead men's flesh and features are perfectly preserved; nor has their clothing perished to any noticeable extent. . . . We were particularly impressed by the nature of the wounds which had caused their death. In nearly every case, the Russians had been hit in the head or in the neck. . . .

Every sort of stuff, books, pamphlets, note-books, steel helmets, maps of the world, and all the paraphernalia imaginable lies about still. In the silence of this forest and the deep snow, it is a strange and melancholy scene.

We were much interested by the way in which the men were living round battalion headquarters:

In each case a tent is built round a growing tree, which acts as a tent pole. The sides of the tent are of cardboard squares, about 3 ft. square, and these are excellent for keeping in the heat. There are timber supports holding the cardboard sides, making the height of the tent about 3 feet at the outer circumference, and the roof is made, tentwise, by timber slats and cardboard—the height in the middle is enough to stand up comfortably. The roof is covered on the outside with pine branches, making a perfect camouflage.

The door of the tent is a sliding cardboard panel. The tent is heated by an iron stove, with an iron tube running through the roof to carry away the smoke. The stove is, of course, kept going with timber and serves both for heating and cooking. The atmosphere is splendidly warm—but not too hot, as there is sufficient ventilation made in the roof, and of course the door can also be opened if necessary.

On the floors of the tents there were palliasses and bedding of different kinds. They also used the leather-covered spring seats from the Russian lorries and waggons. Great numbers of horses had been captured, but most of them had to be destroyed as they were dying of starvation.

The Major was a quiet, sallow man of middle height and slight build. He spoke no English but he told his story to Magill in detail, who translated it as he went along:

Although he had taken this amazing part in a wonderful victory, having in effect destroyed two Russian divisions with his handful of men, he had no easy contempt for his adversaries.

Although they did not seem to understand the forest life, they were beginning to learn. At first, they made no attempt to give their men any warmth or protection (all fires were forbidden); they merely halted in the snow. The most they did was to make a very rough shelter out of green branches. Now they were—so far as the patrols could observe—making a sort of shelter in their 'laagers' and doing some digging and building of huts. (All this, of course, they can do with complete confidence, as the Finns have no aeroplanes on this front and their few guns are not allowed to fire, except in the event of a mass attack by the enemy.) They were also learning to ski, but were not yet expert. They were extremely brave and indifferent to death. And, of course, there was no end to them. If you destroy one division, they bring up another.

But they had little initiative. They are, after all, slaves—not free men. This he repeated, more than once. It was clear that to Major Kari's mind death was preferable to enslavement.

We had reached Kari's headquarters at about 7.30. We returned to the road junction and went on by car to Captain Harola's position. Harola was a very attractive man with a charming smile, fearless, sincere, and with a great sense of humour.

He was particularly pleased that General Toompo should have told us of the exploit where 6 or 7 Finns on patrol had shot 42 Russians and captured 2 out of a total of 44. These were his boys and he regarded the feat rather as a keen housemaster would regard a considerable performance by his [team] in an interhouse match.

We went round his support positions where the men were resting, cutting wood or cleaning equipment. We also saw his one battery— four French 75s—well camouflaged among the trees.

We took at last an unwilling farewell of Captain Harola and his officers.

I felt a real cordiality and friendliness. Nor were these men unreasonable or unwilling to recognise the difficulty of England's position. Any bitterness at being abandoned to the Russians will be against the Swedes and Norwegians.

Seldom have I seen troops with such a high morale as these splendid
Finnish soldiers. We got back to Kajaani deeply impressed. On arrival,
we found a telegram from Colonel Serlachius, saying that owing to the
almost desperate situation on the Isthmus it was impossible for me to
go there, or for the Field-Marshal to see me. It was suggested that I
should try to rejoin Lord Davies, who was now better. He had
collected all the necessary information and was on his way to Vaasa.
He would wait for me there.

The next two days were taken up in long and rather wearisome
journeys. The Russians were making a continuous series of attacks on
the trains, hoping to dislocate the entire system. Nevertheless, in spite
of long halts and continuous air raids, there was no confusion or
panic. In the first six hours we travelled only about sixty kilometres.
Sometimes we would find a station on fire and sometimes we were
bundled out of the train by recurrent air-raid warnings. Fortunately,
on Wednesday the 21st there was a raging wind and a snow blizzard
which, it was hoped, would reduce the air attacks.

Air raids were soon to become familiar to us all at home. Meanwhile, the procedure adopted by the Finns gave us a foretaste of what
we should be called upon to endure:

This has been a day of waiting, always enlivened by a number of air raids
and all that this involves. All day . . . the Russians have been attacking the
junctions and even the small stations on this line. The Finns have at present
nothing to oppose to it other than sheer courage. The ordinary procedure is
this. When the 'air-raid warning' (*halytys*) is given, if you are in a town of any
size, this is done by sirens like ours (giving a 'warbling' note) or by the factory
hooters. In some of these small towns there have been eleven or twelve such
warnings in the course of a day. Your procedure then is (*a*) to stay in your
home and go on with your work or pleasure, or (*b*) to go to the cellar, or (*c*)
to go to any dug-out that may be in the square or other public place. (These
dug-outs, incidentally, are only splinter-proof. Some of the worst casualties
have been caused by direct hits upon them.) Or (*d*) you may retire to a
neighbouring piece of wood and stand under a tree. When the air raid is over
or the 'all clear' given, usually the church bells are rung.

The system of giving the alarm was primitive:

As there is no listening apparatus available, the only method of telling
what the Russians are doing is by actual observers, stationed round the town,
or by telephone (where these are intact) from neighbouring points.

Incidentally, it should be noted that nearly everyone now wears a white costume to make them as invisible as possible. Troops and civilians alike wear these protective clothes. Sometimes they are made like long cloaks, with a hood like a monk's cowl; sometimes they are in two pieces like pyjamas.

By 6.30 p.m. on 21 February we had reached Riihimäki, where we had to stay until after midnight.

We found, nevertheless, a restaurant open, full of troops on leave or returning from leave, where an excellent meal of sausages and potatoes, [with] either beer or coffee, was served. [An] incident which . . . amused me here was that on asking for the lavatory, I was informed by the porter (Lieutenant Forelius translating) that I must do my business outside, as there was unfortunately a dud bomb in the gentlemen's cloakroom, as yet unexploded.

At 1 a.m. on Thursday morning we got into another train and finally arrived at Vaasa at 2.30 in the afternoon. I said goodbye to my guide, Forelius, with some emotion. He was a fine man. At the Consul's house I found Lord Davies and a number of other officers and civilians interested in organising the volunteer forces.

This was the end of our visit to Finland. Although I knew in my heart that the Finnish resistance could scarcely be prolonged, I still hoped for a miracle. I have retained for the rest of my life a vivid memory of those gallant and fearless people.

In the afternoon, Lord Davies and I left Vaasa by aeroplane for Sweden. The temperature was now warmer. Looking down upon the Gulf of Bothnia we could see the great fissures and cracks in the ice, with occasional strips of open water. It seemed, therefore, that the frozen road would not be in use for much longer. After my experiences in Finland, it was strange indeed to come to Sweden. We left a country struggling for its very life. We seemed to pass into a very different world.

On arrival in Stockholm I got a message from Victor Mallet, our Ambassador, asking me to the Embassy. He showed me a message from 'Rab' Butler, Under-Secretary of State for Foreign Affairs, suggesting that I might usefully spend a few days in Stockholm and in Oslo, in order to see people of importance and get what impressions I could of their points of view. In view of this, Victor thought it right to show me various files containing Foreign Office telegrams and his own messages. I was also able to read a full account of the *Altmark* incident, which had taken place on 16 February, and the various diplomatic exchanges which had followed. Some rumours had reached us in Finland, but no details. The decision of the British Government to stop the German ship *Altmark* in Norwegian territorial waters and release a large number of British prisoners on board had been hailed with delight at home. In Norway, and indeed in Sweden, it had been received with rather mixed feelings, in which the satisfaction of the peoples was matched by the alarm of the Governments.

At 4.30 in the afternoon, Victor took me to the Ministry of Foreign Affairs for an interview with the Minister, Christian Günther. In his view,

the primary objective of Swedish policy must be to avoid entanglement in the World War, and all questions must be regarded with that overriding consideration in mind.

He thought that the assistance which Sweden had given and was still giving to Finland had been underrated in Britain:

For instance, the Swedish Army had deprived itself of half its anti-aircraft guns and a large proportion of its anti-tank guns; in fact these latter had been responsible for holding up the attack on Salla; secondly . . . even if the Swedish Army were to go to the assistance of the Finns, this would by no means necessarily enable the war with Russia to be brought to an end.

He went on to say that the biggest military force that the Swedes could possibly send without totally depriving their country of any means of defence would be of the order of two or three divisions. M. Günther did not think

that the Germans would regard the sending of Swedish troops to Finland as an act which would bring German retaliation. That was not his fear. His fear was that since the Swedish military support would not be conclusive, sooner or later Sweden and Finland would have to seek further support. This could only be from England and France and it would be this second stage of the war with Russia which would bring German retaliation. In other words, while he thought the Germans would be prepared to see Sweden assist Finland with her Army, they could not allow English or French troops to come to the aid of Sweden and Finland for fear of the effect upon the supplies of iron-ore.

The question then arose as to the attitude which Sweden would take towards an Allied expedition to assist the Finns. For instance, how would he regard a movement through Narvik and, from that base, through Sweden? On this he was quite definite. He would consider this as a breach of Swedish neutrality to which they could not give consent. Even the use of Petsamo, which involved no breach of Swedish neutrality, M. Günther regarded with alarm. I pressed the question as to what he thought would be the reaction by the Germans if these moves were made. M. Günther replied that 'Germany would retaliate by an attack, not on Sweden, but on Finland'. I expressed doubt as to whether the Germans would agree to being accessaries to the Bolshevisation of Finland and would give military aid to that purpose. But M. Günther was unshaken. He thought that

Germany would probably represent her invasion of Finland as an effort to secure a reasonable settlement of the Finno-Russian dispute.

We next turned to the question of the Swedish trade in iron-ore with Germany. He believed the British Government had overestimated its importance:

There was always a danger that Germany would demand that all Swedish-British trade should stop, and this would be much more detrimental to our interests as well as to those of Sweden. The Germans were after all in a position to enforce their demands because they could move more rapidly and in greater strength than the Allies.

Here indeed he was to prove right.

It was clear that M. Günther strongly favoured an early peace between Russia and Finland as the only way out. He also thought that 'the Russians might stop at something approximating to their original demands, at any rate for the present'. I could not help reminding him of what had happened to Czechoslovakia—first Munich, then Prague —but he did not accept the parallel.

My conclusion on all this was that, whereas the Swedish Government was in favour of the maximum possible support being given to Finland, either by Sweden herself or by the Allies, the overriding consideration must always be that nothing should be done which would lead the Germans to take part and thus involve Sweden in the general war.

During my absence from London there had been a certain development in the attitude of France and Britain. Although military supplies actually released were disappointingly small and the actual deliveries

smaller still, yet the mood was more favourable. The French were
growing equally keen on opening up a Finnish front. Plans for the
attack on Narvik were already being made, and the relief of Finland
and the cutting-off of the Swedish ore became part of a dual policy in
which Édouard Daladier, the French Prime Minister, was especially
active and Chamberlain more than acquiescent. I had the first indication of this development in a talk at the British Embassy on the
afternoon of the 23rd, when the Press Attaché, Peter Tennant, came to
see me:

He seemed somewhat confused by the new instructions which had arrived
from London, instructing the British Legation to give all possible publicity to
the help which England was giving to Finland. This being entirely contrary
to all previous instructions—which were to do everything to keep this as secret
as possible—he seemed a little uncertain as to the way in which this new
policy was to be carried out and as to the tone of any articles which he ought
to write or have written.

Our doubts were resolved when, on the next day, the British Minister
to Finland announced that the Allied plan would amount to 20,000 to
22,000 men, and, a few days later (28 February), an assurance was
given to the Finns by our Minister in Helsinki that these forces could
be made effective by the end of April, if not before.

The next morning, 24 February, I had a very painful interview with
Eljas Errko, the Finnish Minister in Stockholm, whom I had met on
my way through Stockholm on 12 February. He was very pessimistic
and aggrieved, in sad contrast with the buoyancy and optimism of his
mood when I had first met him:

He seemed in a very agitated state. He took me into his room and told me
that he had very bad news. He did not really seem in a suitable condition for
any long talk, but I thought that in this mood he might speak more frankly
than later, and I therefore waited. After a long pause, in which he held his
head in his hands, he looked at me suddenly and said, 'Well! What is your
country going to do? The Swedes will do nothing more. It is finished. It is
decided.'

He added that M. Günther had at last given him categorical confirmation of the decisions recently announced by the King, that
Sweden did not intend to intervene in the Finnish War. He continued
with deep emotion:

We must know what you are going to do. If Sweden will not help us and you cannot, what are we to do? Are we to have our whole country destroyed?

I came away convinced that the Finnish Government must now consider the possibility of a negotiated peace.

Lord Davies left for London on the afternoon of the 24th. He would carry to our Government all the information that we had been able to collect, and he would be able to confirm in detail the Finnish needs. I decided, in view of Butler's telegram, to stay a few days longer and then go on to Oslo.

On the next day, Sunday 25 February, I went to see M. Errko again, at his own request, at 4 p.m. He was bitter about the Swedes and the long delay and uncertainty in which his country had been kept. Although the Swedish help in material had been large, it had always been grudging.

It was like extracting a tooth. Why could not they say exactly what they were prepared to do in material and in men? Even the number of volunteers authorised was never definite.

Similarly with the British. Why could not they say definitely what help we would give in material or men? Then Finland could frame her policy accordingly.

When I asked him what he meant by 'framing a policy', he replied:

Well—decide what to do, when we know what help we shall or shall not receive. But even from England we get contradiction and uncertainty.

He continued:

They would quite understand if England decided she could do no more. But unless the Finnish Government could know definitely the extent of England's support and assistance, it was impossible to frame a policy. Once more I asked, 'What does frame a policy mean? Does it mean, negotiate a peace?'

M. Errko's fat frame shook with emotion. He threw up his hands and exclaimed, 'Yes—I suppose so.'

Although agitated and depressed, M. Errko retained throughout the interview his charm and his attractive smile. He said goodbye to me with deep feeling. I was much moved, realising the terrible situation in which he and his countrymen were placed.

The next day, I had an audience with Crown Prince Gustav Adolf of Sweden, who received me with characteristic affability and graciousness. It was clear that, although sympathetic to giving every possible assistance to Finland, he did not differ in any way from the Foreign Minister.

He stated quite frankly that Sweden did not want, at any cost, to be involved in the Western War. 'We have everything to lose and nothing to gain.'

I replied, 'Like us.' He asked me what I meant, and I replied that we had everything to lose and nothing to gain by war, but that somebody had got to stand up to Hitler's attempt to dominate Europe. He laughed—and said that he supposed this was so.

M. Boheman, the professional head of the Foreign Ministry, told me two anecdotes:

The Swedish F.O. is much amused by the Russian Ambassadress's self-created difficulties over the bombing of a Swedish village by Russian aeroplanes.

Madame Kollontai first admitted, with tears in her eyes ('She wept in my arms,' said M. Boheman), that the Russians had bombed the town; that it was of course a pure mistake; that they would pay full compensation for damage.

Later on, the Russian Government officially denied that any Russian aeroplanes had been in the vicinity and said the whole story was a complete fabrication. . . .

He also told me a curious example of Hitler's confidence and grandiose conceptions:

He has placed a colossal order for Swedish granite, to be supplied after the war, of a sufficient scale to rebuild half the towns of Germany!

From Stockholm I went on to Oslo, where I heard much the same story. My chief impression was the extreme nervousness on all sides. Everyone was really at heart pro-English, but was frightened of the Germans. On 1 March I reached home.

Meanwhile, events were moving quickly. In the last days of February the Finnish position on the Isthmus had seriously deteriorated. Although on 2 March Daladier announced that, if they received a formal appeal from the Finnish Government, the French were ready to send 50,000 volunteers from the French Army and 100 bombers to arrive by the end of March, there was still no clear pronouncement as to what would happen in the event of Norway and Sweden refusing to allow their transit.[2] The true reason for this last offer was the growing pressure of public opinion, especially in France. But by now it was too late. The Russians had broken through the Mannerheim Line and a withdrawal had to be undertaken, although it never became a rout. By the beginning of March the line was back as far as Viipuri. The Russians then put forward proposals for an armistice, more favourable than the Finns might have hoped. They threw aside the puppet 'Government' of Kuusinen which they had set up and paraded before the world. This indicated that they did not mean to seize the whole of Finland. As was only natural, the Finns made one last desperate effort—an appeal to Germany for help. But the Germans were not disposed to give them any aid and advised them to accept what terms they could get. These indeed proved onerous but not absolutely destructive. The whole of the Hanko peninsula, all of the Karelian Isthmus, including Viipuri, and territory on the northern shore of Lake Ladoga must be surrendered and a heavy war indemnity paid. On 9 March, Field-Marshal Mannerheim had to tell his Government that his situation was now wholly untenable. The Finnish Government accordingly accepted the Russian demands. A peace was signed on 12 March, and fighting ended a day later.

The first days of my homecoming were melancholy. I was obsessed by the Finnish tragedy. Yet there was nothing which our committee could do now but wait upon events. Naturally I had welcomed the French offer of 2 March, but I knew that it was too late. Most unfairly, after Finland's collapse there was a tendency in the British Press, not altogether unfostered by Government sources, to give exaggerated accounts of the assistance that had been afforded by Britain, and to blame the Finns for their surrender. This I felt to be grossly unjust. In spite of these excuses, British public opinion was disturbed, and the House of Commons shared the general sense of unease. Everything to which we had so far put our hand seemed to have failed. All those countries which we had guaranteed or tried to help appeared doomed to disaster. It was in this mood that a two-day debate, ostensibly on the place on 19–20 March.

I had prepared my case with special care and had every reason to progress of the war, but largely centred upon events in Finland, took

[2] According to Churchill, Daladier made this offer without prior consultation with the British Government: Churchill, *The Gathering Storm,* p. 453.

believe that the Speaker would call me, in view of my recent return
from Finland. Chamberlain delivered an able opening speech—robust,
forthright and effective. But he made a number of statements which
were, to say the least of it, equivocal. A week before, in reply to
questions, he had said:

The Finnish Government have made repeated requests for materials, and
every one of these requests has been answered. . . .[3]

Shortly before the debate, *The Times* had circulated an exaggerated
account of the amount of material which had been sent to Finland by
France and Britain. I was therefore not wholly unprepared for the line
that the Prime Minister would take. But I did not think that he would
repeat it in quite so precise a form. Nevertheless, he reaffirmed his
previous declaration. 'No appeal,' he told the House, 'that was made
to us by the Finnish Government remained unanswered.'[4] He then
gave a long and detailed list of items involved. All this was very
effective. But his account of the Supreme War Council and the
preparation of the proposed expedition was less convincing. The
question of the probability of Norway and Sweden agreeing to the
passage of troops through their territory remained obscure. Nevertheless, I felt, while I was waiting, that the Government had, by a skilful
use of the Press on the previous day and by the Prime Minister's
speech, done a good deal to weaken the moral position of the Finns
and even cast a certain doubt upon their good faith and courage.

I was called at half-past seven—not a very good time. But the House
filled up and remained full. I spoke for nearly forty minutes—a longer
period than I normally allowed myself. I was conscious of an extreme
hostility from the Front Bench and, what was unusual even in my
previous deviations from the party line, from some of the Whips.
There had even been considerable pressure to prevent me from
speaking. Nevertheless, I look back to this occasion—the last in which
I was to address the House from the back-benches—as one in which I
had the rare experience of starting with a hostile audience and
winning it over to my side. Nor was Chamberlain's wind-up successful
in dissipating the effect. I noticed that at no time during the day were
Churchill or Eden present on the Front Bench, and this made my task
easier.

[3] *Hansard,* 13 March 1940.
[4] Ibid., 19 March 1940.

I knew from my close contacts with the Finns, both during the war and since the armistice, the exact figures of munitions supplied. With all allowances for the difficulties of transport, it was a sorry story. What alarmed me and some of my friends with whom I discussed this affair was that the delays, uncertainties, indecisions and vacillations did not appear to us to have been based on any hostility or timidity, so much as upon mere incompetence. In order to get the support of my audience, I began very quietly, disclaiming any desire to criticise the Government for their failure to rescue Finland from her fate. At best, I said, it was a difficult and hazardous enterprise, in view of the geographic and diplomatic obstacles. Nor did I think that the Finns were disposed to blame us. They understood that we were engaged in a war for our lives which would probably develop into the most terrible and bloody in our history. Indeed, I felt there was a strong argument for never regarding the Finnish affair as any part of our business or an area of operations which we could usefully exploit. In the matter of munitions, I could not resist saying:

We cannot, alas, supply a margin out of our superfluities, but only out of our deficiencies, deficiencies caused to some extent by our own folly in past years. . . .[5]

I had already asked that the discussion should be held in secret session. This having been refused, I went on:

. . . I am conscious of the extreme difficulty that every Member has in open debate in time of war, in avoiding the pitfalls that surround him. On the one hand he feels it a duty, if he is to add anything to the debate, to speak frankly and truthfully. On the other hand, he is only too conscious of his obligation to say nothing to injure the national interest. . . .[6]

I then described what I called 'the first act'—the three months' war—drawing on my own personal experiences. This had a good effect on the House, who were interested and touched by the picture which I was able to paint of the sufferings and courage of the Finnish people. I did want, however, to clear up certain misunderstandings. The Prime Minister had laid great stress upon the request made to the Finnish Government that they should make an open appeal for help. The French Prime Minister, Daladier, had even threatened them that, if they did not do so, they would be abandoned after the war. I asked the

[5] Ibid.
[6] Ibid.

British Government to repudiate this statement, which seemed, even if it was only meant to force the issue, ungenerous. Moreover, by the time the offer was made—at the beginning of March—it was too late.

As regards war material, in view of the statements made in the British and French Press, the public might well wonder how, with such substantial deliveries, the Finnish resistance collapsed so suddenly. The Prime Minister had repeated again that no appeal remained unanswered:

I do not know in what sense he used the word 'answered', and whether he used the word in the sense that the call was answered and the appeal was acceded to. . . .

I think the general impression is that they were not answered in the sense in which a letter is answered but that, as a whole, these requests were acceded to. That is a very different picture from the one which was given to me, and which I shall try to show presently—by General Walden and the Minister of War when I was in Finland. They gave me the impression of a series of appeals for large quantities of materials, appeals which fell almost entirely at first on deaf ears, and were followed at last by materials which were sent always in too small quantities and always too late. . . . I recognise that there was necessarily great delay between the time of the material leaving England and the time when it could reach the field of battle. We know what difficulties of transport there are today to which the Prime Minister referred. But there was almost equal delay between the authorisation of the material by the War Cabinet and the date at which it was actually dispatched.[7]

I then began to deal with the figures item by item. There was some protest at this by individual Members. But I reminded the House that the Government had refused a secret session, had quoted figures themselves and must not now object to the other side being put:

The public have read in these announcements in the Press enormous figures of the release of these materials, but is it generally known that although 148 aeroplanes were ultimately released—and that is the Prime Minister's figure today, and he told us quite frankly—only 101 were sent? I am not speaking now of numbers reaching Finland, but of numbers leaving England. Is it realised that of these 101, only four left England in December; only 44 in January; and only 27 in February; and the others were made up in March?

I do not think the general public knows, but as the Prime Minister has produced these figures I am entitled to deal with them. Is it generally known that we were unable to send any anti-tank guns at all when the Field-Marshal

[7] Ibid.

asked for 100? A number of anti-tank rifles were sent and left England about 28 February. No one could be quite sure when they would arrive; but they were surely sent very late. We could only send 25 howitzers out of the 150 asked for; only 30 field guns out of 166 asked for, and these were dispatched one month after the request. . . .[8]

There was a very peculiar situation as to small-arms ammunition. The Finnish Government had large numbers of cartridge caps on order with English manufacturers in the summer of 1939. Before the outbreak of the European war these orders were postponed, but as a matter of courtesy by the Finns, since no Order in Council had yet been issued. When the Russians attacked them, the Finnish Government said, 'At least send us this material which we ought to have had in June and of our own free will surrendered.' But, here again, the delays and formalities had prevented any deliveries until the last moment:

. . . there is general talk in the Press about the generosity of the Allies in parting with their war material. The generosity, of course, consisted in allowing the material to be sent at all in time of war and not in the terms on which it was sent. In two cases—I think of certain aeroplanes—these were gifts, and generous gifts, and nothing was asked in payment except the packing and delivery costs. In all the other cases payment was made either in cash, or under the Export Credits scheme—that is to say, 15 per cent in cash on delivery, and the rest in bills over a period of years carrying an interest of 4 per cent. When we remember that Finland is the only country that has not defaulted upon its debts and, unlike this country, continued to pay interest on her American debt, her credit was pretty high, and although I recognise that no official statement has ever been made with a contrary suggestion, I doubt whether the general public recognises that with the exception of two cases the whole of this war material was sold to the Finns on an ordinary commercial basis.[9]

This statement seemed to shock most Members and, in order to anticipate a Government excuse, I added:

It may be said that the true reason for this procedure was that it was advisable that this material should become Finnish property in London, in order to facilitate its movement through Scandinavia. That, however, would equally apply to the part of the materials which was a gift. It would become Finnish property by gift or purchase, so that that point is not vital.[10]

[8] Ibid.
[9] Ibid.
[10] Ibid.

I turned next to the question of men, whether volunteer or regular. A small volunteer force could clearly have only a token effect. But a good deal had been made of the offers put forward at different times, and both the French and British Prime Ministers had suggested that it was the Finnish refusal in March to make a formal public demand which led to their unexpected collapse. This, of course, was false. A public demand might have exactly the opposite effect on the Swedish and Norwegian Governments, who had hitherto connived at the passage of munitions and some volunteer forces through their territory. They might be forced to refuse overt permission to what they had overtly agreed.

Finally, we must realise the German pressure which was exerted as the Finnish military position became more desperate. The Germans made it clear that, if the Finns persisted in a hopeless struggle, they would raise no objection to the Russians demanding the frontier of 1809—that is, the absorption of the whole of Finland.

We must do justice to the Finns, who had put up a heroic resistance. The lack of material; the lack of any certainty of Allied troops being prepared to force a passage through neutral territory in the likely event of Swedish and Norwegian objection; the almost hopeless military situation with which they had to deal, surely must make us all agree that the Finnish Government had taken the only possible course, and that the lustre of their fame should not be dimmed by malice or misunderstanding. I ended with a passage which was in a sense prophetic:

As to the general lessons of this episode, I do not know enough of the strategy of war to know whether on the whole we have gained or lost. . . . But it does, I think, throw a piercing light on the present machinery and the method of government. The delay, the vacillation, changes of front, standing on one foot one day and on the other the next before a decision is given— these are patently clear to anyone. The moral of the history of these three months to be drawn for the future is, to use the phrase of Burke, 'a proof of the irresistible operation of feeble counsel.'[11]

The Whips put up one or two tame Tories to try to answer me, but with little effect. The debate ended in a scene between Chamberlain and me. The figures which I had given had made a considerable effect in the House, and the Prime Minister's winding-up of the debate was

[11] Ibid.

almost entirely devoted to trying to rebut them. With his great authority and relying on the almost blind support which a large part of the Conservative Party still gave him, he was able once again to cloud the issue. Nevertheless, a sense of confusion and mismanagement over the whole Finnish affair remained strongly in Members' minds. When the same melancholy story was repeated a few weeks later in the Norwegian campaign, the Finnish incident was not forgotten. What for many months the country had consciously or unconsciously sought was a single directing hand over the whole field, or at least a powerful team of a few colleagues operating from the centre and controlling all the work of Service and civilian departments to a single end. One of the main reasons for the fall of Chamberlain's Government was that he had not armed himself with any adequate machinery for the conduct of war. Himself a supreme peace administrator, interested above all in social reform and internal problems, he was wholly at sea and floundered desperately as a War Minister.

CHAPTER FOUR

The Scandinavian Campaign and the Fall of the Government

THE Finnish collapse was fatal to Daladier, the French Prime Minister. He had identified himself with those forces in France which were especially anxious to help the Finns, partly from genuine sympathy, partly from hatred of Soviet Russia and partly with the vain hope that the war might be kept away from French territory. On 21 March a new Government was formed under the leadership of Paul Reynaud, his chief rival, who was destined to preside over the administration until the fall of France.

Although the effect on Chamberlain was not so serious, his authority was shaken by the confusion and tardiness of the measures taken to help the Finns.

Yet another small country had become the victim of aggression, and the Western democracies had been unable to bring effective help. Whatever the complicated motives which inspired the various Allied decisions to assist the Finns, the end of it all had been another failure. The public was perplexed and uneasy. In default of other news, the debate on Finland's capitulation was widely read and discussed. I could tell from the large correspondence I received that although the Prime Minister had maintained himself in Parliament without serious difficulty, there were many people of every shade of politics who were deeply disturbed by the way in which the affair had been handled. Chamberlain tried to counter these anxieties by a confident speech which he delivered early in April at a party gathering.[1] In this he committed himself to an unfortunate phrase. He was persuaded that time was on our side and that as the months passed, the strength of the

[1] The Central Council of the National Union of Conservative and Unionist Associations, 4 April 1940.

Allies would increase and that of Germany would decline. 'Hitler,' he exclaimed, 'has missed the bus'.[2]

On the day of the Finnish acceptance of the Russian terms (12 March), 'the British Cabinet decided to revive the plans for military landings at Narvik and Trondheim to be followed at Stavanger and Bergen as part of the expected help to Finland'.[3] However, when the news came of the end of the Finnish War, these forces were dispersed. Two divisions were sent to France, thus reducing the troops readily available when the decision was later taken to move into Norway. On 28 March the Supreme War Council met in London. Two decisions were taken, both overdue. Both were concerned with offensive operations for which Churchill had long been pleading. The first was to lay mines in Norwegian territorial waters and thus prevent the movement of iron-ore from Narvik to Germany in German ships. All these months this traffic had gone on undisturbed by the British Navy because it was within the three-mile limit. To mine these waters was strictly contrary to international law. Yet it was intolerable that our blockade should thus be evaded. In spite of the technical breach, intervention was fully justified. Similar action had indeed been taken in the First World War. The name under which this plan was known was 'Mining the Leads'.

The second was a more original but equally ambitious project, the code name for which was 'Royal Marine'. Churchill, with the help of his own advisers, had worked out a scheme for dropping mines by air into the Rhine at a large number of different places and thus disturbing and perhaps altogether destroying a traffic vital to the life of Germany. Both these proposals had been long debated. The first had been put forward by Churchill in September 1939, in the first days of his return to office. It was subjected to long and indecisive arguments in the Cabinet and was only agreed after seven months' discussion. The date was fixed first for 5 April, and then 8 April. The second, although at last accepted in principle in Paris, was lost in the terrible weeks that followed the invasion of France. Whatever might have been the outcome of 'Royal Marine', the mining of the Nor-

[2] Readers of General Spears's *Prelude to Dunkirk* (London, 1954), p. 99, will recall that by a strange chance Churchill, on the same day, in private conversation applied the simile to the Allies. 'Nous allons perdre l'omnibus,' he observed to his French hosts, who one hopes grasped the general meaning.

[3] Churchill, *The Gathering Storm*, p. 453.

wegian territorial waters could have been undertaken without any difficulty or German reaction in the winter months. By a strange chance it was ultimately begun on the very night that Hitler had fixed for the invasion of Norway. Seven months is too long a delay in war between conception and execution of a minor tactical exercise.

No doubt the *Altmark* incident, followed by all the talk about aid to Finland, had been a warning to Hitler. While the British and French hesitated, Hitler prepared and carried out with lightning speed the seizure of Denmark and the invasion and occupation of every important port in Norway. This was on the night of 8–9 April. The German troops moved up in the empty iron-ore ships and even reached Narvik. There followed a hectic period when many conflicting plans were put forward. The Allied Governments could scarcely fail to respond to Norway's appeal for help. Churchill wished to concentrate upon an attack on Narvik. This, in his view, was the great prize, and if a force could be established there, not only would there be an important gain in intercepting the iron-ore traffic and directing it to the Allies, but there would also be at least a base on Norwegian territory where the King and his Government could be installed, and the work of resistance carried on and developed. Thus Norway might perhaps play a role in the discomfiture and ultimate defeat of Hitler similar to that of the Peninsula against Napoleon.

With such aims in view, the Cabinet now agreed to the launching of an amphibious expedition. The convoys left our shores on 12 April with every prospect of success. Following Captain Warburton-Lee's sharply contested and heroic action in the Narvik Fiord, Admiral Whitworth was able to exterminate the remaining German destroyers and supply ships, and he confidently reported that the town itself could be seized with a relatively small force. Unfortunately, everything went wrong with this expedition from the start. The organisation of command was ineffective and, according to our later ideas, primitive. Admiral Lord Cork, a gallant and intrepid officer, was in sole command of the naval forces. But General Mackesy had complete authority over the Army. There was no Commander-in-Chief appointed to the expedition as a whole until it was too late. Meanwhile each commander received his directives from his own Chief of Staff. Mackesy was careful, cautious and orthodox. He thought an assault upon the town, although occupied at that time by a very small number of German soldiers, was too hazardous to be attempted. Lord Cork fumed and raged upon his flagship, while for four whole weeks an army of almost 20,000 men, which had landed at Harstad on the island of Hinnöy, watched impotently a steady increase in the German garrison at Narvik. Only on 12 May, when Lord Cork was given complete command, was an attack launched at the head of the fiord. Narvik was taken on 28 May, but by then the full flood of war had been let loose upon the Western Front. With the threat to the Allied armies caused by the German onslaught, it became impossible to keep a force in the north of Norway which might still play a decisive role in stemming the flood through France. By general agreement it was decided that an evacuation was necessary. To achieve this, the capture of the port as well as the town was essential, and this was easily accomplished, although with some loss. Eventually, by 8 June, 24,000 troops, French, British and Polish, with large quantities of stores and equipment, were successfully re-embarked.

I have anticipated, so far as Narvik is concerned, the end of the sad story. The main drama was played out elsewhere. On 13 April the Cabinet, in spite of the doubts expressed by Churchill and Oliver Stanley (Secretary of State for War), decided upon an immediate effort to seize Trondheim, the ancient capital of Norway. Here the Norwegians might be rallied. Here an effective base might be formed for a serious war in Norway. The invading German forces were still slender and had not reached so far north in any strength. We might beat them to the post.

Orders were given to prepare to force an entrance by a concentration of naval strength. It would be another, but a successful, Dardanelles. After further examination, the plan for a direct assault was soon abandoned. The naval risks were thought to be too great, and the landing of troops in the harbour to be consequently too uncertain, and too costly. On 18 April, the decision was taken to invest Trondheim, and for this purpose to develop into major attacks the minor subsidiary landing which had already taken place without opposition at Namsos, and a new one at Andalsnes. The first was 100 miles north of Trondheim, and the second 150 miles to the south. In each case these larger operations proved wholly unsuccessful, although carried out with conspicuous gallantry. The conditions were indeed bad. The snow, sometimes melting, sometimes frozen again, was a great handi-

cap. There was little or no air support possible. It became necessary
therefore to issue orders for evacuation, and on 1 and 2 May both
these areas were abandoned. The withdrawals were accomplished
without undue loss.

So ended, except for the operation at Narvik, the Scandinavian
campaign. We had little indeed to show for our efforts, except heavy
losses by land and sea. Yet, had we known, there was one result which,
in the light of coming events, might have cheered our hearts. Our
naval losses were severe, but tolerable. Our general naval superiority
was not reduced; it was enhanced. The effective German fleet had
been reduced to one 8-inch cruiser, eight light cruisers, and four
destroyers. Thus, though some of their major ships could be repaired
in due course, the German Navy was out of action during the vital
summer months, when Hitler, after the conquest of France, was
threatening the invasion of Britain.[4]

When the news came of the German invasion of Norway and the
occupation of Denmark, a wave of anger swept the country. In
Churchill's words, it was obvious that Britain had been forestalled,
surprised and outwitted, in spite of our overwhelmingly superior naval
strength. I well remember the debate on 11 April. It fell to Churchill,
the only Minister in whom many of us had any real confidence, to bear
the brunt of failure. He succeeded in calming the House for the time
being; but he could not dispel the deep underlying anxiety. Churchill's friends felt particularly unhappy, since all our hopes for the
future rested upon him. When a few days later the proposed attack on
Trondheim became known, expectation again rose high. Private Members had little information except from the Press and from our
contacts with Ministers. The Press, as so often, were far too optimistic
and so, to be frank, were some of the Ministers themselves.

When, at the beginning of May, the news of the evacuation of the
Trondheim expedition broke, the first reaction of M.P.s was one of
incredulity. It was followed by a growing sense of indignation. For
myself, and I think for many of my friends, the chief concern was the
probable effect of these disasters on Churchill's position. Many of us
had long reached the view that it was essential for the conduct of the
war to find a new Prime Minister and a new Government. This feeling
was not confined to the House of Commons. At the same time,

[4] Ibid., p. 519.

considerable pressure began to be brought from worried constituents. Even those Conservative Members who had hitherto been most loyal began to waver.

After Churchill's speech of 11 April, I had attended a meeting of Lord Salisbury's 'watching committee'. This comprised peers and M.P.s, representing the most diverse elements in the party. The view was strongly put forward that it was impossible for Churchill to carry out at the same time the duties of First Lord of the Admiralty and chairman of the Military Co-ordination Committee. Lord Salisbury undertook to convey this opinion to the Prime Minister. No doubt it was also reported to Churchill. A happy combination of courtesy and integrity with great experience made Lord Salisbury a deeply respected figure and an admirable chairman of a body representing different points of view. The Prime Minister, no doubt at Churchill's request, agreed with us and himself took the chair of the Military Co-ordination Committee throughout the whole campaign in Norway. The subsequent announcement on 6 May that Churchill was in future to be the sole 'spokesman' of the Services before the Cabinet satisfied nobody. In the first place it was obscure. What did 'spokesman' mean? Was he to be Minister of Defence? What was his authority? What were his powers? In any case, it was too late for the Scandinavian campaign.

After the Trondheim failure became known, pressure increased day by day. My friends and I were suspicious of the obvious desire of the Government's apologists to throw the whole of the responsibility on Churchill. They had at least the certainty that he would never seek to repudiate his full share.

All the dissident groups, especially that which met under Amery's chairmanship, were by now determined on a change of Government. But from my friendship with Churchill and my close contact with Brendan Bracken, it was clear to me that Churchill's loyalty and sense of duty would ensure that he would stand firmly by Chamberlain and urge him to fight on as long as he could command a majority; and so it proved. Nevertheless, since we felt sure that the Government could not last for long, we were increasingly concerned lest Churchill's close involvement with this disastrous campaign should militate against his choice for the supreme position which we knew that he alone could fill in the days that lay ahead.

On 2 May there was a meeting of the all-party group of which

Clement Davies was the chairman, at which it was decided that we would use the two days of the Whitsun adjournment, 7 and 8 May, for a showdown. There was some talk of persuading Attlee, as Leader of the Opposition, to put down a vote of want of confidence. Fortunately, he himself decided against this course. For although the debate was likely to develop, it would be much easier for Conservatives to speak freely, and to vote or abstain, on a motion for the adjournment. These are perhaps small Parliamentary niceties, but they are important. In this case they were probably decisive.

In the days immediately preceding the debate, Admiral of the Fleet Sir Roger Keyes was busy in the lobbies. He was in a state of violent emotion because he regarded the unwillingness of the Navy to force its way into Trondheim harbour as an act of timidity, if not of cowardice. Remembering a similar mistake, as he thought it, in the Dardanelles campaign, he could scarcely contain his anger at this repetition of a fatal blunder. He told me that he meant to speak, and to attend for the purpose in the full uniform of an Admiral of the Fleet. His appearance would certainly be impressive; but since he was a hesitating, not to say almost tongue-tied, orator, I was not sure what the result would be. He did not, however, ask my advice about his costume but about the form of his speech. I urged him to disregard the formal rules of the House and to compose a short speech containing exactly what he wanted to say; to write it out; and to deliver it from the text. This he did, with immense effect.

There have been many accounts of these two historic days—7 and 8 May. Some have been written by participants, some by onlookers. It was certainly a decisive debate, for it altered the history of Britain and the Empire, and perhaps of the world. There have no doubt been greater speeches made in the long history of Parliament, though few of such effect. Normally, at least in recent years, our 'full-dress' Parliamentary debates are in the nature of oratorical or argumentative displays, intended not to sway votes inside the House so much as to influence opinion outside. These are contests of which the immediate result is more or less certain. But on this occasion everything was in flux. The issue would, of course, turn on the votes of Conservative Members. How many would vote against the Government? How many would abstain? What promises or what proposals would be made behind the scenes or on the floor of the Chamber which might influence the event? Who would speak? Even this was not known for certain, except, of course, that Chamberlain would make the opening and Churchill the concluding speech.

I have sometimes heard suggestions that the House of Commons might be persuaded to introduce a system of proxy voting, such as the House of Lords abandoned many years ago. A young Conservative Member recently spoke to me about this, and seemed to favour the idea. I could not help observing that it was a good thing we had not had such a system in 1940, for we might have lost the war. In this debate, at any rate, Members were swayed—whether by argument, or by emotion. If their proxies could have been given to the Whips, the issue—and all that was implied in it—must have been different.

I listened to almost the whole of the two days from my seat high up below the gangway on the Opposition side of the House. These benches had been allocated to the Conservatives because of their large numbers. I found them convenient, whether for speaking or observing. For I was opposite and not behind the row of Ministers. All through the tense and fluctuating discussions, I was consumed by two desires. First, the Government must fall. Secondly, Churchill must emerge as the new Prime Minister. As the debate proceeded, I became more and more certain about the first of my hopes, but less confident about the second. The House was full throughout the two days, except for short periods when some dull speaker gave us an opportunity to resort to the lobbies or the smoking-room to compare notes and impressions. The Prime Minister opened. Some thought he would announce the formation of a Coalition Government; but most of us were clear that the Labour Party would not serve with the majority of his present colleagues and probably not acquiesce in his continuing leadership. But he contented himself with a factual account of recent events. He was rudely and unfairly interrupted, in a manner that was distressing and unworthy of a great occasion. There were continual cries of 'Who missed the bus?' Chamberlain's speech, which in form was logical and clear, did not rise to the greatness of the occasion. Perhaps the most important point which emerged was that Churchill's new position, briefly announced the day before, did, in effect, provide him with a Chief of Staff (General Ismay), a small staff of his own, and the power to give 'guidance and direction' to the Chiefs of Staff. Lloyd George immediately asked if he would remain in charge of the Admiralty as well as undertake these new duties. The reply was that it would depend upon Churchill's own wish. This seemed a very happy-go-lucky way of constructing a new machine for the direction of war. Besides, there were enough survivors of the First World War or active participants in the Second among Members of Parliament for the notion to seem absurd that a general could at the same time command a corps and a division. However, one thing had become clear. Churchill had not been directly responsible for the Norway operations except as First Lord and, collectively, a member of the War Cabinet and Military Co-ordination Committee. This gave his friends some relief.

Nevertheless, in spite of its failure to rise to the level of events, Chamberlain's speech was not unskilful. He tried to lower the temperature, and to some extent succeeded. But if he allayed some apprehensions, he raised no enthusiasm. He referred obscurely to the possibility of changes in the character and structure of the Government, but had nothing positive to announce. The leaders of the Opposition parties, Attlee and Sinclair, followed on expected lines. If they said little calculated to attract hesitating Conservatives, they said nothing likely to repel them. But there were two speeches delivered that day which helped to make history. Keyes excited the House with his attack on the Admiralty and his claim to be speaking for the fighting and 'sea-going' Navy. Whether the decision not to force our way in Trondheim Fiord was right or wrong, this speech revealed what Members already suspected—an alarming absence of fixity of purpose and of co-operation within the Services.

If the Admiral's speech was moving because of its simplicity and sincerity, Amery's speech was the most formidable philippic which I have ever heard delivered by a former Minister against a lifelong friend and colleague. For Amery's whole political career had been centred on Birmingham and the Chamberlain tradition was in his blood. His hero had been 'Joe'—the great Radical-Reformer and Imperialist, who commanded, in his prime, a passionate loyalty from his devoted disciples. Like Austen and Neville Chamberlain, Amery had held for over a quarter of a century a Birmingham seat. All these men had sat in Governments together. If Amery had been excluded in 1931 (when the MacDonald–Baldwin Government was formed), he had seemed to bear no rancour. On the great India controversy he had given valuable help to the Government. On other matters he had often been a critic—but a constructive critic.

It is one of the mysteries of politics why Amery did not ordinarily command a greater authority and reach a higher, perhaps the highest, position. Hard-working, well informed, a ripe scholar, imaginative and passionately sincere, he had a far better grasp of world affairs than all the Hoares and the Simons put together. He also had what many lacked—courage, physical and moral. He knew the Empire intimately and was on terms of close friendship with the leading Imperial statesmen. He had travelled exhaustively in Europe, and had friends in every country. He had a grasp of the fundamentals of great problems which few of his colleagues could boast. He was small in stature, but combative and persistent, like a well-trained terrier. He was, at this time, well liked in all parts of the House; his advanced views on social welfare and his progressive ideas had especially attracted many Labour Members. In his own party both the Right and the Left wings admired him. By the speech he was to make on this day, 7 May 1940, he effectively destroyed the Chamberlain Government. This is no exaggeration. In the course of the two days there were many contributory elements to the final issue. But it was Amery's speech—logical, powerful, unanswerable, with one blow after another mercilessly delivered—that seemed to me decisive. Point after point was hammered home, with ruthless iteration and almost ferocity. Thus, when the peroration came, it did not seem forced or exaggerated, but inevitable. With rare skill, Amery put into the frame of a quotation the thought that was forming in every listener's mind. What Cromwell had said to the Long Parliament, this Parliament and the whole nation wanted to say to a succession of mediocrities:

You have sat too long here for any good you have been doing. Depart, I say, and let us have done with you. In the name of God, go!

Leo Amery's speech marked the culmination of his career. There was some talk, in the hectic days that followed, that he might be the most acceptable successor to Chamberlain. Halifax was tarred with the Munich brush, at least to some extent. The Socialists still distrusted Churchill, as did many of the Conservatives. Amery had been out of office since 1929 and so had, like Churchill, a clean record. If Amery heard of these rumours—as he tells us he did[5]—he showed no sign of disappointment or discouragement when the final choice was made. He no doubt would have liked a place in the War Cabinet and to have

[5] Amery, *The Unforgiving Years, 1929–1940*, p. 370.

been intimately connected with the conduct of the war. Nevertheless, he accepted the India Office without hesitation and carried out his work, which became more and more arduous as Japanese aggression approached the subcontinent, with quiet efficiency. It was the end of a long political life in which he might reasonably have hoped for even greater distinction. But Amery was a sincere and selfless patriot, gifted with the courage to meet public disappointments and private sorrows with equal dignity.

When Members met together, in the smoking-room and the lobbies, or adjourned to the clubs, there was little difference of opinion about the course of the first day's debate. Supporters of the Government could minimise the Admiral's speech as irrelevant and theatrical, but no one could deny or underrate the extraordinary speech which Amery had delivered, far beyond his usual form. For he was often prolix or monotonous, with a curious sing-song, parsonical intonation. Tonight there had been clarity; indignation; anger; but all clothed in simple and compelling language. On the Government side there was one speech delivered that day which had moved the House. Arnold Wilson had joined the Air Force, in spite of his age—he was fifty-five—as a rear-gunner. He was a man of distinction and achievement, at home and abroad. He had always been a sincere 'Chamberlainite'. He appealed to the fairness and generosity of his fellow Members, in words which, if not very persuasive, were simple and honourable. He was soon to be killed in action and I felt that he knew it would be so. Apart from this, no real defence had been forthcoming. Oliver Stanley, Secretary of State for War, 'wound up' for the Government. But his witticisms, usually agreeable to the House, did not suit the mood of his audience and fell flat.

It was apparent that night that even the strongest supporters of the Government were doubtful of its survival. But how was the change to come about? Would there be a division? On the motion to adjourn for Whitsun, this was unusual. My own contacts with Clement Davies made me sure that there would somehow be a division. It would be folly for the Opposition to miss the chance—unless, perhaps, they shrank from the responsibility—of success. But, in reality, it was touch and go. Even the usually militant Hugh Dalton was doubtful, fearing no doubt that a vote would tend to consolidate the usual Conservative supporters and rally them to the Government.

Dalton, with whom I was on good terms, especially since the Munich crisis, told me that the Labour executive would meet in the morning to decide what course to recommend to their party. I reported this to the Salisbury group, which also met during the morning of 8 May. Just before luncheon we heard that the Opposition had decided to demand a vote.[6] Before this was actually known, Lord Salisbury had expressed the view that Conservative critics should abstain in the event of a vote. But most Members were beginning to feel that this was too weak a protest. Amery's words were ringing in our ears. Meanwhile the Whips, as was their duty, had been hard at work. Apart from the normal methods of appeal or persuasion, a new approach was made by the Prime Minister's closest adherents. Before the debate was resumed, individual members of the dissident groups were approached and told that if they would vote for the Government in the division, the Prime Minister would see them the next day and discuss their requirements in a generous spirit. A drastic reconstruction of the Government was indicated. Naturally, those to whom this offer was made let their friends know of this development, but most of us thought it was too late. The Government could have been reconstructed at the beginning of the war, or at Christmas. Simon, Hoare and all that lot must go. Sir Horace Wilson must disappear from Downing Street. The Prime Minister did not seem to realise the depth of feeling which had been stirred, or the growing belief that he was unfitted to be head of a Government in war-time.

Our chief anxiety concerned Churchill. We knew he had determined to stand loyally by his colleagues and would close the debate as the spokesman for the Government. We were determined to bring down the Government, and as every hour passed, we seemed more likely to achieve our purpose. But how could Churchill be disentangled from the ruins? If the chief issue of the first day had been the overthrow of the Government, the chief anxiety of the second was the rescue of Churchill. The first had virtually been achieved by Amery. To the second several speakers were to make their contribution. Herbert Morrison's speech was chiefly notable for his announcement that the Opposition intended to demand a division. He asked for a

---

[6] A small majority on the executive took this view, which was endorsed by the Parliamentary Party: Hugh Dalton, *Memoirs: The Fateful Years, 1931–1945* (London, 1957), p. 305.

vote which should 'represent the spirit of the country'. At this, Chamberlain, who had already made his opening speech, was led to make a most unlucky intervention:

I say to my friends, and I have friends in the House . . . I accept the challenge. I welcome it indeed. At least we shall see who is with us and who is against us, and I call on my friends to support us in the lobby tonight.

These were unfortunate phrases, and seemed to treat a national crisis as a party or even a personal issue. Subsequent speakers did not fail to exploit the mistake.

Nevertheless, Morrison, in spite of his general strictures on the Government, had tried to spare Churchill. Similarly Duff Cooper, who had resigned from the Cabinet at the time of Munich and now announced his intention of voting against the Government, recalled past issues as well as the present crisis:

Tonight, we shall no doubt listen to an eloquent and powerful speech by the First Lord. . . . I almost wish it was going to be delivered from the now empty seat which he used to occupy below the gangway. He will be defending with his eloquence those who long refused to listen to his counsel, who treated his warnings with contempt. He will, no doubt, be as successful as he has always been, and those who so often trembled before his sword will be only too glad to shrink behind his buckler.

But it was Lloyd George who made the strongest effort to protect Churchill from the impending disaster. He had already, on the previous day, elicited the fact that Churchill had not been appointed to his new position of a sort of embryo Minister of Defence until after the end of the Norwegian campaign. When, in his speech on the second day, Lloyd George suggested that Churchill was not to blame for all the recent disasters, Churchill at once rose to accept full responsibility, 'I take my full share of the burden,' he declared, not without heat. But Lloyd George answered with a sally which reduced the whole House to laughter:

The Rt. Hon. Gentleman must not allow himself to be converted into an air-raid shelter to keep the splinters from hitting his colleagues.

Although Lloyd George's speech contained, as usual, some gems, such as 'Hitler does not hold himself answerable to the Whips or to the Patronage Secretary', yet I felt his final attack was too bitter. He revived the sympathy which many Members were beginning to feel for Chamberlain, suffering from such a series of blows.

He has appealed for sacrifice. The nation is prepared for every sacrifice, so long as it has leadership. . . . I say solemnly that the Prime Minister should give an example of sacrifice, because there is nothing that can contribute more to victory in this war than that he should sacrifice the seals of office.

These were cruel words. Moreover, as Amery records,[7] they struck a false note. Curiously enough, Lloyd George had been with difficulty persuaded to speak. It was only after Chamberlain's acceptance of the Opposition challenge on the second day that he made up his mind. He can have had little time to prepare; but his speech was one of the most powerful which he had delivered for many years. It was to be almost his last.

During the evening I saw Churchill in the smoking-room. He beckoned to me, and I moved to speak to him. I wished him luck, but added that I hoped his speech would not be too convincing. 'Why not?' he asked. 'Because', I replied, 'we must have a new Prime Minister, and it must be you.' He answered gruffly that he had signed on for the voyage and would stick to the ship. But I don't think he was angry with me.

At 9 p.m., in one of the upstairs committee-rooms, the decisive meeting took place. The Conservative critics met under the chairmanship of Amery. Another group, consisting of thirty or forty Members, under the leadership of Herbert Williams, had, we were told, decided to hold their hand, in view of the offer of a reconstruction of the Government. But we unanimously agreed to vote—and to vote against the motion. So the die was cast. All we had now to do was to listen to Churchill and pray that he might at least emerge from this ordeal unscathed.

His speech was confined almost wholly to the facts of the Norwegian campaign. He was much interrupted, but was not disturbed by this; indeed, I thought he welcomed it. But there was nothing he could do except to carry out his duty loyally. He did not attempt to excuse, but was content to explain. By now it was clear that all those operations by sea and land had suffered from our inferiority in air power. Nobody, in any event, could blame Churchill for this, since in

7 Amery, p. 367.

the years before the war he had pleaded for rearmament in the air, in season and out of season.

He ended with an appeal for unity. This was not the time, he said, to take so grave a decision as to refuse confidence to the Government that was conducting the war:

Let pre-war feuds die; let personal quarrels be forgotten; let us keep our hatreds for the common enemy.

These words certainly expressed his deepest sentiments, both then and throughout the war.

The division was the most tense that I have ever known. There can have been nothing like it since the division on the second reading of the Home Rule Bill in 1886. But that was an internal crisis. Now it was the whole future of Britain and the Empire which was at stake. When the Whips marched in with David Margesson on the right, we knew that the Government had won. But by how much? The Chief Whip read out the figures, in an even voice. Ayes 281, Noes 200. The House was staggered—for the normal majority was 240 or more. Now it was only 80-odd. The Opposition cried 'Resign!'; the loyal Government supporters sat dazed, though they raised a cheer as the Prime Minister left. 'Josh' Wedgwood (a stalwart if somewhat eccentric Labour Member, with a fine record of gallantry in the First World War) started singing 'Rule Britannia'. I tried to join in. But as neither of us could sing, it was not a very successful effort.

As the evening wore on, and Members collected in the smoking-room, the news was put round that Chamberlain had been persuaded to continue in office. Indeed, I soon heard that this was Churchill's advice. But the next day the figures were analysed. Forty-three Conservatives had voted against the Government. Eighty or more had abstained, or were absent unpaired. It was surely now clear that a new head of a new and truly National Government could alone meet the nation's need.

On the day following the great debate (9 May) events moved quickly. In the morning, before the House re-assembled, the all-party group met, with Clement Davies in the chair. Many new adherents attended. A resolution was passed by a large majority in favour of a new Government comprising all three political parties. In the afternoon those Conservative Members who had voted against the Government met under Amery. The chairman tried to restrict the discussion to principles and avoid personalities. But it was not possible to prevent some of us from expressing our views on this vital question. I spoke out strongly against Halifax, who was being canvassed as the next Prime Minister, and in favour of Churchill. I had made the same plea at a meeting of Lord Salisbury's committee earlier in the day. Naturally the Whips and the Prime Minister were fully informed of all these proceedings. Indeed, Amery's group issued a statement to the Press declaring the general view—that we would support a truly National Government, chosen by merit, under whatever leader carried the greatest support.

Rumour was rife. Some said that Chamberlain would stay. Others declared that Halifax would succeed him. Others again believed that nothing could resist Churchill's claims. It was thought that the Labour chiefs leaned towards Halifax. Churchill's long and active career had brought him many enemies as well as devoted friends. Halifax was a more neutral figure. Chamberlain too undoubtedly preferred Halifax. But the decisive meeting, although we did not know it, took place that afternoon. Churchill and Halifax's biographer have described it in full, although Churchill implies that it took place on the morning of 10 May, whereas there can be no doubt that it took place in the afternoon of the 9th. Chamberlain, Halifax and Churchill met in the Cabinet room. When the vital question was put, Churchill's silence— rare for him, as he observes—settled the matter. In any event, the tremendous drama in Europe which was now to be unfolded must have made Churchill's succession inevitable. If Halifax had hesitated on the 9th, he must have known the next day that, with all his qualities, he was no man to ride the storm which was now to blow at hurricane force.

I remember late on the night of 9 May meeting Brendan Bracken. He was guarded in what he said; but he seemed happy and assured me that I could be happy too. On the next day (10 May) came the staggering news of Hitler's invasion of Holland and Belgium. Chamberlain's first reaction was that it was his duty to stay at the helm. All the confusion of a change of Government must surely be avoided. But he was soon dissuaded, and by the end of the morning it was clear that a National Government must be formed and that it could only be formed under a new Prime Minister. Attlee and Arthur Greenwood induced their executive to take a decision to join, to be later confirmed by the Labour Party in full conference. They had favoured Halifax, but would accept Churchill. At 6 p.m. that evening, Churchill saw the King and accepted his commission. He was to hold it for five tremendous years.

After the emotions of the two days' debate and the various private discussions and meetings on the next day, to be followed by the momentous news that burst on the world the morning of 10 May, we were all too exhausted to do more than wait. The House had adjourned, but the clubs were full. I did my best to do my own work in the office, but it was hard to remain calm; furthermore, Brendan Bracken telephoned me from time to time. On the morning of the 10th he was furious at Chamberlain's attempt to stay on. 'It's like trying to get a limpet off a corpse,' he declared, with a mixture of metaphor that in no way obscured his indignation. But it was a momentary hitch. At last, we had Churchill.

There was one final difficulty. Churchill, with characteristic magnanimity, had offered Chamberlain the Leadership of the House and the post of Chancellor of the Exchequer. No doubt he also wished to ensure the support of the Conservative Party, a large part of which was devoted to Chamberlain and had been staggered by his fall. But the Labour leaders, when they heard Chamberlain announce this appointment in his farewell broadcast on the night of 10 May, would have none of it. Great pressure was brought on Churchill and a serious crisis seemed to threaten. Unhappily, in the need for speed or for some other reason, Churchill had not informed his new Labour colleagues of his determination to retain Chamberlain in these high posts and as a member of his War Cabinet.

Our Conservative group was equally incensed. Finally, Lord Salisbury intervened and advised Churchill to alter his plan. It was agreed that Chamberlain should become Lord President instead of Chancellor of the Exchequer, remaining in the War Cabinet. Churchill would himself lead the House, with Attlee as his deputy.

So the new Government began to be formed. The names of the leading Ministers were announced on 11 May, and the rest followed in the course of the next few days. It proved indeed to be a broadly based administration, ranging, in Churchill's words, from Lord Lloyd of Dolobran on the Right to Miss Ellen Wilkinson ('Red Ellen') on the

Left. On the commemoration medal which he gave at the end of the war to all his colleagues who had served under him at any time in the five years, he called it 'the Great Coalition'. Nor was the claim unjustified.

The new Prime Minister sent for me in the course of the next day or two and offered me a place in this proud company. I was to go to the Ministry of Supply, as Parliamentary Secretary to Herbert Morrison, the new Minister. Would that be agreeable to me? It would indeed; and so it was decided.

Thus came to an end for me, after some sixteen years, the carefree although sometimes frustrating irresponsibility of the back-benches. It was not until twenty-four years later, of which all but the last few months were spent in office or on the Opposition Front Bench, that I was to leave the House of Commons. Forty years is enough.

CHAPTER FIVE

Arming the Nation

AT the very moment that Churchill was forming his administration, the German tide was rolling through the Low Countries into northern France. Within a few weeks, the British and French armies were separated and driven back. Although, by what seemed almost a miracle, the greater part of the British Expeditionary Force (over 300,000 men in all) was withdrawn across the beaches of Dunkirk to form the nucleus of a new army and to fight again, practically the whole of their equipment was lost. By mid-June the French armies were facing defeat, and before the month was out were forced to accept a capitulation, more complete and more humiliating even than that of 1870. Britain and the countries of the Empire, which had rallied to her aid, thus faced a triumphant Nazi Germany, now joined by Fascist Italy which, with characteristic prudence, only entered into the fray when Mussolini believed the fighting to be over. For over a year, Britain and the Empire stood alone. In August and September 1940, the battle for the mastery of the air was fought out over our island. Repulsed by the skill and devotion of the R.A.F., the Nazis postponed their plans to invade Britain. The indiscriminate bombing of British cities and ports followed, and grew in intensity throughout the autumn and winter until the early summer of 1941. On the seas, the Royal Navy began slowly to master the first attack of the U-boats, which had threatened to cut off our lifelines, only to face a renewed onslaught in the winter and spring of 1942–43: the Battle of the Atlantic.

With almost all Europe in Hitler's hands, it was only in Africa that British armies were engaged. Here, General Wavell, fortified by the daring dispatch of tanks from a beleaguered and threatened Britain, drove back the Italian forces at the end of 1940 and in the early months of 1941. These successes and our naval victories over the Italians at Taranto and Matapan gave us some gleams of hope in a hard winter. The United States showed the same determination to keep out of war as it had done a generation ago; yet the legal barriers to our import of war material were relaxed or ignored. As our funds began to run out, the import programme became more and more uncertain until sustained by the institution of Lend-Lease in the spring of 1941. All this time Russia was still delivering munitions and raw materials to Germany. In October 1940, the Italians invaded Greece. The Greek armies put up so gallant a resistance that in April 1941 Hitler had to come to the help of his confederate, Mussolini. British forces, at great risk, were sent to help the Greeks. But they could not withstand the German pressure and had to be withdrawn, first from the mainland and finally, in early June, from the island of Crete. In these fierce struggles, heavy losses were suffered on both sides.

About the same time, a British offensive in the Western Desert failed. The Germans, under Rommel, had now taken charge, with powerful armour and air support from African and Sicilian bases. General Wavell had been replaced by General Auchinleck. On 22 June 1941, Hitler launched his onslaught against Russia. Churchill, intent only on the destruction of Nazism, immediately announced that we should give the Soviets all possible aid. Thus, after a year of isolation, Britain had at last an ally.

On 7 December 1941, the Japanese attacked the United States fleet in Pearl Harbour. Simultaneously, they descended upon Malaya. Two months later, Singapore, with some 85,000 British and Commonwealth troops, was forced to surrender. The Japanese seized and held for some time the mastery of the Pacific. Germany declared war on America. Thus from the beginning of 1942 we knew that the issue was certain. However long and bitter the struggle, the resources of the British Empire, Russia and the United States must in the end overwhelm Germany, Italy and Japan.

The results of America's involvement took time to develop. Meanwhile, the hazards of war in North Africa turned once more against us. The partial success of Auchinleck's offensive at the end of 1941 was reversed six months later. In June 1942, Tobruk, with some 35,000 British and Imperial forces, went the way of Singapore. By July, Rommel was at the gates of Egypt. Confident of the victory of the Axis, Mussolini arrived in North Africa equipped with a white charger for his ceremonial entry into Cairo.

These events marked the lowest point in our fortunes and put the greatest strain upon our morale. In the first year, when we stood alone, we had been sustained by a sense of exhilaration and spiritual exultation. It was our proudest hour. But as the months dragged on, even after the entry of Russia and America into the war, everything still seemed to go against us. It needed stout hearts to resist some degree of 'alarm and despondency'. Yet within a few months the picture was to be reversed. Rommel's advance was halted by the first battle of Alamein. In the second battle of Alamein, in October 1942, Generals Alexander and Montgomery won an outstanding victory. Their armies were soon moving steadily westwards, in pursuit of the enemy. This, as Churchill records, marked the turning of the hinge of fate. It might almost be said, 'Before Alamein we never had a victory; after Alamein we never had a defeat.'

At the western end of the Mediterranean, an Anglo-American force under General Eisenhower landed in Morocco and Algeria on 8 November 1942, and was to press on slowly but surely to meet the British Army advancing from the east.

By the end of 1942, therefore, the first phase was over. Hitler had failed to subjugate Russia. British war production, after all the initial difficulties, had reached its highest rate of efficiency in organisation and output. The great resources of the United States were at last harnessed to the cause.

It was against this tremendous background of events that for two and a half years I lived and worked as an Under-Secretary in Churchill's great Coalition, a small cog in the most powerful machine of government that has operated in our history. For the greater part of this time—some twenty months in all—I served in the Ministry of Supply, which was the hub of the vast mechanism of armament production.

At the Ministry of Supply, I served three Ministers. It was a remarkable experience, for they were men of very diverse backgrounds and qualities. The first was Herbert Morrison, the second Sir Andrew Duncan, and the third Lord Beaverbrook. They all treated me with real kindness. But I used to say that with one a Cockney, another a Lowland Scot and the third a Canadian, I never heard a word of English spoken correctly from the Minister's chair. Their working habits were significant. Morrison started work not too early, but went on fairly late. Duncan started very early, but left off at a reasonable time. Beaverbrook worked all round the clock—but preferred, on the whole, night to day. Morrison and Duncan were typical of the homes from which they sprang. Beaverbrook was a unique phenomenon, *sui generis*.

Morrison had all the characteristics of the Cockney. He was tough, imaginative and resilient. He seemed a little dazed at first by the range of his new responsibilities. As he has written himself, 'Supply was hardly a post to run after.'[1] Nor was it altogether suited to his special qualities or experience. I doubted if he really understood the problems which confronted us, for he had no practical knowledge of business or production, or of the management of labour. However, he set about his task with vigour and courage. As an administrator, Morrison was diligent and open-minded. In addition, he was always fair and consequently trusted by those who served him. His chief contribution during his short period was to bring in Sir George Gater to help Sir Arthur Robinson, the original Permanent Secretary, one of the great figures of Whitehall but now an ageing man. He also gave loyal support to the officers charged with the main production departments. But he was really out of his depth, and was not unwilling to move.

Morrison gave me my first lessons in the art of publicity, which was quite new to me. The most important person in his private office appeared to be the Public Relations Officer, a figure of whom up till then I had never heard. Ours was a very intelligent man called Samuel Leslie, who had helped Morrison at the London County Council and was to move with him from post to post. I did my best to second his efforts to keep our Minister in the lead, for he was subject to a good deal of cross-fire between Ernest Bevin, the powerful Minister of Labour, and Beaverbrook, the somewhat anarchic head of the newly-formed Ministry of Aircraft Production. I remember in the first few days going with Morrison to a large assembly of the Press who had been hurriedly collected in a neighbouring theatre. Morrison made them an admirable speech, full of encouragement and enthusiasm, and it was here that he launched his famous slogan—'Go To It'. This was later to be followed by its sequel—'Keep At It'. (Cynics afterwards observed that a more appropriate motto for our Ministry might have been 'Get Away With It'.) He gave his audience nothing very tangible

[1] Lord Morrison of Lambeth, *Herbert Morrison: An Autobiography* (London, 1960), p. 178.

but left them with an impression of urgency and determination, which was useful.

At the beginning of October 1940, following Neville Chamberlain's resignation through serious illness, Churchill made some important changes in his Cabinet. These involved the transfer of our Minister, Herbert Morrison, from Supply to the Home Office, now renamed the Ministry of Home Security. For this post his talents and experience were eminently suited. His knowledge of London, like Mr. Samuel Weller's, was 'extensive and peculiar'. His work at the London County Council had familiarised him with the people and institutions of the great city of which he was proud to be a native. His gifts for administration found full room for their exercise in his new office. He created the National Fire Service; organised the fire-watchers; introduced a new form of shelter; and by these and similar methods did much to maintain the morale of the population. Herbert Morrison was a very endearing chief, and we had grown fond of each other. In later years, these feelings were never weakened or distorted by political controversy. I was very happy to be the means of his moving, at the end of a long and distinguished career in the House of Commons, to the calmer atmosphere of the Second Chamber.

Morrison was succeeded by Sir Andrew Duncan, a man of a very different temperament. Duncan was a typical Lowland Scot—cautious, diligent, orderly, unimaginative, but efficient. I was to work with him until June of the following year, and I learned to admire his good judgement and his grasp of detail. Duncan had not long been a Member of the House of Commons, but he quickly learned its moods. He took infinite trouble in seeing Members and listening to their complaints. Thus, if he were not always able to satisfy their requests, at least he left them with a sense that they had been fully consulted. During the latter part of his administration of Supply, criticisms against the Ministry were growing in strength and diversity. Although many were wide of the mark, some, especially where directed against the failure of our tank production to meet the Army's needs, were not altogether undeserved.

In June 1941, Duncan went to the Board of Trade. Great was the emotion at the Ministry when we heard he was to be succeeded by 'the Beaver'. Until the war, I had hardly known Lord Beaverbrook except

for certain contacts in 1930,[2] but this acquaintance, for it was little
more, had never developed. For the next seven months I was to be his
Parliamentary Under-Secretary; his sole representative in the House of
Commons; and closely associated with his most important tasks. Certainly Beaverbrook's appointment caused anxiety and some concern
among the leading officials of the Ministry. Yet combined with this was
a touch of pleasurable excitement, and even ironical satisfaction. We
had so long suffered from—or at least complained about—the raids
which the Ministry of Aircraft Production had made upon us under
his leadership that it seemed a happy twist of destiny's wheel by which
we should now become the beneficiaries of his independent and
unconventional methods.

His first action was typical. He took a great dislike to the offices
which we occupied and from which we overflowed all over London.
Our buildings, although new, were dismal. Next door to us was
'Naboth's vineyard', Shell-Mex House, modern and well appointed,
with everything that was required for the Minister's comfort and our
own, including a balcony where Beaverbrook could indulge his passion for sunbathing. Part of it was occupied by the Iron and Steel
Control, and after a short and sharp engagement it was decided to
leave them or rather to degrade them to the basement. But the rest of
the building we quickly occupied, consolidated and defended. Nor did
we relinquish our hold upon our previous quarters. All this was done
with a speed and a ruthlessness which commanded, if not the approval, at least the admiration of us all. Then began to flow in the
Minister's private office and personal supporters. Noted industrialists
were introduced, some of whom had served the Minister in his
previous department. There was a general sense of bustle, excitement
and even confusion.

Much has been written about Beaverbrook's life as a journalist and
as a politician. He rightly has his place in almost every book of
memoirs and history covering the years of his long, active and strange
career. I felt instinctively that he was a man whom it was wise to treat
with a certain aloofness, for there were aspects of his character which I
found distasteful. He had a streak of vindictiveness and even cruelty.
But he was equally capable of extraordinary kindness, and often his
kind actions were towards those from whom he could gain no personal

[2] *Winds of Change*, p. 240.

advantage and who could never repay him in any form. His charm could be, if he chose to exert it, almost irresistible. All men, I suppose, have in their moral make-up good and evil. Yet most of us are, to be frank, of a somewhat indeterminate nature. Beaverbrook sometimes seemed almost a Jekyll and Hyde. Some saw only the evil in him; others saw only the good.

To exchange the position of a private Member of Parliament for that of a Minister, even of the second rank, involves a great psychological readjustment. As a back-bencher, one is an observer of all events and developments in every part of a wide field, mixing in the clubs and the lobbies with friends and gossips, and uninhibited by any specific responsibilities. But a junior Minister, especially in a highly technical department, suddenly finds himself cut off from all his normal interests, with scarcely time to find out what is going on, and concentrating upon the detailed work that is allotted to him day by day. This, of course, is doubly true in war-time; for we soon settled down to a régime of almost intolerably long hours without holidays, and with little social intercourse. A Cabinet Minister, of course, receives the official telegrams and memoranda, and whether in the War Cabinet or not, would at this period be tolerably informed of what was taking place in the military campaigns and the outside world. But junior Ministers were not shown these except where they affected their departments. I found myself, as the days passed, more and more immersed in the complexities of my work, and with fewer and fewer contacts outside the Ministry.

Hence we junior Ministers much welcomed the opportunity for meeting friends and exchanging news which attendance at Westminster afforded. But, except on notable occasions—such as those when Churchill was to deliver one of his great speeches—I went little. Many of the Parliamentary questions in the House of Commons were answered by the Minister. It was only in June 1941, when Duncan was succeeded by Beaverbrook, that this duty fell exclusively to me. Sometimes, however, inter-departmental committees, in which I represented my chief, made a pleasant change from the narrow circle of the Ministry. The first of these to which I was sent remains vividly in my mind. We were not vitally interested in the agenda, but I had nevertheless carefully studied my brief. I was anxious to do well and explained my concern to our Second Secretary, Sir William Palmer.

He gave me admirable counsel, which I have never forgotten. 'Don't on any account say anything,' he advised, 'or you might start a hare.' Volumes could not say more.

It took me, I must admit, some little time to learn my way about the Ministry—to grasp the full picture of what we were trying to do, and unravel the complexity of the instrument with which we had been provided. The Ministry of Supply had come into being only after a long political struggle. The agitation for its formation had begun in great debates in 1936, with Churchill one of the chief protagonists. It was not until three years later, after many hesitations, that the Government had yielded. At the end of April 1939, after the final collapse of the policy of appeasement, the necessary legislation was introduced. As a result of this long delay, the first Minister—Leslie Burgin—was not chosen till July, and the new office could not be organised until a few weeks before the outbreak of war. The department had, therefore, hardly time to settle down in its new form before the end of the 'Twilight War' and Hitler's onslaught on Western Europe.

The structure and functions of the Ministry had been based on pragmatic considerations rather than any logical or symmetrical plan. The Admiralty continued to control directly the greater part of its own production. The Air Ministry, and subsequently the Ministry of Aircraft Production, were responsible for the manufacture of aeroplanes. The Ministry of Supply, therefore, like the Ministry of Munitions in the First World War, was, as a producing agent and as far as concerned the chief items of weapon manufacture, mainly responsible for the needs of the Army. Nevertheless, in addition we had the duty of providing some of the most vital groups of weapons and ammunition for all three Services. These were anti-aircraft guns, automatic guns of all calibres, and rifles. Apart from the guns, the small-arms ammunition for the Air Force involved a large number of specialised types of great complexity and was a constant source of anxiety. However, in spite of these important inter-Service requirements, it was the Army which, broadly speaking, was our chief customer, and it was upon War Office departments and traditions that the Ministry had been founded.

Whereas the Navy had had its own long-established relations with specialised firms, in addition to the Royal Dockyards, and the needs of the Air Force had been to a considerable extent foreseen by Lord Swinton, during his pre-war period as Air Minister, with the 'shadow factory' plan, the Army had been until recently the Cinderella in the rearmament pantomime. When Hitler's aggressive policies could no longer be obscured, decisions were taken to step up the size, and therefore the needs, of the Army at a phenomenal and indeed quite unrealistic rate. In March 1939, the Army Estimates contemplated six Regular divisions, of which two would be armoured, and thirteen Territorial divisions. In April it was decided to double the Territorial divisions, making thirty-two in all. In September, soon after the outbreak of war, the Cabinet accepted fifty-five divisions as the target. However long it might take to raise and train the men, to provide modern weapons on this scale from the resources available was indeed a formidable task. Nor was there any firm foundation on which to build. For in the earlier years, both the Army and munitions production had fallen to very low dimensions. The March Estimates—nineteen divisions—were thought to be almost unattainable. What about fifty-five?

For many reasons, partly because the private manufacture of arms was so frowned upon in many political quarters in the period between the wars, the modest requirements of the Army were provided for, at any rate so far as sophisticated weapons were concerned, from two main sources. First, the Royal Ordnance Factories; secondly, a number of firms, of which Vickers, B.S.A., I.C.I. and a few others were the chief. The structure, therefore, of the Ministry had to be cast in a form suited to the facts. The Royal Ordnance Factories, as they grew to formidable dimensions, began to rely largely on private enterprise to manage their extensions, especially in the filling factories. Yet they remained responsible in one way or another for a high proportion of the whole output, even at its peak. By the end of the war there were forty-three Royal Ordnance Factories, employing over 300,000 people —20 per cent of the estimated total number of hands employed on Ministry of Supply contracts.[3] In addition, from 1940 onwards agency factories were begun on the same basis as in the First World War, in which the buildings, plant and machinery were supplied by the Government, and private firms were invited to operate them on a fee

[3] M. M. Postan, *British War Production* (London, 1952), p. 424.

basis. By March 1945, this had reached considerable dimensions.[4] Guns, of larger or smaller calibre, constituted only a small part of the whole. In addition to Vickers and I.C.I., a number of private firms, some of long standing, held substantial contracts for the production of explosives and small-arms ammunition.

Yet broadly speaking, the problem that presented itself was how the enormously increased demands which had been placed upon the Ministry in recent months, soon to be aggravated by the losses in France, could be met from existing resources or from the field in which contracts had up to now been placed. The problem was even more difficult than that which Lloyd George had had to face. During the long siege warfare of the First World War, guns and, above all, shells were the main requirement. These were eventually produced in large numbers by mass-production methods. Now we had to provide an ever-increasing variety of highly complicated weapons as science became more and more harnessed to the needs of ever-changing techniques. There was only one way. It was necessary to expand the list of main contractors for articles which they were capable of handling, or could be taught to undertake. It was of equal importance to devise and supervise a prodigious development of sub-contractors and sub-sub-contractors to make parts and components even for sophisticated final products. Now began the search for capacity, the adaptation of tools, the obtaining and training of labour, as well as novel arrangements for its care and comfort.

All this time we looked anxiously across the Atlantic for help. In the weeks just before the fall of France, the future of the large contracts for materials and munitions which had been placed in America by the French Government began to be discussed in Whitehall. Since these mainly affected our department, Morrison asked me to handle them on his behalf. In the next few days a plan was made for the transfer to British account of these important items. This was the first occasion on which I met Jean Monnet. Later in the war I was to see a great deal of him, when he came to Algiers. Monnet was already a whole-hearted 'European' and has since proved one of the ablest exponents of the European concept. He has remained a devoted friend of Britain.

Still larger questions of American supplies soon began to require

[4] At that date the Ministry of Supply had 159 agency factories, the Ministry of Aircraft Production 87, the Admiralty 19:ibid., p. 434.

our attention. In the early months of the war substantial orders had been placed in the United States by the Ministry on what was called the 'cash and carry' basis. Before the outbreak of war, the Neutrality Act required the President to place an embargo on the shipments of arms to any of the belligerent nations. An embargo which sounds fair and unbiased in principle can prove anything but impartial in its application in practice. This had proved to be so with the embargo on arms to Abyssinia in 1935.[5] For while the aggressor is fully prepared, the victim of aggression is likely to be in a state almost of nakedness. Moreover, the strict enforcement of the embargo would have nullified Britain's command of the sea. The ban was finally removed at the end of November 1939 and munitions of war could be obtained on a strictly cash basis. But 'cash and carry' meant what it said; and by the autumn of 1940 it was becoming clear that the pressure on our dollar reserves would soon become intolerable. So far, we had paid for everything which we had received. But there were very heavy commitments ahead, and we wanted to place further orders. We had already paid or committed over $4,500 million in cash; we had only $2,000 million left, the greater part in investments, of which some were marketable and some could only be sold at give-away prices.[6]

In this predicament, which seriously threatened our capacity to carry on the war against Germany, the understanding and sympathy between Roosevelt and Churchill saved the situation. The President devised the Lend-Lease plan, which he was finally able to carry through Congress by March 1941. From this moment we knew that shortage of dollars would not prevent us from maintaining our struggle, even alone. Although in 1941 we still had to pay cash for nearly everything we obtained from past orders, for those placed under the new system, no money would pass.

Churchill rightly called Lend-Lease 'the most unsordid act in the history of any nation'. It certainly was welcomed in our Ministry because it opened to us a great new field of supply without long disputes with the Treasury. But there was another side to it which we scarcely then realised. America was not at war, and the President had still to justify the supply of goods without payment by rigid applica-

5 *Winds of Change*, p. 382.
6 Winston S. Churchill, *The Second World War*, vol. ii: *Their Finest Hour* (London, 1949), p. 493.

tion of the rules. There was a very strict system of accepting Lend-Lease requirements. Nor could these produce results for a considerable period. Actually the increase in British imports from the United States in 1941 proved almost negligible. Throughout 1941 we still were paying cash for most of the weapons and munitions which we obtained, because these were purchased under the old system. In the end we got what we wanted, and some of the supplies, like the Sherman tanks, were worth their weight in gold. But, in the long run, we paid a high price for saving the world from Nazi tyranny. Our dollars came in fact to an end and we ceased, for the time being, to be an exporting country. We sacrificed our own future to protect the future of civilisation.

In those weeks of May and June 1940 there was a sense of awe and excitement which gripped the whole nation. At first, we still had hopes that the hole which the German armour had pierced might be blocked, and a firm line formed and held. I remember one night dining with General Spears at a small party at which Léon Blum, a former French Prime Minister, was present, and he made us feel quite optimistic about the chances of successful resistance. But as the weeks passed, such news as trickled back grew steadily worse. On 29 May, I, like every other member of the administration of whatever rank, received a printed circular from the Prime Minister which I have long preserved among my cherished possessions. It ran as follows:

STRICTLY CONFIDENTIAL

In these dark days the Prime Minister would be grateful if all his colleagues in the Government, as well as high officials, would maintain a high morale in their circles; not minimising the gravity of events, but showing confidence in our ability and inflexible resolve to continue the war till we have broken the will of the enemy to bring all Europe under his domination.

No tolerance should be given to the idea that France will make a separate peace; but whatever may happen on the Continent, we cannot doubt our duty and we shall certainly use all our power to defend the Island, the Empire and our Cause.

W.S.C.

But the German attack proved irresistible. It soon shattered and divided the Allied armies. The British commander and the home Government were faced with the alternatives of a doubtful evacuation through the available Channel ports or something like annihilation.

No one who did not live through those weeks, followed by the drama of Dunkirk, can fully understand the haunting anxieties of those at home or the sense of relief as the numbers of those successfully evacuated began to mount up. There was scarcely one of us who had not close relations or friends whose lives were at stake. All the British pride in their historic mastery of the sea was stirred by the accounts of the great flood of ships, ranging from vessels of the Royal and Merchant Navies to the tiniest of amateur boats, which took part in the rescue. When we heard at last that almost the whole Army had been successfully brought back, it seemed to most of us that a crushing defeat had become something of a victory. Yet as Churchill said, 'Wars are not won by retreats, however successful'.

At the same time we were doomed to watch another spectacular, and still more tragic, contest—the battle for France. Apart from the tactical situation, which was growing daily more hopeless, the morale of France and the French Army had been destroyed by bad leadership over many years. Churchill and his colleagues did not hesitate. In loyal fulfilment of their moral obligations, they sent back what troops could be hurriedly got together, to take their place yet again on French soil with their French comrades. To many this must have seemed fool-hardy; the contribution that we could give was small and the chances of the French Army being able to recover slenderer still. Thus we had to face a second evacuation and a second loss of lives and equipment which took place in the final phase at the end of June.

On 21 June the telephone rang in my small flat in London some-time between 5 and 6 a.m. It was the duty officer calling. Would I come immediately to the Ministry? When I got to my room I found Dr. Gough, our scientific adviser, and one or two officials. With them was a young man of somewhat battered appearance, unshaven, with haggard eyes, wearing a dirty old trench coat and flannel trousers, yet distinguished by a certain air of grace and dignity. After we had shaken hands, he was quick to explain his purpose. He had brought with him, indeed he had in the taxi-cab outside, a large consignment —some £4 million in value—of industrial diamonds. He had also brought something called heavy water, and some French scientists. I did not know at the time what heavy water was, and I was too confused to inquire. But there was more to follow. 'I've got a party,' he said, 'with more of this stuff waiting on the coast somewhere near Bordeaux.' This assortment, as far as I could make out, consisted of more heavy water, a great number of machine-tools and more scientists. 'Here,' he said, 'is a large-scale map. I have told these chaps to be hiding on the spot marked. Send a ship over and flash lights as I have arranged, and everything will be all right.' All this, of course, soon passed out of my hands. The Minister arrived, and the First Lord of the Admiralty was consulted, and all the dispositions were made at what is called the highest level. But I can never forget those early hours and my talk with this strange man with his combination of charm and eccentricity. Later, I was to know him better. But this was my first introduction to a truly Elizabethan character.

In the autumn of 1939, Lord Suffolk, who had had a very varied career—soldier, farmer, scientist—was unable on medical grounds to rejoin the Army. He was employed by the Ministry of Supply as liaison officer with the Minstry of Armaments in Paris. He soon won the confidence of those with whom he dealt, and when the débâcle was approaching he determined on his course without hesitation. Raoul Dautry, the Minister, was a stout-hearted man and did what he could to help. Armed with an introduction from the Minister, Suffolk set about his adventure. He knew that large stocks of industrial diamonds had arrived in Paris from Antwerp, Brussels and Amsterdam ahead of the invasion. The bankers in whose vaults these were stored seemed quite ready to leave them there for the Germans to seize. This was not Suffolk's idea at all. Brandishing M. Dautry's visiting-card, and supported by his own pistols and those of his private guard, he was able to collect large quantities of diamonds for removal. He had also got hold of the heavy water that had come originally from Norway and had been sent to France before the German attack. He rounded up a number of French scientists with whom he was working and persuaded them to come to Bordeaux, giving them an assurance, in which hope prevailed over certainty, that their passage to England would be arranged. On arrival at this port, he found the situation steadily worsening and the means of transport very difficult. He went aboard a French battleship, whose officers in those uncertain days were still pro-Ally, and obtained a machine-gun and an escort. But the chances of getting a ship were remote. He spent the next three days haunting the docks in the hope of persuading a French skipper to take the risk. On the fourth day he spotted a British collier, S.S. *Broompark,* which was chugging slowly up the estuary, ignorant of what was happening. The captain and the crew were naturally only too anxious to get away as quickly as they could, and the diamonds and chemicals were stowed aboard. Part of a large consignment of American machine-tools, which had just arrived at Bordeaux, were also seized and loaded, as well as some of the scientists. All the rest of the valuable property and personnel were concentrated on a point along the coast, carefully marked upon the large-scale map which this resourceful man had brought with him. He had persuaded his party to stay at a particular spot. When a British ship appeared and gave flashlight signals in accordance with his instructions, they would be taken off. And so it proved. A British destroyer was sent, and all went according to plan.

Later, I attended a conference over which Morrison presided. Lord Suffolk repeated, in a rather detached manner, his strange story. Such a character as Suffolk must have seemed very remote to Morrison. He could not make it out at all. He seemed chiefly concerned as to the battle which would soon rage over the machine-tools between himself and Beaverbrook. But to meet in real life a mixture between Sir Francis Drake and the Scarlet Pimpernel was something altogether out of his world.

On returning to England, Suffolk devoted his knowledge to the problem of bomb disposal. With the help of our scientific adviser, he formed the first experimental field unit. The highest priority was soon given to the bomb-disposal squads. Indeed, by the end of the war more than 50,000 unexploded bombs of various kinds had been dealt with in Great Britain. Suffolk's experimental squad had to learn how to immunise the fuses and open and empty the bomb. This, of course, was a work of extreme difficulty and danger. He was employed on this task for nearly a year after his return from France. It was particularly hazardous, partly because of the many unknown types of fuse involved and partly because many of the bombs were in very dangerous positions. To quote the citation for his posthumous George Cross:

the occasions on which he did so successfully are too numerous to record, but that Lord Suffolk fully appreciated the risks he was running is evinced by the fact that on many of these occasions he cleared everyone away from the danger area and proceeded to operate alone. He exposed himself daily to danger, and knew it. . . .

In the end, fate claimed its victim. On 12 May 1941, Suffolk and his team took an unexploded bomb to the marshes in the south-east of London to investigate a certain novel type of fuse. The bomb exploded, and he and his comrades were all killed. He was thirty-five years old.

The 20th Earl of Suffolk was a direct descendant of one of the greatest of Elizabethan families, and many of the qualities of reckless, exciting living seemed to have passed to him from those times. But perhaps he also gained something from an admixture of blood on his mother's side. The progeny of an English aristocrat and an American millionaire turned out very well with Churchill; and so it was with Suffolk. He may have owed as much to his grandfather, Levi Zeigler Leiter, the Chicago wheat baron of the 1890s, as Churchill to Leonard Jerome. I have had the good fortune in my life to meet many gallant officers and brave men, but I have never known such a remarkable combination in a single man of courage, expert knowledge and charm.[7]

The British Army left behind in France, in the evacuations of May and June 1940, the equivalent of the equipment of eight to ten divisions. These losses included 880 field guns, 310 guns of larger calibre, some 500 anti-aircraft guns, some 850 anti-tank guns, 6,400 anti-tank rifles, 11,000 machine-guns, nearly 700 tanks, 20,000 motor-cycles, 45,000 motor-cars and lorries. In addition, great dumps of ammunition were abandoned. We were faced therefore with a formidable short-term, in addition to our long-term, programme. Having shipped to France almost everything we had, we now found ourselves not only alone, but unarmed. With great difficulty, equipment for two divisions was scraped together. But we now had to provide the vital material to meet the urgent and immediate threat of invasion. It is to the everlasting credit of the Prime Minister and his colleagues that, even when facing this supreme test, they sent out convoys of tanks and munitions to save the Middle East. But, for the moment, most of us had our eyes on the Channel.

Local Defence Volunteers, renamed and ever memorable as the Home Guard, had to be supplied with uniforms, infantry weapons of

[7] I am indebted to the *Saturday Evening Post*, 28 November and 5 December 1942, and the *Reader's Digest*, May 1943, for refreshing my memory with some of the details. See also K. Hare-Scott, *For Gallantry* (London, 1951).

some kind and ammunition. The Americans sent us, in response to Churchill's appeal, a large consignment to meet our immediate needs. We watched anxiously the arrival of every precious ship. We received half a million rifles, not of .303 but of .300 calibre, and therefore involving a fresh complication for our Ministry. Fortunately, about 125 million rounds were included in the parcel, which might, it was calculated, give every Home Guardsman at least a sporting chance. We got, too, 55,000 'tommy' guns and 895 of the old French 75-mm. guns with ammunition—only a thousand rounds apiece—but with no limbers, thus creating another headache for our Director-General. While these were on the way, we had to 'make do' by rapid production of grenades of any and every kind, Sten guns, Smith guns and similar weapons. We even went so far as to make an appeal for shot-guns, and a special cartridge was quickly produced by I.C.I. to provide a bullet which might hope to find its target without exploding the barrel. The response to this request was tremendous. It was in this atmosphere that these first weeks of my ministerial life were passed. Since the needs of the Air Force were rightly given the first and overriding priority, we found ourselves often frustrated by this friendly (and sometimes not too friendly) rivalry in our struggle to meet the essential needs of the small forces, professional and amateur, now assembling to defend their native soil.

A great deal has been written about Beaverbrook's contribution to the Battle of Britain, and some critics have tried to minimise his work. The answer is simple. Almost as soon as the Battle of France was over, the Battle of Britain began. Four hundred and fifty-eight operational aircraft were lost in France between 17 May and 1 June—more than the current production could replace. Beaverbrook's vital decision was to concentrate all the available effort—material, tools, spare parts, skilled and unskilled labour—upon five types: Wellingtons, Whitley Vs, Blenheims, Hurricanes and Spitfires. Everything was sacrificed to get the maximum number of these into the air and to keep them there. Every form of material and equipment for these machines was given an overriding priority both inside and outside the field of the Ministry of Aircraft Production's formal authority. The justification of all this lies in the result. On the Battle of Britain the future of Britain and indeed of the world depended. The battle was won by the narrowest of margins. But it was won. Moreover, in spite of the tremendous loss of machines, from May to September production rose more than enough to cover their deficiencies—at least in material. 'Fighter Command emerged from the battle in the autumn with more aircraft than it had possessed at the beginning.'[8]

It is true that the rapid adjustments and improvisations which the situation forced both upon the Ministry of Aircraft Production and to a great extent upon the Ministry of Supply (for we had to produce the necessary flow of guns and ammunition) was a source of future trouble. But if all these things had not been done, there might have been no future to trouble about.

The Battle of Britain started on 8 August and lasted till 15 September. The heroic combats in the air between the champions on either side were accompanied by German attempts to destroy the fighter bases. We still keep this day, 15 September—and I hope will always keep it—in commemoration of our victory. Perhaps the most anxious moments were towards the end of August, when on a certain day the British losses were so large as to make it necessary to risk our last reserves.

7 September is a great day in my memory, for then we were told that the invasion was imminent. The signal 'Cromwell' was given, and with this password flying from mouth to mouth and the church bells ringing, the Army came to instant readiness and the Home Guard stood to arms. We waited for the great moment. But the Germans shrank from the test. On 17 September, as we now know, Hitler postponed invasion 'until further notice'. Yet the danger of invasion continued for a long time, and Churchill and the Chiefs of Staff had to take the necessary precautions for many months to come. But whatever military experts might advise, the public felt that the moment was over, and that whatever might happen Britain would never be forced to her knees by a foreign invader landing on her shores.

I have preserved two records of this heroic period, both characteristic of the author. The first was a notice issued in similar terms to that of 29 May 1940, and circulated to all Ministers of whatever rank:

On what may be the eve of an attempted invasion or battle for our native land, the Prime Minister desires to impress upon all persons holding responsible positions in the Government, in the Fighting Services, or in the Civil Departments, their duty to maintain a spirit of alert and confident energy.

[8] Postan, pp. 116–17.

While every precaution must be taken that time and means afford, there are
no grounds for supposing that more German troops can be landed in this
country, either from the air or across the sea, than can be destroyed or
captured by the strong forces at present under arms. The Royal Air Force is
in excellent order and at the highest strength it has yet attained. The German
Navy was never so weak, nor the British Army at home so strong as now. The
Prime Minister expects all His Majesty's servants in high places to set an
example of steadiness and resolution. They should check and rebuke expres-
sions of loose and ill-digested opinion in their circles, or by their subordinates. They should not hesitate to report, or if necessary remove, any officers
or officials who are found to be consciously exercising a disturbing or depress-
ing influence, and whose talk is calculated to spread alarm and despondency.
Thus alone will they be worthy of the fighting men, who in the air, on the
sea, and on land, have already met the enemy without any sense of being outmatched in martial qualities.

Winston S. Churchill

4th July, 1940

The second, sent round on 19 August, that is, in the middle of the
Battle of Britain, is equally typical. It ran as follows:

To do our work, we all have to read a mass of papers. Nearly all of them are
far too long. This wastes time, while energy has to be spent in looking for the
essential points.
  I ask my colleagues and their staffs to see to it that their Reports are shorter.
  (i) The aim should be Reports which set out the main points in a series of
      short, crisp paragraphs.
  (ii) If a Report relies on detailed analysis of some complicated factors, or on
      statistics, these should be set out in an Appendix.
  (iii) Often the occasion is best met by submitting not a full-dress Report, but
      an *Aide-mémoire* consisting of headings only, which can be expanded
      orally if needed.
  (iv) Let us have an end of such phrases as these: 'It is also of importance to
      bear in the mind the following considerations . . .', or 'Consideration
      should be given to the possibility of carrying into effect . . .'. Most of
      these woolly phrases are mere padding, which can be left out altogether,
      or replaced by a single word. Let us not shrink from using the short ex-
      pressive phrase, even if it is conversational. . . .

If the great war messages have their honoured place in history, this
last admonition will always be relevant. I still like to think of
Churchill sitting down on that August day, while the fate of Britain
was in the balance, to remind us of the value of brevity.
  After the Battle of Britain came the 'Blitz'. Having failed to

outmatch the Royal Air Force in combat or to put their airfields out of action, the Germans changed their tactics. They now attempted to reduce the great cities and their populations to a condition of destruction and despair. They began with London, partly by day but increasingly by night. The first intense phase lasted from 7 September for more than six weeks without intermission. After that, while giving London a short respite, they made a series of attacks on the great towns—Coventry, Cardiff, Bristol, Birmingham and many others. This was followed by an attempt to put the chief ports out of operation. On London the attacks lasted, with little interruption, all through the winter and spring of 1940–41, culminating in the violent onslaughts of early May.

Everyone who lived in London through the Blitz has his own memories of personal incidents in which he was concerned. I confess that to me the most unpleasant part of the whole affair was the blackout. Creeping about in the dark was a most disagreeable nightly experience. We junior Ministers were not provided with motor-cars; in any case one could not have felt justified in taking out a driver while the raids were on, unless for some special duty. My sight is not good; and although I did not range far, only from the Strand to a club in Pall Mall or St. James's Street and then to my own flat in Piccadilly, I recall with distaste the need to grope along in the murky darkness, only occasionally illuminated by the flash of guns. Early in November I was unfortunate enough to be run into in the darkness by a taxi. It was altogether, I have no doubt, my own fault; but once more I was lucky, as so often before and since. I was much bruised, but no bones were broken, and after a few days I could go back to work. But it gave me a shock, for I was 'knocked out' for quite a little time.

I was lucky, too, on the night the Carlton Club was destroyed.[9] I had gone in about 8 o'clock on my way home from the Ministry. There were a good many bombs dropping and, since by now our guns had begun to operate in some force, quite a lot of shrapnel. So instead of going on further, I thought I would turn into the Carlton, in Pall Mall. I went into the large morning-room and was sitting in one corner talking to David Margesson, Victor Warrender, and one or two other junior Ministers, when suddenly the whole ceiling seemed to collapse about us. A bomb had struck the cornice in the far end of the room.

[9] 14 October 1940.

Had it come straight through we should no doubt not have escaped. Groping our way out towards the hall, we found some members coming out of the dining-room, where another bomb had fallen. Among them were Lord Hailsham and his son, Quintin; and, as Churchill records, the father was carried to safety by the piety of the son. Although there must have been over a hundred members and servants in the club, there were no casualties from the attack itself, although one man was killed by a piece of falling masonry on his way out. This almost miraculous escape of the Tories was a source of much cynical congratulation from our Labour and Liberal friends.

Margesson and I went to look for his car, but that had been destroyed. We then thought it was time for dinner; so we crossed the road to the old Carlton Hotel (which was still standing, although destroyed later on in the Blitz), where we thought we could comfort ourselves with food and drink. We were received in a very doubtful, not to say suspicious, manner by the *maître d'hôtel,* who in normal times was well known to us both. When we looked in one of the looking-glasses we could see the reason. Our hair, faces, and clothes were completely blackened with dirt and smoke. We gratefully accepted the offer of a bathroom. By that time it was getting pretty late, so I made my way to Pratt's (in Park Place, St. James's), where I found my brother-in-law, Eddy Devonshire. While we were sitting there, someone came in to say that his house, No. 2 Carlton Gardens, was on fire. We thought we had better go along there. The fire was gradually got under control, and later we were able to go in and carry out some bits of furniture and other effects (Fortunately, the more valuable pictures and pieces had been moved to Derbyshire.) We piled these, with the help of various willing hands, in the little garden outside the door, and I managed to get some tarpaulins from Macmillans in St. Martin's Street with which to protect these possessions against the rain. The next day, my wife and one of her sisters arrived with a lorry. There was some trouble about an unexploded bomb; but they succeeded, with feminine pertinacity, in getting permission from the police to carry these effects away. The house was gutted and has only recently been restored by the landlords, the Crown Estates.

Morrison, at the beginning of the Blitz, was anxious about my safety and wanted me to sleep in a large underground shelter under our office at one corner of which he had a bed, screened off from the vast dormitory. I tried it one night, but did not like it at all. I therefore remained faithful to the rooms in No. 90 Piccadilly, which I had taken some years before. My wife was in the country in the cottage, and the younger children away at school; my son was in the Army. The only trouble about my little flat was that it was in the mansard roof at the top of the house, and the noise of the German bombers prowling around was rather distracting. One night, however, this difficulty was resolved. I had been working late and then gone to get some supper at Pratt's Club. When I let myself in at 90 Piccadilly, I found a note for me in the hall, left by the servant who looked after us. 'Your rooms have been blown in. I have put some things in Mr. ———'s room.' This was a flat on the ground floor. Here I found pyjamas, dressing-gown, slippers, the property of the owner of the flat, neatly arranged, with toothbrush and glass set out and towel folded in the traditional way on the washstand. This excellent man remained at his post throughout the Blitz. On this particular night the 'In and Out' Club (we were next door) had been partially destroyed. I was able, fortunately, to move into a flat on the first floor belonging to Hugh Walpole, which he kindly allowed me to use. Here I remained until I went to North Africa at the beginning of 1943.

Occasionally I could get to Sussex for a Saturday or Sunday evening. It was a remarkable sight to stand outside our door and watch the attack on London: the searchlights, the flash of the guns, and the glow of fires. A surprisingly large number of bombs were dropped in our neighbourhood, presumably by wounded German aircraft going home and unloading, or by some unwounded ones which may have preferred not to face the barrage. I worked out afterwards that we had on our estate about one bomb to every ten acres; but there were no casualties except a cow and a pheasant. I entered these in the game-book in their proper place, the cow under the heading 'various'.

Woolwich Arsenal and borough suffered a great deal. I remember one particular night at Woolwich most vividly. I thought I had better show myself there occasionally and I arranged to go down one evening with Sir Charles McLaren, the Director of Ordnance Factories, a splendid character—the best type of Scottish engineer. The bombing was heavy, but there was no sign of panic. All possible precautions had been taken. During the attack we sat in the chief officer's room, in the company of many other engineers who all seemed to be Scots and talked unconcernedly of their experiences in different parts of the world. It was a real Kipling scene. The consumption of whisky and the wealth of anecdotes were on an equally generous scale. When the raid seemed over, everyone got to work to assess the damage and make plans for the next day.

My duties required me to travel a good deal during these months. It so happened that I was in Cardiff on the night of a vicious attack. I had given a talk to our Regional representatives and others, and was being entertained at supper at one of the hotels. The bombing began during or just after our meal and lasted for some hours. It was indeed a memorable scene, with the crashing bombs; the fires; the Castle and the great Cardiff public buildings silhouetted against an apparently burning city. The damage was considerable; but once again there was no panic, and everyone seemed to know what to do. I was also at Bristol on the night of a heavy attack. Here the Lord Mayor had arranged a formal dinner in my honour, with many guests. The bombs began just as I rose to make my speech in response to his toast. I asked him if I should cut it short. He seemed not only pained but shocked at the idea. I therefore continued for my full twenty-five minutes and honour was satisfied. Sir Hugh Ellis, the Regional A.R.P. Commissioner, slipped out to see to his organisation, and we afterwards went round to his operational headquarters. Later in the evening the Lord Mayor took me to the Mansion House where we spent the night in the wine cellar. There was a bed for me between bins of Bristol Milk, and another where the Lord and Lady Mayoress reposed. When the noise slackened, I felt cramped in my surroundings and went to my room to finish my sleep. The Lord Mayor was a fine character—a railwayman, a strong trade unionist and a tremendous patriot.

As the attack on London developed, the Germans began to rely as much on incendiary as on explosive bombs. I was at the Ministry on the Sunday night when the City of London was burned. On this night, of course, the City was almost empty, and the fire-watching arrangements had not yet been perfected, or had been neglected. But it seemed inexcusable that such an important area should have been left without proper precautions. As our own fire-watching got organised, we all took our turns. There was a very good post on the roof of the Ministry where one could see all that was going on. A kind of sentry-box had been erected, which gave protection from shrapnel, and except for a direct hit (the chances of which were minute) it was really a very safe place. Sometimes I would go along to see my brother Daniel, who spent most nights at St. Martin's Street, in charge of the fire-watching. The top two floors of Macmillans had some years before been converted into additional space for stock. My brother used to say with a wry smile that there were some very slow-selling books there, and he doubted whether any German bomb could get through them.

The human memories of those days are unforgettable. The vast population of London was wholly unprotected, and so were their little houses. Yet such was the efficacy of the Anderson, and later the Morrison, shelters that the fatal casualties were relatively small. But the scenes of suffering and loss were heartbreaking. The courage with which everyone turned up at their jobs, both in the factories and in the offices, was remarkable. I often used to talk, when I went early to the office, to the cleaners. Most of them lived in the East End, which was being terribly knocked about. Many of their houses had gone; sometimes their neighbours or friends or relations had been killed or wounded; but they were always there on the job.

In the Ministry, our chief anxiety during the Blitz was the loss of production. Yet even after the worst raids the factories were manned and working within a few days. Actually, the total effect of bombing proved less serious than at one time seemed likely. Nevertheless, in addition to the losses in human life, great interruptions were caused, and some vital plants, including a major part of Woolwich Arsenal, had to be moved elsewhere. There were many arguments about dispersal, which necessarily involved some immediate reduction of output. Some of our plants could not be moved without immense difficulty; others could be more easily dealt with. We adopted a policy of moderate dispersal. In the long run we ended up with our capacity increased rather than reduced.

Over the country as a whole, although we suffered heavy losses of buildings and sometimes severe casualties, we soon found that the tools survived very well. Although the tables were turned and the massive attacks of the Air Force on Germany delivered a weight of bombs far greater than we ourselves had experienced, we learned after the war that somehow or other life was carried on even under those conditions, and that the loss of output was less than we expected.

In the early stages of the long battle, a lot of working time was lost, both in offices and factories, by the system of air-raid alarms which had been adopted at the beginning of the war. But in this matter, as in countless other details, the Prime Minister was quick to take action. A new plan was soon introduced by which the 'alert' was given as a first warning, and spotters on the roof of the buildings or in other prominent positions only sounded the 'alarm' when the enemy were approaching. On the alert, you did nothing; on the alarm, you went to ground. This, of course, covered daylight attacks, which continued intermittently throughout. Before the amended regulations were introduced, much time had been wasted. There was, no doubt, some additional risk, but the change was welcomed by everyone. The spotters were generally known as 'Jim Crows'. Whether they were effective or not in giving timely warnings, they certainly helped to keep everybody at their jobs. I remember asking our man on the Ministry roof what he considered his instructions to be. 'Well, sir,' he said, 'when I sees 'em over the Coliseum I rings me bell.' At any rate, after the first humiliating experiences of being driven from our rooms into a basement for long periods, this new machinery was very welcome.

Whitehall suffered heavily in the Blitz, and preparations were very properly made to move the Cabinet and a nucleus of vital departments into various strongholds which were being rapidly constructed. In fact they were not used, except, of course, the new Admiralty fortress which was an operational headquarters. This building, which still graces, or defaces, Horse Guards Parade, was popularly believed to follow the principle of an iceberg, with five-sixths of it or more underground. It was quickly christened 'Lenin's tomb'.

10 May marked the culmination of the raids on London. It was on this night that the House of Commons was destroyed. I went down early the next morning to see the damage. The bomb had fallen right through the roof, but it was still possible to get through the voting lobbies. I picked up a charred Order Paper, which I still have, and a few other souvenirs. Many years were to pass before the House of Commons was to return to its old quarters. We were moved first to Church House and afterwards to the House of Lords. When the time came to rebuild our own Chamber, it was reproduced in exactly the same form as before.

The 'Blitz' now came to an end, at least till the summer of 1944, when Hitler's 'secret weapons'—V.1 and V.2—were at last revealed. It was indeed fortunate that they were not perfected sooner. Meanwhile, although our casualties—43,000 killed and 51,000 dangerously wounded[10]—were grievous, Hitler's assaults on Britain had failed in their main purpose.

Hitler—although we did not know it—was soon to turn to other projects. Alone we had won the Battle of Britain; alone we had withstood the Blitz; alone we were facing the renewed U-boat menace. Other trials were still ahead of us. But we were not to be alone for much longer.

Meanwhile the routine work of the Ministry went on. The immense range and scope of its duties is revealed by a rapid glance through the Parliamentary questions. The collection of railings (repeated almost every week); the Flax Control Board; the uses of glycerine; the provision of sawmills; the utilisation of waste leather; the sales of newspapers in the street; the future of the organ-building trade; the likely yield of the woolclip; the collection of kitchen waste (a special favourite); the provision of steel helmets for Home Guard, nurses and midwives; the Plastics Control; the size and safety of timber stocks; the collection of binoculars; paper for printing books; the cotton price controls; the production of cement in Northern Ireland; the alleged continual larceny of molasses; the supply of newsprint for Polish periodicals; the production of munitions in India; the possibility of paper-making out of straw; the supply of caustic potash; the use of paper for Christmas cards; the provision of children's nurseries for married women workers; the salvage of rubber; the use of home-grown timber; the principles of quantity surveying; the use of railway workshops for munitions; the future of woodworking firms; the supply of toilet paper; substitutes for timber; the ironstone deposits of Sussex; the salvage of bottles; the Area organisation and its utilisation; scientific research; the requisitions by the Ministry of material on the Welsh highland railway. These taken at random are an assortment of the number of questions, small and great, for which we had to provide an answer.

Both Morrison and Duncan left me a good proportion of Parlia-

[10] Winston S. Churchill, *The Second World War*, vol. iii: *The Grand Alliance* (London, 1950), p. 42.

mentary questions to answer. When Beaverbrook took over control, all
these necessarily fell to me. I began to learn the technique, which I
had watched others practise for so many years, and how to avoid the
various pitfalls. One gallant officer in July 1940, when invasion was
expected every day, kept asking me about the supply of grenades 'of all
sizes'. 'Is the Minister satisfied?' he demanded. This is a very old catch.
'My right honourable Friend,' I replied, 'is never satisfied. As far as the
question of grenades is concerned, I would describe his mood as one of
qualified optimism.'

Apart from the natural anxiety of Members to secure efficiency,
there were also a number of difficulties which unhappily revived old
party controversies or infringed on strongly-held political doctrines.
On the one side, it often became necessary for us to use our war powers
to change the management of a factory. The plant might be good, but
the management poor. If even after putting in one or two outside
advisers to assist there was no improvement, then we had to resort to
the final step of throwing out the existing management and installing
a controller. Sometimes—though seldom—either because of the financial weakness of the firm or for some other reason—we were obliged
to use our powers for the compulsory purchase of the equity. Both these
courses, as can be imagined, were distasteful to many Conservative
Members, and I had to defend them in debates against forcible criticism. Equally, we soon found it necessary to seek private-enterprise
management for the new Royal Ordnance Factories that were coming
along with such rapidity, and this policy was very distasteful to the
Socialist Members, both in the Government and outside. For some
reason they believed, with almost religious fervour, that the success of
an R.O.F. was a proof of the triumph of nationalisation. To hand over
these new establishments to private management was a confession of
the failure of Socialism in practice. Indeed, before a face-saving solution was devised, the question actually had to be submitted to the War
Cabinet.

The organisation for production, which we had inherited from the
previous Government and which was based upon a long tradition, had
suffered from one disadvantage which critics were not slow to exploit.
Whatever might be the different methods to overcome the jealousy
and rivalry between the different Ministries, sometimes a Production
Council of the Ministers concerned with an independent chairman,

sometimes renamed a Production Executive composed of the Ministers themselves, these were really expedients which could only work effectively by personal goodwill at the centre and all down the line. On the whole, in spite of the strong idiosyncrasies of different Ministers, the system worked successfully, especially in the early years. But as labour and materials became more and more scarce, and industrial capacity had been successfully taken up by the efforts of all the departments, the need for some central control became increasingly apparent. In all the debates from June 1940 till the spring of 1942 this theme was developed by our critics.

Unfortunately, although the Production Executive set up in January 1941 was in control of almost everything in the country—labour, tools, plant, material—it was not always in effective control of itself. For the Minister of Aircraft Production, Beaverbrook, normally refused to attend and sent his Parliamentary Secretary in his place with somewhat negative instructions. An attempt was made to deal with this by a brilliantly devised tactical stroke. In future, the place of meeting would be Lord Beaverbrook's room. This rather cornered him at first; but he was soon able to find a way of escaping by the back door. There is a story that he did once pay some attention when the discussion was about the likely shortage of some minor but vital metal. But he slipped out in the middle. The talk dragged on from one subject to another; and when the committee broke up, they found Beaverbrook sitting in his private secretary's room on the long-distance telephone to America. Warned by the information he had received, he was hastily buying up all available supplies for the benefit of his own Ministry. This story may be apocryphal, but is certainly characteristic.

An organised opposition especially concentrating on production problems began to show itself from the very first months of Churchill's Government. Emanuel Shinwell made his first appearance in a role which he was to fill throughout the war. Since he had not been willing to join the Government in a minor position, the part which he decided to play was perhaps the most useful and constructive that was open to him. His speeches were always critical—even acid—but generally well informed and interesting. His mistake was that he was too sweeping in his condemnations and thereby weakened the effectiveness of his major points. Bevin, who disliked him intensely, was sharp in his replies.

One of the leaders of this group was Clement Davies. He, too, had not been given any place in the administration and therefore assumed the role of candid friend. The merit of his speeches was that they were fluent. The fault was that they were intolerably long. Associated with these critics, the most persistent came to be Dick Stokes, the Capitalist-Socialist Member for Ipswich, and Austin Hopkinson, an Independent who, although he practised something like Christian poverty, did not combine with it the virtues of Christian charity. Others who took the same line were George Garro-Jones, later an Under-Secretary at the Ministry of Production; Hore-Belisha, a powerful speaker but handicapped by his own record; Thomas Horabin, an able engineer of radical opinions; and, an incongruous member of such a group, Lord Winterton.

As the months passed, Winterton and Shinwell began to hunt closely together and became inseparable companions in the chase. Winterton, gaunt, awkward, angular, who combined a long record of undistinguished administration in minor positions with a curious, almost childish, egotism, was nevertheless something of a favourite. There was an endearing quality about him. He had entered the House as a very young man before the First War, and retained his engaging immaturity until the end. As this tall, ungainly figure strolled through the lobbies with Shinwell running at his feet, one was inevitably reminded of Don Quixote and Sancho Panza. At this time, a popular play had been running under the title *Arsenic and Old Lace,* and these two figures—the agitator and the aristocrat—were quickly dubbed by this appropriate nickname. They were occasionally supported by Sir John Wardlaw-Milne, who from his position as chairman of the Select Committee on National Expenditure, which delved with commendable if tiresome zeal into all our records, was well placed to add a critical note. In general, however, he reserved himself for larger issues.

Whatever the attractions in principle of a single Minister of Production to whom all other Ministers would be subordinate, the difficulties in practice were considerable. There were the individual characteristics of men like Beaverbrook and Bevin, both powerful, determined and highly individualistic in their approach. Moreover, the range seemed too vast for one man properly to control. Churchill was I think right in resisting the pressure for a single command until two years had passed. Moreover, even when armament production had reached its peak and the organisation of all the various Ministries was as near perfect as it could be made, the Minister of Production, Oliver Lyttelton, when he came to be appointed in March 1942, had a different task from that which faced Ministers in the early years of the war. By now, it was not so much a question of adding to the totality of production as of a single control in order to decide the shape of the programmes now that no further increase seemed possible and, above all, to speak with a single voice as representing Great Britain with the American and Russian allies with whom we had soon to deal.

A similar development took place with regard to the direction of labour. In November 1940, Ernest Bevin had absolutely resisted any idea of compulsory labour. But almost exactly a year later he was to introduce and carry through Parliament the National Service Bill, which in fact directed labour, male and female, by compulsory powers. All the same, I think Bevin was right. The time had not yet come. Nor were the factories ready. Bevin was indeed a fine man, one of the most vital and outstanding personalities I have known in a long life. With his great frame, his powerful jaws and his commanding presence, he was cast in a heroic mould. At one period in the various permutations and combinations in the central control, I became subordinate to him in respect of my chairmanship of the Industrial Capacity Committee. I found him a most loyal and lovable chief. He could fight hard, but he bore no rancour.

During the early months of 1941, the sense of strain between Beaverbrook and Bevin became more and more apparent. This was a clash more of personalities than of principles. Beaverbrook wanted things done in his own way. 'Organisation is the enemy of improvisation' was a favourite saying of his; and a printed poster to this effect was hung up in his room alongside his denunciation of committees. But, of course, he did not take all this more than half seriously. Nor would Bevin easily give way on anything which he regarded as a point of principle. Their temperament and outlook were wholly different. With all his bigness of heart, Bevin, who could understand and work with an ordinary Conservative politician, found the elusive character of Beaverbrook difficult for him to grasp. Beaverbrook, in return, could not refrain from teasing his solid opponent who seemed often slow in his reactions and ponderous in his movements. Bevin was the bull with many taurine qualities; Beaverbrook was the matador. As so often happens, the matters really in dispute were few and could easily have been resolved.

Beaverbrook's health was also at this time very precarious. When I got to know him later I realised how terribly he was affected by the asthma to which he was a martyr. Sometimes sleep became quite impossible for him for days on end. We were none of us therefore surprised when on 1 May Beaverbrook retired from the Ministry of Aircraft Production. He remained, however, in the War Cabinet as Minister of State. John Moore-Brabazon was appointed in his place.

On 22 June, the German attack on Russia was launched. From the point of view of our Ministry, Churchill's unhesitating decision to range Britain as an ally of Russia led to still further demands, in order to supply an immense range of weapons, ammunition and materials to the hard-pressed Russian armies. Churchill was quick to move. On the day after the German attack on Russia he began planning for aid to our new ally in every possible form. Within a few days large ministerial changes were announced. Lyttelton left the Board of Trade to become Minister of State in Cairo, remaining a member of the War Cabinet. Duncan left Supply for the Board of Trade, and Churchill persuaded Beaverbrook to return to active and executive office as Minister of Supply. Apart from his services in sorting out the many problems surrounding the production of tanks, the next few months were to be the most active and fruitful in his whole career. He became the indispensable representative of Britain in the complicated negotiations between London, Washington and Moscow. His visits, East and West, were to be of historic importance. He became an essential pivot in the Grand Alliance.

Beaverbrook's method of working was peculiar but, in its strange way, effective. He brought in many of his trusted colleagues, some of whom had worked with him in M.A.P. In the higher control of the tank organisation he made some rapid and drastic changes. In general, he left us alone practically the whole day. I was able to do my own work, and so were the heads of all the different departments, up until some time between 6 and 7 o'clock. There was then a conference in the Minister's room. Although everybody seemed to talk at once and there was an appearance of confusion, actually a lot of things were very quickly settled. There was a generous supply of refreshment. At about 9 or 9.40 p.m. he would usually ask a few of us to dine with him at the Savoy. Later, he had a small dining-room put into the Ministry. After dinner the work continued: sorting out the major problems and making further decisions. About midnight or 1 a.m. we would break up. On what we used to call our 'rest night', the Minister had been summoned for dinner to No. 10.

'The Beaver's' arrival was in itself a thrilling event. Now, in July 1941, after nearly two years of war and fourteen months' hard slogging work at the Ministry, it was fun to be in close and daily contact with this extraordinary man.

As soon as the Minister was installed, he asked which tasks I thought most urgent. I told him that apart from minor improvements and an increased sense of urgency in all our undertakings, our main trouble lay in the production of tanks and their armament. We must have better protection and heavier guns.

After Lord Beaverbrook was appointed to the Ministry of Supply I was the Ministry's spokesman in the House of Commons. The biggest and most testing debate in which I had yet taken part in my short ministerial career took place on 9 and 10 July. I had to wind up for the Ministry on the first evening.

The discussion divided itself into two separate streams—questions relating to the Ministry of Supply itself and questions relating to the general organisation of production Ministries, of which the Ministry of Supply was one. I was able to give a great deal of detailed assurance on points raised—such as the extent to which our factories were working two or three shifts; the best strategic use of our limited supply of skilled men so that the maximum of unskilled labour could be absorbed; on time-saving methods of placing orders; on the development of new inventions. On the other question, in which the House was much interested, the machinery of government, I could not from my junior position contribute much to the argument. But in an attempt to turn the issue a little, I said that although it had been commonly alleged that the priorities given to the Ministry of Aircraft Production had caused some confusion in the early part of 1940, I could not give a final judgement on that point. I continued:

I have not been able to consult my Noble Friend, but I feel no hesitation in giving to the Committee a positive assurance that from now on, at any rate, this special bias in favour of the Ministry of Aircraft Production is not likely to continue.[11]

As 'the Beaver' had taken over Supply only a few days before, the House found this assurance both acceptable and entertaining.

On the main theme, I pointed out that the movement towards a centralised machine of production was going on all the time and had in fact gone further than people recognised. There were three methods by which we had been developing this. First, by the central purchase of stores by one department on behalf of all. People did not seem to recognise how far the responsibility of the Ministry of Supply went beyond responsibility for the Army. The second method was the system by which, though contracts remained in the name of the three Service Ministries, the planning was done by one Ministry on behalf of all—what might be called a centrally controlled plan of production. The third method was the allocation of raw materials which had been going on successfully for eighteen months. I ended my speech as follows:

> We have been faced with the task of converting the whole economic organi-
> sation of the country from a basis on which it was regulated by the pull and
> push of the price system to an economy in which every consideration must be
> subordinated to the maximum production of weapons of war.[12]

That evening I received the following letter:

My dear Harold,
    May I send you my warmest congratulations on your speech in the House today.
    On all hands I hear immense praise of it as a most splendid Parliamentary performance.
    I count myself a most fortunate Minister in having so able and persuasive an advocate in the House of Commons.
                                   Yours ever,

                                              M.B.

This was typical of Beaverbrook. In all the months that I worked with him dealing with great and critical issues, in spite of the high demands of his untiring work and his physical disabilities, it was the same story. I realised more and more how wisely he used the technique of praise and encouragement. Many people have wondered why it was

[11] *Hansard,* 9 July 1941.
[12] Ibid.

that Churchill depended so much upon Beaverbrook and drew so
much comfort from his company. I think the reason was simple.
Although he had many faults, Max Beaverbrook radiated strength,
authority, determination and energy. When things were bad or pressures heavy, when allies were difficult or operations went wrong, he
seemed from his own vitality to have the power of recharging Churchill's batteries.

At the beginning of August 1941, the Prime Minister left on the
Prince of Wales for a meeting with Roosevelt, the first of many
meetings destined to take place in the next four years. The rendezvous
was Placentia Bay, Newfoundland. During the voyage he thought it
would be useful to have Beaverbrook with him to deal with the whole
question of American supplies to Russia. Churchill, in his own words,
'dreaded the loss of what we had expected and so direly needed.'[13]

Churchill went by sea; but in order to be there in time Beaverbrook
had to go by air. So dramatic has been the development of air travel in
the last twenty years that it is difficult now to realise the tremendous
strain which long journeys of this kind then entailed on elderly
commanders or statesmen. The bomb rack of the bomber of those days
was often the only available place for the passengers. There was no
pressurisation. It was dangerous to fly at more than some 10,000 feet
without oxygen, which was not always available. It was intensely cold,
and only by the help of heavy furs was it possible to survive. To fly the
Atlantic required a number of stops, first in Ireland, then in Iceland,
and by the time the traveller arrived he was apt to be in bad shape. For
a man with Beaverbrook's physical disabilities these journeys were
particularly trying.

Beaverbrook and Averell Harriman, the President's trusted adviser,
went on by air to Washington on 13 August and did not return to
London until the 24th. Beaverbrook had done much to stimulate the
Americans' productive efforts and 'to raise their sights'. In spite of all
the risks involved, he became an ardent advocate of giving all possible
aid to Russia. In the middle of September he set out on a new journey,
again accompanied by Harriman. His directive from the War Cabinet
was to arrange a long-term supply programme for the Russian armies.
They went by sea from Scapa Flow to Archangel, and reached Moscow
during the last days of September.

[13] Churchill, *The Grand Alliance,* p. 383.

Beaverbrook's consultations in Moscow lasted from 28 September until 1 October, and resulted in the signature of what became known as the Protocol. This agreement, jointly signed by Molotov, Beaverbrook and Harriman, was our Bible. We were pledged to carry it out with scrupulous and literal devotion. It was certainly a striking document. It set out in detail all the items of aid which we were prepared to give from British and American sources. The burden which lay upon Great Britain made a heavy inroad upon our reserves of armaments, materials and stores. There were some counter-requests from us of a modest kind; but the total figures of what both the United States and the United Kingdom were pledged to supply were indeed formidable. Even before the September meeting, Churchill had agreed to send over two squadrons of Hurricanes and other supplies as a symbol and a foretaste of what we would do. From the point of view of our Ministry, of course, whether these supplies were to be made available to our own forces, military and civil, or whether we must hand them over to the Russians was not a matter for our decision. It was our business to produce the goods. It was for the authorities higher than us to decide upon their allocation. But natually this new burden stirred us on to new efforts, all the more as we were in daily consultation with the Service departments. They felt, in Churchill's words, that 'it was like flaying off pieces of their skin'.[14]

The dispatch of aid was incredibly rapid. On 6 October, Churchill was able to inform Stalin that a 'continuous cycle of convoys, leaving every ten days' had been arranged.[15] Twenty heavy tanks and 193 fighters would reach Archangel on 12 October. By 6 November, as many as 260 heavy tanks, 100 Hurricanes, 200 fighters, as well as a number of Bren carriers, anti-tank rifles and ammunition, and 2-pounder guns would arrive. Other tanks had been shipped to go through Persia and a consignment from Canada to Vladivostok. All that was without regard to American supplies and came from our stocks. When we remember that Japan was becoming increasingly menacing, and the new dangers which must soon confront us in the Far East, these first instalments of a long series were both prompt and generous.

It was our task to go through the agreement item by item and decide

14 Ibid., p. 402.
15 Ibid., p. 418.

how and when the undertakings entered into could be fulfilled. The procedure which the Minister adopted for this purpose was unconventional but, in spite of its apparent confusion, proved rapid and effective. He collected into his large room a huge conference of Army, Navy and Air Force officers, together with all the different representatives of the supply Ministries involved. Since he liked operating by remote control, he made me the organiser of different groups and subcommittees. With the help of the Permanent Secretaries of the Ministries concerned an agenda was drawn up, with the subjects divided into their appropriate compartments. Senior officers and civil servants sat at a series of tables, not unlike a village whist drive, where they discussed how these onerous undertakings could be carried out and the effect upon our own position. From time to time, as when the Master of Ceremonies declares a change of trumps, they were seen to move from one table to another. These confabulations lasted for several days, or rather nights, since, if I remember aright, they began about 5 o'clock in the evening, when all of us had done our preparatory work, and went on until the early hours of the next morning. The normal procedure was to continue until 9 o'clock, when the leading figures retired for dinner, and sandwiches and other refreshments were served to the rest. The conference was then resumed and ended between 2 and 3 a.m.

On one occasion the question of medical supplies came up. The Minister, who hovered about like a host at a party between one table and another, chanced to intervene while these large requests were under consideration. He turned to me and asked, 'Who deals with these?' I replied, 'You do, Minister.' He said, 'What do you mean? It's nothing to do with us.' I said, 'Yes, Minister. All medical stores are under the Ministry of Supply.' 'I don't believe it,' he answered. I stuck to my point. 'Well, anyway, what are we going to be about it?' I said, 'There is a very efficient civil servant in your employ who deals with all this.' 'What's his name?' 'His name is Warburton.' 'Where is he?' 'He is probably in bed. I didn't expect to get so far tonight, or I would have warned him to be here.' 'Well, send for him.' So at about 9.30 p.m. the Minister's Rolls-Royce was duly dispatched to the suburb where this official resided. We adjourned for dinner; and some time just after midnight, when the various conferences had passed on far beyond the subject of medical stores, the door opened and the new arrival was ushered in. Warburton was an extremely efficient but rather conventional civil servant of the best type. Generally he was meticulously tidy, but he had been hauled out of bed; had dressed hurriedly; had been bundled into the car; and with his dishevelled look reminded me of the days when as boys we used to go into 'Early School' with an overcoat and scarf concealing the inadequacies of our toilet. 'This is Mr. Warburton,' I said. Lord Beaverbrook greeted him with his usual charming and hospitable manner. 'Will you have some champagne?' 'Oh, Minister, it is rather late for champagne.' 'Oh no, give him some champagne. Well, look at this list. What are all these?' 'These particular items, Minister, are soporific drugs.' 'What are those?' said Beaverbrook. 'Well,' said Warburton, 'they are commonly divided into three main groups, with various divisions and subdivisions. In the first main group might well be placed the barbiturate drugs. These can be ranged into. . . .' 'Oh God! For God's sake take him away! Give him some more champagne! But take him away! I can't stand it!' So poor Mr. Warburton was given more champagne and hurried out of the room to be put back into the Rolls-Royce and landed in Purley in the early hours of the morning.

Beaverbrook never saw him again; but it was my duty to deal with this admirable servant of the Crown and I felt considerable delicacy was required. However, everything went off all right. We fulfilled this part of the Protocol to the last grain, supplying among a mass of medical stores all the drugs which were the cause of the Minister's impatience. Warburton never referred to this episode in conversation with me. I think he was not sure whether it had ever happened or whether it was a nightmare. This was one of the minor incidents which made life at the Ministry of Supply after Beaverbrook came so eventful. But it did not detract from the hard, steady, slogging work which he got out of those who served him, never sparing himself and always driving on towards his goal.

In these long days and nights, days of careful scrutiny in each department and nights of hard bargaining, we finally arrived at a series of decisions as to the timetable for fulfilling the heavy burdens which the Harriman-Beaverbrook mission had undertaken at Moscow. But the story did not end there. I took no part in the planning of the delivery of all these supplies, except on one or two occasions, when I attended in Beaverbrook's absence specially convened meetings presided over by the Prime Minister to determine the organisation of the convoys. The terrible losses involved remain for ever as a proof of the sincerity with which Britain, at heavy cost, carried out her undertakings. Our part in the Ministry was to see that the material was available, but we could not shut our eyes to the dangers involved in trying to dispatch it all to Russia through the only route then available before the Persian railways were developed—that is, the sea route from Britain to Archangel. That we never got a word of thanks from our sullen allies did not detract from the enthusiasm with which everyone concerned set about the task of aid to Russia.

While all this work was going on, the pressure inside and outside the Government continued. Beaverbrook maintained his somewhat isolationist position, partly to annoy Bevin and partly because he disliked any interference with what he conceived to be his own authority. I did my best during this period to pour oil on these troubled waters, for, as Chairman of the Industrial Capacity Committee, I had a dual loyalty. One of the chief controversies was over the distribution of labour. Beaverbrook was keen to achieve his own purposes and was not disinclined to use unofficial channels. Bevin complained of his 'unauthorised and underhand' activities. I spent a considerable amount of time in trying to find various compromises. As early as July, Bevin had objected to the operations of a newly-appointed official, whom Beaverbrook had employed for the independent recruitment of foremen in Lancashire. Bevin told Beaverbrook that this gentleman's efforts would be 'likely to cause great confusion and resentment'. He added, 'Our officers have had discussions and are taking steps to clear up the mess. But the fact remains that it is a mess about which I must enter the strongest possible protest.'[16] Beaverbrook handed me this letter with impish delight and asked me to reply to it. But I could only rely on evasions, for Beaverbrook was determined to use his own recruiting organisations for special labour which he thought he needed. All this was particularly disagreeable to Bevin, who had an orderly mind.

Another dispute arose about the final authority over raw materials and machine-tools. Here, undoubtedly, the Minister of Supply was under obligation to act on behalf of all the departments and to act fairly. Through the autumn and winter the battle raged furiously.

[16] Letter of 25 July 1941.

Lord Portal and I tried to find some solution. I still retain the concordat which we drew up. But the truth is that Beaverbrook evaded every meeting held to discuss these problems and was determined to pursue his own somewhat piratical methods. He was an agile antagonist and made rings round Bevin.

The attempt to carry on the higher management of war production by committees had been remarkably successful. But we had now reached a point when these matters could no longer be dealt with without a change of system. There was a real need for a single authority. Pressure for a decision, inside and outside Parliament, was becoming increasingly effective and damaging to the Prime Minister's position. In October the Government was under heavy fire. Accordingly, on 28 October, I sent a minute to Beaverbrook:

A Production Ministry (to include Labour) is absolutely necessary.

1. It is a political necessity. Dark days lie before us; the House of Commons and the nation are dissatisfied with the present Production arrangements.

2. It is a practical necessity. I have watched for eighteen months (and taken part in) all sorts of plans and subterfuges to evade the straight issue. All our troubles flow from trying to substitute interdepartmental committees for a head.

When we have a head, all the other parts of the body will work harmoniously together. That's the whole story—except to add that there is only one man in the country who will be accepted for a moment as head—yourself.

To this he made a characteristic reply, gracious but evasive.

Throughout November the agitation continued. On 8 December 1941, Parliament was summoned to face a new enemy. Following Pearl Harbour, Britain declared war on Japan. New measures, at home and abroad, were urgently needed. At home, these included a National Service Bill, introduced and carried through all its stages in December. This, in effect, reversed all Bevin's previous declarations and instituted a system amounting to universal and compulsory service, for men and women, for civilian as well as military duties.

If one long-defended position had to be abandoned in the field of production, what about the other? Was it not now, at long last, necessary to concentrate authority in the hands of a single Minister?

While these discussions were proceeding, there came the heavy blow of the loss of the two battleships in Eastern waters—the *Repulse* and the *Prince of Wales*. Our people are accustomed to setbacks, even disasters, on land. All through history we have had to bear them without flinching. But a defeat at sea is another thing. I well remember the gasp of agony—not despair, but humiliation and almost incredulity—when this news reached us on 11 December.

For a while things had gone better in the desert. General Auchinleck, with some reluctance, attacked on 18 November. In spite of some confusion and disagreement among the commanders, the attack achieved a considerable success. Bardia and Halfaya were taken, and 14,000 prisoners captured. But our advantage was short-lived. By the end of January we had suffered a serious set-back. Once again our tanks were said to be at fault.

From the middle of December until the middle of January 1942 Beaverbrook was in America. When he returned I warned him that the political situation which I had foreseen was now developing. The Press and the public were becoming more and more restive. The disputes between Bevin and Beaverbrook were well known, and some action must be taken to bring them to an end. I was becoming increasingly persuaded that a Ministry of Production was now necessary. Towards the end of January, with my Minister's approval, I therefore circulated a memorandum on this subject, which is described by the historians of war production as follows:

The crux of this proposal was the subordination of the Ministers of Supply, Aircraft Production, Shipbuilding, Works and Buildings, and perhaps others, to the new senior Minister. (The Minister responsible for shipbuilding was to be a Civil Lord of the Admiralty.) The Minister of Production would receive the programme from the Defence Committee. He would have control of the factors of production—materials, tools, and labour—and would allocate them to his subordinate Ministers, who would be directly responsible for carrying out the programme. The staff of the Ministry would be composed primarily of the staffs taken over with the controls and from the Ministry of Labour. The basis of the organisation would be a programme staff, built up by taking staff from the Ministry of Supply and the War Cabinet secretariat. Mr. Macmillan's proposal proved to be only the first essay in a complex and many-sided attempt to frame a new and final system of controlling production.[17]

This, of course, would lead to a head-on collision with Bevin. But it was the only logical conclusion and either Beaverbrook or Bevin had to take the post.

[17] Scott and Hughes, p. 431.

At the same time I began to press Beaverbrook that it was his duty to accept the position of Minister of Production. This had become all the more essential after Pearl Harbour and the American entry into the war, which immediately brought about the need for a complete co-ordination of strategy and supply between our two nations. For this purpose the two Governments soon agreed on setting up the 'Combined Chiefs of Staff', sitting in Washington, with full representation of the British Chiefs. So far as munition supplies were concerned, the Americans appointed one man to preside over the whole sphere—Donald Nelson. We therefore had to have a single individual responsible for the whole of British production, to act both in Washington and in Moscow on behalf of Britain and on equal terms with Nelson.

The next two or three days proved decisive. On the night of 2 February, Beaverbrook told me that he intended to accept the position of Minister of Production. The full scope of his new powers was a matter still to be settled. He would like War Transport to be included in his group, and it was probable that Lord Leathers would agree. Labour was another matter, and was still unresolved. On 4 February, the creation of a Ministry of Production, and the appointment of Lord Beaverbrook to this office, were announced in Parliament. Sir Andrew Duncan was to come back as Minister of Supply. Thus a long controversy came to an end, and once more Parliamentary pressure seemed to have gained a notable success. It is true that the full plan was never implemented, and that another year was required for the new Ministry to find itself. Once more the official historians have correctly analysed the situation:

During this time the conception of the new instrument changed from that put forward by Mr. Macmillan, first to that of a co-ordinating office staffed rather along the lines of an expanded Minister's private office than along those of a Government department; and secondly to something which had elements both of a controlling department and of a co-ordinating office.[18]

Beaverbrook also told me that he would not be allowed a representative in the House of Commons. Since his would be a supervisory function, he would be supported only by a small but expert staff, rather than by the full complement of a normal Ministry. A Parliamentary Secretary might create jealousy among the other Ministries. It would be arranged that one of the supply Ministers would answer

18 Ibid., p. 432.

questions and speak on his behalf when necessary. This was a great grief to him because it meant that we should no longer work together. But he had spoken to Churchill about my future. Churchill had agreed that I should be appointed to an office where my chief was in the House of Lords. The next morning, Churchill sent for me. He explained the situation which had developed and asked me to go as Under-Secretary at the Colonial Office. Since Lord Moyne held this post, I should be as well placed as at present, from the Parliamentary point of view. In addition—and this touched me greatly—he told me of his intention to recommend me to be appointed to the Privy Council. At this time this was an unusual honour to be given to a junior Minister.

I made my round of farewells and finally left the Ministry of Supply on 5 February 1942. Thus ended a period of service—testing, exacting, and challenging—which had lasted since the Churchill Government was first formed in May 1940.

But the difficulties were, alas, by no means resolved. In the course of the next fortnight, Beaverbrook asked to see me on several occasions.

He had moved into No. 12 Downing Street and was using the large room usually occupied by the Whips. I was distressed and shocked by his appearance. His usual ardour and vigour seemed to have been drained out of him. During these days he was a lonely and rather sad figure. He had had no difficulty about the Ministry of War Transport, since the Minister, Lord Leathers, had welcomed the chance of operating under his general supervision. But the battle of Labour was not going well. Bevin was resisting, and Bevin's power in the Cabinet, in the House of Commons, and in the political world was greater than Beaverbrook's. He was a more influential figure in the Labour Party than Attlee, its official leader. Beaverbrook told me that he would either have to agree to some concordat, by which Bevin's independent control of Labour would continue, or throw in his hand. I urged him strongly, in spite of the logical arguments with which I had been pestering him for months past for placing the control of the allocation of labour under the Minister of Production, not to press his demands to the extreme point.

Some historians have regarded the matter as a mere conflict of political power; and that Churchill was in no position to stand out against Bevin, who had a great following, even to secure the con-

tinued co-operation of his friend Beaverbrook.[19] Churchill, on the
other hand, regarded Beaverbrook's final resignation of his new post,
after holding it for only a fortnight, as the result of a complete
breakdown in his health. He did not feel that he could face the new
and great responsibilities which he had assumed.

From my recollection of Beaverbrook's bearing and appearance
during this anxious period, I am convinced that Churchill's is the true
explanation of his apparently wayward moods and vacillations.
Beaverbrook had undergone tremendous strain for twenty arduous
months. His exertions at the Ministry of Aircraft Production were
almost superhuman. His recent journeys to Washington and Moscow,
under the harsh conditions of travelling in war-time, had affected him
severely. His asthma had grown daily worse. The frame had become
too weak to sustain the flame of his spirit. I am sure that if he had
been in full health he would have carried on, partly from his devotion
to Churchill and partly from his sense of duty. He did, in fact, accept
on 10 February a compromise with Bevin on the question of labour.
But he felt the need for peace and rest. Nine days later he resigned.

I knew that Beaverbrook's departure from the Government would
be welcomed by his enemies, regretted by his friends, and misunderstood by the general public. I had grown to understand something of
this strange man during these months. If he was something of an
enigma, he was always exciting. If there were aspects of his character
which repelled, there were others that were intensely attractive. While
I served him and until the end of his life I received from him nothing
but kindness, and was never asked to make any kind of repayment in
any form. Perhaps I was fortunate; but this was my experience.

[19] A. J. P. Taylor, *English History, 1914–1945* (Oxford, 1965), p. 543.

CHAPTER SIX

The New Allies

IN the course of 1941, two events took place which in addition to their effect upon the outcome of the war have left a permanent mark upon the structure of the modern world. The first of these was Hitler's decision to launch on 22 June, without warning and without even the usual excuses, a full-scale attack upon Soviet Russia— 'Operation Barbarossa'. The German invasion of Russia on a wide front set in motion a series of developments, tactical and strategic, which determined the character and issue of the war itself and formed the mould into which the life of Europe has since been poured. Similarly, the treacherous Japanese attack on the American fleet in Pearl Harbour on 7 December brought the United States reluctantly but inescapably into war not only with Japan but also with Germany. America now entered upon, and has never abandoned, a leading role in world affairs.

By the end of 1941 it became certain that Germany, in spite of her enormous military and economic resources, would sooner or later yield to the combined strength of the British Empire, Russia and the United States. The defeat of Japan would follow. More than three years of anxiety and loss, with the ebb and flow of battle, were to be endured before final victory could be won. But after our alliance, first with Russia and then with America, we could feel no doubt about the ultimate issue. Long and bitter as was the path we had to travel, Churchill was right in feeling that this was the turning-point. 'Many disasters, immeasurable cost and tribulation lay ahead, but there was no more doubt about the end.'[1]

Yet if we were to enjoy welcome relief, we could not escape the inevitable political and economic consequences. In the first flush of enthusiasm, we thought only of the recruits to our ranks. As the

[1] Churchill, *The Grand Alliance*, p. 540.

months and years passed we began to grasp the full implications of the
new balance of forces in the world. The revolutionary changes of this
century, the opening phases of which I have already described,[2] were
now to proceed at an accelerated rate.

The alliance with Russia was to bring us many immediate problems.
Although the Soviet Government under Stalin had equalled if not
surpassed the mistakes made by pre-war administrations in the countries of Western Europe, the British people, conscious of their own
errors, were ready to forget the past. For like French and British
statesmen in the years before the war, Stalin had allowed nations vital
to his defence to be eaten up by the Germans, one by one. It is true
that he had gained much from the secret clauses of the Molotov-
Ribbentrop Pact made two years before. Yet all this time, Russia had
continued to supply Germany with materials and munitions on an
ever-increasing scale. Like so many people who are not themselves too
scrupulous, Stalin proved strangely credulous about the scruples of
others. He seemed up to the last moment to have had faith in Hitler
honouring his agreement. There was no lack of warnings, from many
sources. But, like Chamberlain, Stalin persisted in his policy of appeasement. Like Chamberlain, he was angry when he learned that he
had been the dupe of his own wishful thinking.

Even while the German divisions were moving into place upon the
Russian frontier, express trains from the Far East were expediting the
supply of rubber up to the very eve of the attack.[3] (These supplies had
soon to be made good at great sacrifice from British sources.) There
were many other evidences of Stalin's fear of offending his German
friends. In the course of May 1941, the Belgian, Norwegian and even
the Yugoslav envoys were dismissed from the Russian capital. The pro-
German Government of Rashid Ali in Iraq was recognised. Massive
deployment of German troops upon the frontier could hardly have
escaped detection; yet as late as 14 June, the famous Tass dispatch was
published, denying the widespread rumours in the British and foreign
Press of an impending war between Soviet Russia and Germany. The
statement added: 'Despite the obvious absurdity of these rumours,
responsible circles in Moscow have thought it necessary to state that

[2] In *Winds of Change.*
[3] General Thomas of the German War Ministry, quoted by Churchill, *The Grand
Alliance,* p. 326.

they are a clumsy propaganda manœuvre.' It is difficult to assess how far this was wishful thinking and how far Stalin seriously intended to convert his agreement with Hitler into an even firmer alliance. If it had become essential for the German economy to be sustained by large-scale contributions from the Ukraine and from other Russian terri-tories, there is little doubt that these could have been obtained by peaceful means, supported by bellicose threats. Russia would have complied with almost any demands. A significant revelation of the degree of pliancy which the Russians had reached lies in Molotov's pathetic complaint on the German declaration of war. He turned to the German Ambassador and said, 'Do you believe that we deserve that?' This is the true language of appeasement.

But Stalin's bungling, which allowed the Russian armies to be overwhelmed and Moscow and Leningrad almost captured, was neu-tralised by an unexpected turn of events in what must have seemed a subsidiary front—the Balkans. It may even have caused the postpone-ment of 'Barbarossa' from 15 May to 22 June. No wonder Hitler flew into a rage over the Yugoslav *coup d'état* in March 1941, which made in necessary for him to detach the troops earmarked for Leningrad and Moscow to deal with the situation in Belgrade. No wonder he never ceased complaining of the incompetence of his Italian allies, which forced him to rescue them in Greece. Here, indeed, the decision to dispatch British troops on the almost hopeless task of succouring Greece perhaps had its reward.

Hitler may have believed that there would be forces in Britain which on ideological grounds might hesitate to grasp in friendship the bloody hands of Bolshevik revolutionaries. If so, he was not the first nor the last to underrate the practical approach to questions affecting our own vital interests which is traditional in our country. The British reaction to Churchill's lead was unhesitating. Naturally, the ex-treme Left, Communist or semi-Communist, was quick to respond to the new situation. The moderate Left was also swayed by a certain sympathy for the achievements since the fall of Tsarism in 1917 of what was believed to be a working-class system of Government. But the idea that the Conservatives, however great their distaste for the principles and practice of Communism, would be foolish enough not to welcome the prospect of some 120 German divisions being locked in mortal combat with their allies of yesterday is much to underrate their

intelligence. When a thug has you by the throat, you are not disposed
to quarrel with the moral character of any man who becomes, willy-
nilly, mixed up in the brawl. We did not look at the time to the
implications of the new groupings. Whether it was altogether to our
taste to have the Russians as allies was not the question. It was, in our
isolation, an apparently heaven-sent stroke of luck. The only doubts
which the British people had (and these were shared by informed
military opinion) were whether the Russian armies could withstand
the German onslaught. Their poor showing in the Winter War in
Finland had led to their real value being under-assessed. Furthermore,
it was the general view that Stalin's purges of the 1930s had thrown the
Russian military system into great confusion. This may have been
thought by the Russians to justify the policy of appeasement. Just as
the supporters of Munich argued that it had given us another year for
rearmament, so a similar defence was later developed in Communist
circles to explain the Molotov-Ribbentrop Pact of 1939. Hitler may
also have been deceived both by overestimating the effect of the purge
and by the apparent failures in the Finnish war.

Our chief anxiety in those decisive months was not over the long-
term implications of our co-operation with Bolshevists, but whether
the Russians could survive. In the first weeks of December the attack
on Moscow began to grind to a halt, and the Russians were even able
to make some counter-offensives. Meanwhile, so great were the efforts
which we made to give all possible aid that our immediate strength
was undoubtedly diminished rather than increased. Since we had been
promised all the output of munitions which America could achieve
beyond her own requirements, everything that America was now to
supply to Russia came out of our expectations. Of course, in the long
run we were great gainers; but in the short we were faced with new
hazards and reductions of our power to fight the important battles
with which we were soon to be faced.

The immediate burdens upon us were onerous. Apart from the large
supplies—guns, tanks, ammunition and stores of every description—
there was the heavy and dangerous duty of the convoys, where the
losses incurred were painful. Nor was there much apparent gratitude
from the Russians. Even the tragic fate of the convoy PQ. 17 in the
summer of 1942, when twenty-three ships were sunk out of thirty-six
that left Iceland and all their crews perished in the icy sea, drew little

sympathy from Moscow. The northern route in midsummer, with its perpetual daylight, became too dangerous, and convoys had to be postponed until September. This involved further losses, convoy PQ. 18 losing ten ships out of thirty-seven.

But, even had the British people realised the grudging spirit in which our allies treated these prodigious efforts to supply them, they would still have taken a practical view of the value to us of another enemy to Hitler. Some may have hoped that from this new alliance there might result some softening of the fundamental aims which govern Russian policy. But Soviet policy did not change after victory. Communism and Imperialism remained the double-edged weapon of expansion over Asia and Europe alike.

With a strange lack of any understanding of all other peoples than themselves, the Soviet Government began immediately to make demands for the opening of a 'Second Front'. It did not seem to occur to them that the Second Front had disappeared in the summer of 1940 with the collapse of France—a process which they had watched without any apparent discomfort or dismay, although no doubt they would have preferred to see the countries of Western Europe locked for a longer time in a mutually destructive struggle. Anti-British propaganda had continued with unrelieved bitterness up to almost the day of the German attack. Yet they began to clamour for an immediate descent upon the French coast or, alternatively, for impossible and hare-brained schemes of sending twenty-five divisions to Archangel! This cry was soon to be taken up through their friends in Britain, and became an increasing embarrassment to the Government. Our Left-wing politicians, including the Communists, who had been very unwilling to help their own country when it stood alone and in dire peril, underwent an extraordinary conversion when Soviet Russia was attacked by Hitler. Up till then, they had been neutral, if not pro-German; but when the order was given they executed a smart 'about turn'. Not only did they become partisans of the war against Hitler, but they demanded immediate operations to relieve the Russians without the slightest knowledge of the difficulties involved. Just as Stalin and his Ministers never had the smallest appreciation of the problem of landing large forces across tidal seas against strongly defended coasts, so did these agitators fail to appreciate the losses which would have been involved in any premature attempt to launch an attack upon

Western Europe. Fortunately, Churchill had both the courage and the
determination to resist these pressures, whether from his new allies in
Russia or from the sudden converts in Britain.

But more difficult were the political questions which were soon to be
raised. First, and most delicate, was that of Poland. It was, after all,
our guarantee to Poland which had been the occasion, if not the
ultimate cause, of the Second World War. How then were we to accept
the fourth partition and disintegration of Poland, the deportation of
hundreds of thousands of Poles, and the injury done to every tradition
of Polish life? The Poles in exile were naturally suspicious as the
pressure began to grow. Although Britain, and afterwards America,
resisted the Soviet demand for immediate recognition of the new
situation, in the end we were not powerful enough to establish a
genuine democratic régime in Poland. When the war ended, the
tragedy of Poland was to be one of the blots on the fair face of
victory.

The Russian insistence on the frontiers of Peter the Great soon led
to the disappearance of the Baltic States. Here again, in spite of great
pressure, Churchill and Roosevelt stood firm in principle. But here,
too, in practice the absorption and Bolshevisation of these hitherto
independent peoples had to be accepted.

Finally, Finland. After their victory, not content with the terms of
the Peace of Moscow, the Soviet Government never relaxed their
hostility or their demands. They vetoed the organisation of a Scandinavian alliance (which might, incidentally, have proved to their
advantage later). In August 1940 they formally annexed the Baltic
States, greatly to the alarm of the Finns. In June they made claims, not
included in the treaty, regarding the installations which the Finns had
removed from Hanko. They began to sink Finnish merchant ships.
They required the restoration of Finnish State property taken from
Karelia. They insisted upon the expulsion from the Government of
Vaino Tanner, a Social Democrat and a man of great quality and
courage.

All this happened in the course of 1940, and it is hardly a matter of
surprise that the Finns yielded to the German insistence upon the
right to pass through their country into occupied Norway—the so-
called Transit Agreement made in September 1940. Early in 1941, the
Russians cut off all supplies to the Finns and thus forced them to

Harold Macmillan with Winston Churchill at Casablanca, January 1943.

With Lord Davies in Finland,
February 1940.

With Herbert Morrison, Minister
of Supply, May–October 1940.

Lord Beaverbrook, Minister of Supply,
June 1941–February 1942.

SUN [DAILY HERALD]

Cartoon by George Whitelaw.

"H'M. SO THE BEAVER'S TAKEN OVER ALREADY...."

General Henri Giraud and General Charles de Gaulle with President Roosevelt and Prime Minister Churchill at Casablanca.

General Charles de Gaulle.

Major General George S. Patton
and General Noguès.

Taking the salute at Algiers, St. Joan of Arc's day, May 9, 1943. Marcel Peyrouton, General Giraud, General Georges Catroux, Macmillan, Morse, Maurice Couve de Murville.

The visit of 'General Lyon,' June 12, 1943. Macmillan, Admiral Sir Andrew Cunningham, Air Marshal Sir Arthur Tedder, King George VI, General Dwight D. Eisenhower.

Luncheon party, June 5, 1943. *Seated*: Catroux, de Gaulle, Churchill, Giraud, Anthony Eden; *standing*: Jean Monnet, André Philip, Macmillan, General Georges, Field-Marshal Sir Alan Brooke, Cunningham, René Massigli.

Air Chief Marshal Sholto Douglas, Macmillan, General Walter Bedell Smith, Robert Murphy.

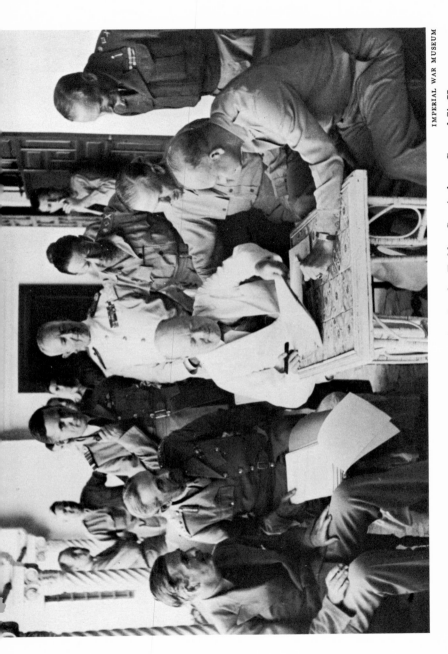

Churchill and the war leaders in North Africa. Eden, Brooke, Tedder, Cunningham, General Sir Harold Alexander, General George C. Marshall, Eisenhower, Field-Marshal Sir Bernard Montgomery.

King Victor Emmanuel and Marshal Badoglio.

General Sir Harold Alexander.

Andrei Vyshinsky

Marshal Tito, Churchill, Dr. Subašić.

General Sir Humfrey Gale,
Macmillan,
General Alexander.

Robert Murphy and Macmillan at Cassibile, near Syracuse, August 1943.

FIELD-MARSHAL LORD ALEXANDER

With General Alexander at Cassino.

The Cairo Conference. *Seated*: Chiang Kai-shek, Roosevelt, Churchill, Madame Chiang; *standing*: Sir Alexander Cadogan, unidentified, Eden, Steinhardt, John G. Winant, Macmillan, Wong Chung-hui, R. G. Casey, Lord Killearn, Major Sir Desmond Morton, Averell Harriman, Douglas.

Churchill and Archbishop Damaskinos in Athens, December 20, 1944.

With General Oliver Leese in the Republic of San Marino,,September 1944.

Peace-making in Athens, December 26, 1944. Churchill and Eden are seated to the right of Archbishop Damaskinos; Alexander and Macmillan are to his left.

become entirely dependent upon Germany for their economic survival. The Finnish Government, therefore, found itself faced with a cruel dilemma. They made every effort to remain neutral and so informed both the Germans and the Russians. Nevertheless, fighting broke out. The Finns refused to take part in the assault and siege of Leningrad, but in their search for a better line of defence, desired to move forward into Eastern Karelia. It would have been wiser had they accepted at least the 1939 frontier. Once more Churchill did his best. He tried, by a personal message to Marshal Mannerheim, to persuade him to stand on the old frontier and not to succumb to the temptation to try to annex Eastern Karelia, in spite of the strong grounds which the Finns had for their ambitions. The British Government, although sympathetic, finally decided to yield to what seemed the larger interest—the defeat of Hitler.

So it came about that, in December 1941, to my great sorrow, Britain declared war on Finland. I have always thought that this was an error. It had little practical effect. Its only object was to appease the Russians. But was this gesture necessary? The American Government did not remove their diplomatic representation and did all they could, as the war proceeded, to assist Finland to disengage. Finally, in July 1944, the climax approached. As the Germans began to retire the Finns were left almost alone. Great new Russian attacks were launched upon them, which were repelled with the same heroism as in the winter of 1940. Marshal Mannerheim, who was now persuaded of the need for disengagement, was able to create a military situation in which a peace, hateful and wounding but not dishonourable, was ultimately negotiated.[4] The end came with the ceasefire of September 1944. Harsh as were the terms and heavy the burden of reparations which were demanded, Finland has paid her debts and succeeded in maintaining her independence. All her small neighbours—Estonia, Latvia, Lithuania—which had emerged from the First World War, have been sucked back into the great Russian mass. Poland has become dominated by the Communist system and in spite of significant developments in recent years has remained a satellite of Russia. Finland, alone of all these, has retained her freedom.

In these early years, however, difficult as the Russians were as allies

[4] Marshal Mannerheim, *Memoirs,* trans. Count Lewenhaupt (London, 1953), pp. 491 ff.

and ungenerous as their attitude towards us remained, all this was
hidden from the British public. Nor could the Government be blamed
for putting first things first. The survival of any form of Western
civilisation depended upon the defeat of Hitler and to that end almost
everything had to be sacrificed. Yet the seeds of trouble were sown.
Nor were the dangers ahead ever absent from the minds of our leaders.
Churchill records how in June 1942 the Russian territorial ambitions
caused him much concern, and the pressure grew as the war continued.[5] The American people, with characteristic impetuosity, became ardent converts to pro-Russianism. A wave of sympathy spread
over the whole country. Admiration for the courage and tenacity of
the Russian Army was particularly strong among the American forces.
Although the State Department held out on the question of Finland
and the Baltic States, the President himself began to suffer under the
illusion, common to statesmen, that by some special qualities of his
own he might be able to 'tame the Russian bear'. A passage in a letter
of his to the Prime Minister on 18 March 1942 is symptomatic:

By the time you get this you will have been advised of my talk with
Litvinov, and I expect a reply from Stalin shortly. I know you will not mind
my being brutally frank when I tell you that I think I can personally handle
Stalin better than either your Foreign Office or my State Department. Stalin
hates the guts of all your top people. He thinks he likes me better, and I hope
he will continue to do so.[6]

This fancy grew upon him and was to have disastrous results in the
closing stages of the war.

In any event, if Hitler's attack on Russia and its failure marked a
turning-point in the war, British-American acceptance of Russia as a
full ally 'settled the fate of the world for many years to come'.[7]

If the relations between Japan and the United States had been
steadily deteriorating during the summer and autumn of 1941, no one—
least of all the American Service chiefs—had the slightest expectation
of anything like the sudden attack on the American Navy lying in
Pearl Harbour. For them it was, in every sense, a bolt from the blue.
For us it was a gift from the gods.

Prolonged negotiations with Japan had taken place in Washington

[5] See also *Winds of Change*, p. 14.
[6] Winston S. Churchill, *The Second World War*, vol. iv: *The Hinge of Fate* (London, 1951), p. 177.
[7] Taylor, *English History, 1914–1945*, p. 529.

and at one time it appeared that some kind of *modus vivendi* might be reached. The Japanese naturally wished to take advantage of the European war without themselves becoming embarked on too dangerous adventures. They had already seized French Indo-China and were anxious to bring their operations in China to a successful end. The diverse and delicately balanced forces which directed Japanese policy hovered long upon the brink. The decision of the American Government in July 1941 to ban virtually all normal trade with Japan had been loyally followed by the British Government and the Dutch Government-in-exile. Yet since this ban extended to oil supplies as well as to most other raw materials, the Japanese were faced with a situation which threatened gradual strangulation. It was the ban on oil which may well have persuaded the Japanese Navy, generally regarded as favourable to moderate policies, to agree to take the plunge.

All through the late summer and autumn months the anxieties of the British Government grew. Russia might be defeated, and Hitler free to turn again to the final assault upon Britain. Our Far East possessions were under dire threat from Japan. Yet we had no choice except to follow American policies. After all, we were largely dependent on their active assistance for continuing the war in Europe. We knew we had the sympathy of the President and those immediately around him. For Roosevelt had for many years been awake to the dangers of Hitler and his dreams. With consummate skill he had guided a Congress and people who were still isolationists by tradition. He had persuaded them, step by step, to amend or allow him to disregard the neutrality legislation in Britain's favour. He had effected the exchange of the West Indian bases for the fifty destroyers—obsolescent, but essential to our needs. He had maintained guard over half the Atlantic against the German submarines. He had solved our pressing financial problems by the institution of Lend-Lease. Yet he was by no means all-powerful. Congress was still suspicious. There had been the greatest difficulty in carrying or renewing compulsory military service. Churchill therefore had to be careful. He must not appear to be trying to coax the Americans into war; for the most wounding accusation that could be made against an American politician was that he had been cajoled by the sly enticements of the subtle 'Britishers'.

It was therefore difficult for us to influence the policy towards

Japan, where American opinion had been deeply stirred by the invasion of Chinese territory. It could be argued that, in the situation into which the Japanese Government had drifted, the embargo of July almost forced them to break out of the ring in some direction, unless they were prepared to accept the American terms—that is, withdrawal from the mainland of China.[8] From our point of view, locked as we were in mortal combat in Europe and the Middle East, a little bit of appeasement in the Far East might not have done us any harm. Yet we dared not propose any course which would have drawn upon us the moral reprobation of the American Government and people. But suppose Japan were to break out upon Dutch or British territory. What would the American Government do? Churchill must have thought that he knew what his friend the President would wish to do. But what would he be allowed to do? In the Guildhall speech (11 November), Churchill declared that if the United States failed to find ways to preserve peace in the Pacific and became involved in war with Japan, the British declaration would follow 'within the hour'. Yes, but what if America did not become involved? What if the Japanese were wise enough to seek their outlet purely at the expense of the Dutch, whose own country was now in Hitler's power, and of the British, whose prospects seemed at the time dark? The Americans made no sign, in private or in public. No parallel declaration to Churchill's was vouchsafed, secret or overt.

These terrible anxieties were relieved by Pearl Harbour. The destruction of a large part of the American Pacific fleet was indeed tragic, and would have its corresponding effect upon the claims of American production to replace the losses. But at any rate the Japanese attack decided the question of war or peace. The whole of the American people were incensed by what seemed to them a mean and treacherous blow without even the decencies of a formal declaration of war. Churchill naturally did not hesitate to seize the opportunity. With the full approval of the Cabinet he announced Britain's immediate declaration of war against Japan.

But there was still another danger which was in all our minds. What would Germany now do? Hitler cannot have been especially pleased with the Japanese who, in spite of their general commitments to Germany and Italy, had made no move to help since the Russo-

[8] Taylor, p. 531.

German war began. We now know how acutely concerned the Russians were as to the final Japanese decision. It was regarded as one of the greatest triumphs of their Secret Service when they could be told beyond a doubt of the Japanese Government's determination, in spite of the pressure from the extremists, to remain neutral, or—if they decided on war—to choose the Pacific rather than Siberia.[9] Germany must therefore have felt a sense of grievance over the hesitancy of her allies in the summer, when a Japanese diversion against Russia, even if limited, might have had decisive results. All this made it uncertain what Hitler would do. However, all our doubts were set at rest. America could not—even had she wished—stand by and watch Japanese onslaughts on Malaya or Indonesia. She was herself the victim of Japanese aggression in its most brutal form. Germany, without waiting for Washington, decided to support Japan with a declaration of war against the United States. A recent historian has commented: 'Hitler's declaration of war was a romantic empty gesture . . . [it] ranks second only to Pearl Harbour as a service to Great Britain.'[10] The hesitations of Roosevelt and those who thought with him were thus removed. They knew well the strength of the neutrality feeling among their countrymen, based upon the old traditions of American isolationism. They knew also the strong resistance that there would be against an unprovoked declaration of war against Germany. Now both Japan and Germany had, on their own initiative, declared war upon the United States. To this situation of fact the American people, once the die was cast, would rally with the enthusiasm and tenacity which they have always shown at every great crisis in their history.

President Roosevelt, more far-seeing than most of his compatriots, had long recognised that the changing conditions of the modern world were making obsolete the old concepts of American foreign policy. While there were many who clung to the tradition that the New World should by every possible means escape from entanglement in the Old, the more enlightened thinkers had begun to realise that the world had shrunk since the pioneer days. In the past, long voyages, by sail or even by steam, across 3,000 miles of ocean were a practical barrier and a powerful defence. In the First War, largely owing to the

[9] F. W. Deakin and G. R. Storry, *The Case of Richard Sorge* (London, 1966), pp. 218 ff.
[10] Taylor, p. 532, n.1.

folly of German policy and the ruthless extension of the U-boat warfare without regard to neutral susceptibilities, the Americans had been drawn in during the concluding stages. But if they had acted, they had also reacted sharply. President Wilson's attempt to take the lead in the Paris peace negotiations was not popular. By a tragic combination of obstinacy and vanity, he was unable to secure the ratification by the Senate of the Treaty, or American adherence to the League of Nations, which he had done so much to promote. Thus the tradition of isolation had been re-established, together with out-of-date concepts appropriate to a colonial and undeveloped country—high tariffs, protection, mercantilism. Roosevelt had seen the collapse of the American economy, which it was impossible to separate from the general state of European and world prosperity. Isolation, insulation, separatism—all began to wear thin. Nevertheless, so great was the reluctance of the American people to be involved once more in a European struggle that it was only by the most skilful management that Roosevelt, perhaps the supreme politician of his age, was able, step by step, to bring aid to the British people in their need. It is doubtful whether he could ever have brought Congress and the nation to join in a second war against Germany had it not been for the Japanese attack and its consequences. To Far Eastern dangers the Americans were more susceptible. They were alarmed, perhaps unduly, about the weakness of their undefended western seaboard; and now, by Germany's action, they were, whether they wished it or not, automatically involved in war in Europe.

To Roosevelt, Britain owes much. Churchill, from the beginning of the war, set himself out to win the President's confidence. His correspondence with him began after the outbreak of war, in 1939. As First Lord, he concealed from Roosevelt nothing of his thoughts or of the problems with which we were confronted. When he became Prime Minister, these contacts grew deeper and more intimate. Nevertheless, President Roosevelt's response was by no means as warm or as open as Churchill believed. Certainly there were prejudices deep in the President's soul which made him suspicious of British policy. With all his apparent sincerity and charm, there lay behind the outward show of friendship a feeling of hostility—perhaps even of jealousy—of the great Imperial story of the Old Country. The British Empire was a bugbear to him. Without any precise knowledge, he would lay down the law about Indian and colonial affairs; and the liquidation of the British Empire was, whether consciously or unconsciously, one of his aims. An example of this can be found in the continual pressure upon us to end the preferential system, and to weaken any ties, whether material or sentimental, by which the Empire was bound together.

I have frequently observed that this inherited antipathy to 'colonialism' is most marked among the oldest families in the United States, especially in New England. To affect suspicion of Britain is perhaps a kind of unconscious, almost nostalgic, tribute to history. Some of my Boston friends, for instance, never seem to be able to forget that unlucky business about the chests of tea. However this may be, the President was no friend of the British Empire. Nor did he understand the clearly defined and steadily pursued procedures by which we had long planned to bestow, by gradual means, first political education and then political independence upon those races for whom we held responsibility. In almost every joint declaration of policy, the Cabinet had to watch, and if possible eliminate, some dangerous phrases. This prejudice, sometimes with unhappy results, extended to monarchical institutions in many countries.

In the early days of the alliance, most of this lay concealed. The happy co-operation between the President and the Prime Minister was fortunately matched by the harmonious working of the machinery which they devised for the purpose of conducting the affairs of the alliance, whether in the sphere of operations or of supply.

While the Russian alliance therefore brought us a welcome diversion, the American alliance brought us an almost fraternal partnership. To me, with my American blood, it was a thrilling emotion. I only wished that my mother had still been alive to see and glory in the merging of the hopes and aspirations of the people of her adoption and the people of her birth.

As the war proceeded, and as the forces of the United States began to grow in strength and armaments until they became a preponderating part in our alliance, American political influence naturally grew correspondingly. Britain, with all her efforts, was a small country. She had undergone trials much more testing than in any war in history, and had exhausted more of her inherited wealth and strength. Her foreign assets were dissipated; large parts of her Empire had been torn from her and overrun. Even with their reconquest, the old prestige could not be re-established. Nevertheless, the American alliance was the solid base on which victory must be built, however long, however difficult the road might be. For the moment, we did not look far beyond the present. But largely under Roosevelt's guidance, and through the influence of the great company of men of all parties and of varying traditions in his own country which he gathered round him, it was clear that after the Second World War there would be no going back. The United States must now become not merely the richest country in the world, enjoying the most highly developed industrialised system, combined with a vast reserve of raw materials of all kinds, but having stepped into the world arena would not again retreat like Achilles into his tent. There might be from time to time suggestions or threats of 'agonising reappraisals'. But these would be passing moods. The virile American people would receive and carry the torch. They would stand as the defenders of Western civilisation and traditions. They would be true to their destiny.

CHAPTER SEVEN

The Colonial Empire at War

TO exchange the heat and bustle of life at Shell-Mex House under Lord Beaverbrook for the cool dignity of the old Colonial Office in Downing Street was a curious experience. Indeed, it was like going into another world. For twenty-one months I had worked under heavy pressure, day in, day out, with scarcely a break. The hours were long, the atmosphere hectic, and the sense of urgency all-pervading. The office in which we lived was an early example of that style of building to which we have now become accustomed. The outer walls enclosed the necessary square feet of floor space, divided into appropriate partitions according to the rank and status of the prospective occupier, but that was all. There was neither character nor sense of tradition. Low ceilings and monotonous fenestration were the rule. To go from this into the Victorian environment of the great block of buidings—Foreign Office, India Office, Colonial Office—which constituted the centre of Whitehall, each with its vast and lofty saloons, noble staircase, tessellated passages, huge fireplaces and sumptuous marble chimney-pieces, great mahogany desks and antique chairs, was indeed a strange transition. I had formed the habit of getting very early to my office and leaving very late. This practice seemed somehow a little out of place in my new surroundings. Fortunately, I brought with me John Wyndham, who had been my private secretary at the Ministry of Supply. His combination of efficiency and humour gradually began to remove certain prejudices which I sensed at the beginning. Somebody asked me at the time how best to describe my experience. I remember saying that it felt like leaving a madhouse in order to enter a mausoleum. But this was really unfair to both.

In the Ministry of Supply, I had served three Ministers in twenty-one months. In the Colonial Office, I was to act in the same capacity to three Secretaries of State in ten months. All were friendly and sympathetic, in their very different ways. But, in the end, I began to hanker for a command of my own.

I had known Lord Moyne, although not intimately, during the many years that he sat as Walter Guinness in the House of Commons. There he had proved a popular and efficient Minister. He was one of the best Financial Secretaries that I can remember, at a time when this position was of outstanding importance in the daily work of government. Always courteous, always well informed, with an indefinable and somewhat elusive charm, he commanded respect and affection. Unhappily, only three weeks after I joined him, the political situation required another reshuffle of posts. Beaverbrook had gone out. Cripps had to come in. As a result, Moyne's post was needed—a decision which he loyally accepted.

On 22 February, Moyne was succeeded by Lord Cranborne, but since Cranborne had been called to the House of Lords, my position as sole representative of my department in the House of Commons was not affected. With Moyne, I had a relationship which had not been given the chance to ripen into comradeship. Cranborne was one of my oldest friends from school and university days. We already were doubly connected by marriage, and during this summer my son was to marry one of his nieces. Our partnership lasted until 22 November, exactly nine months. No man could have wished for a more delightful or generous chief. It was also pleasant to share the same point of view and to be able not only to face the anxieties but to enjoy the humours of our work together.

Unfortunately, my knowledge of the Colonies was very limited. As a private Member, I had concentrated my interests on economic and social affairs at home and, in the last years before the catastrophe, on foreign policy. I had made no study of Colonial affairs and knew very little about the structure of the Colonial Empire or the methods by which it was governed. There was much to learn, although the conditions were somewhat forbidding. Apart from the vast caverns of the Colonial Office building, where light seldom penetrated and ghostly steps echoed down the lofty corridors as in the aisles of some great cathedral, the organisation struck me, in my ignorance, as somewhat antiquated.

The Office was staffed by a devoted set of civil servants, recruited on the same lines as the Foreign Office before its amalgamation with the

Diplomatic Service. Just as young men who joined the Foreign Office would stay in London through their whole career without going abroad, except for an occasional holiday, so the staff of the Colonial Office, with rare exceptions, had seldom visited or served in any Colony. It was a small, tightly-knit Ministry, manned by intelligent and conscientious officials. If it was not inspired by the same kind of ruthlessness to which I had recently been accustomed, I now realise that the pace at which we were trying to work for a few months or years in the war-production Ministries could not be sustained through a lifetime of Whitehall. In any case, I must pay tribute to the kindness and sympathy which were extended to me. Many, especially among the younger men, welcomed my attempts to introduce a greater spirit of dynamism into our work.

Until my last weeks at the Colonial Office, Britain was passing through a period of deepening anxiety. On the political front there was an undercurrent of discontent, both in Parliament and in the country. The confusions over the Ministry of Production and the ensuing Government reshuffle had added to the general sense of uncertainty. The sinking by air attack of the two battleships, the *Prince of Wales* and the *Repulse,* on 10 December 1941, had been followed by large-scale Japanese landings in Malaya. On 15 February 1942, a few days after I began work in my new office, the surrender of Singapore, where General Percival and 85,000 British troops capitulated, was a staggering blow to British prestige in Asia and Africa. Our losses now included Hong Kong, the Straits Settlements, the Malay States, North Borneo and Sarawak, as well as some of the smaller islands in the Pacific. Burma was soon to follow, a military disaster only redeemed by General Alexander's masterly rearguard action. All these misfortunes, together with the evacuation of Dutch territories and the threatened loss of all Indonesia, faced us in the Colonial Office with a new and critical situation. Ceylon seemed likely to be the next target. Not only would a great possession of the Crown fall into enemy hands, but—on the material side—the last major source of natural rubber might disappear.

The next calamity was the fall of Tobruk on 21 June, with the surrender of 33,000 men. This was a grievous and altogether unforeseen blow. For the first time during the life of the National Coalition, a formal vote of no confidence was placed upon the Order Paper of the

House of Commons. It is true that Churchill had challenged his critics to come into the open, for he was anxious for a firm decision. This critical debate took place in a tense atmosphere. Auchinleck's battle in the desert had gone wrong and all our conquests lost. The Army, after suffering heavy losses of men and equipment, was back in the old positions defending Cairo, and the battle for Egypt was actually being fought while we were arguing. Sir John Wardlaw-Milne opened, and spoke with his customary pomposity but with considerable effect. The motion expressed a lack of 'confidence in the central direction of the war'. There are some men who have made a reputation by a single speech. It was reserved to Sir John to destroy his by a single sentence. He was getting on well enough in his argument against the Prime Minister's determination to combine with his own office the functions of Minister of Defence. He demanded their separation, and the appointment of a strong figure as Chief of the Chiefs of Staff. But when he came to propose that the Duke of Gloucester should be appointed Commander-in-Chief of the British Army, his speech collapsed. He lost the House and happily for Britain he lost his motion. Had the motion been carried, it could only have meant the supersession of Churchill. But the seconder, Sir Roger Keyes, made it abundantly clear that such a result was the last thing he desired. It was the Prime Minister's advisers—especially his naval advisers—whom he wished to remove. No one but Churchill could weather the storm. In the famous debate which led to the fall of the Chamberlain Government, the gallant Admiral had asked my advice and shown me what he proposed to say and how he should say it. This time, without a friendly pilot, he was as dashing as ever but seemed to steer a somewhat uncertain course.

All the usual critics took part, including Winterton, Hore-Belisha, Clem Davies and Sydney Silverman. It was on this occasion that Aneurin Bevan launched a specially virulent onslaught on Churchill, using the bitter phrase, 'The Prime Minister wins debate after debate and loses battle after battle.' But Wardlaw-Milne's strange mistake, and the contradiction between him and his seconder, blunted the attack from the beginning. Even after two full days the critics could not reconcile their differences. I heard a great part of the debate, which took place on 1 and 2 July, including Churchill's two-hour defence, which he reserved to the end. In a courageous and closely argued speech, he brought the House back to a sense of realities. It was one of his finest efforts. We all knew the tremendous burdens which he was carrying and the disappointments he had suffered. I had chanced to have some words with him outside the House, and sensed the resolute decision which he had reached. He would be Prime Minister, in the full meaning of the title and carrying the full responsibilities of his office. If this was refused, he would resign. This he stated, without equivocation, to the House. He was in no mood to be reduced to a position which Asquith had refused in 1916, whereby the actual direction of the war would be handed over to some unnamed super-man, leaving the Prime Minister as a kind of Public Orator. Once more, even at this low point in our fortunes, Churchill dominated the House and was rewarded by an overwhelming expression of confidence. The figures in the division were 476 to 25.

Yet all through the spring and summer months one disaster followed on another. The morale of Parliament and of the nation was not high. The perils of 1940 had not shaken the British people or its representatives. But the continued misfortunes of the winter of 1941 and the spring and summer of 1942 were harder to bear. Although Auchinleck, by the beginning of July, had managed to stabilise the line, it was not until the last days of October that his successors, Alexander and Montgomery, were able to launch their counter-attack and to win the triumphant victory of Alamein in six days of hard fighting. Then, indeed, the tide was seen to have turned.

However, in times of stress, it is a great comfort to be fully employed, and I had indeed plenty to do in my new department. At first I found the field so diverse as to be somewhat confusing. The territories under our care stretched over the whole globe. There were fifty-five in all, comprising 60 million inhabitants of different races, religions and in different stages of development. They varied from West Indian islands, advancing rapidly to something like self-government, with three hundred years of connection with Britain, to newly-occupied areas like Nigeria, where modern civilisation was only in its early stages. They included mere coaling stations, now turned into military bases, like Aden, and great historic peoples of ancient culture, occupying large areas like Ceylon. Whether from the point of view of administration or political progress, or social advancement, or war production, the contrasts, apart from the size of our responsibilities, were at first baffling.

The immediate task of the Colonial Office and the Colonial Governments could be summed up in a single sentence—the mobilisation of all the potential resources of the Colonial Empire, both of men and of materials, for the purposes of war. We had lost 60 per cent of the tin production of the world and 90 per cent of the rubber production, together with a large proportion of wolfram, lead and other minerals. In addition, we had been deprived of important sources of food, especially sugar, tea, rice and oilseeds, and threatened with further losses. We therefore needed to increase Colonial production for war purposes on an immense scale. We had to develop mineral production. We had to push up the production of meat, hides, palm oil, ground-nuts, and all the rest. We had to use the methods and inculcate the spirit which had animated us at home in the last two years. From Kenya we needed sisal, as well as more refined crops, such as pyre-thrum. From other parts of Africa, the main requirements were groundnuts, palm kernals, palm oil and—to a smaller extent—rubber and tin. To Ceylon we looked for rubber and tea. To stimulate exports we needed a proper programme.

Cranborne asked me to take care of economic and trade questions, whether of import or export, and to these I devoted my chief energies, keeping close contact with old friends in the Ministries of Supply and of Production. In order to create the necessary organisation in Lon-don, we were forced to expand our Economic Section into a small supply department. We were fortunate in being able to house it in Dover House. In fact, the Ministry of Works tried to fob us off with a decaying building in the Horseferry Road. But John Wyndham dis-covered that the Scottish Office had departed to Edinburgh 'for the duration' and he succeeded in seizing this beautiful house—Lord Melbourne's home—in my name. We had learned something from Beaverbrook.

With regard to rubber, output in Ceylon was stepped up by all possible means. We enlisted the help of planters and experts from Malaya, with mutual advantage. In East and West Africa, neglected rubber plantations were revived, and abandoned areas, mainly in Tanganyika, were restored. Wild rubber was tapped on a large scale and prices fixed to attract the maximum production. We hoped by all these energetic means to fill the gap before the great production of synthetic rubber in the United States came to help the joint war needs of the Allies. The campaign proved very successful and all our targets were reached.

In minerals generally, our customers were the Ministries of Supply and Aircraft Production. They needed bauxite, wolfram, tin, graphite, copper, zinc, mica, manganese, chrome, iron ore and industrial diamonds, and the suppliers were scattered through the Gold Coast, Sierra Leone, Nigeria, Northern Rhodesia, Ceylon, British Guiana, and Cyprus. Production was often not the main problem, but transport, both internal and external. Locomotives were almost as precious then as diamonds, and as rare.

The shipping position had a particularly serious effect on the Colonies. We were striving to increase production. But how were we to get enough shipping to transport the exports and to bring to the scattered territories sufficient imports to sustain and stimulate their populations? The attack of the U-boats was becoming daily more menacing. The Americans, who had not yet adopted systematic convoys, suffered grievously. British and Allied losses for the first six months of 1942 were 3 million tons greater than the ship-building output. Yet all the time more and more shipping was required. Fortunately, by May 1942, the American losses and new building were equalised; and the same position was reached by August as regards Allied losses and construction. Nevertheless, the situation was to remain serious until the end of the year. The convoys in aid of Russia added to the toll. As a result, the total import programme for Britain for 1942 had to be reduced to something of the order of 25 million tons, in contrast with the 30 million or more which we had previously managed to secure. Every effort had to be made to reduce non-essential imports. Equally important was the increase of local food production. In West Africa, we concentrated on rice, vegetables and dairy produce. In East Africa, where we had both the white planter and the African peasant economy, our chief need, in addition to the important crops for export, was to increase the growing of wheat, maize, rye and other foodstuffs, including rice. The West Indies had over many generations depended upon a main export crop, sugar. In normal times, the needs of the population in terms of wheat, flour and meat were met by imports. To economise shipping, it was now necessary to diversify agriculture, both in the large estates and in the small-holdings. This was done throughout the whole Caribbean area, and similar steps were taken in Ceylon, Mauritius and Palestine. Even in the rocky and barren territory of Aden, the cultivation of vegetables, fruit, and other crops was promoted by the Agricultural Officer on a considerable scale for the benefit of the garrison and people of that vital outpost. Every ton of food that could be grown in a Colony saved a ship to bring it. Every ton of food that could be moved from one Colony to a neighbouring Colony saved shipping. Every ton of food grown in East Africa and moved to the armies of the Middle East saved the long haul round the Cape. I used a phrase during a speech in the House of Commons which was taken up afterwards by the Press: 'The farmer is the best shipbuilder.'

One of our main anxieties at this time, which directly affected nutrition standards at home, was the shortage of fats. Production, therefore, of palm oil, groundnuts and the like was a matter of prime importance to the Ministry of Food. We were able to use the old Cocoa Control Board, now renamed the West African Produce Control Board, for this purpose. But the arrangements had to be co-ordinated with the Free French and the Belgian Government-in-exile, who were responsible for the big producing areas in the Belgian African empire and in French Equatorial Africa, which had rallied to de Gaulle. Most important of all, perhaps, we had to agree on a common attitude as regards quantities and prices of commodities sold to the Americans. A battle raged over the whole summer and autumn on a simple but fascinating economic issue.

Our Ministry of Food took the line that maximum production is obtained by raising prices. They also insisted that the whole of the price should be passed on to the producers. The Governor of Nigeria, Sir Bernard Bourdillon, one of our most experienced administrators, supported the opposite view and was sustained by the local representatives of the United Africa Company and by Mr. Samuel, the London manager. Their arguments were simple. Since there was no hope of increasing the present quotas, either of consumer goods or of 'consumer durables' (like bicycles) for Africa, the inevitable result of increasing prices would be to add to the existing inflation. These Colonies were already flooded with money, without any corresponding increase in the goods that money could buy. Raising the price, which in this case the customers demanded in the hope of increasing production, would have precisely the opposite result. We already had experience with cocoa, where we had managed to take advantage of the very high world price, keeping the difference between what the Board received and what they paid to the producers as a nest-egg for the future. We wanted to extend this procedure both on economic and on practical grounds to other commodities. It was impossible to apply, as in Great Britain, direct and indirect taxation, which had at least the effect of keeping inflation in check. Our plan was, in a sense, based on what were known at home as 'post-war credits'. In our country, these sums withheld from current wages were to be paid to individual wage-earners after the war. In West Africa, the difference between the full price and the price we paid to producers was to constitute a kind of collective post-war credit for the benefit of the population as a whole. By the end of the war, the total reached many hundreds of millions and became the basis of the great capital expansion in Africa in the post-war years.

The fact that we had to settle with the Belgians and the French added to the complications of this argument, which was fiercely contested. It brought me into close touch with René Pleven, who was responsible for the colonies in the Free French organisation. I found him a man of great charm and firmness of character, and easy to deal with once I had got to know him. He was straightforward and never went back on any arrangements to which he had consented.

My discussions with Pleven brought me, for the first time, into contact with General de Gaulle. He invited me to call on him at his headquarters in Carlton House Terrace, and in a short, rather formal conversation expressed his thanks for the sympathetic way in which we had approached the problems of the African territories where the Free French flag flew. I was struck by the intimate knowledge which he showed of our negotiations with his Colonial Minister, Pleven. Shortly after this I attended a small dinner at the Travellers' Club, given by Charles Peake, the Foreign Office representative accredited to the Free French movement. On both occasions the General was in his most gracious mood. I was soon to see something of the sterner side of his character.

War, with all its horrors and losses, leaves behind it some gain. Much of the material progress which the Colonial Empire in its new form has been able to make is due to the impetus given during these fateful years.

I cannot claim that I then foresaw, and I think few would have done so, how rapid would be the political evolution of the various Colonies after victory had been achieved. Yet I had, during these months, the first glimpse of what the post-war problem would be. Even then, I realised that the position of the adventurous and valuable pioneers of such a Colony as Kenya would sooner or later be imperilled. I put forward a scheme for the local Government to buy up the freehold of the larger farms, preserving the present owners as managers or tenants, and for the purchase of the smaller farms, with a view to their resale to Africans, for the land hunger was already showing itself. I still have the draft of a plan on these lines. I admitted that it would be expensive, but I doubt whether it would have been as expensive then as it has since proved. Like almost everyone else, I believed that the evolution towards self-government would be a slow process, with a longer period of education than ultimately proved possible. It came rapidly, far more rapidly as the result of the war than it would have done without so great a convulsion. It was later my duty to take some part in the various stages of the transformation of a Colonial Empire into a free Commonwealth. But even at this time I could not but see something of the changes which must come. Now that they are almost complete, they have constituted—for good or ill—perhaps one of the most dramatic of the revolutions of the age through which I have lived.

In the stress and strain of war, it was difficult to give concentrated attention to these essentially post-war questions. Yet the drafting of the Atlantic Charter, which referred to 'the right of all peoples to choose the form of government under which they will live', had already caused a good deal of trouble. President Roosevelt, like President Wilson, was fond of generalisations. The British tradition is more practical, and we were already considering the positive steps in the evolution towards self-government of the different territories, having regard to their history and background.

The American entry into the war brought us, of course, precious comfort and the certainty of victory. But it brought also a number of anxieties and inconveniences of a lesser order. On the political side, President Roosevelt began to take a personal interest in the Colonial question, especially in the Caribbean area. Apparently unconscious of conditions either in Harlem or in the Deep South, he expressed concern about the low standard of living in many of the West Indian islands. One of the difficulties of our sugar Colonies in this area had been, and was to remain, the extreme protectionism of American policy. In the American market, Cuban sugar enjoyed a degree of protection which amounted almost to monopoly. At the same time, the State Department under Cordell Hull, the American Cobden, was always protesting against Imperial Preferences and our bulk buying of Colonial sugar. It seemed to us another case of their attention being concentrated on our poor mote, with singular unconsciousness of the size of their own beam. However, it was clearly right to seize the hand held out to us, whatever the motive. Accordingly, we accepted the proposal for an Anglo-American Caribbean Commission. In order to facilitate its work, a permanent representative of the Colonial Office was appointed to Washington. It was my first lesson—soon to be applied in a wider field—in the art of allowing the Americans to take the lead, in the hope of getting results agreeable to our common purposes.

In this connection, it is worth recording a talk between the Colonial Secretary and John Foster Dulles in July 1942:

I had a conversation yesterday with Mr. Dulles, an eminent American, who has long been interested in the Colonies. . . . [It] related to the attitude of American public opinion regarding the British Colonial Empire. He said that we should realise that deeply embedded in the mind of most Americans was a fundamental distrust of what they called 'British Imperialism'. He did not attempt to defend their point of view. On the contrary, he went out of his way to say that in his opinion no nation had ever done a greater work among backward peoples than the British had during the years since the Battle of Waterloo. But it was, he said, a fundamental fact that we had to take into account. It was not based on any knowledge or reason. It was purely instinctive and inherited. . . . He therefore thought that it was utterly futile for us to attempt to conduct propaganda about our Colonial administration in the United States. Such propaganda could, in any case, only touch a small fringe of the population and it would be generally disbelieved. The only way in which we could remove this deep-seated prejudice would be to invite the co-operation of the United States in the development of our Colonies after the war. . . . They were merely concerned with the welfare of the indigenous populations and the development of the material resources of the territories. . . . If there was to be co-operation between Britain and the United States in the future peace and prosperity of the world, it could not be done on a basis merely of sentiment, for such sentiment would never be enduring. It could only be on the basis of a task to be done. No ideal would more appeal to the American people as a whole than the advancement of backward peoples. If the British and the Americans could combine in such a work, especially in Africa, a solid foundation for future co-operation would be laid.

In later years, when Dulles was Secretary of State, we often discussed these ideas. By then things had moved along a different path. But I blame myself for not having tried to do something positive along these lines.

The end of my partnership with Cranborne was now approaching and would soon confront me with a difficult choice. The unconscious instrument of my small and unimportant entanglement in these perplexities was Sir Stafford Cripps. Cripps was indeed a strange man. Before the war, while he enjoyed a high reputation and a most profitable practice at the Bar, he had allowed himself to drift further and further to the Left until he was finally expelled from the Parliamentary Labour Party. He believed in Socialism and Internationalism and would no doubt have professed orthodox Marxism had he not somehow combined his revolutionary notions with a deep Christian faith. His Labour colleagues did not know what to make of him at all. He actually wanted to carry out in practice the dangerous doctrines to which they gave verbal assent in principle. This shocked them deeply. Moreover, with his Jacobinism went an attitude of spiritual superiority which infuriated them. Many Conservatives had an equal dislike and even fear of him, for he delighted in insulting their most cherished beliefs. When one got to know him better, as I was later to do, he proved a delightful companion and seemed just another figure in the long line of English eccentrics. At the same time, it must be confessed that Cripps was something of a bore. As Herbert Morrison wrote in his memoirs:

The ability not to annoy the Prime Minister and to get on with the strong-charactered and diverse personalities among his colleagues was not, unfortunately for him, the perquisite of Sir Stafford Cripps.

He adds, with perfect fairness:

Churchill undoubtedly admired Cripps's mental powers. He disliked his lack of sense of humour and his often hardly-concealed attitude of mental superiority.[1]

[1] Morrison, *Autobiography*, p. 215.

On his return from Russia, where he had been British Ambassador, Cripps had leapt into a sudden notoriety and popularity. This was in the winter of 1941-42 when the Government's prestige was low. His extreme Left-wing opinions, expressed in the most violent terms before the war, were forgotten. The Russians were now the heroes; and Cripps, quite falsely, was believed to have enjoyed a position of special influence with the Soviet Government. Of course, anyone who knew the Marxist contempt for 'Democratic Socialism' realised that this could not be true. Cripps, at best, might have been described as approaching a Menshevist mentality. Nevertheless, at this time he was the beneficiary of the popular sentiment towards our new allies. Accordingly, Churchill offered him the Ministry of Supply, with the idea that he would serve in the galaxy of stars to be presided over by the new Minister of Production. Cripps refused this post unless it carried with it a seat in the War Cabinet. He must have known that this was an impossible demand for Churchill to concede, for the whole purpose of the new plan was to secure a single War Cabinet Minister responsible for all war production. When, however, Beaverbrook withdrew, fresh arrangements had rapidly to be made. Oliver Lyttelton was brought back from Cairo, where he had been acting as Minister of State, and appointed to Beaverbrook's place. He proved a most capable and effective Minister. Cripps obtained the coveted seat in the War Cabinet, and was made Lord Privy Seal and Leader of the House of Commons. He held the position for some nine months, until even the war-time House of Commons revolted against his magisterial attitude.

One would have thought his duties reasonably absorbing. But accustomed to detailed and exacting wrestling with precise problems, Cripps seemed to have no power of relaxing. A man ought perhaps to enjoy a balanced and genial temperament to withstand the temptations of a non-executive post. An active and diligent man can easily be tempted into criticising and interfering with his colleagues or framing large but unrealistic plans. This is just what Cripps did. In September 1942 he began to worry Churchill with a quite unworkable scheme for the reorganisation of the system for directing the war. He wanted to see appointed three men of equal calibre to the Chiefs of Staff to act as super-heads of the Joint Planning Staffs. He wanted also in each theatre of war a Commander-in-Chief over the naval, land and air forces, responsible to the War Planning Directorate. Churchill has called this a planner's dream.[2] It was really a planner's nightmare. Nor did it take any account of the fact that the British and American Governments had already decided upon the structure which was to govern all their efforts, not only military, but economic. This was the Combined Chiefs of Staff, side by side with which sat the Combined Boards. Moreover, in the operations just about to be launched in French North Africa, a supreme Commander-in-Chief had already been agreed upon—General Eisenhower.

All this restiveness was really a sign of Cripps's inability to detach himself from detailed work and to sit back a little from administrative problems. In the same way he made a bad leader of the House of Commons. He was never willing to let it alone. If a Leader of the House and his Whips are assured that there are sufficient trustworthy Members on the premises to carry through the Government business, they should be happy. If business ends early, they should rejoice, and go off and dine at the club with their friends. But Cripps was never really happy unless everyone was working, and he had no club and few friends. He was much concerned, therefore, if Members began to slacken in their attendance, quite forgetting how many of them were either in the Services or in some form of war work. He lectured them for their absence from debates, and this they found intolerable.[3] That comfortable, respectable and largely middle-class Members of moderate means should be subjected to the ineffable superiority of this rich and aristocratic revolutionary was more than they could bear.

In a thoroughly disgruntled mood, Cripps offered his resignation at the end of September 1942. I heard some rumour of this from Cranborne, but thought little of it or its likely results. I had certainly not admired the schoolmaster's tone which he affected as Leader of the House and felt that his departure would be no grave loss. The supreme battles of the Eighth Army in the desert were preparing in Egypt and the Anglo-American armada was about to sail for North Africa. A political crisis at a moment when everything was still apparently going wrong and there was at last a hope that everything

2 Churchill, *The Hinge of Fate*, p. 498.
3 Morrison, p. 215.

would begin to go right would be a tragedy. Cripps patriotically agreed to postpone his resignation, at least for a few weeks.

In the course of November Churchill was able to persuade Cripps to remain in the Government and wisely offered him an office where his administrative talents and his power of organisation would have full play. It was clear that a Minister of Cabinet rank was required in Washington to preside over the manifold activities of the various British missions on finance and supply. For this he made an admirable choice—Colonel J. J. Llewellin, an old friend, with whom I had worked in close harmony on war production. This made the office of the Minister of Aircraft Production available, since Llewellin had succeeded Moore-Brabazon some months previously. Thus Cripps was safely encased in this demanding post for the rest of the war. But, as I was afterwards to learn when I was forming or re-forming Governments myself, when one piece is moved in the delicate design of an administration, corresponding reactions follow, down to the humblest pawn.

The appointment of Herbert Morrison to the War Cabinet in Cripps's place involved no change of office but was greatly to Morrison's taste. Unhappily for me, Cranborne was persuaded, partly because his health had not been good in recent months and partly because his role as Leader of the House of Lords involved a heavy task, to accept the vacant post of Lord Privy Seal, previously held by Cripps. As a result an appointment had to be made for Secretary of State for the Colonies. The choice fell on Oliver Stanley, who had held no position since the fall of the Chamberlain Government in May 1940. Stanley had been a friend, and indeed an intimate friend, in the early Parliaments in which we had sat together. He had been a collaborator in a little book called *Industry and the State* which was published in 1927.[4] Moreover, as boys at school used to say, 'We knew each other at home'. We stayed with each other, shot each other's pheasants and enjoyed much the same society. Nor had I at all resented his steady climb up the ladder of political success in the Baldwin and Mac-Donald régimes. Sometimes we had had little Parliamentary skirmishes, but these were never ill-natured or such as to injure our friendship. Under the Chamberlain Government, when personal

[4] *Winds of Change*, p. 173.

feelings began to be affected by political disagreements, there had been a certain strain between us. At the time of Eden's resignation he was clearly deeply disturbed, as were other of the younger members of the Cabinet, but he did not move. There was much talk of younger Ministers protesting, but nothing happened. Similarly, after Munich, I thought that he and others would be sure to follow Duff Cooper's example. Again there was smoke but no fire. This was due not to want of courage, for Stanley had shown plenty of these qualities in the First World War, but to a certain diffidence and lack of self-confidence. Since he had held high office in the Chamberlain Government, Churchill's omission of him in May 1940 was marked. He had for the past two and a half years been working in the Joint Planners' Staff with the rank of colonel. Churchill's decision to bring him back to office was no doubt partly due to his personal regard for one of the most agreeable and intelligent men it has been my fortune to know; partly inspired by a desire to secure a powerful group in the Conservative Party, the Stanley interest; and partly based on his high opinion of Oliver's gifts and qualifications.

In any walk of life or in any office I should have been happy to work with Oliver Stanley, but for the particular tasks in which I was now engaged I looked forward with some apprehensions to the prospect. With Cranborne I had a chief with whom one might disagree; but the discussions would be clear and the points at issue defined. Once a decision was taken, action would follow. At the same time, he was willing to devolve considerable authority upon me and give me full support upon a large range of activities. I had thus obtained a position far different from that ordinarily belonging to a Parliamentary Under-Secretary. I had made myself, with Cranborne's full approval, the head of the Economic Department. I had settled it in its own establishment and organised its work at home and abroad. I was, in addition, the sole representative of the Colonial Office in the House of Commons. Now I was to lose all these advantages. After over eighteen months with my Minister in the Lords, first with Beaverbrook and then with Moyne and Cranborne, I had a feeling that I was being reduced not only in status but in power. Decision and action, sometimes drastic action, were not likely from the new régime. There would be a charming and happy relationship; and a pleasant and easy life. But it would be something of an anti-climax. Moreover, since Stanley was a superb parliamentarian, I should find myself unwanted in the House of Commons, as well as gradually becoming impotent in the department. All this filled me with dismay.

Some of the newspapers felt that the Colonial Office ought to be represented in the House of Lords which, embodying so much experience and service throughout the Empire, had a claim to the services of one of the Colonial Office Ministers. It was rumoured by the Lobby Correspondents that in order to meet this situation I should be offered a peerage. At the time I was fortunately able to avoid this fate and I hope, if I live long enough, to escape from it altogether. A few days later, this was contradicted by others who thought that I 'might have quite a long way to go in the House of Commons'. This was a curious episode to look back upon, since I had more than another twenty years to go.

After some reflection, I decided to talk over the question of my future frankly with Churchill. But I was wise enough to have a preliminary discussion with Bracken. During these weeks things were not going very well in North Africa. In spite of the success of the landings, the Darlan episode had caused the Government much trouble, both with the British public and with our American allies. Churchill was occupied to the full, and Brendan did not feel that it would be wise to draw at this moment upon my accumulated reserve of friendship in the Churchill Bank. I showed him a letter of resignation I had drafted, which I still have in my possession. Brendan strongly advised me to wait.

Brendan Bracken has been regarded by many as a somewhat mysterious character in British life. I first met him in the 1930s when he had become associated with Eyre and Spottiswoode, a leading firm of printers and publishers. He afterwards moved into high business circles. With his red hair and white face and his extraordinary range of knowledge covering the most improbable fields (he was the leading expert on schoolmasters and bishops), he was a strange arrival in the City and the House of Commons. He had attached himself to Churchill during the worst period of Churchill's eclipse and gave him the most devoted support in the darkest days. Some people feared Brendan, and thought him an adventurer. In fact, he had a sweet and lovable character. He was full of charitable instincts, which he translated in a quiet and unobtrusive way into reality. But his importance at this stage was his close friendship with Churchill, to whom he would speak with absolute and often outrageous frankness. On thinking it over, I felt Brendan's advice was both disinterested and wise. It certainly turned out to my advantage that I had not offered my resignation at this time, but decided to swallow my pride and be patient. On such small issues do the fortunes of life depend. Stanley was appointed on 22 November. As it turned out I had only one month to wait.

PART TWO

The Mediterranean Campaign

January 1943-May 1945

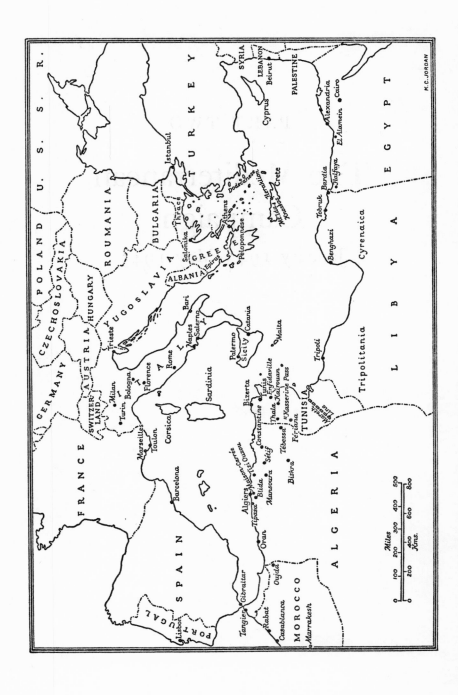

Introduction

THE Mediterranean campaign was destined to prove the first and most successful expression of Anglo-American co-operation in every sphere—military, political and economic. The burden of the defence of Egypt, with the cruel ebb and flow of desert warfare, had for two hard years been sustained by the British alone. It is true that the generous supply of American armaments, especially the dispatch of the Sherman tanks at a critical moment, had proved an important contribution to ultimate success. But it was by British and Imperial troops, under British generals, that the decisive victory of Alamein[1] had been won, a few weeks before the Allied landings in North Africa.[2] By the middle of December, the pursuit of the German and Italian forces had brought the Eighth Army well into Libya, and Tripoli had been gained on 23 January 1943. These British forces, after their triumphant sweep of conquest, were soon to be placed under a single Allied command, and operations over this vast area to be continued as an Anglo-American undertaking until the end of the war.

Though the old Middle Eastern Command—now of much reduced extent and significance—remained a purely British responsibility, the main decisions throughout the Mediterranean area were for nearly two and a half years to be taken by a Supreme Allied Commander, subject to the joint authority of the Combined Chiefs of Staff and under the ultimate control of the American and British Governments. The command structure, to be followed throughout the campaign, was based on the model agreed upon by London and Washington for 'Torch'—the Allied landings in French North Africa. It was to set the pattern for the supreme assault across the Channel in 1944—the famous 'Operation Overlord'.

[1] 23 October 1942.
[2] 8 November 1942.

There is no parallel in history for such a partnership. It stands unrivalled and unequalled.

Often in the past allied armies have fought side by side, as in the First World War. Sometimes, although not commonly, troops of various nations have been placed under a single commander. But the organisation of A.F.H.Q.[3] was unique, in that there was a completely integrated staff in which British and American officers served, not as representatives of their own nations, but as members of a single team. The success of this experiment was largely, if not entirely, due to the confidence created by General Eisenhower, the first Commander-in-Chief. The same sense of fairness and manliness radiated from him as from such great commanders in history as Marlborough and Wellington. Nevertheless, although the system continued unchanged throughout the long campaign, from the landings in the autumn of 1942 to the final German surrender of May 1945, there were definite and sometimes acute divergences of view between the two allies. Sometimes these were reflected downwards from London and Washington; sometimes they came upwards from conditions created on the spot.

I shall not deal with the military aspects of these problems except where they impinge on political questions. Something, however, must be said of the fundamental difference between the American and British conception of war. Broadly, the Americans felt that you should find a convenient place to fight the main forces of your enemy of the moment, and regarded a battle as somewhat in the nature of an athletic contest, without much regard as to what would happen afterwards. The British tended to take a more sophisticated view; war is a continuation of policy, and policies and purposes may fluctuate and change. This difference underlay the long struggle between the President and the Prime Minister; the President wished to fight and defeat the Germans in France and later in western Germany, while the Prime Minister hoped to achieve victory not merely by the liberation of French metropolitan territory but by a rapid advance through northern Italy and Austria, and thus end the war in positions far more favourable to the Western Allies in the situation which was likely to develop.

Naturally, these conflicting points of view did not emerge until after

[3] Allied Force Headquarters—the title of General Eisenhower's command—was continued under his successors in the area, Generals Wilson and Alexander.

the final defeat and ejection of the Germans from Africa. There then arose, in an acute and urgent form, the question of the invasion of Sicily and Italy. The Americans were anxious about further commitments which might prejudice operations in France; the British were attracted by what was called 'the soft under-belly' argument, as well as by the possibilities which the defeat and surrender of Italy might open up in Central and Eastern Europe. Apart from these military and strategic issues, I must frankly admit that Anglo-American co-operation was sometimes put to quite a severe test by the fact that we disagreed on many of the political aspects of our immediate problems. Yet it survived all these pressures. If it had not been for the broad-mindedness of Robert Murphy, my American counterpart, and the generosity of General Eisenhower, we might have got into serious difficulties from the start. But Murphy and I made up our minds that it was our task not to magnify the differences of view held by our principals, but to try to minimise them, or at least allow solutions to be worked out on the spot without too much friction. I much deplored Murphy's departure in the summer of 1944. His successors were charming and admirable men; but they did not carry so much weight in Washington.

In North Africa, the Americans had made the initial contacts before the landings, and were consequently somewhat hampered by the promises they had held out in many quarters in order to facilitate their task and minimise the risks involved. But there was no real agreement at the highest level as to how to handle the wider French problem. This, of course, reflected Washington's long wooing of Vichy and London's support of de Gaulle. The arrangements made with Admiral Darlan, though apparently justified from a military angle, brought a sharp reaction in both countries. After Darlan's assassination, the Americans supported Giraud. The British remained partisans of de Gaulle. How this conflict was resolved, and what were the subsequent effects of all this on the future of France, I shall describe in due course. In these months, I learned my first lesson in this sort of diplomacy. If we were able to get our way in the end and allow our favourite to win, this was partly because the Americans naturally do not like throwing good money after bad. When they realised that Giraud was a horse very much in the second class, which would never even win a Selling Plate, they scratched it.

The same dichotomy, though perhaps in a form less generally known to the outside world, ran through our occupation of Italy. The Americans were anxious to remove the King. For some inscrutable reason, they believed a republic to be better than a monarchy. I felt very much the opposite, and made every effort to preserve the monarchical principal and give it a fair chance. I still think that if this had been done and the American pressure had not been so violent, the Italian plebiscite might well have gone in favour of the monarchy. This, I believe, would have been to the advantage of the Italian people. Here, certainly, was another source of friction.

If there were divergences in the Allied approach to the political problems of France and Italy, they were not so grave as to cause any serious disturbance in public opinion in either country. They were, after all, minor in relation to the overriding purposes for which we were linked—the destruction of the dictatorship and the restoration of freedom throughout the world. Moreover, largely owing to the sense of team spirit which permeated A.F.H.Q. and all the subordinate commands, first under General Eisenhower and then under his successors, no real injury was done. Differences were not exaggerated or exacerbated. On the contrary, they were as far as possible minimised and smoothed over. When we came to the case of Greece, it was not possible to avoid full publicity, with some corresponding damage.

The Greek affair was one of the strangest episodes in the Allied campaign. The British, as the Germans retired, went into Greece with a small force, bringing with them the exiled Greek Government. For a few weeks all went well. But when the Communists broke into open revolution, this British force and the Greek Government found themselves besieged in Athens. The Americans, supported by *The Times* and some Left-wing opinion in Parliament (but not by Ernest Bevin, who was staunch and loyal throughout), refused to give any assistance to their British allies, even in their acute danger. They acquiesced in the dispatch of British and Indian troops, who ultimately restored order, defeated the Communists and made possible the negotiation of the Peace of Varkiza, by which some measure of tranquillity was restored to Greece. This expedition—amounting to some three divisions—was sustained from a joint Anglo-American headquarters. But no American officers were allowed to take any part at A.F.H.Q. or in

Greece, either in the planning or in the execution of the operation. The Americans were, therefore, neutral and in some cases rather conspicuously neutral. It is a great tribute to the skill of Field-Marshal Alexander in this embarrassing situation, as well as to the real sense of comradeship of American officers who resented the position in which they found themselves, that this whole affair, lasting over a period of several months, was carried through without any deep cleavage and without impairing full co-operation in the joint Italian campaign. Once more, this was a testing time for me and for my devotion to Anglo-American unity.

When we turn to Yugoslavia, paradoxically enough, the Americans supported the Right-wing resistance groups and we supported the Left. This was not due on our part to any theoretical or subjective feelings, but was based upon the view that Tito, Communist or not, harassed the Germans with our assistance bravely, continuously and effectively. Mihailović, on the other hand, who was the darling of the Americans, seemed to us to have lost any real local support and to be correspondingly inactive, or only engaged in fighting other Yugoslavs. There were, no doubt, certain rivalries between the British and American Special Operations officers, which reflected themselves in the State Department and the Foreign Office. But here again, rather as in the case of General Giraud and General de Gaulle, the Americans after a time accepted our point of view on the same practical grounds which had influenced us. There were moments of tension and difficulty. They were overcome largely by the spirit of co-operation at Headquarters which had dealt with much graver problems. In the event, when at the end of the war we suffered considerable embarrassments, caused by Marshal Tito's occupation of Venezia Giulia and Carinthia and the dangerous position in Trieste, the Americans gave us full support with great good humour, although with sometimes embarrassing zeal.

These thirty months were full of incidents, sometimes grave, sometimes gay. They constitute a remarkable record of joint and individual effort and determination, with a series of perplexing problems in every field of endeavour. The story is one of which our two nations have a right to be proud. It was indeed a lucky chance for me to be privileged to share in the failures and the triumphs of these heroic days; to work with and for outstanding military commanders; to be brought into close association with many remarkable characters; to see something of leading statesmen in many European countries; and, above all, at critical and vital moments, to observe in operation the two great figures who presided over our fortunes and were the acknowledged captains of our crusade—Roosevelt and Churchill.

CHAPTER EIGHT

The French Schism

MORE than a generation has passed since the sudden and unexpected collapse of the French Army before the German onslaught, with its cruel consequences for the French people. It may, therefore, be convenient to remind the reader of the sequence of events in the two and a half years that passed before the Allied landings in North Africa brought a new crisis in French affairs.

The German offensive began on 10 May 1940. Less than three weeks later there had followed the evacuation from Dunkirk. On 10 June, believing that Britain would now be forced to surrender, Mussolini declared war, in the jackal hope of obtaining some easy morsels. As the Germans advanced, the French Government was forced to leave Paris, and the Prime Minister, Paul Reynaud, sent a last desperate message to President Roosevelt appealing for immediate aid. If Hitler occupied France, declared Reynaud, France would 'cease to exist'. The British Government, with complete fidelity to their engagements, had meanwhile sent back into France all the troops that could be collected to help in the final defence. But all was in vain. On 13 June the French Government asked for formal release from the undertaking entered into on 28 March, that neither country would make a separate peace. This request was refused; and every effort was made by Churchill and his colleagues to persuade the French to continue the struggle. The Germans entered Paris on 14 June, the French Government having moved by successive stages first to Tours and then to Bordeaux. Marshal Weygand, who had replaced Gamelin as Commander-in-Chief of the disintegrating French armies, refused to negotiate an armistice unless the necessary orders were given from the Government itself; in other words, he demanded a political and not merely a military surrender. This put formidable difficulties in the way of those stalwart members of the French Government who wished to follow the example

of Belgium, where the Government had gone into exile, leaving the
Army to capitulate. With the great French Empire at their command
and protected by the overwhelming strength of the joint British and
French fleets, the Government might well have moved to North Africa
and continued the war from there. But those in control had little
stomach for this or any other fight. On 16 June, the French Government renewed their request to their Allies. At least, they pleaded, let
them ask what the armistice terms would be. Our first inclination was
to agree, provided that the French fleet was placed outside German
control and that we were consulted as to the terms. A message to this
effect was prepared but finally withheld in favour of another, embodying a much more radical and generous concept.

On 15 June I attended a dinner at the Reform Club, in which I
found myself unexpectedly in a somewhat varied company. If I remember right, they included the French Ambassador, Charles Corbin,
Lord Halifax, Leo Amery, Robert Vansittart, Arthur Salter and Clem
Davies. There are others whom I do not recall, for it was a considerable gathering. Leo Amery had prepared and circulated a paper
setting out, in this desperate crisis, a bold and revolutionary plan, by
which France's remaining strength, moral and material, might be
rallied to a determined resistance. It involved nothing less than a
complete union between France and Britain.[1] There had no doubt
been prior consultation between some of those present. Even so, it
seemed extraordinary that so vast and novel a proposal should obtain
unanimous support.

The next day, the Cabinet considered this proposal, and their
deliberations resulted in the drafting of a formal document, the
famous 'Declaration of London':

. . . The two Governments declare that France and Great Britain shall no
longer be two nations, but one Franco-British Union.

The constitution of the Union will provide for joint organs of defence,
foreign, financial, and economic policies.

Every citizen of France will enjoy immediate citizenship of Great Britain;
every British subject will become a citizen of France. . . .

This manifesto—hardly remembered now—was approved by the
War Cabinet and by the leaders of all three political parties. As a

[1] I have this historic document still among my records. It is dated 14 June.

demonstration of unity, Attlee and Sinclair were invited to meet with Reynaud by Churchill's side to discuss the proclamation and urge its acceptance.

We hoped that this tremendous offer, not limited to the immediate future but intended to endure for all time, would rally the French Government and secure Reynaud's position. We also hoped that large French forces would be evacuated to British territory or to North Africa to carry on the war under the authority of the French Government and with the support of the French fleet. Alas! It was not to be. The proposal, which would have involved prolonging the war, inside and outside France, did not attract the defeatist and defeated majority of French Ministers. Reynaud resigned; and on the authority of the French President, Albert Lebrun, a new administration was formed by Marshal Pétain.

During the hectic days that followed, Churchill sent a moving appeal to Pétain and his Ministers, urging them not to hand over the fleet. In reply, various assurances, more or less satisfactory, were given. Admiral Darlan—the professional head of the French Navy—at first said that he would move the fleet to safety. But when he entered the new Government as a Minister, he became subject to the defeatism which flowed from the old Marshal and his circle of friends. In Churchill's words, 'France had been rotted from within before she was smitten from without'. The armistice negotiations were completed on 22 June, and resulted in the surrender of the French Army and the division of the country into two zones, Occupied and Unoccupied France. On the previous day, a number of Deputies and Ministers had left for North Africa, in the hope of setting up a French Government that would fight on from an imperial base. But General Noguès, Governor of Morocco, seized them and returned them to France. At least one of these brave men was later executed, and others imprisoned. But they had done their best to redeem the honour of their country.

With regard to the fleet, the Germans had devised a particularly subtle plan. The ships were to be collected in specified ports and there demobilised and disarmed under German or Italian control. The French Government thought—or persuaded themselves to think—that by these conditions they had satisfied their undertaking to their British allies. But there was no security of any kind that these ships would stay disarmed. It was clear, indeed, that the Germans, by avoiding the actual demand for the surrender of the fleet, which would probably have been followed by orders to scuttle the ships, had contrived an ingenious method of obtaining control. Sooner or later the fleet would have been manned by German or Italian sailors.

Yet it was vital to us that this great armada should not become an effective force in German hands. Our future—perhaps our survival—depended upon its immobilisation or destruction. The one great gain of the Scandinavian campaign, with all its failures and disappoint-ments, had been to put the German fleet out of the picture, at least temporarily. But the French Navy was both large and modern, includ-ing some of the finest and most up-to-date units. They had to be dealt with as far as lay in our power. This in some cases was effected without the tragedy of our being forced to attack an old friend and ally. The ships in British ports were seized without difficulty. In Alexandria and Martinique, they were immobilised after negotiations. In Casablanca, the *Jean Bart,* a ship of great importance, was still unfinished. But in Oran, with the exception of the battle-cruiser *Strasbourg,* which escaped to Toulon, the ships had to be destroyed by a British attack. This was on 3 July, and was followed by a French air attack on Gibraltar. At Dakar, in one of the most unhappy episodes of the war, the *Richelieu* was damaged and put out of action. The ships in Algiers escaped to Toulon, where they joined the main French fleet, and there remained, with the exception of a squadron which later reached Dakar, until November 1942—a prize and a threat.

These sad events naturally created great bitterness in the French Navy, and no doubt to some extent among the people of France, dazed and confused as they must have been by the fate that had befallen them. But these harsh decisions were right and indeed inevitable. For Britain, now fighting alone, depended for her life on the command of the sea. The invasion of our island seemed imminent. Even after the Battle of Britain in August and September of 1940 the danger remained for another year or more. Had the French fleet become an effective instrument in German hands, our chances of survival, already precarious, would indeed have been low.

On 1 July 1940 the French Government moved from Bordeaux to Vichy, and a few days later formal diplomatic relations with Britain were broken off. The United States, being a neutral power, both recognised the new French Government and sent an Ambassador, Admiral Leahy, who was to play an important role. Later we were able to restore some unofficial contact through the Canadian Chargé d'Affaires, Pierre Dupuy, who arrived at Vichy in November. Informal negotiations could also be carried on, when necessary, between the British and Vichy Ambassadors in Madrid. Meanwhile, Lebrun, the last legitimate President of the Third Republic, an amiable but ineffective character, disappeared finally from the scene on 11 July. Marshal Pétain became formal head of a mutilated and humiliated France. Into the feeble and trembling hands of this aged but still respected figure had passed at least the semblance of power.

Churchill, who never lost hope of the French, tried to promote 'a kind of collusive conspiracy in the Vichy Government whereby certain members . . . will levant to North Africa'.[2] But there was little chance of this. The Admiralty were worried that Vichy might go so far as to enter the war against us, and it was believed that both Admiral Darlan and Pierre Laval were pressing this upon the Marshal. These fears were increased by the Pétain-Hitler meeting at Montoire on 24 October, when the principle of 'collaboration' in the war against the United Kingdom was agreed between this ill-matched pair. A few days later, Paul Baudouin, a Right-wing defeatist with a bad record, was succeeded as Foreign Minister by an even more deplorable figure— Laval.

The official French attitude towards Britain at this time was one of mingled anger and disappointment. Vichy had reckoned that the early defeat and surrender of Britain would salve their own conscience and bring the war to an end. Yet those obstinate islanders, with character- istic stupidity, were persisting in a hopeless resistance, morally and materially injurious to France. They even encouraged a few French traitors, led by a junior officer called de Gaulle, to challenge the legitimate authority of the Marshal and appeal to the older traditions of the great French Army and people. At the same time, the British blockade was imposing unnecessary hardships. Vichy appealed to Washington, which was inclined to help over this matter by pressure on London. But the demands for imports were so excessive and so evidently German-inspired that London was able to temporise and

2 Churchill, *Their Finest Hour*, p. 450.

finally reject various requests, in return for which Vichy offered
nothing either in France or in the French Empire.

In the middle of December, the dismissal and arrest of Laval seemed
encouraging to some, for his successor, Pierre Flandin, was a man of a
better type. Moreover, although Laval was released on German intervention, he was not immediately reinstated. He had to wait another
eighteen months for the opportunity to bring his perfidy to the highest
degree of perfection.

Slowly the year 1940 drew to its end. The Battle of Britain was
fought and won in the air. The civilian population had suffered and
survived the bombing. The expected invasion across the Channel,
though still threatened, had not yet materialised. All this time, France
lay helpless and hopeless. Nothing came from French Ministers except
deceit. The Marshal's administration had become a feeble imitation of
Teutonic and Italian dictatorships. The proud revolutionary motto on
every public building had been torn down or defaced. Liberty, Equality, Fraternity were no more to be an inspiration of the French people.
Yet the defeatists and traitors were a small if active minority. There
were countless men and women, inside and outside France, who
mourned in silence their country's dishonour.

But one man had taken the lead and others soon rallied round him.
General de Gaulle left for England on 17 June 1940, immediately
after the resignation of Reynaud and Pétain's appointment. He had
been Under-Secretary of State for Defence in Reynaud's Government.
He had won some fame as the exponent of novel views of war.
Although of minor military rank—a two-star amid all the galaxy of
five-star generals—he enjoyed a considerable reputation in French
military circles. On 18 June he broadcast an appeal from London to
all Frenchmen to fight on. Five days later, the 'Provisional French
National Committee', which he formed, was recognised by the British
Government 'as representing independent French elements determined on the prosecution of the war'. This formula was strengthened
by an agreement on 7 August between the British Government and
the London Committee. Material assistance was to be given to the Free
French, as they were to be called. Terms and conditions of service for
French units or individuals, including de Gaulle's acceptance of the
overall British command, were settled. Although the British Government could not in such a document guarantee unconditionally the

post-war integrity of France and her empire, they undertook to do their best to this end. This attitude, which we had maintained in every other case of an ally overrun by Germany or Italy, seems to have sown, quite unnecessarily, the dark seeds of suspicion in de Gaulle's mind. But at present, all was plain sailing.

De Gaulle then set about a bold and imaginative attempt to rally the French Empire. Some of the minor colonies, such as French Oceania and the small French possessions in India, declared their allegiance at once, to be followed by New Caledonia. In Indo-China, Catroux, the Governor-General, was sympathetic to de Gaulle but could not carry the local administration with him and was replaced by a pro-Vichy Governor. However, during 1940 and 1941 Indo-China was gradually absorbed by Japanese aggression. In August, Leclerc and Boislambert were sent out as emissaries to French Equatorial Africa, and by the end of the month Chad, Gabon, the Middle Congo, the Cameroons and Ubangi-Shari had declared themselves for the Free French. Some small military operations against the Italians on the Chad-Libya border were actually begun, which were to culminate two and a half years later in the arrival of Leclerc and his troops to make contact with the British Eighth Army.

But these, although valuable, were not the largest or the most important colonies. North and West Africa remained the great danger and the great prize. The British–Free French assault on Dakar at the end of September 1940 was a complete failure. The Free French troops were received with violent hostility by the Vichy civil authorities and armed forces. It now became clear that a civil war between Frenchmen had begun, which would continue with traditional bitterness. The illusion that the French authorities and populations throughout the French Empire were anxiously waiting to be rescued from German domination was shattered. Most of all, it seemed, did they resent 'liberation' by dissident Frenchmen. The war was over. Why could not they be left alone? All that de Gaulle could do immediately was to give some formality to his movement. A Council of Defence of the Empire was formed, with nine members, some of distinction and experience. A manifesto, published in November, defined the Free French attitude to the Constitution and the Third Republic. It was de Gaulle's contention that the Vichy Government was acting *ultra vires* and had no legal authority. He and his Council regarded themselves as a provisional authority, to be answerable to a representative assembly when such a body could be freely elected by the French people.

So, by the end of 1940, the two streams had become clearly defined. The Free French, under the leadership of de Gaulle, repudiated the legality of the armistice and regarded the Vichy régime as having no constitutional or legal power; stood for the honour of France and the integrity of the French Empire; and were ready to respect their engagements to their allies as best they could and to uphold the glorious traditions of the French people until that dawn which must some day follow the long night of darkness and sorrow. On the other hand, there was metropolitan France, divided into two parts, one occupied by the German Military Government, the other under a Government which owed its existence to German power and could only live by a feeble attempt to introduce into French life a pale reflection of the worst elements of Nazi and Fascist systems.

Throughout 1941 and 1942 the Vichy Government degenerated into ever greater subservience to their German masters. It is true that Marshal Pétain put up a dogged resistance, so far as he was able, to any deviation from the literal interpretation of the armistice terms. Nevertheless, the emergence of Darlan in February 1941 as Vice-President and Foreign Minister was a sign of the increasing weakness of the Marshal's position. When in the spring of that year the Germans wished to use Syria in order to support Rashid Ali's anti-British movement in Iraq, Darlan readily complied. Accordingly, in May, German and Italian aircraft began to arrive in Syria—then a French mandated territory—in large numbers. There was no alternative left to us but to launch an attack in order to restore the military situation and to defend ourselves on that dangerous flank. This took the form, once again, of a combined action by the Free French and the British forces. Once again, as at Dakar, the Vichy forces were almost more hostile to their French brethren than to the British. After a short conflict the situation was cleared, and Syria and the Lebanon were firmly in our hands. The responsibility for this treachery was rightly ascribed to Darlan and was not forgotten in the following year.

In April 1942 Laval returned to office and about this time fresh dangers threatened us in Madagascar, where it was feared that the Japanese might seize the important harbour of Diégo-Suarez. It was therefore decided to occupy this invaluable base and, if it were feasible, the whole island. In this case, in view of past experience, the expedition was purely British.

This operation, launched in May 1942, was successful in its first objective, and an opportunity was allowed for the Vichy Governor to rally to the Allied cause. But once again the tradition of obedience proved too strong. Not until the beginning of November was the Governor forced to accept our terms, which left the civil administration of the island in French hands. This affair was yet another discouragement to those who believed that, as the war proceeded and the entry of the United States into the struggle seemed to assure ultimate victory, French authorities, civil and military, would have a change of heart.

Eden certainly had little expectation of any improvement. He had successfully prevented various American efforts to induce us to allow considerable imports into France in spite of the blockade. But as these negotiations proceeded, even Washington was dismayed at the continual trickery shown by Vichy. In conversation with Admiral Leahy, Laval argued that it was possible to reach an understanding with Germany which would result in a lasting peace, but that a Russian and British victory would mean Bolshevism in Europe.

Churchill, with his mind fixed on the North African expedition, was still hopeful. With characteristic generosity, he could not believe that Frenchmen had sunk so low as their actions and pronouncements seemed to show. He almost sought to excuse them. After all, what could they achieve in their weakness except to avoid the complete German occupation of France by a policy of conciliation of their German masters. 'They had endured Oran, Dakar, Syria, and Madagascar, the British blockade and British air raids with the least possible show of anger . . . allowance should be made for the "unnatural conditions prevailing in a defeated country with a government living on the sufferance of the enemy".'[3]

Thus Churchill still hoped against hope that the French fleet might sail to Africa and that, overtly or covertly, Vichy or its local officials might welcome the arrival of British and American troops. But Eden maintained his view. It was true that the vast majority of Frenchmen,

[3] Sir Llewellyn Woodward, *British Foreign Policy in the Second World War* (London, 1962), p. 113.

whether in Occupied or Unoccupied France, desired an Allied victory.
But they were impotent.

General de Gaulle's reputation, in spite of many difficulties, had
steadily improved in the minds of the British public. His occasional
outbursts of temper and obstructiveness were known only in the
highest circles of Government. His movement seemed to be developing
on constructive lines. He had created in October 1940 a Council of
Defence of the Empire, and a year later had reconstituted his original
Committee into a kind of Cabinet. Many of his supporters were
distinguished and able men and fresh adherents were reaching him all
the time. One of the consequences of Hitler's attack on Russia was to
strengthen his position. Diplomatic relations between Vichy and Moscow were ruptured. The Russian Ambassador at Vichy, Bogomolov,
was transferred to London as the Russian representative with the
French National Committee. Within France, the Communists ceased
to oppose and began to co-operate with the resistance movement. In
spite of the hostility of the Americans, who distrusted both the
General's methods and what they believed to be his political objectives, Lend-Lease was extended to the Free French in November 1941.
Although Free French troops re-established themselves in the islands
of St. Pierre and Miquelon, off the south coast of Newfoundland, in
December of the same year, in defiance of American wishes, the ill-
humour created in Washington by this episode was soon overcome.
Moreover, after Pearl Harbour, the United States wished to benefit
from the use of bases in French Oceania. Consequently, in March
1942, the American Government recognised the F.N.C. as being in
effective control of the French Pacific and their representatives were
admitted to the Pacific War Council of the Allies. In April, the United
States equally recognised the Free French authority over French
Equatorial Africa. All through 1942, de Gaulle's position in relation to
the resistance movement inside France improved. The scattered groups
began to coalesce, and look to the Committee in London as their
authority. A National Council of Resistance, formed by Jean Moulin,
who parachuted into France in 1942, was gradually built up. The
Gaullist movement, originally called 'Free France', was now formally
renamed 'Fighting France' ('La France Combattante'), a symbol of
their hopes of playing their full part in the ultimate liberation of their
country.

De Gaulle's position at the time of the Anglo-American landings in North Africa can be briefly summed up. He was in effective control of all the French Empire, except North and West Africa, Indo-China and the Caribbean. Madagascar was about to be placed under his jurisdiction. He had, indeed, obtained in two years of struggle a prestige and an authority far greater than seemed possible when he came to England as a fugitive and an exile in those crucial days of June 1940.

Why then did Churchill accept the decision not only that Free French troops should be left out of the Anglo-American invasion of North Africa, but that all information regarding the expedition should be withheld from General de Gaulle and his Committee? Churchill was conscious 'of the gravity of the affront which de Gaulle would have to suffer by being deliberately excluded from all share in the design'.[4] On the other hand, Churchill knew that it had only been his persuasive powers which had induced the Americans to abandon a premature attempt to land in France in favour of the North African adventure. In order to bring them along, he had accepted American command and the American character of the expedition, in spite of the fact that the greater part of the forces to be supplied, whether by sea, land or air, were British. The British had to admit that their experience at Dakar and in Syria gave weight to the argument that the Allies would be more likely to be welcomed if Free French forces were excluded. The Americans were adamant in their determination to keep de Gaulle out of the picture.

If the Free French troops were not to be used, there arose the second question as to how and when de Gaulle was to be informed. Security was vital. There was a general belief in Whitehall that there had been previous leakages of operational secrets from Free French sources. Whether this was true or not, there was no sense in taking unnecessary risks. Churchill therefore undertook the task of informing de Gaulle on the night before the landings, and he did his best to comfort him by the assurance that it was because 'Torch' was primarily an American enterprise and must be executed with the greatest possible secrecy, and not for want of British goodwill towards the French National Committee, that they had not been included. He also added, to sweeten the pill, that the final transfer of Madagascar to Free French administration would take place before the end of the year and the

---

[4] Churchill, *The Hinge of Fate*, p. 542.

appointment of the Gaullist General Legentilhomme as Governor-General would be announced immediately.

The policy of the State Department during the period before America was at war with Germany, that is until December 1941, was understandable. It was indeed to the general advantage that they should maintain close contact with the Vichy Government and be informed of every fresh German demand and every new Vichy surrender. The instrument which they chose for their purpose was certainly not ideal. Admiral Leahy was one of those men who, although unable to converse with any Frenchman in intelligible French, believed himself the supreme exponent of the French mentality. Even the keenest members of the Admiral's group had their doubts about his fitness for this post. The reports that he sent were not helpful and his attitude throughout was unfavourable to the British Government. But the American administration also suffered under the delusion, to some extent shared by the American people, that they were especially popular in France. The British, after centuries of rivalry and war, were hated. The French, owing to Lafayette and the wars of the eighteenth century, were traditional friends of America. Moreover, the long-expressed preference of many American travellers for Paris over any other city was supposed to have considerable political influence. Paris was the spiritual home of the American tourist, and it was popularly believed that it was to Paris that every good American hoped to go when he died.

All this had a powerful influence on the Secretary of State, Cordell Hull, and, combined with his genuine love of liberty and democratic equality, helped to make him deeply suspicious of de Gaulle's alleged autocratic tendencies. The State Department, therefore, supported by the President but for different reasons, continually hankered after some co-operation with Vichy. They suspected de Gaulle of trying to use the war and his British and American allies to force himself upon France after its liberation. They were sceptical of his often repeated declarations regarding the provisional character of the F.N.C. and its determination to hand over its authority to a freely elected French Assembly.

The American Government, relying upon the reports of their agents, who had been operating for many months in North Africa, believed that the leading figures in the French administration, as well as many of the important military and naval chiefs, would welcome the landings launched under American command as a step towards the liberation of metropolitan France. The plan included sending in to take the lead in this movement a distinguished figure—General Henri Giraud, who had been taken prisoner in the early months of the war but had lately escaped and was lying hidden in the south of France. Great hopes were placed upon his personal prestige.

The situation in relation to de Gaulle was delicate in the extreme, but had the expedition gone as was hoped and had Giraud's authority been accepted in Algiers and the other North African territories, no serious damage would have been done. After all, Giraud had not quarrelled with de Gaulle. He had had no opportunity of doing so, since he had only just escaped from a German prison camp. He bore no responsibility for the armistice or for any of the sins of the Vichy Government. Whatever might be thought about his capacity, nothing could be said against his character. His record was pure and unblemished. Moreover, his military service in North Africa had been successful and distinguished.

Unhappily, the Allied landings at Casablanca, Oran, and Algiers were opposed with varying degrees of vigour, and when Giraud arrived in Algiers expecting to take over the Supreme Command, the first reactions were discouraging. His reception was cold and hostile. None of the French commanders would admit his authority or accept his leadership. General Mark Clark, Eisenhower's second-in-command, was therefore forced to report to General Eisenhower at his headquarters in Gibraltar on 10 November that Giraud had proved a broken reed. The only possible course, if the fighting was to be stopped and casualties reduced to a minimum, was to reach as rapidly as possible some agreement with Admiral Darlan, who either by chance or calculation happened to be in North Africa at the time of the Anglo-American assault. He had arrived on 5 November with the ostensible purpose of visiting his son, who was lying dangerously ill in a hospital in Algiers. Both Darlan's seniority and his position in the French Government assured to him all the loyalties of the Vichy French. It is possible that if he had not been in Algiers, Giraud might have had some chance; but with the presence of Darlan, all—or nearly all—the admirals, generals, governors and their subordinates looked to him for leadership as their superior officer. There was no time for

Eisenhower to consult Washington or London. Darlan himself hesitated; but strongly pressed by General Clark, he finally agreed to give
the order for a general cease-fire throughout North Africa. ' "In the
name of the Marshal" he assumed complete authority throughout the
French North African territories, and ordered all officials to remain on
duty.'[5] His orders were obeyed, and as the result of what became
known as the Darlan-Clark Agreement, the Allies became established
without opposition in Morocco, Algeria, and the greater part of
Tunisia. In addition, General Boisson agreed to bring over French
West Africa.

The Agreement, in its full form, was signed on 22 November 1942.
It created provisional machinery for administering the whole region
and set out in detail the rights and powers of the Allied Commander-
in-Chief. Although it was amended by later negotiation, it long
remained the legal basis regulating and justifying the Allied position.

Events in metropolitan France followed rapidly. The landings took
place on 8 November. On the 9th, the Germans, with Vichy approval,
started to send troops into Tunisia, where Admiral Esteva, the French
Resident-General, accepted Vichy's instructions. The whole of France,
in breach of the armistice, was occupied by the Germans on 11
November, and Darlan was quickly repudiated by Pétain. His orders
to the French fleet to leave Toulon and join the Allies were ignored.
On 27 November, by the courage of a few officers, the Germans were
prevented from actually seizing the ships. In their curious confusion of
mind, gallant sailors like Admiral de Laborde, who was fanatically
anti-British and refused to accept Darlan's orders or yield to his
appeals, nevertheless foiled the Germans by arranging that the whole
fleet should be scuttled. One battleship, two battle-cruisers, seven
cruisers, twenty-nine destroyers and torpedo-boats, and sixteen submarines were among the seventy-three ships of the great French Navy
which were sunk in port.[6]

De Gaulle's reaction to the Darlan-Clark Agreement was swift and
understandable. In a circular letter to his chief administrators and
commanders, he made it clear that the elimination of the 'guilty men'
who had taken their orders from Vichy was an essential condition for
his co-operation with any French authority in North Africa.

[5] Ibid., p. 558.
[6] Ibid., p. 563.

The British public and a great part of the British Government were upset and angry. They regarded with contempt the figures who had brought France so low, whether before the war or since, whether members of the Vichy Government or outside its formal ranks. They despised those men and woman of the Right whose fear of being deprived of their wealth by the growing strength of the Left had led them consciously or unconsciously into defeatism or pro-Germanism. Yet our public opinion equally realised that the Communist Party, here in Britain so weak in numbers and influence, was in France an important political element. They too had betrayed France. So long as Russia was neutral, the war was a sin against humanity. Only when Russia was attacked had the Communists rallied to the Resistance. Nevertheless, while condemning these two extremes, we all felt a deep sympathy for the mass of the French people. De Gaulle and the Free French movement we admired. We saw with pleasure the firmness in the early days soon after the armistice of many of the French Servicemen and some of the distant colonial authorities and populations. But we were frankly disturbed and astonished at the hostility clearly shown to de Gaulle by so many Frenchmen. We could not understand why the Free French had been greeted with bullets and shells instead of with cheers wherever they had gone, as at Dakar or Syria. Why was de Gaulle thought a traitor and not a saviour? We failed to grasp the curious sense of discipline which requires absolute obedience to an immediate commander. This is the natural and perhaps the understandable refuge of a people who have suffered one change of régime after another, with constantly changing loyalties.

The public had accepted with reluctance Churchill's adherence—some thought subservience—to President Roosevelt's leadership in the planning and execution of the landings. But when the agreement with Darlan was made known, there was an explosion. Eden, in a message to Washington, said that the British people felt that a brilliant military episode had been tarnished and tainted. Lord Strang went so far as to say that the President was losing the moral leadership of Europe.[7] But Churchill, who shared to the full the British disappointment at what had happened, with his usual magnanimity stoutly defended General Eisenhower's decision, and was not prepared to sacrifice the fruits of his long wooing of the President and the

[7] Lord Strang, *Home and Abroad* (London, 1956), p. 73.

American Chiefs of Staff. He was looking not merely to the immediate political situation in Algiers. His eyes were straining towards Italy, towards Greece and Turkey, to the liberation of Central and Eastern Europe. It would indeed be folly to sacrifice the future, in which everything depended on his power to keep the President's confidence and support.

During the next few weeks controversy raged fiercely. Even Churchill had to admit the 'rising tide of opinion' around him. As the days passed, the emotions aroused seemed to recall the passionate controversies of Munich. The Press led the van; but Parliament and the public were not slow to follow. The crucial debate was held in secret session on 11 December, a month after the landings. Churchill defended General Eisenhower loyally. He argued the case on purely military grounds and succeeded by the sheer weight and power of his argument in changing opinion in the House. Nevertheless, although criticism began to die down, there was an undercurrent of disappointment and disquiet throughout the country.

Meanwhile, the American people and Press were almost equally hostile to the Agreement. They were in general not unfavourably disposed towards de Gaulle. They had no friendly feelings towards Vichy, and no use for Darlan, Laval, or even Pétain. Although some of de Gaulle's performances seemed to them strange and inexplicable, on the whole the American people, themselves strong individualists, liked to see a man standing up for himself. It was no matter to them if his seizure of the French islands of St. Pierre and Miquelon had caused concern in the State Department and upset old Cordell Hull.

The American administration, from the President downwards, was swayed by more complicated and divergent motives. The President believed, erroneously as it proved, that if the expedition were regarded as an American adventure, it would meet with little or no resistance. He also took the view that the only thing that mattered was to beat the Germans and that almost any means were justifiable if they contributed to that end. Like the American generals, he gave little weight to the political consequences. What would be the ultimate effect in Europe of sustaining the corrupt and despised Vichy crowd was as unimportant to him as what might be the result later of concessions to Moscow. His approach to politico-military problems was generally tactical rather than strategic.

On Christmas Eve 1942, Darlan was shot in the entrance to his office in the Palais d'Été in Algiers and died within the hour. What was the motive and who were the instigators of the assassin, who was tried and executed two days later, became a matter of much subsequent dispute. The assassination at least put an end to one part of the controversy:

Darlan's murder, however criminal, relieved the Allies of their embarrassment at working with him, and at the same time left them with all the advantages he had been able to bestow during the vital hours of the Allied landings.[8]

Unhappily, the succession was to lead to new French divisions. General Eisenhower, faced with the immediate problem, acted in the only way which seemed open to him. He called together the leading French notables and secured the election of Giraud to fill the vacant place. Thus General Giraud became High Commissioner for French North and West Africa, with the title of Commander-in-Chief, Civil and Military.

On Christmas Day, the day after the murder, de Gaulle suggested a meeting in North Africa for discussions. Giraud replied evasively. He declared that the time was not yet opportune, and proceeded to exercise his new functions without any relation to the Gaullist movement. De Gaulle was deeply wounded. He felt that Giraud's appointment had been made under Allied pressure and confirmed by a so-called 'Imperial Council'—actually a junta of Vichy administrators who had first accepted with varying degrees of reluctance Admiral Darlan's orders and then bound themselves by a military convention with General Eisenhower. These proceedings de Gaulle regarded as derogatory to France.

As the result of these startling events, crowded into seven short weeks, the French became even more divided than before. Three groups now emerged with differing loyalties.

There were those in metropolitan France, living under German domination and owing at least a nominal allegiance to Marshal Pétain's shadowy Government, and to a great extent still under the influence of the strangely powerful tradition that surrounded the Marshal's name. This 'mystique' which he enjoyed was incomprehensible to non-Frenchmen.

[8] Churchill, *The Hinge of Fate*, p. 578.

There was a second group, comprising leading administrators and soldiers, sailors and airmen in North Africa, who had hitherto been loyal to Pétain, but now felt themselves entitled to accept first Darlan's and then Giraud's authority. Apart from the pressure of events, by which they were constrained, they comforted themselves with the thought that the occupation of *all* France was a breach of the armistice and had, in fact, destroyed the Marshal's freedom of action. Thus was evolved the doctrine of 'le Maréchal Empêché', which was to prove serviceable in salving many uneasy consciences. These people were by no means penitent about their past defeatism. Nor were their hearts always changed when they changed their coats. Among the French population in North Africa, the Anglo-American invasion had been received with mixed feelings. Many of the 'colons'—especially the rich farmers and industrialists—saw with some dismay the prospect of war being brought into territories where they had so far been able to live in comparative ease and comfort. Their trade with southern France would be cut off. Their properties would be requisitioned. They and their homes would become a target for enemy bombing. Of course, there were others whose welcome was warm and genuine. Up to now they had believed, with a sort of resigned faith, in the Marshal. But, without bitterness against him, they were ready to follow first Darlan and then Giraud.

Finally, there was the third group, who had rallied to de Gaulle, some by joining him in exile, some by bringing over large parts of the French Empire, and others by their resistance in metropolitan France. In North Africa itself there were many keen Gaullists, soldiers and civilians. It was to their leaders that the American agents had looked for the *coup* which was to deliver Algiers to the Allies. These now found themselves degraded, and in many cases either in prison or in hiding. The Darlan-Clark Agreement had been a bitter and cruel blow to these gallant men. While they might doubt the wisdom of some of de Gaulle's actions, they recognised him as the splendid leader of resistance and the true upholder of the honour of France.

The situation at Allied Force Headquarters when I arrived at Algiers after the assassination of Darlan could be summed up as follows: General Eisenhower, for purely military reasons, had accepted Darlan as the man who could deliver the goods. In this, he had the powerful support of Admiral Cunningham, the Allied naval chief.

Darlan might be a scoundrel, as the British said; or a traitor, as Pétain now said; or guilty of many crimes against France, as the Gaullists said. But he had this in his favour. He had stopped the opposition to the landings and thereby saved many lives. He was also one of those men who seemed to justify the notorious, if cynical, definition of honesty: 'Once bought he stayed bought'. The murder of Darlan had been a terrible shock to Allied Force Headquarters. But Giraud seemed to be an acceptable—indeed the only—substitute. Nevertheless, in their hearts they knew that if trouble was to be avoided, sooner or later some plan must be devised to bring about a reunion of all the forces inside and outside France prepared to work with the Allies for final victory. Meanwhile, what mattered was not so much the politics of Algiers as the difficult and frustrating campaign in Tunisia.

CHAPTER NINE

Allied Force Headquarters

D URING the evening of 22 December 1942, the Prime Minister sent for me. He asked how far I had followed affairs in North Africa since the landings. I replied that I had only done so in a superficial way, by reading the newspapers and so forth. I was, however, aware, from my contacts with General de Gaulle's organisation, of the indignation which had been caused by the Allied agreement with Admiral Darlan. Unluckily, I had not been able to attend the secret session, where the Prime Minister had explained and defended the decisions taken on the spot. Churchill then began an exposition of the military and political situation; although the former was encouraging, the latter was distressing and confusing. The House of Commons had been satisfied, at least for the moment, with his defence of General Eisenhower's action. But the public and the Press were disturbed. Nobody could understand how it was that the Western democracies, engaged in a struggle to defend freedom and honour, should shake the hand of such a traitor to their cause as Admiral Darlan. Nevertheless, the expedition, as he had told the House, was under American command and the Americans held the prime responsibility. The landings, if strenuously and persistently opposed, could not have succeeded without very heavy casualties. Darlan had at least put an end to the fighting. It was too crude an explanation to regard him as a man of no principles. Like so many of the French after a long history of revolution and unstable régimes, he was obsessed by a sense of loyalty to his immediate commander—in this case, Marshal Pétain. The recent German occupation of southern France, in breach of the armistice, would no doubt release many other French officers and civil servants, besides Darlan, from their fancied obligations.

Churchill went on to explain that, encouraged by the delay caused by these political events, the Germans had been able to occupy Bizerta and were sending in heavy reinforcements; but there was still a good chance of pressing forward within the next few weeks, so that the First (British) Army, under General Anderson, might reach Bizerta and Tunis, while the Eighth Army, under Montgomery, occupied Tripoli. In any case, the military considerations were supreme, for the prize was great—the liberation of all North Africa from German and Italian control. While fully accepting that the command of the North African expedition was American, we had the right and the duty to express our opinions, especially in the political sphere. There was already a Foreign Office official, and an admirable one, on Eisenhower's staff. But he had not sufficient rank or influence. The Cabinet was determined that it should now be represented at Eisenhower's headquarters by a ministerial colleague.

I naturally soon began to see the purpose of these preliminaries. Their object was not merely to treat me to the pleasure of being admitted into the picture of Churchill's political and strategic plans, but to lead to an offer to become at least a participant in this unfolding drama. I tried to control my impatience as he came gradually to the point. There should be a Minister at Allied Force Headquarters, now set up in Algiers. He would be of Cabinet rank, though not a member of the War Cabinet. He would be entitled to report direct to the Prime Minister. His status would be roughly parallel to that of the Minister of State in Cairo. But there was an important difference. The Middle East was a purely British concern, and all executive power was in the hands of the British military and civil authorities. In North Africa, the command was American. The Headquarters were staffed equally by British and American officers, but the American general held the final responsibility, subject only to the Combined Chiefs of Staff in Washington. A Minister of State, therefore, although his rank would be similar to that of the Ministers now operating in Cairo (R. G. Casey)[1] or in British West Africa (Lord Swinton), must depend on the influence that he could exert upon the Supreme Allied Commander. Although the debate in the House of Commons had done much to satisfy Parliamentary opinion, and criticism in and outside the House had been temporarily quietened, there was still an undercurrent of hostility and dismay. Moreover, although the command was

---

[1] Later Lord Casey; successively Minister of State, Middle East; Governor of Bombay; Minister of External Affairs, Australia; Governor-General of Australia.

American, it was well known that the greater part of the armies, navies and air forces engaged were British. It was essential that the British Parliament and people should feel that they had more say in future developments. Here was a post of great potential significance. It would bring its occupant into the very centre of world events. Although it would entail secondment from the House of Commons, the chosen Minister could still keep his seat. It would be an adventure of a high order. This post was at my disposition. I replied at once that there was no need to hesitate—I would accept it immediately and gratefully. Although the Prime Minister insisted that I should take a few hours to think it over, and send a formal reply the next day, the conversation proceeded on the assumption that the matter was settled.

Churchill then gave me a copy of the full text of his speech in the secret debate, which proved very valuable, for I had little knowledge of the background of this affair. He asked me when I would leave for Algiers. I replied, 'Tomorrow, or rather the day after tomorrow.' That seemed satisfactory. Would I go in uniform? He had known of my hopes of getting back into the Army at the beginning of the war. Now they could be satisfied. I would be at the seat of war. I thought a moment and then replied, 'No, sir, I don't think I will go in uniform.' 'Why not?' he exclaimed angrily. 'Are you ashamed of your uniform?' 'No, Prime Minister, but I think among all those generals, admirals and air marshals an infantry captain formerly in the Reserve, even of the Grenadier Guards, would not cut a very impressive figure.' Churchill calmed down and reflected. 'I see your point,' he said. 'You mean that between the baton and the bowler there is no middle course.'

So it was arranged. One of the private secretaries was sent for and told that the matter was settled. But the Prime Minister was reminded that he had not yet cleared it with the Americans, and the necessary steps were set in motion. No announcement could be made until President Roosevelt knew and agreed. However, there was no doubt at all in my mind that the Prime Minister intended to press his point to a conclusion.

On the morning of the 23rd I sent my formal acceptance to Downing Street and, learning that there must be some delay before the announcement, I went down to spend Christmas in the cottage in Sussex and to tell my wife the wonderful news. Before doing so, I informed John Wyndham and asked him to come with me to Algiers.

He at once accepted. On the afternoon of Christmas Eve, we heard on the wireless that Darlan had been assassinated. A wave of disappointment swept over me. I rang up John in London to find out what people were saying and to ask if any information could be obtained from the private office at No. 10. Although he and I were not actually cast, as in a Shakespeare play, for the roles of First and Second Murderers, I feared that the fact that Darlan had been eliminated might so simplify the French situation that a new Minister would not be needed. After a little reflection, I decided that the wisest course was to do nothing and hope for the best. I had now become tremendously excited by the wonderful prospect opening out. I could escape from a subordinate ministerial and Parliamentary post at home, which seemed to offer few prospects, into a position where I would be operating completely on my own. Above all, I should be if not at the Front at any rate near it. Although neither I nor the Prime Minister had really the slightest idea what I was going to do, I would do it with the utmost diligence and perseverance. Surely the cup could not be snatched from my lips at the last moment merely because a young man had assassinated Admiral Darlan. There must be plenty of other difficulties and confusions which would have to be cleared up, even after the removal of the leading figure. There were.

Further telegrams passed between the Prime Minister and the President on 27 and 28 December. As a result, the announcement of my appointment as Minister Resident at Allied Headquarters in North-West Africa was given out from No. 10 on the afternoon of 30 December and was in all the newspapers on the 31st. The Press was encouraging in its welcome both to the new post and to the selection of the man chosen to fill it. On the same day I was granted an audience by King George VI. Although I had some acquaintance with the King, it was the first time I had been received as a Minister. In the last day or two I had done my best to find out something about the situation in Algiers. I had enjoyed the advantage of an hour's talk with the Deputy Head of the Foreign Office, Sir Orme Sargent, and had read through a large file of telegrams. But when I talked with the King, I had my first experience of the extraordinary diligence and accuracy with which successive occupants of the Throne make it their task to study all the details of the manifold problems which it is their duty to master.

On the night of 31 December, accompanied by John Wyndham,

Miss Campbell—my admirable secretary of the Colonial Office—and another young lady whom John had collected (Miss Williams), we left upon our mission in a Hudson aeroplane which could take a few passengers and a small amount of essential luggage. At Brendan Bracken's request, we gave a lift to an American journalist, Miss Virginia Cowles.[2] We stopped at an airfield in Cornwall and took off again for Gibraltar just before midnight in the last hours of 1942. France being wholly occupied by the Germans, our course took us in a wide circuit over the Atlantic and back again. In the exhilaration of new and thrilling fields of effort, we disdained the discomfort and extreme cold of our journey. Miss Campbell, under the general impression that Africa was always hot, wore, I remember, a little round straw hat as a kind of symbol. We had two typewriters, stolen from the Colonial Office, and these proved a wise provision, as we would have been helpless without them, and they were as jealously guarded as gold at A.F.H.Q.

I now began the practice, which I continued to the end of the war, of sending letters home to my wife at certain intervals, usually through the confidential bag. These amount to something like a diary for the whole two and a half years of the campaign.

We got to Gibraltar about noon on Friday [1 January]. No incidents and a very smooth and comfortable journey. But it was an early start in the morning and a very rough and cold bed in a hut the night before.

The girls and John stood the journey well. Miss Campbell is a practised traveller and knows all the tricks—pockets full of chewing gum and raisins. Miss Williams is more timid, but pretty and soon gets help from any soldier or airman, as required.

We stayed the night at Gibraltar. Mason-MacFarlane (the Governor) very friendly. The best thing about Gibraltar is a cask (mark you, a cask) of sherry standing always in the drawing room and available at any time.

Lord Gort was there on his way home for some leave. A very pleasant dinner in semi-viceregal surroundings—all the things we have forgotten in England—five or six courses, sherry, red and white wine, port, brandy, etc.[3]

The next morning we flew on to Algiers, where I was met by Hal Mack,[4] a member of the Foreign Office who had been on Eisenhower's staff from the early days of 'Torch' planning. He took me to lunch and

2 Now Mrs. Aidan Crawley.
3 7 January 1943.
4 Sir Henry Mack.

gave me, as briefly as possible, a general outline of the local state of affairs. It was obvious that everyone was pretty jumpy as a result of Darlan's murder. He also warned me that I was to see General Eisenhower at 4 o'clock that afternoon, but that since neither Washington nor London had informed him of my appointment, of which he had only heard by chance on the wireless, this first meeting might be rather sticky. However, there was nothing to be done about it, and I was duly taken to Allied Force Headquarters, which were established in the Hôtel St. Georges, on the top of the hill, in the main highway of Algiers. The hotel was a modern building, decorated in an imitation Moorish style. It was guarded by a formidable array of sentinels and an elaborate system of passes. This was my first meeting with Eisenhower. Although it was an inauspicious start, our relations were destined to ripen into a close comradeship and friendship, and to last over many years of war and peace.

The General made no attempt to conceal his feelings. 'Pleased to see you,' he said, 'but what have you come for?' I tried to explain that I thought my appointment had been arranged between the President and the Prime Minister. 'But I have been told nothing of it. You are a Minister, but what sort of a Minister are you?' 'Well, General,' I said, 'I am not a diplomatic Minister; I am something worse.' 'There is nothing worse,' he replied. 'Perhaps you will think a politician is even more troublesome,' I said. 'Well, I don't know about that. Perhaps so. But anyway what are you going to do?' 'I will just do my best. I shall be told and will be able to tell you what are the feelings of the Prime Minister and his colleagues on anything that comes up.' 'Oh,' he said, 'but I have got a fine man in Hal Mack who does that.' 'I am afraid that Mr. Mack will be wanted elsewhere, and you will have to rely upon me. I can tell you I have at least one advantage over you all. I know nothing whatsoever about the political problems here. I shall have to learn.' 'Well,' he said, 'there's plenty to learn.' But, naturally offended at the rather casual manner of my appointment, the General did not give me much help. The conversation began to languish. Happily, I thought of my own background and I began to ask him whether he knew my mother's home state. 'What do you mean, your mother? Why should I know that?' 'My mother was born in Indiana,' I said, 'at a little town called Spencer. So I am a Hoosier.' This disclosure gave him obvious pleasure, and after that we got on better.

I could soon see that the General was a man of rapidly changing moods. But it was also clear that he was naturally open-hearted and generous. He began to unbend, and treated me for an hour or more to a full account of all the difficulties and problems in the political aspect of affairs. He had clearly been hurt by the hostile criticisms of the British and American Press about Darlan and the political arrangements which had followed. 'I can't understand,' he exclaimed, 'why these long-haired, starry-eyed guys keep gunning for me. I'm no reactionary. Christ on the Mountain! I'm as idealistic as Hell. Now that poor Darlan has been killed,' he went on, 'we've got this Giraud, and no one can attack his record. We have made Giraud the boss. Of course we're going to make changes. We are going to get a new Governor for Algeria. It's a guy called "Pie-row-ton". They tell me he's a fine guy.' But in any case the Allied armies must rely on these Frenchmen, and the greater part of them were Pétainists at heart. The first need was to keep the country calm and to see that the hundreds of miles of difficult and dangerous communications between the ports and the front line were kept intact. This was his 'priority' duty and he intended to perform it. Much depended on the Arabs remaining quiet. There must be French administrators who understood the Arab problem and could help him in this aspect of the military campaign. The whole population must be kept under control and our job was to try to damp down politics until Tunis and Bizerta could be captured and the Germans thrown out of North Africa. Then there was the question of the French Army and its loyalties. All this seemed to me very sensible and was set out in a series of idiomatic and forcible sentences. He introduced me to the Chief of Staff, Bedell Smith, who would always be ready to receive me and with whom I should mainly deal. Nevertheless, he himself would be available if I wished to see him.

The interview therefore ended better than I had expected. But, as I subsequently learned, I had already in my innocence been guilty of a grave error. The guy 'Pie-row-ton' turned out to be Marcel Peyrouton, who was already on his way, but whose appointment caused a storm of protest in the British Press and was anathema to the Gaullists. Although he had the merit of having quarrelled violently with Laval, he was a typical Vichy politician with a doubtful record. The Foreign Office had, I believe, been warned by Mack that this project was in the air, but I received no instructions to try to alter the decision. Moreover, I must confess that all this meant nothing to me even when I discovered the true name of the Governor-elect. But it was a serious mistake and was to cause a great deal of trouble. At a later stage, when our arrangements for close and loyal consultation on all political questions were perfected, such an error could not have occurred.

I came away encouraged by at least one thing. It was clear to me that in General Eisenhower ('Ike' as he was already known to all the world) as our leader we were indeed fortunate. Even at this first meeting I sensed the inherent goodness and firmness of his character. If sometimes impetuous, he was always fair. I felt that his natural antipathy to the idea of a British Minister of Cabinet rank, who might make trouble for him in all sorts of ways, could be overcome. If I would play the game with him, he would do the same by me. As days and months passed, I learned more about Ike and began to feel for him real affection as well as respect. Meanwhile, the first hurdle had been faced and surmounted. 'Beedle' (General Bedell Smith) made me welcome and immediately showed the same willingness to treat me with confidence if I would do the same by him. With these two men I was to live on terms of increasing intimacy for many months. Bedell Smith's too early death removed from the scene a sincere friend of Britain. 'Ike' happily remains.

The next day I paid a formal call on General Giraud. He was already installed in the Palais d'Été, a viceregal residence, with a massive guard and a large number of personal aides-de-camp and political assistants, mostly soldiers. He received me gravely, and at first somewhat stiffly. It was not in his nature to be anything but correct, at any rate at the beginning of an interview. However, this attitude soon changed into a more cordial mood, as he found my knowledge of French adequate, both for speaking and, more important, for listening. I had the story of his exploits in two wars; of his adventurous escapes; of his hatred of politics in any form and his determination to disregard all such unworthy considerations in favour of war. His blue eyes, his noble stature, his fluent and almost classical French, his obvious sincerity—all these struck me forcibly. But they could not conceal, even at this first meeting, his unsuitability for the difficult and complex task which he had assumed. He was no doubt a gallant cavalry leader and an adequate divisional commander. As Civil and Military Head of all French North Africa he was clearly out of his depth. That he possessed an engaging and endearing personality was equally evident.

These interviews were duly recorded and transmitted to London. But they did not seem to take me much further.

Mack had to return within a few days, and Bob Dixon[5] was to come out for a short time to help me pending the arrival of Roger Makins,[6] who had been appointed as my adviser. Meanwhile, I confess that I felt somewhat at a loss as to what to do. The first problem, as in all such situations, was physical. How to live and work? On leaving General Eisenhower's office, I was taken by Hal Mack to see Bob Murphy, political adviser to General Eisenhower and personal representative of the President. This again was my first meeting with a man who had already played a notable part in trying to secure French agreement to or connivance at the Allied landings. The details were of course unknown to me at the time except in the vaguest outline, but I realised that Murphy had been a remarkable operator in the secret work which he was engaged upon during the months before 'Torch'. Nevertheless, his hopes were, to a great extent, disappointed. His friends, such as General Béthouart and General Mast, and many others who were favourable to the Allies and awaiting an opportunity to join the anti-Vichy forces, as well as those who were friendly to de Gaulle and his movement, were repudiated. Giraud, after all the efforts to contrive his escape from France and arrange for him to be brought by submarine first to Gibraltar and then to Algiers, proved to have no authority. Murphy had therefore been forced to recommend, or at least acquiesce in, the agreement with Darlan, and the retention of all the old Pétainist administrations throughout the French territories.

I had sensed that there was hostility to Murphy in many quarters in London, but it seemed to me on reflection vital that we should work closely together, and that I should gain his confidence. The first thing was to get somewhere to work, and I was determined that any office I could obtain should be next door to my American colleague.

John and I had some rooms at the Hôtel Aletti down by the harbour and were starting gradually to organise our life. It was very cold and rained a good deal:

Hot water from 7.30 to 8.30 a.m. only. Bed hard; bottom sheet wet, no top sheet but coarse blanket. No fire or heating of any kind.

[5] Sir Pierson Dixon, later British Ambassador in Paris.
[6] Now Lord Sherfield. British Ambassador in Washington, 1953–56, Permanent Under-Secretary of the Treasury, 1956–59.

A naval mess takes pity on us and we lunch and dine with them. Nowhere to sit after dinner, except at dining table or upstairs in one's room in heaviest overcoat available![7]

Within a few days, we were able to acquire a couple of rooms in the same building (in the Rue Professeur Curtillet) as that in which Murphy's office was placed. Murphy welcomed me with generosity. If at first there was some awkwardness, we soon learned to understand each other. We became and have remained firm friends.

There is no paper, no pens, pencils, typewriters, filing covers—and, of course, no steel cabinets or tin boxes or anything. So all our documents have to be carted about with us wherever we go, which is a great bore, especially as the hotel is [a long way] off. . . .

However, we have our [two] typewriters. . . . We have corporals to guard us and we have a car—a fine Buick—with a corporal to drive. We also have a corporal on a motor-bike in front. And today they have produced a Union Jack and put it on the car. Thus pride defies security.[8]

The next problem was to get out of the hotel into some kind of a house. This presented considerable difficulties. Meanwhile, a number of telegrams began to come in and a certain pressure was developing that I should do something to justify my existence. I was indeed fortunate to have with me so wise a counsellor as Hal Mack during those first days. He was an easy-going Irishman of equable temperament and of great ability, with sufficient seniority to show considerable independence of Foreign Office control. He lived in the same villa as some of the leading officers, British and American, and was on the best possible terms with them all. He showed me great kindness by introducing me to the various villas in which similar messes were placed, and I was soon to be a welcome guest at all of them. What he called the rigours of the North Africa campaign could best be mitigated by generous consumption of liquor, particularly gin, which seemed to be readily available and at a very low price. He heartily agreed that I must resist the temptation to show undue activity. In spite of their apparent change of heart after our first meeting, I knew that Generals Eisenhower and Bedell Smith, and indeed all the American officers, were suspicious of my appointment and would resent any premature attempt to influence their decisions. Nor could Murphy have really

[7] 7 January 1943.
[8] Ibid.

welcomed my arrival. All of them had been indignant and upset by
the hostile reaction to the Darlan-Clark Agreement and the lack of
understanding of the actual situation with which they had been faced.
They had been even more shaken by the assassination of Darlan just as
things were beginning to settle down. Admiral Sir Andrew Cunningham[9] ('A.B.C.' as he was known by everyone) had taken pity on me
soon after my arrival and had given me the benefit of his wise advice.
He was to prove a stalwart friend in all the troubles that were to
follow. But I could see that he too was doubtful as to what I could
usefully do, and was prone to resent the fact that British critics had
fastened upon the political difficulties instead of recognising the
outstanding naval and military successes. He had been Eisenhower's
strongest supporter all through the negotiations with Darlan. He was
indeed Aaron to his Moses. Moreover, as I was subsequently to learn,
since Darlan was after all an admiral and there was a strong trade
union feeling among all admirals which bound them together, 'A.B.C.'
could not understand why we had not accepted an admiral who had at
least delivered the goods.

I therefore made up my mind to spend the next few weeks doing as
little as possible except socially: to listen and learn; to accept all the
invitations to luncheon and dinner which were so generously given to
me; and not to worry General Eisenhower, but to take the opportunity
of the Chief of Staff's kindness to drop in and see him from time to
time, usually towards the end of the day. If I could once overcome the
British and American suspicion of politicians and gain their confidence, I might be of some use. I must also win Murphy's trust and
make him regard me as a colleague and not as an opponent. All this
could best be achieved by a policy of masterly inactivity. Bob Dixon
had now come to join me, and he in his turn accepted this plan. On
the whole it was justified by results. The only grave disadvantage
which followed was having allowed the appointment of Peyrouton to
take place without protest.

The physical difficulties of our life were rapidly dealt with by
Wyndham:

John has devoted himself solely to the task of trying to get us a house to
live in. We hope to get a villa. We have seen one or two excellent ones. But

9 Admiral of the Fleet Lord Cunningham of Hyndhope.

how can they be obtained? By registering. How is that done? By the American Army authorities. What, for a British civilian Minister! Well, then, by the British Army authorities. What, for a civilian! Well, by the French authorities. Ah! that is better, but M. le Préfet is away—he is indisposed. The Préfecture only opens one hour a day—by bad luck always during an 'alerte'. How can work be done during an 'alerte' with bombs and guns and so on?

However, John has—or thinks he has—overcome all these difficulties and obtained for us a rich and sumptuous villa.[10]

In addition, the owner of the house would herself remain in certain rooms and provide a housemaid and a cook. This was a notable triumph, but involved of course a security risk, and military policemen and what-not were accordingly allotted to us. General Gale, the British head of all our administrative side, proved a splendid ally and even provided us with a batman. But there were other needs.

There is the 'batterie de cuisine'. There is not a saucepan, teapot, kettle, kitchen knife or anything like it in North Africa. Our linen, our towels, scrubbing cloths, table linen, blankets, pillow cases, glass, silver, etc., where is that to come from? John has solved it. From the Fleet or the Merchant Navy. A huge list of articles has been seized from a [sunk] P. & O. liner and is waiting on the docks (pray Heaven it will not be bombed) to be taken to the villa when the final negotiations are complete.[11]

An equally important question was that of food.

There is *no* food to be had, except in the black market, and there is a sort of self-denying ordinance (very rightly) that English and Americans should not compete with the inhabitants for what little food there is. So we must have rations. Yes, easily said, but not so easily done. Army rations or Navy rations? And who is to pay? On whose vote will it be borne? Will an M.P. ask a question at the Public Accounts Committee? All these questions John is coping with. He sees Admirals and Commodores and tells them what we want. We never see him (except at meals), and, while we are making slow progress with political questions, he is in sole charge of this much more vital aspect of our mission.[12]

Finally, at Admiral Cunningham's suggestion, we drew naval rations and gin at naval rates.

During these days we were not wholly inactive. I had many talks with Murphy, who generously shared with me his long experience and

[10] 7 January 1943.
[11] Ibid.
[12] Ibid.

knowledge of all the background. Although he naturally defended his own policies, I thought him singularly objective and fair-minded. Even at this rather difficult time, before we had learned to understand each other, he was helpful and forthcoming. I had one or two conversations with the Chief of Staff, to whom I handed, under instruction, a long and not very illuminating memorandum from the Foreign Office. But I made no attempt to see General Eisenhower again. On one occasion the four of us met together at his request. It led to a curious and somewhat poignant assignment.

During these weeks following the murder of Darlan the political situation in the city of Algiers had deteriorated seriously, and the security position was alarming. Moreover, the reports from the other provinces were not reassuring. In Algiers, many different contending groups of Frenchmen, with all the bitter hatreds which civil strife and division bring in their train, were eyeing each other with sullen animosity. Although Darlan's assassin had been executed within two days, nominally under Giraud's orders but in fact by the decision of General Bergeret, Chief of Staff to Darlan, this rapid action was itself a cause of new suspicions. It was known that Henri d'Astier de la Vigerie, already implicated in an attempt at a subversive movement in the town on 8 November, was still at work. Henri, as well as his brother, General François d'Astier de la Vigerie, who had arrived on 19 December on a visit of exploration, was a leading Gaullist. It was widely rumoured that a plan had been concocted for pressure to be put upon Darlan to abdicate his position and either join or help to form a representative administration under a restored monarchy. It was even asserted that it was because of Darlan's refusal to comply that Bonnier de la Chapelle, confident that his act would have the approval of monarchist and clericalist forces, and that he would be regarded as a national hero, had assassinated him. General Bergeret's rapid reaction, under Giraud's protecting authority, prevented the development of this conspiracy. So at least it was rumoured in Algiers at that time. The Comte de Paris, claimant to the French throne, had gone from his farm in Tangier to Rabat, and was now said to be in Algiers. The possibility of a *coup* on his behalf was thought by the Allied Headquarters Intelligence to be a real and imminent risk. At the same time, the republican and Gaullist elements were in ferment. Although many of them were in hiding or in prison, an outbreak was possible by these disappointed patriots which the Vichy administrators would be only too happy to quell—an action at which General Giraud would easily be persuaded to connive. All this would not only embarrass the military situation (the dash for Tunis was now reaching a crisis) but would lead to a fresh wave of indignation in Britain and America.

It was strongly recommended to General Eisenhower, and supported by his Intelligence staff, that at least one source of trouble should be removed. Accordingly, it was decided that General Giraud should be told that the Supreme Allied Commander, in accordance with his rights under the agreement between him and Admiral Darlan, must request the French High Commissioner (Giraud) to secure the removal of the Comte de Paris from French North African territory. Since this seemed a delicate and unpleasant task, it was to be entrusted to the civilian representatives, who thus came into their own in a big way. The duty of delivering this message was delegated to Murphy and myself. I welcomed this for two reasons. It was the first official acceptance of my position as something more than an observer. It entrusted to me, at least in part, a quasi-executive function. Secondly, it enabled me to act officially in partnership with my American colleague, Murphy. It was the first of many occasions when we could make it clear that we would wherever possible work together and not allow ourselves to become the victims of separate intrigue by any French faction.

So we had to go along to the Palais d'Été, brave the line of sentries, heavily armed and trigger-happy, and request a formal meeting with General Giraud, now the effective 'Head of State' throughout French North Africa. The interview was short and rather tragic. How strange it seemed, indeed how impudent, that Murphy and I should go to a French general to secure the expulsion from a French territory of the descendant of the longest line of kings in Europe.

We had worked out our little piece; it was as short as possible and merely gave the danger of public unrest as the reason for General Eisenhower's request. My colleague spoke first from our agreed text. I followed him briefly. General Giraud answered with dignity. 'It is not for me,' he replied, 'to say anything about the present whereabouts of Monseigneur. But you can assure General Eisenhower that the wishes he has expressed through you will be met.'

By this time our little staff was beginning to function. I had Bob Dixon with me in the place of Mack, and we had acquired, in addition to Miss Campbell and Miss Williams, a couple of cipher clerks. An 'archivist', the official title for someone who keeps the documents, was on his way. We were poised for the next developments, whatever they might be.

But the somewhat desultory discussions of our many problems were soon to be brought to a dramatic close. We should be forced to make up our minds and give collective advice to our chiefs, if at all possible, for the news had reached us that a great conference was to be organised in Morocco, where the President and the Prime Minister, under the code names of Admiral Q. and Air Commodore F., would meet, with a suitable court—Ministers, Chiefs of Staff and other notabilities. Decisions would have to be taken, agreeable to both these potentates. We must now concentrate our minds on being able to give agreed advice on behalf of our own chief, General Eisenhower. The telegram imparting this exciting information reached us on 12 January. On 15 January, just a fortnight after my arrival, I was to set off to go nearly seven hundred miles in another direction. Certainly all this looked like being more fun than sitting at home in the impressive but dreary surroundings of Whitehall. I had been right to be patient; but this reward was something beyond my wildest dreams.

CHAPTER TEN

The Casablanca Conference

BEFORE starting on our journey to Morocco, I decided to hold a Press conference in Algiers for the British and American correspondents. The lack of any news from the Front, combined with the great distance of Headquarters from the scene of military operations, had directed the minds of the Press representatives more and more into political channels. Yet a rigid censorship of all political news had been set up in the previous December and was still in force. This had been imposed by Allied Force Headquarters, without consultation with Murphy, ostensibly to prevent French officials in North Africa from joining in a public quarrel. But since its result was to keep the British and American public ill-informed about affairs, both before and after the murder of Darlan, it certainly added to the growing hostility and suspicion. General Eisenhower, in his own memoirs, says frankly that this application of censorship to the political news, which lasted for only six weeks, was an error.[1] Curiously enough, very few of the correspondents attacked me about this matter. Because of my recent arrival and my somewhat anomalous position, I could perhaps hardly be held in any way responsible. At the end of the meeting the matter was raised and I promised to see what could be done. When by pure chance the censorship was lifted a fortnight later, my stock naturally rose.

I had thought a great deal about the wisdom of holding this Press conference, but it proved both fortunate and well timed. My chief object was to state publicly my support for General Eisenhower's original decision to implement and confirm the Darlan-Clark Agreement. There was no doubt at all that if Darlan had not been persuaded to give the necessary orders for the cease-fire, there would have been tough fighting both during and after the landings, with heavy

[1] Dwight D. Eisenhower, *Crusade in Europe* (New York, 1948), p. 131.

casualties. The French Army, although ill-equipped, was by no means negligible. It comprised some 125,000 men. Both the Army and Navy were loyal to their chiefs, and the resistance would have been determined and prolonged.

Whatever the rights and wrongs, it was important to remember that the North African expedition would no doubt be the prologue to the story of the years ahead of us in Europe. We must learn the lessons from the unexpected events which had happened. I went on to declare that whatever mistakes had been made, and no doubt they had, there was only one mistake which would be fatal. This would be to allow any rift or division between the British and American forces and authorities, either here in North Africa or in the world outside. I was determined not to allow myself to be made an instrument for such a purpose. I had been, even in a few days, immensely struck by the sense of comradeship and co-operation which General Eisenhower had himself created among the British and American officers and troops under his command. The use of Darlan had of course been distasteful. But that phase was over and General Giraud was a man of a quite different character and background. Nevertheless, there were a number of things in Algiers and throughout North Africa which needed to be put right—the laws against the Jews, and the imprisonment or degradation of a number of well-known Allied partisans who had done their best to help in the landings, ranging from distinguished generals, like Béthouart, to the humblest individual among the 8,000 political prisoners in the old Vichy camps.

Furthermore, it was our duty to work for a rapid agreement between General Giraud and General de Gaulle. The sooner satisfactory arrangements could be made, the better pleased the British and American people would be. I had every hope that a *de facto* French administration could then be set up, which would clean up some of the wrongful acts and remove the survivors of a bad régime. Meanwhile, I expressed the view—too sanguine, as it proved—that co-operation between the two generals was in sight.

During the lull in military operations, this conference created much interest in the British and American Press. It achieved my main purpose. By a strong defence of General Eisenhower, I felt that I had gone a long way to win his confidence and that of his Chief of Staff. By refusing to allow myself to be used as an instrument to create trouble and by making it clear that I would work closely with my colleague

Murphy, I took the first step towards making effective the policies which I knew my Government wanted. By the frank acceptance of the many things that were wrong in Giraud's administration, not from malice but from incapacity and lack of political experience, I was able to bring steady pressure upon General Eisenhower to demand reforms. Lastly, as I appeared to have done nothing at all in my first weeks, these public declarations put the British Resident Minister as it were 'on the map' and registered his existence. It was a risk; but it came off, and proved a useful preliminary to the difficulties which were soon to confront us at the Casablanca Conference.

I had learned enough from my talks with Murphy to realise that his sustained and intense efforts to seduce the leading French authorities from their adherence to Pétain, which had been spread over many months, had in effect failed. Murphy (then Counsellor of the American Embassy at Vichy) had negotiated in the winter of 1940–41 an agreement with General Weygand, who had been appointed 'Delegate-General of the French Government in North Africa', a newly-created post. Although the Murphy-Weygand 'accord' had been agreed in principle in February 1941, it was not finally made effective until June. Under its terms, substantial amounts of materials of all kinds—petrol, cotton goods, tea, sugar—were to be supplied by the Americans to French North Africa. In return, a number of American observers were to be admitted as 'control officers' to scrutinise the passage of these goods to French and Arab consumers and to ensure that they did not reach German hands. The agreement had not been popular either in Britain or in America. It was 'appeasement' of Vichy. It implied a substantial breach of the blockade—at that time the main British instrument of warfare against the Axis powers. But it had this important advantage: the control officers could, and indeed did, become something more than observers of the flow of materials. At a later stage, they were in effect intelligence agents, charged with winning over or subverting the French authorities, building up resistance movements, and organising a Fifth Column in preparation for the Allied landings. Murphy had been given the charge of all this by the President. For many months before the landings he was the intrepid and resourceful leader of a movement which, in spite of the disappointments and complications, made a substantial contribution to French confusion and Allied success.

In approaching this formidable and dangerous task, Murphy and his agents had made innumerable contacts throughout the area. Their approach was twofold: partly to influence officials, civil or military, who were believed to be anti-German and patriotic; partly to recruit unofficial individuals and organisations, ready to operate 'on the day'.

In the first category, the most important were the soldiers and administrators. Murphy believed from his talks with such fine officers as General Mast, commanding XIX Corps in Algiers, and General Béthouart, who had won a considerable reputation in the Scandinavian campaign and now commanded a division in Casablanca, that he could create a situation where the Allied landings would be received amicably by a great part, if not all, of the French and colonial military forces. He believed that General Juin would join in this movement. His contacts with Admiral Darlan in Vichy many months before led him to think that Admiral Fénard, Darlan's naval representative in Algiers, would be sympathetic. If only Noguès would come over, all could be well in Morocco, where his influence and authority were paramount. He was well known to be a man without any great fixity of purpose. He was indeed the Vicar of Bray of the French Army, and would follow the line of least resistance. He might even 'deviate into disinterestedness' at the right moment. But would he take the lead? These, and others in various official positions, formed the first group on which Murphy's plan depended.

The second category was more diverse and naturally included—as such movements always do—men of very different types and qualities. Some were honourable and patriotic, like René Capitant, the Gaullist leader in Algiers. They included such men as Colonel Vanhecke, leader of the 'Chantiers de la Jeunesse', 30,000 strong, and Dr. Abouker, leader of the Jewish groups. Others were of more doubtful antecedents and motives, attracted partly by hope of gain, partly by love of excitement—born adventurers.

The first part of the plan failed completely. The fact that Darlan was in Algiers in the first days of November, whether by chance or by design, rendered negative all the efforts of those in authority—such as Mast in Algeria and Béthouart in Morocco—who stood by, or tried to stand by, their word. Juin, for example, hearing of Darlan's presence, exclaimed characteristically 'Darlan outranks me' and meekly accepted his orders. Noguès even succeeded in putting Béthouart under arrest. Thus serious opposition was met at all the points where the Allies landed.

The unofficial resistance began hopefully. The key places in the city of Algiers were seized in accordance with the plan. The telephone exchange was occupied by Gaullists and other important installations were taken over. But when the Army and the 'Garde Mobile' stood by the local authorities, these gallant young men were unable to hold their ground. As Murphy explained to me, at one point in that dramatic night of 8 November he, too, had the curious experience of first informing the leading French generals that they were prisoners in the hands of his friends, and then finding himself a prisoner in his turn.

This total collapse of the plan—whether depending on the change of sides of leading French commanders or on the success of the Fifth Column—was a terrible disappointment. But it was also a complete justification for the decision to settle with Darlan. He alone could deliver the goods, and he had indeed delivered them. Algeria followed him at once. All Tunisia would have conformed, had the Allied armies been able to move forward with sufficient speed. Noguès, and with him all Morocco, was brought over. To no one else except Darlan would the redoubtable Boisson have yielded—and this meant French West Africa and the long-coveted Dakar. Of course, there were important political consequences, the ill effects of which it was now our duty to reverse.

During these few days I had been able to form some estimate of Murphy's character and also of his difficulties. I knew, of course, that in the Foreign Office he was regarded with considerable suspicion, which Hal Mack's telegrams, although fair and objective, had not been able to dispel. In the British and especially in the American Press, he had been subject to violent attack. Curiously enough, as one of his colleagues had recorded, the things for which he was most criticised bore no relation to the facts. He was pictured by the extreme American commentators as a sophisticated 'man of the world'—a reactionary, almost a Fascist. In fact, he was a man of simple origin, whose career had been based on merit and not on influence. 'Far from being pro-Nazi, he had good personal reasons to detest them, aside from any ideological aversion. His wife had been rudely treated by some arrogant Nazis when he was stationed in Germany, and the resulting dispute had caused the German Government to ask for his recall.'[2] In Britain, many believed that because he was a Roman

[2] Kenneth Pendar, *Adventure in Diplomacy* (London, 1966), p. 20.

Catholic born from Irish immigrants he must be naturally anti-British. If this had ever been so, I certainly saw no trace of it in my long connection with him.

Intimately as I came to know Murphy, I cannot improve upon the description of his appearance and personality given by one of his American colleagues:

A tall, thin, strongly-made, but loose-limbed man, who looked younger than his age, which must have been fiftyish at this time. He was clean shaven, with the peculiarly white Irish skin, and a shock of blond hair over clear, blue eyes. In personality he was anything but the 'stuffed shirt' he was depicted in the press. He had a gaiety that brought out gaiety in others, a tremendous gift for friendship, affections that were almost too easy-going and warm. He wanted to, and was inclined to, believe the best of everybody.[3]

So far from being reserved, he was open and forthcoming. He was generous perhaps to the point of indulgence. He was fair-minded, ready to see both sides of a question. Sometimes this led to uncertainty as between two difficult courses for both of which there was much to be said. But this failing is by no means confined to officials of the State Department. It is common to all foreign services, including our own.

Many of the leading figures, military and political, in various aspects of the war have written their own story. Bob Murphy has done the same. I know of no book so fair, so generous and in general so accurate as his own volume of memoirs.[4] It reflects his singularly attractive personality. Naturally, at the beginning of our work together I was a little cautious, and so was he. But I soon made up my mind that the only thing to do was to treat him with complete frankness, and in his own record he has paid a tribute to my sincerity. He always recognised the delicacy of my position. But he has truly summed up our relationship in the words 'we got along famously together'.[5] Some of my advisers felt that I was being unguarded. But I can say with conviction that he never took any advantage of my frankness. I often showed him copies of my telegrams, in and out, and since the system of the State Department for keeping their representatives abroad properly posted was nothing like so complete as the British practice, I was often able to give him valuable information. I

[3] Ibid., p. 19.
[4] Robert Murphy, *Diplomat among Warriors* (London, 1964).
[5] Ibid., p. 206.

could see that he was sometimes in a difficulty because of his instructions on some particular point from the President. But this was not due to any deceitfulness; on the contrary, he did not conceal his embarrassment even when he was forced to be reticent. Moreover, I recognised that he was not altogether in a similar position to my own. I was a political Minister and could express my views frankly and freely to the whole Cabinet, including the Prime Minister. Indeed, since my controversies with Churchill were chiefly by telegram and at a distance, I had some advantage over my colleagues in London in that I was less easily overawed. In the last resort I could resign. But Murphy was a State Department official. If he had his own conflicts of loyalty, they were largely because he had been appointed 'Personal Assistant to the President', who was very apt to send out his orders without consulting or informing Cordell Hull, the Secretary of State. I have worked with a large number of colleagues in a long life. There is no man with whom I had a more pleasant relationship, often in difficult and baffling circumstances, and whose character I grew so quickly both to appreciate and to admire.

There was, however, one fatal flaw in his position. This was not his fault but that of his employers. It would have been far better if at the beginning of January 1943, when the invasion of North Africa had been successfully launched and Darlan's assassination had allowed Giraud's natural succession to power, Murphy had been withdrawn. It was clear that a new phase was about to begin in the relations between the Anglo-Saxon allies on the one hand, and France and the different French groups on the other. Murphy had been primarily employed as the protagonist in a large-scale and ambitious Fifth Column operation. It had been his business, which he carried out with remarkable skill and courage, to make whatever 'contacts' he could, respectable and otherwise, and enter into a whole variety of intrigues and plots in order to facilitate an operation which entailed heavy military risks. In the course of his duties, he had been forced to deal not only with men of high integrity like Generals Mast and Béthouart, but also with more doubtful or hesitating figures like Noguès, Boisson, Châtel and, above all, Darlan. In addition, in the underground part of his work he had had to get in touch with many unreliable and disreputable agents, as well as with keen but sometimes over-enthusiastic patriots. This experience was bound to prove a great handicap to him and his work in the next period. He was under obligations to a large number of personalities, official and unofficial. Apart from being physically and mentally somewhat exhausted by two exceptionally heavy years, he was in a dangerously compromised situation. I, at least, and Roger Makins, my able assistant, had no commitments. We had only to face the perplexities of the present. Murphy was inexorably caught in the meshes of a past which everybody now wished to forget. He had approved and stimulated actions which, however admirable they might seem to us and the Americans and to those who wished for an Allied victory, must have appeared reprehensible to many Frenchmen, with their strict conventions of discipline. He should not have been asked to become responsible for the new and, outwardly at any rate, more normal political situation with which we had now to deal. The President and the State Department would have been wiser if they had replaced him with a man as uncommitted as myself. However, I am very glad that they did not do so; for it would have deprived me of an assistance during this anxious period for which I shall always be grateful, and of a friendship which I deeply value.

One useful step we took together at General Eisenhower's suggestion before we left to meet the great figures now assembling in Morocco. It was clear that, although the Conference was doubtless called mainly to deal with strategic and military plans, urgent political and diplomatic questions would arise. Of these, the most important was that of finding a method of combining in a satisfactory union all French organisations willing and able to fight against the Germans. Murphy and I therefore drew up together a formula which was approved by Eisenhower. We laid down the necessity of bringing about without delay joint political leadership between de Gaulle and Giraud, with a merger between Giraud's North African administration and members of de Gaulle's London Committee. They should, if possible, be reformed into an enlarged organisation to be centred in Algiers. Knowing that de Gaulle had frequently spoken respectfully of Giraud and that an opportunity for a meeting seemed now about to present itself, we felt some confidence about the prospects of success. The principle of our formula was acted upon in due course. It proved a vital stage in the reunification of the various French groupings and the creation of at least a provisional French authority. But it was to take us longer to bring it about than we had anticipated, and to involve many complications, crises, alarms and excursions. It is, however, a tribute to General Eisenhower's wisdom that at this early stage he gave us his full authority to work for our plan. It is equally a tribute to Murphy's objectivity that he was ready to recommend and support it. For he must have known that it would not be an altogether welcome solution, either in the State Department or the White House. Indeed, much to his embarrassment, he was soon to find the President acquiescing in a completely different manœuvre.

On Friday 15 January I duly set off for Casablanca. There was a problem as to how to get there. The R.A.F. at that time was not particularly forthcoming about flying civilians around the area. Nor, to be fair to them, had they many machines suited to the purpose. There were American routine flights, which I afterwards used to a considerable extent, on the famous DC. 3s, taking troops, reinforcements, couriers and so forth from stage to stage along the North African coast. However, General Eisenhower kindly invited me to go in his Fortress. This seemed likely to be a more agreeable method of travelling. It proved, however, to be somewhat hazardous. We flew without incident to Oujda, where we stopped for the General to have a fifteen-minute talk with General Clark. On the way from Oujda to Casablanca I was dozing quietly when I noticed considerable excitement among the passengers and crew. I was told that 'No. 4 motor' had 'acted up and out, but wouldn't quit'. This did not give me much enlightenment, but I observed that the oil from the motor was running out all over the wing, which seemed wrong. However, since there were three other engines, I did not quite see what all this fuss was about. But the captain appeared to think the aeroplane might burst into flames, and we were ordered to put on our parachute equipment and stand by the appropriate exits. Shortly afterwards, another motor 'conked out', which caused additional alarm. However, in the end we glided safely into the airport. I was afterwards told that the propeller shaft had broken and that we were fortunate that the aeroplane did not disintegrate altogether. This was the first disagreeable experience of this kind which I was to have in the campaign. Very soon I was to suffer from a much more serious accident. I was thus to learn that flying in war-time was just one of those occupational hazards to which one must become accustomed. But even at the end of two years, I still found it somewhat disconcerting to look out of the aeroplane as we approached our destination and see fire-engines and ambulances being run out in preparation.

The spot chosen for the meeting between the two great leaders of Western democracy was admirable from the point of view of comfort and beauty. But there were some anxieties among their advisers. For the President and the Prime Minister to disappear from the news altogether for a period of more than a fortnight presented a security problem of one kind. For both to descend upon a part of Morocco until a few weeks previously controlled by the Germans, swarming with German agents, and within range of German bombing attacks, constituted an even graver risk. The first idea had been to meet at Marrakesh, by commandeering the famous Mamounia Hotel for the staffs and housing the two potentates in the famous Villa Taylor. Such were the attractions of this place for Churchill that after the Conference was over he persuaded Roosevelt to go there for a few days' holiday. But Marrakesh had great disadvantages. It was a large Arab city, extremely difficult to police or supervise. It was filled with Axis spies of all kinds, and the problem of physical protection was formidable. Eventually, it was decided to hold the conference at Anfa, a small suburb outside the modern city of Casablanca, which, by a delicious irony, had been the headquarters of the Italian and then the German disarmament commissions. This settlement was a rich man's paradise, centring round a three-storey hotel with about fifty to a hundred bedrooms and appropriate dining-rooms and lounges. The dining-room was on top, commanding a wonderful view of the Atlantic on the one side and the hills and mountains of Morocco on the other. Eighteen villas were taken over at short notice by the American military authorities from the inhabitants. A wire fence of immense strength and solidity was constructed round the area covered by the villas and the hotel, and this formed a kind of Roman camp with a circuit of about a mile.

On arriving without disaster, if not without incident, at the airport, we drove to the camp, which was heavily guarded:

I have never seen so many sentries armed with such terrifying weapons. The rifle is almost forgotten here. There are machine-guns and Tommy guns and sawn-off shot-guns and all sorts of weapons of that kind. Every time you go in and out of the circle you are in danger all the time of being shot. On the other hand, once they recognise who you are, they are apt to turn the guard out and present arms to you. It is difficult to know quite which drill is going on.[6]

The arrangements made for our comfort were superb. The villas were distributed to the leading notabilities—the President, the Prime Minister and one or two others, including, happily, myself. The main staffs were put up in the hotel. A certain rivalry naturally developed between the two groups.

The very smart ate their meals in the villas, and the more ordinary in the hotel. The whole thing was rather like the *Normandie* or the *Queen Mary*. However, the appointments were extremely well made. The whole thing was free, including most excellent food and quantities of drink. Even cigarettes, cigars, chewing gum, sweets, of which the Americans are very fond, and soap, shaving soap and razors—all these were freely distributed. . . .[7]

At lunch, I found that most of the notabilities had already assembled, including the British and American Chiefs of Staff. Later, there arrived, as well as General Eisenhower, General Alexander, Admiral Cunningham and Air Marshal Tedder. General Ismay was in great form with his body of planners. The British had one advantage over the Americans. We had arranged a communication ship, which one could see in the bay, with facilities not only for a vast volume of messages but a great library of information to support the case which our Chiefs of Staff wanted to develop.

The whole spirit of the camp was dominated by the knowledge that two men were there who rarely appeared in public, but whose presence behind the scenes was always felt. These were officially called Air Commodore Frankland, who lived in Villa 3, and Admiral Q., who lived in Villa 2. These titles, which were used universally throughout the period, covered, of course, as has now been revealed, the personalities of the Prime Minister and the President of the United States. . . . I christened the two personalities the Emperor of the East and the Emperor of the West, and indeed it was rather like a meeting of the later period of the Roman Empire.

The two Emperors met usually late at night and disported themselves and discussed matters with their own generals and with each other's generals. And there was a curious mixture of holiday and business in these . . . facinating surroundings.[8]

[6] 26 January 1943.
[7] Ibid.
[8] Ibid.

There was a certain difference between the arrangements made to guard the two great men:

The Emperor of the East's villa [the P.M.'s] was guarded by a guard of Marines, but otherwise things were fairly simple. His curious routine of spending the great part of the day in bed and all the night up made it a little trying for his staff. I have never seen him in better form. He ate and drank enormously all the time, settled huge problems, played bagatelle and bezique by the hour, and generally enjoyed himself. The only other member of the Government present was [Lord] Leathers,[9] and the P.M. had nobody except his secretaries and so on.

The Emperor of the West's villa [the President's] was difficult of access. If you approached it by night, searchlights were thrown upon you, and a horde of what I believe are called G-men . . . drew revolvers and covered you. With difficulty you could get access, and then everything was easy. The Court favourites, Averell Harriman and Harry Hopkins, were in attendance, as well as the two sons who act as aides and, tragic as it seems, almost as male nurses to this extraordinary figure. The President was particularly charming to me. There was a great deal of joking. . . . There was a lot of bezique, an enormous quantity of highballs, talk by the hour, and a general atmosphere of extraordinary goodwill.[10]

Later on, I was to become more accustomed to these gatherings; but they were always remarkable and romantic episodes, illuminating the routine of life.

The whole affair, which lasted for nearly a fortnight, was a mixture between a cruise, a summer school and a conference. The notice boards gave the time of the meetings of the various staffs, rather like lectures, and when they got out of school at five o'clock or so, you would see Field-Marshals and Admirals going down to the beach for an hour to play with the pebbles and make sand castles. Then at night came the meetings of the Emperors and the staffs and great . . . discussions and debates. I thought the P.M. handled the situation with consummate skill. And as I was either at his house or the President's most of the night and had to do my own work by day, you can imagine it was fairly exhausting.[11]

There was one disappointment. Because of his commitments, Stalin could not come, although he sent a courteous reply to the invitation:

The only sad thing about it was that the Russians could not attend. If we had had the Red Emperor as well, it would have made the thing perfect.

[9] Minister of War Transport.
[10] 26 January 1943.
[11] Ibid.

Perhaps at the next meeting, which will probably be in Iceland or somewhere like that, we shall see them all together.[12]

On the afternoon of my arrival (15 January) I was summoned to Churchill's villa, where I was welcomed by the genial secretaries, as helpful as ever. He was in tremendous form and received me in a most friendly way. When we came to discuss our immediate problem, we of course concentrated on the need to arrange a meeting between General Giraud and General de Gaulle. Churchill told me that the President and he were thinking of inviting both of them to come to Anfa in order to meet each other and the heads of the British and American nations at the same time. I expressed some doubt as to this plan, but it was agreed that the question should be discussed later that night at the President's villa.

In the course of the evening, I got a message from one of President Roosevelt's aides, asking if I could call upon the President at 6 o'clock. He offered to lead me through the dangerous approaches and when I got there I found the President in a great bed on the ground floor. He was indeed a remarkable figure: the splendid head and torso full of vigour and vitality; below, concealed by the coverings, the terrible shrunken legs and feet. No victim of disease ever made such a wonderful triumph over physical disability. At the head of his bed was sitting Churchill and, standing to attention like a Roman centurion on the other side, our Commander-in-Chief, General Eisenhower. As I came in through the door, the President threw up his hand in friendly greeting. 'Hallo, Harold,' he called, 'it is fine to see you—fine.' Murphy soon joined us and a short discussion followed about conditions in North Africa. When I left, General Eisenhower came out with me. He seemed somewhat surprised. 'You never told me,' he said, 'you were a friend of the President.' 'Well,' I replied, 'I don't think I am a particular friend, but I have seen him several times in the United States and we have some friends in common.' 'How strange you English are,' reflected the General. 'If you had been American, you would have told me that you were on Christian-name terms with the President of the United States.' I replied, 'Well, I'm not sure that I am—not mutual; but that's just his way of being friendly.' The General seemed still more perplexed. But, curiously enough, this little incident served me well with him.

12 Ibid.

After dinner, I was sent for again to attend a meeting where Air Commodore F., Admiral Q., Murphy and I discussed the question of the invitation to the two generals. I repeated my fears that one or both of them might resent an invitation to meet each other in an Allied armed camp on French territory. After all, they had already sent messages to each other proposing their own meeting. Although nothing had yet been arranged, might they not resent our interference? I thought it indeed probable that Giraud, being a simple soldier, would appreciate the advantages of joining in a gathering of Allied leaders and Service chiefs. I naturally hoped that General de Gaulle might take the same view; but I believed it doubtful. However, it was decided to send the invitations. General Eisenhower was to return to Algiers and convey it personally to General Giraud, while the Air Commodore sent a telegram to Eden, asking for a personal message to be sent to General de Gaulle in the following terms:

I shall be glad if you would come to join me here by the first available plane which we will provide, as it is in my power to bring about an immediate meeting between you and General Giraud under conditions of complete secrecy and with the best prospects. It would be advisable for you to bring Catroux with you, as General Giraud will want to have someone, probably Bergeret.

The same night the Foreign Secretary replied that he was seeing General de Gaulle the next day, and asked whether he might inform him of Admiral Q.'s presence at Anfa. He felt that he would resent it if this news were to reach him from any but official sources.

As I anticipated, the matter did not prove as easy as the great men expected. General Giraud accepted at once and turned up the next day. But a considerable negotiation was necessary before General de Gaulle could be persuaded. Eden was at first forced to report that his arguments had proved unavailing. De Gaulle was unwilling that the future of France should be discussed at the invitation of British and American statesmen in an armed camp wholly occupied by British and American troops. It would be a distasteful prospect. Eden's message came through the night of the 17th and Churchill sent for me at 8 o'clock that next morning. He was filled with indignation at what he regarded as de Gaulle's folly in missing such a wonderful opportunity. Various alternatives were discussed, but it was clear that the right thing to do was to continue our attempt to persuade the leader of the

Free French to change his mind. Any other course would place us in a somewhat humiliating position vis-à-vis the Americans, and would have the most adverse effect both on the resistance movement in France and on public opinion in England. It has often been said that Churchill in his anger was ready to contemplate 'deposing' General de Gaulle from the leadership of the French Committee, and demanding that General Catroux or some other less difficult personality should take his place. I feel sure that this was not seriously considered. It was often Churchill's method to put forward—at least in oral discussion— every possible plan in order to clear his own mind and those of his advisers. But his final judgements were the result of deep study and thought.

After much debate, we decided to send a telegram to Eden, urging him to reassure de Gaulle as to the conditions of privacy and freedom from Allied pressure, in which he would be able to conduct conversations with General Giraud. He was further to impress upon him the folly of missing so favourable an opportunity of coming to good arrangements with all concerned. Meanwhile, a further telegram arrived from Eden. De Gaulle was still in a highly intransigent frame of mind.

At lunch and throughout the afternoon, Air Commodore F., Admiral Q., Murphy and I discussed the problem. I proposed that de Gaulle from a point of view of national dignity might have preferred a direct invitation from General Giraud. After all, de Gaulle had suggested a meeting and Giraud had up till now not taken this matter any further. However, my suggestion was not accepted, and further messages were sent to the Foreign Secretary with renewed arguments to put before de Gaulle.

Meanwhile, I thought something might be done to alleviate the sensitivity of many Frenchmen who might feel some concern about the circumstances of our meeting, which seemed more suitable to conquering armies than to allies. I proposed, therefore, that Churchill should ask General Noguès, still the Governor of Morocco, on whose territory we had arrived without prior warning, to call upon him. I thought this would be a politeness which he and French official circles would appreciate. 'Is he a good man?' asked Churchill. 'Not very,' I said, 'he is rather an equivocal character. "No-Yes" we call him.' 'Why, then, should I see him?' 'Well, until he is superseded, which I should like to see as soon as possible, he is the French official responsible for this territory. He is, after all, the Viceroy of Morocco. It would be a courtesy to invite him.'

And so it was arranged. He was to come at 12.30 to lunch with Churchill. The General duly arrived in good time, but the Prime Minister was not yet up and dressed. After some delay, I brought him into the room where Churchill was sitting, and introduced him. The news of the great Conference had not yet been broken to the world. No doubt General Noguès must have heard some rumours, but nothing for certain or officially. Churchill came at once to the point. 'Vous ne téléphonerez pas à Vichy que nous sommes ici, will you?' Noguès was full of protestations. 'Monsieur le Président, je vous assure de mes sentiments. . . .' Churchill was not impressed. 'Parce que maintenant clair de la lune et très bon pour bombarder.' And then the overwhelming deduction, emphasised with a wave of the long cigar, 'et si on bombardait nous, on bombardait aussi vous'!

Poor General Noguès was thrown into great confusion. In fact, there had been some fear of German raids on Anfa, which was well within bombing distance. Nor was there much doubt in my own mind that messages had already passed between Rabat and Vichy. After these preliminary exchanges, however, the luncheon passed off agreeably enough.

The period of waiting on an answer from London was an anxious one for us. I personally had some sympathy with General de Gaulle's view, that it should not require a British or an American intermediary to bring two Frenchmen together to discuss the affairs of France. Naturally the Americans could not resist the temptation to enjoy our discomfiture. Here was our great hero, the winning horse that we had bred and trained in our stable; and when the great day came it refused to run at all. A lot of jokes were made at Air Commodore F.'s expense which were not altogether to his liking. It was a great relief to us all, therefore, when at midnight on 20 January we received a message from the Foreign Secretary, stating that de Gaulle was leaving England that same evening. Owing to bad weather his flight had to be postponed, and it was not until the morning of the 22nd that he eventually arrived. Whether by accident or design, this incident naturally put a good deal of the limelight on to de Gaulle. Everyone's attention was focused upon him. With his fine sense of drama, he had made it clear that 'Roosevelt and Churchill needed his co-operation at that moment as much as he needed theirs'.[13]

The next few days were especially distressing for the British. To our practical minds, the position which de Gaulle was taking was difficult to understand. We had been locked for two and a half years in a desperate conflict with Germany. Although the entry of America into the war seemed a guarantee of ultimate success, there were many obstacles still to be overcome, many dangers still to be faced, and many grievous losses to be borne. Naturally, British statesmen, like their American partners, tended to concentrate on the immediate problem of bringing Hitler to book. Although the Allies had just succeeded in occupying part of North Africa and our British armies had won a resounding victory in the desert, yet even in this sector there was a tough fight before us, with German air and ground forces pouring in at an ever increasing rate into the Vichy-controlled territory of eastern Tunisia. The British and especially the American leaders were therefore impatient at the theoretical difficulties continually raised by de Gaulle, and attributed to mere intransigence what he regarded as points of principle. This was particularly aggravating for those of us whose sympathies lay with de Gaulle and his movement.

The discussions now began in earnest: between the two generals; between Murphy and myself and one or other of them; and between us all, including the Commodore and the Admiral. Since this was my first experience of high-level diplomacy, I was naturally determined to persevere in the hope of at least some measure of success. Accordingly, I found myself in the embarrassing position of continually trying to persuade Churchill and Roosevelt to give de Gaulle another chance, which he seemed always unwilling to grasp. Draft after draft was put forward, framed by Murphy and myself, in the hope of finding a formula upon which the two generals could agree. It was typical of Giraud, who had no political sense or interest in larger issues, that he accepted each of them in turn without a murmur. It was equally typical of de Gaulle, whose purposes were highly political and whose suspicions had been thoroughly aroused, that he turned them down one after another.

All through these crowded days and nights, Murphy and I hurried from one imperial villa to another to get the agreement of our chiefs

[13] Murphy, p. 216.

to a new proposal, which we then took to the French leaders, without much hope that a satisfactory arrangement could be reached. One fundamental difficulty soon became clear. De Gaulle recognised Giraud as passionately anti-German. But he was not anti-Vichy. He would not move against the servants of Vichy, all of whom were hateful to de Gaulle. He would not agree, as a pre-condition ('préalable') of co-operation, that such men as Noguès, Boisson and Peyrouton should immediately be removed from office. At his very first meeting with General Giraud on the afternoon of 22 January, de Gaulle had delivered a violent diatribe against Darlan and his successors, and poor Giraud was under the impression that he was being blamed for all their faults. During these days, de Gaulle had interviews with both Roosevelt and Churchill, and a number of plans were suggested for a merger between the two French groups. The British-American proposal of a 'Directing Committee', with Giraud and de Gaulle as joint presidents, contained the germ of something which was ultimately to prove useful. But de Gaulle objected that we seemed to be thinking only in terms of an 'Administrative Committee' to govern the Empire and assist in the military campaign, rather than of a 'Political Committee', which could in due course develop into a Government of France. The British indeed sympathised with de Gaulle's view that in the near future a Provisional Government of France should gradually emerge. But this was anathema to Roosevelt and to most of the Americans, who contented themselves with the dogma that for the present 'France had ceased to exist' and that until the liberation of metropolitan France no French authority could come into being without danger to the future. They were convinced that Gaullism would bring with it a new form of dictatorship.

From the very beginning, de Gaulle wanted a Provisional Government, comparable to the exiled Governments which were operating in London. Although it could not claim, like them, de jure legitimacy, yet it could surpass them in de facto power, since all the French Empire could now be placed under a single control. Such a French 'War Government', located in Algiers, would in time become the Government of the Republic. Giraud would be the commander of the Liberation Army, but de Gaulle would be the political leader. By this time General de Gaulle was losing interest in military affairs. He had become and has remained a politician. Our problem was to find at least a temporary compromise.

This part of the Casablanca Conference, which had made a bad start, somehow stumbled along towards a shaky finish. Things were not helped by a dinner which Roosevelt gave in honour of the Sultan of Morocco on the very day that de Gaulle arrived at the Anfa camp. The guests included General Noguès, Churchill, General Marshall (the American Chief of Staff), Murphy and myself. It was a curious and impolitic manœuvre, and Murphy rightly records the sulkiness which Churchill showed throughout. Though this was partly due to the fact that no alcohol of any kind was served, I felt sure that he regarded the President's action as 'deliberately provocative'.[14] The President talked a great deal about colonial aspirations towards independence and the approaching end of 'imperialism'. All this was equally embarrassing to the British and to the French. He dwelt at some length on possible economic co-operation between America and Morocco after the war. In spite of the hostility between Noguès and de Gaulle, no doubt the latter was soon to learn about the President's dinner party and the overtures which he had made to a ruler under French protection. All this added fuel to the fire.

At this time, the position of Noguès was still a strong one. He had completely outwitted General Béthouart, the French patriot who had tried to deliver Casablanca to the Americans, and who was now languishing in prison. Meanwhile, he had brought General Patton, the American commander in the area, altogether under his sway. This eccentric and opinionated officer proved a cause of great trouble to Eisenhower, Murphy and myself. It seemed to me a monstrous thing that General Patton should be so easily impressed by the gay hunting parties and the lavish entertainments which Noguès gave in his honour, and show so little concern at the way in which Noguès was treating the friends of Britain and America. Nevertheless, even Noguès must have been shocked by the President's unguarded talk.

At my first serious talk with de Gaulle, he had made it clear that he would not come to an arrangement with General Giraud unless a decision was taken to dismiss a number of leading personalities connected with the Vichy régime. He maintained this position in discussion with Churchill that evening and with the President. Roosevelt, who had not met de Gaulle before, was in fact considerably impressed by him. But his fears were not removed; indeed, they were enhanced. He was also impatient of de Gaulle's excuse for avoiding

14 Murphy, p. 217.

any positive commitment on the ground that he could not do more than hold discussions, the conclusions of which he could recommend to his London Committee. At the same time, de Gaulle did not conceal his view that the only sensible and effective method of bringing about the devised union was for Giraud and his armies to rally to the Fighting French. Giraud should have the military command and de Gaulle would be the civil chief. In his own words, he would play the role of Clemenceau and Giraud that of Foch. Giraud, although naïve, could not accept this, largely because he was a five-star and de Gaulle only a two-star general. In any case, it was not an acceptable solution for the Americans.

However, during the evening of 23 January, de Gaulle yielded on the point of the Giraudists rallying to the Fighting French. He was now prepared to consider a fusion of his organisation with General Giraud's by setting up a 'Comité de Guerre', with the two generals as co-chiefs, each taking their turn as chairman. He must, however, insist on the exclusion of the men of Vichy and a declaration severing all connections with Pétain. If he could not get this fusion, the best thing would be for the two organisations to be left intact upon the basis of establishing a liaison and entering into an understanding to abstain from propaganda against one another. I felt strongly that although de Gaulle professed not to have much hope in the success of his first solution, this was what he really wanted. At my suggestion, Churchill agreed to back de Gaulle's proposal for a 'Comité de Guerre', although he could not support any 'unreasonable conditions'.

All through that night (23–24 January) we battled on in the President's villa. Murphy began to argue that it was useless to continue negotiating with General de Gaulle, and the President was inclined to share this view. I felt that some further attempt ought to be made to find a formula, and was supported in this both by Churchill and—unexpectedly—by Harry Hopkins, the President's special assistant. Murphy and I therefore drafted another formula which our chiefs approved, and we spent most of the next morning (24 January) trying to persuade de Gaulle to agree to it. It was based upon the principle of a joint declaration, with a view to ultimate fusion. But although Giraud, as usual, was amenable, there was still trouble with de Gaulle. According to his own account, he objected to the draft communiqué because it suggested that he was 'satisfied' with a committee for administering the French Empire. Important as was the distinction in his eyes, all these points seemed to us mere legal niceties, and the more complicated and pedantic the argument became, the more the Admiral and Air Commodore became enraged.

Finally, at noon on the 24th, when any result seemed hopeless and the Conference was about to break up, I went to see General de Gaulle, who always treated me then and afterwards with great courtesy, and asked him to come with me to see the President in his villa. There de Gaulle repeated his regretful unwillingness to accept the communiqué as drafted. At that point, Air Commodore F., who had been saying goodbye to Giraud, also came into Admiral Q.'s room. Having learned that de Gaulle had refused to accept Giraud's draft, Admiral Q. proposed that Giraud should be brought back to see whether the two French generals could not at least be brought to agree on some joint statement which could be announced to the world. Murphy and I then did some quick work. I held on to de Gaulle, while he rounded up Giraud. After a short discussion, it was agreed that the two generals would draw up a new formula in the course of the evening after the Admiral and the Air Commodore had left. But something had to be done to put the seal on this understanding. We had suffered so many disappointments and so many set-backs that I felt that only some public action could prevent any 'backsliding' from this verbal 'agreement to agree'. The chance lay ready to hand. A large conference of the British and American Press had been ordered to assemble in the garden outside the President's villa. Since this was the first news of the meeting between Roosevelt and Churchill, and since the whole great drama of the Conference, now concluding after a fortnight's session, broke unexpectedly upon them, the Press representatives were naturally in an excited and expectant mood. There were some folding doors in the room; as they were thrown open for Roosevelt and Churchill to take their seats on the terrace, Murphy and I almost forcibly pushed out the two generals and made them appear at their side. Two more chairs were hurriedly provided, and the Press conference began. The President and the Prime Minister each made their statements, and then the two generals, in a picture which went round the world, were seen shaking hands with the best approach to a smile that they could manage.

Immediately after this episode, Air Commodore F. and Admiral Q.

left Anfa camp. We stayed behind to try to guide our French principals into a suitable declaration, and waited anxiously for them to carry out their undertaking. Late in the afternoon, the text was handed to me. This joint declaration stated that the two generals had met and discussed and reached complete agreement on the need to achieve the liberation of France and triumph of human liberties by the total defeat of the enemy. The means by which this end would be achieved was by the union of all Frenchmen fighting side by side with their allies.

Allied public opinion interpreted this somewhat original form of reconciliation as implying more real understanding than could subsist between two men of such very different temperaments and characters. In Britain and in the United States, the Press campaign and the public agitation were temporarily calmed. Unhappily, the President persuaded himself that he had won over de Gaulle and would be able to continue to 'manage him'. Murphy and I both knew this to be an illusion.[15] For the real struggle was now about to begin. I summarised the results from the political aspect :

My work consisted of immensely complicated and rather unsuccessful negotiations between the two generals. It was decided at the beginning that a wedding should be arranged if possible. The President at once said this must be a wedding even if it was a shot-gun wedding, and Murphy and I were responsible for making the necessary arrangements between the bride and bridegroom. The bride (General de Gaulle) was very shy and could not be got to the camp at all until two days before the end. I never thought that we would get them both to the church, and, as I warned both the Emperors, the dowry required to make anything of it would be very large. However, as you will probably have seen from the films or the pictures, we got them there in the end, and, partly by chicanery and partly by pressure, forced them to shake hands in front of all the cameras. I hope the result will be of some use. Apart from chaff, I do think it will be the beginning, though only just the beginning, of the loosening-out of a very complicated situation between the various French [groups].

If Roosevelt had deluded himself into the belief that de Gaulle had fallen a victim to his charm, Churchill left the Conference with a certain sense of disillusion about the French problem. He had been disappointed by de Gaulle's attitude, partly because he had not understood his basic position. From an early moment in the war,

[15] Murphy, p. 220.

certainly from the time of American intervention, de Gaulle had shown no great interest in military operations as such. The French were only in a position to act as minor allies. No French general could take a leading role in the planning or carrying-out of the campaigns which lay ahead. French colonial armies, re-equipped by the Americans, could and did play a splendid part both in Tunisia and in the subsequent battles in Italy. But theirs was a subordinate role; they were not protagonists. De Gaulle had no doubt made up his mind that the Germans would ultimately be defeated. Therefore his whole purpose during the rest of the war would be to sustain the spirit of France and to preserve the integrity of the French Empire. He did not accept the dictum that 'France had ceased to exist', even temporarily. The armistice was null and void. The Vichy Government was illegitimate. Only through the movements which had rejected the armistice could the true spirit of France be restored. He thought of the new committee, which was soon to develop, first under the joint consulship of himself and Giraud and then under his sole leadership, as something which should immediately succeed to the Government of the territories which had been or were to be liberated, including metropolitan France. When the time came, this Provincial Government would surrender its powers. But till that time, it must be the only recognised French authority. It must, therefore, not be a mere committee of provincial governors. On the contrary, generals and governors must be subordinate to its authority; and the French military command must be answerable to the civil power, although temporarily working in alliance with or even subordinate to the supreme British or American commanders. In other words, while Giraud and his friends contemplated at most an *ad hoc* organisation, consisting of the actual governors of the territories when they had come over to the Allies, or been liberated by them, de Gaulle was thinking of an authority which, although temporary and provisional, should during these next few years have the right, as well as the duty, to protect the interests of France on every issue. Frenchmen must, above all, ensure that the defeat and capitulation of 1940 did not in any way endanger the revival and continuance of France and the French Empire as they had been in September 1939. In a word, Giraud was a good, sound, worthy man, honourably anxious to help the Allies as a soldier. But de Gaulle had become a statesman in the long French tradition. Such sentiments as gratitude or friendship might play a minor part in his thoughts and conduct. But all must be subordinate to his main purpose—the strength and glory of France, and the French renaissance.

There was a strange sequel to the Anfa negotiations about the relations between the Allies and the French, which became known in our private circles in Algiers as 'the Anfa Mystery'.

In my report to the Foreign Secretary on the situation in North Africa, I gave a full description of what had happened. I pointed out that all we had been able to obtain was a kind of public truce between the two generals, with a private understanding to establish liaison with one another by means of missions to be approved by both parties. I added that it was understood that Admiral Q. had made certain suggestions privately to General Giraud of which the import was not yet known. This was based upon a hint which Murphy had given me of some discussions between the President and General Giraud of which he was not yet at liberty to inform me. I was surprised at this in view of the close co-operation which we had established, but it was clear to me that he was acting under precise instructions.

On 27 January, after we had returned to Algiers, he gave me the text of two documents, both of which had been approved by the President:

The first—described as a résumé of agreements in principle reached with General Giraud—dealt with the re-equipment of the French forces in North Africa, and also stated that the President and Prime Minister agreed that General Giraud should be given every facility for bringing about the union under a single authority of all Frenchmen fighting against Germany. The second document recognised General Giraud as having 'the right and duty of preserving all French interests' until the French people were able 'to designate their regular Government'. The document also laid down that the 'form of relations between France and foreign Powers temporarily occupying French territory' had been 'defined in a letter exchanged between Consul Mr. Murphy in the name of President Roosevelt and General Giraud before the landing'. The details of the understanding were to be worked out by General Eisenhower and Mr. Murphy in the light of conversations already held in Washington with General Giraud's representatives and of the decisions taken at Casablanca by the President, Mr. Churchill, and General Giraud.[16]

[16] Woodward, *British Foreign Policy in the Second World War*, p. 218.

I immediately transmitted the text of these documents to London, where they naturally caused emotion and even anger. Unhappily, as we learned later, not only had the President signed these papers, which dealt, among other things, with the question of rearmament, the monthly quotas of food and the new exchange rate of 50 francs to the dollar, but had accepted phrases which were misleading and indefensible.

Under the political plan, it was agreed between the President of the United States, the Prime Minister of Great Britain and General Giraud that it was their common interest for all the French fighting against Germany to be reunited under one authority, and that every facility would be given to General Giraud in order to bring about this reunion.[17]

I stated my view that the President had not seen these documents until the end of the Conference and under the pressure of business had not realised their true significance. It seemed to me impossible that he had really intended to endorse what was implicit in these memoranda—the sole trusteeship for Giraud. The Foreign Secretary urged me to make a strong protest to Murphy, and to tell him plainly that these documents had to be held in suspense until the British Government had a full opportunity to consider them and make its views known. It was quite impossible for us to accept this concept of a special position for Giraud. Nor could we allow 'the further details to be worked out between General Eisenhower and Murphy', without apparently any reference to the British Government, on the basis of discussions in Washington of which we knew nothing and of decisions in Casablanca of which we had no record. It was completely unacceptable to us that the relations between France and foreign powers, other than the United States, should be regulated by an agreement of this kind.[18] Murphy sympathised with my indignation, and readily agreed to convey the British sentiments to Washington.

Churchill had gone straight from Marrakesh to Adana for a conference with President Inönü of Turkey and his colleagues. When he returned to Algiers on 5 February, he took the matter up himself with Murphy. I did not—and do not—know what approaches, if any, he

[17] Arthur Layton Funk, 'The "Anfa Memorandum": An Incident of the Casablanca Conference', reprinted for private circulation from the *Journal of Modern History*, vol. xxvi, no. 3 (Chicago, September 1954), p. 250.

[18] Woodward, *passim*.

had made to the President. He handled this delicate matter with some reticence and consummate skill. As a result, both Murphy and Giraud were made to accept important modifications in this draft which, when they were finally agreed by Washington after a lapse of nearly four months,[19] rendered them utterly innocuous. One most important change affected the re-equipment of Giraud's forces. It had been an almost open-ended commitment. This was now to proceed 'as may be determined by the Combined Chiefs of Staff'. More important, Giraud's authority as a trustee for French interests was limited to French North and West Africa. Finally, it was made clear that the facilities for French unification should be given not only to Giraud but 'to the French National Committee under General de Gaulle'. In other words, every assistance would be given for a reunion of all Frenchmen fighting against Germany to be achieved under a single authority.[20]

The full story of this curious episode has now been told in detail.[21] The roots of the trouble lay far back. In the original negotiations which Murphy had undertaken in order to facilitate the landings, he had written a letter to Giraud in which he guaranteed that French authority and sovereignty would be in no way interfered with by the Allied armies. But when Giraud was unable to fulfil his part of the terms, these promises were naturally allowed to lapse. The Darlan-Clark Agreement superseded them, and set out in detail General Eisenhower's overriding rights, military, political and economic. After Darlan's assassination, some of Giraud's advisers, with more ambition than judgement, attempted to restore the old position. The chief of these was Jacques Lemaigre-Dubreuil. This man was a wealthy manufacturer of vegetable oil in whom Murphy placed considerable confidence. As an associate before the war of some of the Right-wing pressure groups, such as the Cagoulards, he was distrusted by the Gaullists. But he had certainly taken considerable risks in assisting Murphy's pre-landing schemes. He had now gone to Washington on a military mission and arrived about the time of Darlan's assassination. Encouraged by the fact that Giraud had succeeded as High Commis-

---

19 The formal memorandum was not actually conveyed by Murphy and myself to General Giraud until 28 May.
20 Woodward, p. 219.
21 Funk, op. cit.

sioner for North Africa, Lemaigre-Dubreuil attempted to restore Giraud to the position which had been promised by Murphy in quite different circumstances. After discussions with Secretary Hull, upon whom he made a favourable impression, he was persuaded to return to Casablanca to see what he could do. It was at his instigation that the offending documents were put forward by Giraud and signed by the President. Murphy was merely informed. How Roosevelt could have done this was and remains the core of the Anfa mystery. The simple explanation is probably the right one. The President was in a very happy holiday mood throughout the Conference. He laughed and joked continually and, unaccompanied as he was by any but unofficial advisers, he took without due consideration a course which might have led to permanent difficulties, not only with the French but between Britain and America.

My efforts during the next few months were certainly hampered by the fact that some knowledge of this affair must have reached de Gaulle. It no doubt explained many of the difficulties which were to follow. It was certainly a foolish as well as a reprehensible action on Roosevelt's part, and the use of Churchill's name was unpardonable. From my point of view, there was one useful result. Murphy was tremendously impressed by Churchill's handling of this dangerous situation. For the Prime Minister, on his return to Algiers, was at his best: firm, courteous, without recrimination, and never allowing himself any criticism of the President in the presence of one of his officers, but quietly and conscientiously going through the text and insisting upon amendments which were necessary to turn it from a dangerous into a harmless document. He was able to persuade both Murphy and Giraud to agree to the redraft; and since General Marshall and Secretary Stimson, of the War Department, were as concerned about the military commitments as some of the State Department advisers now became about the political implications, the changes were made and enforced upon Giraud without too much difficulty. Murphy had always been concerned at the President's rather slapdash methods of doing business. Since up till now he had mainly seen Churchill exchanging general and sometimes rather unguarded conversation, he did not realise his extraordinary grasp of detail, and the persistence with which he would pursue his point once he became seized of its importance. I could not reproach Murphy for having kept me in the dark until our return from Casablanca, for he owed a supreme loyalty to his chief and to the strict orders he had received. But he was uneasy and unhappy throughout the incident, and glad when it was closed.

Naturally, the Casablanca Conference primarily affected me on the political side. Nevertheless, Churchill told me from time to time about the progress of the military discussions in which he was deeply absorbed. These he and the British Chiefs of Staff handled with remarkable dexterity. Everyone agreed on the need to drive the Germans out of North Africa as rapidly as possible. Unhappily, the dash for Bizerta and Tunis had failed. General Anderson's troops, although they fought with the greatest gallantry, were too weak and too far from their bases to achieve the hoped-for *coup de main*. The British had originally proposed to put the weight of the 'Torch' attack further east, but because of anxiety about the possible Spanish re-action the Americans were against this plan. The importance of securing Morocco and West Africa was strongly pressed by them. It was clear, therefore, that a skilful and determined effort to bring the campaign in North Africa to an end was the first necessity. Churchill wisely brought General Alexander, then Commander-in-Chief, Middle East, to the Conference. His quiet confidence made a great impression upon the President. The Mediterranean situation had been dramati-cally changed by the victorious advance of the Desert Army. Alexander made it clear that he hoped soon to seize Tripoli and to deploy six divisions on the Mareth frontier by the middle of March. With Anderson's four divisions in the First Army, there would, therefore, be ten British divisions available for the final assault upon the enemy position. Since the Americans would only have two divisions in Tunisia by early spring and since the French colonial divisions, although in a good state of morale, were under-equipped, it was clear that the British must have the right, as well as the duty, to take the lead.[22] As the result of the friendly co-operation of all those concerned and the skilful manner in which Churchill managed the negotiation, the result was to produce a very powerful team to be in charge of the last phases of this part of the campaign.

The armies coming from the east and those from the west were all put under Eisenhower's supreme command. But General Alexander, by virtue of being appointed Deputy Commander-in-Chief to Eisen-

[22] Churchill, *The Hinge of Fate*, pp. 606–7.

hower, became in effect the tactical commander of all ground forces, British, American and French, throughout the area. By a similar arrangement, Admiral Cunningham took the command of all the Allied fleets and Air Marshal Tedder of all the Allied air forces. I have always thought it a remarkable tribute to General Eisenhower's combination of foresight and generosity that he accepted this arrangement not only without a murmur but with enthusiasm. Put into commercial terms, Eisenhower now became the chairman of a company of great power and resources. He had under him, as managing directors of the constituent companies, three of the ablest executives available. He raised no objection to the fact that they were all three British. He thought only of the success of the organisation which had been entrusted to his care. It took a big man to do this.

But what would follow throwing the Germans and Italians out of North Africa? Admiral King, Chief of the American Naval Staff, naturally believed that all resources should be diverted to the Pacific. General Marhall's chief ambition was to build up the necessary strength for an early attack upon metropolitan France, an operation which then went under the code name of 'Round-up'. But this, of course, must be at the expense of any further progress in the Mediterranean. It would delay any hope of knocking Italy out of the war and would, in the present situation of German strength, not yet seriously diminished, prove—in the view of our advisers—a most hazardous adventure.

The British wanted to move forward from victory in Africa to operations in Italy or Greece. Churchill wisely did not try to press his point too far. If the Americans argued that any movement in the Mediterranean would be in the nature of a diversion, the British did not maintain that it should be regarded as more than a wise exploitation of what looked like a favourable situation. After Africa had been cleared, an attack should first be made upon Italy. Once this was agreed, the argument began to turn on the rival claims of Sardinia and Sicily. In the end, Sicily was chosen. Nevertheless, there were some disadvantages in the situation. The Americans, urged on by Stalin, and supported by considerable political agitation in Britain, wanted the 'Second Front' as soon as possible. Anyone who studies the immense resources and the vastly complicated machinery which proved necesssary to effect the successful landings in France, which were ultimately to take place in June 1944 ('Operation Overlord'), will readily agree that a premature attempt could only have led to disaster. To land great armies and supply them over the beaches without harbours, except those artificial substitutes for them which were invented and constructed with immense labour—Mulberries—was a prodigious undertaking. Even when the Germans had been weakened by two years of hammering in Russia and in Italy, it proved no easy task. Churchill certainly did not shrink from the cross-Channel landing as the final knockout blow. But he was anxious for tactical, strategic and political reasons also to secure the liberation of Central and Southern Europe. The Americans consistently resisted this policy, and as a result of this dualism valuable opportunities were lost which, had they been followed enthusiastically, might have been used to our common advantage. Of course, some difference of strategic and tactical concepts between great allies is natural and unavoidable. The remarkable feature of the Second World War was the high degree of mutual understanding, of give and take, of common purpose, which sustained and inspired Britain and America through so many years of continuous struggle in every part of the globe.

There was one further and unexpected result of the Casablanca Conference. When the President addressed the Press on 24 January, I was chiefly preoccupied with my French generals. The sudden announcement by Roosevelt that we would enforce 'unconditional surrender' on all our enemies took me by surprise. This declaration was afterwards a subject of much controversy. It was believed for many years and, indeed, inadvertently confirmed by Churchill, that the British Cabinet had not been consulted. This was not true. It is quite clear from Churchill's telegram of 20 January to the War Cabinet that this phrase had been referred to them.[23] Its use has often been regarded as a great error. It has even been alleged that it prolonged the struggle and made European recovery more difficult. This seems very improbable. Most of us at the time, with memories of President Wilson's Fourteen Points and all the complications which had followed, including German arguments that they had been tricked into an armistice, thought it a fine idea that we should achieve victory without tying ourselves up with all kinds of obligations, many of which might prove onerous and confusing. All the attempts to draft

[23] Ibid., pp. 612–13.

conditions which would satisfy us had so far proved impossible. As
Churchill says, 'They had in fact only to be written out to be
withdrawn'.[24] 'Unconditional surrender' did not mean that we should
try to force harsh or unjust terms upon the German, Italian and
Japanese peoples. It meant that we were not prepared to bargain with
their present Governments; and that until these were deprived of all
power of resistance we would not be ready to face the problems of
peace.

So ended the Casablanca Conference. The Emperors departed for
their short jaunt at Marrakesh and then flew back to their respective
tasks; the great commanders in the field resumed their posts; the
Chiefs of Staff returned to their desks in London and Washington. We
humbler folk went back to Algiers to wrestle with our own smaller but
intriguing problems. For me, it had been a unique experience. Never
had I mingled with this high political and military society or been
made privy to such vast and enthralling issues. And all this in the first
three weeks of my new appointment!

[24] Ibid., p. 617.

CHAPTER ELEVEN

Force X

AMONG the many anxieties which had weighed upon the British Government at the time of the fall of France, none was more painful than that concerning the future of the French fleet. Action was taken, in many parts of the world, sometimes with tragic, sometimes with more fortunate results, to ensure that these powerful naval units should not fall into enemy hands. In the Eastern Mediterranean, the French naval forces, at the time of France's collapse, were concentrated in Alexandria. They consisted of a battleship, four cruisers and a number of smaller ships. After protracted negotiations between their commander, Admiral Godfroy, and Admiral Cunningham, commander of the British Mediterranean fleet, an accommodation was reached which served to immobilise the French squadron at an important moment in the shifting balance of naval power in that area. It was a typically British compromise. The French admiral agreed to discharge his oil fuel, to remove certain important parts of his gun mechanisms and to repatriate some of his crews. The British admiral undertook to see that pay for the French naval officers and men would be forthcoming from British sources. This arrangement was tacitly accepted by the Vichy Government. Meanwhile, Admiral Godfroy's loyalty to Marshal Pétain, with whom he was able to maintain radio communication, remained unshaken. To demonstrate his neutrality, he shut himself up in his ship and lived the life of a recluse, refusing to go ashore. Admiral Cunningham's agreement had some flaws in it, of which the French were said to have taken advantage. We were bound to pay the officers and men of the French ships concerned at the appropriate scale for their rank. It was popularly believed that they exploited this provision by promoting themselves, or persuading the French Admiralty to do so, with corresponding improvement in their own comfort and to the great indignation of the British Treasury. But I can find no confirma-

tion of this widely-circulated story. In any event, for over two years
this situation remained reasonably acceptable to both sides. The officers
and men of Force X (the code name given to this fleet) remained in
their inglorious, but not disagreeable, inactivity.

However, when things began to move in the Western Mediterranean; when one French territory after another had begun to rally
either to Giraud or to de Gaulle; when the great victories of Generals
Alexander and Montgomery began to raise new hopes of ridding
Africa of Germans and Italians altogether, the position of these ships
and their crews began to seem more and more anomalous.

Churchill had certainly not forgotten them. In the autumn of 1942,
before the launching of 'Torch', he proposed to the First Sea Lord that
there should be some powerful additions to the British fleet based on
Alexandria, in order to impress the French with the benefits of siding
with the Allies. 'Superior force,' he declared, 'is a powerful persuader.'
But neither this nor any other manœuvres produced any effect on the
mind of Godfroy. In November, Darlan seemed confident that these
French warships could be brought back, first into an effective technical
condition, and then to the Allied side. But Godfroy obstinately
resisted Darlan's approaches. He argued that at least until the Allies
had conquered Tunisia they could not claim that it was in their power
to liberate France. Although Admiral Godfroy had very different
sentiments about the British from those which inspired Admiral de
Laborde at Toulon, he was equally unwilling to obey any order which
he might receive from Admiral Darlan. Our Admiralty then instructed
the British admiral at Alexandria, now Admiral Harwood, to threaten
drastic action. But menaces of this kind are a double-edged weapon.
Although it seems strange to a landsman, the major threat which ships
of war can use to avoid coercion is to sink themselves either in harbour
or in the open sea. By the turn of the year this had already happened
at Toulon. But in this case, while we regretted the loss of a fine fleet,
we were not incommoded by the blocking of the port. In Alexandria,
in spite of the arrangements which had been made regarding the
disposition of the ships, it was clear that a scuttled fleet would be
something of a nuisance.

At the end of 1942, Admiral Godfroy seemed to have changed his
position somewhat. The Germans had broken the armistice by the
occupation of hitherto unoccupied France. Might it not therefore be

argued that Marshal Pétain was no longer a free agent but under German constraint? In that case, the oath of loyalty was no longer binding—or, as Churchill puts it, 'all bets were off'. If Pétain could no longer act freely, then let his next senior in rank, Darlan, assume the mantle. Admiral Godfroy, therefore, before bringing over his ships, must be assured that the British and American Governments now recognised Admiral Darlan as the supreme French authority. More-over, since he had heard some suggestion drawn from President Roosevelt, under pressure from his public opinion, that the Allied acceptance might be only temporary, he must be assured that Darlan would be recognised and confirmed in his position 'for the duration of the war'. The assassination of Darlan put an end to what might have proved a prolonged and tortuous argument. But it confused still further the question of 'legitimacy', which seemed the dominant issue in Godfroy's mind.

Soon after our return from Casablanca, the future of Force X, among other French problems, began to concern us acutely, and telegrams started to pour in freely from London and Cairo, through Foreign Office and Admiralty channels.

Churchill came to Algiers on 5 February, where he remained for two or three days, mainly concerned with the negotiations with Murphy for the solution of the 'Anfa Mystery'. But the French fleet was never out of his mind; and before he left he gave me firm instructions to do something about it by guile or by force. Accordingly, deeply as we were beginning to be engaged in broader French issues, I found it impossible, especially when goaded by continual appeals from London, to leave the matter of Godfroy's fleet in abeyance.

I had now been joined by Roger Makins, who had taken over from Bob Dixon; and with the arrival of some subordinate staff our little office was beginning to take shape. I could therefore, if necessary, leave Makins in charge at A.F.H.Q. to hold the fort in my absence. By the middle of February, the interchange of suggestions and proposals between London, Algiers and Cairo had reached a point at which it seemed best to set off to Cairo myself and learn what could or could not be done. The Prime Minister and the Admiralty felt strongly that Giraud had now 'succeeded to Darlan's position' and that Admiral Godfroy ought to accept his orders. Cairo took the same view. From what I had been told about him, I felt doubtful as to whether this line of argument would prove successful with Godfroy. At the same time, there would be some delicate repercussions of this thesis on the broader French situation:

I have always argued strongly against the tendency to rely too much upon Giraud for this purpose. In the first place, if we use him . . . to send either an order or an appeal to Admiral Godfroy to rally his ships to the cause, we are clearly asking him to do so as head of a State. I mean just as a General he has no right to give orders to Godfroy. But if as head of a State, of what State? We and the U.S.A. have only recognised Giraud as head of a provisional administration of French North Africa. That means Morocco, Algeria, Tunisia. By what authority then can he give orders to a fleet at Alexandria? Only (and this is *very* delicate) by a more general authority over French interests as a whole, which the U.S.A. seem rather inclined (especially since de Gaulle's behaviour at Anfa) to concede him [and] which H.M.G. is determined to deny him.[1]

In the end, Giraud decided to send not an 'order' but an 'appeal', and we waited to see the result. It had no effect whatsoever. We then decided to play our next card:

I have hoped that it would be possible to get Admiral Michelier—who is the senior French naval officer not in German-controlled France—to take some part in this affair. This was naturally not too easy, as it was after all only in November last that Admiral Michelier fought against the Allied landings at Casablanca.

Meanwhile, he has slowly been coming over . . . first to a modified support and now, I think, to a really enthusiastic co-operation with the British Navy. This change of heart is largely due to Admiral Cunningham, who has managed him very well.

Anyway, after a lot of humming and hawing, Michelier (in association with Giraud but not exactly on his orders) has been [induced] to take the step of sending his own Chief of Staff, Admiral Missoffe, to Alexandria with a message to Godfroy, instructing him to bring over the Alexandria fleet.[2]

It was accordingly arranged that we should start for Cairo, taking with us Admiral Missoffe. My plan was to see Godfroy myself; but we intended to use Missoffe as the chief negotiator. Soon after midnight on Sunday 21 February, John Wyndham and I left Algiers, accompanied by Admiral Missoffe and his flag-lieutenant, in a small

[1] 22 February 1943.
[2] Ibid.

Hudson, provided for us, after some difficulty, by the R.A.F. It was to prove a disastrous enterprise.

I don't know why, but I mistrusted the whole thing from the first. The plane was not fitted for passengers—no seats—but that doesn't matter, and it is quite easy with rugs and flying coats to make oneself happy enough on the floor. But there were no rugs; no arrangements for even minimum comfort; no officer at the airport to receive me. . . .

We were asked to get well forward for the start and to move back *after* she was in the air. As the heaviest, therefore, I went right up into the cockpit . . . next to the pilot. The navigator was in the nose, below us.

We taxied round in the usual way till we got to the far end of the runway. Then we started down it, gaining speed with the usual roar, as the throttle is opened out to full.

To my amazement, at this point, after rising a few feet off the ground, the pilot suddenly began to close the throttle to reduce speed to land again, and to put on the brakes. But he was, of course, too far along the runway to make this feasible. Sitting by his side I could see exactly what was happening and in a few seconds I had two rather clear impressions. . . .

First, I realised the immense pace at which we were going on the ground. . . . You know how when one is in a plane in the sky one gets *no* impression of speed. But racing along the ground (or a foot or two above it) I remember being conscious of tremendous speed.

The second feeling that I had instantaneously was of relief that the accident had come so soon. I felt so strongly that there was going to be an accident that I thought it was as well to get it over quickly. . . .

Of course, it was impossible for the pilot to stop the plane in the space allotted. In spite of his heavy braking, therefore, the plane ran on over the end of the runway into a field or bush or wall or something, gave a kind of stagger or drunken lurch, and then just settled down with a cracking sort of noise, like a child's toy motor. . . .

The shock was not very great, and none of us three in the cockpit was stunned. But immediately—just after one had time to realise that one had survived the crash—the flames began.

The pilot broke open the emergency exit on his left and disappeared through it. The navigator, who during the course of these proceedings had come out of the nozzle and was crouching near the pilot, did the same. Since this was clearly no occasion for a 'Casabianca' business, it was evident that the time had come for me to take what is technically called 'avoiding action'.

But middle-aged and rather portly publishers, encumbered by the weight of their own dignity and a large green Ulster overcoat, trying to spring through a smallish hole about the height of their head, this hole to be reached by scrambling over a confused mass of driving wheels, levers, and other mechanical devices of a jagged and impeding kind, if they are to achieve success in such an operation, must be inspired by a powerful and over-whelming motive. For lesser exertions, such as to enter Parliament, to struggle through years of political failure and frustration, lesser motives may serve. Ambition, patriotism, pride—all these can impel a man and finally bring him within the hallowed precincts of the Privy Council and the Cabinet.

But to do what I did in the early hours of last Monday morning, only one motive in the world is sufficient—FEAR (not Fame) is the spur.[3]

As the aeroplane sank more and more to one side, the aperture be-came more difficult to negotiate. But I decided to make a final effort to get enough of myself through the hole to tip the scale and bring me down on the top of the wing. The flames inspired me and with a great heave I was successful, and emerged burnt but alive. Meanwhile, Admiral Missoffe, his flag-lieutenant, and John Wyndham, who had been at the back of the plane, got out quite easily. It was only I who had been imprisoned in the cockpit. Sliding to the ground, I crawled or lurched as far away as possible. As the others came to my assistance, we were soon able to

look with melancholy satisfaction at our machine burning steadily, with flames darting here and there in the night, until soon the big petrol tanks were reached and up she went with a bang. I say 'melancholy satisfaction'—*melancholy* because there lay burning our hope of getting to Cairo and all our hopes there, *satisfaction* because if this aeroplane must burn, at least we were not inside it.[4]

Somebody had by now produced a stretcher on which I was put and taken to a dressing station. I had some small wounds in each leg, no doubt caused by catching against pieces of metal. My face was badly burnt. As I lay on the ground,

I felt a terrible stinging in my face. But I knew it would really be all right because my spectacles were still on my face (which protected my eyes) and after all, in one's face it is only to one's eyes that one attaches (at my age at least) much importance.[5]

The Admiral, although unhurt, was particularly distressed. It ap-peared that his cap had fallen off or had been left in the plane and that no similar admiral's cap could be obtained, except from metro-

[3] 23 February 1943.
[4] Ibid.
[5] Ibid.

politan France. He walked up and down, wringing his hands, and crying out: 'Ma casquette; ma casquette! J'ai perdu ma casquette.' To this lament, I replied, or so it was alleged, 'I don't care a damn about your casquette. J'ai perdu my bloody face.' This retort, which was soon to echo round Allied Force Headquarters, was thought to be in the best British tradition.

In the early hours of the morning, I was taken to the Maison-Carrée Military Hospital, not far from the airfield. Here I remained for the next few days. At first I suffered from severe shock, and imagined myself back in the hospital at Abbeville, where I had been nearly thirty years before during the Battle of the Somme.[6] But I made a quick recovery and by the second or third day suffered little pain.

They have put a sort of mask over my head—made of bandages and plaster—with I suppose a dressing on the inside. There are slits for my eyes and my lips, but otherwise the mask entirely covers my head, like the members of the Ku Klux Klan. . . . The only discomfort is that it is rather stuffy; but a very ingenious build-up of the mask enables me to breathe through my nostrils. My lips are still rather a bore, because they are very swollen, so that eating and drinking is very difficult. But I think the swelling is already better today. My eyes also ooze in rather an unpleasant way, but I think that will probably get better too. In every other way, I am fine.[7]

I was soon allowed to see a number of visitors. General Giraud's condolences were brought by Commandant Beaufre, his adjutant. Then came Admiral Michelier and Admiral Missoffe.

I amused Michelier very much by telling him that it would soon be all over Algiers that I was a 'Cagoulard'. (The Cagoulards were the French Right wing . . . which was supposed to be [planning] a revolution of the Right. . . . 'Cagoulard' . . . means 'hooded' and everyone here is accused or accuses others of having been a Cagoulard.)[8]

But the great sensation, of course, was the arrival of Sir Andrew Cunningham.

Everyone is tremendously excited. Nobody cares much about a poor old civilian Minister; but an Admiral of the Fleet, with a white hat, and gold from his cuff to his elbow, and 'Flags' with gold all over him; well, you can imagine how my stock has risen.

[6] *Winds of Change*, p. 90.
[7] 23 February 1943.
[8] Ibid.

Incidentally, the Admiral has brought me some very good news of the battle here, which has comforted me. He is a splendid man and absolutely first-class and a most amusing and agreeable companion. He is, of course, not surprised at the failure of the R.A.F. to take anyone safely anywhere. 'For myself,' he says, 'I generally travel American.' This, of course, is just naughtiness and to tease the Air Chief Marshal and others.[9]

By the end of the week I was able to return to our villa, although still in my mask, and even do a little work.

Air Marshal Welsh came to see me today. He was very apologetic. Apparently, the trouble was the mechanic forgot to take the cover off the gadget on the end of the fuselage through which the air passes and operates the speedometer.

[The pilot] could quite well have got this fixed by the navigator while in the air. Instead of that, he did this mad effort to land again and stop.

If I go to Cairo—which I hope still to do—I shall go in a Liberator and I have told them they must make it comfortable for me, as well as safe. I think they will do their best after this effort.[10]

This visit was followed by one from Eisenhower's Chief of Staff, General Bedell Smith.

He is a most charming and excellent fellow, and I am very fond of him. He has helped me a great deal.

Did you know that in the American Army, when a man is wounded he gets (instead of a wound-stripe) some kind of decoration called a Purple Heart? Have you ever heard of anything so ridiculous? Bedell says he thinks he will get me a Purple Heart. I think that would be awfully chic.[11]

On another day, Air Marshal Tedder came for a talk. This was the first opportunity for a serious discussion with him since he had taken over the command of all the British and American air forces. I noted my impression at the time:

Tedder is really a most interesting man. He has that rare quality of greatness (which you can't define but you sense). It consists partly of humour, immense common sense, and a power to concentrate on one or two simple points. But there is something more than any separate quality—you just feel it about some people the moment they come into a room. And *Tedder* is one of those people about whom you feel it.[12]

[9] Ibid.
[10] 25 February 1943.
[11] 26 February 1943.
[12] Ibid.

I was determined somehow to get to Cairo to deal with the question of Force X. Apart from the telegrams of sympathy which kept reaching me from Churchill and other Ministers, I read copies of instructions which were being sent to Casey, in Cairo, and Admiral Harwood, in Alexandria. I was alarmed at the idea that this affair might be taken out of my hands and that rash or premature action might be taken. There was now likely to be a pause in the political situation in French North Africa for two or three weeks. The Gaullist mission, agreed upon at Casablanca, was beginning to collect; but General Catroux was not expected back from Syria until the beginning of March. If, therefore, I could get away quickly, I might hope to be back by the time things began to work up in Algiers. Accordingly, in spite of some protests from the doctors, I started again for Cairo on Sunday 28 February, exactly a week after our mishap.

This time we have a *Liberator*. . . . There are seats fitted—which there were not in the Hudson.

I have been lent a really lovely flying suit—which is very necessary as it is very cold and there is no heating. . . . I have lovely leather breeches, with fur inside, a leather coat, with fur inside, and a hood. This is very nice as it covers my head, which is still in bandages. I have lovely fur-lined flying boots.

Air Marshal Welsh sent these to me—I think as a peace offering. I have a good mind to keep them as a partial compensation for the loss of my own clothes.[13]

In fact I did keep them and have them still.

We reached Cairo about 7.30 the same evening and I was driven to the beautiful villa belonging to Mr. Chester Beatty and temporarily in the occupation of R. G. Casey, who had succeeded Oliver Lyttelton as Minister of State in March 1942. He and Mrs. Casey treated me with extraordinary kindness and seemed not at all disturbed at my strange appearance. This was the beginning of a long and close friendship. It was a wonderful experience to be taken care of in this beautiful and luxurious house and to be treated with such tender consideration. The next day I went to the Scottish Hospital in Cairo and at last my bandages and mask were removed. This was a great relief after ten days of constriction.

[13] 28 February 1943.

My hair is burnt a good deal and has turned a curious kind of porridge colour. My beard was about an inch long (almost white) and has been shaved with extraordinary skill by the hospital barber. My forehead is pink—lovely new skin like a baby. My cheeks are rather mottled—there are one or two places not quite healed. Altogether, it is an odd effect.

I feel pretty well, except I think I am now feeling the effects of a slight concussion—that is, I have a headache each night, and a certain dizziness in the morning. No doubt this will wear off.[14]

Long conferences in Cairo and the discussion of many telegrams filled up the next few days. Unfortunately, I had begun to suffer from delayed shock and was forced to spend a good deal of time in bed. But it was a pleasure to meet again Lord Moyne, who had been my chief for a short period at the Colonial Office. He was now Deputy Minister of State and as charming and mysterious as ever.

By 6 March I felt fit to set about my task. I had told Churchill in one of my telegrams that if I did not persuade Godfroy's fleet to rally sooner or later, I would eat my hat. Happily, this pledge no longer applied, for my hat, together with most of my clothes, had been burnt with the aeroplane.

I went by train from Cairo to Alexandria, accompanied by Admiral Harwood, the hero of the *Graf Spee* battle, now Naval Commander-in-Chief in the Eastern Mediterranean. He was a man of great authority and power, but I found him very much confused by the conflicting advice which he had been receiving on the intractable problem of the French squadron. Admiral Godfroy arrived at Admiralty House at 5 p.m. and after the necessary introductions Admiral Harwood left me. It was a very rare thing for this strange and twisted man to come ashore, and he had only consented to do so after some pressure. The discussion was in French throughout. It was arranged that we should have our first talk at Admiral Harwood's house and that later the same evening we would dine together with a certain M. Fumaroli, a resident in Alexandria, who for some reason had become an intimate friend of Godfroy's.

It was clear that Godfroy had much resented the pressure which was being put upon him by Casey and his staff on Churchill's instructions. He began by launching into a rather excitable tirade against the treatment to which he had been subjected. Casey had tried to cross-

[14] 3 March 1943.

examine him as if he had been a dishonest witness. The report of the interview was quite inaccurate and unacceptable to him. He had been forced to write a repudiation of the statements attributed to him. He was the more surprised because Casey's assistant appeared to be an intelligent man.

The telegram from the Prime Minister was insulting and absurd. As for his interview with Nahas Pasha, he had been treated to a lecture on Egyptian law which no doubt the Egyptian Prime Minister had some qualifications to deliver, as he understood that he had been an advocate of mediocre attainments, but he, Admiral Godfroy, knew enough of the subject to be aware that this statement of the legal position was fantastically incorrect. He knew perfectly well the position of Great Britain in Alexandria under the treaty with Egypt. He could not be browbeaten by such childish methods. After these preliminaries, the Admiral became more reasonable. He had got all this off his chest and instead of making statements began to ask questions.

His chief concern appeared to be the question of the exact status of General Giraud's administration in French North Africa. He had armed himself with a number of quotations from British and American wireless news tending to show that F.N.A. was, in fact, occupied territory. In his suspicious and tortuous mind, he had even twisted the publicity given to the imports organised by the N.A.E.B.[15] into further proof of the economic tyranny exerted by the U.S.A. and Great Britain.

I did my best to describe to him objectively the development of the situation from the first days of the landings to the present time. I explained to him how the original conception of an occupation— necessary, since the landings were at first opposed by the French authorities—had been changed by the agreement made between Admiral Darlan and General Clark. I tried to expound to him the steady development of this relationship into a working arrangement between Allied Headquarters and the French administration, which was gradually taking the form of a normal agreement between allies in the field. I emphasised the respect shown for French sovereignty. General Giraud, as Chairman of the Comité de Guerre, resided at the

---

[15] North African Economic Board. This body had been set up by A.F.H.Q., in agreement with the French, to organise—or rather restore—the economic life of French North Africa.

Palais d'Été with his staff and military guard. His War Cabinet consisted of the heads of the various provinces, with General Noguès for Morocco, Marcel Peyrouton for Algeria, and so forth. I gave him instances of the various agreements which had been freely negotiated between Allied Headquarters and the French administration—for example, the Joint Economic Committee of which N.A.E.B. represented the American and British half, and the French Treasury the French side.

I also gave him other instances: the agreement regarding postal and telegraphic censorship, the agreement regarding radio control, and the agreement regarding the Joint Commission to visit internment camps. All these had been negotiated in the ordinary way by Mr. Murphy and myself on behalf of the American and British Governments with General Giraud and his colleagues.

All this appeared to interest and reassure the Admiral. He seemed to be quite moved when I made it clear to him that, by implication, the term 'Allies' meant to us the British, American and French peoples freely joined together in the war against Germany. Indeed, my membership card of the Cercle Interallié d'Alger, Musée de Bardo, recently organised in Algiers, gave him quite a thrill.

He then asked what would happen if Giraud died. How could a legitimate Government be formed? I replied that it seemed to me that in the Comité de Guerre there was a *de facto* authority which could take the necessary action. But, of course, if and when all the French Empire could come together and a provisional administration be formed to cover the whole field, then the situation would be correspondingly improved and regularised.

This led the Admiral to deliver a rather rambling speech on de Gaulle and Gaullism. He appeared to maintain two opposite views. He disliked intensely the Gaullist movement, which was, he said, mixed up with radicalism and rascality. He also thought that General Catroux could never recover from the infamy of what he had done in Syria. (This, of course, meant the expulsion of the Germans and Vichy French.) On the other hand, he seemed to argue that until de Gaulle and Giraud got together, the French administration would not be sufficiently broadly based for him, Admiral Godfroy, to recognise it. I ventured gently to point out the contradiction involved.

Admiral Godfroy then said he must be quite frank. On the whole, he thought that the majority of his officers wished to rally to Giraud, but they trusted their commander with regard to the timing of such a move. He must find a suitable occasion. He had his orders from his own Government. He could only disregard them and run the risks involved in very clear circumstances. He had thought Toulon would have been the occasion. He wrestled all one night with this problem and made up his mind to act. But he found that his captains would not support him. Thinking it over since, he wondered if he had not been wrong in regarding Toulon as the turning-point, because he felt that after all it was not perhaps the Germans who had broken the armistice but the French in North Africa, by restarting the war against Germany. This was rather disconcerting, as it destroyed the main doctrinal foundation of our thesis. However, I passed it over and asked what opportunities might occur. I suggested two alternatives, from which he did not dissent. The first might be the formation of a French administration representing all those parts of France or the French Empire not in enemy hands. The second might be the end of the Tunisian campaign. The Admiral added two others: the clear indication by some action of the Germans that Marshal Pétain's Government in France could no longer be regarded as legitimate, or the death or resignation of the Marshal. I ventured to add that surely the notorious pressure of the Germans on all France, including the Vichy authorities, must not be disregarded.

He then spoke of the visit of Admiral Missoffe. He had been very glad to see him and to send Captain Garron to French North Africa. He thought Michelier a very decent fellow. He had had him once under his orders and thought well of him. He was prepared to make some preliminary arrangements for putting his ships in order, but he would never take them anywhere except to a French port. He seemed very anxious to know my views as to the capture of Tunisia. At this point the first interview ended.

We dined at 7.30 p.m. at M. Fumaroli's house. Dinner was very long. After dinner, the ladies left in the English manner.

I kept the conversation chiefly on reminiscences of the past, stories of the last war, and assumed as a fact the complete reconstitution of the Anglo-American-French alliance in French North Africa on the lines of the First World War. We discussed partridge-shooting at some length. The Admiral told me that his father-in-law had owned or leased a famous shoot in England. Those were the days when affairs were run by well-bred men, and politics had not fallen into the hands of rascals. Really, Godfroy was a terrible old snob! Then we passed to 1914–1918, its highlights, its moments of despair and of triumph. Hence to the events of French North Africa and to the reconstitution of the alliance. I laid stress on the size and rearmament programme of the French Army, and also on the excellent work of Michelier's squadron in alliance with Admiral Cunningham. We talked of mutual friends, of the harbour at Casablanca and other local topics.

I asked the Admiral if he intended to keep up his contact with French North Africa. He said yes. He would need the assistance of the Navy Department at Casablanca, especially with regard to personnel. I said that I hoped that he would let me know of any help that we could give for postal or telegraphic communication, or air travel, and that I hoped very soon to see the Admiral at Algiers and have a game of bridge with him in the Club. We did not mention precisely the arrangements contemplated for accepting representation of the French North African Naval Department at Alexandria, but it seemed to be implied.

I did my best to play upon the nostalgia in the Admiral's heart. I told him of the considerable number of officers and civilians who were continually coming out of France and rejoining the movement in French North Africa. All this seemed new to him and I think made some impression.

At 9.45 p.m. the car came for me. I drove the Admiral to the quay and left him with many friendly and complimentary exchanges.

I sent an account of this interview to London, together with my conclusions. They were as follows:

1. I do not think you can bully Admiral Godfroy. He is contemptuous of such methods, and especially of the Prime Minister's efforts. He is too sure of himself . . . to submit to being bullied. . . .

2. He has his orders from Vichy and will not go against them until an opportunity arises which he thinks will clearly justify him.

3. He is now (since the renewal of the war by French North Africa) looking forward to such an opportunity and will probably take it when it comes. This will, in my view, be at the moment when the Germans are ejected from Africa, and Admiral Godfroy can sail his squadron through the Mediterranean to a French port.

On my return to Cairo, there was little to be done except to wait for the Prime Minister's reactions, which were not likely to be enthusiastic.

It seems convenient to finish, although slightly out of sequence, the story of Force X. I felt sure that the only possible way to lead this strange man to the conclusion to which, in a sense, he longed to come, was to bring financial pressure upon his officers and men, and to point to the final expulsion of the Germans and Italians from North Africa. The first part of this policy, which I explained to the Prime Minister, was based upon the principle 'Where your treasure is, there shall your heart be also'. The second was about to reach its triumphant climax.

Towards the end of April 1943, I succeeded in persuading Giraud to send an officer to take charge of the supply question affecting Force X. At this time he was confident that it would now not be long before a final settlement would be reached. We meanwhile arranged to warn Admiral Godfroy that he must now look to Giraud's organisation for payments. The British Treasury would continue to provide the funds in accordance with the original agreement, but no payments would be made direct, only through Giraud. Although Churchill still continued to suggest more drastic methods, I was able to resist this pressure, largely with the help of Admiral Cunningham who gave me full support throughout. On 15 May, Godfroy at last came to terms. He still tried to raise some minor political questions, but Giraud made it clear to him that he would cut off the pay unless he would immediately agree to the re-attachment of Force X at Alexandria to the French North African naval forces.

And so at last this long-standing problem reached its solution. Churchill never quite forgave me, or at least pretended not to do so. Towards the end of May we met at Government House, Gibraltar.

He immediately attacked me about Force X . . . and accused me of having disobeyed instructions, to which I retorted that at any rate he had got the fleet. 'No thanks to you,' says he. 'I don't know,' said I. 'You would have blamed me if the thing had gone wrong, so you must give me the credit when it has gone right.' He went on mumbling away about not carrying out his instructions to me.[16]

There was still, of course, some delay in making the ships fit to take to sea, and it was not until August that Admiral Godfroy brought to

[16] 4 June 1943.

North Africa, via the Red Sea and the Cape, one battleship, four cruisers, three destroyers and a submarine.

This episode was an extraordinary example of the wrong-headedness of those who remained loyal to Vichy, and of the special difficulty of dealing with those who were not mere traitors or time-servers. Godfroy was clearly a man of the highest moral standards. He was a tremendous snob, as his conversations made clear. But in a sense, his snobbery was based upon old-fashioned concepts, on what he believed to be a gentleman's honour. He simply could not understand how anybody like our Prime Minister could expect him, or even ask him, to break his oath of loyalty. He hated the Germans and had a deep affection for the English. Indeed, he was half English by birth. But however much he may have suffered from successive French Governments in whom he placed no reliance—he even disapproved of many of Pétain's actions— he was tied by his oath.

Had we attempted to seize the fleet by force, Admiral Godfroy would have given the order to scuttle the ships; and it would have been obeyed. Criticism did not move him. Neither Churchill's appeals nor his objurgations had any effect on him. In the end, the combination of financial pressure and, much more important in my estimation, the triumph of the Allies in North Africa brought him to take, hesitatingly, unwillingly and almost against his conscience, the final step.

CHAPTER TWELVE

After Casablanca

THE pursuit of Force X, with all its exciting incidents, was only an interlude in the major difficulty which now faced us. How was the apparently insoluble puzzle of the relations between the various French groups opposed to the Germans to be resolved?

Before setting out on my first and unlucky mission to Cairo, I reviewed the whole situation with the help of my small but highly efficient staff. We felt it important that, in view of the inevitable delay in achieving a united French administration, the criticisms at home and abroad about the conduct of affairs by the Allies should be met, if possible, by a better understanding of the difficulties.

Owing to the stagnation of the battle for Tunis, many of our newspapers seemed to have forgotten what was the main purpose of our expedition. It was our task to remind them of the realities.

French North Africa must be considered in its strategic role. It is a convenient place in which to fight the Germans; it is the object of our armies to drive the Germans from the territory; and it is the Allied interest to use French North Africa as a convenient springboard from which to attack the enemy in their Continental positions.

The Allies did not land in French North Africa for their health, or to spend an agreeable winter in a sunny climate. It was not a piece of tourism. It was an act of war.[1]

It was obviously the duty of those charged with advising the Commander-in-Chief on political or civil affairs to do all we could to help him achieve his supreme military objective.

The French Army must be kept or made loyal to the cause. The French Administration must be persuaded or instructed to afford all possible

[1] This and subsequent passages are taken from memoranda which I prepared at the time.

facilities. The French and indigenous populations must be kept as far as may be calm and contented. The lines of communication must be protected from sabotage. Labour must be induced to work cheerfully and consistently on docks, roads, aerodromes and the like. There must be neither disorder nor disaffection likely to disturb military operations. Espionage must be put down. Censorship must be operated, of radio, Press, cables, letters, etc., to prevent leakage of military news.

The country remained calm. The railways, docks and public facilities were operating successfully. Communications had not been interfered with. It was true that on a purely theoretical basis the position of the French authority was anomalous. An Army commander, operating in occupied enemy territory, has no choice, at least in the first stages. He must immediately set up a military authority for civil purposes by declaring himself the supreme military governor. But even this, as we were soon to find in Italy, has great disadvantages. To accept direct responsibility for the administration of part or the whole of an invaded country requires a vast army of officials, who are usually ignorant of the background and uninstructed as to the local problems. Indirect government in some form becomes almost immediately necessary. In any case Eisenhower had decided against this plan, which was for obvious reasons inapplicable to a people whom we hoped to restore to full military alliance against the Axis powers. An alternative plan would have been to have treated the French as an ally from the start.

In that case, the position of the Allied forces would be not disimilar to that which the British occupied vis-à-vis the French Government in the last war, when fighting on French territory. That, of course, is the position which the French administration would like to reach. In my view, it would be quite wrong to concede it. It would only have been justifiable if we had landed, as in 1914, on the invitation of a French Government. The very contrary was the case. It could only be conceded at a much later stage, and many conditions precedent would be required, none of which are yet in sight.

Actually, we were following a kind of middle course, illogical perhaps, and difficult to define, but by no means unsuccessful. We wished, at any rate for the present, to maintain this compromise; but it required most careful and skilful handling. The ultimate authority of the Commander-in-Chief had to be kept in reserve like that of a suzerain power. But everything that we wished to obtain from the French administration must be won, if possible, by diplomatic nego-

tiation and not by force. Faces must be saved so long as results were
obtained. When we made demands upon the French for military
purposes, it was relatively easy to get satisfaction.

But where we begin—as in the realm of internal politics, internees, radio
and propaganda of all kinds—to encroach, without so clear a justification,
upon French sovereignty, difficulties occur. We have to rely upon arguments
based upon a more remote interest. We have to say that it is a military
question that there should be political calm. We have to assert that the public
opinion of the U.S.A. and Great Britain must be kept satisfied if the
Governments are to obtain their enthusiastic support in the production and
military fields.

This, indeed, was our most potent weapon in urging political reforms.

It was clear, therefore, that at any rate for the present nothing
should be done to disturb what was working successfully from the
military angle. But we had another problem which, happily, had so far
presented us with no insuperable dangers. These immense territories
had to be administered; and they were very different in character.

Algeria was legally part of metropolitan France; but of course it was
not really French. The European population, French, Italian and
Spanish, was about a million. The Arabs were over six million. There
were, in addition, some 100,000 Jews. In Algeria, nevertheless, with its
large French population, there was a genuine French public opinion.

In Morocco, where the Sultan was still the nominal ruler of the
country, there was a situation not unlike that of a great native state in
India in the old days. The European population was just over 200,000,
the Moslems nearly six million and the Jews 160,000. Apart from the
complications introduced by the character of General Noguès, none of
the normal considerations of European politics applied.

About this time I had a curious visit from General Noguès, who
came to pay his respects and to thank me for the Prime Minister's
party in the Anfa camp. Nothing he said led me to change my opinion
about him. As Slender said of Mistress Ann Page, 'There was no great
love between us at the beginning and it pleased heaven to decrease it
on further acquaintance.' General Noguès sat himself down and with
many compliments expressed his high regard for Churchill, the greatest leader of any country throughout all history. He said how well he
got on with all British officers and men whom he came across (there
were very few in Morocco); how admirably the British conducted

themselves at every level; how experienced they were in the delicacies of politics and the problems of colonial empires. I accepted these tributes without comment and waited for the inevitable second part of his harangue. He went on to observe how in every respect the Americans were the opposite to us. Of the President, he had a poor opinion; the American troops behaved badly and made trouble wherever they went; he had no confidence in their commanders; the Americans had little or no experience of the difficulties involved in Africa; altogether, they were a disaster. When he had finished, I said to him, 'I suppose, General, you are now going to see the American political representative, Mr. Murphy.' He admitted that this was so. 'General,' I said, 'I can spare you the trouble. I will dictate now a note of everything you have said about the British and the Americans. Only, in the first part, where all the praises are given, I shall put "American" instead of "British". In the second part, where all the criticism is made, I shall put "British" instead of "American". Then I shall send a copy up to Mr. Murphy, and it will save you a lot of trouble.' Noguès was rather taken aback and left hurriedly. The story soon spread through A.F.H.Q. and was not without its value in the anxious days that lay ahead. Although it is only fair to say that under Noguès, Morocco had remained quiet, this area did involve us in difficulties, especially from the supply point of view.

In Tunisia, where the battle still raged, the population was over $2\frac{1}{4}$ million Arabs, some 60,000 Jews and 213,000 Europeans.

In the part of Tunisia which is at present in German hands, there is a Mussulman population of importance. This represents in itself a formidable problem. The Germans are conducting a very active propaganda among the Arabs. They have seized a large quantity of goods of all kinds for distribution to the natives. And by every possible means, with (I believe) the active cooperation of the Grand Mufti of Jerusalem, they are influencing them against us. I have already done my best to expedite the formation of a proper Arab Section of the Psychological Warfare Department.

It was very difficult to assess the real feelings of the French people in Algeria. There was a loyal population intensely devoted to France, deriving largely from those French exiles who had preferred to settle in North Africa rather than accept the German occupation of their loved and treasured homes. These had emigrated after the war of 1870 from Alsace and Lorraine. They preserved their customs, their costumes, and their traditions in a way which was both moving and inspiring. These folk were the élite of the French population. But even they were influenced by varying political emotions. They supported Giraud and would in due course support de Gaulle. Nevertheless, it was the keen Gaullists among them who had been our friends and who now, to our shame and distress, were suffering for their friendship. For the rest, the 'colons', whether large or small proprietors, were, like most agriculturists, more interested in the price of their products, in this case mainly the export of wine. Up till the end of 1942 wine had been freely exported to France and they had obtained their immediate import requirements, largely by the deliberate policy of the United States, preparatory to the landings. Now, after a period of nearly three months' isolation from metropolitan France, they were troubled in their views. Export of wine had been cut off. (Later, the Allies arranged to purchase large quantities.) The foolish and oppressive rate of exchange had harassed them. The presence of great numbers of British and American troops naturally had an inflationary effect. Hence the importance of the supply and civil activities of A.F.H.Q., of which N.A.E.B. was the instrument. I had been appointed to the somewhat anomalous position of co-president of this body with Murphy. But the Board was really managed by General Sir Humfrey Gale, one of the most efficient officers I have ever known.

The American and British officials are now shaking down into a harmonious and reasonably efficient team. . . . They are grappling (heroically and stoically, but none the less under extreme difficulties) with their important tasks. I have been very much struck with the high standard of performance—under most disadvantageous physical conditions—of our British team. It is one thing to get through a lot of work in a Government office in London, with all its equipment of messengers, files, boxes, telephones, secretaries and the like. It is another thing altogether to do the same with one (inefficiently operated and maddeningly obstructive) telephone among ten or twelve men, without typewriters, paper, pen, or even ink, and situated with one chair and a desk formed of a piece of packing-case delicately poised upon a housemaid's sink.

These economic difficulties, however baffling, would of course be gradually overcome. But what about the internal situation? How were we to achieve the 'house-cleaning' which our public opinion rightly demanded?

For the present, General Giraud held the field. His character was simple and engaging. Sometimes he seemed to me rather like the White Knight in *Alice,* for he appeared to live only in the clouds. His manners were exquisite, and he spoke that pure and simple French which is easy to follow. But he could be very irritating. Peyrouton, who, whatever may have been his political failings, had a pretty wit, once said to me: 'On connaît toujours la politique des militaires par leurs moustaches. Giraud a la moustache très symbolique, comme le Lord Kitchener.'[2] He certainly resembled Lord Kitchener in his complete ignorance of politics in any form. He too was a general of that old colonial school.

His experience is one of imprisonment and defeat. But these disagreeable accidents have in no way destroyed his confidence in his military knowledge. Those of our high officers who met and talked with him at Anfa will have formed their own view as to the value to be attached to his opinions on military affairs. But I feel sure that they will agree that, like those of many of the older generation of French soldiers, they are largely obsolete. They bear the same relation to modern strategy and tactics, as did the ideas of the German and Austrian generals to the genius of Napoleon.

I am told that he is altogether neglectful of the science which is now called logistics. He does not seem to understand that modern armies cannot 'live upon the country'. And he appears, like M. Stalin, to regard the sea as a minor obstacle, across which troops and equipment can readily be flung, as if across a small stream.

Of course, this was true not only of Giraud but of the great majority of French officers in high command. For the French Army had indeed degenerated from the great days. Before the war, promotion had been intolerably slow. Battalion commanders were men of forty-five or more. Generals of two or five stars were anything from sixty onwards, and the longevity of marshals was notorious and appalling. Nevertheless, the French soldiers were still sublimely convinced of their superiority. In spite of overwhelming defeats in 1870 and 1940 and a very severe shaking in 1914–18, they still regarded themselves as the élite of the military world. The British were only amateurs.

But as we know from sporting analogies, there is no such unimaginative player of any game as the second-rate professional. And that is really what they are.

[2] 13 April 1943.

These views about the French Army were formed after only a short experience, but they were soundly based. I was much interested when, some months later, General de Gaulle expressed almost the same sentiments to me. He felt that a new Army must be created, like the revolutionary army that had sprung to arms after 1789.

As for the morale of the French Army in North Africa, it was difficult to be sure. There were some monarchist tendencies, as there always had been in the colonial forces. But much more dangerous was the hankering after Vichy, strangely enough combined with a contempt for the politicians who had been responsible, in the view of most soldiers, for the collapse of the Third Republic.

While they are uncertain as to what régime should take its place, they do not want to revert to the French Parliamentary system as it operated in the years between the two wars. Moreover, they are genuinely alarmed by the spread of Bolshevism. Quite respectable and decent officers have said to me in my own home: 'The Russians are doing well—too well.' This feeling is being much exploited at the moment by enemy propaganda.

General Giraud, however, whatever may have been his faults, was not affected by these defeatist concepts. He was genuinely anxious to fight the Germans, for whom he felt a passionate hatred. Indeed, when asked his view on any subject, political or economic, he would reply with a disarming smile, with those clear blue eyes fixed upon his interlocutor, 'Mon ami, je fais la guerre.'

In politics, General Giraud affects to take no interest. Nevertheless, he has found himself, by a series of chances or mischances, at the head of an administration. He regards politics as subservient to the necessities of war. But in this (as in all politicians whose sympathies are with the extreme Right) he is really somewhat disingenuous. Even in war, politics cannot be wholly divorced from the conduct of military campaigns. Apart from technical economic problems, of which he is profoundly ignorant, there are the broad questions of the balance of advantage, such as the manpower problem, which cannot (as our experience shows) be settled by generals or admirals alone, but needs examination by a body of mixed experts and resolution by the presiding authorities of the State from an independent point of view. And to say 'Je fais la guerre' is only a phrase. Everything else that he does or leaves undone in the political sphere has its reactions on the war effort. Moreover, under the cover of this sentiment, he perhaps unconsciously, many others round him consciously, while they are nominally making war, are incidentally making admirable dispositions for peace.

But perhaps the greatest disadvantage under which poor Giraud suffered was the recent blow to his pride by his utter failure to rally support when he landed in North Africa. He had put himself under Darlan's orders. He thereby took cover under Vichy and accepted the doctrine of apostolic succession. I had been told by his adjutant, Commandant Beaufre, that the real cause of his failure was a ludicrous mischance. He had landed in plain clothes. His full general's uniform had been packed and sent ahead, but unluckily had been mislaid.

How to make a *coup d'état* in a bowler hat? What a problem! A new uniform had to be procured of five-star general rank, and a precious day lost. In any event, General Giraud lost his nerve on these fatal nights after the disembarking of the Allied forces. *Hinc illae lacrimae.* From this event springs all the timidity, the wobbling, the whoring after the false gods of Vichy, the Right-wing political flavour of the Administration, the pathetic cry for 'order' (always the refuge of the weak man) and the hesitating, vacillating, double-faced policy which has lasted now since Darlan's elevation and assassination.

So I felt that Giraud would never take a strong line. He would talk big; but he would yield to events. And so it proved.

General Bergeret was the first Deputy High Commissioner and Secretary-General—that is, second-in-command to Giraud. He was a charming man to meet and gave every impression of being trustworthy; but he was a hopeless reactionary. Nogués was left to fascinate backwoods American generals with his dinners and hunting parties and to oppress the friends of the Allies. The other members of the so-called 'Imperial Council' were Boisson—correct but unfriendly in Dakar—and Peyrouton, who had replaced Châtel in Algeria. Peyrouton was intelligent, a good administrator and now convinced that the Allies were going to win. But he was not the man for the needs of a renascent France.

A powerful figure in affairs in Algiers was Lemaigre-Dubreuil who, although he had certainly done much to redeem his character by his work to help Murphy before the landings, was much suspected as a reactionary, even a 'Cagoulard'. He had now become Under-Secretary for Allied Affairs. Before the war, we irreverent young Conservatives had given to a number of the less attractive industrialists who sat on the Conservative side in the House of Commons, generally for very safe seats, the offensive nickname of the 'Forty Thieves'. Lemaigre-Dubreuil would have had a high place in this company.

I did not feel that Giraud really liked all these people with whom he consorted, for he was a man of high and honourable ideals and conduct. But he was frightened. He had not forgotten that awful day.

The great General Giraud appeared in person (probably in the third person, which he always employs about himself) and the Army was not impressed, so he comforts himself by what he calls 'politique de perroquet'. He will go slowly. He will act 'progressivement'. (In fact, except under extreme pressure from Murphy and me, he does nothing at all.)

Now, what had we done in these few weeks? We, too, could repeat our well-worn theme, parrot-like, whenever we saw Giraud. British and American public opinion was anxious and disturbed. We had gone to war to bring freedom, not tyranny, to Europe. It was all very well for Giraud and his friends to say they too were anxious for an understanding with the Gaullists, but there were obvious conditions which de Gaulle must demand.

First—and an essential prerequisite of fusion—there must be an absolute break with Vichy and Vichy traditions. Secondly, certain high officials must be removed; not a great number in all, but important both in themselves and as symbols of action. Thirdly, more civilian elements must be introduced into the administration at all levels. Fourthly, the political prisoners and internees must be set free. This was urgent. I knew as well as General Giraud that among the 8,000 held in prison camps, scattered through the desert, sometimes in very bad conditions, there were felons and criminals, as well as harmless Jews or keen sympathisers with the Allies. I was to have this confirmed in rather a macabre way a few weeks later. I was told at a luncheon party by a French officer, presumably Gaullist, who had been released, that in a prison with him was a Spaniard who had been convicted of shooting a man and eating his arms. I could not help observing to a fellow guest that he (the French officer) kept his hands in his pockets. This seemed to amuse him greatly. Nevertheless, in spite of some exaggeration, the prison camps were a scandal and must be dealt with. Fifth, the laws against the Jews, which were of purely Vichy origin, must be repealed. They offended every canon of decent behaviour. They were among the worst of the horrors which the Nazi régime had brought into Europe. Finally, the various Vichy and 'Fascist' organisations of different kinds must be cleaned up.

Summing up therefore at this time the result of the first few weeks: while the first vital need—a firm and calm basis for the battle—had been secured; while the economic problems, although serious, had not proved insuperable; there was little to show as yet on the political front. The whole atmosphere from top to bottom remained tainted with Vichyism. While we had made some progress with the release of individual political prisoners, there was still a long way to go. On the other matters, there had been much talk but little done. Moreover, every day, there were disturbing incidents.

For instance, decorations—Croix de Guerre with Palms—are given to brave French soldiers. For what? For resisting the landings. And how—by fighting English and American soldiers? Not even that—which (from one point of view) is a brave and meritorious act on the part of the individual soldier. No. For shooting two de Gaullist or pro-Ally irregulars who were helping to guide our troops.

There was another, even worse, scandal.

The Lafayette Squadron of the Air Force is solemnly re-equipped. Much music by French and American bands; speeches by French and American generals; and then—two of the newly constituted Squadron get into their machines and fly off. Where? To Tunisia? To bomb Sicily? To attack Sardinia? No. They flit to Marseilles, quickly, there to rejoin the Marshal, their wives, or maybe their mistresses. You would imagine that such an incident would cause a good deal of stir. But so far, except for an 'enquiry' which has been ambling along for over three weeks, nothing has been done. The famous—or infamous—General Mendigal still commands the French Air Force. The Americans are a gentle and forgiving people. I only wish these two rascals had flown off with two of the Spitfires which General Giraud wheedled out of the Prime Minister (with my aid, I confess it) and I feel sure that *verbosa et grandis epistola* would have come from Downing Street.

The arrival of the first Gaullist emissaries certainly encouraged the expectation that something was going to happen. Yet I feared that the sense of relief was only temporary. If the liaison should not prove fruitful, or relations were broken off, a very serious situation would follow. Political agitation might take a dangerous form. British prestige, in particular, would be gravely affected. Yet in spite of all these discouragements, the plotting, counter-plotting and the sense of frustration, 'calculated to sap the vitality and depress the spirits of a platoon of Mark Tapleys', I felt that some small progress had been made.

President Roosevelt, and to some extent the Prime Minister, had often expressed their anxieties about the future of France. The official formula was that 'the people of France must be free to choose their own form of government after the liberation'. But I felt that this would some day have to be translated from a theoretical into a practical basis.

All history shows that Governments and forms of government are not chosen in the void. Only the Abbé Sieyès was under such an illusion. Everything that is done or left undone during the remaining period of the war will clearly have its effect. If a large, victorious and well-equipped French Army re-enters metropolitan France, whoever has the command of such an army will obviously be in a very important position. He will be to some the saviour, to others the potential oppressor of the French people. If he comes, with a largely black army, he will not have to worry about the political views of his army. If he has been surrounded by men of the Right, anxious, perhaps from genuinely patriotic motives, not to put back the weak Parliamentary régime which brought France so low in the years before the war, but to build an authoritarian régime of some kind, whether under monarchist or republican form, there may be reproduced in France that very situation which has led to such disasters in Spain.

The Left and even the moderate forces in France herself will swing more and more to Communism as the only reply. The forces on which de Gaulle leans and hopes to rally will become more and more extreme 'Left'. And from the *coup d'état* of the Right and the civil war which may be provoked, there will follow equally bad results for Europe as a whole and Great Britain in particular. Our people will be split by the same bitter division of which we had the foretaste in the Spanish affair.

It is therefore not only a French but a British interest, on a long view, that there should be a real de Gaulle–Giraud fusion now.

I went on to add in the same memorandum:

It is vital that such a fusion should be based upon a broad and central political foundation; that it should try to rebuild a faith in liberal and democratic ideas; that it should admit frankly the pre-war betrayal of democracy (and we perhaps can help by openly and humbly confessing our own sins); that it should nevertheless try to recover the *élan* which once inspired the free peoples; that round this theme the authority of any provisional administration of the French Empire should grow; that from this source it should take its sustenance.

Only thus do I see the possibility that France can save herself, and incidentally Europe, from disaster.

Meanwhile, certain changes had taken place at A.F.H.Q. which favoured my purposes. A Political Council was formed, presided over by General Eisenhower and attended by the Chief of Staff (Bedell Smith), Murphy and myself, together with our assistants, Roger Makins and Sam Reber, a most admirable and liberal-minded official who had come to help Murphy. This committee normally met two or three times a week and more often when required. It was of great value in helping to form a common British and American policy. Eisenhower himself took a leading and constructive part.

In addition, by the end of February not only had the advance guard of the Gaullist mission begun to appear, but more important, on 26 February, Jean Monnet arrived from Washington. He had come nominally to discuss French rearmament; but he was destined to take a leading part in the evolution of the French political situation. Monnet was already a well-known figure in the higher circles of Government in Washington and London. I had met him in the summer of 1940 in connection with the French contracts which we took over at the time of the fall of France. He had not joined the Gaullist movement publicly or privately. But he was strongly anti-Vichy and a sincere patriot. He was known, moreover, to enjoy the confidence both of Churchill and of Roosevelt. He was actually a member of the British Supply Council working in Washington. Many influential Americans, including Harry Hopkins, had a high regard for him. It was the President who persuaded Monnet to go to Algiers (with or without the approval of the State Department), and his authority with both French sections began immediately to grow. He was trusted by Giraud. At the same time de Gaulle realised that Monnet's main purpose was to work for French unity.

This remarkable man has played, in a quiet and unassuming way, a vastly important role in the life of France. For many months I worked closely with him in Algiers. I both gave him my confidence and received his. Some of my American friends felt by the end of this critical summer that Monnet had in a sense deceived them. Since he was sent out by the American Government, many of them felt he should continue

THE BLAST OF WAR

to support the main American thesis. This was that no central French authority, recognised as such and able to talk on equal terms with the Governments of the United States and Britain, should be allowed to come into being.

Monnet's chief efforts were directed to two main purposes. First, that whatever 'administration' or 'Government' came into being, it should not be based upon personal rule, but on Cabinet responsibility. Secondly, he strongly maintained that after the liberation of metropolitan France some constitutional method of procedure should be used. There should be no imposition of a dictatorship.

At that time the old 'loi Tréveneuc' of 1872, by which the surviving members of the local councils (Conseils-Généraux') should form a kind of constituent assembly, was still in force. To many, including Monnet, its application seemed the right course. But as time passed and it became apparent that such a method strictly adhered to would prove impracticable—largely owing to the disappearance of the individuals concerned—Monnet realistically accepted the need for some adaptation of procedure.

France owes much to Jean Monnet. His work at Algiers was absolutely vital to any solution. He was the lubricant, or even catalyst, between the two bitterly opposing factions. His work in France after the war proved to be the foundation of the great prosperity which France has now attained. But he was an equally good friend to the British and American Governments and peoples. He never swerved from his concept of the close co-operation that should exist, during and after the war, between the New World and the Old. In his long and brilliantly effective labours for the European movement, he has never deviated into a narrow or particularist view, either of France's position in Western Europe, or of Britain's place as a European power. Many tributes have been justly paid to him. For my part, I learned to know him intimately in these hectic months in Algiers and I have never swerved in my opinion of his qualities, both intellectual and moral.

Equally encouraging was the improvement in the military situation. There had been a difficult time in mid-February when Murphy and I saw General Giraud on the two urgent issues of the political prisoners and the persecuted Jews. We chose an unhappy moment, when the German counter-attack had temporarily broken the American line.

Thala was attacked, Tébessa was threatened, and General Giraud explained to us—in great detail and with some relish—that in his view the network of Allied communications in western Tunisia as well as the chain of aerodromes on the plateaux of eastern Algeria, from Biskra in the south to Télergma in the north, were in danger. General Giraud could not conceal a certain enjoyment of the tactical advantage which this situation had placed in his hands. Although he promised that something should be done about the prisoners and the camps, he bridled over the mention of Jews, in whose fate, according to him, our Governments were chiefly concerned because so many of our newspapers were owned by Jews! He would give us no satisfaction about the changes in the administration and the removal of the Vichy characters. He ended the interview by launching into a tirade about the failure of the Allies to arm the French troops, who were evidently to be assigned a purely defensive role.

It is true that on this last issue, owing to the unlucky promises made at Anfa, which still had somehow to be straightened out, Giraud had some legitimate grievance. Moreover, there had been some difficulty about civilian supplies. The food situation was deteriorating, and we had to draw heavily on American and even more heavily on British sources. There was, of course, a good deal of hoarding of grain, especially in Morocco. Indeed, it was said that an American battery engaged in live shell practice in the desert had found to their amazement that when their missiles exploded, great clouds of grain were thrown into the air. They had unluckily struck one of the many store-rooms, some of them dating from Roman and even pre-Roman days.

At no time did I feel more depressed than after this inauspicious interview on 19 February. Yet within four weeks, the 'New Deal', as it came to be called, was an accomplished fact.

On that same day General Alexander came to see me. He was leaving for the Front to take over his command, which he assumed formally on 20 February. I well remember the calm and confident way in which he explained to me what seemed to have happened at the Front. While there was no panic at A.F.H.Q., there was real alarm. Within a few days Alexander reorganised the order of battle. The Second American Army Corps had suffered a heavy defeat at the Kasserine Pass. But under General Alexander's quiet and efficient

control, by the end of February the line was wholly restored. Some
necessary delay must no doubt be faced in the formulation of the plans
for the final battle to eject the enemy from North Africa. But meanwhile British prestige rose high, partly from the splendid fighting
qualities displayed by our First Army, partly from the admirable way
in which Alexander had met the difficult situation, and still more from
the generous and diplomatic temper in which he had handled the
matter so as not to ruffle the feelings of our allies. All this had a
considerable reaction on General Eisenhower, the most generous of
men, and to some extent assisted me on the political aspect of affairs.

Meanwhile, on our front, within four weeks of the wholly negative
discussion which Murphy and I had with Giraud, the position was
suddenly and dramatically changed.

In the afternoon of 6 March, Murphy and I were formally and
ceremoniously informed that it was propsed to repeal *in toto* the
legislation which discriminated against the Jews. On 10 March we
were told that more far-reaching measures had now been agreed which
would be announced formally on 14 March in a speech by General
Giraud. On 16 March, General Bergeret and Jean Rigault resigned,
and the next day eight ordinances meeting almost all our demands
and giving legislative effect to the New Deal were officially promulgated.
Never, since the age of miracles, had a conversion been so rapid, so
thorough, or so apparently inexplicable.

All this was done by Giraud himself. He did not consult the
governors of the provinces. They were presented with a *fait accompli*.
Peyrouton, who was too intelligent to change his position too rapidly,
but moved with a certain dignity and grace, let it become known that
he was now a 'moderate New Dealer'. Noguès acquiesced without
making any difficulty. Boisson, who was able, hard and honest, made it
clear that he did not like it at all.

The vital point was General Giraud's speech, and we were consulted
as to the draft.

We were given a text on Saturday at 5 p.m. Work on it continued till the
early hours of Sunday morning. It was delivered at 6 p.m. on Sunday
afternoon.

The scene was quite impressive. The hall was well filled (about 500–600)
and the audience of Lorrainers and Alsatians. Murphy and I arrived together
at 5 p.m. and were put in the front row of the platform, next to two empty
seats—these being left for Giraud and Bergeret (with cards). There was a

musical performance till about 5.45 when Giraud arrived, attended only by an A.D.C. The chair prepared for Bergeret was hastily removed—and by this, of course, I knew that his resignation had been given. Peyrouton and Boisson were on the platform. Noguès had already returned to Morocco.

Giraud's speech was delivered (after a preliminary presentation of bouquets and cakes by small children and their appropriate osculation) in a simple and soldierly style, with no attempt at oratorical effect. The whole thing lasted under half an hour and was very well received by the audience.

After the meeting there was a Gaullist demonstration in the streets. I'm afraid Giraud was rather upset by this (or so he told me when I called on him the next day).[3]

The speech, followed by the announcement of the resignations of the most disliked Ministers, had considerable effect in the world Press. On Tuesday 16 March, a formal invitation to de Gaulle through Catroux was issued to the Press. It was correctly sent to General Catroux, who had now arrived in Algiers as the head of the Gaullist mission. Actually, Giraud's speech had contained an appeal for French unity and a thinly veiled overture to de Gaulle.

The changes in the administration, few but symbolic, and the publication of the new decrees completed the operation. The effect was all the greater since it was cumulative. In four days the obstacles had been cleared from the path leading to the union of all Frenchmen fighting against the Axis.

General Catroux, who never allowed himself to be rushed, after a short visit to Algiers had departed for the Levant. It was therefore not until his return that any real progress could be made.

Nevertheless, it was the New Deal and all that it implied which laid the foundations for negotiations between the Giraudists and the Gaullists. If they were not to reach a conclusion without many critical and anxious moments, that was all in the day's work. But at any rate, I felt that we had started along the road to fusion.

Before starting on the next phase of the French problem, I was fortunate in having a short change of scene. General Alexander invited me to stay a few days with him at his headquarters. It was indeed a welcome respite from the atmosphere of intrigue and confusion which surrounded us in Algiers. Makins and I left by aeroplane on the afternoon of 20 March and arrived at Alexander's headquarters after an uneventful flight.

[3] 19 March 1943.

The next day Alexander and I left early for a drive to different parts of the Front, stopping at the various headquarters of corps and divisions.

It was a very interesting experience. First I saw a great deal of the country in which the fighting is taking place and got a real idea of the terrain—an extraordinary sequence of great mountains and mountain passes leading into extensive plains.

Next, it gave me the chance of an uninterrupted and very valuable talk with Alexander about many problems of this and future campaigns, and of the many complicated problems which arise.

Lastly, it enabled me to learn something of the character of this very remarkable man. He has quite extraordinary charm. He has made simplicity the rule of his life. The whole atmosphere of the camp is dominated by his personality—modest, calm, confident.[4]

I was particularly impressed by Alexander's methods. We stopped at the headquarters of General Omar Bradley, commander of the Second Corps, which were in the railway station at a place called Fériana. He showed us upon the map how the battle was progressing, and there were certain dispositions and movements of troops of which I could see General Alexander did not altogether approve. By a brilliant piece of diplomacy, he suggested to his subordinate commander some moves which he might well make. He did not issue an order. He sold the American general the idea, and made him think he had thought of it all himself. This system, which he invariably pursued, made Alexander particularly fit to command an Allied army. Later, when he found himself in the Italian campaign controlling the troops of many countries, he developed this method into a remarkable technique. If Montgomery was the Wellington, Alexander was certainly the Marlborough of this war.

On the Sunday—or rather on the Saturday night—began the great battle which is now raging—with varying success. It is of vital importance. But I must say I have every confidence in Alexander bringing it off, if any man can. During Sunday, we drove over the country, saw a few officers, visited some . . . Roman remains (in which Tunisia is very rich). He neither asked for nor received messages or news. When we got back in the late evening, he showed neither anxiety nor nervousness.[5]

[4] 21 March 1943.
[5] Ibid.

During dinner, a message was brought in which was Montgomery's report of his first attack on the Mareth line. He did not open it till the end of the meal. A few other telegrams arrived and a few orders were quietly given. For the rest of the evening, after listening to Churchill's broadcast, we chatted about politics, sport, architecture, Roman history and the like.

On the 22nd we returned to Algiers to the daily round of telegrams, meetings, luncheons, dinners and rumours which constituted our life there. The next few days were ones of waiting.

Yesterday (Thursday the 25th) there was a tremendous funeral ceremony in the Cathedral . . . Colonel Baril had been killed in an air accident. He was a remarkable and quite charming man, with whom I made great friends. He is a great loss to France and to us. It was through his work (largely) that the landings at Sidi Ferruch (near Algiers) and at Blida were practically unopposed, and he would have been a useful link in the de Gaulle–Giraud negotiations, since he had the respect and affection of both sides.

The funeral was a terrific ecclesiastical and civil ceremony—with speeches, march past of troops, etc. The British detachment (Irish Guards) took everyone's breath away, so splendid was their bearing.[6]

We were still waiting for General Catroux's arrival from Syria.

No doubt there will be some tricky and anxious moments, but I feel in my bones that we shall bring it off in the end. I think both sides are beginning to realise that the people of France will never forgive them if they go on squabbling while France is in agony.[7]

The news from the Front remained good.

The battle of Mareth has been very severe, but I felt great confidence in Alexander and Montgomery and I gather that the air support was really tremendous. If only we can get fine weather, the aerodromes will dry up and allow our air superiority to be used to the full.

If we can bring off a really resounding defeat of the Germans and Italians, the moral effect here will be tremendous. For there are still many hesitant Frenchmen, oppressed with the sense of defeat and almost mesmerised by German power.

Meanwhile, there is every day some improvement in things here—some rascal dismissed and a good man put in his place.[8]

The New Deal was beginning to work.

[6] 26 March 1943.
[7] Ibid.
[8] 31 March 1943.

CHAPTER THIRTEEN

The Path to Union

WHILE steady and indeed commendably rapid progress was being made in implementing General Giraud's New Deal on the legislative and administrative side, no parallel steps were being taken to make necessary changes in the command of the armed forces and in the highest ranks of the provincial Governments. The whole administration was still weak and centred far too much upon Giraud's personal authority. Nevertheless, certain improvements were made. The appointment of Dr. Jules Abadie as Secretary of the Interior, in succession to Rigault, was welcome. Dr. Abadie was a distinguished surgeon of liberal opinions and was said to be already sharpening his knives with a view to the necessary operations upon his section of the Government. Two days later, on 25 March, Maurice Couve de Murville was made Secretary-General in succession to Bergeret. It is a tribute to the former's breadth of view that on arrival from Spain he was ready to take a position under General Giraud. The British Treasury informed me that they had the highest opinion of his intelligence and his probity. He has since had a distinguished career under de Gaulle. We made then a friendship which has continued through many years. René Mayer became Secretary for Communications. This appointment was novel in two respects. In the first place, he was a Jew; and, secondly, he was an expert in the matters with which he was to be entrusted. On 27 March, M. Muscatelli, who had been one of our supporters at the time of the landings and had been removed from his position as Director of Police after the Darlan murder and for some time confined to prison, replaced Temple as Prefect of Algiers. Since Temple's appointment dated from Laval's time, this change had considerable significance. On the same day, Lemaigre-Dubreuil and all his staff handed in their resignations; which, somewhat to their surprise, and much to their chagrin, were immediately accepted. This by no

means ended Lemaigre-Dubreuil's activities, although they were temporarily transferred from the political to the social field.

All this had a considerable effect in strengthening the administration. If changes had been made at the same time in the Governors of
Algeria, Morocco and West Africa, public opinion would have been
satisfied and de Gaulle's complaints and hesitations fully met. As
usual, however, Giraud moved too slowly and too late.

Although great pressure was brought upon de Gaulle in London to
reach a rapid accommodation with Giraud, he held out for a specific
reply to the important memorandum which he had communicated to
Giraud on 23 February. This document, which was published on 12
March, set out his conditions. The armistice must be repudiated. In all
French territories, the old and fundamental freedoms must be restored, subject, of course, to military necessities. There must be
freedom of thought, free meeting of trade unions, and the equality of
all citizens before the law. The release of those improperly imprisoned
must be carried out with increasing speed. All the laws passed under
the influence of the Nazi occupation of France must be regarded as
null and void. Finally, it must be made clear that any authority acting
for the French people during the war accepted the principle of an
election based on universal suffrage after the liberation of France. De
Gaulle also suggested that, in addition to the provisional central
authority, it would be useful to create a consultative council which
might draw its representatives from resistance groups, former Deputies
and perhaps from universities and trade unions.[1] De Gaulle, therefore, not unreasonably, responded to Giraud's New Deal speech by
asking for a specific answer to his memorandum.

All this time, increasing numbers of the Gaullist mission, as well as
other Frenchmen, were arriving in Algiers. Perhaps the most striking
was Colonel Pechkoff, with his splendid row of medals and his one
arm. This officer was said to be the natural son of Maxim Gorky. I
remember thinking that, if so, his mother must certainly have been
Ouida, for if one could imagine a blend between these two literary
styles taking human form, it would certainly be best incarnated in the
person of the gallant Colonel. The newcomers included many who had
grievances against de Gaulle or had quarrelled with him. Among these

[1] Charles de Gaulle, *Mémoires de Guerre: L'Unité, 1942–1944* (Paris, 1956),
pp. 92, 446.

were Admiral Muselier and some of his officers, together with more severe critics like Cambon and Comert.

General Catroux finally returned and called to see me on 30 March. This remarkable Frenchman played a unique role at this troubled time. Calm, reasonable, infinitely patient, he was indeed a friend on whom we could all rely. He already had behind him a distinguished career, chiefly in the French Colonial Empire. He was a five-star general. He could therefore talk on equal terms with Giraud. He enjoyed the admiration and affection of de Gaulle, but was by no means blind to his faults. If de Gaulle went too far or was too intransigent, Catroux would be firm as well as persuasive. De Gaulle knew that he could not push Catroux beyond a certain point without risking his resignation—an event which at that time would have been fatal to him and his movement. Catroux did not believe that progress could be very rapid. But he seemed confident that on the basis of his long friendship with Giraud he could gradually persuade him to adopt a reasonable position.

In our anxiety for quick results, perhaps many of us did not altogether realise the fundamental difference between the position of the French National Committee and that of Giraud and his friends. As de Gaulle has brought out in his own account of these days, however regrettable political questions might be in the middle of war, they were of paramount importance: 'It is not our fault if France is . . . undergoing a virtual revolution at the same time as being at war.'[2] He was determined to see a strong and independent French Government in being when liberation came. He even believed that without such a Government the liberation of France would merely mean exchanging German domination for Anglo-Saxon.[3]

Giraud could not see the importance of this aspect of the problem. All he thought necessary was a provisional central authority consisting of the governors and perhaps other nominees of the two sides. While he was soon to agree that he would only have the same powers as the other president or presidents (if there were to be three in all), he still demanded a position of real supremacy. For Catroux could not, at this point, persuade him to abandon his proposed double role of co-president and also Commander-in-Chief of the forces. Given these

2 De Gaulle, p. 452.
3 Ibid., p. 95.

posts, he would not object to de Gaulle acting as chairman of the
Central Committee. But de Gaulle felt that this plan gave Giraud too
much power. He now proposed to come himself to Algiers for personal
discussion. This request, for some reason, was something of a bomb-
shell at A.F.H.Q. Even Monnet felt that a most difficult position
would arise if de Gaulle were to arrive in the present state of the
negotiations.

During discussion at our Political and Economic Council, the
Americans were strongly against de Gaulle being allowed to come to
Algiers at this stage. The Battle of Tunis was about to reach its crisis
and nobody wanted public demonstrations in Algiers until it had been
won. Catroux himself felt indignant at not being allowed to continue
the negotiations quietly. He even threatened to throw in his hand. At
the same time, I was very doubtful of the wisdom of any action by the
Supreme Allied Commander which actually prohibited de Gaulle's
arrival. I felt this would be attributed to the old distrust and even
malevolence on the part of the Americans. We therefore sent on 3
April, after much discussion, a message which was a plea from General
Eisenhower, from one soldier to another, not to complicate the situation until the military operations now moving rapidly to their culmination had been concluded. We had moreover to deal with the
problem of General Catroux's possible resignation. I seemed to me the
best plan would be to persuade Catroux to go back to London and
talk to de Gaulle; but this at the moment he was unwilling to do.

On 6 April I found the situation at headquarters one of violent
indignation. De Gaulle had published a communiqué implying that
he had been prevented by General Eisenhower from coming to North
Africa to conclude a French union. This resulted in very hostile
criticism of Eisenhower in the American as well as the British Press.
The Chief of Staff felt that we had badly let down Eisenhower and
expressed his opinions in strong and idiomatic language. I therefore
went to see Catroux the same night. He repeated his protestations that
he would have nothing to do with the 'politique' which General de
Gaulle seemed to be following. He would not associate himself with a
visit from de Gaulle, the object of which seemed to be to stir up
political animosities, to hold public meetings, to stimulate demonstrations and all the rest. I told him that General Eisenhower and the
British and American Governments had taken on themselves the

responsibility for avoiding a rupture between him and de Gaulle and he must therefore play his part. After some reflection, Catroux agreed that it was his duty to go to London. Accordingly he left Algiers on 8 April. During the next few days the feelings of the American Army Command cooled down.

Giraud's new suggestions which Catroux took to London were not immediately acceptable. But they showed an advance. De Gaulle rejected them, still demanding the formation of an authority for all territories which had been or would be liberated, including metropolitan France, to which all French forces should be answerable. He repeated his view that all generals, governors and even the Commander-in-Chief himself should be under the orders of this authority. In other words, the new system must function in the normal democratic way; officials, civil and military, must obey the instructions of Ministers. Finally, he repeated his demand for the dismissal of what he called Vichy 'capitulators and collaborators'.

Thus when Catroux returned on 18 April there was little sign of progress except a conciliatory, if somewhat patronising, message received by Eisenhower from de Gaulle sending his congratulations and good wishes for the battle then in progress. Catroux remained calm, and on 21 April Eisenhower somewhat surprisingly informed me that he proposed to tell Catroux that so far as he was concerned de Gaulle could come to North Africa at any time he liked. On this Giraud—as always in a period of crisis—left for the Front and did not return until Easter Sunday, 25 April. The following day, Easter Monday, he asked me to call at the Palais d'Été. He was in a stubborn, egotistical and even defiant mood. He had made a complete tour of the Front from north to south—three busy days. He was gratified to find that all the ideas which he had put forward for the conduct of the battle had been acceptable to General Alexander and the other generals. He had also explained to them in detail his views on the next operation, which we called 'Husky' but to which the French referred quite unblushingly by the name of the country concerned. All his plans had received ready acceptance on the part of the British commander, by whose attitude he had been delighted. I suppose that he had misconstrued General Alexander's good manners and his respect for age and experience.

He then proceeded to argue about de Gaulle's demands that the armistice should be regarded as null and void. He had never gone as far as this. He accepted the armistice as a fact. He was not responsible for it, but he accepted it. But it had come to an end in November 1942 when he, General Giraud, denounced it. 'I did so,' he cried exultantly, 'when I instructed the troops to fire upon the Germans in Tunisia.' I observed that General de Gaulle had done the same thing three years ago. But this was swept aside. However, the real points of difference did now emerge. De Gaulle wanted a Government like a pre-war Cabinet. Giraud wanted the ultimate authority to remain with the Commander-in-Chief. He must control economic and financial matters which had their effect on the conduct of the war. He went on to say that our Prime Minister, Churchill, was Commander-in-Chief. I demurred at this. 'Oh yes, it is so, for I know. He showed me all his maps at Anfa.' I replied that Churchill was Minister of Defence and if that was what Giraud meant by Commander-in-Chief, there was no reason why such a Minister should not sit in the Cabinet. In that case, he would give the Cabinet's orders to the appropriate military—and in some cases even civil—commanders. But Giraud regarded all this as really an attack upon his authority. Nor did he agree with de Gaulle's views as to what should happen after the liberation of France. He believed there should be a military Government followed by a meeting of the Conseils-Généraux. Finally, he could not abandon those high officers like Boisson or even Peyrouton, whom he did not regard as traitors. I said I thought this could be a matter of negotiation when the time came to form a new administration. We then discussed the question of the inner council which Giraud wanted to see formed, like our War Cabinet. If he was to be Commander-in-Chief, then he would presumably give the position of Président de Conseil to de Gaulle. 'No, no,' he said, 'that is impossible. De Gaulle is fifteen years younger and only a general of the second grade.' I replied that Pitt was Prime Minister of England when only twenty-four years of age.

He concluded with a harangue in a majestic manner about the French Army. The Army had fought splendidly in spite of its weakness. He had 450,000 men, one-third of them French. How could he persuade them to accept de Gaulle at all? They had no sympathy with what de Gaulle had done. I observed that this surely did not apply to the younger men of the Army or to civilians. But Giraud insisted that he knew the Army and that they were all for him. As to civilians, their views in war were not important. He had held the line in Tunisia. He had held it when the Americans had collapsed before the German counter-attack. He clearly regarded himself as responsible for the tactics and strategy of the present operations. He did not want a civil Government, wasting money upon Ministers and portfolios. Why should he give in to de Gaulle, who after all had only 12,000 men? Altogether Giraud was in an excited and quite intransigent mood on this night. It was the usual result of his visits to the Front. Happily, although he was subject to these emotions, he was quick to change. I told him frankly that if he demanded both the positions of Président de Conseil and Commander-in-Chief, that is in effect 'Commandant en Chef Civil et Militaire', he would not be supported by public opinion; certainly not in Britain. Why were we such Gaullists in Britain? he demanded. I replied that de Gaulle had stood by us when we had not a friend in the world. He had held French Equatorial Africa. If Boisson had done the same, we could have been in North Africa a year earlier.

I ended by declaring that our people had long memories and did not like to abandon those friends who had stood by us in the hour of need. At this he was touched; for he was a generous, if not very intelligent, man. He understood our feelings and respected them. But he, too, had a duty to perform; the danger was Communism, and he would not yield to it.

During this interval, Murphy and I had become the joint chairmen of an international commission investigating the problem of the prison camps. The work of cleaning up this situation was not an easy one; but gradually we made good progress. We even managed to get the Mexican Government to accept 3,000 Spanish Republican internees. Prisoners belonging to Allied countries were released and either repatriated if their countries were not in Axis hands, or allowed to join their respective armies on British soil. Thus, in spite of the difficulties, the numbers came down; and, if I remember aright, by the end of this operation only somewhere between one and two hundred had to be kept in prison as definite criminals. All the rest were dealt with in one way or another. This question had caused a great deal of feeling in Britain and Parliament until it was resolved. As usual, when the grievance was removed, nobody bothered any more about it, and we got no particular thanks.

With very few exceptions, the British Press and public regarded the clash between Giraud and de Gaulle as a mere question of personal ambition. Only a few realised that there was a serious conflict of principles. The personal question nevertheless played an important role. Giraud, after his unpromising and frustrating talk with me on Easter Monday, suddenly changed his views and on the 27th handed to Catroux a new memorandum, together with an invitation to de Gaulle to meet him either at Biskra or Marrakesh for a quiet discussion. All this was in a different mood from that in which he had orated to me. It was obvious that either as a result of my arguments or because of Monnet's pressure, Giraud had once more changed his ground. The memorandum in itself showed considerable progress, although, as I expected, de Gaulle immediately raised difficulties about being asked to come to some 'hole-in-the-corner meeting'.[4]

The next few days were spent in an interchange of telegrams of the style to which we had become accustomed in an Algerian crisis. However, as usual,

a period of frantic activity was succeeded by a period of comparative calm. It certainly appeared that the starters in this particular race had a difficult task. General de Gaulle is one of those horses which either refuse to come to the starting gate at all, or insist in careering down the course before the signal is given, or suddenly elect to run on a racecourse different from the one appointed by the Stewards of the Jockey Club. There is something almost comical in the alternation between his refusal to accept an invitation to come to North Africa and his insistence upon arriving as an uninvited guest. It seemed that the consummation of French union must depend upon some happy moment when he was both invited to the feast, willing to attend it, and complaisant about the rendezvous.

In spite of the delay, I still felt fairly confident, for after all not only did Giraud's memorandum set out quite laudable principles, but a clear intimation had been given that Giraud would now be prepared to concede to de Gaulle the position of joint president of the General Council, or War Cabinet, which was to be formed.

On 2 May de Gaulle in a long message declared his willingness to hold the meeting if it could be held in Algiers, and I was about to use my influence to secure that this concession should be made when the atmosphere was once again darkened by a speech which de Gaulle delivered two days later, on 4 May. This constituted a wounding attack on Giraud in bitter and sarcastic terms. When the speech was

[4] Ibid., pp. 467–9.

discussed at a conference which Murphy and I held with Giraud, Catroux and Monnet, the outlook seemed rather black. However, Giraud's temper seemed completely restored when he lunched with me the following day. The icy disapproval of the night before melted easily in the genial warmth of two French princesses whom I had taken the precaution of inviting.

As he left the house, he pointed to the sky and said, 'Du calme, mon cher ami, et du courage—surtout, du calme.'

We now had to prepare the reply to be made to de Gaulle's last telegram, since the ball was now, as it were, in Giraud's court. Whatever else was clear about this document, it was soon apparent that Giraud was not to be allowed to write it. His function was to swallow it. I remember observing at this conference that whatever they might feel about the tone of de Gaulle's speech, they could not break off a negotiation simply on the ground that one politician made an offensive speech about another. I told them that in my country this was almost the recognised procedure, preliminary to forming a coalition Government. Although this seemed rather to shock Murphy, it amused Monnet. I also told them that for a great country to remain divided because no one could decide whether a negotiation for a National Government should take place in London or Brighton seemed absurd.

If you fear de Gaulle and want to call the whole thing off, you must break on a question of principle. Make him accept your principles—especially the two you think vital, namely:
1. Cabinet government *not* personal government.
2. No attempt to form a Government for post-war France but the proper constitutional procedure according to laws of the Republic.
If he accepts these points, let him come to Algiers. If he doesn't, don't let him come at all.[5]

The war news now began to have a decisive effect. On 7 May, the American Second Corps entered Bizerta and on the same day the British First Army occupied Tunis. Back in Algiers an imposing ceremony took place. Giraud, supported by Catroux, formally accepted from Eisenhower a large quantity of new equipment for the French Army. On the morning of Sunday the 9th, St. Joan of Arc's

[5] 5 May 1943.

Day, although we missed her spiritual descendant, a great procession took place of the new war material.

During these days of waiting, everyone became very excited except Catroux, who remained characteristically calm. At last, partly as a result of long disappearances by Monnet and myself to the quiet seaside resort of Tipasa, with its Roman city and wonderful bathing, the required document was produced. We were very anxious that this reply, which was ultimately agreed on 17 May, should be short and even, so far as a political paper can be, snappy. It must bear publication.

If it was to be intelligible to the British and American people, it would also have to be understood by General Giraud. In this dilemma it seemed necessary to ask de Gaulle only to reply to two points. It was a close-run thing. General Giraud was so disturbed by de Gaulle's activities that he had actually prepared a document in fact breaking off the negotiations. Yet by the evening of the 17th a final reply was officially given by General Giraud to Murphy and myself.

Accordingly, on the 17th Giraud's reply was dispatched. It was the work of Monnet and, to some extent, of myself. It was sent by Giraud reluctantly and without enthusiasm. It did not really correspond with the General's feelings, but it sufficed. In effect, Giraud's proposals were as follows:

An Executive Committee should be set up in Algiers as soon as possible, to control all matters now handled by F.N.C. London and C.-in-C. Military and Civil Algiers. Among other functions, it should organise a National Consultative Council and a Committee of Resistance. There should be a dual presidency and collective responsibility. The Committee should function only until such time as a Provisional Government could be set up in France. 'We are not and cannot be the Government of France.'

At this very time, an event took place which made us all feel renewed sympathy for Giraud. He had just heard that the Germans had carried away his married daughter and all her children. She was living in Tunis, her husband being an officer in a North African regiment. He could get no news of her, and this was a terrible and tragic blow at this critical moment. Really, there seemed to be no limit to the pettiness and cruelty of the Germans.

After we had sent off this last offer, it was clear that Catroux should

himself go to London to explain it. On the 19th I made up my mind
that I would accompany him. I felt that we should never improve
upon Giraud's proposals—a Cabinet with collective responsibility and
a joint premiership with de Gaulle. Catroux would no doubt have
more influence upon de Gaulle than any other man. But I felt it
important that the British Government should also bring the maximum pressure to bear. After all, we were paying enormous subsidies to
the Gaullists and we had, therefore, the power, as well as the duty, to
influence de Gaulle's decision. Eden agreed with my suggestion, and
accordingly I set out with Catroux on this mission of peace on 21 May.
But before that there was one really memorable day on which all the
mists and confusions of Algiers were dissipated by the sun of victory.
For on 13 May the Tunisian campaign was brought to its triumphant
end.

Since my visit to General Alexander's headquarters he had found, as a
result of the Eighth Army's attack on 24 April, that the Enfidaville
position was too strong to be overcome without heavy loss. He therefore transferred three divisions from the Eighth Army to the First
Army's command. On 6 May the culminating attack was launched,
supported by a supreme effort from the Allied air forces with 2,500
sorties in one day.[6] At the same time a complete blockade by sea and
air was established.

  By 8 May the circle was complete, the armies from east and west
having joined hands. It was only a matter of days before the end came.
On 13 May General Alexander was able to report to the Prime
Minister that the Tunisian campaign was over and all enemy resistance had ceased. Thus the disappointments and delays of the early
months of the year were now gloriously obliterated. Hitler, with
characteristic obstinacy, had poured troops into the steadily diminish-
ing area still in his control. The final result therefore involved not
merely the loss of the last hold of the Axis powers in Africa, but was a
serious blow to some of the finest German military and air formations.
The magnitude of the victory which ended the war in Africa is best
summed up in Churchill's own words to the United States Congress.

  The African excursions of the two Dictators have cost their countries in
killed and captured 950,000 soldiers. In addition nearly 2,400,000 gross tons of

  [6] Churchill, *The Hinge of Fate*, p. 692.

shipping have been sunk and nearly 8,000 aircraft destroyed, both of these figures being exclusive of large numbers of ships and aircraft damaged. There have also been lost to the enemy 6,200 guns, 2,550 tanks, and 70,000 trucks. . . . Arrived at this milestone in the war, we can say, 'One continent redeemed'. . . .[7]

At no time, perhaps, in the whole of the Second World War did the prestige and power of Britain stand so high. British armies had cleared the treacherous Italians out of East Africa and liberated Abyssinia. British armies, after two years of fluctuating fortune involving tragic and almost despairing moments, had gained the decisive victory at Alamein. In the forces moving from the west, British troops still predominated. The American Air Force had of course given immense support to the R.A.F. But here again it was under British leadership that the Germans were outmatched. It was under a British commander that Allied naval forces had completed their encircling and blockading task. As a result of Hitler's strategic error we found ourselves with an enormous booty. General von Arnim had been captured. The prisoners were said to number about 250,000, 150,000 of whom were German. Thousands of guns, tanks, vehicles and other weapons had been taken. Many of our own prisoners had been released.

Owing to the modesty and charm of General Alexander and of the other British officers—Tedder and Cunningham—the Americans felt no jealousy, but rather shared with brotherly affection in the mutual congratulations by which each nation saluted the other's prowess. No less credit was due to General Eisenhower, the Supreme Allied Commander; for it was under his authority and through his guidance that the whole Allied forces were welded together.

Although the minds of all these men and their planning staffs had already been turned to the next operation, the conquest of Sicily, it was felt that there should be a fitting celebration of this outstanding victory. Accordingly, a review was organised which proved a remarkable and unforgettable spectacle. It was the happiest kind of parade, for all the troops who were not wanted for duty were in the audience; and the audience comprised also the whole civil population, European and Arab alike. A few civilians were invited to take part—Makins and I, Murphy, Reber and Jean Monnet. Murphy and I stood at the back of the saluting base. Eisenhower, with true courtesy, had placed

[7] Ibid., p. 714.

Giraud at his side and immediately behind them stood Cunningham, Alexander and Tedder. Each side of the platform was guarded by a Churchill tank.

Leaving Algiers at 7 in the morning we all reached Tunis about 10 o'clock. Our procession from the airfield to the saluting base was led by the great notabilities of the Allied armies, navies and air forces. But since they were in closed cars they were scarcely recognised. At the end of the queue came the representatives of the civil power—Murphy and I—and it was generally conceded that the honours of this part of the day went to us.

At the end of the procession of closed cars and unseen generals came an open 'command car' (a sort of superior jeep), and perched upon this, as in a Roman chariot, were Murphy and I. Immediately in front of us were the flags of our respective countries—the Stars and Stripes and the Union Jack—and (since we had the flags and were the only people who could actually be seen) I can tell you that our procession through the streets of Tunis was like driving through Stockton on Polling Day.[8]

Murphy, although a career diplomatist and inexperienced in the art of popular elections, began to enjoy these new sensations.

Every street was packed; every window in every house was packed; every roof was packed. When the people saw our flags, they cheered and waved and threw flowers. We cheered and waved and kissed our hands to the ladies on the roofs and in the windows and on the street. It was a magnificent progress. Troops presenting arms; people cheering. It was much commented on. If ever I am forced out of English public life, I shall certainly put up for Mayor of Tunis.

About 30,000 troops took part in the parade, which lasted over two hours. The atmosphere was very cheerful, like a jolly football crowd. First came the French—Zouaves, Tirailleurs, Moroccan and Algerian native troops, and the Foreign Legion.

The procession was led by a detachment of Spahis, making a brave show with their white horses, red cloaks, red leather saddles and drawn swords. As they passed the saluting base they rose in their saddles.

The men made a splendid show, but their arms and clothing were sadly out of date—antiquated rifles, torn cloaks, slippers or bare feet. The Moroccan Goums, who had fought very well and very murder-

[8] 20 May 1943.

ously, received an enthusiastic reception from our troops. Everyone realised what a brave performance they had put up through all these hard months with such poor equipment and material.

After the French came American regiments, representing the American Second Corps. They were led by a fine brass band.

In contrast to the French, the American equipment and clothing is almost indecently rich. Every private soldier has a pair of lovely brown leather shoes with rubber soles. (Incidentally, you cannot march in rubber soles—I mean from the dramatic or review standpoint.) He also has a pair of leather gloves which would cost me a fiver in England; he has a wonderful kind of golfing jacket, a splendid helmet, lots of gadgets hung round, and is altogether a very expensive fellow who has cost his national treasury a lot of money.

The Americans marched well and got great applause, and everyone seemed happy and pleased.

By that time an hour or more had passed and I thought that we would have a small British detachment and then all would be over. But for once the British had decided to put on a really dramatic display which would take everyone by surprise. After the Americans had passed there was a slight pause. Then, coming from far off, a faint sound of pipes. Somebody had collected together all the available pipers from the First and Eighth Armies. Scots Guards, Irish Guards and all the Highland Regiments were represented. When they approached the saluting base they broke into slow time. Then they countermarched—each line wheeling and passing through—one of the most effective of all drills, and then in due course broke into quick time and marched away into the distance with the sound of pipes gradually dying away. Another pause, just long enough for us to wonder whether there had been some hitch; and then the British Army marched past, 14,000 men in all, each division and brigade led by its general and his staff, each battalion by its colonel.

In a long file they came, formation after formation, regiment after regiment, unit after unit.

Unlike the French and Americans the British were in drill, not battle, order—shorts, stockings and boots, battle blouses or shirts with short sleeves—no helmets (forage caps and berets). The helmet gives a soldier the look of a robot. . . . With the forage cap or beret you can see his face—his jolly honest, sunburnt, smiling English, Scottish or Irish face—relaxed now, not worn or harassed as men look in battle—and confident and proud. All these brown faces, these brown bare arms and knees, these swinging striding outstepping men—all marched magnificently.

Just before the saluting base (a very old parade trick) there was stationed a band. This of course got all the men marching at their best before they reached the saluting point.

My mind went back to Kitchener's Army and the Battle of the Somme. I had always thought that these were the finest British formations that had ever taken the field. But now I had to admit that the First and Eighth Armies were just as good. These men seemed on that day masters of the world and heirs of the future.

After the Infantry, the guns, armoured cars and tanks, Derbyshire Yeomanry leading. . . . Guns and tanks polished and shining; the great trailers for the guns, the lorries, the cars—a magnificent and Roman progress. With our troops, Colonel Leclerc's regiment of Free French (who came from Lake Chad) and refused to march with the French, preferring English for companions. (Incidentally, the two kinds of French troops—Gaullists and Giraudists, now that there are no Germans to fight, will soon start a civil war amongst themselves, unless my mission to London is successful.)

At last the parade ended and we all moved off for a sumptuous luncheon at the Palace of the French Resident-General.

The *only* subject (almost embarrassingly so) of conversation among *all* the French and Americans was the British parade.

I must say that they were all very generous. Giraud said that when he had seen the Eighth Army at Sfax, he thought they must be unique. Now he had seen the First Army he realised that it was as good. He said that in his whole life he had never seen such a body of men. All that old Ike (Eisenhower) could do was to say ecstatically to me and others (and repeat it the next day) that he had never believed it possible to dream of having such an honour as to command an army like this. Really, it has been a grand day.

It ended with a courtesy call on the new Bey of Tunis, the late one having been recently deposed. Here all the military notabilities received medals of various degrees of splendour. My parcel included the insignia of some exotic order. The remarkable feature of it was that the colours were the same as the M.C.C.'s. It was destined to give me a lot of trouble, for not knowing the rules about political Ministers receiving foreign decorations I took it home and left it in the cupboard of the nursery of the cottage which we now occupied. I thought it would do well for charades. A long correspondence followed with an official at the Foreign Office ordering me to send it back. I could only suggest that application should be made to my wife. After several months the exasperated official wrote to tell me that he had not succeeded in getting her to answer any of his letters. I suggested that he should either telegraph or telephone; but this must have been contrary to some protocol, and nothing more was heard about the question.

Eisenhower kindly gave me a place in his aeroplane back to Algiers. As we passed Bizerta we saw approaching the first convoy to attempt the Mediterranean passage since 1941. It had left Gibraltar a few days before, and was to reach Alexandria without loss. To look down upon this great armada was indeed to see a striking proof of what had been at last accomplished. I turned to Eisenhower and said, 'There, General, are the fruits of your victory.' He turned to me and said, smiling through his tears, for he was deeply moved, 'Ours, you mean, ours— that we have all won together.'

On the next day, 21 May, after talks with Cunningham, Murphy and Monnet, and a short call on Giraud, I went to see Eisenhower at noon. He was as usual very friendly. He gave me a Flying Fortress to take Catroux and me to England and bring us back: 'Come back as soon as you can. I don't want to be without you.' Eisenhower fully agreed with the urgent need to bring the present political situation to a close. Paradoxically, victory had increased the danger of incidents between the Gaullist and the Giraudist troops and the need for a quick settlement.

Without a common enemy, the forces of both French groups began to drift apart. De Larminat's Fighting French division from the Middle East was said to be actively recruiting in Tunis by offers of higher pay, advances in rank and other inducements. According to our information the French troops were in any case overwhelmingly Gaullists.

On the day after I left Algiers (22 May) there was a fresh complication. An ill-timed message was sent to de Gaulle from the Central committee of Resistance in France recognising him as the sole leader of French resistance. This was given wide publicity in the Algiers Press. However, somehow or other, Murphy and Makins managed to gloss this over, and Giraud was comforted. But he was quite immovable when Murphy called upon him on the 24th and asked for the dismissal of General Mendigal, an active Pétainist, much distrusted by the Allied Air Command. Giraud, while never fully understanding constitutional problems, was always very sensitive about individuals. It was, therefore, vital that we should persuade de Gaulle to accept Giraud's proposal without more ado. Any hesitation would certainly have resulted in a final breakdown.

Although I had the help and sympathy of Eden, as Foreign Secretary, the absence of Churchill in Washington was a considerable handicap. He had gone for most vital discussions on war strategy. His purpose was to persuade the reluctant Americans to exploit the situation in the Mediterranean and to follow up the impending occupation of Sicily as rapidly as possible. To this end he used all his skill and energy in exposition and argument. But as he himself says:

A very stern mood developed in Washington about de Gaulle. Not a day passed that the President did not mention the subject to me. Although this was done in a most friendly and often jocular manner, I saw he felt very strongly indeed about it.[9]

Churchill himself shared some of these apprehensions; but his main difficulty was that he feared that the continued support of de Gaulle would lead to an estrangement between the British and American Governments. These views he transmitted, in forcible terms, to his colleagues in the War Cabinet. Eden told me that they had unanimously agreed that a break with de Gaulle would now be fatal. Everyone had been very brave in the Prime Minister's absence![10] They also pointed out, basing themselves upon my own advice, that the chances of French union were now growing and that it would be a terrible error to throw away the opportunity at this critical moment. Churchill accepted this and was prepared to await the outcome.

Catroux presented the arguments for an immediate acceptance of Giraud's offer with his usual lucidity at a meeting at which I was present. Afterwards, de Gaulle received me alone, and I did my best to add my counsel with such powers of persuasion as I possessed. De Gaulle was in a calm and even benevolent mood. Nor, indeed, could there be any possible reason for refusal, since he had clearly gained the main points of principle for which he had contested so long and so

[9] Churchill, *The Hinge of Fate*, p. 716.
[10] The Earl of Avon, *The Eden Memoirs: The Reckoning* (London, 1965), p. 386.

strenuously. On 24 May, therefore, he sent a friendly message to Giraud accepting his two conditions. In return, it was arranged, with the approval of Giraud himself and of General Eisenhower, that de Gaulle should come to Algiers immediately. The date was fixed for 30 May.

On my return journey, I stopped again at Gibraltar, where I found Churchill and all his staff, together with General Marshall. They had arrived the night before from Washington. I went in to see the Prime Minister, who was in bed. After the little wrangle about Force X,[11] he went on to tell me about all the difficulties he had encountered in Washington, with daily and almost hourly attacks by the President and other Americans upon de Gaulle. But I thought he seemed relieved that we had surmounted the first hurdle and that we could now proceed. I took Catroux in to see him, and he was exceedingly polite to the General. We all went on to Algiers—Churchill, General Marshall, and a number of other notabilities. As before, Churchill stayed in Admiral Cunningham's villa, and in this genial atmosphere it was a relief to listen to thrilling plans for future military operations instead of our tangled political disputes. Eden joined us at Algiers the next day. Luckily, Churchill's talks with Marshall had gone very well, and he and Eden were in a relaxed mood and treated their visit as something of a holiday. On the other hand, General Georges had just been brought from France. This elderly survival of the old French Army was a friend of Churchill's, and he had been brought out at his special request to assist Giraud. Eden rightly summed him up as 'a reactionary old defeatist'.[12] He certainly was to cause me a good deal of difficulty during the next few months.

De Gaulle's arrival went off successfully. He landed, characteristically, in a French aircraft on a small landing ground under French control. He brought with him René Massigli and André Philip, who were his two nominees to the Committee which was now to be set up. Pierre Billotte and Gaston Palewski came on his personal staff. He was met by Giraud, and the two generals drove off together to the Palais d'Été. It was not till the next day that I heard from Monnet an account of what had taken place since de Gaulle's arrival. Monnet had had a long talk with him on the evening of Sunday 30 May, lasting for

[11] See above, p. 228.
[12] The Earl of Avon, p. 388.

some three hours. According to him, de Gaulle's mood seemed to vary from comparative calm to extreme excitability. He was clearly very hostile to the Americans and, to a somewhat lesser extent, to the British. In the course of conversation, he observed that the Anglo-Saxon domination of Europe was a mounting threat, and that if it continued, France after the war would have to lean towards Germany and Russia.

On the following morning Giraud, de Gaulle, Georges, Monnet, Massigli and Philip met together. Georges and Monnet were Giraud's nominees; de Gaulle had brought Massigli and Philip. They were supposed to constitute the new Executive Committee. Catroux was also present by general agreement. There was no agenda and no secretary, and the proceedings were mismanaged from the start. Giraud opened the proceedings by asking if anyone had anything to say! This gave de Gaulle the opportunity for a long and discursive speech involving a violent attack on the whole management of affairs in North Africa. He was especially bitter on personalities. 'We must quickly,' he declared, 'get out of this *marasme.*' It was an indispensable condition that Boisson, Peyrouton, Noguès, Generals Mendigal and Prioux, as well as Admiral Michelier should be dismissed. Georges, it seems, followed with a rambling and largely irrelevant reply. It was obvious that de Gaulle was infuriated at finding opposite him an elderly general who had opposed the modernisation of the French Army and who had then led it to utter disaster. Georges was equally indignant at the attitude of the young colonel who had proved him to be wrong. This antagonism was at the bottom of much of the trouble that followed in the ensuing days. Giraud spoke in a conciliatory way, but little progress was made. Monnet wisely observed that the first thing to do was to form the Committee. He added that if it would be of any assistance, he might say that, so far as he was concerned, when the Committee had been formed and got down to consider appointments, he would himself be in favour of radical changes. He would accept most, if not all, of de Gaulle's demands. Catroux naturally tried to build a bridge, and after more discussion de Gaulle stated that the matter could not now be taken any further, and he would see Giraud privately at 3 o'clock that afternoon. Another meeting of the seven had been called for 5 p.m. but had subsequently been cancelled.

I am afraid I could not resist telling Monnet that he had behaved foolishly in not calling attention to the fact that there was no motion before the Committee. What he ought to have done was to move that the seven individuals present should constitute the Executive Committee charged with French interests and asked somebody to second his motion. Then at least some progress would have been made. Monnet regretfully agreed and blamed himself for not having taken this line. However, there was little more that I could do that night. We would have to start the next morning. Accordingly, at 8.30 a.m. on 1 June I went to see Giraud. He began by congratulating me warmly on my appointment as Viceroy of India, about which there had been some rumours in the Press. I disclaimed that this high honour was to come to me; and after some further conversation on neutral topics, he came to the real point. He gave an account of the previous day's proceedings which tallied with that already given me by Monnet. At the meeting between him and de Gaulle at 3 o'clock, the latter had repeated his statement that he could not work on the Committee unless the men whom he named had first been dismissed. He also informed Giraud that he did not propose to call upon General Eisenhower; he was not acquainted with the General. In due course he would show the British and Americans their true position. I naturally gave Giraud the same advice I had given Monnet—that at the next meeting a motion should be proposed, to be carried or defeated. I did not think that de Gaulle and his friends would vote against the motion constituting the Committee. That would put him in a ridiculous position. I warned Giraud that when the Committee had been formed, some, if not all, of the objectionable figures would have to go.

At noon on the same day Murphy and I called upon de Gaulle. This was an interview of a very different kind. De Gaulle was at his best, and my colleague was much impressed. He set out his deep feelings in a powerful and even noble way. Naturally there were some harsh phrases. But it was clear to us both that here was a more powerful character than any other Frenchman in or outside France.

De Gaulle began by expressing his views as to the character of a French administration. It should be, if not a Government in name, as near to a Government as possible in effect. The central committee should consist of the necessary number of Ministers or Commissioners to carry out the work. There would, therefore, be the joint Presidents, a Minister of Finance, a Minister for the Colonies, a Minister for Transport, a Minister for Supply, a Minister for the Army, a Minister for the Navy, a Minister for the Air and a Minister for Foreign Affairs. There would also have to be Ministers for Justice and Education. It would probably also be desirable to have on the Committee a Minister representing the interest of the Moslems. This should make ten or eleven in all, but it was essential if the work was to be done.

When asked by Murphy whether the Executive Committee had been formed, he said that this had not been done. He expressed his disappointment at the attitude taken in the discussion the day before. He gave a somewhat different version from those we had already heard, because he said that his disappointment was shared by Philip, Massigli and even Catroux. With regard to the proposed composition, he expressed great surprise that General Georges had been brought out of France by the British for the purpose of putting him on this Committee. Georges was an old gentleman, quite incapable of working as was needed today and, moreover, associated with the defeat of France. Monnet was a good man, but more of an internationalist than a Frenchman and would be most useful in that aspect of affairs. In the course of conversation, he explained that he had made it a condition that the following should resign: Peyrouton, Boisson, Noguès, General Mendigal, General Prioux, and Admiral Michelier. He wanted this done immediately. We said that this could be done after the Committee was formed. But he reiterated his concern at the resistance to the resignation of these men, whether before or after the Committee was formed, which was put up by Giraud and Georges. He admitted that the others did not take his view.

De Gaulle said that many Frenchmen and others did not seem to realise that France was going through a period of revolution. An immense gulf was fixed between the period before the defeat and the present time. Just as the royalist army after 1789 was torn in conflict and divided loyalties, so had the French Army been. It must be renewed by the spirit of the revolution. It must be officered by young and untried men. All these outdated generals must be got rid of.

At the same time, on being pressed, de Gaulle seemed to think that the matter would be arranged; indeed, certain discussions were now going on. He did not give any sign of breaking off negotiations and going back to London. But it was clear that he did not regard himself as committed. He spoke of himself as a separate power; and indeed the appearance of his villa was like the court of a visiting monarch. He further asked Murphy to arrange for him to call upon General Eisenhower. He apologised for not having done so before, but he had no liaison officer through whom these appointments could be made. He also asked me to arrange for him to visit General Alexander and Air Chief Marshal Tedder.

De Gaulle talked about the proper place for the French administration. The central authority must be removed above the atmosphere of colonial politics. He therefore hoped it would be possible to find a town—Blida, Castiglione, or perhaps Constantine—to which they could go. In this atmosphere life would be simpler and more work could be done.

De Gaulle repeated that his desire for the removal of the half-dozen officers and officials he mentioned was not vengeance; but France expected new men for the new work that lay before her. She would not understand a Government of old men associated with defeat. He had no intention of allowing himself to be imprisoned in an Executive Committee. He was quite quiet and rather pleasant throughout. His arguments clearly had considerable effect upon Murphy. On leaving, he took Murphy by the arm and said, 'Why do you not understand me? Why do you always interfere with me? It is a mistake France will not understand, why your politicians are against me. I represent future France, and it will be better for us all if you support me.'[13]

Later in the evening Catroux came to see me. He had done his best to persuade de Gaulle not to insist upon the resignations as a preliminary to the formation of the Committee, because he would have a majority on his side as soon as it was formed. In order to relieve his doubts, he had obtained Monnet's positive declaration of support. He had seen de Gaulle several times during the day, but he seemed unwilling to reach a definite conclusion. In spite of these uncertainties, Catroux still hoped for a successful outcome. The day ended, therefore, in an atmosphere of qualified optimism. But the next day was to be one of a combination of tragedy, high comedy and even farce. In the end the situation became so fantastic as to produce a reaction towards some common sense.

The new dispute, which at one moment threatened to be fatal,

[13] 4 June 1943.

centred round the debatable personality of Peyrouton. At about 9 p.m. on 1 June, Peyrouton sent a letter to de Gaulle, placing his resignation as Governor-General of Algeria in his hands, and asking for an appointment as a captain in the French forces. De Gaulle, without consulting Giraud, immediately accepted this offer, gave instructions that the Secretary-General (Gonon) was to carry on the Government of Algeria temporarily, and promised Peyrouton a position in the French forces of the Levant. At 11 o'clock, de Gaulle's Press officer gave the correspondence to the Press. The General then wrote a letter to Giraud, telling him what he had done. This letter was delivered at the gates of the Palais d'Été about 1 a.m. the next morning. Meanwhile, some time after 11.30 p.m., Peyrouton wrote a second letter on this occasion to Giraud, in more or less similar terms. The time at which this letter was written was in dispute; but it was certainly not delivered to Giraud until the early hours of the morning. Giraud also accepted the resignation and promised Peyrouton an appointment in the Army. This interchange was given to the Press at 3 a.m. By this time, Giraud had received de Gaulle's letter. He then wrote two letters to de Gaulle. In the first, he expressed his astonishment at the manner in which de Gaulle had dealt with Peyrouton's resignation, and proposed a meeting at 10 o'clock the following morning. The second was clearly an unaided effort and was couched in the wildest language. He accused de Gaulle of seeking to introduce into France a political system on the Nazi model. He demanded a public disavowal of his pretensions before any further discussion took place.

By now Giraud had completely lost his head and had become convinced that de Gaulle was intending to organise a 'putsch' against his authority. He accordingly appointed Admiral Muselier as a member of his Cabinet to maintain order in Algiers, and called in a number of colonial troops. Giraud also believed the story that there were up to 3,000 of General de Larminat's troops on leave in Algiers for the purpose of supporting de Gaulle in a *coup d'état*.

We heard garbled versions of this story in the course of the morning of 2 June, and the peacemakers immediately set to work. Murphy and I first called upon Giraud, who gave us a substantially correct version of these curious events. We did our best to calm him down and urge upon him that the matter should be handled in a correct way. The right thing was to hold a meeting and to elect a Committee. This, after all, had been agreed in the letters exchanged between himself and de Gaulle before the latter had come to Algiers. He should act in accordance with his offer and get the Committee into being. On leaving the Palace, we met outside a number of leading figures, including General Georges. I had a short word with him, but he was clearly not going to help. This led Murphy to express his regret that Georges had ever come to Algiers. We next saw Gonon, who told us that he believed Peyrouton had yielded to extreme pressure from the Gaullist party. A hint had probably been given to him that if he would resign quietly he would be looked after, but if he was obstructive no one could answer for the consequences.

When I got back to my villa, I found that de Gaulle had asked to see me, and the meeting was fixed for 4 o'clock that afternoon. He began by saying that he could not understand the extraordinary atmosphere with which he was surrounded: the calling-up of the Goums, the appointment of Admiral Muselier in charge of police and other measures, as if there was going to be a civil war. He laughed the whole thing off and said it was quite ridiculous. I told him that I thought the atmosphere of suspicion on both sides was very regrettable and even absurd, but I told him frankly that he was only saying about the Giraudists what they were saying about him.

De Gaulle then discussed the Peyrouton incident. I said I thought Peyrouton was greatly at fault in sending his resignation to de Gaulle when he knew the Committee had not been formed, and when he was the servant of Giraud. I also thought de Gaulle was wrong in accepting it. He said he had accepted it because he was the head of the French National Committee and he took it that Peyrouton, by writing to him, acknowledged his authority. I said that was a bit thin; and what would he think of a man who had served him for five months and then sent in his resignation to the head of another group or party. De Gaulle replied, 'That is just the kind of man Peyrouton is! I have always told you all along he was a rascal.'

However, he told me that in spite of everything he was going to make another attempt, and that a meeting of the seven was to take place at 5.30 that evening, to see whether they could end up by forming the Committee. I said that I was delighted to hear it. This gave me an opportunity to appeal to him not to miss so great a moment in his own career as well as in the life of France. I asked if I might speak quite frankly to him, and whether he would mind my speaking in English as it would be easier. He said he did not mind; he could understand.

I told him that I, like many other of my countrymen, had fought in the last war; I had been wounded on French soil on three occasions; I had lost many of my best and dearest friends in that struggle. We formed an affection for France which had never been broken. In my country I had been a Member of Parliament for sixteen years, and had strongly opposed the policy followed by the leaders of my party, Baldwin and Chamberlain. I had separated from them and joined Churchill and others in the demand for rearmament in the years from 1937 onwards. I also told him that I thought his views on social matters were probably very like mine. In Britain we believed that great advances could and ought to be made in social legislation. In my country, as in his, there were old men who looked backwards rather than forwards to the future. We needed young men with young minds. Many people in my walk of life had quite realised that the future in my country would be wholly different after the war. Great wealth would pass away. Property would be regarded as a trust, for the general benefit. We hoped to see the transformation from one society to another without revolution or disturbance, and it depended in my country, as in his, on whether men of progressive opinions could work together and inspire the necessary changes. I told him that I had followed all his ideas and actions with sympathy and admiration; that I realised his impatience on finding old men and old minds still in control; that I understood the difference between my country and his, because we had not been subjected to such terrible pressures as had weighed upon France; we had not suffered a great defeat and the sense of shame that followed that defeat. Nevertheless, I implored him to take courage; not to miss his opportunity to join honourably with Giraud in this national administration. I felt sure that as the weeks and months went by he could, without straining the law, or acting in any way unconstitutionally, obtain for himself and those who were with him the reality of power. He could build up a strong machine for war which could also be available for the reconstruction of France in peace; but that if he missed this chance he would merely condemn France to further divisions now and the prospect of civil war in the future. I ventured to make this appeal, not as a diplomat, as I was not a diplomat, but as one man to another; we were both of the same age and had something of the same ideas.

The General listened patiently to this harangue and said (after asking if he might reply in French) that he would pay full attention to what I had said. He had always felt that I had understood him, and he promised to weigh all this very carefully before allowing a break to come. He found it terribly disappointing to find himself surrounded by such an antiquated point of view. I said that disappointments were made to be borne and obstacles to be overcome, and I had every confidence that he would play his role in an honourable manner. On that, he then left with every appearance of good feeling and friendliness.

Later the same day, Murphy and I called together on Catroux. We found him sitting in his garden, cool and elegant as ever. Murphy complimented him on his self-control and said he was the most patient man in the world. To this, Catroux replied that he had not lived up to this reputation, as he had lost his temper earlier in the day. Nevertheless, he seemed to have fully recovered it, and it was clear that in spite of all the difficulties he would do everything possible to see that the Committee was constituted, because he realised it would mean the reality of French union. He confirmed Gonon's account of the motives by which Peyrouton had been actuated. But when he got de Gaulle's very formal letter he went off on another line and wrote to Giraud. As Catroux observed, it was not without an element of comicality that Peyrouton, accused by the extreme Gaullists as being a traitor, had been offered a commission in the Gaullist army in the Levant. I asked Catroux who could replace Peyrouton as Governor of Algeria; to which he replied that he thought he would have to take the position himself, combining it with a seat on the Committee. I reminded him that it was important, when drafting the rules, to frame them in such a way as to make this possible. Finally, Catroux said, 'Well, I will go on, but it is very exhausting.'

During the whole of this day the city was buzzing with rumours and great excitement prevailed. There was talk of a Giraudist 'putsch' and a Gaullist 'putsch'. But eventually all this nonsense was to end with the definite decision to forget about these follies and to hold a meeting of the Committee the next morning, with the purpose of reaching a conclusion. Murphy and I agreed that the best thing we could do was to strike a note of optimism and confidence. So at 7 p.m. we held a Press conference. Whatever might be the effect upon the Press of the world, we were sure that our action would help to bring pressure upon all the divergent French elements. After the Press conference I went to Admiral Cunningham's villa to dine with the Prime Minister. Of course he had heard about the row, but I was able to reassure him. He saw that I was in a state of considerable exhaustion and with characteristic kindness did not press me. 'Anyway,' he said, 'you have done your best. No one can do more.'

The next day,

we were all somewhat exhausted by recent events; and after a morning at the office, I took [Eden] out to Tipasa where we bathed and lunched. While we were having lunch we got a telephone message to say that the seven French stars had met and formed themselves into a definite constellation.[14]

In the evening Massigli came to see me and left with me the statement of the new Committee which was to be given to the Press. He told me that an official Note would be presented jointly in London and Washington by the Fighting French and the Giraudist delegations, announcing the formation of the new central authority and asking for recognition. He also informed me of Catroux's appointment as Governor-General of Algeria, and various other changes, which would be made in a manner broadly satisfactory to de Gaulle. The two generals had embraced at the end of the meeting, thus ending a French political crisis on the classic model. For myself, I felt naturally much relieved. At any rate, whatever storms might lie ahead, we had reached one definite point in our journey. Massigli incidentally told me that de Gaulle had been deeply moved by what I had said to him the day before and had expressed great pleasure at the sympathy and understanding which I had shown.

I gave a dinner for the Foreign Secretary that night, the guests at which included a number of British and American officers.

After dinner, we were sent for to 'No. 10', where we found General Eisenhower, Air Chief Marshal Tedder, Admiral Cunningham, General Montgomery. We passed a very interesting and delightful evening, and the conversation lasted well into the early hours of this morning. The Prime

[14] 4 June 1943.

Minister seemed to be delighted at the turn in French affairs, and I think he has also reached a very satisfactory settlement of other questions with the Americans.

The settlement, in effect, meant that after the occupation of Sicily the mainland of Italy would be attacked. This was the plan upon which Churchill had set his heart.

I told Admiral Cunningham that the invitations should now be sent out for a luncheon party which he proposed; this duly took place the next day. There were present the Prime Minister, the Foreign Secretary, the C.I.G.S. (General Brooke), and myself, together with Giraud, de Gaulle, Catroux, Georges, Monnet, Massigli and Philip.

The party appeared to pass off very well. After lunch the Prime Minister made a short speech without rising to his feet. He was himself sincerely moved, and so were his audience. He referred to his first knowledge of the French Army and people thirty-five years ago, when he attended manœuvres under General de la Croix. From that time onwards he had formed many friendships with French statesmen and soldiers. He had never wavered in his friendship and admiration for France, the French people and the civilisation which they had made. Nor had he wavered in his political support; even in bad times, when some of his own countrymen seemed to be turning away, he had been loyal to the French connection. He had seen with the deepest sorrow the distressing years through which France had passed after she was overwhelmed by a brutal enemy; but he had seen with equal admiration her revival and renaissance. He believed that on this historic day, when all French people were united once more, prepared to take up in loyal co-operation with their allies the struggle against the enemy, our hearts could well be glad even amongst so much sorrow. He pledged himself to continue to the full the loyal support which he had given; he equally pledged his Government and the people of Great Britain and the Empire. Then he asked us all to rise to our feet and drink the toast of 'la belle France, la France victorieuse'.

Giraud made a short and very suitable reply, referring to the uplift in all French hearts which had been caused by the landings in North Africa and the successful conclusion of that campaign.

De Gaulle then delivered a very well phrased and really moving little speech, chiefly about the Prime Minister's personal attributes. He referred to the three years during which he had seen the English people passing through terrible times. One judged individuals and people more by how they stood bad times than by their behaviour in times of prosperity. In prosperous times, friends were easily come by; but in times of trouble one found the true value of individuals and of countries. He would never forget the inspiration the British people had given him.

Eden then spoke shortly, referring to the need for Britain and France to hold together after the war for the reconstruction of the things in which they mutually believed—freedom, tolerance and the rights of the people to enjoy their own lives.

Georges replied with a few remarks, in which incidentally he referred to Joan of Arc, which caused some merriment, the Prime Minister exclaiming that it was not we but the Burgundians who were responsible.

All the speeches were in French, the Prime Minister speaking that vigorous idiom, drawing widely from both French and English vocabularies, in which he excelled. After the luncheon, the whole party was photographed together, and finally a picture was taken of the Prime Minister with Giraud and de Gaulle. All this—both the entertainment and the photographs—was on rather a happier note than the famous photograph at Anfa. Something had been achieved in four months.

The British Press was enthusiastic about this French union, although some struck a note of warning. My part in it was generously recognised; one paper referred to my having been assisted 'by a good knowledge of French, and an imperturbability which it is almost impossible to rattle'. Perhaps this was the foundation of the legend of 'unflappability' which was to serve me well many years later. But I was certainly to have need of this quality within a very few days.

CHAPTER FOURTEEN

The Road to Recognition

I MMEDIATELY on its formation, the newly-established French Committee for National Liberation applied for formal recognition by Britain and America. Unhappily, the début of the Committee was not brilliant. On 8 June, the question of the command, organisation and control of the French armed forces was under discussion. Tempers soon began to rise. De Gaulle was demanding that he should be the Commissioner (or Minister) for Defence on the British model, with the Chiefs of Staff for the three Services under him. Giraud, realising the threat to his authority as Commander-in-Chief, was said to be angry and excited and talking of resignation. But by the usual Algiers paradox, it was de Gaulle who resigned.

On 10 June, Giraud asked to see me. He showed me a letter which he had received from de Gaulle, complaining that the Committee was apparently poisoned by suspicion of himself, was harking back to Vichy ideas, and was trying to surround him with an atmosphere of 'putsch'. No progress could be made with his ideas because the simplest proposition appeared to require an interminable argument before any decision could be reached. In the light of his duty towards France, he could not take the responsibility of remaining in such a body. He had therefore tendered his resignation both as co-President and as a member of the Committee.

Churchill had returned to England on 5 June, and some of us had enjoyed a pleasant weekend's holiday in the mountains. So we were ready for the new crisis, although we had not expected it so soon. While I was speaking to Giraud, General Georges came in. He began to complain of de Gaulle's behaviour on the Committee, which he called 'brutal and indecent'. The smallest thing seemed to excite him to a frenzy. For instance, whenever the name of Marshal Pétain came up, as it must often do, he found that it caused the most violent reaction from de Gaulle, which he could not understand. Meanwhile, Giraud sat at his desk, writing in his own hand a reply accepting de Gaulle's resignation. Both generals seemed delighted at the way things were working out. They asked me what I thought of the position. I said that I was afraid my brain did not work as quickly as the brains of Frenchmen, and I would like some time to think about it. I begged them to take no decisive action without careful consideration.

I thought that the result of de Gaulle's resignation would be very grave. They rather pooh-poohed this; but I said, 'Well, it would not be so grave in three or four months' time, when the Empire has been closely knit together under the new Committee, when all the problem of the English agreements has been resolved. To whom will the Governor of Madagascar and of French Equatorial Africa look? From whom will Larminat and Leclerc take their orders? And what will the Free French fleet and aviation do? It is too early to expect them to accept loyally the new Committee. If this resignation took place after three, or preferably six, months, things would have settled down, but I see in this the danger of very grave events and a complete break-up of the French Empire. It will be worse than if the union had not been made at all, that it should fail in eight days.' All this seemed rather to impress the generals, and they thought they would think the matter over.[1]

Monnet then came into the room and supported my pleas. Catroux next arrived, and at this point I thought it best to retire and leave the four Frenchmen together. I had only one card now to play—a court card. King George was about to make a visit to North Africa. But this was a closely guarded secret. The code name under which he was to travel was that of General Lyon; the visit was known as 'Operation Loader'. In the circumstances, I thought myself justified in informing first Giraud and then de Gaulle. I made this the reason for my visit to the latter on that afternoon, and I told him that at the luncheon on the following Sunday, to which he had been good enough to accept an invitation, not I, but General Lyon, would be his host.

De Gaulle had many complaints, some of them justified. The delay in the arrival of his friends from London, which was the fault of the American command, had annoyed him. He was not unnaturally suspicious of their motives. He also had some complaints about Churchill's speech in the House of Commons about the status of the F.C.N.L. and the importance of Giraud retaining the military com-

[1] 10 June 1943.

mand. I explained that this was merely a general review and not a formal diplomatic reply to the Committee's request for recognition. We dealt with one or two other points, and then he observed that this was all very interesting but it might not interest him much longer. He could make no progress. He was surrounded by old men with old-fashioned ideas. He wanted to make a modern Army, but Giraud wanted to keep the Army that had been beaten. He was hampered at every point. I begged him to be patient. The Committee had only lasted a week. It must take some time to settle down. He said it was all 'embêtant'. I said that he had always found that Englishmen were 'embêtant'. He had now realised that many Frenchmen shared the same characteristic. Anyway, I would always be at his service, night or day, if he wished to see me. He thanked me and said with a smile:

'If I am no longer in the Government, will General Lyon wish to invite me?' I replied that I felt sure that General Lyon would be glad to see a Frenchman who had done so much for England in the hour of her greatest need and had stood by us when we were alone. This seemed to please him. . . . He accompanied me downstairs and saw me into my car.[2]

It was of course necessary to report these new troubles to London and Washington. Although strongly stimulated by Roosevelt, Churchill's reaction was comparatively mild. It reached me on 11 June in the following terms:

There can be no question of our giving recognition until we know what it is we have to recognise. See St. Matthew, chapter vii, verse 16: 'Ye shall know them by their fruits. Do men gather grapes of thorns, or figs of thistles?' Indeed, the whole chapter is instructive.

You are quite right to play for time and let de Gaulle have every chance to come to his senses and realise the forces around him. We play fair with him if he plays fair with us and with France.[3]

When this telegram reached us, it was late at night. We were tempted to reply in the same vein. After much research, a suitable reference was found in some rather obscure but relevant verses in the Book of the Revelation. We therefore sent back a message thanking the Prime Minister for his advice, but adding 'See Revelations, chapter ii, verses 2–4 inclusive'. The quotation ran as follows:

[2] Ibid.
[3] Winston S. Churchill, *The Second World War*, vol. v: *Closing the Ring* (London, 1952), p. 156.

I know thy works, and thy labour, and thy patience, and how thou canst not bear them which are evil: and thou hast tried them which say they are apostles, and are not, and hast found them liars:

And hast borne, and hast patience, and for my name's sake hast laboured, and hast not fainted.

Nevertheless I have somewhat against thee, because thou hast left thy first love.

The last line was so appropriate that it hit the mark. Desmond Morton, Churchill's personal assistant, told me later that he happened to be with him when the message arrived. When the Bible had been sent for and the passage looked up he was for some time speechless with rage. However, he was forgiving, and contented himself with instructions that this Biblical correspondence must now cease.

However, in spite of mutterings and rumblings, and a lot of critical messages reaching my colleague and myself from the President and the Prime Minister, the King's visit now began to dominate the scene. He arrived on 12 June, secrecy having been well preserved. He brought with him Archie Sinclair, Secretary of State for Air, and P. J. Grigg, Secretary of State for War. On the first evening, the King, although very tired, gave a dinner party at which Eisenhower was present. This went off very well.

The King had had a bathe and a sleep and was in excellent form. He was very good with Eisenhower, who was himself in excellent shape—interesting, amusing, not too shy or too much at ease—in fact, the real natural simple gentleman which he is.

After dinner, in the chief sitting-room of the villa, the little ceremony took place to which Eisenhower had looked forward with great and genuine pleasure. The King took the General a little apart . . . and presented him with the G.C.B. with a few very well chosen phrases.[4]

The King asked me what he was to do about the luncheon for the French. He had been advised by the Prime Minister not to hold it unless they were behaving well. Were they behaving well? 'No, Sir. Some have resigned; others are threatening resignation. I can't say that they are behaving well.' What then, asked the King, were we to do? 'Sir,' I ventured to reply, 'I would advise you to go on with the luncheon. It may do good, and it can do no harm.' He laughed at this,

[4] 12 June 1943.

and in fact the party was a great success. The guests consisted of Giraud, de Gaulle, Catroux, Murphy and myself.

After luncheon, de Gaulle asked me how I intended to spend the afternoon. I said I would probably motor to Tipasa and bathe. He asked if he could come with me and alone.

So I had three and a half hours of driving, walking in the ruins and continuous talk with this strange—attractive and yet impossible—character. We talked on every conceivable subject—politics, religion, philosophy, the Classics, history (ancient and modern) and so on. All was more or less related to the things which fill his mind.[5]

I still remember with pleasure this curious episode. I bathed naked in the sea at the far end of the Roman city; De Gaulle sat in a dignified manner on a rock, with his military cap, his uniform and belt. Then we had a nice little supper at the inn with the excited *patron*.

It is very difficult to know how to handle him. I do my best and I know that he likes me and appreciates having somebody whom he trusts and with whom he can talk freely. I think I have persuaded him to stay in the Committee for the present and give the thing a chance. (But I'm afraid he will always be difficult to work with.) He is by nature an autocrat. Just like Louis XIV or Napoleon. He thinks in his heart that he should command and all others should obey him. It is not exactly 'Fascist' (an overworked word), it is authoritarian.[6]

Meanwhile, the French crisis slumbered. In the evening of 15 June, de Gaulle and Massigli came round together to see us. It was rather a useful conversation on the question of the French military reorganisation. All my sympathies were with de Gaulle; for obviously a proper ministerial system should be set up with proper ministerial responsibility. The difficulty was to find any functions for the Commander-in-Chief.

President Roosevelt, who had never welcomed the formation of the French Committee and would have been very glad to see it collapse, sent formal instructions to General Eisenhower to prevent any control by de Gaulle of French military affairs in North and West Africa, since this would seriously jeopardise the safety of the Allied forces and operations.

[5] 14 June 1943.
[6] Ibid.

The British and American Governments (the President leading, the P.M. following) object to de Gaulle having authority over the Army at the moment, because they have no real confidence in what he might do.[7]

A new situation now began to develop which in the end proved very helpful to me. In spite of the prejudices against de Gaulle, such opinions were not really shared by Eisenhower or Bedell Smith. Both of them, as well as Murphy, were beginning to feel that Giraud was really no good. He was stupid and vacillating, always 'preferring the discomforts of a fence to the horrors of a decision'. Since Americans hate throwing good money after bad, they were preparing to abandon him. Nor had they any sympathy with the President's views about the imminent collapse of the French Empire. No doubt 'colonialism' was a bad thing, and this would be changed after the war. But, regarding their immediate problem as purely a military one, they began slowly to move towards the position which they finally reached in August, when they gave strong advice in favour of accepting de Gaulle and the F.C.N.L. and recognising that body as in effect the Provisional Government of France. The progress towards this conclusion was slow but steady. I had but to let it develop.

Meanwhile, I was in an embarrassing position because both de Gaulle and Massigli had put to me some awkward questions. Was there a personal agreement between any Allied Government and General Giraud as regards the rearmament of the French forces? Was the execution of this agreement dependent upon the form and structure which might be assumed by the central French authority? Was General Giraud justified in claiming, as he was claiming, that he had a blank cheque from the Allies to maintain whatever position seemed best to him? These were not easily answered, except in general terms, because of the dark corners of the Anfa Mystery.[8] General Eisenhower was all the time receiving strong telegrams from the President and I had a similar series from the Prime Minister. He showed me his and I showed him mine. It was like a nursery game, and I could usually say 'Snap' with a Churchill to a Roosevelt message.

General Eisenhower then said, 'What do you think I should do?' I said that as he observed from my telegrams, my instructions were to give him absolute support in carrying out the President's instructions. He said, 'Oh yes. But, as

[7] 15 June 1943.
[8] See above, pp. 206 ff.

a friend, what would you advise me to do?' I said that that was quite a different question and that I thought we might interpret these instructions in our own way. Finally, he sent a very sensible reply to the President, which he dictated in front of us. He asked me to suggest amendments and I made a few.[9]

It was therefore decided that Eisenhower himself should try to settle the matter simply and quietly. He asked the two generals to meet him at his villa (which he thought to be more tactful than at A.F.H.Q.). The meeting took place on the morning of 19 June. No one else was present except the Chief of Staff.

Massigli, Murphy and I were sitting in another room in the villa, in case we were required. This plan was in order to emphasise the purely *military* character of the intervention. Since it was impossible (in the view of Washington, supported by London) to avoid any intervention at all, I was very anxious to make it more acceptable to the French by insisting upon its military and probably short-term aspects. The real demand of the Allies may be boiled down to this:

(a) There is to be a Commander-in-Chief of French forces.
(b) The C.-in-C. is to be in effective control of these forces.
(c) Any reorganisation system must not take away the C.-in-C.'s effective control.
(d) The C.-in-C. must be able to carry out the existing military agreements and give us the use of railways, dock and harbour facilities, etc.
(e) For the present, Giraud is to be C.-in-C.

All this—which on the face of it is an interference with French sovereignty—we justify on the ground of our enormous military commitments here and the impending operations.[10]

The interview was naturally cold and unfriendly. Yet one of its chief results was that Eisenhower seemed impressed by de Gaulle's powerful personality; he had never seen him in action before. The demands of the Allies were perhaps reasonable in so far as they required an effective control of the armed forces, even during reorganisation. The military agreements with regard to the use of railways, dock and harbour facilities and the like should be implemented. But the method was almost insulting to the French, and could only be justified by fundamental distrust. Yet in view of the immense risks involved, for every port in North Africa was vital to the success of the Italian expedition, itself hazardous, it was a difficult dilemma for

[9] 18 June 1943.
[10] 19 June 1943.

the Allies to resolve. De Gaulle was strong, but uncertain; Giraud was reliable, but weak. After the generals had left the villa, we wisely decided that Eisenhower's requests should be put into the form of a written memorandum to be given to the two generals, and circulated to all members of the French Committee. This would at least avoid exaggeration and misunderstanding. But there was obviously going to be a big row.

Before this was due to explode, I was able to enjoy an exhilarating and memorable experience. For I had been invited by the King to accompany him on his visit to Malta.

There had been many and animated discussions as to whether the King should go by air or by sea. The arguments of the Air Force were strong, but the Navy were equally determined. In the end, the King's wish to go by sea prevailed. But there was certainly a greater risk involved. At about 10 p.m. on 19 June, we sailed from Tripoli in the cruiser *Aurora* with an escort of destroyers.

The Admiral [Cunningham] kept teasing me that it was on my advice that the trip had been undertaken, since constitutionally the King can only take the advice of Ministers. I kept telling him that this was my reason for coming, so that we should all sink or swim together!

Actually, I think that neither on the trip over (on Saturday night) nor on the return trip (on Sunday night) did any of the naval officers sleep at all. And I am sure they were all pretty relieved when the cruiser got back to Tripoli early on Monday morning.[11]

I went up on the bridge soon after 7 a.m. on Trinity Sunday morning. It was a glorious sunrise; and there was a nice cool breeze which lasted all day. We soon passed the minesweepers which had been busily at work to make all secure.

At 8.15 the King came on the bridge; a special little platform (like a pulpit of the old three-decker type or as in some modern Nonconformist churches) had been constructed for him. . . . Here he stood alone, in white naval uniform. As we steamed into the Grand Harbour, a slow passage lasting at least three-quarters of an hour, all the cliffs and forts, filled with troops, sailors, airmen and civilians, thundered out a tremendous welcome. It was really a most moving sight. On the old castle of St. Angelo were rows of sailors and marines. On all the other vantage points were infantry, gunners, airmen, Boy Scouts, Girl Guides and the dense eager crowds of the civilian

[11] 19–21 June 1943.

population. Whenever possible, there was a choir or a band. Slowly we steamed into the inner harbour and found our berth—and still the cheers and flag-waving and tears of emotion and excitement.[12]

Since we civilians did not take part in the King's procession, we saw only the start. But the great square in Valletta Harbour, packed solid with applauding humanity, was a memorable sight. The King drove for two hours in the morning from town to town, and in the evening visited the aerodromes and other parts of the island.

We ran into the Royal progress on our way to Verdala Palace (where the luncheon took place) and in the afternoon at various other points. Flowers, flags, confetti—and all the people, usually led by their clergy, with religious banners and emblems outside each church and crowding every square.[13]

The news of the King's visit had only been given out at the Masses in the various churches that very morning. Yet the whole population turned out.

That night we sailed for Tripoli, arriving early the next morning. When it was all over, we were glad that the decision had been made to go by sea, in spite of the risks of submarines, mines and air attack. Mussolini had called the Mediterranean 'Mare Nostrum' ('our sea'). Under Providence and by the valour of all his forces it had been cleared for our King.

When we got back to Algiers we found, as I had expected, a pretty complicated situation. The F.C.N.L. had met that same morning (21 June) to consider General Eisenhower's written requirements. The discussion lasted all day. A formula was found the next day which, although fundamentally unsatisfactory, met the immediate difficulty. The moderates on the Committee, with our full support, persuaded the two generals to agree to this compromise. A permanent Military Committee was to be set up, including both generals, 'with responsibility for the unification, organisation, and training of the armed forces. The National Committee would be responsible for the general direction of the French war effort and would control all the French forces: General Giraud would be Commander-in-Chief in North and West Africa, and General de Gaulle in other parts of the French Empire.'[14] I felt that if this rather tenuous structure could last for a

[12] 20 June 1943.
[13] Ibid.
[14] Woodward, *British Foreign Policy in the Second World War*, p. 221.

few weeks or months it would do. Our chief purpose was to allow the conception of French union gradually to become too strong to be overthrown.

In the course of the next evening, I heard that de Gaulle was now determined to force the issue on Boisson. The situation of this officer was peculiar.

To the de Gaullists, he is a double-dyed traitor; to the English, mildly antipathetic owing to the memories of 1940; by the Americans greatly admired.

The President, unfortunately, is . . . determined to see Boisson kept in his position and therefore there is every reason to expect a new row. . . . Anyhow, I undertook to see Massigli early on the next morning to see if some compromise could be arranged. (I am in some difficulty, since I personally think the President's demands outrageous, but I am instructed to support them. Fortunately, General Eisenhower shares my view and is trying to get some compromise out of the White House.)[15]

René Massigli was from now on to play, in alliance with Catroux, a most valuable role. I had already in the few weeks since I had met him formed a high opinion of his intelligence. I was soon to be equally impressed by his wisdom. Admittedly, he was often difficult to understand, whether speaking in French or in English, especially when he was in a state of some emotion. But his good humour, his determination to find a solution to all problems, however difficult, and his fundamental loyalty to the alliance made him at this time a key figure. The friendship which I formed with him was to last through all my relations with the French in Algiers and to be continued through many years of active co-operation. It remains as firm as ever.

On 24 June, there was a review of the French troops held in the morning in honour of the King. Eisenhower rang me up soon afterwards to tell me that Giraud had informed him that Boisson had sent a telegram offering his resignation. Giraud had immediately replied accepting it, without consulting de Gaulle or any member of the Committee. This seemed a strange affair, since Giraud had now committed exactly the fault with which he had formerly charged de Gaulle in the matter of Peyrouton. When I saw Giraud the talk ran along familiar lines.

The old boy was in capital form. He said that things were not going very well but that he had everything well in hand. He told me that Boisson had resigned, but that he (Giraud) had refused the resignation. I expressed some surprise, because I thought he had accepted it. 'Oh yes,' he said, 'but that is unimportant. Now I have refused it.' (I found myself, like Alice, repeating to myself: important, unimportant, refused, accepted, accepted, refused, unimportant, important.)

Apparently, immediately [Giraud] got back from the review, after his few words with Eisenhower, he sent off another telegram to Boisson refusing to accept the resignation.[16]

When I went to see General Eisenhower to tell him the situation, he was as agreeable and understanding as ever. We both felt that if we could somehow get over this fence we might at last be in the straight. Perhaps this was an optimistic view, but one had to retain some optimism in Algiers or else go mad.

Within the next few hours, the Boisson crisis came to a sudden end. Nobody quite knew why. But the main credit was due to General Eisenhower, who expressed his own opinions quite firmly to Washington. The President, after his outburst on the subject of the French command, on which his messages had been violent and unreasonable, now began to lose interest. His first instructions to the General had been to demand Boisson's retention. He even went so far as to threaten to send American troops and warships to Dakar if Boisson was removed. But all this was previous to Boisson's resignation. Murphy very wisely advised his Government that if, as seemed true, Boisson insisted upon resignation, it would be most impolitic to keep him in office. While the White House stormed, the Committee behaved with dignity and great good sense. They informed us officially that Boisson had resigned and had been asked to remain at his post until a successor had been found. The Americans then insisted that any successor must be *persona grata* to them. The Committee prudently responded by putting forward one name only: Pierre Cournarie, the French Governor of the Cameroons, a man of good background and unexceptionable record. This nomination was reported by Murphy to the President, who made no reply. On 1 July, therefore, the Committee confirmed the nomination. A few days later the President sent a message concurring, but reminding the Committee of the Allied interest in Dakar, and reserving his rights. This, in effect, was a climbdown. Another hurdle—this time of American construction—had thus been successfully surmounted.

[16] 24 June 1943.

The little episode illustrated not only the political weakness of Giraud, but also the folly of the President in basing his policy towards France on the support of individuals rather than principles.

After the Boisson squall there was a welcome period of calm. Apart from a minor difficulty over the position of Admiral Michelier, whom it was proposed to remove, there was little trouble. Admiral Cunningham was concerned about Michelier, because he had got him well in hand. But he was disliked by the Americans since he had opposed their landing at Casablanca; moreover, he was a confirmed Vichyite and Pétainist. He had, indeed, actually signed the armistice. But, of course, he was a member of the Admirals' Club.

On 2 July, Giraud left for America, an unwise action on his part since it left the field open to de Gaulle. But when I went to see him off at the airfield, he was in tremendous form, 'like a schoolboy leaving for the holidays'.[17] I confess that I felt equally relieved.

The heat at this time was very oppressive, and everybody's nerves suffered. But Murphy and I were chiefly distracted by the mass of conflicting and sometimes foolish telegrams which reached us from Washington and London.

I only wish the U.S. and H.M.G. would give official recognition to the Committee. I do not seem able to get the true position understood at home—or rather, I think they do understand but are unwilling to press Washington. The Americans here (Eisenhower, Bedell Smith and Murphy) are absolutely sound now. . . . All I have to do is to follow in their footsteps, making polite noises of agreement with their ideas. But their conversion has not yet spread to Washington![18]

Roger Makins had been on a short visit to London and returned on 8 July.

His visit has been very valuable and my mind is a good deal cleared. It seems that most of my colleagues have put their confidence in my refusing to obey my instructions from the P.M. too literally and in the chance that I should be able to straighten things out. I really think it is a bit mean of them. They might summon up enough courage to speak up in the Cabinet from time to time.[19]

[17] 2 July 1943.
[18] 5 July 1943.
[19] 8 July 1943.

Amid these various and sometimes distracting problems, the date fixed for a new and exciting operation was now rapidly approaching. The invasion of Sicily—'Operation Husky'—was timed to take place on 10 July. On the previous day I went to see de Gaulle and told him that the attack would start in the early hours of the following morning. I had no instructions to do this; I thought it wiser not to ask for any, or to consult anyone. But it seemed to me very discourteous to let the General learn the first news from the wireless or the newspapers. He seemed genuinely to appreciate being told about the operation, and was deeply interested in any details which I might be able to supply of its magnitude and ultimate objectives. De Gaulle was in good heart, for he had had a very successful visit to Tunis and a splendid reception. He felt that the internal situation was improving and the Committee getting down to work in a realistic way. On this, I reminded him of his despondency a few weeks ago. But of course he had many complaints about the external position. He could not understand why he was consistently attacked both in the American and the British Press; the Americans were treating him especially badly. For instance, they were refusing his nominee, Henri Hoppenot, as Governor of Martinique. The story was circulating that they had kept Giraud two days in Puerto Rico in the hope of sending him to take over the island, but that this plan had been dropped owing to the danger of his finding a very poor reception. I laughed, and reproved him for reverting to his suspicious mood; to which de Gaulle replied, 'One must be suspicious when one is surrounded by troubles.' Nevertheless, throughout this interview he was friendly and confident. Everything would turn on the question of recognition; for the delay in according this by the British and American Governments was bitterly resented.

By 14 July, the French national holiday, Giraud had not returned. A great *défilé* took place throughout Algiers, and the French units, newly equipped with American uniform and material, made a favourable impression on the public. Here at least was some tangible result of the alliance. Murphy and I were on the platform with the members of the French Committee, still 'unrecognised'. De Gaulle took the salute, accompanied by General Juin, representing Giraud. When the review was over, I went to see the Chief of Staff, Bedell Smith. After hearing his views I decided to send a telegram to London, recapitulating all the arguments for recognition. It was really quite absurd to continue withholding this formality. It was both silly and ungracious. Moreover, it tended to weaken the conception of a constitutional Committee with collective responsibility, which it was our whole purpose throughout to achieve.

> If you take the worst view of de Gaulle (as the White House and State Department do), what could do more to elevate his position in French eyes than to try to snub him and what could do more to weaken Giraud than to invite him to Washington? All history teaches the same lesson. The French are just as insular and proud a people as the English. And we preferred a Dutch king who was maladroit, and two Hanoverian kings who could not speak English, to the charm and attraction of all the Stuarts—and why? Because the Stuarts depended on France for money, arms and political support. But of course the Americans do not read—or at any rate comprehend —history.[20]

Later the same morning, there was a tremendous meeting in the square which de Gaulle addressed with a fine speech, well delivered, a good voice, enough humour, some epigrammatic points and an eloquent peroration. The crowd was rapturous. But Giraud was still in Washington.

So the French affair drifted on. At any rate, I felt that I was now getting the Prime Minister's sympathy and help.

> There is still a refusal by the President to recognise the French National Committee. But the P.M. has sent a really wonderful telegram, urging him to do so. I am told by Rooker (who has come out this week as Counsellor on the *French* side), that he did seven drafts of it before sending it. It is witty, convincing, pleading, loyal—all at once. I feel it must have an effect. Also, the successful start of the Sicilian campaign will tend to increase the P.M.'s prestige. For it is he alone who has stood for the Mediterranean policy, and stage by stage has carried the Americans along with him, in spite of fierce technical—especially naval—resistance.
>
> I had also a very nice personal telegram from him, explaining his position and difficulties and approving my actions. I hear from Murphy that the State Department are beginning to waver. Eisenhower and Murphy continue to plug in telegrams about this (I got Ike to send another from Tunis) and I think the cumulative effect will gradually wear down the prejudice of the President and Cordell Hull.[21]

[20] 14 July 1943.
[21] 21 July 1943.

On the evening of 27 July I called on Giraud, who had returned from America four days previously, after stopping briefly in London.

I'm afraid that his visits to Washington and London have had a disastrous effect upon him. His natural, if naïve, conceit has been enormously increased. He thinks (perhaps with some justice) that the Americans have promised their material to him personally. He has, however, quite misunderstood the President's and Cordell Hull's game. His vanity is such that he really believes that they are interested in him as a statesman and general. Of course, they are only interested in him as a convenient instrument to (a) injure de Gaulle, (b) break up the French Union.[22]

The same day Massigli came to see me, after a short visit to London. He was in good heart, and had been impressed and even touched by the courtesy and friendliness of his reception. Although he naturally deplored the delay in according recognition, he understood our own difficulties.

The game which the White House and the State Department are playing is obvious. They hope by delaying recognition to excite a nervosity and lack of confidence of the Committee in itself. Then they hope that Giraud will (as a result of the promises or half-promises made to him in Washington) take such a stiff line on military questions as to provoke a dissolution of the Committee.

When that happens, the non-recognition of the Committee will have been a bull point for them and they can go back to supporting Giraud as Lord of French North Africa and a willing tool of the American Government. If the President knew how much this policy is disliked and even despised by the American Army here, I think he would get a rude shock.[23]

On 29 July the F.C.N.L. discussed, once again for the whole day, the problem of military reorganisation, but made no progress.

Giraud put up a plan yesterday which left him:
(a) joint Prime Minister;
(b) Commander-in-Chief of all troops, navies and air forces, both in North Africa and elsewhere (i.e. absorption of de Gaulle's forces).

No place at all for de Gaulle (except a rather shadowy consultation on a 'Planning Committee'). He seems to have told the Committee that in Washington he had been promised equipment as an individual, not as President of the Committee. This plan was unanimously rejected by the Committee.

In order to reach agreement, de Gaulle today made three proposals, each of which Giraud turned down:

[22] 27 July 1943.
[23] Ibid.

(i) Giraud to be C.-in-C. De Gaulle to be Minister of Defence, each also to be joint President. A small *War* Cabinet to adjudicate any differences.
(ii) Giraud to be C.-in-C. (and joint President), a civilian to be Minister of Defence.
(iii) Giraud to be Minister of Defence and C.-in-C. but to resign from joint presidency. . . .

Giraud is now threatening to resign from the Committee, apparently relying on the Americans to support him as a sort of dictator.[24]

I did not take all this too tragically, for by now I had been through many of these crises, and we had always managed to reach at least a temporary solution. Murphy agreed with me that we should not intervene at present.

By this time, my staff, as well as my responsibilities, was growing. We still had the original founder members—John Wyndham and myself, together with the invaluable Miss Campbell and Miss Williams. Roger Makins, who was my chief adviser, had now been joined by Harold Caccia to look after Italian affairs, and John Rooker for France. Tom Dupree had come as Press Attaché. I had, in addition, two young men, John Addis and Eric Duncannon.[25] Miss Eden had also arrived as Makins's secretary, Sergeant Brown as archivist, two corporals as chauffeurs, and, most important of all, Mr. Harnett of the Treasury, who somehow or other provided the money to pay for our growing expenses.

At the same time, social life in Algiers was now becoming more and more exacting. The lesser Gaullists and Giraudists, who had started by keeping apart, were now getting together, and the distinctions appeared to be social rather than political. Many pretty young ladies had arrived to charm us, and some aristocratic old ladies to entertain us. The only difficulty was that with all the British and American officers and civilians, as well as the French officers and politicians and their wives, it meant a dinner or luncheon practically every day. This was a considerable strain, especially as the weather got hotter. One evening we had a dinner organised by Eric Duncannon, to which some of his attractive young friends were invited. One of them I called 'the Kodak Girl'—too smart to talk. It was a large party, including Dr. Abadie, now Minister of Justice, a man of high quality but more suited to the dignity of the Athenæum Club than to the mixed company of our

[24] 29 July 1943.
[25] Lord Duncannon, later Lord Bessborough.

villa. So it was rather heavy going. However, the evening was relieved by an American colonel suddenly observing to Mme. Abadie, 'Est-ce que vous êtes procuresse? Je veux procurer une jeune dame pour des leçons.' Mme. Abadie looked a bit surprised, but replied calmly enough, 'Oh, non. Il fait beaucoup trop chaud.' It transpired that the gallant colonel wanted lessons in the French language![26]

On the last day of July, a new compromise was reached, which de Gaulle wisely accepted, for it was greatly to his advantage. He was to be the sole President of the F.C.N.L.; in other words, sole Prime Minister. But he and Giraud were to sign all orders jointly. The Military Committee would be superseded by a Committee of National Defence, and the late dualism of command was to be abandoned. Giraud was still to be Commander-in-Chief, but on the understanding that if and when he took over any active operational command he would cease to be part of the Government.

> Everyone agrees that the compromise (or plan) announced today is a very good one and that de Gaulle has taken a wise decision. In the long run, he stands to gain, because Giraud will concentrate more and more on *military* questions, leaving the *political* questions in de Gaulle's hands. At last he is beginning to learn a little patience.
>
> I do not see how the President can hold out now.[27]

We were now all set for the recognition, although it was actually to be delayed until 26 August. There were naturally one or two flurries; but I felt quite able to deal with them.

On 8 August, with Eisenhower's agreement, I went to London, partly to discuss the everlasting question of recognition but also to deal with some urgent Italian problems. With my larger staff, I could now feel sure that any new troubles could be adequately dealt with in my absence. On the French side of my mission, as I explained fully to de Gaulle and Massigli, the ball was no longer in our court. It was understood that the matter of the final recognition would be discussed at the forthcoming Quebec Conference between the President and the Prime Minister. Churchill was naturally disinclined to quarrel with our American friends over de Gaulle. Nor was he willing to allow any dispute over this matter to upset his close relationship with the President. But Eden took a different view. They debated this question throughout July and August by spirited minutes. The Foreign Office

[26] 30 July 1943.
[27] 31 July 1943.

felt that both the President and the Prime Minister seemed to leave out of account the damaging effects in France, present and future, if the question of recognition remained unresolved. At the same time, Churchill began to be influenced by my reports concerning the views which Eisenhower and Murphy now expressed, both of them advising immediate acceptance of the Committee's request. Telegrams passing in the course of July between Churchill and Roosevelt did not advance matters much. Everything had to be left till Quebec. I was able to tell the French that Churchill was going to try to settle with the President a satisfactory formula of recognition. There, for the moment, the matter rested. At Quebec Eden argued this point strongly with Secretary Hull but failed to persuade him. However, he made it clear that if no agreement could be reached, each of the two Governments must use its own formula. Roosevelt wanted a 'limited acceptance' of the Committee and to avoid the term 'recognition'. But this was quite unacceptable to us. Finally, two slightly different formulas were adopted. Accordingly, on 26 August Murphy and I called upon de Gaulle with our two texts. Rather unexpectedly, he made no complaints as to the terms but seemed genuinely delighted at the happy result of all our efforts. We then went to see Giraud, who took a polite, but detached, interest in the matter and told us in some detail about his war strategy for the early conquest of Southern Europe, without sufficient landing craft or logistical support. While delivering this discourse, he looked more like the White Knight than ever.

In the evening of this dramatic day, which marked the end of a long contest, Murphy and I, assisted by Massigli, held a Press conference for the British, American and French Press.

M. Bonnet, Minister of Information, in the chair. Massigli did very well and, much to my delight, found himself in the position of defending the British and American texts, explaining away the differences, skating over the weaknesses—all in the best style of a skilled H. of C. debater answering supplementaries. He really did awfully well and Murphy and I had very little to do except come in at the end and supplement it.

I made a joke—which went all right—and a sentimental appeal—which seemed to go also—and I think we have done the trick so far as what goes out from here is concerned.[28]

[28] 26 August 1943.

The British 'formula' recognised the F.C.N.L. as ' "administering those French overseas territories which acknowledge its authority, and as having assumed the functions of the former French National Committee in respect of territories in the Levant". The document noted "with sympathy" the desire of the Committee to be regarded as the body qualified to ensure the administration and defence of all French interests. The British Government intended "to give effect to this request as far as possible, while reserving the right to consider in consultation with the Committee the practical application of this principle in particular cases as they arise".[29] The American formula was less forthcoming in form, but it proved sufficient.

Thus was another milestone safely passed. De Gaulle now found himself Prime Minister of what was in effect the Provisional Government of France.

[29] Woodward, p. 224.

CHAPTER FIFTEEN

The Italian Surrender

I T has been necessary, in order to give a coherent account of the
evolution of the French political situation, at least to the point of
recognition of the Provisional Government, to anticipate the
march of events. While we were occupied with the minor but to us
enthralling problems of Algiers, vast military struggles were taking
place in many diverse areas of the world.

While the Casablanca Conference was meeting in Morocco, the epic
story of Stalingrad was being unfolded. In December 1942, the German Sixth Army was surrounded, and in the course of January and
February eliminated. This first major defeat of Hitler was as plainly
the turn of the tide on the Eastern Front as the Battle of Alamein
and 'Operation Torch' had been in the West, and the American
conquest of Guadalcanal in August had marked the beginning of the
counter-attack in the Far East. The end of the Tunisian campaign,
with its overwhelming defeat of the German and Italian forces, was to
be followed by an ambitious German offensive against the Russian
Army. This, beginning in July, was bitterly fought for nearly three
months. Faced with the desperate German effort to deal a knockout
blow to the Red Army, it became more and more essential to make
whatever contribution was possible in the West German divisions.

Even the most confident supporters of the view that the only
effective way to strike at the heart of Hitler's position was by means of
landings in France had to admit that there was no question of these
being possible until the spring or summer of 1944. Churchill had
explained to me, both at Casablanca and Algiers, his earnest desire to
exploit the expected victory in Tunisia as rapidly as possible. While
the Americans were suspicious that too great an entanglement in the
Mediterranean would delay what they regarded as the decisive assault
in France, General Marshall and the Combined Chiefs of Staff,

SWITZERLAND

AUSTRIA

VENEZIA
TRIDENTINA

CARINTHIA

VALLE
D'AOSTA

VENEZIA
GIULIA

Udine
Ljubljana Gap

•MILAN

Gorizia

Piave R.

Trieste

Turin

Venice

R.Po

Istria

Fiume

Genoa

Modena

Pola

YUGO-

Bologna

Lugo

Ravenna

Imola

Faenza

SLAVIA

La Spezia

Loiana

Forlì

Futa Pass

Cesena

Pistoia

Rimini

Lucca

San Marino

Riccione

Pisa

R.Arno

Coriano

Pesaro

Florence

Urbino

Leghorn

Arrezo

Ancona

Siena

Perugia

Assisi

ADRIATIC SEA

Orvieto

L.Bolsena

Terni

R.Tiber

Vis

Pescara

Civitavecchia

ROME

Fiumicino

R.Liri

R.Sangro

Anzio

Cassino

Foggia

R.Garigliano

Caserta

Bari

CORSICA

APULIA

Ajaccio

NAPLES

Vesuvius

Sorrento

Salerno

Brindisi

Taranto

Grottaglie

Lecce

SARDINIA

Tyrrhenian

Sea

CALABRIA

Palermo

Strait of Messina

Mt.Etna

Bizerta

SICILY

Tunis

Catania

Cassibile

Syracuse

Pantelleria

Allied Line in Autumn 1944 ∘∘∘∘∘∘∘∘
„ „ „ August „ +++++++
„ „ November 6 1943 •••••••••••

Miles
0 20 40 60 80 100
0 40 80 120 160
Kms.

Valletta
Malta

Lampedusa

K.C.JORDAN

strongly supported by the British Chiefs of Staff, accepted, at least for
the immediate future, Churchill's proposal. History will perhaps record that the persistent suspicion of the American leaders, that
Britain wished somehow to avoid the risk of direct landings in
Normandy in the hope of striking at Germany through 'the soft under-
belly' of the Mediterranean countries, resulted in the failure to exploit
the victory of Tunis with the speed which might have been expected.
Our forces were certainly short of aircraft and, above all, of landing
craft. In addition, five divisions were already earmarked to return to
England, beginning on 1 November. Undoubtedly, had the means of
landing more rapidly and at different points on the Italian mainland
been available, we might have been spared the tedious and expensive
battles from one defended mountain position to another. The Press in
both England and America were to show a certain impatience after the
conquest of Tunisia. I remember Bedell Smith complaining to me
that they seemed to think that American and British soldiers were
capable of performing miracles. 'Jesus Christ may have walked upon
the waters, but I guess our boys can't do the same.'

In the course of July, the American Secretary for War, Henry
Stimson, arrived in Algiers. He made it clear in discussion with
Eisenhower that although the Americans had yielded to the British in
1942 by agreeing to the African expedition, and again at Casablanca
by accepting the plan to attack Sicily, and were now ready once more
to agree to a limited invasion of southern Italy with the main purpose
of capturing valuable airfields, he did not feel that any more British
schemes in the Mediterranean ought to be allowed. Nor were matters
changed by the first Quebec Conference in August. The President
made up his mind to hold the British to their agreement not to divert
to the Mediterranean any forces earmarked for the invasion of France.
This commitment, in spite of Churchill's efforts to obtain some additional assistance for Alexander, was scrupulously observed. It is in the
light of these handicaps that Alexander's military reputation must be
judged. Whether or not the overall strategic concept was right, either
militarily or from the wider political angle, is a question to which,
perhaps, no final answer can be given. But it involved many disappointments and set-backs. The capture of Rome, confidently expected
for the autumn of 1943, was thus delayed until June 1944.

Although no formal directive was given to me until the middle of
June, when I was instructed to play the same advisory role to the

Commander-in-Chief in Italian affairs as I had with regard to French, I became gradually involved from early February. For many months, Italian and French problems occupied my time almost equally, and as the weeks passed, the new prospects became more and more enthralling. They also brought me into closer contact with General Alexander who, under Eisenhower's supreme authority, became the effective commander of all the Allied armies, first known as XV Army Group and at a later stage as Allied Armies in Italy—A.A.I.

Although the attack on Sicily had been authorised at the Casablanca Conference, no one really knew what was to follow. Nevertheless, in one form or another it seemed likely that we should be attacking Italian territory; either by seizing Sardinia; or the toe of Italy; or, more boldly, by landings in the Bay of Naples, or even north of Rome. From my point of view, therefore, it soon became necessary to join in the massive preparation of the civil side which was being worked up by London and Washington.

I welcomed all this, for I hoped that there would come a moment when the French troubles would reach a final solution, and I could myself move to a new sphere. Alas, my estimate of the time involved was not altogether correct. It was not until the end of 1943 that I was able to hand over my French duties to Duff Cooper, first Ambassador to the French Provisional Government. Even after that event, I became involved in the many problems between the French Government and the Mediterranean Command.

Meanwhile, the planning for the invasion of Sicily, which had started before the Battle of Tunis was over, was soon proceeding at full pressure. When Grigg, the Secretary of State for War, was visiting us in June, we went frequently to General Alexander's camp, which was in a pine wood above the sea about thirty miles from Algiers. In this attractive spot his planners were hard at work.

The General was as delightful and interesting as ever. He is really a first-class man. The more I see of him, the more I like him. I am very flattered, because I have been elected a member of his mess, to go and live or eat whenever I like both here and throughout the campaign. That is a high honour.[1]

My talks and conferences with him and his staff continued throughout June in spite of our French preoccupations. I often went to his camp

[1] 14 June 1943.

or he came to dine with us in our villa. This experience was to prove
of the greatest value later on.

Little as I knew of the detail of military and naval affairs, I recognised that the invasion of Sicily was a formidable undertaking. Some
of those who were soon to criticise the delay had no conception of the
problems involved. Apart from the strong position of the high ground
round Mount Etna, which was to prove a considerable obstacle, the
operation was one of the first magnitude. Some experience on landings
had been gained in North Africa. Similarly, the lessons learned in
'Husky' were to prove of enormous value in the planning of 'Overlord'
for the following summer.

In the initial assault nearly 3,000 ships and landing-craft took part, carrying
between them 160,000 men, 14,000 vehicles, 600 tanks, and 1,800 guns. These
forces had to be collected, trained, equipped, and eventually embarked, with
all the vast impedimenta of amphibious warfare, at widely dispersed bases in
the Mediterranean, in Great Britain, and in the United States.[2]

The Fifteenth Army Group, consisting of the Seventh United States
and the Eighth British Army (the First British Army having now been
merged with the Eighth), was under Alexander. Tedder, as before,
commanded the whole Allied air force and Admiral Cunningham all
the Allied navies. Whereas 'Torch' had been primarily an American
affair, in 'Husky', as in the Battle of Tunis, there was an equal partnership.

The proportions of the armies available in July were: British, eight
divisions; United States, six. Air: the United States, 55 per cent; British, 45
per cent. Naval, 80 per cent British. Besides all this there remained the
considerable British armies in the Middle East and in the Eastern Mediterranean, including Libya, which were independently commanded by General
Maitland Wilson from the British headquarters at Cairo.[3]

Fortunately, the problem of command presented no difficulty. All the
British commanders were only too happy to serve under General
Eisenhower as Supreme Allied Commander; and Eisenhower had
acquired such a great affection for and confidence in Alexander,
Cunningham and Tedder that he too not merely accepted but wel-
comed this command structure.

The days before the attack on Sicily were an anxious time for all,

[2] Churchill, *Closing the Ring*, p. 24.
[3] Ibid., p. 25.

especially for us civilians, who could do so little except pray for the success of the greatest joint operation that had ever been launched in history.

'D'-day—the day on which our hopes and fears have been pinned for weeks. I could not sleep very well—nor any of us, I found—for we were all thinking of the huge concourse of ships and their precious human freight. . . . Considering that this Armada started from Alexandria (in the east) and English ports (in the west), it was a pretty remarkable performance.

The weather conditions were not too good. There was a heavy swell and a 25–40 [m.p.h.] north-west wind. This did not worry the landings in the south-east very much, but was very troublesome for the south and south-west beaches. In all this during the first days, including the landings, I think only three merchantmen, one hospital ship (bombed with its full lights burning—a pure act of treachery), one American destroyer and a few landing craft were lost.[4]

I had already decided to establish myself in a forward position in Tunis where I would be near the operational commanders, and where Eisenhower also had a small villa. We were lucky to find a splendid spot at La Marsa, just outside the town. I had previously sent John Wyndham with Sergeant Brown to find a place to live and open up an office. He did this with his usual efficiency. Accordingly, I left for Tunis with Harold Caccia on the morning of 10 July.

We are living in part of the old 'Consular Residence'. We have got one wing in operation—it consists of a large sitting-room, with a lovely domed roof, a large dining-room, which we use at present as a sort of hall, three or four bedrooms, some servants' rooms for clerks, chauffeur, etc., and an office. This wing is more or less self-contained and has its own entrance. In the middle of the house is a large central hall—about 60 ft. and about 20 ft. in height. It is a really lovely room, with a fine marble floor, tiled walls and a splendid painted ceiling. Outside is a large covered terrace—about 80 ft. by 30 ft.—and the other wing leads off the hall. In this wing are three nice drawing-rooms. The ceiling of the terrace is very fine—rather faded—but of good Arab style. I think my wing is the oldest part of the house—probably in Arab times the women's quarters. The tiles on the walls of the dining-room are very beautiful. This also has a domed ceiling, with charming Arabesque traceries.[5]

This house was a gift of the Bey of Tunis to Queen Victoria at a time when British influence in Tunisia was predominant. It had ever since

[4] 10 July 1943.
[5] Ibid.

been used by the British Consul, except during the German occupation, when it was a divisional headquarters. I was pleased to find a good library of English books untouched, including Disraeli's novels.

John came up by car and got it all ready and scrounged or stole some furniture. We have some nice rugs which were sent by two leading Jews (M. Henri Smagda and M. Lévy Despas) in recognition for what I am supposed to have done for the Jews since I came to North Africa!

The other wing served as ante-rooms for the Officers' Mess, which was in the large hall. The terrace formed a pleasant place for lounging and gossiping. General Alexander had his headquarters behind the Residence, occupying the extensive garden and some paddocks with tents and caravans.

This forward post proved the best spot that we had yet found, and it was with reluctance that I made the frequent return visits to Algiers which duty and the French problem demanded. There was splendid bathing, and when General Alexander was there, he and I used to bathe every morning at 7 a.m. There was also very good sightseeing, for the remains of Carthage were only a few miles away, with its Roman theatre, amphitheatre and ruined aqueduct.

The North African Economic Board, which had already done splendid work in Algeria and Morocco, was functioning with equal efficiency in Tunisia. But there were many problems to be decided, and I found a good deal to do in this field while waiting for further news.

The High Command now began to gather at Tunis. The Battle for Sicily, although hard, was going well. Naturally, after the first rapid advance there was to be a hold-up in the high ground round Mount Etna. But Alexander, who arrived from Malta on 17 July, seemed satisfied.

He is really a remarkable character—his simplicity, modesty and firmness make up a most charming and impressive whole. Like so many men of his responsibilities, he is dependent on a simple but complete faith in the certainty of victory and the guidance of Providence. He told me an interesting thing about the landings. When they were all in Malta—Eisenhower, Cunningham, Tedder and he—waiting up through Friday night and in the early hours of Saturday morning, they were all much disturbed by the quite unexpected (and for the time of year almost unprecedented) phenomenon of the gale. The wind varied from 25 to 40 miles an hour and they worried terribly about the effect which this might be expected to have on the landings. In point of fact, it proved a double advantage. First, the enemy were certain no possible disembarkation could be attempted on such a night. One of the captured Italian generals described it as a 'pyjama night', i.e. they had thought this a perfectly safe night for a good sleep. Secondly, the sea, driven by the wind, carried the landing craft safely over the many treacherous sand barriers which otherwise might have proved a serious impediment.[6]

Unhappily, the storm seriously affected the airborne landing. The 1st British Airborne Division was to be landed largely in gliders borne by American aircraft, and with the high wind these plans went sadly wrong. The casualties were very heavy among this gallant force.

Life in Tunis was very pleasant.

It is rather like a large country house. You come to meals and otherwise attend [to] your own business. There is plenty of quiet amusement available—sightseeing, bathing or just agreeable conversation with the other guests. A cloudless sky, a dark and lovely sea, a slight breeze, a perfect August day, a cool night. No fuss, no worry—and a great battle in progress! This is never referred to but is understood to be going on satisfactorily. . . . The conversation is the usual tone of educated (and there are some *very* well-educated) Englishmen—a little history, a little politics, a little banter, a little philosophy—all very lightly touched. . . . It is a strange and fascinating experience. Very occasionally, an officer comes in with a message for the 'Chief'. After pausing sufficiently out of politeness for the conversation in hand—the campaign of Belisarius, or the advantages of classical over Gothic architecture, or the right way to drive pheasants in flat country to show them well, or whatever it may be—General Alex. will ask permission to open his message, read it, put it into his pocket, continue the original discussion for a few more minutes and then, perhaps, if the message should call for any action, unobtrusively retire, as a man might leave his smoking-room or library after the ladies have gone to bed, to say a word to his butler, fetch a pipe or the like.

I have never enjoyed so much the English capacity for restraint and understatement.[7]

It was certainly a great comfort to be out of the hot town of Algiers, with its crowded harbour, large apartments, villas and slums, all jostling together, and the semi-fashionable society of over- and under-dressed women, politicians, journalists, businessmen, hangers-on of all kinds—a kind of imitation capital. In Tunis, although the society was

[6] 17 July 1943.
[7] 18 July 1943.

almost exclusively male, it was quiet and, in spite of the heat, pleasant
for work. The rooms in my old Arab house were wonderfully constructed and remained comparatively cool without any of the modern
apparatus. Sometimes we went to dine with friends. General Clark,
now commanding the American Fifth Army, had a splendid villa and
managed to have some female company to entertain us. The d'Er-
langer villa was occupied by General 'Tooey' Spaatz, Deputy Allied
Air Commander, and he shone with the reflected glory of this luxurious and somewhat exotic house. One day, with great daring, we gave a
party ourselves, chiefly to entertain the staff of the Consulate and the
British civilian community. There were also a number of Maltese
whom we roped in. Some of the younger officers of the staff came to
help us, and although there was a sirocco blowing from the south, the
party was voted a great success. Alexander looked in for a few
moments, which gave enormous pleasure. On another evening we had
some very enjoyable singing, given by a concert party of Italian
prisoners, mostly Sicilian and Neapolitan.

They played concertinas and sang a number of duets, trios, choruses, etc.,
both sentimental and comic. They seemed very happy and contented.[8]

At Tunis, Alexander began the practice of inviting me to his
morning conference in his War Room, where all the maps were
available, and the latest information of the campaign was given by one
of his officers. This privilege was accorded to me, whenever I was in or
near his H.Q., until the end of the campaign.

Bedell Smith, Eisenhower's Chief of Staff, was at this time a little
perturbed at the high proportion of British officers on Alexander's
staff. It did not seem to him 'sufficiently integrated'. I promised to talk
to Alexander about this, but told Bedell Smith, quite frankly, that he
must supply some better American officers if they were to be taken
seriously. As a result, he sent Alexander as deputy a splendid American officer who has since achieved, and shone in, the highest posts.
This was General Lemnitzer. We all loved 'Lem' at first sight.

On Sunday night, 25 July, I dined with General Mast, now Governor of Tunisia, our old friend of the November landings. I had
succeeded in persuading the Secretary of State to obtain the award of a
D.S.O. to this officer, who was highly delighted by this recognition of

[8] 19 July 1943.

his services. On getting home from the dinner, I was reading in my room when Commander Martelli, who was on the Intelligence Staff, rang me up with the news of Mussolini's fall. I went along to the mess, but nobody was up except Billy Scott.[9] We had much trouble in making the wireless work, but at last we got the midnight news (no doubt B.B.C. Overseas), which confirmed the fact that he had either resigned or been dismissed, but gave no details.

I wondered whether it was worth while waking up General Alexander but decided against it. I felt it would infringe the good manners of their mess, where . . . the war is not allowed to impinge on conversation and social amenities. So I went—very cheerfully—to bed. . . .[10]

The next morning I bathed as usual at 7 a.m. with General Alexander. 'I told him about Mussolini—he seemed pleased!'[11]

At 8 a.m. General Eisenhower rang up and asked me to come over at once to his villa. He was in a state of considerable excitement and full of plans and ideas for exploiting the situation created by Mussolini's fall. So far we had no very clear picture of what had happened in Rome except that Mussolini had gone. The story of Mussolini's fall and the complicated plots and counter-plots has been now fully told. It seems that there were two conspiracies, the first within the Fascist movement itself, the second emanating from the royal palace. A formal meeting of the Fascist Grand Council called at Count Grandi's insistence ended with a humiliating vote which demanded that the King should resume the command of the armed forces which he had previously surrendered to the Duce. Strangely enough, it seems that Mussolini was not unduly disturbed by this inauspicious and prolonged debate. When he went the next day to the palace, the King, who with the help of Marshal Badoglio and his Minister of the Royal Household, the Duca d'Acquarone, was operating a separate but parallel conspiracy, had made careful arrangements to depose and arrest the dictator whom he had tolerated for so many years. The Duce, with a certain naïvety, had fallen into the trap, and had—temporarily, at any rate—disappeared from the scene.

All this, of course, was only gradually revealed to us as the various

[9] Captain Lord William Scott, M.P. for Roxburgh and Selkirk, 1935–50.
[10] 25 July 1943.
[11] 26 July 1943.

emissaries of peace began to arrive. The announcement made by Marshal Badoglio after taking office merely stated that so far as Italy was concerned the war would continue. Having now been appointed by the King as head of the Government, he appealed to the Italian armed forces and population to obey the orders of the new administration. But the phrases used were perfunctory and uninspiring; and it was evident to us that the plain interpretation of Mussolini's departure was the right one. The Italian people wanted peace. Their problem, indeed their terrible dilemma, was how to get it. Alas, there was no easy way out for Italy. Two-thirds of the Italian Army was situated outside the boundaries of the Kingdom, in the Balkans or in the south of France. On the Italian mainland itself there were only some twelve Italian divisions. Even at the end of July, the German strength amounted to eight divisions. It was soon to be decisively augmented. Furthermore, the number of German agents in key positions in the central Italian machine was alarming. According to one of the Italian emissaries with whom we were soon to make contact, it was as high as 10,000. Most of these were believed to be in Rome. Nor had the Badoglio Government any great authority. Badoglio certainly had a considerable name and reputation, but he was an old man—the 'Pétain of Italy'. No young or vigorous elements seemed to be included among those he chose to serve at his side.

What was the Allied position? According to Alexander's estimate it was unlikely that Sicily would be completely reduced before the middle of August. Plans had been made for an attack upon the Naples area to be carried out at the earliest possible moment thereafter. But with all the difficulties of assembling landing craft and air cover, there was no hope of this new expedition sailing until some time in the first half of September. Even then it would be a dangerous and hazardous operation. It was in these circumstances and against this background that we discussed how best we could use this dramatic event—the fall of one of the two great dictators—to facilitate our military enterprise. Two proposals were put forward. The first was that General Eisenhower should deliver a broadcast message to the Italian people, emphasising that in requiring 'unconditional surrender' we did not mean to impose dishonourable terms. Secondly, it was clearly a matter of the utmost urgency that Eisenhower should be in possession of some definite terms that he could put forward on behalf of the Allied

Governments if an approach were to be made. At this stage we found ourselves at Allied Force Headquarters without authority and without instructions. It is true that an Allied committee in London had long been preparing a complicated draft of some forty clauses and had sent this to the United States Government for their consideration and approval. But no decision had yet been reached. Moreover, the fatal flaw in this document was that it assumed that an Italian Government which wished to capitulate would be in a physical position to do so without reckoning with the Germans.

I was asked to draft telegrams to the two Governments on both points. The first, as to a declaration to the Italian people, was sent off the next day. On the second point, a telegram was sent on the following day to the Combined Chiefs of Staff suggesting ten simple conditions to be imposed if the new Italian Government should make any request for a military armistice before the actual invasion of the mainland took place. These ultimately became the basis of the famous 'short terms'.

As may well be imagined, there was a considerable flow of telegraphic communications on both these points. In the upshot, although the two great principals, Roosevelt and Churchill, did not much like the idea of propaganda declarations by General Eisenhower, the text of his proposed announcement was approved, and the message was duly broadcast on 29 July. We even succeeded, though with great difficulty, in obtaining consent to the terms of a military armistice should it be needed.

One of the most crucial points in these 'short terms' was the question as to what we should ask the Italian Government to do about the German forces in Italy. With the balance of forces as they were, it was clearly out of the question, before any Allied landing on the mainland, to demand that the Italian Government should immobilise and hand over German forces on Italian territory. After much coming and going it was decided that all we could properly ask was that the Italian Government should 'use its best endeavours to deny to the Germans facilities that might be used against the United Nations'.

The 'short terms' were purely military articles. But General Eisenhower was instructed to make it clear, if approached, that more elaborate and comprehensive demands would be presented, covering political, economic and financial questions. The 'long terms'—a planner's dream and a general's nightmare—were a matter of negotiation between the State Department and the Foreign Office.

Naturally, to us on the spot, all this elaborate procedure seemed remote from realities. However, during the first three weeks of his Government no direct approach was made by Marshal Badoglio. He did his best to establish his authority and to remove some of the most objectionable Fascist characters. He did what he could to curb the impatience of the Italian people for peace by harping on the impossibility of Italy accepting 'unconditional surrender'. Yet, just as the Russian people in 1917 wanted peace, and only peace, so the Italians now cared little about Fascism, or the King, or Badoglio. All they wanted was peace. Unhappy people! They were for nearly two more years to endure the cruel agonies of war.

I returned to Algiers with General Eisenhower, and we awaited anxiously the response of our political chiefs. Many new and perplexing problems began to harass us with increasing rapidity during these anxious days. On 28 July I recorded:

A very long and difficult day. I was at the office from 8 a.m. to 8 p.m. A series of telegrams pouring in and out. We are now trying to keep two balls in the air at once—France and Italy. Each is in a critical position.[12]

The next day was equally hectic but not unsatisfactory in the end.

I spent from 9 to 12 going backwards and forwards between my own office and A.F.H.Q., and conversation with General Eisenhower and Bedell Smith. . . . Poor Eisenhower is getting pretty harassed. Telegrams (private, personal and most immediate) pour in upon him from the following sources:

    (i)   Combined Chiefs of Staff (Washington), his official masters.
    (ii) General Marshall, Chief of U.S. Army, his immediate superior.
    (iii) The President.
    (iv) The Secretary of State.
    (v)   Our Prime Minister (direct).
    (vi) Our Prime Minister (through me).
    (vii) The Foreign Secretary (through me).

All these instructions are naturally contradictory and conflicting. So Bedell and I have a sort of parlour game in sorting them out and then sending back replies saying what *we* think ought to happen. As this rarely, if ever, coincides with any of the courses proposed by (i), (ii), (iii), (iv), (v), (vi), or (vii), lots of fun ensues. But it gets a bit wearing, especially with this heat.[13]

[12] 28 July 1943.
[13] 29 July 1943.

We held a meeting at noon with the propaganda experts to try to tie up a policy regarding Italy.

Fortunately, we have in this field two admirable men—intelligent, humorous and loyal. These are [Charles] Jackson (Am.) and Dick Crossman (Brit.).[14]

Alexander had left Tunis and gone to Sicily. He invited me to join him at his camp, but with so much activity on both the French and Italian fronts, I had to remain with Eisenhower.

So far as Italy was concerned, our plan was simple. We have given the Italians a little respite from bombing. We sent from the H.Q. quite a 'soft' message. We said, 'Well done, King. Well done, people. You have got rid of Mussolini and Fascism. That's grand. Come now and do the necessary.'

If (as I think probable) Badoglio tries to stall, and we get no overture, direct or indirect, we should (after a very short interval) turn on the tough stuff—we should say, 'Well, a week's gone by. What is the King doing? What is Badoglio up to? Get on or get out. You have been idle, so we must be busy. We shall bomb Genoa, Naples, Bologna, Milan, Turin, Rome. And it will *not* be our fault. It will be the fault of the *King* and *Badoglio*.'[15]

This policy got us into great trouble at home, with frequent outbursts from the Prime Minister. Meanwhile we were still waiting for the result of the final battles in Sicily. As I recorded at the time, 'Propaganda can be a splendid means of exploiting victory, but it must follow, not precede, victory.'[16]

The next day, 4 August, we were still without fresh news of the fighting, but the telegraphic warfare with London and Washington continued without intermission.

I spent rather a difficult couple of hours with the C.-in-C. and Chief of Staff. Ike is beginning to get rather rattled by their constant pressure of telegraphic advice on every conceivable point. Also, the sirocco is still on and we are all getting . . . on edge, so that incidents unimportant in themselves are magnified —mountains out of molehills.[17]

In Sicily, Catania fell on 5 August, and the end seemed to be approaching. But even so there were internal troubles, minor but irritating:

[14] Ibid.
[15] 30 July 1943.
[16] 3 August 1943.
[17] 4 August 1943.

. . . the B.B.C. has been guilty of some frightful 'gaffes' which have upset the Americans terribly. They said the other day that the Seventh Army had 'nothing to do except walk through Sicily, eating melons and drinking wine'. This caused a terrific 'shemozzle'.[18]

On the same day:

. . . after a long conversation on a number of rather difficult problems relating to Italy and the future, Ike said to me, 'I wish you could get the P.M. to see my point of view—or, at least I wish I could get a really clear idea of what he wants.'

Unfortunately, there have been a number of minor incidents which have caused irritation (quite naturally) on both sides. The P.M. thinks that Ike is too fond of 'propaganda' and makes too many 'statements' and 'proclamations to the Italians'. On the other hand, we have the great propaganda machine here, with the most powerful broadcasting apparatus in the world, and it seems a pity not to use it.[19]

Amid all these difficulties and uncertainties, General Eisenhower pressed me to go back to London and try to find out what was really happening. I left Algiers as soon as transport could be arranged and arrived at Prestwick early on the morning of Sunday 8 August. A few days spent at home enabled me to appreciate much more clearly the anxieties and hopes of my colleagues in London, and to give them a picture of our local difficulties.

The short armistice terms were settled at last, and, although diplomatic negotiation was still going on about the 'long terms', there was no doubt at all that General Eisehower now had authority to treat with the Italians if the approach came from reputable sources. I was also able to do something to explain to the Ministers in London Eisenhower's anxieties and difficulties and to plead that he should be given more latitude. The Prime Minister sent a generous and soothing telegram to Eisenhower from Quebec. As a result, when I saw the General on my return to Algiers at the end of the week he was in a more relaxed mood.

The tragi-comedy of the Italian surrender developed through a number of distinct acts and scenes. First there were the 'feelers'. These began a few weeks after Badoglio's accession to power. During this phase, the Marchese d'Aieta, the new Counsellor of the Italian Lega-

[18] 6 August 1943.
[19] Ibid.

tion, had a tentative conversation on 3 August with the British Ambassador at Lisbon. On the 6th, Signor Berio, Counsellor in the Italian Ministry of Foreign Affairs, talked in similar terms to the British Consul-General at Tangier. The chief difference between these two inquirers was that the former made no mention of peace terms, while the latter alleged that he was authorised to negotiate with any British officials in Tangier, or with a representative of General Eisenhower. From Greek sources we learned that the Nuncio at Berne had made approaches. In addition, a certain Signor Busseti called on our Consul-General in Barcelona, claiming to be the bearer of a formal communication from various political parties of the Left. Since the Tangier contact seemed the most promising, our Consul-General at Tangier (Joe Gascoigne) was authorised on 13 August to give the following answer: 'Marshal Badoglio must understand that we cannot negotiate but require unconditional surrender, which means that the Italian Government should place themselves in the hands of the Allied Governments who will then state their terms. These will provide for an honourable capitulation.' He was also instructed to remind Signor Berio 'that the Prime Minister and the President had already stated that we desired that in due course Italy should occupy a respected place in the new Europe when peace has been re-established, and that General Eisenhower had announced that Italian prisoners taken in Tunisia and Sicily would be released provided all Allied prisoners in Italian hands were released'. Signor Berio seemed rather disappointed with the reply but said he would forward it to Rome. All these somewhat tentative gropings were soon to be replaced by something more solid. The first dove, or pair of doves, was about to take flight.

General Castellano, Chief of Staff to General Ambrosio, and Signor Montanari of the Italian Foreign office called on 15 August upon Sir Samuel Hoare, now British Ambassador in Spain. Castellano was a professional soldier who had served in the Army before Mussolini's seizure of power. He therefore belonged, like Badoglio, to the old guard. He was on his way to Lisbon, under cover of an Italian delegation which was to accompany a party of Chilean diplomats and consuls to be exchanged in that city with a number of Italian officials who had left Chile when that country broke off relations with Italy. They had a block visa for this purpose. General Castellano brought with him satisfactory credentials. For he had a signed introduction from Sir

D'Arcy Osborne, our Minister at the Holy See, vouching for him as a representative of the Italian Government. This was confirmed by a telegram from Sir D'Arcy, in which he stated that he himself held a signed statement from Badoglio authorising Castellano to speak on his behalf. There was no doubt therefore that he enjoyed such authority as the Italian Government itself possessed.

Eisenhower, Murphy and I awaited our instructions with growing impatience. On the morning of 18 August these duly arrived from the Combined Chiefs of Staff. Two officers from A.F.H.Q. were to be sent immediately to Lisbon to establish contact with General Castellano. Eisenhower decided to send Bedell Smith, the Chief of Staff, and a British officer, Brigadier Strong, then the head of the Intelligence Section. They were to leave by aeroplane at 2 o'clock that afternoon. The rest of this hot morning was spent in an atmosphere of amateur theatricals. They must go in a British civilian aircraft. Civilian papers must be provided. They must be dressed in civilian clothes. For if they were to arrive openly in Lisbon the international Press and the German Secret Service would be on to them in a moment. Fortunately both officers had fairly common surnames. By juggling with the Christian names and photographs, passable papers were produced before lunch-time. Even so, there was a *contretemps* about the Chief of Staff. Murphy took the view that he would do better to use the American diplomatic passport which had been given to him for some previous journey. This seemed to me a bad idea, for he was referred to as 'Bedell Smith' and his next of kin was given as the Adjutant-General of the War Department, Washington—a strange relative for a British commercial traveller. However, when they got to Gibraltar, the Governor provided him with a satisfactory British civilian passport and quite easily arranged for Portuguese visas for both him and Strong. I took a patriotic pleasure in the fact that the British had proved professionals at this game, at which we were so often regarded as amateurs. The clothes for these officers presented no insuperable difficulty, but produced some slightly comical effects. I shall never forget Bedell sporting an appalling Norfolk jacket which he had somehow purchased in Algiers and some grey flannel trousers which fitted him very ill. He had obtained some kind of dubious hat with a feather in it; but I persuaded him to remove this, saying that no British traveller of whatever class would walk about with this unusual decoration. Kenneth Strong did not find the civilian tailors of Algiers to his taste, and was similarly decked out in a very improbable costume. However, they got through and returned without incident.

When they met the Italian emissaries, they found a situation somewhat different from that which they had expected. Bedell Smith had begun by saying that he understood that General Castellano had come to signify the acceptance by the Italian Government of 'unconditional surrender' and proceeded to give him the terms of the military armistice—the 'short terms' as we called them. But this was not by any means the Italian idea. They were not so much concerned with the terms of an armistice as with the conditions for a new alliance. Castellano made it clear that they envisaged a complete reversal of Italian policy: they wished to abandon their German allies and join the British and Americans. This would be a new 'combinazione' and, he trusted, a very happy one. Fortunately we had had some hint of this, and the Chief of Staff had in his possession a form of words to meet the occasion. While not committing us to any promise to the Italians, the formula he used pointed out that the better they behaved and the more they impeded the Germans, the more it would stand to their credit in the future. This was really the beginning of what became the accepted phrase 'working their passage', and merged finally into 'co-belligerence'. On their side, the Italians hoped that all this would put them in a better position for the ultimate peace, and we knew it. On our side, we wanted to get their help, particularly to obtain an unopposed landing, and to sabotage and delay German communications in the very difficult operations which lay ahead of us; this they guessed. Nevertheless, in spite of these amenities, our representatives made it quite clear that the Italians must accept the military terms before any question of their amelioration in practice could be considered. Since the exchange of Chilean and Italian diplomats could not be effected for a few days, there was some unavoidable delay. Castellano could not travel separately without a special visa, thus calling attention to himself. He could not therefore hope to arrive in Rome before 25 August at the earliest; perhaps later. He was accordingly given till midnight of 30–31 August to convey his answer by the special wireless arrangements which were to be laid on between Rome and A.F.H.Q. Would the Italian Government accept the military terms of the armistice? That was the vital question on the answer to which all depended. Eisenhower appealed to me to help about the channel of communication between Algiers and Rome. Again, it was through British means that this essential service was established and maintained throughout the coming weeks.

I have sometimes thought that the comparatively long period—ten days—which we allowed them to make up their minds may have given the Italians the impression that the date of our landing on the mainland was some way off. This perhaps influenced their subsequent judgement and actions. But it was unavoidable.

Since there now seemed an interval before the next act in this melodrama, I gladly accepted Alexander's invitation to pay a visit to Syracuse. The Battle of Sicily had now been won. The island had been taken in thirty-eight days. It had been defended by more than thirteen divisions—400,000 men in all, of whom nearly 100,000 were German. It had been attacked by thirteen divisions, and in view of all the difficulty of the long coastline, the heavy fortifications with pill-boxes and wire, and the defensive advantages of the country with its steep valleys, cliffs and gorges, this rapid victory was a remarkable achievement. The Allied casualties were 31,000 killed, wounded and missing. The enemy was said to have lost 170,000 men.

Harold Caccia and I left in the early morning of 21 August.

It was rather fun coming over the sea, past Pantelleria and Lampedusa, and to land in Europe. Since we were driven out of Greece no British troops have fought in Europe . . . it was quite a thrill to land on European soil.[20]

We arrived at noon at the General's headquarters at Cassibile near Syracuse. As usual his staff were in tents, this time in a series of walled orchards. 'Alex. himself lives in his usual two caravans—one his office, the other his private quarters.' I explained to him immediately on my arrival the situation which was developing. After luncheon, at his request, I gave a general account of it to the leading members of his staff.

Harold Caccia and I are in the guest house—called 'the White House'. This is a delicious little farmhouse which Alex. first took over for his own use when he arrived in Sicily. It was too small for a H.Q. . . . and it is kept as a guest place for favoured guests. There is another camp, called Fairfield, for those less honoured or less welcome.

[20] 21 August 1943.

This farm consists of two good sitting-rooms and a large kitchen. It has all been cleaned (whitewashed, etc.) and makes a most delightful little place. Behind the house is a vineyard, and round it a delightful kitchen garden; and the estate consists of orange, olive, almond groves—tomatoes, grain, etc., being planted between the trees.

Outside the farm, there are the usual outhouses . . . a huge old olive to sit under (with large fig trees as well) which completes the picture. Every morning and evening the donkey works away by going round and round pushing a pole. This works a sort of 'sandy-andy' which lifts the water from a deep well into a little reservoir or tank, from which it overflows into the elaborate system of irrigation with little ditches and channels which was described by Theocritus and Virgil and no doubt dates from the very earliest times. It is a pleasant, soothing sound—a sort of click of the machine, followed by the swish of the water.[21]

We slept in tents in the olive grove behind the farm with camp beds and sleeping bags which we had brought with us. In the afternoon the General took me in his jeep for some sightseeing to Syracuse. First the Cathedral, a seventh-century A.D. church built round the fifth-century B.C. Greek temple, with all the great Doric columns incorporated into the Christian building. Then to the Greek theatre, one of the most beautiful surviving theatres, where Aeschylus is said to have produced the *Persae;* then to the stone quarries where the poor Athenian prisoners of war (survivors of the ill-fated Sicilian expedition) were incarcerated.

On 23 August we flew back to Algiers. By this time, before the first doves had been able to return to the stranded ark of the Italian administration, two more doves had been released.

On 24 August the Italian Government, becoming anxious no doubt about the delay in the return of General Castellano, decided to send out a second mission to Lisbon. This consisted of General Zanussi, chief assistant to General Roatta, and a certain Signor Lanza Di Trabia. To establish their good faith, they brought with them General Carton de Wiart, a British prisoner of war. Zanussi's instructions were to proceed, if possible, to London. But the British Ambassador was unwilling to assist Zanussi since he thought it would complicate the negotiations already in train with Castellano. However, Zanussi was hidden in a flat belonging to one of the staff and told to remain there for the present.

[21] Ibid.

Meanwhile, London and Washington had at last agreed on the forty-two clauses of the full instrument of surrender. It was a formidable document, containing detailed political, economic and financial provisions and putting almost every aspect of Italian affairs into Allied hands for an indefinite period. The British Ambassador, in accordance with his instructions, delivered these harsh conditions to Zanussi on the morning of 27 August. After a cursory reading of the text, the General, while admitting that he had no alternative but to place these demands in the hands of his Government, was constrained to observe how deeply he regretted the decision to force Italy to so public and so humiliating a surrender. The 'short terms' they might easily accept, for they were in essence a military armistice; but the longer document now given to him would present much greater difficulty. He therefore urged that the time-table arranged between General Smith and General Castellano should be retarded to give his Government more time for consideration. He also warned the Ambassador that the German strength in Italy was building up, and a serious—perhaps uncontrollable—situation was developing.

In Algiers we had also received from independent sources the news of the daily increase of German forces. All the commanders concerned, British and American, were united in their opinion that the military difficulties involved in the proposed landings in the Naples area were so great that it was scarcely possible to exaggerate the value of an armistice concluded before the expedition was launched. All were therefore partisans of the 'short terms'.

I strongly urged this view on London. If the introduction of the 'long terms' were, as I feared, to cause such difficulties as to preclude the signature of the armistice, we ought to be content with the 'short terms' already communicated to Castellano. A very confused reply reached me from Attlee on behalf of the War Cabinet, Churchill being still away. They and their advisers hankered after the long terms, which were the result of months of careful planning. If military exigencies absolutely required it, we could sign the shorter document, but on the clear understanding that this should be regarded as a military convention and that it should be replaced as soon as possible by the comprehensive and complete terms of surrender. Eisenhower characteristically called this 'a crooked deal'. For my part I decided, come what may, to use my own discretion. Anyway, Sicily was quite a long way from Whitehall.

The attitude of my colleagues in the Government who wanted us to impose these almost brutal terms at all costs, without regard to the military situation, did, I confess, surprise me.

I wish some of them would come and try landing on a defended and mined beach out of a barge, in which one has been three or four days at sea (and sick half that time) in the middle of the night![22]

The next urgent point was to ensure that the plans for Castellano's reply should be adhered to. He, of course, was only concerned with the military armistice. Meanwhile there was the problem of how to dispose of Zanussi and his friend. Unlike Castellano, they had brought no introduction from either British or Italian authorities and carried no credentials. It was finally decided to take them to Algiers, where they were put in one of our S.O.E. camps under the command of Colonel Dodds-Parker. It was thus hoped to keep the whole thing secret. All these events were exciting, if confusing. The plots, counter-plots, and cross-plots were increasing day by day. Amidst this atmosphere of mystery, it became increasingly difficult to give instructions to our admirable propaganda team. Dick Crossman had, I think, an inkling of what was happening.

A very able chap and working splendidly. The Americans (rather unexpectedly) like him although . . . he is a Socialist (which usually terrifies them).[23]

But what line were we to take towards the Italian people—hard or soft, or alternating?

Since these days coincided with the final arrangements for the formal recognition of the French Committee, they were fairly hectic. However, I had time to call and see Zanussi and Di Trabia at Dodds-Parker's camp. They were really quite an engaging couple. We bathed with them before dinner and spent a very agreeable evening in their company. Although they had no formal documents, they protested their good faith which they seemed to think we must take as evident from their open and disarming countenances. Incidentally, they gave

[22] 5 September 1943.
[23] 25 August 1943.

us their own account of the fall of Mussolini. 'It was like one of your Shakespeare plays,' Zanussi kept explaining. 'There was a plot, and then inside the plot there was another plot. There was Grandi's plot—and then there was the King's plot. Poor Count Grandi! He is a very intelligent man—yet he was sadly deceived. He made the first plot. He thought everything was fixed. He would succeed Mussolini. But when he came to "collect" he found the King and Badoglio had made another plot. Each, you see, had deceived the other. Of course, we are absolutely truthful and would never deceive you; but still it is strange. One would have thought that Grandi was an intelligent man.' We were amused by this attempt to demonstrate their complete honesty of purpose and method.

It was now 29 August, and the vital date was approaching. Zanussi was induced to write to Castellano urging him to go to Sicily and to complete the arrangements for the surrender on the 'short terms', of which he had a copy. Zanussi's letter would be taken to Rome the next day by Di Trabia. Zanussi himself we would keep in Algiers. He would be safer there. At the same time, the comprehensive terms which had been given to General Zanussi in Lisbon were now taken away from him. We did not want these to be used as a pretext for delay.

One fresh complication was imposed upon us by our masters. In spite of the supreme importance of secrecy at this moment, I had received instructions on the evening of 28 August to communicate to the French an abstract of the comprehensive surrender terms and, to crown it all, to invite them to be present at the signature! Similar communications were apparently to be made to a number of other Governments, including the Commonwealth Governments. We protested, but in vain. With pardonable misgivings, Murphy and I made our joint communication to Massigli at noon on 29 August. We were at pains to insist that the whole thing was 'hypothetical'. No question of signature on any document had yet arisen, and the utmost secrecy must be preserved. This incident was, however, symptomatic of the lack of any sense of reality that prevailed in London.

30 August was a day of suspense. At midnight, the time-limit with Castellano ran out. What was to be done? General Eisenhower rightly thought that the best thing was for Bedell Smith, Murphy and myself to go to Sicily and to take Zanussi with us. At the same time arrangements were made to bring Castellano to Sicily with all speed. If, as we

hoped, he arrived on the 31st, we at least would be there at Alexander's side to make the critical decisions. So on 30 August we set out. We were, as usual, hospitably received in Alexander's camp. After dinner he explained for our benefit the essentials of the military problem. London seemed to think that this campaign would be a walkover. But what were the facts?

The operation, he told us, was a dangerous gamble, because such inadequate Allied forces had been allocated to it. The Germans already had some nineteen divisions in Italy, built up during the month since Mussolini's overthrow. The Italians had sixteen divisions, who might jump either way. But Alexander said he would have only three to five Anglo-American divisions for our initial landings, to a maximum build-up of eight divisions over the following two weeks. So Italian co-operation must somehow be obtained immediately.[24]

Whatever the orders from Roosevelt, Churchill, Attlee, or anybody else, the obvious thing to do was to forget about the 'long terms' and arrange an immediate signature of the short military terms. We should even go beyond that. We should accept and welcome Italian co-operation. This was our only hope, in a desperately dangerous situation.

I was deeply impressed by Alexander's note, not of alarm, but of calm and logical precision. I made up my mind that no telegrams from London or anywhere else would prevent me from getting what he wanted if it was humanly possible to do so. Murphy, a stout-hearted comrade in times of need, supported me loyally.

Castellano duly arrived, accompanied by Montanari. A long discussion took place at which neither Murphy nor I was present. Nor did Alexander himself take part. It was thought wiser to keep the talks on a purely military basis, under the Chief of Staff's direction. At the end of the discussion it was decided to arrange for all the Italians, except Castellano, to go back to Rome. They undertook to try to persuade their Government to accept the terms of the military armistice.

The Chief of Staff, with the full support of Murphy and myself, decided, temporarily at any rate, to suppress the longer and more formidable document. But it was becoming clear that what mattered to the Italians was the relative power of the Allied and the German forces. This was more important than words or texts. On the same evening, at a conference in General Alexander's caravan, it was decided to recommend to Eisenhower that an airborne division should

[24] Murphy, pp. 236–7.

be sent to land near Rome and thus bolster up the morale of the Italian divisions in the neighbourhood. This plan, if agreed, should be communicated to the Italians by the methods which we had set up. The next day Eisenhower telegraphed his approval.

The story of the airborne division is indeed a sad one. When some days later the Italians returned to Rome after accepting the armistice, they were assured that this division would arrive, and help them to seize and hold the city. General Ridgway, the commander, and his deputy, General Maxwell Taylor, were both men of courage and determination. But they had their doubts about this venture. More-over, the airborne troops would be needed for Naples. But Murphy and I argued

that failure to go through with the operation would destroy whatever chance there was of organised Italian military co-operation and especially of the six divisions they had promised. It also would look like bad faith on our part. Ridgway finally growled that he would agree only if the two double-damned political advisers went to the Rome landings in the first place. Macmillan and I had not thought about this but suddenly the suggestion seemed exactly right. 'It's a deal,' we told Ridgway.[25]

A little later Eisenhower and the majority of his staff supported the venture and Taylor was given the dangerous duty of going to Rome to see for himself. Murphy tells the rest of the story:

As soon as the project was definitely approved, Macmillan and I informed Eisenhower that, by agreement with Ridgway, political advisers would be in the lead plane. The General replied, 'That's good. Send some of your men who really know their way around.' Macmillan explained that we were not planning to send anybody; we intended to go ourselves. Eisenhower looked at us for a moment, and then said dryly, 'Well, all right. There's nothing in the regulations which says diplomats are not expendable.'[26]

Apart from the adventure, which would have been thrilling, both my colleague and I believed that enormous political gains might be won. Unluckily, at the last moment when we were all set to go, a message came from Maxwell Taylor that the Italians had withdrawn their support owing to the movement of German armed units into the Rome area. The Italians were now doubtful as to whether they could control the airfields. How far this information was correct no one will

25 Ibid., p. 242.
26 Ibid., pp. 242–3.

ever know. But whatever the rights and wrongs, the failure to risk the airborne division proved a fatal impediment to our hopes for the early capture of Rome and added enormously to the difficulties of the long struggle from one end to the other of the Italian peninsula.

While we were waiting, we lazed about in our pleasant orchard, trying to remain at least outwardly calm. Meanwhile one of my staff, Tom Dupree, was having a little adventure of his own. When passing through Lisbon, General Zanussi had deposited at the Italian Embassy two packets containing a lot of useful information about the Germans, including their order of battle. Prunas, the Italian Minister in Lisbon, was a reliable man, and a keen supporter of Italy's making peace with the Allies. Once again my office organised quite a nice bit of work. A number of messages were sent, in not too secure a code, by which it appeared essential for my Press Attaché to go to Lisbon on urgent Ministry of Information business. However, Tom had a better idea himself and after various precautions to cover his tracks he decided to be a Spaniard. In this guise he presented himself at 8 o'clock on 1 September in the Italian Embassy. He obtained the two packages from the trembling hands of Signor Prunas, and delivered them safely at A.F.H.Q. the next day.

On the morning of 2 September the Italian delegation reappeared. But they now stated that they had no authority to sign the armistice terms. They wished only to discuss plans for the landings of the airborne division and to carry on military talks. The negotiations were of course in the hands of Bedell Smith, representing Eisenhower; but Alexander was the senior officer on Italian soil, and it seemed to me that in this emergency he must take action. I therefore sent a message to his camp—a little distance from ours—to suggest that the moment had come for a display of firmness. He entered into the spirit of the thing with enthusiasm.

After a little time his cortège arrived, with a number of officers, all in parade order. The guard turned out and presented arms. He himself wore a well-pressed tunic, beautifully cut breeches, highly polished boots with gold spurs, and a gold peaked cap. He sent for the Italians and received them with a correct but cold dignity, contrasting noticeably with the rather too familiar terms which had now been established between the Italians and Eisenhower's representatives. There was no shaking hands, no interchange of civilities. He expressed

his amazement at the behaviour of the Italian delegation. Were they
negotiators or spies? Let them make up their minds—and immediately. They had been sent back to obtain the necessary authority to
sign. They should not have returned without it. It was a breach of
faith, for which they and their friends would surely suffer. He carried
out this little play-acting with great aplomb and, remounting his car,
he and his little procession retired with some ceremony, the guard
turning out for the second time. But the General was as eager as all
the rest of us to hear the result. The Italians retired to their tent for
consultation. Our tent was behind it. The only way by which the
General could reach us, unseen by the Italians, was—after leaving the
orchard at the far end—to creep round outside the wall till he could
climb over it to join us. This he did, with schoolboy delight. But the
circuit was very long, and it was very hot; and his boots, although very
smart, were very tight. Finally he reached us, and together we awaited
anxiously the result. The Italians continued for some time to discuss
their problem with eager volubility. At last, they requested a further
meeting with the Chief of Staff. They formally announced their
decision to ask immediately for authority to sign, and to meet all
General Alexander's demands. A message was accordingly sent back
through our wireless link. The authority must be given and confirmation deposited with Sir D'Arcy Osborne, and he must acknowledge its
receipt.

While we anxiously awaited the reply, messages kept arriving from
home asking what arrangements were being made for representatives
of Governments of the Dominions and other United Nations to attend
the official ceremony. I kept sending back protests at this folly. We
were not yet sure about the short terms—indeed I feared that the
Italians on the mainland had begun to realise our military weakness
and the difficulty of landing troops in sufficient force. There was no
hope of getting the long terms. But my protests had no effect; and I
could only hope that what I had now learned to call 'logistical'[27]
reasons would prevent these ambassadors from arriving. Actually
General Theron, of South Africa, did turn up; but he soon understood
the situation and behaved with great good sense. He readily agreed to

[27] Soon after my arrival in Algiers, I asked what 'logistics' meant. One of my staff
sent me the following note: 'Logistics is an American term. It is short for Q, like ele-
vator for lift.'

the formula that he had not been there at all; meanwhile he was a welcome and agreeable guest.

The next day, 3 September, was one of ups and downs. The vital telegrams to Rome had got through in a rather garbled form, and it was not until about 4 o'clock that the final reply reached us. It ran as follows: 'General Castellano is authorised by the Italian Government to sign acceptance of the armistice conditions. The declaration which you asked for [i.e. from H.M. Minister at the Vatican] will be delivered today.' The remaining formalities were quickly completed. It remained only to discuss how the armistice should be announced. It was finally agreed that Generals Eisenhower and Badoglio should announce it at 6.30 p.m. on the day, to be called X-Day, before the landings. We, of course, were unwilling to give them the precise date when the invasion would take place, for the risks were too great. But if they would listen each day to the B.B.C., on the vital morning there would be broadcast two talks about Nazi propaganda in the Argentine. This would be the signal; the armistice must be proclaimed that evening. Meanwhile, it would be convenient, before we parted, to interchange texts of what Eisenhower and Badoglio would say. (This was Kenneth Strong's idea, and was to prove invaluable.)

Montgomery's armies were now beginning to move across the Straits of Messina, and no very serious German opposition was encountered. But the attack on Salerno and the attempt to capture Naples was a much more serious affair. The earliest possible day for launching this was the night of 8–9 September. On the 4th, I returned to Algiers with Murphy, Bedell Smith and other officers. During the short interval, the situation in Rome worsened and the German grip began to tighten. At 11 o'clock on the morning of 8 September, the Chief of Staff rang me up to say he had received a message through our sources that the Italians now wished to call the whole thing off! The plan for the airborne division had been cancelled, and German forces were in command of the Rome area. According to Badoglio, the announcement of the armistice was no longer possible. Nor could he guarantee any airfields. General Maxwell Taylor, who had gone to Rome, confirmed this pessimistic account of the military position. He reported that the Germans had 12,000 troops in the Tiber area and that the Panzer divisions had been reinforced by detachments to a total of 24,000 men. All supplies of gasoline and munitions to the Italian divisions had been stopped. They were therefore virtually immobilised. The new 'combinazione' had met with a considerable set-back.

Eisenhower was in Bizerta, but in view of this unexpected development we decided to send a message to him and to the Combined Chiefs of Staff saying we felt we should go through with the plan as agreed, which at least would create the maximum confusion to cover our operations. Eisenhower fully accepted this advice, and a strong message was sent demanding that the Italians must stand by their signed undertaking. It was also agreed that Murphy and I should see Massigli and de Gaulle to inform them of the situation. By 5 o'clock we got encouraging messages from the President and the Prime Minister. Accordingly, Murphy and I called on Massigli and gave him the news of the military armistice. As I rather expected, this filled him with dismay. The surrender of Italy was fine. But the French Committee had not been informed. I told him the outline of the whole strange and tangled story, partly to show how difficult it would have been to consult him at every stage, and partly to underline the importance of secrecy from the military point of view. It was a help to be able to add that we had not even been able to keep the Commonwealth Governments fully informed. I also told him quite frankly about what was happening at the moment and the possibility that even now the Italians would repudiate the armistice. At 6 o'clock we went on to see de Gaulle with the same news. With a certain sardonic humour, he congratulated us that the war between our countries and Italy was at an end. France, of course, was still at war with Italy, as his Government was not a party to the armistice. I did not take this too seriously, but ventured to observe that, as a soldier, he would understand the need for secrecy. To this de Gaulle replied, 'I am not a soldier.' I was tempted to ask why he dressed himself up in a peculiar and rather obsolete costume which surely no one would choose to wear unless it was imposed upon him by military necessity.

The critical hour was now approaching. At 6.30 I went down to the office of the 'psychological warfare boys'. We began with Eisenhower's broadcast, which had been recorded. Then we waited, in breathless excitement. What would come out of Rome Radio? After a few minutes' silence and a short consultation with Murphy, the order was given. Marshal Badoglio's declaration was read. Never did I bless any man more sincerely than Kenneth Strong. It was his foresight which saved the situation. Marshal Badoglio's words came over fine, at least from Algiers. We felt a little unhappy about this deception, but what else could we do? We waited on hopefully. It was a relief when at 7.45 Rome Radio broadcast the announcement of the armistice and Badoglio's statement in precisely the terms agreed. So the Italians kept their word. The delay was due to the confusion and danger in Rome, not to bad faith. Indeed, the King and Badoglio had been forced to precipitate flight, to avoid falling into German hands. On this terrible night they motored through the German lines to Pescara on the Adriatic coast, where they embarked on an Italian cruiser for Brindisi. They left with only a small group of officers and courtiers, without luggage or effects. The Germans closed in immediately, disarmed all Italian troops in the Rome area, and started to move their divisions south of the capital. There was an armistice, but no peace.

Warned by Alexander's explanations, Murphy and I were fully aware of the true military position and only anxious lest our people at home would think that the armistice meant that Italy was in our hands. Of course it merely meant that our campaign in Italy began under more favourable conditions. Already we felt sorry for the Italians in their terrible dilemma. They were indeed to pay a heavy price for their long years of submission to Mussolini and Fascism.

But the advantages of the armistice were certainly substantial. The surrender of the Italian fleet, which was loyally carried out, was a real gain. Landings became possible in Calabria and Apulia, and a rapid retirement of the Germans followed in that area. Moreover, the moral and material consequences of the defection of an ally were not inconsiderable. If a long and difficult struggle still awaited us, the Germans were now fighting, as in Africa, a desperate and prolonged rearguard action. In any event the war in Italy was assuming the proportions of a Second Front and to that extent gave substantial relief to the Russians.

During these anxious days the battle was proceeding with full vigour. The build-up of our divisions was slow, and reinforcement was much more difficult for us than for the enemy. At the same time, the Eighth Army was moving rapidly up from the toe of Italy to join the hard-pressed Fifth Army. By a remarkable stroke Taranto had been seized, and this fine harbour fell into our hands. This was an achievement of the Royal Navy. With 6,000 men of the British Airborne

Division on board, our ships steamed into the harbour and captured it. There was no opposition or protest. The Navy also gave splendid help in the Salerno and Naples area. To this end, when a naval bombardment could be of assistance, Admiral Cunningham never hesitated to risk his capital ships. By 19 September the position, which had been precarious and even alarming, began to improve. The German counter-attacks were finally repulsed, and more and more of our troops got ashore with their essential supplies. By the beginning of October the port of Naples and the Foggia airfields were safely in our hands. These were great prizes.

Meanwhile, by a remarkable *coup*, the German parachutists had succeeded in rescuing Mussolini. From now on there would be a rival Italian Government, with gradually shrinking territory and authority as the war proceeded, but still with a certain nuisance value. However, in the end it was perhaps no disadvantage. Mussolini would have been a great embarrassment to us if he had fallen into our hands alive.

Murphy and I, after our disappointment over the airborne division, now felt that we should somehow get to the mainland of Italy. Fortunately we were able to persuade Eisenhower that it would be a good thing to go and find out what was happening. The King and Badoglio were believed to be at Brindisi. But what kind of Italian Government could exist? What should be our relations with it? What was it to do? Was it, above all, an organisation which had any reality? Could it possibly enforce, with the best will in the world, the armistice terms which it had accepted? All these were urgent matters. There was considerable discussion as to the nature of any mission. It was finally decided to make it a 'Service' or 'Military' Mission, with Murphy and me as political advisers.

I thought this wisest, because I have no guidance at all as to the line H.M.G. or the U.S. Government want to take towards the Italian Government. We made a 'Military Armistice' and it's best . . . to have a nominally 'Military' mission.[28]

General Mason-MacFarlane was suggested as head of the mission. I sent the necessary telegrams to the Colonial Office, War Office and the King for his temporary release and he arrived the next day. He had been a good friend and a generous host to all who passed through

[28] 13 September 1943.

Gibraltar during these years. Eisenhower had a high regard for him. But he was to prove an unlucky choice. General Maxwell Taylor, charming, intelligent, and with some knowledge of Italian, was added. Vice-Admiral Power (commanding at Taranto) was told to make whatever preliminary contacts might be possible.

We started from El Aouina aerodrome (Tunis) at 9 a.m. [on 12 September] —the four of us and Bombardier Casey (Mason-Mac's batman) who (I feel) is going to be the real leader of the mission.

The pilot of the Flying Fortress asked us where we wanted to go. We said either Brindisi or Taranto. He said, 'Aren't those in Italy?' We said, 'Yes.' He said, 'I think the Germans have got the aerodromes there.' We said, 'No. We sent a brigade into Taranto on Saturday (or perhaps Friday) and we think they have got Taranto.' He said, 'Yes—but the aerodrome is at a place called Grottaglie, about 20 kilometres from Taranto, and how do you know who has got this?' We said, 'Well, we can go and see.'[29]

We flew past Sicily, leaving Messina and the Straits on our left, and just after noon we saw Taranto. We thought we saw some Italian cruisers and a destroyer and our pilot thought it wiser to sheer off in case they had not heard of the armistice and decided to shoot us down. We were told not to use any wireless for fear of enemy detection. So we circled several times around the airfield, flying very low. There seemed to be a number of undamaged Italian fighter machines as well as some damaged Italian and German planes. Eventually we landed. The crew stood to the guns of our Fortress, and we got out rather timidly and a little self-consciously, wondering what would happen next.

A large number of Italian Air Force came running up and excited conversation ensued. We felt rather like the discoverers of a new continent— with the aborigines gesticulating and gabbling in a strange tongue.

General Taylor has done 'Italian in Twenty Lessons' and was jolly good.

Murphy and I smiled and kept repeating with outstretched and welcoming arms, 'Pace! Armistizio! Armistizio! Pace!' Casey made himself the best understood of all, and

as far as I could make out, he demanded the surrender of the aerodrome, which appeared to be readily conceded.

Our position was now full of interest and opportunity.

[29] Ibid.

. . . we found ourselves in possession of an excellent airfield, some partially destroyed buildings, the embarrassingly loyal attentions of a large number of Italian Air Force, including the Orderly Officer in a purple sash, no transport of any kind, and great difficulty in making a field telephone work. (We were also not quite certain whom to ring up. It seemed hardly correct to ring up the Exchange at different towns and say 'Excuse me—but can you tell me whether your town is in the possession of the Allies or the Germans?') We also had (by a most unusual mistake of the Americans) no food or drink. However, after prodigious conversational and telephonic efforts a colonel was produced who had both a car and some gasoline. Casey and the crew were left in charge of the Fortress. Four of us crowded into a rather small Fiat, and drove to Taranto. We got there about 5 p.m.

What was to be done next? I had already sufficient experience to know that the best thing to do in any difficulty is to ask for Navy House. This turned out sound, for we found

an admiral, a captain, several commanders and junior officers, a system of communication, an officers' mess, a commandeered hotel (with bedrooms and real beds) and a clear picture of the situation.

The Germans had retired one or two days before and were believed to be about fifteen miles away. We had originally brought one airborne brigade and another was now ashore. These had advanced and so a screen had been thrown round the town. The road to Brindisi was said to be cleared of Germans, at least Admiral Power had left by car and had not returned. (This argument seemed to me double-edged, but I said nothing.) The position of Bari was uncertain. The Italian fleet had conformed to the orders which they were given, and things looked pretty healthy so far as the Navy was concerned.

We decided to wait for Admiral Power . . . [who] turned up about 6.30. He gave us an account of his contact with Badoglio and . . . the Minister of Marine. He did not see any other Ministers. He believed the King to be there, but did not ask. He could not form any judgement as to whether the Government as a whole was functioning or capable of doing so.

We decided to remain in Taranto for the night with our hospitable hosts, and to set off the next morning in search of the remains of the Italian Government.

We found them in Brindisi housed in a fine medieval castle, greatly extended in later times, and surrounded by a moat. One side over-looked the harbour, with a wide view of the port. It was a naval establishment of importance. The sailors seemed to be clean and well turned out, and the saluting was good. A smart enough guard was produced for our reception.

We were met by General Ambrosio, whom we understood to be Chief of the Combined Staffs, Army, Navy and Air Force. He seemed neat and efficient but not impressive. After General Mason-MacFarlane had explained our purpose we were taken to see Marshal Badoglio. He was seventy-two years old, and I summed up my impressions at the time as follows:

Honest, broad-minded, humorous. I should judge of peasant origin, with the horse common sense and natural shrewdness of the peasant. A loyal servant of his King and country, without ambitions. He states a case with clarity, in a few words. He is a little like General Georges but with more restraint and dignity. He is a soldier and clearly without much political sense, believing that he has the popular support at the moment and that it can all be concentrated in a military movement without a political side. In this he is a little like Giraud, but with more modesty and less egotism.

The only other officers we saw at this time were General Zanussi, our old friend from Algiers and Sicily, and General Roatta, Chief of the Army Staff. My report about the latter was perhaps harsh, but not very far from the truth:

A good linguist, a travelled and intelligent conversationalist, with tendencies to be a bore. The perfect Military Attaché. I would say that his brains were more developed and effective than his guts.

In addition, we saw the Duca d'Acquarone, the Minister of the Royal Household. He seemed to combine the posts of Keeper of the Privy Purse and Principal Private Secretary. He struck me as entirely devoted to the King and the Royal family.

Our first contacts with these notabilities were somewhat perfunctory, for our chief purpose was to form an impression of the situation. After talks with the Ministers, we lunched with the King and his small staff. To my regret, Mason-MacFarlane took a very hostile attitude towards the King, which seemed to be strange for a British officer. It was perhaps round the monarchy that we could build some kind of a Government. In the afternoon Murphy and I talked again with Badoglio, this time in private. We explained frankly to him the difficulties with which his Government was faced. We told him that

the British and American Press could not forgive the King for his
surrender to Mussolini and Fascism and his long support of that
unhappy régime. Moreover, our Press was reviving all the stories of
Italian atrocities in Ethiopia. We should have difficulty in helping the
Government; but if they would act fairly with us we would undertake
to act fairly with them. With a certain resemblance to some of those
French officers we had lately met, he said quite simply: 'I was a Fascist
because the King was a Fascist. When the King told me to organise an
anti-Fascist Government I agreed to do so. I do what the King tells
me.'

Murphy and I also managed to see the King alone, without the
jaundiced presence of General Mason-MacFarlane. He seemed nervous
and—as well he might be—exhausted. He explained to us how hurriedly they had had to leave Rome to avoid capture by the Germans.
He pointed out that even now there was an Italian ship in the harbour
with steam up, ready to take him away if the Germans recaptured
Brindisi. We tried to reassure him. Murphy asked whether there was
any personal assistance we could give him. Was there anything he
wanted?

After a hesitant pause, he said: 'The Queen has been unable to get any
fresh eggs. Is it possible that we could somehow get a dozen eggs?' That was all
he asked of us, so with a dozen eggs we sealed our concord with the thousand-
year-old House of Savoy.[30]

We also managed to make a call upon Prince Umberto. I found him
agreeable enough and with a certain sort of dry humour.

He observed that he had purely by chance planned to come to Rome on
the day [of] the armistice. . . . Marshal Richthofen came to see him about an
hour before the announcement, and this had not been an easy conversation![31]

There was already passing through my mind the possibility of the
King's abdication; it seemed to me that the Prince could not be held
responsible for his father's decisions or indecisions during the last
twenty years. Perhaps he could play a useful role.

The Italians, of course, were anxious about the status of their
Government and country vis-à-vis the Allies. They were also much

[30] Murphy, p. 247.
[31] 16 September 1943.

concerned with economic and financial matters. An expert called Innocenti was produced at one moment.

The Marshal professed complete ignorance of these; but M. Innocenti was certainly ill-named. I thought him very slick.[32]

Murphy and I now thought we had better try to make our first report. One thing at least we had settled. Marshal Badoglio agreed to give the necessary order for the banks in Taranto to accept Allied lira notes. But since we had

no typists, no transport (except a car which we pinched off an Italian colonel and the driver of which—we call him Wilfred—is loyal to us and seems to stick with us), very little food, and no help of any kind,[33]

it seemed best to get back to base—which was still Algiers.

The next few days in Algiers were very hectic. For 20 September my record is self-explanatory.

Italy, France, France, Italy—a series of problems and telegrams pouring in from London and Washington. Propaganda in Italy meetings; propaganda in France meetings; a French row about Corsica; a French row about our being too kind to the Italians; de Gaulle and Giraud have quarrelled; they have made it up; they want to see me; I refuse to see them, saying I am busy on important matters and leaving again in a few hours, and so on. A *splendid* telegram from P.M. *endorsing our policy* completely, with which General Smith was delighted. *No* telegram from Washington, which infuriates him. Quite a day.[34]

Since we seemed to move continually from Tunis or Bizerta to Algiers and back again, with occasional visits to Italy, we were kept alert.

The British and American Press were suspicious of another Darlan-Clark Agreement. All those whom Eisenhower used to call 'the long-haired, starry-eyed boys' were on the warpath again. But on the night of 23 September a 'Most Immediate' message arrived which delighted us.

Stalin is being very sensible. He is all for the King of Italy (and the Pope if necessary) as long as they will help to fight the Germans. He is much more realistic than our *New Statesman, Daily Chronicle,* etc.[35]

[32] Ibid.
[33] 15 September 1943.
[34] 20 September 1943.
[35] 23 September 1943.

The next difficulty was to get the King of Italy to give a broadcast.

He is too old to let him speak direct into the microphone and anyway we
want to be sure of the speech. We have now managed to get a recording set to
Brindisi and the records should get back here by air today or tomorrow.
There has been a tremendous 'howdedoo' about this. The Italian Ambassadors at Madrid and Lisbon won't do their stuff about Italian naval and
merchant ships in Spanish and Portuguese ports without it. We have already
got . . . letters from Badoglio flown to Madrid and Lisbon.[36]

Our financial coup in Brindisi had a sad ending:

Excited telegram from the P.M. about some broadcast at Bari in which the
King of Italy was referred to as King of Albania and Emperor of Ethiopia!!
(Of course it turned out to be merely a proclamation about currency and the
rate of exchange, of which our mission had written the text but omitted to
see the headings. So the printer had just put in the usual style, out of habit, I
suppose.)[37]

After all, the Kings of England continued to style themselves Kings
of France for many centuries after the loss of the last piece of French
territory. But perhaps that was different.

At 1 a.m. on 27 September, after a long night of conflicting duties, I
sent this telegram to the Prime Minister:

. . . I find it rather difficult at the same time to look after all these details in
Brindisi, to perform my duties at General Eisenhower's advanced H.Q. at
Tunis, and to deal with a French crisis at Algiers. But I do my best.[38]

Churchill was discerning enough to let this protest pass without
comment.

The minds of the President and the Prime Minister were now
moving along more constructive paths. We must make a rapid decision
as to whether Italy was to be treated as the Germans had treated
France—that is, as a conquered country—or whether we were to
advance towards quasi-alliance. It was at this point that the term 'co-
belligerency' first came into use. On 21 September Churchill had
telegraphed to Roosevelt as follows:

The question of giving the Badoglio Government an Allied status does not
come into our immediate programme. Co-belligerency is good enough. On this

[36] 24 September 1943.
[37] 26 September 1943.
[38] 27 September 1943.

footing we should work for the gradual conversion of Italy into an effective national force against Germany, but, as we have said, she must work her passage.[39]

He went on to declare that the principle must be 'payment by results'. Roosevelt was disposed to agree, and wished to instruct Eisenhower to withhold the long-term armistice provisions until things began to evolve.

On my return from Brindisi I had sent a detailed report on the situation, pointing out that since the Italians knew nothing about the long armistice terms, except by hearsay, we were in a position either to withdraw them or to modify them. Unhappily, modification was not so easy because the bureaucrats of the State Department and the Foreign Office in their pride of authorship had already communicated them to the United Nations. The President, having his eye on a future election and a large Italian vote, began to draw back; and Churchill would undoubtedly have followed him. But apart from our own officials, who can sometimes in the last instance be controlled, there was Stalin. It seemed unlikely that he would let us out of the entanglement into which we had got ourselves enmeshed. I was bound in honour to report that I believed that Badoglio if pressed would sign the long terms, possibly with a new preamble and with an understanding—not altogether logical but in the circumstances useful—that the old armistice of 3 September would remain operative. So this distasteful operation became necessary. The chief difficulty, as I expected, was to turn on the phrase 'unconditional surrender'. These words, which held pride of place in the long terms, had been studiously avoided in the short.

Murphy and I set out for Brindisi. The long terms and Attlee's telegram on behalf of the War Cabinet, which I had kept safely locked in my box at Cassibile, must now at last be revealed to Badoglio and the King. The Italian Government had been invited to a meeting in Malta on the 29th. It was now the 27th. It would be useful to go through the agenda. For this purpose our delegation consisted of Mason-MacFarlane, Bedell Smith, Murphy and myself. General Badoglio was accompanied by General Ambrosio and the Duca d'Acquarone. In trying to soften the impact of our new demands, we explained that Article 12 of the military armistice had referred to them, and that

[39] Churchill, *Closing the Ring*, p. 168.

their acceptance naturally followed. The chief reasons, we admitted, were first to satisfy Allied public opinion—weak arguments, since the terms were not published during the war—and secondly, to avoid misunderstanding later on about points of detail. However, General Eisenhower had authority to make such modifications in their application as he might think fit. It was indeed clear that the turn of events and the spirit of the declaration of the President and the Prime Minister had already made some of these provisions out of date.

At our first meeting Badoglio merely agreed to discuss the matter with the King. There then followed a long talk about the other points on the agenda, with particular reference to an Italian declaration of war against Germany. Bedell Smith emphasised the military importance of this, since in its default any Italian soldiers, sailors or airmen captured by the Germans might, with some show of legality, be treated as *francs-tireurs* and not as prisoners of war. On the political side, a declaration of war would impress public opinion and help us to implement, by stages, increasing concessions to Italy, including the gradual modification of Allied military government and the return of Sicily and other provinces to Italian rule. This matter—the declaration of war—must also be referred to the King for decision.

As regards an alliance or quasi-alliance, the Marshal himself seemed to be ready enough to accept the phrase 'co-belligerence'. A formal alliance was not a necessary condition for armies fighting side by side. In the First World War there was no alliance between Great Britain and the United States. They had, in truth, been co-belligerents. Bedell Smith had thought up this argument and was very pleased with it, repeating it many times.

In general, Badoglio indicated that many of the matters on which the Allied Governments wanted satisfaction—the declaration of war; the question of alliance; above all, the broadening of the basis of the Government—could only be effective when the King and Government returned to Rome. Alas, at that time we too thought that Rome would soon fall into our hands, and that the Germans, for sound military reasons, would shorten their line to the positions into which they were eventually driven. But Hitler did not like retirement. He realised the political importance of Rome. As in Africa, he ordered his troops to yield ground as slowly as possible, reinforcing them for this purpose right up to the end. Yet, at this time, the prospect of early entry into Rome dominated much of our planning.

There was another expression in the long terms which gave great concern to the old soldier. The document referred to the right of the Italian people to choose their own system of government after the war. What did this mean—free elections? If so, it was acceptable. Or did it mean that the monarchy itself would be in jeopardy? In any case how could all these matters be decided in Brindisi? Rome was the capital.

On the next day, 28 September, we met again, Badoglio telling us that he could now speak with the authority of the King. What is more, he pointed out that it was necessary to go through once more the forty-two clauses in detail. How I cursed the experts of the Foreign Office. Many of these conditions were already inapplicable. Many of them were beyond the power of the Italian Government to implement. We therefore promised that this general point would be covered in a letter from the Commander-in-Chief to be handed to him on signature. Badoglio once again protested vigorously against the title 'Instrument of Surrender' as well as clause 1(a), stating that the Italian land, sea and air forces wherever located hereby surrendered unconditionally. As I reported to London, he said his objections were more practical than theoretical. The King and he were already being attacked, especially by Mussolini's Fascist friends, for accepting dishonourable terms. The words 'unconditional surrender' had not been included in the short-term armistice. To produce them now, after nearly four weeks, during which the Italians had done their best to carry out the armistice honourably, would be damaging and even dangerous. We said that we would try to meet this point in one form or another, the simplest being a letter from General Eisenhower recognising on behalf of the Governments to which he was responsible the effective change in the status of Italy since 3 September, by which Italy had become a co-operator with the United Nations. As soon as the Marshal left us, we drafted such a letter. It was in effect signed without amendment and given to the Marshal the next day. Our final task had been to ask the King to allow specific reference to the Soviet Union to be introduced into his broadcast. This was agreed.

We all thoroughly disliked the whole procedure, no one more than Eisenhower. But we were forced to go through with it. We left Italy at crack of dawn and flew to Malta. The conference took place on H.M.S. *Nelson* at 11 in the morning on 29 September. General Eisenhower was present, together with the three British commanders, as well as General Mason-MacFarlane, Murphy and myself. Other distinguished officers attended. On the Italian side there was Marshal Badoglio with General Ambrosio, General Roatta, and one or two others. Before the plenary conference there was a long discussion. At last Badoglio was persuaded to sign, on the understanding that his appeal for changes would be passed to the Allied Governments and that he would be handed Eisenhower's letter, to which he attached the greatest importance.

Many other points were covered, including the declaration of war against Germany, which the King wished to reserve until we got to Rome, at that time regarded as not likely to be long delayed. In fact, it was to be made on 13 October. The question of including new members in the Government was discussed at length. The King, it seemed, wished to reward Grandi for his betrayal of Mussolini. The Americans—or rather the President—were pressing for Count Sforza, who had a long and consistent record of opposition to Fascism. The one point on which everyone enthusiastically agreed was to say nothing to the Press.

So ended the Italian surrender. The fall of Mussolini, followed by the collapse of all that Fascism represented, was a signal triumph for the forces of freedom and democracy. But the problem presented by a nation in a state of collapse and wishing to reverse the policy of a whole generation was not an easy one to resolve. Many years later, when the old antipathies and hatreds have become obsolete and forgotten, the difficulties may seem to have been exaggerated. But our people had suffered much and long from Italian truculence and treachery. Our public opinion felt special resentment against the jackal Mussolini and those who had supported or condoned his policies. The transformation from a defeated enemy to something like an ally and friend was a process which was bound to take time. It is to the credit of the military commanders that they were the first to see this necessity. The so-called leaders of public opinion, especially in the Press, were only too prone to blame us for another infamous deal, such as had taken place a year before in North Africa. Generosity to a defeated enemy and the Christian desire to help and sustain a suffering population are often stronger the nearer one approaches the scene of war. Neither the commanders nor the rank and file felt any particular resentment. On the whole they rather liked the 'Eyeties'. Fortunately, the moods of newspapers change very rapidly, almost from one edition to another. Moreover, the long terms were not at that time published.[40] They played no role whatever in the development of the relations between the Allied Governments and Italy. They need never have been written, and all the bother about getting them signed was only a waste of time. Those assembled on His Majesty's splendid ship knew this to be true. Thus the actual ceremony gave no pleasure to any concerned, least of all to Admiral Cunningham, who now had the Italian Fleet safely in Valletta Harbour. However, it was soon over and followed by an excellent and enjoyable luncheon. We then got back to work.[41]

[40] The full Italian terms, short and long, were published in a White Paper (Cmd. 6693) in November 1945, together with other documents.

[41] In Appendix 1 will be found an account of the conversation between the various high officers on board H.M.S. *Nelson* at Malta on 29 September 1943, at 11 a.m., together with General Eisenhower's letter of the same date to Marshal Badoglio.

CHAPTER SIXTEEN

My French Mission: The Last Phase

WITH the coming into being of what was virtually a French Government and its formal recognition by Allied and neutral powers, both Murphy and I felt that our usefulness in this sphere was over. We both thought that we had been too closely connected with the early and somewhat anarchic period to be appropriate ambassadors in the new conditions. We hoped that the new organisation would function as an orderly and responsible Government without the old atmosphere of continuous unrest. In this we were rather too optimistic. Nevertheless, it was certainly right to wish for a change. It was soon agreed that this should be done. Duff Cooper, an old and dear friend, was nominated to be the first British Ambassador. But his arrival was delayed by a number of difficulties and it was not until the first days of January 1944 that I was able to be relieved of my dual functions. Ed Wilson replaced Murphy during November.

These last months were not without the usual number of sudden and violent storms which seemed to blow up so easily in the turbulent atmosphere of Algiers. The abnormal régime which I had found on my arrival on 2 January 1943 had certainly been replaced by a system which, if it were not founded on any firm constitutional basis, was at any rate trying to follow normal democratic and parliamentary procedure. Massigli, with his usual moderation, tried to gloss over the differences between the British and American formulas of recognition, and not to lay too much emphasis on the more liberal terms employed by the Soviet Union. Nevertheless, the long delay was widely resented by the French. As Dr. Johnson wrote in his famous letter to Lord Chesterfield, 'Patronage would have been welcome had it been timely'. Thus a sense of inferiority, especially tragic in the case of a country with so noble and splendid a history as France, still remained. Our success in Sicily was applauded by all our French friends. At the same time there was some disappointment that French troops had not been able to share in the enterprise. Similarly, the signature of the Italian armistice without informing the French, although it could be explained on practical grounds, was another blow to their pride.

In September 1943, a Mediterranean Commission was established. The news that France was to be represented was received with enthusiasm. But this proved short-lived; for the decisions of the Moscow Foreign Ministers' Conference in October involved radical changes. The proposed Mediterranean Commission disappeared, and France was not included in the new European Commission. Fortunately, an Advisory Council for Italy later came into being, although on a lower grade. In this we were able to secure French representation on an equal basis. The extreme sensitiveness of the French was, of course, natural—if rather tiresome. It explained many exaggerations and emotional outbursts which would otherwise have seemed inconceivable.

Towards the end of the year, bitter feelings were aroused by the notorious speech of Field-Marshal Smuts, in which he said that France could now be written off as a great power. I tried to remind the critics that, had they read the Field-Marshal's declaration more carefully, they would have seen that, in his view, Britain also must accept after the war a position of relatively reduced prestige and power. With the growth of the giants of the East and West, would it not be wiser, I tried to argue, for the countries of Western Europe to come more closely together in mutual support?

On returning to Algiers from Tunis on 25 September, I sensed that trouble was brewing. The next morning, while talking with Murphy and Bedell Smith,

a telegram arrived from the P.M., instructing me to tell de Gaulle that 'any alteration in the system of co-Presidents (de Gaulle and Giraud) would overthrow the basis on which the French Committee had been recognised and would have the most serious results'. He also told me to say the same to 'all the members of the Committee who are my friends'.[1]

This, of course, put me in a great difficulty.

[1] 26 September 1943.

If I were to deliver the message, [de Gaulle] would, of course, get very excited over another 'Allied intervention in French affairs' and the chances of a settlement would be much reduced. Or, alternatively, we would be put in a rather ridiculous situation, with no real remedy except to withdraw recognition and undo the work of nine months.

If, however, I were *not* to carry out the P.M.'s instructions and suppress the message, and the affair were to go wrong, I should be told that it was all my fault for disobeying my orders and that the delivery of the 'intervention' would have saved the situation.[2]

I was due to see de Gaulle at 11 o'clock at his invitation. We talked in general terms on the war, the situation in Italy and other matters. He seemed in a cheerful and rather mischievous mood. It soon became clear that he was hoping for an intervention by the Allies as an excuse for beating the patriotic drum with his colleagues. In spite of my instructions, therefore, I merely told him that in my personal opinion a break-up of the Committee through Giraud's resignation would be deplorable.

The question now turned on certain decrees of a complicated and highly technical character. De Gaulle observed that the new decrees had not abolished the co-presidency from the juridical point of view, although it would of course cease from a practical point of view. In other words, he would remain Prime Minister, while Giraud would become a Commander-in-Chief responsible to a civilian Minister. When I saw Massigli the next day he explained that the whole story of the crisis was simple. What was really the issue was the creation of what we would call a Minister of Defence. The new system would gradually deprive Giraud of his importance, but it could not be said to be a formal breach of the consulship system.

There were two issues in which Giraud's conduct of affairs was specially criticised. First, and most important, was his handling of the Corsican affair. On the night of 11 September the news came that the 'patriots' had secured control of Ajaccio. Giraud immediately sought and obtained permission of A.F.H.Q. to send two French destroyers, the *Fantasque* and the *Terrible,* with French troops to help the resistance movement. But the next day he got cold feet and called off his plans. The following morning he recovered his nerve and sent off the expedition. He also dispatched a French general appointed by himself

2 Ibid.

to administer the island under an *état de siège*. At the same time he sent Charles Luizet (curiously enough a keen Gaullist) as Prefect-designate of Ajaccio. But he did not see fit to inform the Committee— or even de Gaulle as co-President—of the action he had taken. The result was a stormy meeting of the Committee on 18 September on the question of principle as between civil and military power. However, a united French front was finally presented to the world. A proclamation was broadcast in the name of the Committee, congratulating the Corsican patriots on their achievement and by implication asserting the Committee's authority over liberated Corsica. At the same time the Committee announced its appointment of Luizet as Prefect of Ajaccio, without disclosing that he had been functioning in that capacity for a week.

There was another even more stupid episode about the Brosset Division. This, formerly the famous Larminat Division, had fought all the way from Alamein with the British Eighth Army. It was supplied with British equipment. Everyone knew that it was one of the best fighting divisions of the French Army. But, in spite of repeated requests, Giraud refused to re-equip it with American arms which were now available. When, therefore, he was asked to nominate a third division to be sent to Italy and chose the Brosset Division, General Alexander was forced to point out that it was quite impossible on technical grounds to put this British-equipped division alongside the two American-equipped French divisions already in the line. A Senegalese division was therefore nominated by Giraud in its place. This was a foolish affair, very damaging to French morale. It looked like a childish and peevish attack upon de Gaulle's veteran troops. It also drew attention once more to the anomalous situation by which the re-equipment of the French Army seemed still to be a matter of personal arrangement between the United States and General Giraud. As a result of this incident, negotiations were begun to regularise the system. But it injured Giraud in the eyes of moderate and patriotic Frenchmen.

I reported to London what was happening, and decided that the best thing to do was to go back to Italy, leaving Roger Makins in charge in the hope that the malady would take its usual Algerian course. On 28 September, while at Brindisi, I got a telegram from him to say that the Algiers crisis looked (after all) like running its normal course. Everyone had quarrelled, everyone had resigned, and everyone had become reconciled in the course of Monday. Giraud claims the victory; de Gaulle has won it. The only thing that matters is that the Americans should not get excited about it in Washington. I can easily keep them quiet at this end.[3]

A Minister of Defence was in fact appointed. By agreement between all concerned the choice fell on General Legentilhomme—a good soldier, very friendly to the British, but not a man of any administrative or political experience.

In view of Italian questions, which were now my main concern, I decided to go to England for a few days for consultation. I got a lift from Field-Marshal Smuts and was in London from 4 to 9 October. On my return to Algiers I found that Anthony Eden had arrived ahead of me. He was on his way to Moscow, for the conference of Foreign Ministers. I unfortunately felt extremely ill—as I had done for some days—and on taking my temperature found it was over 102°. Perhaps it was in this mood that I found the presence of the Foreign Secretary, with his considerable staff, as well as General Ismay with a bevy of staff officers, rather overwhelming.

In this pandemonium, they were all making separate and impossible plans. They would stay here; they would leave at once for Tunis; General Eisenhower would be at Tunis; no, General Eisenhower was in Italy; yes, but he would be returning to Tunis; well, they would go to Cairo and stop on the way at Tripoli, and so on. . . . It soon emerged (when the officer in charge was given a chance to speak):

(a) that the tyre of the York required repair;
(b) that there was no flying round Tunis owing to weather;
(c) that it would not be possible to land at Tripoli owing to weather;
(d) that the bad weather was moving east, and if they wanted to make sure of Cairo, they had better leave very early tomorrow and get ahead of it.[4]

For the next few days I was seriously ill and did not seem to be able to shake off my fever and sickness. Fortunately Colonel Richardson came to see me, and under his care I slowly recovered. This was my first acquaintance with this brilliant doctor, who afterwards became a devoted friend and has looked after me ever since. Richardson thought that I was in a bad state of exhaustion approaching prostration. However, I was able by remaining in bed to do a certain amount of

[3] 29 September 1943.
[4] 10 October 1943.

work and to see a number of visitors. The chief excitement was the appearance of Bogomolov, the new Russian Ambassador to the French Committee.

He has arrived here with twenty-five assistants, but like everyone else he has just got a room in the Aletti Hotel and eats in the American mess. As his standards of living are pretty high, he seems rather annoyed about it.

He has no car yet, so I sent John in ours to fetch him here. He asked John if he had been at Eton. Yes, replies John. Ah! says Bogomolov, a splendid school—a fine tradition—a splendid school, and went on muttering this all the way from the hotel to the villa.[5]

Bogomolov, a large-limbed man with loose clothes, white hands and a fat white face, called to see me and talked at considerable length.

He was very gracious—a little royal even. He talked a little about my stomach and at great length about his own, which requires constant attention and the rarest foods. These last are not found in the American mess or the Aletti and he is rather put out about it.

I did not attempt to do any business, but I did inform him about the Italian declaration of war which had just taken place.

He asked only one question on this. 'Did the Marshal know?' I showed him the Three-Power declaration, signed by Stalin, and all was well.[6]

During this time a large number of telegrams and papers were being sent to me on the subject of liberated France. Although this 'planning' was all very well intended, it seemed to me most unrealistic. I therefore wrote a letter to the Foreign Secretary setting out my views. I felt certain that the French would settle this matter for themselves and in their own way. The whole concept upon which the preparations were being made for the control of 'civil affairs' in metropolitan France seemed to me most dangerous. Surely the right thing was for the F.C.N.L., which was in effect the provisional Government of France, to take over at the earliest possible moment. They, and not British and American officers, were the natural people to administer metropolitan France and to assume full responsibility for its government. I expressed the same opinion to Cordell Hull, who also passed through Algiers at this time on his way to Moscow. General Eisenhower asked me to meet him, and I managed to go, although at this time I was

[5] 13 October 1943.
[6] Ibid.

spending most of my days in bed. The Secretary had come by cruiser to Casablanca and from there by aeroplane. The Americans certainly travelled in great style, even then. Averell Harriman, who accompanied him, had two C.54 machines and the Secretary another two.

I don't know why American statesmen are always so old. Secretary Stimson (Secretary for War) who came through here is over 80. Hull is 74. He is exactly like the portraits of all Americans of the Civil War period—a fine Southern gentleman. His views on internal politics are reactionary and on foreign politics based on the sort of vague Liberalism of the 'eighties' tinctured with personal prejudice. Nevertheless, he is obviously a 'character' [with] his fine head and striking appearance. . . .[7]

When I was ushered into the presence, Bob Murphy was flitting about like a monsignore in a papal palace. There were several doctors in attendance, including a little tubby man who looked like the anaesthetist. Hull was sitting in a kind of semi-darkness, and after an interval observed in his high voice that he had heard a great deal about me. He had been pleased at the co-operation between Murphy and myself, but of course the French were very difficult people. I said that for that reason the best thing to do was to let them manage their own affairs. The Secretary seemed a little doubtful as to the wisdom of this proposition. But about the Russians Secretary Hull was emotional. He thought that the conference of Foreign Secretaries would be of epoch-making effect. In a speech to Congress he had declared:

There will no longer be need for spheres of influence, for alliances, for balance of power, or any other of the special arrangements through which, in the unhappy past, the nations strove to safeguard their security or to promote their interests.[8]

Hull represented an opinion which was to reach its full and tragic development at the fatal Yalta Conference. It was to dominate American policies for the next few years. Meanwhile, it did not make our task easier.

At this time, Admiral Sir Andrew Cunningham left us to replace Sir Dudley Pound as First Sea Lord. I had got to know him intimately, and he had never failed in his sympathy and support. He was of special use to me by the influence that he obtained over the French naval officers and thereby upon quite important elements among the

[7] 15 October 1943.
[8] Murphy, *Diplomat among Warriors*, p. 259.

politicians. Everyone loved him, even if many were rather frightened of him. He left on Sunday 17 October, amid great ceremony. Admiral Sir John Cunningham took his place. Since he had previously been in charge in the Levant, he was to prove of special help to me shortly.

I still could not shake off my depression. The only thing that comforted me was the news of the birth of my first grandson.[9]

During this quiet, almost halycon, weather, de Gaulle came to lunch with me alone. He was in a most friendly mood. There was less complaint than usual regarding his treatment by the Allies, but he still felt he ought to have their full confidence and support. There was only one way to prevent difficulties and even civil war in France, and that was for the Committee of National Liberation with himself at the head to take over the Government at once, as the Germans retreated. Any interval would be dangerous. It would give an opportunity for the Communist Party to seize power. He felt no doubt that he could hold the position until the time came for a properly elected assembly and the formation of a new constitution. If this dangerous interval could be got over, things would settle down. He was the only man who had sufficient authority in France to control the situation. As always, I admired his sense of mission and his ardent faith.

Bogomolov, who called again the next day, took an unfavourable view of the French. He thought their standard of administration very low and their powers of organisation poor. They had already tried to make trouble by playing off each of us against the other, but we must present a united front. Britain, America, and the Soviet Union—these nations alone mattered. I began to wonder whether he too had been at Eton after all.

When I recovered my health I was forced to spend a great deal of time in Tunis or in Italy, leaving Makins in charge in Algiers. But I was back for the first meeting of the Consultative Assembly which was held in the afternoon of 3 November. It was intended to give some democratic basis to the governmental structure and to serve as an outlet for public opinion.

Since, of course, no real elections can be held, the members (about seventy) are partly elected by the municipal and county councils here in North Africa, partly ex-Deputies and ex-Senators who have escaped from France, and partly nominated by the various resistance movements in metropolitan France. Some

[9] Alexander, eldest son of Maurice Macmillan, M.P., born 10 October 1943.

of the last category have not yet arrived . . . their escape is not easy and depends on the various underground methods which we and the French have developed for this work.

The meeting of this Assembly was held in the meeting place [of] the Algerian Council. It is arranged in a semi-circle, like the French Chamber, with the President like a judge, on a sort of elevated platform.

There was a diplomatic gallery, in which I sat, with Bogomolov and Murphy and all the other representatives.[10]

I thought it a moving and imaginative concept, and had no patience with those who ridiculed or minimised the value of this body. Nevertheless, it was to lead to fresh troubles. With the institution of something like a normal Government and an assembly, as representative as the circumstances allowed, the feeling began to be widely expressed that the Committee had too many generals. It was almost a 'junta'. Moreover, Giraud's 'pluralism' was no longer tolerable. He must choose between being a joint President and remaining Commander-in-Chief. The pressure grew, and knowing the views of the President and the Prime Minister on this issue, I realised that it would be difficult to avoid Allied interference. General Georges came to see me on the morning of 10 November. He gave me an unexpectedly objective picture, for he too was beginning to lose patience with Giraud, much as he distrusted de Gaulle.

This was his story. On 6 November François de Menthon, speaking in the Assembly, urged the reconstitution of the Committee to include fewer generals and technicians and more politicians, and made a strong attack upon Giraud. When the Committee met, the general answered with great dignity in a speech which deeply moved the majority of the Commissioners. He appealed to his record. He had fought in the last war, had been gravely wounded and had been taken prisoner. He had fought in this war and had escaped from Germany to continue the fight. He had served to the best of his ability during the past year since the landing in North Africa. He had been condemned to death by Vichy. His wife was languishing in a prison in Lyons. His children had been taken off a few weeks ago to Germany where they were prisoners. He knew that many others had suffered equally; but perhaps there were some among those who prided themselves on having been followers of Fighting France who had not made any

[10] 3 November 1943.

personal sacrifices of a proportionate kind. Georges went on to say that had the vote been taken at that point, the Commission would have voted for Giraud. However, the debate proceeded; and it was decided that it was right that there should be a reorganisation of the Committee. General Georges offered his resignation and so did the other Commissioners. Since under the existing decrees the Committee was the only body empowered to accept resignations or make additions to itself, it was obviously impossible for the whole fifteen of them to engage on the task of Cabinet-making. It was therefore the general feeling that there should be a small sub-committee for this purpose, and General de Gaulle, René Pleven, Adrien Tixier and René Mayer were entrusted with the task. This resulted in a decree which in effect laid down that the Commander-in-Chief must become subordinate to the Government. Giraud thought that the intention was that he should remain co-President until he left to take command of the armies in the field. But this was clearly not the legal meaning of the decree and Giraud ought never to have agreed to it without clarifying this important point.

There was nothing now to be done except to try to find a reasonable solution. Catroux, with whom I lunched on the same day, gave me roughly the same account. But there were certain differences. He stated that at the meeting of the Committee two motions were carried: (1) that all the Commissioners, including Giraud and even de Gaulle, should place their resignations in the hands of the Cabinet-making sub-committee; (2) that the 'pouvoir militaire' should be definitely separated from the 'pouvoir civil'. Giraud accepted both these motions without demur.

Unfortunately, Giraud had not told the Committee that he hoped within a few weeks to take up his command and thereby, under the decree of 2 October, automatically vacate the co-presidency. However, on receipt of Giraud's letter of resignation, it was decided to send a delegation to see him. This in fact was done. When Murphy and I saw General Georges in the afternoon he told us that in his opinion the crisis was over. The deputation, led by Catroux and consisting of Tixier, Pleven, Mayer and some others, had assured Giraud that they had not wished to attack his position in any way; there had clearly been misunderstandings, and they thought the General had agreed to the propositions in full knowledge of their effect. A number of conces-

sions were made regarding Giraud's position as Commander-in-Chief
and it was agreed that a letter should be sent to him by all the
members of the Committee, asking him to remain in that post. Georges
took all this much more lightly than on previous occasions, and as he
left us he said: 'So ends our monthly crisis. The only difference is that
this one came ten days too soon; they usually take place in the week
after the 20th of each month.' He said that he himself would be glad
to resign.

After dinner I saw General de Gaulle. He clearly regarded this affair
as of minor importance. In any event, far too much emphasis was
being laid on Algiers and not enough on France. In reality the French
crisis had begun in 1789 and had lasted until the outbreak of war with
varying temporary systems but no permanent solution. It was his duty
to bring about such a degree of national unity as would make possible
a solution of the social and economic problems of France, without
disorder on the one hand or extreme policies on the other. It was for
that reason that he was so anxious about the position of the Communists and how best to handle them. Once again I ended the day feeling
that de Gaulle stood head and shoulders above all his colleagues in
the breadth of his conceptions for the long term. Meanwhile, he was
clearly the victor in the short-term struggle for power. Giraud, while
remaining for the time being Commander-in-Chief, left the Committee. At the same time Georges resigned or was expelled.

The next day I left for Italy, returning to Algiers on 13 November
to find a new and much more dangerous question. This time it was
one in which the British Government could not help being seriously
involved. For it concerned a major crisis in the Lebanon. The whole
affair seemed to have blown up very suddenly.

The French are committed to the policy of abolishing the mandate and
setting up an independent Lebanese Government, retaining for themselves—
by treaty—only the same kind of position as we have kept in Iraq or Egypt. In
1936 such a treaty was agreed with the Lebanese, but the French Government
fell, and it was never ratified. In 1941, when we conquered Syria and the
Lebanon and drove out the Vichy forces, the Free French troops fought with
us and we [installed] the Free French administration. At that time, Catroux
made the most solemn declarations and did indeed begin to take steps (very
slowly and deliberately) to implement them. Since he left Syria, I think that
his successor has been 'stalling' a good deal. However, the elections . . . did
in fact take place. These caused considerable friction, because Helleu

(Catroux's successor) violently accused Spears of taking part in the elections in order to secure the success of pro-British and anti-French candidates. Spears with equal vigour denied this. . . .

The French candidates were defeated heavily and a Government was formed with Ministers very hostile to the French, pledged to secure the independence of the Lebanon as soon as possible.

Helleu came back to Algiers for instructions and I was told to bring as much pressure as possible on the French Committee to secure his return with a liberal policy.[11]

With typical pedantry, the reality of the problem was complicated by a legal argument about the juridical position of the French Committee. Was the provisional Government the legal successor to the French rights and duties, including the mandate? Since they were not the legal Government of France, could they negotiate and ratify a treaty? Could the mandate be brought to an end with the League of Nations in abeyance?

Anyway, Helleu went back. When in Cairo, he heard that the Lebanese Parliament was in session and preparing a Bill revising the constitutional situation and declaring complete independence. Very naturally, he appealed to them to adjourn the debate until he could get to Beirut to explain the policy which had been agreed in Algiers and to negotiate. Very improperly, the Government refused this. The debate was held, and the amending Bill was passed through all its stages.

Helleu retaliated by arresting the [President and the] Ministers in the early hours of the morning, and closing the Parliament.

From this have started various incidents—riots, shootings, excesses by Senegalese troops, [all] minimised by the French in a most unblushing way, and [emphasised] by Spears in unending streams of telegrams to the Foreign Office, repeated to me.

I had no very clear instructions, but on receipt of this news I immediately had a short talk with Massigli. It was not altogether satisfactory, for the information we were receiving was confused and obscure. But I had my usual confidence in Massigli's wisdom and fairness.

On Monday 15 November I was suddenly ordered to Gibraltar. John and I set out and arrived in the afternoon. There was considerable confusion owing to the bad flying weather between England and Gibraltar, and the non-arrival of a number of expected machines. However, telegrams kept appearing in quick succession, and at 6.30

[11] 13 November 1943.

p.m. I was told to leave Gibraltar at once by launch. So off we went; and a few miles out of the harbour we were put aboard the *Renown*, to be greeted by the Prime Minister, on his way to the Cairo Conference.

The party consisted of the P.M., his daughter Mary, Randolph, Sir A. B. Cunningham (my old friend—now First Sea Lord), Lord Moran, General 'Pug' Ismay, Major Morton, and some others. The Air and Army Chiefs of Staffs and various other notabilities were not in the party, but proceeding by air.

The P.M. was in excellent form and asked a great deal about the French situation. . . . As always, if you maintain a point with energy, he is prepared to listen.[12]

The next morning Churchill sent for me at about 9 o'clock. He was in bed, having breakfast. He kept me enthralled for three and a half hours.

It was really a fascinating performance. The greater part was a rehearsal of what he is to say at the Military Conference; and he is *terribly* worried and excited about this. He naturally feels that the Mediterranean position has not been exploited with vigour and flexibility.

This . . . is due to the extreme rigidity of the combined Chiefs of Staff system, and of our American allies generally. It is, of course, infuriating for Winston, who feels that all through the war he is fighting like a man with his hands tied behind his back. And yet no one but he (and that only with extraordinary patience and skill) could have enticed the Americans into the European war at all.

I feel that he regards this coming [conference] at Cairo as the real turning point and the hardest job he has encountered.[13]

After this, to me, vastly revealing survey of the broad strategical problems, he asked about France and the Lebanon. He was naturally annoyed at Giraud's disappearance from the political field, but of course he knew in his heart that the co-presidency was only a temporary expedient. He was angry about General Georges. I tried to explain my view of the new forces which were rising up—not all of them in de Gaulle's hands and some of them challenging his authority. He turned next to the Lebanon.

I told him that I regarded this as rather a test case. If we handled the affair with some tact, as well as energy, we would get the support:

[12] 15 November 1943.
[13] 16 November 1943.

(a) of Catroux;

(b) of Massigli;

(c) of quite half if not two-thirds of the Committee,

and we could put de Gaulle in a minority of three or four.

But this required avoidance of ultimatums, except if absolutely necessary. I am afraid I also said that I thought as long as *Spears* was in Beirut there would be open and bitter warfare between us and the French. The P.M. did not much like this.[14]

Spears was an old friend of mine. We had worked together at the time of Munich, and I had always found him not only well informed and independent, but a devoted friend of France. Unhappily, he had quarrelled bitterly with de Gaulle about the Levant, and I could not help feeling that he took a rather prejudiced view of the situation now that de Gaulle was in charge. In any case, the French had developed a deep suspicion of what they were pleased to call 'la politique personnelle du Général Spears'. However, there was nothing to be done until we heard Catroux's report—for the one helpful thing was that Catroux had been sent to Beirut to deal with the problem on the spot.

I shall never forget the luncheon on the *Renown*. There we sat with the P.M., surrounded by a large and distinguished company, including among others John Winant, the American Ambassador in London. I was a few places down, but well within the P.M.'s range of fire. He told me that he thought he would send for General Georges as soon as he got to Algiers. He would do this in order to mark his displeasure at the turn of events.

He asked me if I agreed. 'Now give your opinion frankly. You always do, I know, and I very seldom agree with it!' So I said I thought it would be a most deplorable error on his part. 'Very well then, I will do it. I will see him at 6 p.m.' I do not really think it much matters, and he certainly had decided anyway, but I thought I would keep my end up.

During part of the luncheon and the long sitting that followed, the Prime Minister was in one of his rather brooding moods. Of course I knew that he was thinking about the large strategical issues of which he had given me a glimpse in the morning.

Somebody rashly remarked that the Services were better co-ordinated in this war than in the last. The Chiefs of Staffs system was a good one. 'Not at all,' said Winston. 'Not at all. It leads to weak and faltering decisions—or rather

[14] Ibid.

indecisions. Why, you may take the most gallant sailor, the most intrepid airman, or the most audacious soldier, put them at a table together—what do you get? *The sum of their fears.'* (This with frightful sibilant emphasis.)[15]

I felt glad that I was not the only victim of his attack. But I knew, as we all did, what tremendous burdens lay upon him and with what unsparing energy he was determined to pursue his purposes.

We reached Algiers the same afternoon. The Prime Minister wisely decided to continue his journey by sea. I was glad of this, for I knew what an exhausting programme lay before him; Cairo, Teheran, and back to Cairo again. He only delayed the ship long enough to receive General Georges. I did not much like this, but in view of the storm now blowing up around the Lebanon any little flurry on this account would be of minor importance.

In the evening I went with Bogomolov and Murphy to see Massigli and gave him a formal invitation to the French Committee to appoint a representative on the new Allied Advisory Council for Italian affairs. This at least was a little jam to go with the medicine that was now to be administered.

Makins told me what had happened about the Lebanon in my absence. General Catroux had arrived in Cairo and had two interviews with Casey, who had demanded not only the recall of Helleu and the release of the Lebanese Ministers, but their reinstatement in office. On the next day the Prime Minister sent Casey a telegram from the ship saying that the British Government could not wait indefinitely for the release of the arrested Government. That afternoon General de Gaulle made a statement on the situation, in reasonably moderate terms, to a specially summoned meeting of the new Consultative Assembly. I think he was impressed by the liberal opinions which were expressed from several members; at any rate he took the line that the incident was now in the process of settlement.

On 17 November the Foreign Office instructed Casey that if our demands had not been met by the evening of the 18th, he should go to Beirut on the 19th and inform General Catroux of an ultimatum expiring at 10 a.m. on Sunday the 21st. British troops would take over the responsibility for law and order, since they could not allow a dangerous situation to develop at such an important strategic point in the defence of the Middle East as a whole. At the same time I recieved

15 Ibid.

a telegram from the Foreign Office setting out various possible developments, but containing the definite statement 'We are not insisting on the immediate re-establishment of the old Government'. All through the next day a ceaseless flow of telegrams kept arriving from London, Beirut and Cairo. I felt sure that I could secure the reasonable requirements of the British Government from the French if I was given a chance. But I wanted to get them in a way that did not destroy the work of nearly a year in Algiers and which would carry with us all those moderate Frenchmen who were our friends. I did not want a Fashoda, and I could not help thinking that there were some who did.

I also had great confidence in Catroux, for I had long experience of his tact and diplomatic skill. Catroux had, of course, protested against immediate reinstatement of the Ministers, but was in general conciliatory. There was surely now an opportunity for a compromise solution.

On 19 November the French Committee sat all morning. General de Gaulle proposed an intransigent telegram to Catroux, urging him to make no concessions. But after a long debate, it was agreed to allow Catroux to make a settlement upon the lines which he had himself proposed. These were that the President and the Ministers should be immediately set free, and the President urged to form another Government under a new Prime Minister with whom negotiations would immediately be started with a view to a settlement of the larger issues. They also wished to postpone, as a face-saving device, Helleu's dismissal, at least for a few days. In the afternoon of the same day, Casey presented his *aide-mémoire* to Catroux, containing an ultimatum which would expire at 10 a.m. on Monday the 22nd. I had at least got the date of expiry postponed to Monday, on the grounds of the difficulty of communication between Beirut and Algiers, especially for the French. This document, delivered in writing, included the demand that the President and Ministers should 'revert to their status prior to the recent crisis'. I was instructed to give a copy to Massigli without delay.

The situation seemed to me so grave and so threatening to the future of our relations with France that while I showed Massigli the text at 9 a.m. on the 20th, I agreed not to deliver it to him formally until after the meeting of the Committee. This would enable him to argue the question on its merits. Since we had sat up most of the previous two nights receiving 'Most Immediate' telegrams from all quarters, this proved rather an anxious and exhausting day. A lighter tone was introduced by noon by a deputation of Communist Deputies to the new Consultative Assembly. 'They wished to congratulate Great Britain on things in general and the war in particular. A queer world!'[16]

To my great relief, Massigli came to see me at 4 p.m. to tell me that he had carried the recall of Helleu and the release of the Ministers through the Committee. Only de Gaulle and two others had been against it. But at the same time he made an urgent plea for the postponement of the time-limit to allow further discussion of the other questions involved. I strongly supported this in telegrams both to the Foreign Office and to the Prime Minister. But now the Foreign Office went back upon its previous view and I received a telegram telling me that Casey's *aide-mémoire* of 19 November had been formally approved by the War Cabinet and that they could not agree that on the release of the Lebanese Ministers a new Government should be formed. I was obliged to inform Massigli accordingly. I also received on the night of the 20th–21st a telegram saying that the time-limit must stand at 10 a.m. on the 22nd. I could do no more. Massigli, however, managed the affair with remarkable skill. He came in the afternoon to give me the text of the communiqué which the French Committee would issue at 5 o'clock that day. He would also send me a formal letter of protest at the treatment they had received. I attached much greater importance to the first than to the second.

The French decision is rather clever. It makes it *appear* to be done by them *on their own,* or on Catroux's advice. It recalls Helleu; it liberates *and* restores to his functions the President of the Lebanon Republic: it liberates only (and leaves the point of their status obscure) the Ministers. But it does *appear* at least a voluntary decision and does save some face.

I telegraphed all this (and the text of the formal letter) all round. I know there will be further trouble about the reinstatement of the Ministers, but it is a great thing to get this far.[17]

On receipt of this communiqué the British Government also made a gesture of retreat. Since the issue was now narrowed down to the reinstatement of the Ministers, the time-limit would be extended until 10 a.m. on Wednesday the 24th. It seemed to me ridiculous to be

16 20 November 1943.
17 21 November 1943.

talking about an ultimatum on so small a point, and I continued to protest to the Foreign Office. After all, the President and the Ministers had been released, Helleu had been sent back to Algiers, and surely we ought to allow Catroux a little latitude. One other helping of jam was fortunately available. Murphy and I went to see Massigli at 7 p.m. to give him an *aide-mémoire* to say that the British and American Governments now recognised that the Darlan-Clark Agreement was out of date, and were prepared to discuss with the French Committee a new agreement as regards our military needs in North Africa, more consistent with the political situation than the provisional French Government now held. This pleased Massigli, and we agreed on a public statement to be issued at once. Later that night I called on Massigli. I found him rather depressed. Could the time-limit really be enforced about the one point now outstanding—the automatic rein-statement of the Ministers in office? However, in the course of conver-sation he told me in confidence that he had now received a telegram from Catroux strongly recommending this course, and indeed intend-ing to act on his own responsibility unless the Committee actually forbade it.

He asked me whether our ultimatum still applied on this point. I said . . . would it not be better for him not to have an answer until as late as possible? I therefore arranged with him to write him a letter, which would be sent to him during the Cabinet meeting tomorrow.

If he could carry his colleagues to adopt Catroux's proposal and reinstate the Ministers by argument, he would do so. If asked whether there was a British ultimatum on this point, he would say he did not know (my letter not having yet arrived).[18]

The next morning, the 23rd, we carried out our plan.

As agreed, my letter to Massigli was sent down to him at about 11.30 a.m. They must of course be told H.M.G.'s decision, but I should much prefer to see Massigli get his way without reference to it. It will be better for us and for him in the future.[19]

This little conspiracy worked out satisfactorily. After luncheon,

Massigli telephoned to say he had carried the Committee, and the order to reinstate the Lebanese Ministers would be given at once. Would I be sure to send off the necessary telegram at once, so as to avoid the danger of some

[18] 22 November 1943.
[19] 23 November 1943.

mistake tomorrow morning? I gathered that he had *not* had to use my *aide-mémoire* but carried it on Catroux's telegram.[20]

I called on Massigli at his office later in the evening. There had been a debate on foreign affairs in the Assembly which had been on the whole helpful. Moreover, everything had gone well at the meeting. Only de Gaulle, Pleven and Diethelm had been against him. Our scheme had worked well:

> As soon as the session began (10 a.m.) de Gaulle had said, 'Another British ultimatum, I suppose.' 'I know nothing of this,' said Massigli, 'we are to discuss a telegram from Catroux' (which he then produced).
> Massigli is tired and very anxious, but really rather triumphant.[21]

The Lebanese crisis had been one of the most exhausting, for, unlike the previous ones, it had been largely taken out of my hands.

> However, we got through . . . with very reasonable success, since we have got what we wanted without making things too difficult for the French Committee. I have felt real admiration for Massigli and it has been interesting to see the newer members of the Cabinet making themselves felt. . . .
> The only fear I had was that owing to the Lebanese trouble the announcement of Duff's appointment and his American colleague might be postponed. However, this was not done and this was wise. It gave the French more confidence in what I was telling them—viz., that we had no desire to humiliate them. We simply wished, in their interests as well as in our own, a proper solution of the political problems in the Levant.[22]

The next day I left Algiers early in the morning for Cairo. Throughout these days Desmond Morton had been staying with me in Algiers. He was not only a most agreeable guest, but a very useful one, for he was an intimate friend of Churchill and gave me good advice on the best tactics to pursue. He came with us to Cairo. We drove from the airfield to Chester Beatty's villa, where I had stayed with Casey before. For the time being it had become No. 10 Downing Street. We were greeted by the now familiar faces of the entourage. I was at once summoned into the presence. Churchill was, as usual, in bed surrounded by red boxes and smoking the inevitable cigar. He seemed in better form than he had been on the *Renown*.

> He listened with unusual patience to my story of the Lebanese crisis from our point of view in Algiers. He seemed impressed by my arguments that

20 Ibid.
21 Ibid.
22 24 November 1943.

de Gaulle had been prevented from extreme courses by his own people and that this method was much more effective than British and American pressure . . . which merely played into de Gaulle's hands and enabled him to appeal successfully to French pride and sensitiveness.[23]

It had originally been hoped to arrange a conference at which Stalin could be present, and much argument had taken place as to the possible location. Finally, Stalin was unable to agree to go further than Teheran, where Roosevelt and Churchill went to join him, after a preliminary meeting in Cairo. However, the Chinese were glamourously represented by General and Mme. Chiang Kai-shek, supported by a large entourage.

Owing to a leakage in one of the newspapers, the security arrangements were fantastic. It was impossible to move anywhere without passing two or three barriers and showing innumerable passes. The Prime Minister was at Mena House. The President was at the so-called Kirk Villa (the residence of Ambassador Kirk). Other notabilities were distributed in villas or hotels, or lodged in Cairo. The Conference itself was held in the Mena House Hotel, just on the verge of the desert and close to the Pyramids. The weather was splendid, dry and warm, a great change from the bad weather which we had had in Algiers.

As at Casablanca, the photographers were in full force.

The photographs consisted of various groups. First, the GREAT, i.e.
  The President,
  The P.M.,
  The Generalissimo and Madame Chiang.
Next, the STAFFS.

Here there was an indescribable scene—all the American and British officers of whom one had ever heard. . . . While we were standing about in the garden of the villa waiting it was really like a sort of mad garden party in a newsreel produced of Alice in Wonderland. There were, of course, the Chiefs of Staff—General Marshall, Admiral King, General Brooke, Air Marshal Portal, Admiral A. B. Cunningham—with Field-Marshal Dill, General Somervell (U.S.) and so on thrown in. Then the Commanders, Eisenhower, Admiral John Cunningham, Tedder, General Wilson (G.O.C. Middle East) (Alexander was away). . . . Then suddenly in walks Lord Louis Mountbatten, General Stilwell (U.S.) and General Carton de Wiart—all from the Indian theatre of war. In addition, all the well-known figures in the minor ranks: Pug Ismay, Admiral Leahy (President's aide), etc.

After the 'greats' (President, P.M., etc.) [and] their military and naval staffs

[23] Ibid.

[had been photographed], we had the civilians. In this photograph were Harry Hopkins (President's Personal Adviser), Averell Harriman (U.S. Ambassador to Russia), Ambassador Winant, Murphy, Kirk (U.S. Minister in Egypt), etc. Also Anthony Eden, Sir Alec Cadogan, Lord Leathers, Lord Killearn (formerly Lampson—British Ambassador in Egypt), Casey (Minister of State) and myself.

It really was a most extraordinary performance and (I suppose) a useful one.[24]

This was followed by a sumptuous luncheon at the Casey Villa at which Churchill and Eden were the principal figures. There was a lot of talk about the French in the Middle East and some sharp arguments. I thought Churchill was tired, as well he might be, and therefore rather repetitive.

Actually, if one stands up to him in argument I do not think he resents it. And it is amusing to watch how he will take a point and reproduce it as his own a day or two later. He misses very little, although he does not always appear to listen.[25]

After luncheon (which lasted until about 3.30) I went back to Cairo. I had no real work to do, except a preliminary talk on the question of the Levant. I felt that Spears had overplayed his hand. He argued his case with great skill. But surely it is possible to be firm with the French without antagonising them so deeply.

On the next day we had a further discussion, when our policy towards France and the Levant was finally settled and the necessary instructions were sent out to all concerned. I had a bit of a struggle, but Eden was very helpful.

We must make it clear both to the French *and* to the Syrians and Lebanese that we have no desire to see French interests in the Levant overthrown. We have no wish either to eject or (still less) to supplant the French. We wish the pledges for Levantine independence given quite clearly in 1941 to be carried out. This would mean a position for the French similar to that which we enjoy in Iraq or Egypt. Both these countries are now completely independent. We no longer maintain High Commissioners there, but Ambassadors. But we have special treaties freely negotiated, which guarantee to us the special rights which our past and present connections with these countries justify.

As for the immediate method of obtaining this, both the Syrians and (especially) Lebanese must be deflated. They must be told that they cannot rely on us to help them eject the French, only to get a fair arrangement as

[24] 25 November 1943.
[25] Ibid.

outlined. Equally, the French must be told that in this liberal and progressive policy lies their only hope and that they must take this course or their Near East interests must inevitably go under in the end.

We agree, therefore, to get the French and Lebanese (and Syrians) to discuss and negotiate. We will not interfere, unless we are asked to come in as arbitrators by both parties.[26]

General 'Jumbo' Wilson, whom I now met for the first time, struck me as shrewd, intelligent and kindly. He took a much more moderate view of the position and thought that Spears's account had been exaggerated. Apart from these talks on the French problems, it was clear to me that the future of the Mediterranean Command was still uncertain. This naturally involved my own position. Meanwhile, I returned to Algiers and thence to Italy, and it was only when we got back to Cairo on 4 December that this was to be finally settled.

On Monday the 5th, at about 11 p.m., just as I was going to bed in Lord Moyne's house, I got a summons to the Kirk Villa. I had left Brindisi two days before, and it seems that a telegram had been sent asking me to arrange for Vyshinsky, Deputy Soviet Commissar for Foreign Affairs, to come to Cairo to see the President and the Prime Minister on their return from Teheran. Eden rather sadly asked me what I had done with him. Apparently they had thought that this could easily be arranged. I had not received the telegram, and in any case Vyshinsky had left Bari by car for Naples. The reason for trying to get him along was partly as a compliment, since he was one of the most senior Russian Ministers, and partly, no doubt, to help to bring some pressure on the Turks. All this took some time to arrange, and it was after midnight when I was brought into the drawing-room, where I found the President and Churchill sitting on a sofa together. There followed a very curious conversation on similar lines to that I had heard in Anfa. Roosevelt seemed to believe that France could not recover; that Indo-China should not be returned to her control; that Dakar, in West Africa, should pass under American protection, and so on. This anti-colonialism was a strong part of Roosevelt's make-up, but he seemed to have very crude ideas as to how independence could be gradually introduced in the great colonial empires without disorder and with the best hopes of success.

Churchill and I left the President's house at about two in the morning and I went back with him to his own villa,

[26] 26 November 1943.

where we talked of France (he still opposes in argument but accepts in reality a great part of my views), British politics, Russia,[27] the next election, the Mediterranean war, etc. He made a good remark about the Mosley debate. He had inquired by telegram whether any Ministers had abstained or voted wrong. The results were disappointing to him. 'I have made it clear that, as regards the present Government, all resignations will be gratefully received!'

'Does that mean,' said Randolph, 'that anyone can join who wants to?' 'No,' replied the P.M., with a grin, 'but you can join the queue.'[28]

At this time we also had a discussion about the future of the Mediterranean Command. If it was to be united under a single general, should this be Eisenhower, Alexander or Wilson? Would Casey or Macmillan be liquidated? I then heard that Churchill was trying to get Casey to accept the Governorship of Bengal.

At 7 p.m. on 7 December I was sent for by the Prime Minister.

He is tired but triumphant, since at the last moment his policy—his strategical policy—has triumphed. The Far East adventure is postponed, and all will be concentrated (as far as may be) on the Mediterranean and North European campaigns. If reasonable material is made available again for the former we may make some progress even during the winter.

This involves, among other things, amalgamation of the North African and the Middle Eastern Commands, so that the Mediterranean (Italy, Dalmatia, Balkans, Greece, Aegean Islands and Turkey) is regarded as a single strategic problem.

The P.M. explained all these ideas to me. The unification of the Command is settled.[29] An individual has not been chosen, but in any case it will be a British officer. Eisenhower is to go to England, to take the Supreme Command [of 'Overlord'] . . . Bedell Smith may (a) go with Ike, which Eisenhower naturally wants, (b) remain here as Deputy Commander-in-Chief.

The P.M. asked me what I thought of all this and about any views I might have on the organisation of the command. I asked about the political side and he told me that Casey is to go and his place not be filled; so I suppose my area would be extended to the whole Mediterranean.[30]

It was now clear that a British general would soon succeed Eisenhower. The choice would fall either on General Wilson or on General Alexander. The C.I.G.S., General Brooke, was in favour of the former. The Prime Minister asked me to give my opinion, but before doing so

27 See *Winds of Change*, p. 14.
28 6 December 1943.
29 The Commander of the unified command became known as SACMED (Supreme Allied Commander, Mediterranean).
30 7 December 1943.

to talk the matter over with General Brooke. I preferred Alexander because he was a younger man and I had got to know him well. But obviously Wilson was also a very experienced officer. I discussed the matter briefly and rather tentatively with General Brooke, who clearly did not relish my taking any part in the decision. The next evening Churchill sent for me again. He told me to put my views about the Mediterranean Command in writing. Accordingly I sent him a minute in the following terms.[31]

PRIME MINISTER

I have completed the attached paper, in accordance with your wishes, after a talk with the C.I.G.S.

I do not of course know whether General Alexander has the military qualities most suited to the duties of a C.-in-C. in such an organisation. But I feel strongly that these points should be weighed:

1. General Alexander has commanded with conspicuous success Anglo-American forces in the field. He pulled them out of a hole in Tunisia and his reputation stands high in the forces of both nations.

2. He has now learnt the quite difficult art of managing Americans; both the military and civilians have fallen to his charm.

3. He has—so far as I can judge from the talks I have had with him—the art of simplifying problems instead of making them more complex.

4. He has the simplicity of character and the concentration on the sole purposes of war which are needed in a leader and which do not pass unnoticed by the troops.

If, therefore, your only hesitation is not on professional grounds but because you fear he may be wasted and unduly immersed in political problems, I hope you will feel that—if you entrust me with the job—I ought to be able, with Murphy's support on which I can count, to relieve him from any but the more important decisions and thus help to make his task easier.

Harold Macmillan

In the event, the choice fell on General Wilson, and I have no doubt that in the existing state of the Italian campaign it was wise to leave the tactical conduct of operations in Alexander's hands. I was to have a very happy nine months working with General Wilson, for he was intelligent, considerate, and prudent.

We then returned to Algiers to new difficulties. My chief purpose was to patch everything up until Duff Cooper arrived. Churchill had intended to come to Algiers for a short stay before going home. But on

[31] 8 December 1943.

Monday December 13 I got a call from Tunis saying he was laid up
with a bad chill.

Will I arrange with A.F.H.Q. to have a portable X-ray apparatus sent up at
once, in order to ascertain the state of the lung? They fear pneumonia.
Would I and Desmond Morton come up ourselves as soon as possible?

After a terrific morning of telegraphing and telephoning and finding out
whether the frightful weather will allow flying, we discover there is a perfectly
good apparatus at a hospital in Tunis.[32]

By taking the sea route Desmond Morton and I managed to fly successfully to Tunis, arriving in the late afternoon. Churchill insisted on
seeing me that evening, but he seemed weak and drowsy. I escaped as
soon as I could, as I felt sure he was seeing too many people. The next
day was to prove the most distressing and anxious.

The P.M. is definitely worse, and has got pneumonia, and they fear
pleurisy. General Wilson arrived. He is definitely to get the Mediterranean
Command. . . .
The P.M. asked me to discuss with the General the organisation of the
Command and write him a report.
In spite of his temperature (101°) he dealt with this in the evening and
wrote a long telegram to the Cabinet about it.
A rather dreary day of waiting. Moran seems very worried. He is telegraph-
ing all over the place for specialists.[33]

The next day the Prime Minister was definitely worse.

His pulse is very irregular. Brigadier Bedford (a heart specialist) has at last
arrived from Cairo. He seems sensible and gives us comfort. He is giving
digitalis to try to calm the heart. . . .
At last a Colonel Buttle—the great M. and B. specialist—arrived from Italy.
He is an expert on how to give the stuff. He seems clever [and] determined—
just the chap we need. I had a long talk with him and begged him to be firm
and *forbid* telegrams or visitors.
At 6 p.m. the P.M. had a heart attack—what is called 'fibrulation'. It was
not very severe but has alarmed them all. More digitalis is being given. . . .
Lord Moran tells me that he thought the P.M. was going to die last night.
He thinks him a little better as regards the pneumonia, but is worried about
his heart.[34]

This was the worst moment of his critical illness. For those who not
merely revered but loved him it was a terrible time. And what of the

[32] 13 December 1943.
[33] 14 December 1943.
[34] 15 December 1943.

future—Britain and the Empire and the Grand Alliance? How could we face the ordeals which still awaited us without the greatest war leader in our history?

But the next day he was definitely better—his pulse steadier and his lung beginning to clear. The experts seemed to think he was through the crisis.

Since there was nothing more to be done in Tunis, I decided to return to Algiers, where a mass of work was piling up. I saw Churchill before leaving. He was cheerful, although very weak. The news about him continued to remain good on the following days, and by 21 December it was clear that he was on the mend. In the overwhelming sense of relief and gratitude, nothing else seemed to matter.

We had during the next few days one or two minor French difficulties. There was a rather futile argument about the use of French troops—how far they were to be under A.F.H.Q. and how far under the orders of the French Committee. We made some progress on the Lebanon, where both Massigli and Catroux showed themselves as helpful as ever. But now one final row was brewing. It was on the question of the 'purge' or 'épuration'.

Great pressure was being brought on the French Committee, from many quarters, to deal with this question. The Gaullists were determined on the prosecution of people like Boisson, the ex-Governor-General of French West Africa, and Admiral Derrien, second-in-command to Admiral Esteva, who had fought side by side with the Germans in Bizerta. The members of the resistance movement were equally resolved to attack the ex-Vichy Ministers like Pucheu and Flandin. Others no doubt would be brought to justice in due course.

Châtel, who was Governor-General of Algeria when I came, and General Noguès, who was Resident-General in Morocco, had prudently escaped to Portugal. The two admirals, Godfroy, who had sulked so long in Alexandria, and Michelier, who opposed us in Casablanca but subsequently followed Darlan's lead, had already been dealt with by the simple process of placing them on the retired list. No further action had been or would be taken against them, except to prevent them from residing in dockyard towns, such as Bizerta or Casablanca—which did not seem a very serious inhibition. We were left therefore with the five vital cases: Pucheu, Derrien, Boisson, Peyrouton and Flandin—and perhaps General Bergeret.

Pierre Pucheu had been the direct cause of hundreds and perhaps thousands of Frenchmen being handed over to the Germans in Paris. Admiral Derrien might well also be thought an active traitor. I felt that there was little likelihood of pushing things to an extreme, except perhaps in these two cases—unless of course we interfered. Naturally we did interfere.

The Prime Minister was recovering rapidly—almost too rapidly— and a telephone call came to me in the middle of a luncheon party which I was giving in honour of a distinguished Arabic scholar, Professor Hamilton Gibb.

The P.M. was in a most excited mood, roaring like an excited bull down the telephone—which incidentally is listened to by many British and American telephone operators at different stages of the line as well as by all the professional French 'listeners-in'. He has certainly made a remarkable recovery.[35]

Ed Wilson (the newly-appointed American Ambassador to the French Committee) and I had in any case to see Massigli the afternoon of this day (the 21st) in order to receive from him a French draft in place of the Darlan–Clark Agreement. On this front things were moving satisfactorily, and the proposals seemed very reasonable. We took occasion to talk to him about the arrests and expressed the hope that this did not mean the beginning of a widespread persecution. He was obviously worried but thought it was too late to stop the action already taken. The trouble centred round the arrest and imprisonment of Peyrouton, Boisson and Flandin. For Peyrouton the Americans had a direct responsibility, since they had persuaded him to leave the safety of South America and landed him in Algiers in the beginning of the year. For Boisson the President had great regard; Flandin had been a friend of Churchill in pre-war days and, with his usual loyalty, he wished to help him in his fall. He had entertained Flandin in London in 1936 at the critical period of the remilitarisation of the Rhineland.[36]

The next day the Prime Minister began to ring up from Tunis almost hourly about the threatened arrests.

I am sure it is bad for him. He was in such a passion on the telephone today that I thought he was going to have an apoplectic fit.[37]

[35] 21 December 1943.
[36] *Winds of Change*, p. 428.
[37] 22 December 1943.

When Wilson and I saw Massigli at 6 p.m. on 22 December, he told us that, after reporting to the Committee our unofficial talk of the day before, he was authorised to say that the arrests of Bergeret, Pucheu and Derrien had been the natural result of a policy already announced. The Committee had some months ago made known its intention that the Ministers of the Vichy Government and others who had been personally responsible for the persecution of patriots or for military action against the Allies would be brought to justice. Under French procedure there would be a preliminary inquiry by a *juge d'instruction*. Although the Committee would not interfere with the course of justice, they felt certain that the judge would in fact find that there was not sufficient evidence either for an acquittal or for a trial to be held. Thus the preliminary investigation would in fact be adjourned until after the liberation of France. This would apply to all or nearly all these cases. To this we replied that since nobody could tell when this date would be, it seemed very hard if these men were kept in prison or suffered harsh treatment. Surely something much more lenient, like 'résidence surveillée', would be the right course. Massigli told us that this indeed was a matter for the Committee and not for the judge, and he hoped that something on these lines would be possible.

The next day the situation grew worse.

The most extraordinary telegram has arrived from the President to Eisenhower. It says:

'You shall direct the French Committee of National Liberation immediately to set free and discontinue the trial of Peyrouton, Boisson and Flandin.'

This telegram (to Eisenhower, *not* to the American Ambassador) has fairly put the cat among the pigeons. Ed Wilson is furious; Eisenhower is in Italy.[38]

The same morning, after a conference with Wilson, it was agreed that he would telephone the State Department in the afternoon to say

(a) that he cannot accept the position of Eisenhower receiving orders without his (Wilson) being informed.
(b) that he protests against this method of handling the affair, which is obviously intended to cause a final breach.[39]

Meanwhile I had sent a telegram to Eden, and repeated it to Churchill, reminding him that on his instructions I had on 23 October sent to Massigli a well-documented protest with regard to the inhuman

[38] 23 December 1943.
[39] Ibid.

treatment of British subjects in French West Africa between June 1940 and November 1942. I had formally invited the Committee, as trustees for the honour of France, to punish the guilty and compensate the victims. The tortures suffered by our merchant seamen were unprintable. Boisson had tried to deny the allegations, but was later forced to admit their truth. The British seamen's point of view was summarised by one of their number who at the end of the report said to the French authorities, 'Do not forget that your day of reckoning will come. I assure you that several hundred British merchant seamen will watch the news with unbounded interest.' I thought this reminder timely.

Wilson and I saw Bedell Smith the same afternoon. He took a very gloomy view of the position. He did not quite see how he or General Eisenhower could refuse to carry out the President's direct order. But under pressure he agreed to defer action for two or three days.

I had had another telephone conversation with the P.M., who seemed rather alarmed at the avalanche which he had started. I do not think he expected the President to react quite so violently or quite so rapidly.

The President hates de Gaulle and the French Committee. He would seize on any excuse to overthrow them and restore Giraud.

The P.M.'s sentiments are more complex. He feels about de Gaulle like a man who has quarrelled with his son. He will cut him off with a shilling. But (in his heart) he would kill the fatted calf if only the prodigal would confess his faults.[40]

Churchill now telegraphed to the President both about the terms of his proposed communication and the method of its delivery. Bedell Smith (as I was able to tell the Foreign Secretary) agreed with me that the literal carrying-out of the President's orders would precipitate a most serious situation. The Committee would most certainly refuse to obey. Our bluff would be called. But we could not afford to have our bluff called. We should therefore have to take military action to enforce our demands. For this, effective military dispositions must be made. British and American troops must therefore be moved accordingly. I felt sure that Churchill's precipitate action had been due to his illness.

Telegrams (and alas! telephone calls) are coming in at all hours of day and night. (The P.M. even rang up the Chief of Staff when I was in his room this

40 Ibid.

afternoon and said, 'Keep Harold up to the mark. He is much too pro-French. He will not carry out my policy or my wishes. I rely on *you!*')[41]

Much as I loved Winston I felt slightly hurt and really alarmed. So far my telegrams to Eden had not produced any result. I felt a particular grievance at all this trouble arising in the last days, and almost hours, of my tenure of office. This baby ought really to have been firmly put into Duff Cooper's lap. Unhappily, though some of his staff had arrived, no one could yet produce a suitable house for him and Diana to occupy. Until this problem could be resolved he was unable to relieve me of my functions.

Although to our British minds, so long accustomed to orderly and constitutional methods, these semi-revolutionary events were naturally startling, one had to see the point of view of the French. They knew that they could make only a minor contribution to the war. The liberation of France would be by British and American armies. They looked forward to it with desperate longing. But the fact that they could do so little to achieve it added to the burden of bitterness and shame. The one thing they could do at once was to set about a series of State trials. It was to de Gaulle's credit that, with few exceptions, these were postponed. The emotions were partly revenge, partly ambition, and partly the taking of political positions for the future.

I felt very differently about the different men. For Boisson there was little to be said. He was a brutal and cruel man. Bergeret was a reactionary, but with honestly held views. Yet when he was deputy to Giraud he had been very fond of putting other people in prison, and I did not feel that he had a great grievance now that the wheel had turned full circle. In any event, I was informed that the charges against him would not deal with his actions as second-in-command to the High Commission in North Africa, but his alleged betrayal of French interests in Syria. As for the two admirals, they had been reasonably dealt with. The case of Peyrouton was more difficult, for he was in a sense a victim of the confidence he had placed in the President. But in any event, I believed that if we could handle this without a first-class conflict with de Gaulle, there would in fact be no question of any immediate sentences, with the possible exception of Pucheu.

Meanwhile, apart from our discreet talk with Massigli no harm had been done. The President's message was held in abeyance, and I was to

[41] Ibid.

see the Prime Minister the next day. For he now invited me to fly to Tunis for Christmas Day and return the following morning.

In this somewhat anxious though not unhopeful mood we held our Christmas Eve party and dance for all our staff and those of other organisations, like the Economic Board. The next morning, after 8 a.m. Communion, when the church was crowded with troops, I left for Tunis. I drove to the Prime Minister's villa,

and found them all just having sat down to a magnificent Christmas dinner, with soup, turkey, plum pudding—and champagne![42]

This astonishing man, who had been at the point of death a few days before, had presided over a two-hour military conference in his bedroom all the morning. He appeared at the meal dressed in a padded silk Chinese dressing-gown, decorated with blue and gold dragons. Mrs. Churchill, Randolph and Sarah represented the family, John Martin, John Colville and Tommy Thompson the staff. There was Lord Moran, Dr. Bedford and another doctor; General 'Jumbo' Wilson, the C.-in-C. designate for the Mediterranean, Generals Alexander and Gale; Admiral Sir John Cunningham, Air Marshal Tedder; and several others. Eisenhower and Bedell Smith were at the conference, but flew back before the luncheon.

In the best Russian style (and looking in his strange costume rather like a figure in a Russian ballet) the P.M. proposed a series of toasts with a short speech in each case. . . . He proposed mine in most eulogistic terms.

He looked at me a bit sourly, but I think more in sorrow than in anger. After the luncheon, which ended somewhere about 4 o'clock, I managed to escape with General Alexander for a short walk.

At about 5.30, just before the P.M. went to sleep, he sent for me. He was obviously *very* tired, as he had worked all the time since luncheon, dictating a résumé of the military decisions taken in the morning and on a telegram embodying them to his colleagues and the President.

He only kept me for a few minutes. He was very sleepy and I left him, thereby earning a good word from poor Mrs. Churchill, who does her best to make him spare himself.

I gathered from the private secretaries that they had been alarmed at Churchill's excitement, which they attributed to the state of his heart and general health. But he seemed better. At about 8 p.m. there was a

[42] 25 December 1943.

buffet dinner, to which all the officers of the battalion of Coldstream which was providing Churchill's guard were invited, together with other personalities, including General and Mme. Mast. Churchill had his own dinner in bed, but appeared later and in capital form.

At about 11 p.m. he retired to his bedroom . . . and sent for me. He was obviously rather embarrassed and really almost pathetically so. He actually asked for my views and gave me ten minutes' free run to explain the present French situation as I saw it. Then he said, 'Well—perhaps you are right. But I do not agree with you. Perhaps I will see de Gaulle. Anyway, you have done very well.'

Then he took my hand in his in a most fatherly way and said, 'Come and see me again before I leave Africa, and we'll talk it over.'

I was deeply touched, and my love and affection for him came flowing back. His amazing power of recovery, as well as his devotion to work and duty, were beyond belief. He told me about the military conference and all the decisions, which included the final arrangements for the Anzio landings. Now I realised that it was this great and difficult operation which had been worrying him all the time. Our affairs were something upon which he could let off steam. Strangely enough, I think he trusted me to see that nothing very desperate would result.

When I got back to Algiers the next day, I found that the whole situation had been dramatically reversed. A telegram had come from the President, who had completely backed down. There was to be *no* ultimatum, *no* intervention by General Eisenhower; it was to be left to the diplomats to deal as best they could with the problem of the political trials.

The next day there was a meeting in de Gaulle's office. Bedell Smith, Wilson and I attended; there were also present Giraud and Massigli. It was very successful and led to at any rate a temporary solution of the question of the status of the French troops. We soon made considerable progress over the problem of the political prisoners in whom we were interested.

De Gaulle has given us a formal assurance:
(a) that they will be kept in a proper villa, with ordinary comforts and opportunity for exercise, pending the preliminary investigation;
(b) that actual trial will be postponed till *after* the liberation of France, i.e. until a legal and constitutional Government takes the place of the Committee.
General Eisenhower is telegraphing to the President strongly urging him to

accept these assurances. Wilson is doing the same to Hull. I am recommending to Eden and Churchill that we should now let the matter drop. I fear that the P.M. will react a bit, but if the President accepts the points I shall be surprised if the P.M. (after a few angry growls at me) does not do the same.

So that's that. The usual feeling of flatness follows so many emotions.[43]

I felt satisfied that de Gaulle and the older members of the Government were anxious to restrict the purge to the minimum, and so it proved. There was to be a fresh difficulty in March of the following year over the trial of Pucheu. But there was no question of any breach of faith, for he was not included among the list of those for whom the Prime Minister and President were pleading. So ended, almost on the anniversary of my arrival, the last of the many Algerian crises of 1943.

In the New Year, Churchill was able to move to Marrakesh for convalescence. The Villa Taylor soon became a kind of Chequers, and a vast amount of business of all kinds was carried on. He soon discovered that he could easily telephone from there to Algiers, and was regardless of all security regulations. Sometimes he remembered, and indulged in strange and unintelligible precautions. For instance, I got into great trouble for not being able to interpret his desire to have 'the vegetable man' sent to him as soon as possible. My little staff went into conference, without being able immediately to resolve the problem. It was of course President Beneš, head of the exiled Government of Czechoslovakia, who was paying a visit to Algiers. How foolish of us; 'Beans' was the obvious answer.

Churchill bore no rancour; it was one of the most attractive of his characteristics. Accordingly, on New Year's Day 1944, after attending de Gaulle's reception for the Diplomatic Corps, of which I was the doyen, I was called to the telephone to speak to the Prime Minister. Forgetful of recent controversies, Churchill had decided to take my advice; to see de Gaulle and have a frank talk with him in the hope of reaching some basis of permanent understanding. But in his impetuous way he insisted that de Gaulle must come at twenty-four hours' notice. A telegram, not yet received, had been dispatched this morning, telling me to make the necessary arrangements. The telephone call was the first I had heard of it.

The next day at 8 a.m. the resonant voice of the Prime Minister

[43] 31 December 1943.

began to boom from a distance of 700 miles. Why was there no reply to his invitation? What was I doing? At 10.15 I went to see de Gaulle to give him the Prime Minister's urgent invitation.

He received it without much apparent enthusiasm, as I expected; and added that he was very busy and could not of course alter his plans at such short notice. Moreover, the P.M. had lately gone out of his way to insult and thwart him. I, of course, told de Gaulle that all this was beside the point; that here was a splendid opportunity to get things on a better basis and that he *must* accept. He finally said that he would think it over.[44]

Beneš was more amenable and was to leave within a day or two for Marrakesh; but I was anxious about de Gaulle's final decision, so I had a word with Massigli at lunch-time, and asked him to do his best.

The next day the Duff Coopers at last arrived, although their villa was not in good order. They were able to move in, but most of their staff stayed with us.

Winston had been ringing me up all day, in a great state of anxiety and emotion. He told me to cancel the invitation to de Gaulle, since he could not be kept waiting. It was monstrously undignified; I was weakly pandering to the French, etc.

I, of course, told Winston that I would see de Gaulle and cancel the invitation as soon as I could, but that I could not command the exact time for an interview. I would see him by hook or crook today.[45]

All the parties, British and French, which had been given for Beneš had made it difficult to get a time arranged.

Naturally, the P.M. did not really wish to cancel the visit. He only wanted to preserve his dignity and give vent to his feelings on the telephone (to which, of course, the French listen intently all day). He showed his disappointment when I agreed to cancel the invitation, and at the end of each of his calls (three today before dinner) ended by saying he would leave it to me.[46]

When I saw de Gaulle in the evening, to my surprise and relief he was in excellent humour. Before I could say anything, he told me he accepted Churchill's invitation with pleasure; it only remained to fix a date to suit them both. I undertook to send this message immediately; but he kept me for an hour's talk about France, Russia and Czechoslo-

[44] 2 January 1944.
[45] 3 January 1944.
[46] Ibid.

vakia, the future of Europe—all in a very expansive and friendly tone.

> I rang up Winston and gave him de Gaulle's message. He received it with a gasp of surprise, relief, and some disgust into the bargain. But I rang off before he could say much.[47]

The visit was arranged and proved, on the whole, a success.

On 4 January 1944, I formally handed over my functions to Duff Cooper, paying a farewell visit to Massigli,

> who was really charming and said more nice things about what I had done for them than I deserve. However, it was pleasant enough to hear them![48]

I lunched with Louis Jacquinot, the Minister for Marine, a very good fellow. He had a large party of admirals, captains, and commanders, and made a very friendly speech about my services to France.

At this time my health was not good and I had great trouble with a painful skin infection on my hands (no doubt the result of the burns I had suffered). Colonel Richardson wanted me to have a month's holiday; but this was difficult to arrange at the time when the new Mediterranean Command was coming into effect.

Eisenhower had left for Washington and went from there direct to London, so there was no formal farewell at Algiers. He came to say goodbye to me just before he left, and pressed me to come with him to 'Overlord'. But I was now deeply engaged with Italian affairs and looked forward to a widening range of responsibility. In March, while I was in London on leave, the leading military, naval, and air force commanders who had served him in North Africa were able to arrange a dinner in his honour and presented him with a piece of plate. I was invited and asked to speak in support of the toast. As Eisenhower observed in replying, it was happily George II silver; had it been George III he could not have taken it back to America. He was, I think, much moved by our affection for him, but it was well deserved. During this year I had learned to understand and admire his truly noble character. I formed with him a lasting friendship. I did not, of course, at this time foresee that he would be 'drafted' into politics, for which he had always expressed a great contempt. Whatever may be the final judgement about him, either as a soldier or a statesman, there

[47] Ibid.
[48] 4 January 1944.

can be no doubt about his quality as a leader of men. His services to the Allied cause were immeasurable. The experiment of a fully integrated staff, where British and American officers served side by side, was unique. Only Ike could have made it succeed. General Wilson carried on, in full, the tradition of A.F.H.Q. Eisenhower built S.H.A.E.F. on the same lines, and finally established it in N.A.T.O. When big decisions had to be taken, Eisenhower never flinched. The landings in North Africa, when the conflicting news might have made a smaller man hesitate; the attack on Sicily, when an altogether unexpected storm seemed to put the whole operation at risk; finally, the frightful weather at the time of the invasion of metropolitan France: on all these vital occasions the terrible decision rested with him—postponement and perhaps chaos, or to pursue the plan with the prospect of frightful casualties and perhaps defeat. Eisenhower, at all crises, military or political, showed supreme courage.

The experience of watching the growth of something like a responsible French Government out of the chaotic situation which I had found on arrival in Algiers was unforgettable. Although I was to have no further formal dealings with the French Committee, the fact that Allied Headquarters was not able to move into Italy until July 1944 kept me in close touch with the development of French affairs. Far the most fascinating part of my experience was my relations with General de Gaulle. I had no doubt at all of his greatness or of the opportunities which lay before him. It was equally clear to me that in spite of Roosevelt and the State Department nothing could prevent him from becoming the leader of at any rate the first phase of post-Liberation France. For de Gaulle had, in spite of many faults, real genius. Passionately devoted to France, ruthless where French interests were concerned, insular, half revolutionary, half reactionary, he showed then the first signs of the great career which clearly now places him in the front rank of French statesmen.

CHAPTER SEVENTEEN

Italy: Friend or Foe?

FOR over two years I was to be concerned, in one form or another, with the problems arising out of an Allied invasion of Italian soil. Many changes took place during that time, both in the structure and in the objectives of Allied organisations. It may seem to the student of this period that a great deal of unnecessary effort was spent in planning and executing what should have been a comparatively simple undertaking. But one must recall the psychological, as well as the physical, background in order to understand the complications.

There were many separate and often conflicting strands in the tangle of difficulties with which we were confronted. The first was the extent of the operation. As the planned scope of military operations in Italy was gradually extended, new burdens were continually placed on the planners of what were called 'civil affairs'—that is, the administration of the occupied territories and also relations with any surviving Italian authorities.

The second problem was how to regard the Italian people. As friend or foe? As an enemy or something equivalent to an ally? After the armistice, the Italians had no doubt on this matter and were incapable of understanding our slow appreciation of a fundamentally changed situation. They had been for ten years or more closely allied with Hitler and the Nazis. But Hitler was not doing very well; indeed, he had almost abandoned them to destruction and defeat. It was surely sensible therefore to make a new 'combinazione' and to join themselves formally with the Allies. This they had tried to explain to us in Lisbon, in Algiers and later in Sicily. Unfortunately, handicapped by a slower mentality and more rigid instructions, we had seemed incapable of grasping the radical change in affairs and still mumbled out-of-date texts with such words as 'unconditional surrender'. Indeed, in a sense, it was the Italians who had a grievance against us, not we against them. For they would scarcely have ventured on so dramatic a betrayal unless they had thought it could be made effective. The cancellation of the airborne division intended to secure Rome; the failure to liberate at least the greater part of Italy, by a series of landings, east and west; the development of a slow and stubbornly contested struggle through the mainland: all these were producing a lamentable result. Italy, instead of escaping from war as they had hoped by changing sides, was to become the battlefield for a long, destructive and protracted campaign.

Consequently, we were to bring about a division of Italy reminiscent of the centuries during which she had been nothing but a geographical expression. First there was German-held territory, from just north of Naples to the Alps, comprising the most populous and productive areas, industrial and agricultural. Next, Allied-held Italy, from Naples to Brindisi, including Sicily and soon Sardinia. But the advance moved forward with frustrating slowness. Even Allied-held Italy itself was soon to be divided between that part directly administered under the military authorities, and that re-transferred to the authority of the Italian Government. In the forward areas under direct rule there was a vast apparatus, planned for rapid and continuous advance, but now obstructing the arteries and veins of local life. This was the Allied Military Government of Occupied Territories, to be famous, or infamous, under the name of AMGOT. It was soon to be renamed A.M.G. and supplemented by the Allied Control Commission, presiding over areas nominally under Italian control. Both these were amply staffed with British and American officers. Although these two organisations were nominally separate, they had to work—or to be made to work—closely together, for the effective operation of harbours, roads, such railways as remained operative or could be reconstructed, for the supply of minimum civilian needs, including food, and for countless other purposes. Behind these two—A.M.G. and A.C.C.—there lay the appropriate section of A.F.H.Q., growing with Parkinsonian proliferation. Finally, like the gods of Olympus, sometimes beneficent and reasonably quiet, sometimes either hurling their thunderbolts or sending their divine and semi-divine messengers to instruct us, loomed the impressive authority of the Combined Chiefs of Staff, who issued directives in Delphic language, and even themselves were believed to tremble at the occasional intervention of the old gods, their creators, the President and the Prime Minister.

The invasion and occupation of one country by another necessarily bring with them many difficulties and responsibilities. The more primitive nations in the past have solved the former by evading the latter. Conquest has often meant the slaughter of the aged and the mass deportation of the able-bodied, male and female, into slavery. As for the rest, they could be allowed to starve. The Germans followed these horrible precedents of savage times, especially in Eastern Europe. But civilised armies, defending high principles, cannot find this easy way out. They start as conquerors, but soon find themselves trustees. The British armies already had some experience of these problems, but it was chiefly confined to North and East Africa. As various territories had come under our control, it had been found necessary to set up a civil organisation for their care and to maintain the population in as high a condition of material well-being as was practicable. Thus had grown up a body known as O.E.T.A. (Occupied Enemy Territory Administration), from which were drawn many good officers for the Italian enterprise. But they had dealt largely with small, scattered and relatively primitive peoples. Now we were to be faced with the much more difficult task of governing a highly developed country with a European population. Moreover, while Sicily might be expected to be more or less self-supporting, the southern part of Italy was very unproductive. Over the whole area of battle, powerful air attacks and bombardments would no doubt have resulted in large areas without transport, without communications, and without any effective local administration.

Finally, there were divergences of approach between the Allies, which were apparent at an early stage and became more acute after the Italian surrender. As early as February 1943 this argument began and continued throughout all the pre-'Husky' period. On 8 February, General Eisenhower had sent a telegram to General Marshall asking for guidance. He stated that British and American policy would have to be reconciled in advance and he asked three questions. First, what should be our attitude towards the population of occupied territory? Secondly, what should be the character of the administration? Thirdly, what should be the machinery for preparing the necessary plans? These questions were of course repeated to London. While the answer to the first was not too difficult, at least in words—'the population should be treated in a benevolent manner in so far as this was consistent with military objectives'—the answers to the others involved a long and unnecessary dispute between the British and American Governments. At first Washington seemed to claim that since 'Husky' was a derivative of 'Torch', the Americans should continue to have the main responsibility. London replied by defending the opposite doctrine. Britain should be the senior partner, partly on the grounds that we were providing the majority of the forces and partly because we were now entering the Mediterranean, traditionally a British sphere of influence.

The fact that at this time my position had not been formally recognised in this affair did not prevent Eisenhower and his Chief of Staff consulting me frequently and showing me all their telegrams. I also received a vast quantity of instructions and requests for information from London. Personally I thought the argument rather childish. I was opposed to the whole concept of senior and junior partnership. We should be, as under Eisenhower's leadership we had become, comrades on an integrated and equal basis. The really important thing was to prepare an effective and practical scheme of operation. With this in view, I proposed on 12 March that General Alexander should become Military Governor; that he should have an organisation attached to him comparable to O.E.T.A., adapted to meet the conditions of a European country; that the chief officer of this should be British, the deputy American, and the staff Anglo-American. In order to keep the necessary contacts between General Alexander and the Supreme Allied Commander, a small section should be formed, presided over by two officers, of which the senior should be American and the junior British. General Eisenhower should remain the ultimate arbiter, subject to the Combined Chiefs of Staff.

There remained the problem of 'political advice' to the commanders. Washington thought there should be an American Deputy Chief of Staff for this purpose, who would of course engross all authority. The British Government realised that the Commander-in-Chief would have in this set-up no British adviser. I then proposed that I, as Resident Minister, should act as his adviser and therefore interpose some check upon the new Deputy Chief of Staff and his organisation. Here a double obstacle was encountered. In the first place A.F.H.Q., though willing to deal with me, to whom they had by this time become accustomed, were very much afraid of giving me a place in any plan of organisation, since they were terrified of having imposed upon them an American politician, and in particular Mayor La Guardia of New York.

After three months' argument this matter was finally settled. There was to be no 'political Deputy Chief of Staff'. Murphy and I were authorised to continue to do what we had been doing daily, with increasing application, for several months. Our broad scheme was accepted. General Alexander was to be Military Governor. Lord Rennell was to be his deputy, dressed as a major-general. A Liaison Section was set up at A.F.H.Q. under Colonel Julius Holmes, an American, with General Maxwell as his British deputy. The State Department continued to be influenced by two conflicting emotions— one the desire to keep out of any further involvement in European affairs; the other, the belief that the Sicilian population would be better disposed to the Americans than to the British.

After the armistice and the flight of the King and Badoglio, another organ was hastily devised. It was to be called the Allied Control Commission. It had its germ in the appointment of the Military Mission to the Italian Government in September. I had already dispatched Harold Caccia to be my representative on the Military Mission at the beginning of October, and Reber became his American counterpart. A.C.C. was destined to grow alarmingly in size and importance. As A.M.G. began to wane, A.C.C. was to wax. But, for the moment, it was confined to a few rooms in a small hotel in Brindisi, while a large number of British and American officers were being widely recruited to be trained at Tizi Ouzou (an Algerian mountain resort) for their still uncertain functions. On to this already somewhat unwieldy apparatus there was soon to be imposed yet another body, the outcome of the meeting of Foreign Ministers in Moscow, to be called the Advisory Council for Italy. It consisted at first of representatives of America, Britain, Russia and France. Greece and Yugoslavia were later added. We certainly could not complain of lack of interest in our efforts, or shortage of volunteers willing to take a hand.

But grave questions of policy were soon to arise. The American Government and, still more, the President, as the American Presidential election drew nearer, began to take a great interest in the Italians as the friends and relations of a large and well-organised Italian population living and voting in the United States. But they had been gravely shaken by their experience at the beginning of 'Operation Torch'. The attacks on the agreement with Darlan had been even more bitter in the American than in the British Press. The accusation of dealing with disreputable politicians and officials had wounded Secretary Hull's sensitive nature. The American Government did not want to have all this trouble over again. Washington's reply to General Eisenhower's original question, directing that the Italian population should be treated benevolently, responded to one aspect of their political needs at home. But a proviso had been prudently added, requiring that 'active or violent Fascist leaders or declared pro-German partisans should be arrested and removed'. This was, no doubt, for future publication. In practice, like most directives, it was useless.

The leading Fascist figures had disappeared, either into exile or with Mussolini to his rump Government in northern Italy. But what of the rest of the civil and military administration? How were we to treat the admirals, generals, and all the other Service personnel? What about the stationmasters and functionaries on the railways? What about the officials on whose co-operation the efficiency of sewerage and water and electrical systems might depend? I was soon to find that directives are more useful in protecting the writer than instructing the recipient.

Some weeks before the landings in Sicily, I had summed up these divergences as follows:

It is very difficult to plan the political and administrative side, when the military future is so uncertain. And—as in French matters—there is clearly a divergence of policy between the Americans and ourselves.

Broadly speaking, the difference is this. The Americans favour an Allied Military Government of Italy (AMGOT) even if and when the whole or the greater part of the country falls into our hands. We, being more realistic, would prefer to change over as soon as practicable from what might be called *direct* government (AMGOT) to *indirect* control—just as we did here [in North Africa]. . . . In the early stages—especially while military operations continue—you must have *direct* government. But, in my view, as soon as the greater part of Italy falls to us, we ought to try to find some kind of central Italian Government which we could guide and control, but which would relieve us of the almost impossible task of direct administration in each locality. Merely from the point of view of personnel, I do not believe an efficient team can be recruited on the scale required.[1]

The armistice was certainly to favour the British view.

The first test of our planning took place in Sicily. The A.M.G. officers found none of the expected difficulties of dealing with a hostile population. There was no need to detach troops from the attacking forces to maintain law and order. Although there was a certain amount of natural confusion and a comparatively small number of A.M.G. officers could be landed in the first wave,

the genuine friendliness with which Allied troops were everywhere greeted, in spite of the immense amount of suffering caused by Allied bombardments, was astonishing to many of those who had arrived, as they supposed, in the capacity of enemies.[2]

There was no difficulty in obtaining the co-operation of any remaining civilian elements, whether official or unofficial. The plan of relying upon existing police forces, mainly the Carabinieri, to maintain order was completely justified. But there was, in the course of this short Sicilian campaign, a bitter foretaste of the difficulties which were to confront us for many months. Lord Gerald Wellesley observed that the chief function of AMGOT was 'to bury the dead and to feed the living'. The first task was especially urgent in the heat of a Sicilian summer. But with the vast destruction and the ensuing debris it was not always easy. The second was one which was to haunt us until the end of the Italian campaign.

In Sicily, which would normally have been a productive territory, the ration distributed in the weeks before the invasion was sufficient to produce something between ¼ lb. and 7 oz. daily of bread, plus a weekly ration of pasta, often as little as 2 oz. The stocks in the island were low; the farmers had not yet brought in the harvest, which had been a poor one, to the *ammassi*. What had been delivered, had been largely destroyed by military operations. Moreover, the Germans had taken away everything they could carry. Most of the civilian transport had been seized by the retiring troops; what was left was being used by the invaders. Even such grain as was available could not easily be milled, for the mills were mainly worked by electric power and, in the

[1] 16 August 1943.
[2] C. R. S. Harris, *Allied Military Administration of Italy, 1943–1945* (London, 1957), p. 37.

early days, power was almost everywhere cut off. The black market, which had always flourished, grew rapidly. Equal difficulties arose with water, sewage, sanitation and all the rest. Under the fierce bombardments the inhabitants of the towns had streamed away into the hills. Now they came pouring back as the invading armies passed. Nevertheless, though there was no doubt malnutrition, there was no actual starvation. Fruit, nuts and vegetables were fortunately plentiful. In general, the action taken by the Army authorities in support of the civil affairs officers was rapid and effective. There were no epidemics. The only serious diseases were typhoid and malaria, which were more or less endemic. If everything did not go exactly to plan, improvisation and ingenuity succeeded. Certainly, in all the history of war, no invaders have made greater or more genuine efforts to reduce the inevitable suffering of the population involved than the British and American Armies in this first assault upon the Axis powers in Europe.

The situation of Naples, after the September landings, was more serious. Here was a city with nearly a million inhabitants, and the first reports showed that the people were on the verge of starvation, with cholera and typhus having already broken out. Lord Rennell, with the full support of General Alexander, acted quickly; and ample supplies of ordinary stores as well as food were rapidly made available. The rumours of disease proved somewhat exaggerated, but general conditions were alarming.

Food was extremely short, but the most acute trouble was the almost complete absence of water, which in a city of a million inhabitants, more than a half of whom were still in the town, portended serious trouble. In addition to some damage from Allied bombing, the main aqueduct supplying the city had suffered from deliberate German sabotage, which had blown up the main bridge and demolished it in no less than seven places, and all reservoirs, except one small one, had been drained.[3]

Indeed, the people were literally unable to quench their thirst until the prompt action of the Fifth Army engineers relieved their terrible situation. Sea water was soon distilled from the bay, and the secondary aqueduct which was still functioning was immediately taken under control. Within a fortnight all the districts were provided with a moderate supply. But the destruction of sewers and the sabotaging of electric power-mains and sewage-pumping machinery presented a most

[3] Ibid., p. 85.

serious health problem. Furthermore, the absence of soap meant a
danger of louse-borne typhus, and in addition a considerable number
of the population had taken to living in the caves in the most primitive conditions. As regards electricity, everything that the Allies had
not bombed, the Germans had sabotaged. Yet by the end of the month
a small supply of power, strictly rationed according to priorities, was
available.

By some confusion, the imports of grain which had been planned did
not arrive, owing to the failure of the responsible staff section at
Algiers to call them forward in time. Nor had sufficient allowance been
made for civilian needs in the convoys which were due in December
from America. But a reserve of some 10,000 tons had been earmarked
for Rome, and owing to the slow advance, this became available.
British organisations in the Middle East were brought in to help. Yet
in spite of all our efforts during the three months that followed the
landings, 'the population surrounding the Bays of Naples and Salerno
went very short of food, to the point of severe malnutrition'.[4] Transport difficulties were so great that even stocks of food which were
available in the centre and east of Italy could not be brought to
Naples. Everyone and everything depended on Allied shipping. But by
Christmas, the worst was over. The precise relations between A.M.G.
and A.C.C. were, at the end of this year, still being worked out, with
the result that there was undoubtedly some confusion. As usual an *ad
hoc* arrangement was made, and General Brian Robertson, the most
efficient 'Q' officer since Marlborough's Cadogan, was put in charge.
He somehow or other managed to fill the gap. If the Allies had failed
at all, it was not through too little, but perhaps through too much
organisation.

For many months, until the autumn of 1944 when I was given
executive authority, I watched the development of our administrative
machine and did my best to help. I flitted from Algiers to Brindisi,
Naples, or Bari and back again in a series of aeroplane journeys of
varying comfort and speed. The combinations and permutations in
the organisation were certainly perplexing, and sometimes almost comical. At the end of October, the A.M.G. territories were divided into
forward and rear areas, the rear areas being amalgamated with A.C.C.,
and thus coming directly under A.F.H.Q. instead of under the Mili-

[4] Harris, p. 88.

tary Governor; in other words, under General Eisenhower and not under General Alexander. General Mason-MacFarlane, on the principle which had been agreed—that the head of the Commission should be of the same nationality as the Supreme Allied Commander—now returned to Gibraltar. He was replaced by a delightful, but not impressive, American officer, by the name of General Joyce. I recorded my first impressions of him, which were not changed by experience:

Elderly, well mannered, with those peculiar rimless *pince-nez* which the older generation of Americans affect (before the horn-rimmed mode came in). . . . He did not appear to have any particular qualification or any great disqualification for the task which he is to undertake. I should not think he would be difficult to manage.

Under the same protocol, when General 'Jumbo' Wilson succeeded to the Supreme Command in January 1944, Joyce disappeared and Mason-MacFarlane returned.

Meanwhile, we were plunged into Italian politics in a big way. Both in Algiers and in Italy I had naturally come in contact with various Italian personalities. Signor Pazzi and Signor d'Agnoni, claiming to represent a coalition of five anti-Fascist parties, met us at the end of September 1943. These parties, later joined by a sixth, formed the Committee of National Liberation which had been set up secretly in Rome under Ivanoe Bonomi after the flight of the King and Badoglio. Bonomi, like so many Mediterranean politicians, was rising eighty or more. His claim to consideration was that he had been the Prime Minister who had been overthrown by Mussolini a generation before. But a more important visitor arrived on 17 October, four days after the Italian declaration of war on Germany. Churchill has described in some detail his meeting with Count Sforza in London. He had been Italian Foreign Minister and Ambassador in Paris before the Fascist revolution. During the whole of Mussolini's régime he had been in exile. He was undoubtedly a notable figure among the Italians in America. He commanded a good deal of American support and, as Churchill has observed, some of the American Italian vote. Although he began by declaring his willingness to work with Badoglio, it was clear that his ambitions rose higher. However, it was agreed between him and Churchill (or so Churchill thought) that he would work loyally with the King and Badoglio at least until the capture of Rome, when a broad-based Government could be formed.

Murphy and I saw Sforza together. After going into something like a trance for a short period, the Count, in spite of a sore throat and a heavy cold, poured out a continual stream of words. Except on one occasion, when Murphy managed to interject a question, our visitor spoke without stopping for an hour and a half. (What could the meeting with Churchill have been like?) He wanted an Italian Government, for the Allies were trying to do things which ought to be done by Italians. With that, to some extent, we sympathised. He described his conversations with the King, Badoglio and the Duca d'Acquarone, who had shown him private letters from King George VI and the President of the United States, which he considered very improper.

D'Acquarone had even included an appeal to their common aristocratic origins and the class feeling which should link them in comradeship at such a time. Sforza would have none of this, although I have no doubt he was not displeased by the ducal acceptance of the Count's reputedly shadowy claim to the high lineage which his name would imply.

But his main demand was the abdication of the King in favour of the Prince of Naples, 'the only innocent member of the House of Savoy', for he was a child. There were difficulties because of the Italian constitution, but they must be overcome. The Prince of Piedmont would not do; he had accepted Fascism, and he was weak and discredited. But of course Sforza's plan soon became clear. He wanted to get rid of Badoglio by making him Regent and become Prime Minister himself. He was not anti-monarchist; the monarchy should be maintained and the regency would serve that purpose. We asked what would be the effect of the abdication on the armed forces, and at this Sforza showed considerable hesitation. However, he finally said that provided the monarchy was maintained he did not think there would be trouble.

Churchill was insistent that we should do no Cabinet-making until we got to Rome, and at the time this seemed the right policy. But as the months dragged on, it became more and more difficult to maintain.

I went on a visit to General Alexander's headquarters at Bari in the last week of October. In the course of the visit I recorded my impressions:

The political situation seems rather complicated, but I think they all worry unduly about this. All situations have been complicated ever since I arrived at

A.F.H.Q. on 2 January [1943]. But it is no use worrying. One must also laugh.

The difficulty arises from our desire to see a more liberal and broad-based Italian Government. But such party leaders as we can find at this stage are not very impressive. The more well-known figures are in Rome, Turin or Milan. Moreover, some of them refuse to serve under Badoglio, others refuse to serve under the King. Some demand a civilian Prime Minister; others demand, if not a republic, at least an abdication by the King, a renunciation of his rights by the Prince of Piedmont, and a succession by the young Prince of Naples (six or eight years old and in Switzerland) with a regency.

There is a further complication that under the Italian constitution, the Regent ought to be the next of kin. This means the new Duke of Aosta, who is regarded as quite impossible.

Sforza is running an intrigue to force the abdication of the King, to get Badoglio to act as Regent (in spite of the strict law) and to become Prime Minister himself. Badoglio is too loyal, as a soldier, to the person of the King to take the lead in such a scheme. But I think he might accept it if somebody else produced the crisis and I am not sure how far he is working a 'combinazione' with Sforza with this in view.[5]

There was now beginning to develop a general fear that if the Germans were to evacuate Rome, a revolutionary Government would come into being before the Allied armies arrived, something like the Commune in Paris in 1871. In order to obviate this danger, Badoglio wished to send a message to the politicians in Rome through our secret channels appealing to them to hold their hands. But to strengthen his argument he asked General Mason-MacFarlane to give him authority to assure them that the Allies gave full support to Badoglio and the King and insisted on their future retention of power. To my horror the General gave him this assurance, and in writing. In other words, in complete contradiction to the Churchill-Roosevelt agreement, not only were the King and Badoglio to be supported up to Rome, but they were to be sustained by the Allied powers after the capture of the capital. I shuddered to think of the effect on the American and British Press when this document appeared. This would be a super-Darlan! Something must be done. Murphy was with me at Alexander's headquarters, and the next day we set out for Brindisi.

Murphy and I had an interview with Badoglio at 10.30. We found him rather pathetically aged and weakened. He is very unhappy about the armistice terms and the amendments which he hopes to get from the Allies. . . .

[5] 26 October 1943.

In the course of conversation, we were able to get Badoglio talking about the Rome group and the internal political situation. Murphy said that he understood that MacFarlane had given him a document as a sort of 'aide-mémoire' and we should be glad to see it in order to study it. Somehow or other we got possession of the document and managed to leave the room without returning it. It is now in the fire and reduced to ashes.[6]

We were both rather ashamed of ourselves, but Badoglio was a good-natured man and never reproved us. It certainly saved an infinity of trouble.

A day or two later we called on Benedetto Croce at Sorrento. He had been saved from capture by the Germans by our advance troops and was duly grateful. I had never met the great philosopher, although my firm had published English translations of some of his works. This small, gnome-like old man received us with a toothless chuckle, in the library of his handsome villa. His opinions, unlike his philosophy, were clear and definite. He had always been a monarchist. But the King was hopelessly discredited. No one could trust a man who had put a wreath 'on the grave of Mussolini's father, a drunkard at the best'. For a philosopher this seemed to be rather a *non sequitur*, but I did not interrupt. Croce had fallen entirely for the Sforza plan. Badoglio must be Regent and Sforza Prime Minister. Until this could be done there must be an Italian High Commissioner to represent Italy in the Naples area. Croce had little fear of Communism. He thought it was more a fashion than a force. As a proof that Badoglio knew nothing about politics, Croce asserted that he had not even been able to follow a simple work which he had written some time ago on the history of Italy. I thought that perhaps Badoglio had some excuse.

Possibly in deference to my colleague or for whatever reason, Dr. Croce did not make any reference to his extreme anti-clerical opinions. He did not, however, conceal his opinions on those economic questions which he puts into the lower category of philosophic thought. He is a liberal, of the old extreme capitalistic school. He is also . . . rich.

Soon after this, Badoglio made a journey to Naples to try to get anti-Fascist recruits to join his Government, but he failed completely. This produced a difficult situation. The King now asked permission to go himself to Naples to see what he could do. We decided to allow it, but

[6] 27 October 1943.

to tell Mason-MacFarlane not to go himself but merely to send an officer as an act of courtesy.

I do *not* want the Allied Governments to be associated *at this stage* with the dispute, either *for* or *against* the King. Incidentally, I have *no* guidance whatever from London as to H.M.G.'s views about abdication or anything else. General Eisenhower also has no idea of Washington's opinions. . . . Murphy . . . wants us to intervene and dismiss the King. But that is *quite wrong* at this stage. If they can solve their problem without *direct* interference by us it will be infinitely better both for us *and* for them, now and in the future.[7]

The Americans soon began to press strongly for the King's abdication, but I resisted this. It was true the King had failed in his efforts to widen his Government, but there was no need for us at this stage to intervene. I managed to persuade my colleagues that what we should do was to send a clear and objective picture of the situation to London and Washington and let them decide the great issues.

I do not see why great dynastic changes—for good or ill—should be made by a couple of generals, British and American, of limited political experience. This was finally agreed, and a telegram drafted for General Eisenhower to send to Washington to the Combined Chiefs of Staff setting out the position. Murphy was to be free to send his comments to the President and I would do the same to the Prime Minister.[8]

I summarised the position as follows:

The problem *may* be solved by the Italians themselves—without intervention from us. On the one hand, the various political leaders who should join a National Government may agree to waive the dynastic issue, at least for the time being. On the other hand, the King and the Prince may abdicate in favour of the child of six—the Prince of Naples. In either of these events, there is nothing for us to decide.

But I think it more likely that the politicians will maintain their refusal to serve, and that the King will decline to abdicate. He will appeal to Badoglio, as a loyal servant of the Crown, to carry on as present—*without* a broad government. Badoglio will say that he can only do this if the Allies support him in spite of his inability to get recruits to his Government of the kind we should like.[9]

[7] 2 November 1943.
[8] 3 November 1943.
[9] Ibid.

The argument seemed rather balanced. From the point of view of our declared war aims and public opinion at home and in America, it would perhaps be better to get rid of the King. After all, he had given his support to Mussolini. On the other hand,

the military situation is developing only slowly and we have a long tough fight ahead. The Italian Navy is co-operating well and efficiently on sea and on shore, in docks and workshops. The Army, if not fighting, is *working* for us. Practically all the embassies abroad have rallied to the King. This also applies to merchant seamen. We are not sure what would be the effect on all these people of an abdication which was *not* voluntary but enforced.

Interest now began to turn upon the Advisory Council for Italy, to which I had been officially appointed with the title of United Kingdom High Commissioner. I was at the same time to retain my other appointments: Ambassador to the French Government until relieved by Duff Cooper, and Political Adviser to the Supreme Allied Commander in respect of the Mediterranean area. On our return from the Cairo Conference, it was our urgent duty to get the Advisory Council into being in conformity with the decisions taken at Moscow. It was clear that the Russians were going to attach considerable importance to this new body. This was shown by the appointment of Vyshinsky, Deputy Commissar for Foreign Affairs and one of the most powerful figures in the Russian Government. He had just arrived in Algiers and we were all agog to see what kind of a man he would be as a colleague. After some discussion with Murphy, we thought the best thing to do was to start off with a lunch, followed by an informal talk as to procedure. This was duly arranged and took place on 29 November at Murphy's villa. Massigli and Guérin (his Under-Secretary) represented the French, and Roger Makins came with me. We had little difficulty at this stage, although there were one or two points on which the Russians were rather pedantic. I detected a tendency to try to expand the Council from an advisory to an executive character. But nothing with any real bite in it came up in these preliminary talks.

Vyshinsky is a strange personality. Outwardly he is genial, with red fat face and white hair, the image of every Conservative mayor or constituency chairman. . . . The eyes, however, are blue, spectacled—and hard. And behind the geniality and bluff heartiness, I think (even if one did not know his record) one detects a certain toughness. . . . But all the same it is difficult to visualise in him the cruel persecutor of the Russian terror—the scourge of prisoners, the torturer of witnesses, the gloating, merciless, bloody figure of which we read six or seven years ago.[10]

The next day the first formal meeting took place and once again was preceded by a luncheon, given by Bogomolov, the Russian Ambassador to the F.N.C.L., in his newly-acquired and magnificent villa.

Bogomolov is obviously *very* small beer compared to Vyshinsky, of whom he . . . stands in awe.

The luncheon was a miracle in Algiers. Caviare, smoked salmon, Russian bacon, tunny, sturgeon . . . in profusion. Vodka poured, like water, from carafes. Every two minutes Vyshinsky would leap to his feet and give a toast: 'To France and de Gaulle—Winston Churchill—Roosevelt—Democratic Liberties (*sic*)', etc.

Then we all joined in this toast game. Every toast meant more vodka. More vodka meant more caviare and smoked salmon and so on.

The ordinary courses started to arrive by about 2 o'clock and we finally staggered away about half past three, exhausted but enthused with Soviet ardour.[11]

At 4.30 the first formal meeting took place, and as a courtesy to the French we voted Massigli to the chair. The Chief of Staff welcomed the Council on behalf of General Eisenhower, and General Holmes of A.F.H.Q. gave a short account of the formation of A.M.G. and the new conception of the Control Commission—A.C.C. A few questions were asked. No difficulties were made. Some formal resolutions were voted and that was all.

On 2 December the Council left for an inspection tour in Italy. Murphy, Vyshinsky and I started together. Massigli was to join us the next day. We arrived at Brindisi in the late afternoon where we were met by Harold Caccia and Reber, now vice-presidents of the Allied Control Commission. I already felt that the whole thing was becoming top-heavy.

How extraordinary is the military mind! They have constructed in the War Department in Washington and the War Office in London this fantastically elaborate and top-heavy machine, with Chiefs of Staff, sections, sub-sections, sub-commissions and staffed either by [retired] professional soldiers—too [old] to be employed in any operational capacity—or quite good civilians, expert in finance, shipping, coal, etc., whom they insist on dressing up as brigadiers, colonels, etc. Then the whole is put down to govern a few square

[10] 29 November 1943.
[11] 30 November 1943.

miles and (at present) under twelve million people on a strictly military organisational basis, with returns in duplicate, and the incredibly complicated and obsolete internal mechanisms of the two War Departments hopelessly intermingled![12]

At this period the American General Joyce was enjoying his short reign and received us in a most stately but gracious style. We were told that business would begin the next day at 9 a.m. The problem of housing the staff, which Lord Stansgate (formerly William Wedgwood Benn) had now joined, was causing great difficulty. Fortunately, and to General Alexander's relief, we got most of them moved to Palermo. The next morning the Committee met, and after a preliminary statement by General Joyce, the heads of the various sections gave a report on the prospective organisation and duties of their sections. On the whole, this was well done. Harold Caccia, who headed the Political Section, had the most difficult task. For it was clear that the Russians were more interested in politics than in finance or food supplies.

Vyshinsky wanted to know how many Fascists had been tried and how many had been shot. The best that Harold could do was to murmur something about nearly 1,500 in prison—but Vyshinsky obviously thought this a very poor result of three months' work.[13]

Massigli had now joined us and after luncheon we had a formal meeting of the Council at which we discussed two major questions. First, the Russians, basing themselves on Article 37 of the long armistice terms, which were shown to and approved by them before signature at Malta, demanded the right to appoint Russians as members of the Control Commission, and they produced a number of officers as their first appointments. To this, of course, the French immediately reacted and made the same claim.

As the result of interminable talk, we agreed on a formula, viz., that the problem should be reported by us (in Council) *jointly* to General Eisenhower and by *each* of us separately to our Governments, asking for a reply as soon as possible.

I think myself that the French and Russians will realise that it is quite impossible for an executive body to function if it is completely polyglot and I think they (and certainly the French) will be content with three or four places each (out of the 1,000), more as a matter of prestige than anything else.

[12] 2 December 1943.
[13] 3 December 1943.

At any rate, I have recommended H.M.G. to accept a compromise on these lines.[14]

The second question was posed by General Eisenhower. It was

When (after the armistice) the King and Badoglio fled to Brindisi, we thought we must have a sort of 'enclave' under the royal sovereignty, so that the Italians could have a little kingdom (however small) in which the Italian State legally continued. The 'enclave' consists of the four provinces of Bari, Lecce, Taranto and Brindisi.

Here, of course, we sent in AMGOT (Allied Military Government of Occupied Territory) officers to supervise. But in this territory they acted *not* in the name of General Alexander (as Military Governor), giving direct orders and decrees. But they acted *indirectly,* supervising (and removing, by asking the Italians to do so, any undesirables) local Italian officials.

The Control Commission is being got ready to extend this system and it has been our plan that all Italian territory, including Sicily and Sardinia (except a narrow strip in the immediate rear of the armies which will remain under AMGOT) shall revert to the Italian Government, advised and supervised by the Commission.

In other words, we are going to operate *indirect* government (however strict) instead of *direct* government.[15]

Already this was being criticised as a surrender to the reactionary Italians, and we should be still more strongly attacked as the process continued. We therefore thought it wise to fortify ourselves by asking the new Advisory Council, with its French and Russian members, to agree to the return of further territory to the King and Badoglio. I thought that if we could achieve this it would be rather a sell for our Left-wing critics at home, since I would find myself no longer in the bad company of Murphy but in noble comradeship with Vyshinsky. Finally, after much argument, the proposal was agreed by Vyshinsky and Massigli as well as, of course, by the Americans and ourselves. They insisted upon only two conditions for the transfer. First, that only non-Fascist and pro-Allied officials should be employed; secondly, that we should not be indefinitely committed to the King and Badoglio, but only up to the capture of Rome. Since both these conditions were what I wanted, I accepted at once.

But if I thought the question settled I was wrong. Vyshinsky said he must refer the matter to Moscow, and Massigli said the same about Algiers. (Of course I might have known that Vyshinsky will never agree to anything

[14] Ibid.
[15] Ibid.

without reference to Moscow. He has two Ogpu chaps who watch him all the time and I suppose he has to watch his step.) However, both said they would recommend strongly that the decision be in favour of transfer. . . .[16]

At dinner, Vyshinsky was in great form and we had a tremendous argument about politics. Vyshinsky was very much upset about Mosley's recent release from prison, which he regarded as a sinister event. He could not understand why we had not shot him.

He also produced two gems:

'Democracy is like wine. It is all right if taken in moderation.'
'Free speech is all right, so long as it does not interfere with the policy of the Government.'[17]

Neither Vyshinsky nor any other of the Russians, so far as we knew, had ever been out of their own country, and we thought the best thing was to arrange a tour around southern Italy before the next meeting.

The two problems which concerned us at the first meeting were satisfactorily settled within a few weeks. The Russians agreed to the transfer of southern Italy to the Italian Government on 17 December, and on the 24th, at one of our meetings, they agreed to a symbolic representation of Russia and France on the Allied Control Commission. At the same meeting it was agreed to add representatives of Greece and Yugoslavia to the Advisory Council.

On 30 December the Advisory Council went off for another trip. I had to wait in Algiers in order to deal with the last French crisis and to hand over to Duff Cooper, but I joined them a few days later at Palermo. Vyshinsky, with his nine 'stooges' and his formidable and sub-human Lett detective, whose pockets bulged with revolvers and grenades, greeted me with enthusiasm. They had had a very agreeable time in Sardinia. I had sent with them a new member of my staff, Aubrey Halford, who was a highly intelligent young man with the advantage of speaking good Italian and Russian.

Palermo was 'governed' by a certain Colonel Poletti, an American-Italian and Lieutenant-Governor of New York State. He was in his element and seemed to be loving it. The Sicilians seemed to love it too. I think they felt rather proud that one of their kind should have made good in America and now be sent to hand out good things—

16 Ibid.
17 Ibid.

food, clothing, and medical stores—with a kind word and a joke for everyone.

The transfer of Sicily from direct to indirect control, although agreed, was still delayed by a mass of legal formalities, partly in A.F.H.Q., but chiefly in Washington and London. The War Office was one of the chief culprits, turning out regulations, memoranda and plans like a sausage-machine. The Allied Control Commission was also getting out of hand: 1,400 officers and 4,000 persons to administer a small part of Italy. My annoyance at this confusion, with which I had no authority to deal (I could only recommend to the Supreme Allied Commander and to my Government), was compensated for by a fascinating talk with Vyshinsky in the evening. It was difficult when conversing with this man, with his Pickwickian appearance, to realise his appalling history and the frightful responsibility which lay upon him for the deaths of hundreds of thousands—some even say millions —of unhappy people in the great Stalin purges.

He thinks there is little in what he has yet seen in Italy on which to base any strong Italian Government . . . we must wait till something emerges, perhaps in the meantime allowing local and municipal elections and starting the re-education of the people in self-government in this way. (All this is rather amusing in a way. Free Press, free speech, free elections—for everyone else.)[18]

When we got to Naples the next day it was clear what the Russian method of operation was. Vyshinsky had a great team of secretaries, 'contact men', interpreters, and all the rest. As soon as we arrived, most of these disappeared, no doubt to seek out the Italian Communists, only to reappear when it was time to leave.

All that day (9 January 1944) we listened to representatives of the six political parties grouped under the so-called Committee of National Liberation. They ranged from the Right to the extreme Left, and included the Communists. With the translation backwards and forwards, the discussions were tedious and exhausting. It was my turn to be in the chair and I found it hard work.

The Italians talked mostly in an excited fashion, with an irritating Neapolitan twang, but with some fascinating Neapolitan gestures, many of which were new to me. (One of the most interesting consists in clasping your

[18] 7 January 1944.

hands together under your throat and then suddenly shooting out your arms like a swimmer.)[19]

One of the great advantages of travelling with our Russian friends was that wherever we went there seemed to be a good supply of vodka and caviare. On the whole, except for a burst of temper from Vyshinsky when on one occasion the aircraft failed to start, it was an unqualified success. It was clear to me that the Russians were thoroughly enjoying their novel experience.

On the major problems of organisation neither the French nor the Russians took much interest. Before we ended this particular trip we heard that General Mason-MacFarlane, General Joyce's predecessor, was soon to take over again. I thought this might worry the other members of the Council, but they were so used to functionaries of all kinds appearing and disappearing with mysterious rapidity that it did not seem to concern them. At one of our meetings we had the advantage of hearing Badoglio address the Council. He did only moderately well, and seemed rather deflated. Nevertheless, a few days later Vyshinsky told me that he thought Sforza and Badoglio the only two men of any stature. At another meeting we heard the detailed reports of some of the A.M.G. officers concerned in the Naples area. I arranged this, since all kinds of statements had been made by the six parties' representatives, many of them prejudiced, and some definitely untrue. I thought the Council should hear both sides.

Vyshinsky naturally took the opportunity to submit the Allied officers to a good-humoured but merciless cross-examination. One saw, for the first time, the gimlet eye of the State prosecutor replace the Pickwickian benevolent beam. I re-examined after him, and Vyshinsky quite enjoyed the duel. The officers were grateful to me and it really was quite an interesting and exciting end to the day.[20]

Vyshinsky kept assuring me that although he thought the King would eventually have to abdicate, there was no hurry.

On returning to Algiers, I found that the form in which the necessary reservations as to the Allied rights had been drafted by the lawyers in London and Washington was so harsh as to make me unwilling to present the document to the Italians. General Wilson agreed with this view, as did Mason-MacFarlane. Bedell Smith, who

[19] 9 January 1944.
[20] 10 January 1944.

was about to leave for England for 'Overlord', was equally concerned. I therefore drafted a telegram of protest to be sent by General Wilson to the Combined Chiefs of Staff, and telegraphed personally to the Foreign Secretary. I was also to get an opportunity to discuss it with the Prime Minister for I had received a command 'to dine and sleep' at Marrakesh where he was finishing his convalescence.

The P.M. was in a most mellow mood. The de Gaulle visit had taken place the day before and had gone off satisfactorily. This morning there had been a military review, at which de Gaulle and the P.M. had taken the salute. Winston had been much moved by the enthusiasm of his reception.[21]

He went on to talk about Victor Emmanuel and Badoglio. He was all for keeping them at present: 'When I want to lift a pot of hot coffee, I prefer to keep the handle.' He also gave me a long memorandum from the Cabinet about my new position and functions, and asked for my comments. Realising that he was bored with these details, I prepared a much simplified form. He asked me whether I wanted to stay in the Mediterranean or would like office at home. Of course I wanted to stay. It was a unique and wonderful experience for me, and I had enjoyed every moment of it. He agreed, adding: 'Well, in spite of our tiffs, we have got on well together. You have done very well, very well indeed.' The only point in my memorandum which he noticed was my desire to be given some better method of carrying out my duties. To travel by the ordinary 'courier' aeroplane was very exhausting. I thought I ought to be provided with something better. Our arrival in Marrakesh, for instance, had been delayed for five hours merely through the difficulty of getting seats. He was very kind about this and promised to give instructions to the Air Ministry. As a result I was to have far better treatment in the future. Churchill was very charming and appreciative in every way, and bound me more firmly than ever to his service by affection as well as by duty.

Soon after I got back to Algiers, Vyshinsky came to lunch with me. When I repeated to him Churchill's phrase about the handle and the coffee pot, he was delighted.

Since it was necessary to obtain Alexander's approval for the reorganisation by which he assumed full responsibility for both A.M.G. and A.C.C., on 18 January I left Algiers for Naples, where Mason-MacFarlane came to join me. We drove out to Caserta, where we found

[21] 13 January 1944.

the General had just moved into a part of the enormous palace. This was my first visit to this vast building, into which A.F.H.Q. was to move permanently in July and which was to remain our headquarters until the end of the war.

> Everything was in disorder and he seemed (as usual) to have been fobbed off with the worse quarters. (I have a bedroom and sitting-room—or office—reserved for me in the A.F.H.Q. wing and these are most comfortably arranged.)[22]

This must have been an anxious time for the General. For the Anzio landings were about to take place. This operation began hopefully; but for a variety of reasons it was not pressed on by its commanders with sufficient speed and vigour. As a result, the Germans were able to launch powerful counter-attacks and at one moment the situation looked critical. Alexander himself went to take control and restored the position. But the high expectations which had been placed upon this operation were doomed to at least temporary disappointment. The bridgehead was held and the 'build-up' continued. But the 'break-out' proved impossible. Nevertheless, the Anzio forces were to play an important role in the final battle for Rome. Meanwhile the Anzio set-back, together with the deadlock on the Cassino front, was to make the early months of the year a frustrating experience for Alexander and his armies. I saw a great deal of him in my frequent visits during this period. His mood of calm and quiet confidence never changed. Whether the news was good or bad, he seemed to be able to maintain extraordinary self-control. He welcomed my appearances at his H.Q., for I think he found it pleasant to have a man of his own age to talk to about things outside the military world. Whenever I left, he pressed me to return.

If the military position was temporarily static, the political situation was developing. At a meeting of the Advisory Council in Algiers on 24 January, with Vyshinsky in the chair, Massigli presented a formal document demanding the immediate abdication of the King, and asking for Italian warships, merchant ships and other material to be distributed to the French as a compensation for Italy's attack upon France in 1940. I was very indignant at this, and so was Vyshinsky. It was clear that Massigli was ashamed of these outrageous requests, which he had been ordered to present.

[22] 18 January 1944.

Vyshinsky proposed that we should discuss the problem of the King 'at the meeting *after* the next one'—which we hope may be after the capture of Rome.[23]

Alas, this hope was not to be realised; but Vyshinsky's plan at least gave us an interval. At the same time there was better news from London and Washington.

The Allied Governments have accepted completely our view about the 'transfer' document, so I hope this will now go through. It is a great 'climb-down' after all the pages of stuff which they write in London and Washington. But they never face the realities. The real problem is to get an Italian Government to accept the responsibility of even *trying* to govern southern Italy in present conditions, dependent as they are on us for food, transport, fuel and clothing. If Badoglio is too hard pressed he will throw in his hand and this will be very embarrassing for us.[24]

I had now to go again to Italy to get General Alexander's signature— as Military Governor—to the necessary documents. After the formal business he told us something of the Anzio situation.

Alex. was tired, but quite cheerful. The weather has not been quite so kind lately. The wind has been very strong and made it difficult to land the stores, etc., that are required. What they need is an 'off-shore' wind. If it is blowing from the sea it forces the ships forward, as they become lighter with the landing of their cargoes, and therefore there is a risk of them 'broaching'— that is getting stuck on the sand and thus becoming losses. It is really rather wonderful what they manage to do. There is only a tiny little harbour at Anzio (fortunately undamaged); all the rest of the stuff is carried over the beaches, even from big Liberty ships as well as from regular landing craft.[25]

A new crisis had arisen over the meeting of a congress arranged by the Neapolitan Committee of National Liberation, to be held in Bari. A similar plan for a meeting in Naples in December had been forbidden by the military authorities on our advice. But when it was proposed to hold it in Bari at the end of January there did not seem to be any reason to interfere. (Murphy had by now gone back to America on leave and did not reappear until April. He was admirably represented by Reber and Reinhardt.)[26] Nevertheless, this affair was to result in a sudden and unexpected sequel.

[23] 24 January 1944.
[24] Ibid.
[25] 25 January 1944.
[26] Frederick Reinhardt, who had recently jointed Murphy's staff.

Great alarm was caused in London by a signal from Admiral McGrigor in Taranto to the C.-in-C. Mediterranean, which was unfortunately repeated to the Admiralty.

The gallant flag officer at Taranto thought that the congress would perhaps lead the Italian Navy to:
(a) mutiny;
(b) scuttle their ships.
It was not quite clear whether they would adopt this course because:
(a) they were monarchists, and wished to protest against the views [likely to be] expressed at the congress;
(b) they were republicans, and wished to show their sympathy for the said views.
Anyway, Admiral McGrigor's signal caused distress in London and a very foolish message to me from my colleagues.[27]

It certainly seemed unwise to withdraw permission now.

It will be a 'ticket' meeting and I have no doubt uncommonly dull. Croce will open, with at least 1½ hours . . . and I do not believe that there will be any serious disturbances.[28]

I went to see Admiral Sir John Cunningham, now C.-in-C. Mediterranean, to discuss it with him. He was a clever and experienced officer, with a pleasant sense of humour. I ventured to tell him

that although I was quite prepared to accept the view that the Italian fleet would mutiny, I did *not* believe that this would be as a result of the congress at Bari, but rather due to the natural propensity of all fleets to mutiny. This seemed to satisfy him.[29]

Although no doubt the congress was not very welcome to the King or Badoglio, it ended in talk. Any proposals for violent action from the Left were squashed by the Right. The congress confined itself to declaring that the abdication of the King was an essential condition of reconstruction. But the question of the monarchy was by no means quiescent.

The State Department have suddenly gone mad and sent the most extraordinary instructions to Reinhardt, who is acting in Murphy's place. . . . (a) to tell Massigli that they agree with the French Note and that they think the King should be 'removed' at once and a new Government be

[27] 27 January 1944.
[28] Ibid.
[29] Ibid.

formed (apparently on a purely revolutionary basis and without any legal sanction), and (b) to tell the same thing to Sforza.

It would be difficult to imagine any diplomacy more crude or more futile. The French will immediately publish this démarche . . . of course emphasising the fact that they are in agreement with Washington and *against* London in the matter. Sforza—whom we are trying to get to agree (after the usual Italian bargaining) to some compromise—will at once be so puffed up with conceit as to raise his price.

Fortunately I was able to persuade Reinhardt *not* to carry out either of these instructions [without] . . . sending over to consult Reber.[30] Meanwhile, I must telegraph the F.O. and get Winston to take it all up with the President direct and get Reinhardt's instructions changed.[31]

General Wilson at first favoured strong action against the King, but I persuaded him to change his mind and to leave the matter for the President and the Prime Minister to settle between them. Churchill spoke in the House of Commons on 22 February, pleading for delay. He pointed out that the Italian military and naval forces, together with Italian airmen, were now fighting on our side. He was not convinced that any other Government could immediately be formed which could command the same obedience; when the battle for Rome was over we should be free to discuss the whole political situation.

I was now in rather a poor state of health. My own doctor, Colonel Richardson, had himself been struck down with serious illness and returned to England. I felt I must have some leave. My hands were troubling me, and I was suffering from eczema in other parts of my body. I must get home. Accordingly, after consulting London, I left Algiers on 12 February and did not return until 9 March. My four weeks benefited me enormously, though they were not altogether restful. I had many conversations with Ministers and officials at the Foreign Office as well as with the Prime Minister.

I returned to find the situation still confused. As I had warned Churchill at Cairo, the change of command had not been to our advantage.

. . . two things have resulted. . . . First, General Wilson—although a shrewd, clever, humorous and rather cunning man—has not the capacity to make himself liked by the Americans here to the same extent that General Eisenhower was able to attract British sympathy and support. Secondly, the

[30] Reber was in Italy, in the Political Section of A.C.C.
[31] 7 February 1944.

very fact that we have a British and not an American general in command, paradoxically enough weakens instead of strengthening our political position. When General Eisenhower was here, if I could persuade him to recommend to the Combined Chiefs of Staff in Washington a course which . . . was what H.M.G. wanted, I knew that it would go through. The State Department would not venture to intervene against the recommendations of an American general. Or if they did, General Marshall and the War Department would come out in full cry and hunt the State Department to the death. Now all that is changed. The State Department is opposing our policy in Italy as well as elsewhere. And the War Department will naturally not rush to defend a British general.[32]

During my absence Mason-MacFarlane had continued to report growing opposition to the King from Sforza and others and the need for the Allies to intervene. But Makins handled the situation with characteristic skill and persuaded the military commanders, including General Devers, the American deputy to Wilson, to oppose political intervention at the present time.

In the event, as a result of an exchange of messages between himself and Churchill, the President gave firm instructions to the State Department to take no further action affecting any change in the Italian Government, pending such improvement in the military situation as would warrant taking political risks.

We were soon, however, to be faced with a new and entertaining diversion from our Russian friends.

Vyshinsky had gone back to Russia and had not returned; but on 8 March Bogomolov, who had replaced him on the Council, informed Marshal Badoglio that the Soviet Government was willing to re-establish diplomatic arrangements with the Italian Government and to exchange representatives who would have all the privileges and rights of ambassadors.[33] I heard of this move on the day after my arrival in Algiers and immediately reported it to London. In the evening I dined alone with Bogomolov, but I could get nothing out of him. I threw several flies over him, but he rose to none. No instructions had yet reached us from London or Washington.

The next morning General Wilson called a meeting to discuss the problem. We now heard that the Russians, in addition to their diplomatic move, wanted an air base at Bari, giving as an excuse that

[32] 9 March 1944.
[33] Harris, p. 141.

it would be convenient for flying in and out members of their mission to Tito. Two days later the telegrams began to pour in about the Russian move. In the course of the morning of 13 March, Bogomolov came to tell me officially of the Russian decision. I expressed pained surprise, but of course said that I could not believe that Moscow was acting independently and that no doubt it had all been arranged with London and Washington. Perhaps they had forgotten to give us instructions. Bogomolov (keeping as always his eyes on the ground or squinting sideways) said that he had no information.

I asked Bogomolov if there was to be any announcement in the Press. He would give me no guarantee. Of course they have been very clever and have bullied the Italians into announcing it first and will publish their own communiqué a day later.[34]

Lunching with Massigli alone the next day I found him much concerned.

The French are naturally very anti-Italian and correspondingly suspicious of anything affecting the status of the Italian Government.[35]

It was my turn to act as chairman and I therefore insisted upon calling a meeting of the Advisory Council for 15 March. Both Reinhardt and I had pretty stiff instructions and some nasty questions to ask Bogomolov. We kept up the pressure for one and a half hours and got at least some satisfaction.

At first he said that he had no instructions and could not discuss the Russian diplomatic arrangements with Italy. Then—under pressure—he gave us his own view. He pretended (which is quite untrue) that the initiative came from the Italians. Then he said it was a very small affair (like the housemaid's baby—illegitimate but small) and that there would be no interchange of accredited ambassadors or Ministers, but only agents.[36]

It was rather significant that Bogomolov came alone to the meeting. The Russians usually brought six or seven attendants as well as interpreters. He asked that no record should be made of what he had said.

I suppose he is afraid of being shot for disobeying his orders, which were obviously to say nothing at all. Reinhardt and I said indignantly that we must

[34] 13 March 1944.
[35] 14 March 1944.
[36] 15 March 1944.

insist on the minutes recording what we had said. He had the usual right to correct the draft minutes as regards what he said. In order to impress further on him what we said, we undertook to give him the same afternoon an 'aide-mémoire' in writing, which he could telegraph to Moscow.

After all this, we thoroughly enjoyed our luncheon.[37]

There was a considerable concern expressed in the British Press, but the mystery remained and Bogomolov attempted in conversation with members of my staff to play down the whole incident. Nevertheless, news reached us that Prunas (now Under-Secretary in the Ministry of Foreign Affairs) had frankly admitted that this was the beginning of further action by the Russians. There might be other gifts in store, and the Italians certainly expected another move.

General Wilson, on our advice, pointed out to the Combined Chiefs of Staff that he could find no clause in the 'surrender terms' which prevented the Italian action, but the Foreign Office still maintained their power to refuse consent. The State Department also argued our right to control the Italian Government's arrangements with any foreign power, whether Allied or neutral. The consent of the Supreme Allied Commander was necessary and should be obtained through the Control Commission.

For the next fortnight the battle raged. Finally, on 26 March, I again saw Bogomolov who informed me that his Government had presented a memorandum to London and Washington dealing with the incident. He was happy to say it repeated the assurances he had given me unofficially at the meeting of the Council; that is, minimising the incident and the results that might be expected to follow. He again insisted that these arrangements did not constitute normal diplomatic recognition. He now told me that the Soviet representative would be M. Kostylev, who would have the rank of Counsellor, and an Italian agent would be similarly received in Moscow. Kostylev would be under the orders of the Soviet member of the Advisory Council who he hoped would remain Vyshinsky. At any rate the Soviet Government intended to support the Advisory Council in every way.

I had to leave the negotiations to make a visit to Cairo to arrange matters concerning the Mediterranean Command and the responsibility for the Balkan States. But in spite of Badoglio's protestations, it was quite clear to us that he had fallen for the Soviet guile. All we

[37] Ibid.

could do in the end was to accept the fact of the Russian intervention. This incident gave us some warning of what we should have to face from the Soviet Government as the war drew to a conclusion.

The unilateral diplomatic action by the Soviet Government, together with their pressures for facilities for their air force in Italy, were combined with growing activity by the local Communist leaders, soon to be inspired by the return of Palmiro Togliatti, a fully trained and highly qualified Communist. General Solodovnik, the Russian representative on the Control Commission, had intimate contacts with all the local organisations and leaders whom he could influence. Moreover, with great skill the Russians were beginning to exploit the clear differences of British and American policies and opinions. I reminded the Foreign Office of the extent to which the Allies were drifting apart, even in our own area, since Eisenhower had left. The Foreign Office proposed to send out a Foreign Office official of ambassadorial rank. I thought this an excellent suggestion, assuming that he was to take my place as High Commissioner on the Advisory Council; for it was vital that he and his American counterpart, when appointed, should not regard themselves merely as envoys to the shadowy Italian Government, but rather as co-operating loyally with each other and with the Allied military commanders. That should be their chief duty, and if they worked as a team with General Mason-MacFarlane in the same way as Murphy and I had long worked with General Eisenhower and General Wilson, all would be well. Sir Noel Charles, formerly Ambassador in Brazil, was chosen for his post; but I insisted that no announcement should be made until the Americans had done the same. Finally both Sir Noel and Alexander Kirk, from the American Embassy in Cairo, were appointed. I found them both very easy to work with. Charles was a most agreeable and delightful man and accepted the secondary role which was afforded to him. When he got to Rome, Ambassador Kirk ensconced himself in magnificent apartments in the Palazzo Barberini and entertained there on a splendid scale. Meanwhile, he had to content himself with the more modest accommodation which Naples could supply.

But the pressure was building up and the battle still hung fire. The Anzio diversion had temporarily failed. There was deadlock on the Cassino line. I knew from my close contact with Alexander that the new offensive could not begin until early in May. Was it possible to

maintain a completely static political policy for so long? The Prime
Minister continued to fight strenuously for this thesis 'No change until
Rome'. But with the Americans, Russians, French and Italians all
pressing, some apparent progress seemed to me essential. There were
two questions: that of the King, and that of bringing the six parties
into the Government under Badoglio. But would the parties be willing
to serve under the old Marshal? On this point Togliatti, acting no
doubt under instructions from the Russians, was to throw his weight
in favour of the immediate formation of a six-party Government,
without demanding any change in the premiership.

On 23 March, when I was in Cairo with General Wilson to discuss
Balkan affairs, I heard that owing to Mason-MacFarlane's weakness,
largely due to approaching physical collapse and Bogomolov's intrigues, things were on the boil. Eden asked me to return to Italy as
soon as possible.

Much to my delight, Murphy, who had been in America since the
end of 1943, unexpectedly returned. He had been offered some post as
liaison officer between the State Department and the White House
which he had very wisely managed to avoid.

His first reason was a wise [reluctance] to appear to be taking Harry
Hopkins's job from him while he was away (for this work of trying to arrange
matters between the President's office and the State Department was rather
Harry's speciality). His second was a natural unwillingness—as a 'career'
diplomat—to commit himself so intimately to an administration which has
not very long to run.[38]

He was to remain with us until he went to General Eisenhower as
main political adviser for 'Overlord'—a post to which he was eminently suited. I gathered from Murphy that the President had found
the winter trip to Cairo and Teheran very exhausting. He had
returned very tired and was not in a good state of health.

Unfortunately Harry Hopkins—on whom the President depends greatly—
has been seriously ill, with two dangerous internal operations from which (if
he recovers at all) he will be incapacitated for some time to come.[39]

This was bad news, for I always regarded Harry as a good friend and a
great help in untangling apparently hopeless knots. Murphy told me
that the President was still very anti-de Gaulle, but would of course in

38 7 April 1944.
39 Ibid.

fact yield to the realities of any situation. On Italy he was very keen to have something to show politically before the Presidential election. Roosevelt had agreed to Churchill's formula of waiting for the capture of Rome, but very reluctantly. I felt that it would help relations if we could get some forward move in Italy. We could not really resist much longer. After talking it over with Noel Charles, I sent my recommendations to the Prime Minister. The six parties were now moving rapidly towards the idea of entering the Government. I felt that we should take advantage of their mood, if a Government could be formed without interference on our part and without prejudice to the political position of the monarchy. I accordingly sent a telegram to the Prime Minister urging that this opportunity should not be missed. All that mattered to us was to ensure that the new Government should bind itself firmly to an acceptance of all the obligations entered into by its predecessor. Secondly, they must agree that the monarchical question should be postponed until the whole Italian people could be freely consulted—that is, after the end of the war. If we could get these two conditions, it seemed to me a positive advantage to allow the new Government to be formed on a wider basis. I also promised to do my best to keep out Sforza, at least from the post of Foreign Minister.

The Prime Minister replied immediately approving our proposed course of action, saying:

. . . I do not mind very much whether the King retires now or waits till Rome is taken so long as Umberto is created Lieutenant and Badoglio remains at the head of the Government.

Armed with this support, I proposed the necessary resolutions to the Advisory Council, which were approved, Bogomolov merely reserving his official confirmation until he could hear from Moscow.

The situation was rather intriguing because the instructions being given to the Communists had now reached our ears.

. . . the whole situation has been largely changed by the Communist move. Under orders from Moscow, they have let it be known that they will enter a Government *without* raising the question of the King and the monarchy. . . . But this Communist position makes the liberal and moderate parties very uncomfortable. On the one hand, they long to enter the Government and would hate to see the Communists and Socialists collar all the best jobs and all the power; on the other hand, they have made so many speeches and uttered such brave words, that a lot of the latter would need to be eaten if they were to come along and join Badoglio. It is, therefore, in my view necessary for a sufficient gesture to be made by the King—whether abdication, or a regency, or a promise of a regency—for the other parties to enter a coalition Government immediately, without too much loss of 'face'.

This . . . should (I think) be treated as the central [problem]. The effects on British and American opinion are important, but secondary. If we can obtain a 'broad-based democratic Government' by a comparatively modest move by the King, we are not entitled to demand a drastic one merely to please American voters.[40]

Things now began to move rapidly. There were in effect two plans. First, the King's plan, put to him originally by an Italian politician called De Nicola, which had become more or less known in political circles.

Under this plan, the King would announce *now* his intention of appointing Prince Umberto as 'Lieutenant-General of the Realm' or Regent *after* the taking of Rome.

There are certain points to be tied up, even under this plan. For instance, the King appointed a Lieutenant-General of the Realm in the last war (when he was at the Front). It must therefore be made clear that the appointment is final and irrevocable. What is to happen if the capture of Rome is long delayed—and so forth.[41]

But there was a second plan which was in a sense a variation of it. The party leaders, except the so-called Liberals, would be happier if the King would make the appointment now instead of waiting to implement it. Others were asking that the Prince should not have full authority, but only an honorary position, all powers being delegated to some other body. I had no precise instructions, but I agreed to give my support to the second plan, if the King would agree.

Accordingly, Murphy and I called on the King in his villa at Ravello at 11 a.m. on Monday 10 April. We were accompanied by Noel Charles and General Mason-MacFarlane. Old age had not deprived this monarch of any of his subtlety in negotiation and ingenuity of mind. He immediately greeted us with the question as to whether there was any news of the battle and when we hoped to take Rome and drive the Germans out of Italy. By arrangement, Murphy was to open the discussion. He developed his theme with considerable force and skill.

He told the King quite frankly the view of American opinion about himself as an individual and his conduct of Italian affairs during recent years. He said

[40] 8 April 1944.
[41] Ibid.

that as the King was bound up in the American mind with Fascism for twenty years and with the guilt of having declared war against his old friends, it would be better for the preservation of the monarchy if the King would declare his intention to abdicate at once, or at least retire immediately in favour of the Prince by appointing him Lieutenant-General.

As agreed, I supported this proposal with a few words in what I thought was appropriate language. To have to say hard things to a man many years one's senior is never a pleasant situation. It was all the more distasteful to one who was brought up on monarchical principles to have to say them to a person who had for forty years exercised the royal authority.

The King affected to be very much surprised. He thought we had come on a courtesy visit. He showed great alarm and some indignation. In a rambling manner, which I think was more put on than genuine, he spoke to us of the losses of his subjects caused by our bombing of Rome and a number of other rather irrelevant topics. We subsequently heard that he had been perfectly well informed of the object of our visit and was merely trying to gain time. He said he must consult on such a matter with his Ministers.

Murphy and I then retired to the Villa Cimbrone—Lord Grimthorpe's beautiful house which was now used as a rest camp for officers—where we were staying. A message was brought to us about lunch-time to say that the King must ask for forty-eight hours to make up his mind. As the Junta—the representatives of the six parties—was meeting on Wednesday the 12th, we said that was too long. He must make a decision within twenty-four hours.

Meanwhile, General Mason-MacFarlane, who had gone to see Badoglio in Salerno—the Italian Government was now mainly centred in this delightful town—sent us a message that the Marshal had been rung up by d'Acquarone and had assured him that if asked his opinion he would urge His Majesty to accept the British and American proposal. Badoglio also said that the Communists and Socialists had already decided to join the Government, but the Social Democrats and Liberals were waiting to see what action the King would take. If Badoglio could get four parties, the Government would be sufficiently representative, for the Party of Action and the Labour Democrats had very little following.

At noon the next day (11 April) the Duca d'Acquarone came to see us and said that the King had given much thought to what we had told him and that he was prepared now to bind himself by making an immediate announcement. D'Acquarone produced a text, which ran as follows: 'I have decided to appoint my son, the Prince of Piedmont, Lieutenant-General of the Realm. The formal transfer of power will take place on the day on which the Allied troops enter Rome.' If we were prepared to accept this formula the King would see us at 4 o'clock in the afternoon, accompanied by Marshal Badoglio, and bind himself formally to abide by it.

This was rather an ingenious suggestion of the King's and was in fact a compromise between the two plans. Murphy strongly protested and demanded an immediate transfer. I contented myself with giving as much support as was consistent with my undertaking to Murphy without getting too much involved. At 3.30 in the afternoon Badoglio arrived and argued strongly in favour of the King's original plan. He said that his only interest was to preserve the monarchy, and the King also was thinking not of himself but of his dynasty. It was a mistake in politics, especially when dealing with Italians, to make all the concessions in a single gesture. They were soon forgotten and no thanks were given. He himself felt very doubtful as to whether in any event the monarchy could be saved. But by the King's scheme something could be done now, and Badoglio thought the politicians would accept it. When we got to Rome the Prince would actually take over. This would give an opportunity of summoning a new Government. Fresh interest and fresh emotion would be caused. There was still another card to play: the King might abdicate definitely in favour of his son. In the last resort, Prince Umberto could himself abdicate in favour of the young prince. Badoglio was therefore in favour of the policy of small concessions doled out little by little. I could not help smiling to myself at this; it reminded me so much of Giraud's 'politique de perroquet'.

Murphy and I then retired to confer and I persuaded him that we should take the following line: we should ask Badoglio to see the King and say that we still felt that it would be in the interests of the monarchy to take the plunge, but we would not put any pressure on him as representatives of the Allied Governments. We were there to advise him, not to force him. We were not Prussians. We were not exercising our power as representing conquering armies. We were giving him what seemed to us the best advice. If he refused it, and a Government could not be formed, then a further concession would have to be made and he would be robbed of the advantage of a voluntary gesture. He must decide. Badoglio gave this message to the King, and at six o'clock Prunas, who had been with him all the time, returned with the decision. The King had listened, he said, to our arguments, and had now put forward another suggestion: that a sounding be taken as to whether a Government could be formed on the present plan, and if in two or three days it was found to be impossible, he would reconsider the position.

We naturally said that this was the worst proposal of all, and we could not accept it. It would have the disadvantage of delay; the King would be bound to nothing; he was even trying to evade the concessions he had made; and he would not be pledged to any decision. We must ask him to give further consideration to his position. Prunas said he would inform the King accordingly. In reply we insisted that he should return by 10 p.m. with the text of the proposed declaration, to be read on the wireless and given to the Press. Prunas duly came back with the draft. I thought it not strong enough. I did not wish to alter the more or less inoperative paragraphs, but I insisted upon an insertion of more definite phrases. The King must say 'I have decided to withdraw from public affairs' and there must be also included the words 'This decision is final and irrevocable'. Before we left to motor back to Naples we heard that these words had been approved. The vital paragraphs were as follows:

> Putting into effect what I have suggested to the Allied authorities and to my Government, I have decided to withdraw from public affairs by appointing my son, the Prince of Piedmont, Lieutenant-General of the Realm.
> This appointment will become effective by the formal transfer of power on the day on which Allied troops enter Rome.
> This decision, which, I firmly believe, furthers national unity, is final and irrevocable.

Although this was not what Murphy had wanted for the American public and the forthcoming elections, it was really good enough. Anyway, he stuck by it with absolute loyalty, and at our Press conference the next day valiantly argued that the arrangement marked a substantial advance and should be regarded as acceptable to American public opinion. He was confident that it would lead to the formation of a broad-based Government.

There was one amusing sequel. At 6 o'clock on the afternoon of 13

April, Bogomolov asked to see me. I had rather expected that he would want to know what Murphy and I had been up to during the Easter holidays, and would register a protest against our unilateral action. But butter would not melt in his mouth. He came to tell me merely that his Government had approved our resolution of 8 April, which he had referred back to them, and hoped that I would soon be able to lunch with him again. I had done so the week before, when the fare had been: caviare; hors d'œuvres (vodka); soup; macaroni; fish; chicken; lamb; Neapolitan ices and cakes; cheese; fruit; various wines; coffee; liqueurs. I had felt rather concerned in view of the fact that the people of Naples were living on the bare minimum of subsistence. However, it was not for me to raise any objections. I was now only relieved at the Russians taking so well what we had done. Both Churchill and Eden sent me congratulatory telegrams at the successful conclusion of the royal episode.

Badoglio's six-party Government, in which he remained Prime Minister and Minister for Foreign Affairs, was composed as follows: the Service Ministers were unchanged—Admiral De Courten (Navy), General Sandalli (Air) and General Orlando (Army). The five most prominent political leaders became Ministers without Portfolio. They were Croce, Sforza, Rodino, Togliatti and Mancini. The other offices were divided up equally among the six parties, with Ministers and Under-Secretaries balancing each other. The Government's first step was to give in writing two undertakings which the Allies demanded. These were, first, to accept all the obligations towards the Allies entered into by the previous Government; and second, to pledge not to reopen the constitutional (i.e. the monarchical) question 'until such time as the whole Italian people were in a position freely to express their views'. Both these undertakings were required from all successive Italian Governments until the conclusion of the peace treaty.[42] Churchill was pleased at our work, chiefly because Badoglio remained Prime Minister and Foreign Secretary, and Sforza was only one of five Ministers without Portfolio. More important, the Ministry of the Interior was given to a Christian Democrat and not to a Communist.

Noel Charles had now succeeded me on the Advisory Council and

[42] Harris, pp. 143–4.

Ambassador Kirk was soon to take Murphy's place. Alexander persuaded me to go with him to Italy and stay with him for a few days. We lived on his train just outside Caserta. In the mornings I attended the War Room for the routine review of the position. Most of the day we spent driving to different parts of the Front. One day we lunched with General Anders, commanding the Polish Corps. This was my first opportunity to meet this remarkable soldier. I could see that, although he and his men loyally carried out their engagement to the Allies, memories of Poland, fear for her future, and equal hatred of Russians and Germans were not far removed from his thoughts. One thing struck me as most moving when we reached his headquarters in the morning.

The trumpeters played a curious and appealing call, which ends suddenly—broken off in the middle of a musical phrase. We were told that this is always played at noon. It commemorates a trumpeter who was calling the people of Cracow to muster against the Tartars. As he was playing an arrow pierced his throat. Ever since . . . this call is played at noon, in memory of the Poles' long struggle against barbarism and urging them still to fight in the same cause. It always ends on this broken note.[43]

The history of this corps was truly remarkable. Recruited largely from eastern Poland, they had been imprisoned in Russian internment camps in 1939 after the Molotov–Ribbentrop Pact and the defeat of Poland by Germany. When Germany attacked Russia they were at last set free and after incredible adventures they marched (like the Greeks in Xenophon's *Anabasis*) until they finally reached Palestine. Now they had re-entered Europe in Italy.

At this time our life was immensely cheered by the arrival of my wife from London. She was to stay for four months, first in Algiers and then, when we moved, in Naples. She enjoyed her time and certainly gave a great deal of pleasure to others with her simplicity and charm.

There was a sharp argument between A.F.H.Q. and London and Washington about the proposals of the State Department to declare Rome an 'open city'.

The British Chiefs of Staff and F.O. had sent a waffling telegram (F.O. particularly feeble) and I had a good deal of trouble in [showing] that our chief interest was not so much the desire to *attack* Rome while in German

[43] 24 April 1944.

hands, but to *use* the city when we had captured it. We must be very careful not to *tie* our hands.[44]

I asked what the expression 'open city' meant, and I was amused to find, when the lawyers were consulted, that it had no meaning and was not used in the Hague Convention of 1907. In the event, as is well known, the damage to Rome by the Allies was very small since our attacks were confined to the area of the marshalling yard outside the city.

General Wilson moved to our forward headquarters at Caserta on 24 May. On the 26th there was a full meeting to discuss what was to be done on the capture of Rome.

> General agreement was reached on procedure.
> (*a*) There will be no formal entry into Rome. General Alexander is very anxious that the capture of Rome should be treated militarily on its true basis. The battle is for the purpose of destroying the German Army, and any triumphs should be delayed until that object is completed.
> (*b*) General Johnson will act as Governor on behalf of General Clark of the American Fifth Army. He will be accompanied by 'S' Force, who will carry out all their duly appointed tasks, and the A.M.G. officials will also work under him. At the end of the first phase A.M.G. will take over and the second phase will begin.
> (*c*) The position of the Italian Government was discussed. It was clear to me that General MacFarlane has already largely put himself under an obligation to Badoglio and the Prince. I do not like it at all.[45]

On 1 June I saw Mason-MacFarlane.

> He has at last insisted on the King carrying out his decision to retire from the throne and appoint his son Regent. It appears that [he] is still trying to wriggle out of his engagement. I have also persuaded MacFarlane not to allow him to go to Rome and not even to go to Naples. I told MacFarlane that if the King makes any nonsense he should put him in an aeroplane and send him to Kenya.[46]

On 4 June the Allied armies entered Rome. We had an Old Etonian dinner at Algiers and sent the following telegram to Alexander:

> Many congratulations on the successful development of your battle and all good wishes for its exploitation.

[44] 16 May 1944.
[45] 26 May 1944.
[46] 1 June 1944.

It was moreover thoughtful of you as an old Harrovian to capture Rome on 4 June.[47]

To this he replied, 'Thank you. What is the Fourth of June?' This was sent *en clair* through A.F.H.Q. signals and much intrigued the Americans.

The King duly signed the document creating his son Lieutenant-General of the Realm, and on 8 June Prince Umberto and Badoglio, together with seven members of his Cabinet—one from each of the six parties, and Count Sforza—were flown to Rome. Badoglio held a conference with the Roman Committee of National Liberation in the presence of General Mason-MacFarlane. This committee was presided over by Bonomi and he brought with him a representative of each party including Alcide De Gasperi for the Christian Democrats and Pietro Nenni for the Socialists. It was clear from what emerged that Badoglio had either been outmanœuvred or had bowed to irresistible pressure. He had in any case to offer his formal resignation to the Regent. He was now persuaded to retire, as indeed he had long wished to do. Bonomi became Prime Minister, and Count Sforza Minister for Foreign Affairs; otherwise the new Government was much the same as the old one. But these changes caused an explosion in London. A violent telegram reached me from Churchill expressing astonishment at the result. He could not understand why I had left this matter to Mason-MacFarlane, who had no authority to 'connive at the transference of power from Badoglio'. Italy was a conquered territory and the Italian Government could only administer the provinces re-assigned to them under strict Allied control. Badoglio was the only man with whom we had entered into a binding relationship.

I had already warned both Mason-MacFarlane and Noel Charles of the inevitable result of allowing the Badoglio Government to go to Rome instead of sending for the Italian politicians to come to Salerno.

When they rejected my advice, I warned the F.O. They preferred Charles's views. Incidentally, Mason-MacFarlane has of course been obliged to let the Government party stay on in Rome. Will he ever get them out again?[48]

More trouble followed. General Mason-MacFarlane, in order to try and rescue something,

[47] 4 June 1944.
[48] 9 June 1944.

took it upon himself, without any instructions from the Combined Chiefs of Staff, to express the opinion that the appointment of Count Sforza as Foreign Secretary 'would not meet with much approval on the part of the Allied Governments', a step which provoked protest from Washington to London on the part of the Acting Secretary of State, who complained, with every justification, that his Government had not been consulted. The United States Government, indeed, later went so far as to request General Wilson to inform Signor Bonomi that General Mason-MacFarlane's views did not represent those of the Government of the United States, to which the appointment of Count Sforza as Foreign Minister would be entirely agreeable.[49]

All this was just French politics in 1943 over again. Actually, although the management of the Italian affair was certainly fumbling, the result was quite good. Bonomi was a respectable head of the kind of Government that we wanted. The introduction of people like De Gasperi and Giuseppe Saragat added strength to the administration. What perhaps was insufficiently realised was that New York State was the key state in the coming Presidential elections, and Sforza claimed to swing many thousands of votes.

Unhappily, all these difficulties had a very bad effect upon poor Mason-MacFarlane's health. Although he struggled manfully against the effects of an old spinal injury, at the end of June he could not carry on. I persuaded him to go home on sick leave and announce his resignation on grounds of health. He was succeeded as Acting Chief Commissioner by an American officer, Captain Ellery Stone, U.S.N.

The Allied Governments withheld their recognition of the new Italian administration pending consultation with the Advisory Council, but of course all this was only 'face-saving'. As soon as the Council were satisfied that the two essential conditions had been accepted, authority was given for the formal entry of the new Government into office.

At this point a new and unexpected problem arose which entailed my return on a short visit to London. It was a convenient moment; for the liberation of Rome and the formation of the Bonomi Government marked the end of the first phase in the Italian problem. We had travelled a long way from the orchard at Cassibile and the Italian surrender.

[49] Harris, p. 202.

CHAPTER EIGHTEEN

'Operation Anvil'

THE whole world was thrilled by the news of the liberation of Rome. The expulsion of the barbarians from the most famous of all cities was greeted with enthusiasm by every nation, friendly or neutral. But Rome was not the real, and certainly not the only, objective.

. . . knowing Alex's plans, I am much more interested in Part II of the battle. He has a real chance of destroying the German Army during the coming weeks.[1]

On 6 June the first accounts reached us of the landings in France: 'Overlord' was launched at last.

I had already, from our frequent meetings and close association, some inkling of the ambitious plans which were forming in Alexander's mind. His own staff, General Harding, General Robertson and General Joe Cannon (U.S. Air Force), were already at work on the details.

The great problem of strategy now has to be settled. A. gave me a copy of his appreciation. He wants to strike east—but I fear the C.C.S. will insist on a movement west. The problem of the future of Alex. and his armies is a grave one. It seems a terrible pity . . . to leave unused or break up the armies in Italy, which are now a great fighting instrument, confident in themselves and their commanders.[2]

At this time, General Marshall, the American Chief of Staff and the most powerful figure in the United States after the President, was visiting Italy, accompanied by General Arnold, head of the United States Air Force. In the course of the various functions that were given in their honour, I began to feel that some of the American 'top brass' were not altogether unsympathetic to Alexander's plan. There was, of

[1] 5 June 1944.
[2] 17 June 1944.

course, a doctrinal objection to having anything to do with the Balkans. Indeed, I remember General Marshall asking me at one of these dinners, 'Say, where is this Ljubljana? If it's in the Balkans we can't go there.' I told him it was practically in Austria and he seemed relieved.

After a formal dinner given by General Eaker (U.S. Air Force) in Marshall's honour on 17 June, I had a long talk with Alexander. He was very anxious for me to go to London with General Gammell (Wilson's Chief of Staff) and see the Prime Minister. He felt that I might be able to put the case before him more effectively than could be done by telegram. I protested that this was out of my sphere; but naturally I would do anything to help so long as General Wilson agreed. I went off immediately to see Wilson, and after obtaining his approval had a further talk with Alexander on his train outside Caserta. For more than an hour he explained the tactical and strategical aspects of his plan with his usual simplicity, but with greater vigour and enthusiasm than I had ever known him display. He showed me his personal telegram to the Prime Minister, which was couched in strong and even eloquent language. In this message he had pointed out that Kesselring's Tenth and Fourteenth Armies were now a beaten force, although not yet eliminated from the field. The Germans intended to hold the Apennine position—a front of 180 miles—with the equivalent of ten to twelve divisions. Alexander declared that provided his present forces were left intact he should be able to split the German Army in half and destroy the German forces in Italy. There would then be nothing to prevent him marching on Vienna unless the Germans should send at least another ten or more fresh divisions against him. If they were to do this, nothing could be of greater assistance to 'Overlord' and the fighting in France. He went so far as to declare that here was an opportunity of inflicting such a defeat on the German Army as might have unpredictable results, and that such a chance must not be missed.

Accordingly, with the approval of the two commanders, and in my desire to do everything possible to assist Alexander, I set off on an undertaking far outside even the most liberal interpretation of my functions.

There has been much controversy in many of the histories of the war about the alleged resistance of Churchill to the invasion of Western Europe. The Americans are represented as being ready to trust everything to the landings in France. Churchill is said to have continually tried to postpone them in order to exploit in their place Mediterranean and Balkan opportunities. Churchill has made it quite clear that this was not so. He accepted, and unequivocally supported, the great 'Overlord' plan. But partly from the strength or obstinacy of his nature and partly from his clear grasp of the possibility of nurturing the Mediterranean without starving the French campaign, he was not willing to accept so rigid an application of the overall strategic doctrine as to exclude the winning of additional prizes if they could be obtained without injury to the major concept. Hence 'Torch', 'Husky', and 'Avalanche'—North Africa, Sicily, and the Italian mainland. It is true that at the meeting at Teheran many months before it had been agreed that the operations in Normandy should be assisted by landings in southern France. But the situation had now changed very much. The weakening of the armies in Italy before the end of 1943, in order to assign them to 'Overlord', had reduced Alexander's forces while Kesselring's had been strengthened. The original time-table had been delayed. 'Anvil'—the proposed landings in the south of France— could not be mounted in any case until mid-August.

Churchill has told the whole story of this conflict in his history of the war.[3] In this authoritative and fully documented account, all these great issues are expounded with the full authority of one of the protagonists. It may be of interest to add a contribution from a humbler angle, not so much to revive an old controversy but partly because of the light it throws upon the various participants, and partly in view of subsequent developments in Europe.

I did not feel that anyone who had not been in close contact with General Alexander could sufficiently realise the growth in his authority and confidence in himself. The fact that his plan was put forward so firmly and with such a certainty of success meant more from him than from almost any other commander. He is not a man given to overstatement or boastful phrases.

Undoubtedly, if the landing craft and troops had not been removed so remorselessly and so prematurely—as we thought—in September 1943, the Italian campaign would have moved at a very different rate.

To the general public the winter campaign in Italy seemed unduly drawn out; to those who knew the facts it was a miracle that he could do so much with such small resources.

[3] Winston S. Churchill, *The Second World War*, vol. vi: *Triumph and Tragedy* (London, 1954), chap. 4.

The choice was now clear. It lay

between 'Anvil' (in the South of France) and an operation eastwards to cross the Rivers Po and Piave, seize Trieste and the Istrian Peninsula, and march through the Ljubljana Gap, threatening Vienna.

Three American divisions had already been removed from General Alexander's forces and put into training at Salerno for amphibious operations. Another American division and four French divisions were to follow—eight divisions in all. At the same time, 70 per cent of the air force operating in support of the Battle of Italy was to be removed. The strict instructions of the Combined Chiefs of Staff, therefore, seemed to be

to halt upon the Pisa—Rimini line, make no attempt to force the Apennines, and leave the Apennine positions, the valley of the Po and the famous strategic strength of the 'quadrilateral' in German hands; in other words, to call off the Italian campaign at the very height of its success.

The Wilson—Alexander alternative plan we called for convenience 'Operation Armpit'. Before I left Algiers it had been fully set out in a telegram to the British and Combined Chiefs of Staffs by General Wilson. It was true that this communication was nominally addressed to General Eisenhower, since the task of deciding which was the best tactical and strategical method of support to 'Overlord' had been entrusted by the Combined Chiefs to Eisenhower and Wilson. Put in more vulgar language, they had passed the buck to these two generals.

General Gammell and I arrived in London on the afternoon of Wednesday the 21st. We were not without encouragement, especially from the thought that General Marshall had not been as hostile as might have been supposed.

At 4 p.m. I saw Eden. He expressed some surprise at my arrival, but I explained the situation.

6—9.15 p.m. The Prime Minister received me at 6. He was in bed in the Annexe. He began by saying, 'I think I [should] tell you that the Foreign Office are rather annoyed at your coming without permission.' I said that I had sent a telegram. Of course I had left at short notice. He went on to say: 'I must also tell you that I am very pleased you have come. You are not a servant of the Foreign Office. You are my servant and colleague and you must do whatever you like.' This seemed a very auspicious start.

In the course of a long discussion, I was able to get Churchill to see the picture as we saw it in the Mediterranean. He had been much impressed by Alexander's personal telegram but seemed uncertain as to what move to take. Later in the evening, Eden joined us. At first Churchill wanted to call a meeting of the British Chiefs that night. But it was wisely decided to allow General Gammell to put General Wilson's paper before the British Chiefs, to discuss the points fully with them, and to have the meeting on the next evening. This would give time for consideration. Accordingly, at 10.30 p.m. on Thursday 22 June, the meeting was held. All the British Chiefs were present as well as the Foreign Secretary. General Gammell and I were invited, to represent the Mediterranean Command.

The Prime Minister opened the subject in a very ingenious way, not committing himself definitely either for or against 'Anvil' or for or against 'Armpit'. He asked me to put forward the plan as I understood it, and more generally General Alexander's enthusiasm and confidence. This I tried to do. It was clear that the Chief of the Air Staff was very much attracted, [being] against breaking up the Air Force and using it in two theatres. The C.I.G.S. seemed more uncertain, and the First Sea Lord look little part in the discussion. After the meeting broke up, the P.M. kept me till about 2. a.m. He is clearly getting very worked up and interested in the immense strategic and political possibilities of 'Armpit'.

On Sunday 25 June, I was summoned to Chequers. It was on this day that Churchill finally produced a draft paper which was printed by the late evening. It was a powerful statement of the case for the consideration of the British Chiefs. He spent most of the day composing it and at the end seemed very exhausted.

Sitting in the drawing-room about six o'clock [he] said, 'I am an old and weary man. I feel exhausted.' Mrs. Churchill said, 'But think what Hitler and Mussolini feel like!' To which Winston replied, 'Ah, but at least Mussolini has had the satisfaction of murdering his son-in-law.' This repartee so pleased him that he went for a walk and appeared to revive.

We were to have left England on the 26th, but Churchill wished us to stay and await developments. A telegram arrived from the American Chiefs, objecting in rather peremptory terms to General Wilson's telegram to General Eisenhower in which 'Armpit' had first been put forward. Late on Monday the 26th, the British Chiefs sent a reasoned reply, setting out their preference for 'Armpit' on the lines of Churchill's paper. By the evening of the 28th, the American Chiefs' reply arrived.

It was not only a brusque but even an offensive refusal to accept the British plan. It so enraged the P.M. that he thought of replying to the President in very strong terms; but after consideration it was decided that the British Chiefs should reply formally that they could not change the advice that they were giving to His Majesty's Government to whom they had the duty of giving the best professional opinion which they could form.

Late on the night of the 28th I saw the Prime Minister, who had rewritten his paper, of which he gave me a copy.[4] He thanked me for the comments which I had written at his request on his first paper, and decided to telegraph his revised paper to the President with an appeal for further thought. Churchill was very anxious on every ground to continue the Italian battle. At least we must cross the Pisa—Rimini line and seize the Po Valley. Even if further exploitation towards Trieste were not possible this summer, the opportunity should be left open for the following spring. Nevertheless, in spite of this splendid State Paper, one of the most well-argued documents that I have ever read, I got the impression

that, in view of the heavy contribution of the American forces to the European campaign and the general situation, we should have to give in if Eisenhower and Marshall insisted upon 'Anvil'. We can fight up to a point, we can leave on record for history to judge the reasoned statement of our views, and the historian will also see that the Americans have never answered any argument, never attempted to discuss or debate the points, but have merely given a flat negative and a somewhat Shylock-like insistence upon what they conceive to be their bargain.

I left London that same night and reached Algiers the following morning. When we told our story, 'Jumbo' Wilson was kind and appreciative but did not anticipate success.

On 1 July I left Algiers early in the morning for General Alexander's forward camp on the shores of Lake Bolsena.

I found General A. as quiet and imperturbable as usual. After a short rest we went for a trip on the lake in a motor-launch, which affords him great pleasure. We landed on a small island which we visited and admired, and in the cool of the evening returned in time for dinner. I explained to him the situation, gave him the papers to read, and enjoyed as usual the pleasure of the quiet, calm and slightly retired atmosphere of General Alexander's camp.

Late that night a personal telegram arrived from the C.I.G.S. to General Alexander saying that he had little hope of our succeeding.

[4] It is printed as Appendix D to Churchill, *Triumph and Tragedy*.

The next day, 2 July, Alexander, realising the unlikelihood of 'Arm-pit' being approved, began to revise his plan and to search all the Mediterranean to see whether, despite the reduced forces at his command, he might be able at least to carry out the first part of the original 'Armpit' plan.

This will involve combing the Mediterranean for 'air', taking some risks on the seas by reducing coastal command sweeps, perhaps reducing S.O.E. use of 'air' to Greece, Albania and Yugoslavia, taking risks in the Middle East by reducing the defence divisions at least by one, perhaps by two. If there is to be a revolution in Palestine, I do not think it will be till after the war and we could borrow a division from there anyway for two months. We could take an Indian division from Iraq and perhaps borrow another Indian division during the monsoon period, scrape some odd troops out of Malta and Gibraltar—two battalions—and replace them with Home Guard from Eng-land, search the Middle East for dock companies, repair shops, etc. . . .

I proposed that now we had got one Italian division at the Front doing reasonably good work on a quiet sector of the line, an effort should be made to raise another two divisions.

In this and in other ways it might be possible, by taking considerable chances in different parts of the Mediterranean, by holding those parts of the line where the attack is not to be made with the least good troops, yet to concentrate sufficient striking power to bounce the enemy out of the Gothic Line (Pisa-Rimini), cross the Apennines, cross the Po, seize the 'quadrilateral', and be in a position to exploit in any direction, particularly eastwards. In the event of 'Overlord' and 'Anvil' becoming something of a stalemate, it would then be possible to have a very hopeful line of development for next year, whereas if this is not done, and 'Overlord' and 'Anvil' both get sealed up, the situation might be really serious and the possibility of bringing the Germans to a defeat correspondingly reduced.

A message now came from the Prime Minister, asking Alexander to return immediately to London. We had a free afternoon which we employed in visiting Orvieto and admiring its beautiful cathedral with the famous Signorelli frescoes in the southern aisle. We returned to the lake for another trip in the motor-boat, and a bathe before dinner.

The decision in favour of 'Anvil' was finally accepted by Churchill. We were by now in a weaker position and more dependent upon the financial and military strength of our ally. For Churchill, the decision —and especially the way in which it was conveyed—was a bitter blow.

For me, this excursion into higher strategy, although unsuccessful, was a fascinating experience.

I was . . . well received by the Prime Minister. I reached a very clear understanding of his methods of work, and I think more real friendship with him in his difficulties than I had before. It has been interesting to see the working of General Wilson's mind, his loyalty to his nominal subordinate, General Alexander, and also to watch General Alexander's self-control, dignity and determination in a situation which must upon the fact of it have proved . . . disappointing to his hopes.

The immediate consequences of the decision were serious, not only on the material strength of the armies in Italy, but to some extent upon their morale. Something seemed to have gone out of the campaign. In the middle of September, on one of my visits to Alexander, I found him calm but tired, and even strained.

He feels rather bitterly the neglect by the powers that be of his campaign and the lack of support which he has received. Even on the basis that everything was to be sacrificed to the operations in France, a more determined effort to take up a little help would have meant a great deal to him. He has lost seven divisions (to 'Anvil') and 70 per cent of his air force. But a single airborne brigade, or a division from M.E., would have made all the difference. As it is, the Germans have 26 divisions against his 20 (which include Brazilians and Negroes) and have in the Gothic Line a naturally defensive position almost stronger than that at Cassino.

However, he still feels that he has a chance of achieving a break-through, in spite of all the disadvantages of his position.[5]

Never did I admire more Alexander's self-control and loyalty. He recognised the wonderful effort that Churchill had made to support him, and took satisfaction in the unanimous approval of the British Chiefs of Staff of the plan of his grand design.

'Anvil' was now re-christened 'Dragoon', partly, no doubt, in case the enemy had learned the meaning of the code word and partly to satisfy British feelings. Even a later effort of Churchill's, to switch the attack to the south-west coast of France, was unacceptable to our Allies. Actually, 'Anvil' had little or no effect upon the campaign in France. Indeed, it may be that more German troops could have been immobilised by the threat of this diversion than by its execution. But, like a stone thrown into a pool, the results of this almost unilateral

[5] 15 September 1944.

American decision have been of ever-widening importance. The burden of countering the ill effects has fallen largely upon the American people.

A break through the Ljubljana Gap and a march into Austria might have altered the whole political destinies of the Balkans and Eastern Europe. In his arguments against this bold concept, Roosevelt had insisted on the fact that Stalin had been told about the landings in southern France at Teheran, a year before. It would be wrong to go back on this decision. But, in the first place, the tactical question was one purely for the British and Americans. Secondly, so far as strategical implications were involved, was it not clear that the Russians wished to keep the Allies in Western Europe, and did not welcome a break-through into the central and eastern countries of the continent? But apart from Roosevelt's desire, at that time, to please Stalin at almost any cost, nothing could overcome the almost pathological suspicions of British policy, especially in the Balkans. Within a few months these were to exercise a baneful, and nearly fatal, influence over the future of Greece.

Thus were sown the seeds of the partition of Europe, and the tragic divisions which were destined to dominate all political and strategic thinking for a generation. Although Churchill has described the 'Anvil' story fully and dramatically, he has not dwelt unduly on its implications. But through all these years I have looked back on this decision of June 1944 as one of the sad turning-points of history.

CHAPTER NINETEEN

From Algiers to Caserta

THE changes agreed upon between Roosevelt and Churchill at Cairo made no formal alteration in the relative functions of A.F.H.Q. and the Middle East Command. Nevertheless, they marked the beginning of a process by which the power of Cairo began to wane and that of Algiers to wax. This indeed was natural. The very successes of the British forces operating originally from Cairo and primarily intended for the defence of Egypt and the Canal had brought them far from their base. The victorious armies led by Alexander and Montgomery had joined with the Anglo-American forces which had landed in French North Africa. Operating under a single command, the British and Americans had inflicted an over-whelming defeat on the enemy in Africa with the victory of Tunis. Together they had liberated Sicily; together they invaded Italy. All these operations were presided over from Algiers, not from Cairo. At the same time General Eisenhower's departure for 'Overlord' deprived us of a commanding personality. He took with him General Bedell Smith, his Chief of Staff, and several other distinguished British and American officers. When therefore General 'Jumbo' Wilson and his Chief of Staff General Gammell—a British officer with little or no ex-perience of working with allies—arrived in Algiers, they were con-fronted with a delicate situation. It was of vital importance to retain American confidence. Murphy was away. Duff Cooper and Ed Wilson, as British and American representatives or Ambassadors to the French Committee, were new to their work and had no experience of the pe-culiar political structure of the Allied command. At the same time, with the American strength in men and materials becoming now more nearly matched with the British and soon to be predominant, it was clear that full co-operation was more than ever essential.

Keenly as they resisted being drawn into action in the Eastern

Mediterranean and above all the Balkans, the Americans disliked being kept in the dark. It was vital to keep them informed of all that was going on throughout the whole area. In due course, in spite of the objections and dangers, the responsibility for affairs in Yugoslavia, Greece and other Balkan countries gradually but inevitably began to pass from General Paget in Cairo to General Wilson, first in Algiers and then in Caserta. The reasons were obvious. We had the supplies, the troops, the bases and the airfields. Naturally, the problems involved often became the cause of much anxiety and sometimes conflict between London and Washington. Sometimes they bore a curious likeness to the disagreements on French affairs. It was therefore our local task to soothe frayed tempers and find practical solutions by invoking and maintaining the vast store of Anglo-American goodwill which was General Eisenhower's most valuable legacy to his successors.

Throughout January and February 1944 the question of my own future was discussed at home, and various and elaborate draft directives were composed. At the end of January, I was told to give political advice on all countries under Wilson's command, except Turkey. I naturally asked for some staff, some information, and even some ideas as to what the British government wanted. But then a silence followed. As an instance of the strange working of the mind of the Foreign Office in London, about this time Roger Makins was woken up in the middle of the night in Algiers. It was a 'Most Immediate' telegram. An agreement must be made without delay with Marshal Badoglio on some matter or other—not of great actual importance. Roger replied to this with some humour as follows:

Badoglio is in Brindisi; Harold Caccia is in Salerno; General Mason-MacFarlane is in Sardinia; the Minister is at Marrakesh; Halford is in bed. With due regard to these difficulties as to personnel and location, I will carry out your instructions with the utmost rapidity.

When I was in London in February, I had some discussions with both Churchill and Eden. But I soon realised that they were too hard pressed to bother with my problems. At one moment I thought my job would prove unworkable and even impossible. But at any rate it would be great fun. Soon things began to straighten themselves out. I had discovered by now that the chief thing was not to ask too many questions. When I was in Cairo at the end of March it was agreed, without any difficulty, that general responsibility for Yugoslavia, including the control of our missions, was to come under General Wilson. Lord Moyne—now Resident Minister in Cairo—was positive as to the wisdom of this on broad practical grounds. Moreover, since we could not operate without the Americans knowing what we were doing, it was much better to have them in with us at every point—at least to share our information, even when they might not wish to be associated with our decisions. This could only be done at A.F.H.Q. The Foreign Office was at that time insistent that Greece should remain under Cairo and Moyne. This seemed sensible; for what remained of the Greek Army, together with the Greek Government, were in the Middle East and could clearly only be controlled from Cairo. However, after September 1944, when the Greek Government moved to Salerno in Italy, it was natural that Greek affairs should be transferred to General Wilson's authority. With Bulgaria and Roumania we had at first little to do. Later on, provisional Ambassadors to their 'liberated' Governments turned up at our headquarters and we became a sort of launching-pad for their dispatch. Thus in spite of a natural tendency of the Foreign Office to regard my operations with some distrust, inevitably I became charged during 1944 with an ever growing range of responsibilities.

With the appointment of Duff Cooper, I was relieved of any direct functions in respect of the French except in so far as their actions might affect the interests of the Supreme Allied Commander. However, until we were able to move from Algiers to Naples towards the end of July 1944, in spite of continual flying about the area, my main headquarters were still at Algiers. It was therefore inevitable that I should be drawn to some extent into French affairs. I worked closely with Duff Cooper, who proved in every way an admirable colleague.

The first difficulty that arose was on 10 March over the arraignment of Pucheu. The trial was the sole subject of interest and debate in Algiers when I returned from my visit to England.

Pucheu put up a very fine performance. He is clearly a clever but unscrupulous man. Rough justice will, I think, be done if he is shot. But it will have a bad effect on de Gaulle's reputation and the Committee generally. I think de Gaulle would like to pardon him but will be afraid of the resistance movements. To them Pucheu is a double-dyed traitor.[1]

[1] 10 March 1944.

General Wilson was somewhat concerned as to the effect of the trial upon the French troops under his command. I told him frankly that I did not think there would be any reaction, since Pucheu was a civilian. If they started to try soldiers and sailors it might be another matter. Indeed, the case against Admiral Derrien was very strong and I was worried about this prospect. Pucheu was deservedly condemned to death and shot. The repercussions were negligible.

A much more difficult problem appeared to be the question of negotiating a new agreement for the control of French forces, and this was complicated by Roosevelt's reluctance to recognise the F.C.N.L.'s authority in metropolitan France. Massigli, in the course of a discussion with me on the affairs of the Advisory Council on Italy, plunged into a bitter attack on the President.

I am afraid the Americans are muddling their French policy and dragging us behind them. I quite see the difficulty of H.M.G. standing up to them at this delicate moment, but I am afraid it is going to make a very bitter feeling against us in France. The trouble is that this does not really hurt the Americans after the war; but with the growing power of Russia I feel that we must depend upon France and other Central European countries to work with us.[2]

Early in April a new French crisis blew up. The agitated telegrams were repeated to me when I was at the Villa Cimbrone in Italy. The action of the French Committee in approving and publishing, without consultation with Giraud, an ordinance appropriating to the President—that is, de Gaulle—the final authority in matters relating to organisation and employment of the French armed forces, had led Giraud to announce his decision to resign his office and retire to private life. With characteristic loyalty, he had signalled to General Juin, who was in command of the French troops fighting in Italy, his instructions to serve with undiminished devotion with the British and American forces. General Devers, the American second-in-command at A.F.H.Q., saw Giraud and tried to persuade him to alter his decision. General Wilson, on my advice, telegraphed the Combined Chiefs of Staff giving his view that part of the reason for the trouble was the resentment of the French at the grudging political recognition which they had received, especially from the Americans. In conversation with Duff Cooper, Giraud maintained his determination to retire. Murphy

[2] 29 March 1944.

saw Juin who was quite firm that although Giraud's departure was regrettable it would have little effect. I felt it unnecessary to return to Algiers, having complete confidence in Makins. But I did send him the following message:

1. Giraud has been an unconscionable time dying. Let him die.

2. But stick to JUIN. His views seem very sensible, and I believe he knows the Army well.

3. I am sure Ambassador Cooper will take it all calmly. I do not know what Ambassador Murphy will say, but let General Wilson know that in my view Giraud's departure will be no real loss.

4. Please show this to Ambassador Cooper.

As I expected, Duff Cooper took the affair very calmly. De Gaulle was determined, however,

to put an end—once and for all—to the conception that Giraud, as Commander-in-Chief, has a kind of extra-constitutional position and has private agreements with the Allies which are not within the purview of the F.C.N.L. This started in February [1943] at Anfa. It has finally perished fourteen months later.[3]

A few days later I was back in Algiers and dined with de Gaulle, who was in a smiling mood.

He seemed quite satisfied with Cordell Hull's latest declaration on the French Committee's position in metropolitan France.

About Giraud, I think he genuinely deplored his refusal to accept the honorific post of Inspector-General. But he was quite firm in his determination to remove him from active command. I am bound to say that I think he is right.

After dinner, I called round to see Duff Cooper and told him of my conversation.[4]

On 18 April I went with Lord Gort, now Governor and C.-in-C. of Malta, who was staying with me for a few days, to pay our respects to Giraud at the Palais d'Été. This was almost his last day in the Palace, which he had first occupied on 24 December 1942 after Darlan's assassination. He had then been complete master of the situation— 'Commandant en Chef Civil et Militaire'. To this little farewell party General Wilson and Duff Cooper also came. General Georges was present, witty, cynical and strong-minded as ever.

[3] 6 April 1944.
[4] 13 April 1944.

Giraud behaved with the dignity which makes one forgive all his failings. There was no reference in all the talk and cross-talk (for an hour) to any recent event. It was just the interchange of reminiscences about the last war and the first year of this war—such as you would hear in the United Services or the Naval and Military Club.

We had a great guard of Spahis—swords, red cloaks, white horses and much music to see us in and out of the palace.

I think Giraud really appreciated the visit and it was pleasant to feel that this sad little ceremony had something of dignity and personal quality at the end.[5]

Nevertheless, it was painful to see the last stages in the career of a man who with all his faults was honourable and true.

A few days later, I had a chance to visit the French troops in Italy. I went with General Alexander in his open car.

The line was very quiet; a little desultory shelling of roads.

The French here show up much better than in Algiers. Here they are keen and well on the way to recovering their confidence.[6]

There was no doubt at all that no one was 'thinking of the old 'un'— that is, regretting Giraud.

The question as to the control of the use of French troops and their organisation was unexpectedly and quietly settled. I admired both the skill with which General Wilson handled some minor points and the good sense of General de Lattre de Tassigny, who conducted the negotiation. French affairs remained quite, so far as I was concerned, until 15 May, when two events took place. The French Assembly voted that the F.C.N.L. should now be called the Provisional Government of France. Although I knew the Americans would react against this, I could see no objection. Indeed, it was merely officially accepting what was now a proved fact. More important was de Gaulle's formal denunciation of the Darlan–Clark Agreement. This at first caused some anxiety, but we at A.F.H.Q. decided to take no official notice of this statement, which was made in the course of the debate. We were already engaged in revising the Agreement and there was no reason why we should not continue with the discussions. I strongly advised London to stall on this matter and leave it to us to handle locally. For public consumption, we stated that General Wilson's Chief of Staff, General Gammell, was already in touch with the French Chief of Staff

[5] 18 April 1944.
[6] 22 April 1944.

on this matter and that there was no repudiation of the *de facto* arrangements. What was much more worrying to me from the point of view of economic and military needs was the French action in calling up far too many men in North Africa, both Europeans and natives from farms and workshops. Production was more important to us at this time than military manpower. I persuaded General Wilson to take this matter up with de Gaulle.

The French have also got into great difficulties with their wheat and cereal situation generally. Five days' supply in Tunisia, a week in Algeria—and the harvest not yet in. They have twice been wrong in their calculations already this year. They have borrowed over 30,000 tons from us . . . (and they ought to be an *exporting* and not an *importing* country in F.N.A.). . . . It is a pity they pay so little real attention to the French Empire about which they talk so much.

I suppose the truth is that the metropolitan French (and especially the Government) are thinking about nothing but France. It is as if an exiled British Government were sitting at Nairobi. The English settlers would hate them as bitterly as the 'colons' hate the whole set-up here. The 'colons' are as anxious to be 'liberated' from the French as the French are to be liberated from the Germans![7]

On the top of other miscalculations and muddles came the locusts. I had never witnessed before the extraordinary phenomenon of the mass flight of these unpleasant creatures. They darkened the sky for days, nor could any effort keep them out of the house, as they got through the doors and curtains. They had now gone to the sand to lay their eggs.

It is *vital* to have the bran ready for the poisoning campaign when the hoppers hatch out in a month to six weeks from now.

It was finally agreed

to lend them some more wheat, on the condition that they got a good bran extraction from their present and this new stock. For the rest, they must tighten their belts and live on vegetables till the harvest. We also decided to tell them the Allied plans for feeding France. Then, if they are really hoarding or stockpiling here for metropolitan France, they may be prepared to produce these hidden quantities, knowing in detail our generous plans for France when liberated.

One matter was settled at this time which marked the development of our economic relations with the French authority. Immediately

[7] 20 May 1944.

after the landings in November 1942, General Eisenhower had set up an organisation known as the North African Economic Board to deal with the complicated issues of import to and export from the large territories now under his control. This Board was one of the most successful of all the Allied undertakings in North Africa. Murphy and I acted as nominal presidents, but the real work was done under General Gale and a fine team of British and Americans, sometimes in uniform, sometimes in civilian clothes, who devoted themselves to these complicated tasks.

It was certainly a fascinating task. In no field was Anglo-American co-operation so genuine and so effective. Many were the difficulties which we overcame. Amid many troublesome political and military crises, this work, which was hardly noticed at the time and has not since been sufficiently recognised, was a triumph of sensible co-operation.

One of the most moving events at this time was the arrival from Barcelona of the *Gripsholm* with British and some American repatriated prisoners. My wife was then in Algiers, and we went together to meet the ship. We found the men in remarkably good heart considering their grievous wounds and long imprisonment.

A number of Tees-side and Tyneside lads—one Stocktonian. They were really wonderful to talk to. One sergeant said, 'The Germans are getting very timid now, sir; very timid indeed!' I could not quite discover how they showed this; presumably a less harsh treatment of our prisoners.[8]

At the beginning of June I had a long talk with Murphy, who was distressed at the fact that London and Washington were not as close as they had once been.

The honeymoon stage between the President and the Prime Minister is over and the normal difficulties and divergences, inseparable from staid married life, are beginning to develop. This all has its effect upon the Americans in this theatre.[9]

I could not help agreeing with him about the changed position, and this was all the more distressing because of my affection for Murphy and the fact that we had always worked so closely together.

On French affairs, the President remains quite intransigent. Bob complained to me about Duff Cooper's failure to inform him or Chapin (the U.S.

[8] 20 May 1944.
[9] 5 June 1944.

Chargé d'Affaires) of the British invitation to de Gaulle to go to London. It was the first time in twenty months that there had not been complete confidence between American and British diplomats in Algiers, etc. I did my best to explain it away, as due to the rush of business, but I do regret the incident very much.[10]

But Murphy remained as good a friend as ever.

Meanwhile, 'Overlord' had been launched; and in spite of the rather childish arguments which had developed in London with de Gaulle, the excitement and enthusiasm of the French in Algiers was growing day by day. While I was in London towards the end of the month, I put up my plan to the Foreign Secretary, that the Committee should move from Algiers to France as soon as practicable; that it should broaden its base; that it should summon the notabilities of France to form a Consultative Assembly and reaffirm the constitutional procedure already approved in Algiers.

In the end, all these matters were resolved without my further intervention. It is, however, an inescapable fact that the treatment by the British and especially by the Americans of France's claims both then and earlier has never been forgotten by de Gaulle. Nor, to be just, has he ever ceased to be grateful to those of us who tried to help during these critical and creative months.

On 21 July, A.F.H.Q. moved to Caserta from Algiers. A few days before our departure all the members of the French Provisional Government called to say goodbye to me. I thought this rather a touching attention, and the speeches made, though too flattering, were agreeable. I had a final personal call from de Gaulle. We gave a huge cocktail party at the villa for all the Diplomatic Corps, all our French friends, official and unofficial, and British and American officers— soldiers, sailors and airmen.

Dorothy and I travelled in General Wilson's aeroplane, with a small staff and a vast quantity of luggage, including a parrot. During the journey the parrot laid an egg, which was regarded as a good omen. The General came to stay in my villa at Naples, bringing his A.D.C., his Sudanese servant and his Annamite servant, but not his kit, which was lost. It was all rather tiring but very enjoyable. Most of the lorries and cars broke down, including the Supreme Commander's. Our villa at Naples was 'staffed with Italian servants (about eight or nine in

[10] Ibid.

number) and their friends and relations (almost eighty or ninety in total). Our English servants had gone to Caserta, except one sergeant and one batman.'[11] We all dined that night with Admiral Sir John Cunningham (now C.-in-C. Mediterranean) at the magnificent Villa Emma, the famous home of Sir William and Lady Hamilton.

So ended, definitely and finally, my official residence in Algiers, after eighteen months of a varied, sometimes hectic, but always enjoyable experience. So, also, for practical purposes, ended my connection with French affairs, for the rapid progress of the campaign was soon to lead to the liberation of Paris and the re-establishment of a French Government. Algiers returned to its old status as a colonial city.

Yet for me, as for many British and American officers and men, Algiers remains the symbol of the first great achievement of Anglo-American co-operation and the restoration of a free and renascent France.

From July 1944 until the end of the war our official headquarters were in the Palace of Caserta. I had been there for the first time in January and had soon established a forward post for my own use. This astonishing building is familiar to many visitors to the Naples area. It will certainly be well remembered by thousands of Allied officers and men who served at one time or another in these extraordinary surroundings. When I first saw the palace in January it was occupied by General Clark's Fifth Army headquarters.

The house (built about 1760) is larger, I believe, than Versailles. There are four great courts, 3,000 or more rooms and so on. The garden leads up the hillside and is filled with fountains, statues, watercourses, etc. The canal pond is used by General Wayne Clark (Fifth Army H.Q. are also here for the time being) to land a Moth aeroplane on (fitted with floats).[12]

The garden was in a state of considerable confusion, but we could see how beautiful it must have been with its many fountains and fishponds, lakes, orchards, and temples. The Bourbon Charles III, King of the Two Sicilies, has certainly left an extraordinary monument. For over two years it was destined to house many thousands of officers and men from Britain and America, with the P.X. shops and Allied messes, and all the rest of the paraphernalia of invading armies,

[11] 21 July 1944.
[12] 27 January 1944.

in the halls intended for the courtiers of the eighteenth century. At the
far end of the garden there was a charming hunting lodge occupied by
General Wilson, and later by General Alexander; and in the little
village I had a tiny cottage in which I could stay the night when
necessary. But I had also the villa in Naples, twenty miles away.
Although the journey was often tedious owing to the great mass of
transport moving up and down the road, it was pleasant to get back in
the hot evenings to the beauty of the Bay. My villa—Carradori—was
at Posillipo, not far from the so-called Rosebery villa and near to the
Villa Emma.

Although my aeroplane journeys to Algiers were now no longer
necessary, I was to have plenty of flying, to Rome, to Bari, to Cairo
and later to Greece. But it was a relief to be more or less settled in one
place. Soon after our establishment at Naples, where my wife remained for a short period, we had the excitement of a visit from King
George VI. He arrived punctually at the aerodrome on the afternoon
of 23 July, and the same evening Admiral Sir John Cunningham gave
a dinner at which 'Jumbo' Wilson and I were the only other guests.
Sir Noel Charles and Sir D'Arcy Osborne had dined at my villa with
my wife, together with Roger Makins and Harold Caccia.

The King expressed a desire to see them and they were sent for. As the
Villa Emma is only five minutes by car from Villa Carradori, we expected
them at once. But there was a long delay, at which His Majesty seemed vexed.
It was finally discovered that they had arrived at the Villa Emma but had
been sent about their business by Admiral Dundas (Chief of Staff), who
thought they were ubiquitous Press correspondents! They finally arrived
. . . and a very merry evening continued till quite late.[13]

The next day there was a great reception in the banqueting hall in the
centre of Caserta Palace, where a large number of officers of all services
and nations, as well as civilians, were collected. The King walked
round the circle shaking hands with each guest, who was presented by
the Section Leader, since of course General Wilson could not know
them all.

After the luncheon His Majesty left for the airfield. He was to be in
General Alexander's care for several days to make a tour of the Front
and to see, and be seen by, the troops. On 31 July the King reviewed
the Canadian Corps, to which ceremony I had the good fortune to be

[13] 23 July 1944.

invited. The display was splendid—an old-fashioned drill parade—
and the troops enthusiastic. After luncheon with the Canadian officers
we drove back to Cassino where General Alexander explained the
whole battle.

The next day I was sent for to the Villa Emma and the King kept
me for an hour. Once again I was impressed by his retentive memory
and detailed knowledge of all that was going on.

He was immensely amused by an incident which took place early this
morning. The King of Italy (as we discovered a day or two ago and as I had
informed the King yesterday) came to Naples about ten days ago without
asking anybody's leave and set himself up in the Villa Rosebery.

Unfortunately I forgot to inform C.-in-C. Med. and the picket boat (which
patrolled all night outside the Villa Emma) arrested a suspicious-looking
couple who were fishing from a small boat just off the villa, in the early hours
(about 5.30 or 6 a.m.). These proved to be the King and Queen of Italy. They
(or rather the Queen) protested vigorously and the noise woke up the King of
England, who put his head out of the window.

The King naturally asked what all the row was about.
'Says he's the King, sir.'
'What King?'
'The King of Italy, sir.'

(A regular *Rose and the Ring* scene.)
Finally, the Queen of Italy produced an enormous visiting card (of Alice in
Wonderland proportions) and gave it to the naval lieutenant.

The young officer's report (with the card) amused the King enormously and
he kept the card as a souvenir.[14]

After this incident it seemed to me unwise that the King of Italy
should remain in Naples, and we persuaded him to return to Ravello.
The next afternoon King George left.

His Majesty was in the highest spirits till the end. It has been a really
happy and successful visit.[15]

Since all the time we had a good deal of our own work to do, these
visits were a little distracting. However, they added greatly to our
enjoyment.

Operational control for British efforts to help Tito's resistance movement in Yugoslavia was transferred from Middle East to A.F.H.Q. on

[14] 1 August 1944.
[15] 2 August 1944.

21 March 1944. The Americans were kept informed, but were not
actively involved.

Nearly three years had passed since the German attack on Belgrade
and the capitulation of Yugoslavia. King Peter and his Government
had been evacuated first to Cairo and then to London. In 1941 a
guerrilla movement was begun by Mihailović and the Serbs. These
were known as the Chetniks. They were loyal to the King and the
Yugoslav Government-in-exile. British liaison officers were sent to
assist them, but they were never very active in harrying the Germans,
and later were suspected of collaborating with them. In the autumn of
1941 Tito and his Communist Partisans began their operations. But it
was not until May 1943 that British liaison officers were sent to Tito.
In September of that year Fitzroy Maclean arrived to head the mission,
a task which he performed with conspicuous skill and success. When
the Italian collapse came in the autumn of 1943, the Italians in
Yugoslavia were disarmed by Tito's Partisans, who thus became very
strong. The Chetniks, the followers of the monarchy and the legitimate Government-in-exile, were relatively weakened. In November
Tito set up a provisional Government and formally deprived the
Yugoslav Government of all its rights. Shortly afterwards, at the
Teheran Conference, all the Allies agreed to give maximum support to
Tito and his Partisans. This was accepted with some reluctance by the
Americans, and there soon began to develop a situation not unlike
that which had existed in French North Africa. The Americans tended
to support Mihailović, although they had agreed to the Teheran
decisions. Murphy was concerned at the consequent developments. I
used to tell him all I knew, and from time to time he would express his
anxiety.

Of course (under O.S.S. inspiration), he [Murphy] inclines to Mihailović,
and cannot follow the P.M.'s pro-Tito policy. But it is a great thing to get
him interested. I have always felt that we should try to bring the Americans
into Balkan affairs. And I feel equally sure that the way to do it is through
A.F.H.Q. (which was started by Americans and has a genuine Allied
tradition) rather than through M.E. Cairo is suspect—it is somehow connected
in their minds with Imperialism, Kipling and all that.[16]

By December of 1943 the most informed British opinion was that
the Partisans would eventually rule Yugoslavia and that the monarchy

[16] 5 June 1944.

had little future and had ceased to be a unifying element. At the same time the area was one of the greatest military importance; for Tito's forces, adequately supported, were capable of detaining a very large number of German divisions, greatly to the advantage of the Italian and later of the French front.

Churchill explained in the House of Commons on 22 February 1944 the reasons for our support for Tito, who had now nearly a quarter of a million men operating in one way or another under his control. King Peter was still unwilling to disavow Mihailović, and the Royal Government's authority seemed to have faded almost to nothing. Nevertheless, by a curious paradox in view of the Teheran decisions, Yugoslavia's representative on the Advisory Council for Italy was still chosen by the Yugoslav Government in exile. I remember formally welcoming M. Smilganić in this capacity. At this time Philip Broad was acting as Counsellor to the British Embassy to the Yugoslav Government, the Ambassador being Ralph Stevenson. But since the Yugoslav King and Prime Minister had gone to London and the Government was a very shadowy kind of affair without any authority except perhaps in parts of old Serbia, I arranged for Broad to be moved on to my staff and to operate at Bari. Broad served me for the rest of the war, sometimes at Bari and sometimes at Algiers, with admirable loyalty.

The Foreign Office were naturally concerned at the delicacy of the situation. We had officially recognised the Yugoslav Government in London, to which our Ambassador was accredited, while all effective work was being done in Bari with the mission under Fitzroy Maclean's command, supported by Bill Deakin and Randolph Churchill. In spite of this theoretical difficulty, things soon began to get working on a practical basis. While the Prime Minister at his end was doing his best to bring about a reconciliation, or at least a working agreement, between King Peter and his adherents and Tito and his supporters, we at our end continued to give every possible support in material and money to Tito. From the spring of 1944 on we ceased to give any but the slenderest help to Mihailović.

Although Churchill pressed the King to get rid of his Government, he was not able to persuade him to do so until 17 May, when the King formed a new administration under a Croat leader, the Ban of Croatia, by name Dr. Subašić.

A few days later General Wilson and I went to Bari to look into the whole organisation, and while we were there, on 28 May,

came the news of the German attack upon Tito's headquarters. It appears that the attempt to capture him and Randolph—which would be the greater prize it would be difficult to say—failed by a hair's breadth, the Marshal having escaped to the hills some two hours previously.[17]

Marshal Tito, driven from Yugoslavia by the Germans, suddenly turned up on 4 June at Bari.

Woken up in the middle of the night by a 'Most Immediate' saying that Tito had had to leave Yugoslavia and was now at Bari. I think it is of great importance that he should leave Italian soil as soon as possible, and after consultation with General Wilson we sent a message to say so.

After a meeting at 9.30 in the morning we also decided to send Maclean immediately to Bari. The proposal is that the Marshal should go to the island of Vis, which has already been taken from the Germans by joint action of British commandos and Partisan troops. He will then be on Yugoslav soil and not a refugee. Broad seems to think that he will be able to control the movements of his Partisans more effectively from Vis than if he goes on the mainland, but I am not sure what the psychological effect will be. In some ways it may be helpful because it should increase our hold over him.[18]

At this point I was informed that Subašić had appealed to Tito for a meeting. The proposal was that King Peter should go to Malta and remain there for a few days, while Subašić, now Prime Minister of the Royal Government, should go to Vis with Stevenson to open negotiations. The King was now prepared to appoint Tito the supreme military commander in Yugoslavia. It was hoped by this means and with the offer of funds which were still the property of the Yugoslav National Bank that some accommodation could be reached.

On 11 June the Yugoslav party arrived in Algiers.

There were eight of them altogether. The King, the Ban, Ralph Stevenson, Colonel Bailey and the King's A.D.C. were brought up from the airfield . . . [to A.F.H.Q.].[19]

General Wilson was not available till the afternoon, so I brought the party to my villa (my move to Caserta had not yet taken place) and gave them lunch. When General Wilson joined us,

[17] 28 May 1944.
[18] 4 June 1944.
[19] 11 June 1944.

it was decided that the King should [go and] stay in Malta until the right opportunity arose, and that if possible Stevenson and the Ban, after a short visit to Bari for the purpose of seeing M. Topalović, General Mihailović's Political Adviser, and various other Yugoslav notabilities, should proceed to Vis. If Tito was willing to come out to see General Wilson at Caserta, the whole party would return and the King would or would not be produced at a suitable moment from Malta according to Tito's mood.

I saw the King off at the airfield.[20]

I was careful to give Murphy and the Americans full information as to what was happening, for I was conscious that considerable tension was likely to build up over what they would regard as the unilateral handling of this affair. Later I was relieved to find that Washington and Moscow had been informed of the general plan from London.

Meanwhile we had useful talks both in Algiers and Bari as to some plan for an accommodation between the two groups of Yugoslavs. On the 16th, I heard that Subašić and Stevenson had seen Mihailović's representative at Bari and had gone on to Vis, the King remaining at Malta. Randolph Churchill was now in our party, I having persuaded General Wilson to give orders for him to be taken out of Yugoslavia. He was naturally indignant at this, but I felt sure this was necessary.

I did not want him captured and perhaps tortured by the Germans partly for the P.M.'s sake and partly because I felt sure he knew too much. Anyway, he has not had a bad time since he came out. He has been to Rome, interviewed the Pope . . . and generally enjoyed himself. It was finally arranged that he should go to England on leave and then return as a British liaison officer to Bosnia.[21]

Some progress was achieved and a provisional arrangement, which appeared not unsatisfactory, was made between Subašić and Tito. Subašić accepted Tito's estimate of the strength of the Partisans in Serbia and concluded that Mihailović must be abandoned. Tito, in turn, was willing to accept the principle that the peoples of Yugoslavia should be free to decide the question of the monarchy and the constitution at the end of the war. Meanwhile, Tito would nominate two members to the Royal Government. He assured Subašić that he did not intend to introduce a Communist system or impose a party line. While many of us were not convinced that Tito would be able, even if he wished,

[20] Ibid.
[21] 16 June 1944.

to implement this undertaking, from the point of view of our immediate military needs the position looked not unhopeful.

When I was in London in June on the question of 'Operation Anvil', I had some talk with the Prime Minister on the situation in Yugoslavia. Fitzroy and Randolph, who were in London at the same time, strongly supported the view that Britain and King Peter must put their whole weight behind Tito's movement. Although the Foreign Office was still worrying about the position of the Chetniks, in fact much of this argument was in vain. Events were destined to settle the future.

On my return to Naples, I saw a number of British officers who had been with the Chetniks and these naturally felt that unless some drastic action was taken, civil war between the two groups of partisans would become inevitable. On 11 July, a telegram reached us to say that Marshal Tito was after all not prepared to pay his proposed visit to Caserta. This was probably due to his unwillingness to meet Dr. Subašić again and perhaps his growing sense of his own strength. At the same time, it was clear that all was not going well with Subašić's new Government. The old Serb Party was making as much difficulty as possible, and in the United States the Yugoslav Ambassador, Fotić, was particularly troublesome. The next day Fitzroy Maclean arrived and told us that the Partisan General Velebit had received instructions from Tito to leave immediately for London with two nominees for Subašić's Government. This looked more hopeful; and Murphy and I called to see Subašić in the little villa allotted to him in the village of Caserta. He was certainly of a genial and optimistic character, since he began by observing that the political sky seemed almost completely clear. When we told him that Tito had refused to come to the meeting, he showed no disappointment but observed, 'It is just a little cloud; it will pass.'

Interchange of telegrams between London, Washington and Caserta became, as usual, rather confusing. It appeared that Tito was sending his own representatives into Serbia and these included Ranković, Kardelj and one or two others. These two were known to be doctrinaire Communists and considerable powers behind the scene, the first a Serb, the second a Slovene. Subašić and the other Yugoslavs who were at Caserta now determined to return to London.

The jovial Ban came to dinner on Saturday night. He was in excellent form, all his good humour restored, full of enthusiasm and hope and with many stories of the battles of the last war and of the struggles and trials of this. His general idea is to return to London, bring what influence he can upon the old Serb Party, chiefly mobilising the King and the Court, then perhaps pay a visit to Moscow and, with the blessing of Stalin and the merit of having made a pilgrimage to the Holy Places of Marxism, suggest another meeting with Tito. This he thinks will ease Tito's position, who is clearly suspect by the extremists in his own party and might be fatally injured by the reproach of having sold out to the moderates and the King.

On 16 July a message arrived, saying that Tito had informed the officer in charge of our mission that he was thinking of coming over to Italy and would like to meet General Wilson. Churchill, who was planning to visit Italy, was very keen to see Tito.

Tito arrived in Naples on 7 August. Churchill was expected within a few days.

[Tito] had a military talk with S.A.C. and has gone to see General Alex.— by plane. Either he was genuinely frightened, or he wanted to stay in Rome, or he was sick because he had eaten and drunk too much of S.A.C.'s lavish entertainment. In any case, he absolutely refused to get into the aeroplane to come back. He has gone to Rome (? to see Bogomolov) and will not return till tomorrow [by car].[22]

On 9 August Tito returned from Rome and

came to lunch at the villa in Caserta. He was accompanied by two of his staff officers and [an] interpreter, and also by . . . Fitzroy Maclean. I told the latter that I was not prepared to have Marshal Tito's personal bodyguard standing in my dining-room during lunch. I thought [he] might explain to the Marshal that this was not the custom among gentlemen in our country. A firm position proved successful. The bodyguard stood in the passage.[23]

Tito made a very favourable impression upon me, and our talk was simple and clear.

He is quiet, well behaved, interesting and seemed reasonable. I think he is very much on his best behaviour. It is difficult to form an estimate of his quality. He obviously has character and power of command. He is shorter, stockier, and even fatter than I expected, but he has a certain dignity which is impressive.[24]

[22] 7 August 1944.
[23] 9 August 1944.
[24] Ibid.

The Americans behaved very well. They

cannot resist any social figure, and in spite of their natural leanings to General Mihailović, have taken Tito to their bosom. An immense dinner was given by General Eaker in his camp, with bands playing and drink flowing freely. The Marshal seemed duly impressed by the wealth and magnificence of the American display.[25]

It was difficult to keep Tito occupied while waiting for the Prime Minister, but I was able to tell him that he was coming two days earlier than expected and would be available the next day. My wife took him out rowing in a small boat in the Bay of Naples, but he must have been very hot in his thick uniform and gold braid.

I . . . informed him that Dr. Subašić would be coming with some of his advisers for discussions with the Marshal. Tito took this quite well and seemed quite happy about these arrangements. It is clear that he is looking forward with great pleasure to seeing Mr. Churchill.[26]

The interview finally took place on the morning of Saturday 12 August at the Villa Rivalta where the Prime Minister was staying.

Marshal Tito arrived at noon and a conference took place between the Prime Minister and Tito. The only other persons present were Bob Dixon, who took notes of the proceedings, and two interpreters. I gather that the talk went fairly well, but had not really broached the realities. There was a luncheon after the conference at which I was present.[27]

I felt sure that Tito meant to be in full control at the end of the war.

As I had feared, the situation did not develop very satisfactorily. Tito began to make trouble on his side, and the King's Government showed a lack of reality. On 2 September Subašić appealed to Tito, suggesting the creation of a united Government, but Tito sent a frosty reply. Early in September I saw one of Subašić's Ministers and urged upon him the need for an immediate amalgamation of the armed forces and for Subašić to go himself as quickly as possible to Yugoslavia. The British Government then tried to get Soviet support for the pressure on Tito for a united Government, but the situation began to worsen. Tito even alleged that the Allied Command was aiding

25 10 August 1944.
26 11 August 1944.
27 12 August 1944.

Mihailović; but this we strenuously and truthfully denied. Churchill sent a personal message of protest at this accusation. Tito next maintained that the time was not yet ripe for the formation of a united Government. The Russian drive into Yugoslav territory, which soon began, clearly strengthened the keen Communists among the Partisans. Maclean gave us his view of the situation:

> He anticipates that when the European war is over Tito will proceed to hold an election or plebiscite on the Russian plan. (He does not think there will be much of a civil war, for Mihailović will be on the run and Tito's power, with a Russian army at his side and the splendid equipment which we have given him, will be very strong.)
>
> This election will result in the 100 per cent return of all the 'party' men and Government nominees. They will proceed to elect a Constitutional Assembly and so on, and the Federal Union of Yugoslavia will come into being, based on the principles already enunciated by the National Committee of Liberation.
>
> The King will be ignored and also the Subašić Government. If Subašić and his friends arrive in Yugoslavia, they will not be shot. On the contrary, they will be asked to join the Government.[28]

The question of recognition by the Great Powers would then arise. Russia would give enthusiastic and immediate recognition, sending an Ambassador with a large and impressive staff.

> What will Great Britain and America do? If we hum and haw and recognise the King's Government (either with Subašić if he proves loyal to the King or with another if Subašić deserts to Tito) as the *de jure* Government of Yugoslavia, but compromise by sending an 'observer' or an 'emissary' to Belgrade, we shall miss our opportunity, throw away all the goodwill we have built up painfully over a long period, and of course push Tito into the arms of the Russian bear. He may not be too anxious for that suffocating embrace. But (if he is cold-shouldered by the U.S. and Great Britain) he will have no alternative.[29]

This thesis, which Maclean put forward at General Wilson's meeting on 25 September, struck me at the time as convincing. I could not help feeling that the decision about 'Anvil' had gravely weakened our hope of obtaining our objectives in the Balkans. We should soon be starting to send representatives to Roumania and Bulgaria to discuss relief and other matters. But the Russian military presence and our

[28] 25 September 1944.
[29] Ibid.

absence must necessarily put us in a very secondary position. Nevertheless, as the year progressed, arrangements for relief when the time came were made with Tito's Government and not with the Royal Government, contrary to the preference of the Combined Chiefs of Staff. The Moscow talks in October 1944, which resulted in a general agreement as to equal influence between the Western Allies and Russia in Yugoslavia, seemed hopeful. But I felt strongly that if any progress was to be made it would be necessary for us to abandon the King.

Mihailović, who may still have felt that he had some American support, now sent a message to Wilson asking us to abandon Tito and all the arrangements made in Moscow. Naturally we sent a firm refusal. As a result of discussions in Serbia between Tito and Subašić, agreement was reached that there should be three Regents as well as Ministers who would organise a constitutional plebiscite. Tito's administration, meanwhile, would have the full legislative power. By 1 November it was agreed between Tito and Subašić that there should be a constitutional monarchy but that the King should not return until a plebiscite had been held. This seemed a hopeful turn of events. 'Things certainly seem to be much improved by the Moscow Conference. Pourvu que ça dure!'[30]

It looks as if (owing to the Moscow Conference) a Subašić-Tito agreement will go through. The only danger is that Winston will get up in arms about the proposal to appoint three Regents. He has a most remarkable fondness for kings. But really it would be a terrible error to sabotage the very hopeful development because of King Peter. I do not believe there is any chance of this poor boy regaining his throne whatever we may do. And it is far more important to avoid civil war in Yugoslavia and strengthen British influence there. Both these things we have a good chance of doing at the present time.[31]

The supplementary agreement between Tito and Subašić was signed on 7 December, and it was now for Churchill and Eden to persuade the King to accept. They told him quite clearly that he must do so, pointing out that Tito was in effective control and that no British Government would intervene by force to reinstate the King. Unconvinced, the King released a Press statement of his objections; but the British Government rightly decided that the agreement must stand

[30] 5 November 1944.
[31] Ibid.

and that the King be ignored. Tito was not distressed at this development, for he considered that it had damaged the King's prospects ir-
revocably.

By the end of January 1945 Stalin was urging recognition of the
united Yugoslav Government, but the Americans were doubtful. The
King now dismissed Subašić and his friends. But we stood firm and
finally Subašić and his colleagues left for Yugoslavia at the beginning
of February. King Peter finally endorsed the formation of a Regency
Council, and both it and the new Government took office at the beginning of March.

Thus by the end of the campaign we seemed, in spite of all the
difficulties, to have achieved a fair measure of success. Both Stevenson
and Maclean carried out their task with patience and skill. If the
subsequent history of Yugoslavia took a different course, we could not
blame ourselves—we had done our best. Once again, the differences of
emphasis in London and Washington were unfortunate; yet they were
not a major factor. Events took control. The Russian presence in the
Balkan States at the moment when the war ended proved decisive.

In November 1945 the elections for the Constituent Assembly were
held. Subašić had by now resigned and the various pro-Tito parties
campaigning as a National Front won an overwhelming majority.
This was followed by the recognition of Tito's Government by both
Britain and France. The Constituent Assembly at the end of November proclaimed a republic—the Federal People's Republic of Yugoslavia. The constitution was modelled upon that of Soviet Russia.
From that day began what the Left, by the strange misuse of language,
call a 'people's democracy' and ordinary people call a totalitarian
State. In April of the following year (1946) the United States gave its
recognition. In the following month Mihailović, who had come into
the hands of the Government, was tried and shot. If only General
Alexander had been allowed to follow his strategic plan in the summer
of 1944, how different the story might have been!

CHAPTER TWENTY

The New Deal for Italy

N EARLY twelve months had now passed since the Italian surrender had been followed by the improvised status of co-belligerency. Yet the question remained. Was Italy still to be treated as a defeated enemy, subjected to the strict conditions of unconditional surrender? Or was she to be accepted as an ally in the struggle against Germany?

Had the military campaign moved more rapidly, the political issues would have been easier to resolve. Even after the capture of Rome, the German forces were successfully regrouped into strong positions. The capital of Italy was taken, but Kesselring's armies escaped. It was not until the end of August 1944 that the summer offensive began.

During these weeks I saw much of Alexander, who took me entirely into his confidence. I was able to understand both his hopes and his frustrations. Although he was gradually able to advance his line, so that by the late autumn the battle front ran from north of Rimini to south of Spezia, thus freeing the important harbours of Ancona and Leghorn for military and civil supplies, yet the prize just escaped him. Without superiority in numbers and met by the skill of the German commanders, 'Alexander's offensive failed, by the barest of margins, to achieve the success it deserved'.[1]

While the battle was at its height, he asked me to come to his advanced headquarters some three miles from Siena.

As usual, the General has found a lovely spot, in a little wood, in rolling country, with farmland and vineyards all round. My billet is in a farmhouse (taken over as a guest house). The General is . . . in his caravan. The mess and ante-room are in tents. The customary air of quiet efficiency pervades the camp.

General Alexander looked, however, rather tired. . . .[2]

[1] Churchill, *Triumph and Tragedy,* p. 111.
[2] 15 September 1944.

But he was still hopeful of the break-through. The next morning I attended, as usual, the morning conference. Some advance had been made by the Fifth Army on the Futa Pass, commanding the Florence–Bologna road, and some by the Eighth Army on the Rimini front.

But the Germans are fighting desperately and are reinforcing their left. General Leese has now nine German divisions against his seven. It is a race against time . . . since the weather will break soon and with the rivers in spate the mountain line will be impassable till the spring.[3]

We motored to Florence where at Fifth Army Headquarters we found General Gunther—the Chief of Staff—hopeful but anxious. At a little village called La Trellia, north of Florence, we climbed to the top of a hill and then to the top of a high tower. The whole great Apennine range was stretched out in front of us; and for two hours with glasses and maps we watched the fierce battle which was raging.

The main effort of the Fifth Army troops was concentrated round the Futa Pass and an attack was in progress upon a certain Monte Catria (5,600 ft. high) to the south-east. This proved partially successful, but the miracle to my mind is that any progress can be made at all in ground so wonderfully adapted to the defence.[4]

One feature of this form of warfare, where the defence held such strong positions, struck me forcibly.

The great use of smoke makes it difficult to follow a modern battle even from such a vantage point as ours. The smoke screen is the infantryman's only hope of approaching such strongly held positions, and apart from the smoke bombs and shells fired by supporting artillery, he uses his own mortars for this purpose.[5]

On our way home we stopped in Florence. The Duomo, Baptistery, Giotto's tower, Palazzo Vecchio, Loggia di Lanzi, Santa Maria Novella—all these were quite uninjured. The bronze doors of the Baptistery were walled up and safe. But all the bridges were destroyed (except the Ponte Vecchio). No Allied shell or bomb fell in the city, but only on the marshalling yards outside. Those were Alexander's orders. All the destruction was German.

[Alexander] is very proud of the fact that so far in this campaign he has succeeded in saving Rome, Florence, Pisa, Siena, Assisi, Perugia, Urbino from

[3] 16 September 1944.
[4] Ibid.
[5] Ibid.

any except minor damage and that wantonly inflicted by the enemy when retiring. The General has a reputation for his anxiety to spare the lives of his men. He is as careful of the arts.[6]

He was clearly not confident about the issue of the battle. He would win ground; he would hold large German forces engaged, greatly to the advantage of the battle in France. But he would not entirely destroy the German Army until next year's campaign.

In this situation it was natural that Italians of all classes should be restless and unhappy. With a certain naïvety even the politicians had believed that by abandoning their allies and surrendering to their enemies they could save Italy from the miseries of war. They had underestimated German tenacity and strength and overestimated British and American power, in view of vast commitments east and west, to devote sufficient forces to a rapid conquest of the peninsula. It can be argued that from the military point of view the more divisions the Germans poured into Italy the greater the relief to General Eisenhower and the Allied forces soon to operate in France. In a sense Hitler repeated in Italy the mistakes he had already made in Tunisia. Nevertheless, these considerations were of little comfort to the Italians. Accordingly I felt convinced that something must be done to bolster their morale. If it was not yet possible to make a final peace and a full alliance, could we not do something to make a reality of the phrase 'co-belligerent'?

The economic situation in Italy was indeed distressing. Inflation had begun on a big scale and, as we were to find later in Greece, was easier to diagnose than to cure. In early May of 1944 I prepared a paper on the economic problems of southern Italy which dealt largely with the monetary question, and E. H. M. Lloyd, a British official of great authority, was sent to give us advice. From our occupation of Sicily in the autumn of 1943 to the spring of 1944, notes to the value of some 2,000 million lire had been issued in the liberated areas. The older and barbarous methods of warfare, which involved living on the country and letting the inhabitants starve, at least avoided the problem of monetary inflation.

. . . one just cannot disguise from oneself the fact that, to the extent to which the Germans follow the medieval system of looting without payment,

[6] Ibid.

they nevertheless do far less injury to the economic structure of a country than the modern method of looting by which invading armies pay for what they need in paper money which they have been careful to manufacture before their arrival.

The money injures the economic structure of an occupied country more than rapine.[7]

An Allied Anti-Inflation Committee was appointed. One unanimous recommendation was an increase in the bread ration, which was still at only 200 grammes. The central point of an anti-inflationary policy was believed to be to raise the ration to 300 grammes and thereby break the black market. As a result the farmers would be more likely to bring in the harvest to the *ammassi* instead of disposing of it illegally. If we could get hold of the Italian harvest we ought to be able to keep people on a better standard and yet save Allied shipping. There were therefore two purposes—humanitarian and financial—in the contest on which we now embarked with the Combined Chiefs of Staff. First was our desire to feed those people who could not afford to buy on the black market, and secondly, we hoped to hold or even break the inflation by preventing wages from rising on the basis of black-market prices. It was calculated by some of our experts that the actual consumption in Italy at that time averaged something like 300 grammes of bread and pasta, only two-thirds of which was legitimately obtained. On 31 May we had a great meeting of the Economic Section where Lloyd's report was discussed and adopted.

Lloyd's arrival has been, of course, an absolute Godsend, and the ginger that I tried to apply some weeks ago could not have been effective without his coming. He has been both tactful and intelligent and of course drafted the greater part of the reports.[8]

Accordingly, General Wilson authorised on 8 June a temporary 300-gramme ration to operate from 1 July. Since in the previous year only 20 per cent of the harvest had been collected for official distribution, we confidently expected that with a larger ration allocation something like 50 per cent should be available for distribution. The Chiefs of Staff were quick in their comeback and demanded postponement. A telegraphic contest followed. Nevertheless all the Italian officials and Allied officers had been notified; there was no alternative but to

[7] Letter to Sir Desmond Morton, 10 April 1944.
[8] 31 May 1944.

proceed. General Wilson was rather too easily upset by the censures of the Combined Chiefs—or rather those issued in their name. I therefore backed him up strongly in London, pointing out that all the British and American experts on the spot had agreed that this was a wise 'anti-hoarding and anti-inflationary measure'. In my view the hypotheses upon which the Combined Chiefs of Staff were working were wrong and the deductions false. In the circumstances I felt that General Wilson deserved praise, not censure, for a bold and timely action which all economists with experience of the problems created by modern war would have approved.

All through this controversy the ambivalent position of Italy remained one of the causes of our difficulties. Was the Allied policy to squeeze the Italians for all we could get, or was it to win their gratitude for the post-war Europe? Were we to be avenging or ministering angels?

I was rather shocked when at the end of July I was told from London that the Italians should be made aware that their troubles were their own fault; first, because of years of unsound policy, and secondly, because Italy had declared war on us and that was the only reason we found ourselves now on Italian soil. These reproaches were true, but neither generous nor constructive.

At any rate General Wilson's confidence in his advisers and his own courage was soon to be justified. I was asked by the Secretary of State and the Chancellor of the Exchequer to give some account of the effect of the new ration in Naples. On 19 July I was able to report that

Black market bread has fallen from 160 lire to 60 lire; flour from 300 lire to 40 lire per kilo. This should certainly make it easier to resist inflationary rises in wage levels.

After the problems of consumption came those of production. The anomalous position of Italy made it impossible for Lend-Lease funds to be made available either to the Italian Government or to the Control Commission on her behalf. This was an enormous gap, later to be filled by new American legislation.

The next great trouble was power—especially electric power. The Germans had destroyed everything as they retired. Although we had been able to make some repairs, there was naturally considerable competition for any productive capacity that could be made available.

The armies wanted as much as possible for their immediate needs. The Navy had succeeded in getting some of the naval arsenals into operation. With the help of General George Clark (General Gale's successor) I worked out a plan by which both the Italian Government and the Control Commission could operate on a system, however primitive, based on our own Ministry of Supply at home. I accepted that the first need should be to serve the military objects of the Allies in the broadest sense; but civilian production was vital also. No priorities should be absolute. We needed to maintain a contented population and to avoid unnecessary imports and shipping. As far as the civilian population was concerned the primary needs to which production must be related should be food and fertilisers, clothing, housing and transport. The well-established naval and military factories in the back areas (Taranto, Brindisi, Naples) should be operated like ordnance factories or Royal Dockyards. Factories temporarily operating in the forward areas would of course be under the Army authorities. But all other establishments should be controlled by the A.C.C. in conjunction with the Italian Ministries. Thus, largely by the help of General Brian Robertson, this system gradually became operative. But it was a long and difficult process.

Although my authority was still only that of 'Resident Minister' and adviser to General Wilson, I found both Captain Stone, the acting head of the Commission, and all the members—British and Americans —friendly and co-operative. Our only trouble was that the Economic Section was not well treated by Washington. A series of representatives were sent, but none of them ever seemed to stay for more than two months. It was also clear that in spite of the complaints which Washington afterwards made that the British had too much authority in economic affairs, the American choice fell upon men who would be useful campaigners for the vital Presidential election rather than effective colleagues in the struggle with Italy's problems. This weakened the whole section, in which they held the chief posts.

The Economic Section has never had a chance. First Grady came from America, stayed five weeks and then returned to the States and was absent nearly five months. He returned for a month . . . and then retired. After him came Brigadier-General O'Dwyer, a New York lawyer and a purely political appointment. He is a Democratic leader in New York State. He has now

gone back to the U.S., presumably to campaign for the President. He was
unexpectedly sensible, but of course fundamentally ignorant. His second,
Antolini, is another political appointment. We have no British second-in-
command of the Economic Section, though we have men on the various sub-
commissions. Some of these are fairly good, others distinctly poor.[9]

The politicians came as brigadier-generals, saw for a few weeks, and
went back to conquer in the wards in the vital states, especially New
York.

Meanwhile there had been developments on the political front. In the
spring of 1944, the Foreign Office, prompted by Marshal Badoglio's
request for Allied status, had put forward a proposal for some positive
action. They suggested that the Allies should be ready to abolish the
armistice régime and sign a preliminary peace treaty as soon as they
were 'satisfied that the military position permitted this' and 'the
Italian Government had sufficient authority to speak on behalf of the
Italian people'. This plan was no doubt partly stimulated by the
forthcoming attitude of the Russian Government, who had already
sent an Ambassador. Although Generals Wilson and Alexander approved this course, and I also gave it my support, it was not at first
enthusiastically received by the State Department. Nevertheless, by the
time Churchill arrived in Rome in August they had moved cautiously
in the direction of some concession. I then put forward the idea of
something that might be called a *modus vivendi*, and this was discussed at length at a long meeting held on 22 August in the British
Embassy in Rome. We were all, of course, conscious of the difficulties
involved in a formal peace treaty, for there were many issues to be
decided when the war was over, above all the question of the Italian
colonies and the disposal of the fleet.

The meeting was held on a boiling-hot day and lasted from 2.30 to 7
p.m. In addition to Churchill and myself, there were present Sir Noel
Charles, Roger Makins and Bob Dixon, the latter representing the
Foreign Office. There were really two issues, one concerning our own
internal organisation and the other more fundamental—what ought to
be done to help Italy both in the economic and the political field?
During these long discussions,

Winston was like a dog worrying at a bone. But his peculiar method does
succeed in eliciting the truth—and throwing over all those sort of bureaucratic

[9] 14 September 1944.

Foreign Office proposals which sound all right but are quite obviously unworkable.

Bob Dixon struggled manfully with his brief. His task is to elevate Charles
and liquidate your humble. But Winston would have none of it. When
Charles cried out piteously, 'But what am I to do?', he replied, 'What do
Ambassadors ever do?' He was very scornful of the title 'High Commissioner'
when he realised that Charles had *no* executive functions and that his diplomatic functions were confined to being Ambassador to a shadow Government.[10]

The Prime Minister went on to suggest that any new policy on which
we might agree should be discussed at the forthcoming Quebec Conference. He thought that I ought to be the instrument for carrying it
out.

He wants me to be head of the Control Commission and run the new
policy. He will *not* have a treaty, but he wants a steady process of relaxation
of control. This, he says, is the task of the politician, not the diplomat.[11]

On the substance of the discussions, Churchill was quite ready to
accept that Italy should be regarded as 'a friendly co-belligerent and
no longer an enemy State'. Accordingly she should be relieved from
the application of the Trading with the Enemy Act, thus allowing
some revival of exports and an inflow of currencies. If the Americans
would agree, she should enjoy the benefits of UNRRA. An increasing
measure of responsibility should be handed over to the Italian administration. The details would be gone into at Quebec.

Churchill seemed completely tireless during this visit. The day after
our long meeting he had an audience with the Pope at 11 a.m., a Press
conference at noon, where he made a friendly and informative statement, luncheon with the Prince of Piedmont, and an hour's discussion
with the Italian Government.

He thus saw in one day all forms of power—spiritual, regal, governmental—
and the fourth estate of the realm.[12]

His versatility and devotion to duty were extraordinary and he
appeared to enjoy it all like a boy. I was very glad that he had seen all
the members of the Italian Government, thus forestalling the criticism
that would certainly have resulted, here and at home, from his seeing
only the political 'Right' (Bonomi and Badoglio).

Immediately after Churchill's visit, a party of British and American

[10] 22 August 1944.
[11] Ibid.
[12] 23 August 1944.

trade union leaders arrived to study the progress of affairs. Apparently
Ernest Bevin organised the trip, in the hope that they could teach
Italian labour leaders about the proper way to run free trade unions. I
was particularly pleased to receive the British members, Tom O'Brien
and William Lawther, with whom I formed a lasting friendship. The
Americans were Balzani and Antolini who, unlike our pair, could
hardly speak English but spoke excellent Italian.

They have already caused some excitement by giving Press interviews on
the day of their arrival, imputing the worst charges against A.C.C. and all its
officials, and alleging that the British are trying to turn Italy into a colony.[13]

The British and American Ambassadors tried to persuade the military
censors to stop this article, but the officer concerned very wisely
refused.

[The account] would have reached New York in due course, and the papers
would have had a splendid headline 'British General Tries to GAG American
LABOUR!'[14]

While awaiting further political developments, I managed to get
away for a few days to the Front. This I was always anxious to do,
partly because it made such a refreshing change from the life at
Headquarters; partly because the generals liked to see somebody from
another world and to hear the news; and partly because I was so
anxious to know whether there was any chance of the battle proving
decisive.

Accordingly, I arrived at Alexander's forward camp, passing
through Siena, at about 1 o'clock on 21 September. I found General
Infante, a former divisional commander in the Italian Army and now
principal A.D.C. to Prince Umberto, the Lieutenant-General, exchanging reminiscences of the Western Desert with Alexander.

The General seems in good spirits. After a very heavy day's fighting
yesterday in which the Americans at the Futa Pass and the British on the
right suffered heavy casualties (3,000 . . . in the 56th Division), good progress
is being made. Rimini is taken and there is a good hope that the slogging
match is drawing to an end and that the enemy will not be able to take much
more punishment.[15]

13 29 August 1944.
14 Ibid.
15 21 September 1944.

Alas, they were to slip out of the noose, if only by a hair's breadth. Early the next morning, 22 September, we left in two 'whizzers' to visit the Eighth Army, now commanded by General Leese. The forward headquarters were just over the Coriano ridge, a few miles south of Rimini. First we went to the Canadian Corps, commanded by General Burns, who were in excellent form and very pleased with their success. Their armoured divisions, together with the New Zealand armour, were beginning to cross the Marecchia river, which runs through Rimini, and were advancing in the plain.

The two generals and I drove to the Fortunata feature already captured and watched the battle for the crossings of the river to the east. We already had some bridgeheads at Rimini. We then drove in jeeps to Rimini.

> The town is rather badly damaged, but not irreparably. There are some lovely Renaissance buildings as well as some of earlier date. Naturally, since the place was only taken yesterday, it presents a pretty depressing appearance. But I feel sure it will 'clean up' better than it now appears.
>
> One great difficulty with these partially destroyed buildings is to prevent further deterioration with the bad weather and rain approaching. But the Fine Arts Sub-Commission of A.C.C. are helping the Italians and have done splendid protective work.[16]

Practically the whole population of Rimini had fled, mostly to San Marino, already full of refugees. Then we drove over the river and watched the armour going forward. The Germans were shelling pretty heavily and putting up a very strong delaying action. Later, we got back to General Leese's headquarters. General Alexander left by 'whizzer', and I spent a pleasant evening with Oliver Leese.

> I had a very comfortable caravan, with some excellent gilt furniture. This had been specially 'liberated' for the use of King George when he came.[17]

The next day we left early by jeep, General Leese driving. We covered the whole Front, by various lateral roads, and at different distances from the actual front line. Things were on the move, and everywhere the General was received with smiles and greetings.

> He is indeed a very popular figure and I told him that he conducts the whole affair like an election campaign. It is a remarkable contrast with the

[16] 22 September 1944.
[17] Ibid.

last war. Then a general was a remote, Blimpish figure in white moustache, faultlessly tailored tunic, polished boots and spurs, emerging occasionally from a luxurious château, and [riding] in his huge limousine Rolls. . . . Now an Army Commander is a youngish man, in shorts and open shirt, driving his own jeep, and waving and shouting his greetings to the troops as he edges his way past guns, tanks, trucks, tank-carriers, etc., in the crowded and muddy roads, which the enemy may actually be shelling as he drives along.[18]

It had been necessary to occupy San Marino, and troops of the Indian Division and Scottish Brigade were employed for the purpose; but every formality was observed.

This tiny republic is a somewhat absurd mixture of old and new. We were received by one of the Co-Regents—who wore white gloves and a very long swallow-tail coat (like a *maître d'hôtel*)—and by the Cabinet. (We assumed that there was only one swallow-tail coat between the two Co-Regents and that they can therefore only function one at a time.)[19]

After an exchange of courtesies, the General and I were led up to the Council Chamber.

The town hall is 1850 Gothic—rather like the hall at Balliol—and the product of one of San Marino's chief exports, viz., the sale of titles. This building, together with a great part of the medieval town that crowns the rock, was largely built by an American lady. This benefactress also put in a water supply. For these—especially the last service—she was suitably rewarded by the title of 'Duchessa d'Acqua-Viva'!

After a ceremonial wine-drinking and a few speeches, the Co-Regent began to open up on the question of compensation for damage by bombing and so forth within his State. Fortunately at this moment the pipers began to pipe vigorously in the square outside and allowed me to escape from this awkward problem under cover of their deafening sounds. However, this dispute dragged on for many years before it was finally settled.

In the midst of this confusion,

the Divisional Commander of the Indian Division turned up with plans for a counter-attack on a hill nearby, where a furious battle was raging some 2,000–3,000 yards away.

The whole scene was really fantastic. The Co-Regent and his swallow-tails discussing compensation; the General and I making polite con-

[18] 23 September 1944.
[19] Ibid.

versation amid the din of the pipes and the guns; and the battle going
on quite close to us. From our great height we could look down on the
foothills and the river and watch the fight.

At the end of September, to my deep regret, Roger Makins was
taken from me. I gave a farewell party in our splendid suite of offices
at Caserta with its Bonapartist pictures, the attendance at which was a
great tribute to the position which Roger had won for himself at
Allied Force Headquarters. Over a hundred people came, and the
servants played up by producing great quantities of food and drink
and by not getting too drunk themselves. After my party, we went to a
select dinner given by General 'Jumbo' Wilson and his staff in the
hunting lodge in Roger's honour.

It is naturally a great loss—even a great grief—to lose Roger. He has been a
most loyal supporter in all my difficulties and a most agreeable companion
and friend. I think it is a tribute to both of us that we have lived together for
nearly two years, like subalterns in a company mess, without quarrelling (and
Roger's temperament is more highly strung than mine). The inspiring thing
about him is his standard of work. He is *never* satisfied with the second best.
And this goes through the office and inspires the others.

It will be a great change. Kit Steel will, I think, be agreeable and efficient.
But he has not that rapier-like brain, combined with that almost monastic
devotion to duty, which makes Roger such a unique figure in the public
service.[20]

After the second Quebec Conference, further discussion on Italy
took place at Hyde Park, President Roosevelt's home, and a statement
signed by Roosevelt and Churchill was published on 26 September.
The Hyde Park Declaration recognised that the Italian people during
the past twelve months had shown their will to be free and their desire
to fight on the side of the democracies and take a place among the
United Nations. The President and the Prime Minister wished to
encourage those Italians who stood for a political rebirth and would
give them a more significant role in the defeat of the enemy by placing
larger responsibility upon the Government. An increasing measure of
control would be gradually handed over to the Italian administration.
The name of the Allied Control Commission should be changed,
dropping the word 'Control' (this came to be known as muting the
middle C). The British High Commissioner and his American coun-

[20] 29 September 1944.

terpart would be full Ambassadors. The Italian Government would be asked to send representatives to Washington and London. UNRRA would send medical aid and other essential supplies. The first steps would be taken to restore the Italian economy, partly as a military measure and partly to employ Italian resources to the greatest possible extent. The Allies would help as far as possible to repair electric power systems and the railways and provide motor transport. They would supply engineers, technicians and industrial experts to assist in this work. The Trading with the Enemy Act would be modified. Finally, the Allies looked forward to the day when all Italy would be free, and free elections could be held. Both on the political and on the economic side, this Declaration was well received in Italy, as well as in Britain and America. But it led naturally enough to renewed pressure both on and from the Government for immediate action. Bonomi was insistent in urging me to work out the details as rapidly as possible.

As part of these changes, my appointment was also agreed, and formally announced on 10 November. I became Acting President of the Allied Commission, the Supreme Allied Commander being the President.

Meanwhile the Italian Government sent a memorandum demanding immediate alterations in the whole system of the Commission, including the introduction of Italian representatives to the Commission itself. They also demanded that the Commission should consist chiefly of civilians and that the Allied officials attached to the spurious Italian Ministries should be withdrawn. These, and other proposals, went beyond the policy laid down by the Declaration. My immediate purpose, therefore, on taking office was to persuade the two Governments to agree to work out a directive to myself, and in October I sent a full draft of my proposals.

Month after month the discussions raged about this unhappy document, but I was able to implement many of the decisions on my own responsibility. There were many practical things to be done. I was able by the end of the year to abolish the Political Section of the Commission, in order to allow the Ambassadors to function normally. The problem of the North loomed over us more and more. Instructions were sent to the S.O.E. and O.S.S. officers to persuade the partisans to preserve law and order as the enemy retreated, and particularly to protect public utilities from sabotage by the Germans. On 17 November, important discussions took place as to the integration of the partisan committees and their relation to the Government.

But most important of all, from the practical point of view, were the economic developments. The President, in the throes of his political campaign for re-election, began to make more and more generous interpretations of the Hyde Park Declaration. Up to now, the bread ration had been increased to 300 grammes only for liberated Italy. General Wilson not unnaturally inquired whether the President's promises meant that the 300-gramme ration should immediately be implemented to cover all liberated Italy as the armies advanced. This would sooner or later require greater imports. The Chiefs of Staff, presumably not being influenced by the needs of American politicians, remained unmoved, or rather maintained a firm but significant silence. Finally, at the end of October, the President stated that he assumed the responsibility for inviting General Wilson to increase the ration; Churchill immediately countered by informing Roosevelt that since he had assumed the burden he must now find the ships.

There were a number of matters upon which American policy was proving somewhat embarrassing, not least the President's declaration on 10 October that the United States would provide Italy with the dollar equivalent of the Allied paper money "issued up till now and hereafter' to United States troops in Italy. A similar British concession would have placed an impossible burden upon the British Treasury. All that we could undertake to do was to allow Italy to use for imports, so far as shipping allowed, the sterling equivalent of any exports which they made to Britain or the sterling area. With the continuous flow of complicated and sometimes conflicting instructions from the various departments in Washington and London, it soon became clear that the position should be regularised. It was accordingly arranged that I should go to London at the end of November to seek the agreement of my colleagues, and after full discussions with the officials concerned go to Washington, in order to try to settle the many questions which were still obscure. At any rate, the Presidential election would by then be over.

Before leaving, I was granted an audience with the Pope, which my new position seemed to require. Sir D'Arcy Osborne arranged this, and the private audience was fixed for 10.30 a.m. on the 18th. Sir D'Arcy introduced me and then retired. Pope Pius XII was sitting at a desk near the door. He rose to greet me, shook hands and put me in a chair next to the table.

He began to talk in English, but I had been warned that he speaks more fluently in French, so we soon changed into that language. In spite of the considerable experience which I have now had in recording conversations, I find it difficult to give a very accurate account of what he (or I) said. Many subjects were touched upon—in quick, bird-like quiver from one to another. I think I cannot have listened with great attention, since I was thinking of so many other things—the Pope's appearance, voice, gestures; the room; the occasion; the long history of the Papacy; and the queer chance that brought me into the Vatican—a long way from St. Martin's Street and further still from Arran![21]

His Holiness seemed depressed about the world, as well he might be.

He spoke of Communism, infidelity, misery. He lived much in Germany, knew England, and of course Italy was his home. For all he grieved, especially Italy, torn by faction and ruined by the disasters of war. He spoke of our Prime Minister with respect, almost awe. Of our King, with affection. Of the loss to the Church of England by Archbishop Temple's premature death. But I found it difficult to say much or remember what I said. . . . The Pope went on, sadly, from one point to another. The chief impression on my mind all the time was the extraordinary contrasts—the vast edifice of outward magnificence and beauty—St. Peter's—the Vatican—the unending suites of rooms, the rich furniture and vast store-house of wealth . . . then a sense of timelessness—time means nothing here. Centuries come and go, but this is like living in a sort of fourth dimension. And at the centre of it all, past the papal guards, and the noble guards, and the monsignori and the bishops and the cardinals and all the show of ages—sits the little saintly man, rather worried, obviously quite selfless and holy—at once a pathetic and a tremendous figure.
He gave me a little medal—and a sort of unofficial blessing. Later he sent round a Count something or other with another and better medal, and a message of great goodwill.[22]

I arrived in London on Saturday the 25th. Our formal work was to start on the Monday. General Wilson, who had been appointed to succeed Field-Marshal Dill in Washington, had arrived on a visit from Caserta and came to see me at my room in the Cabinet offices. He was to be made Field-Marshal, a well-deserved promotion. Wilson was a splendid man to work with, loyal and honourable. But the change of

[21] 18 November 1944.
[22] Ibid.

command meant that General (now Field-Marshal) Alexander would become SACMED, and this delighted me.

The next week was taken up by various meetings at the War Office and the Treasury. By the following Monday, 4 December, my Cabinet paper was ready for a joint meeting of the various official committees. I saw the Prime Minister at luncheon on the same day and told him that things were going well. Nevertheless,

the whole supply and shipping question for Europe has been opened up by these Italian proposals. And the shipping position is desperate, partly because the German war was expected to end by 31 December 1944 and partly because of the Germans holding on so long to the French ports, and partly by the large liberated areas to be looked after without the war ending. All the calculations have gone wrong and there is an estimated shortage of at least 5 million tons during the first quarter of 1945. Moreover, the Americans are insisting on diverting more and more ships to the Pacific war. And the more successful their operations, the longer become their lines of communication and the greater becomes their demand for ships. It is a vicious circle.[23]

My paper had been approved and was circulated to the Cabinet. There seemed no doubt that it would be accepted, and I fully expected to leave for Washington before the end of the week. Meanwhile, as always seemed to happen when one left only for a few days, two new rows had begun in Rome. The first trouble was a crisis in the life of the Italian Government.

It ran true to form—almost Algerian form. The prestige of the Government had been lowered by a number of incidents. The lynching of a witness at the Caruso trial and the drowning by the mob of one Carreta, a former Governor of the Regina Coeli prison, with the police impotent or sympathetic, were regarded as incompatible with the high claims which the Allies were trying to meet by the 'New Deal'. Trouble gradually spread among the Ministers.

A series of intrigues and manœuvres on the part of the parties of the Left—in which the hand of Count Sforza was also plainly discernible—and their attempt to gain a preponderance in the more important Cabinet offices finally induced Signor Bonomi on 26 November to tender his resignation.[24]

Following the correct procedure, the Lieutenant-General of the Realm consulted with Orlando and Toretta, the prospective presidents of the

[23] 4 December 1944.
[24] Harris, p. 214.

Chamber of Deputies and the Senate. The party leaders met together as a Committee of National Liberation without their chairman, Bonomi, who agreed to absent himself. They elected Sforza as chairman. They then decided that a coalition Government could not be formed by Bonomi unless the Ministry of Foreign Affairs was entrusted to Sforza. The fat was now in the fire. Sforza was like a red rag to a bull to Churchill, and I sometimes felt that Roosevelt, who had a great sense of fun, used this Italian politician like the matador's cloak to infuriate his colleague and friend. At any rate, when a delegation of three of the party leaders, De Gasperi, Saragat and Cianca, who had all been members of Bonomi's Government, asked Sir Noel Charles whether the British objections to Sforza were still effective, Charles could only reply that any improvement in our relations with Italy would be impossible if Sforza were appointed.[25] This of course was based upon instructions from London and was, however unwise, an expression of a view, not a veto. I telegraphed on my own to Steel to make the position clear. Sforza had been actually appointed Ambassador in Washington, and if only the Italian storm had broken after he got there everything would have been all right.

One aspect of this affair pleased me:

At any rate the Italian crisis has given us an example of how the new system works. The Allied Commission as an Anglo-American body takes no part unless it receives direct orders to do so from the Combined Chiefs of Staff. The British and American Ambassadors act independently (and in this case unilaterally), each representing the views of their own Government.

This procedure was adhered to strictly, and neither I nor my deputy, Commodore Stone, nor any member of the Control Commission expressed any opinion on what was regarded as a purely Italian question. Nevertheless, the incident was unfortunate, especially at a time when our relations with America, both in Italy and elsewhere, had lost some of the initial enthusiasm of the early years of our co-operation. It even raised old Croce to protest. But nothing could shake Churchill. He disliked Sforza and distrusted him. The Americans protested, but with so many other dangers about to confront us, including the German counter-attack in the Ardennes, after a sharp interchange of telegrams between the State Department and the Foreign Office, and further recriminations between Edward Stettinius, now the American

[25] Ibid.

Secretary of State, and the Prime Minister, the matter was allowed to drop.

In the end, Bonomi achieved a considerable triumph. The Action Party, so called, not only demanded Sforza as Foreign Secretary, but also criticised Bonomi's perfectly correct action in offering his resignation to the Lieutenant-General of the Realm instead of to the Committee of National Liberation. They were joined in this protest by the Socialists. Neither of these groups had any serious following. Paradoxically enough, the Communists thought all these objections ridiculous, and Bonomi was thus able to form a four-party Government and emerge strengthened from the crisis. Sforza was not made Minister for Foreign Affairs. The two powerful figures were De Gasperi, the leader of the Christian Democrats, and Togliatti for the Communists. With these secured, Bonomi was in a strong position. The authority of the Christian Democrats was indeed enhanced, and with the second Bonomi Government began their long domination of Italian politics.

Although the Italian crisis continued for a number of days, the new Government was formed on 12 December and lasted without change until June 1945, when a new coalition was formed, including all the parties. The dangers of civil war or revolution, which many pessimists had foreseen, were thus successfully avoided.

The second row was even more reminiscent of Algiers. While I was negotiating in London on the details of the Italian New Deal, I read a telegram about the threat to arrest and try Marshal Badoglio as part of the Italian 'purges' which had been going on in a not unduly vindictive way for some time. I discussed this telegram with Sir Orme Sargent and suggested that we should ask the Americans to join with us in intervening on military grounds. It was obvious we could not allow Badoglio to be imprisoned or executed, but I did not see why the Americans should not carry some of the responsibility. On 7 December, Eden told me that the State Department, although friendly, was unwilling to interfere. But I thought we should stick to our point. If we said we would not intervene alone and seemed to mean it, I felt we could shame the Americans into taking their share. Even Ambassador Kirk would not like to see the old Marshal shot outside his luxurious palazzo. In the end, as so often in these disagreeable affairs, it fell to the British to shoulder the burden.

Noel Charles, in a telegram which reached us on 5 December, gave

the whole story. The Marshal had called and asked for his advice. At
the instigation, as he believed, of Sforza, he was about to be arrested
and put on trial. What should he do? Should he stay in his house in
Rome or take refuge with friends in the country? Charles immediately
undertook to consult the Allied authorities. Kirk took the view that on
no account should we take any measures 'until the worst happened'.
Such in his opinion was 'our democratic position'. Churchill, of course,
reacted rapidly and characteristically. He sent a message to Charles,
holding him personally responsible for the Marshal's safety and sanc-
tuary in the British Embassy or some equally safe place. After all, the
Marshal had signed the armistice and the various documents upon
which our whole position in Italy depended. He could not be brought
to trial without the approval of the two Allied Governments. Our
military honour and that of the high admirals and generals with
whom he had faithfully dealt was clearly involved.

Charles acted accordingly, and the Marshal was safely lodged at the
British Embassy. Then came the necessity for consulting the Americans. But in the absence from Washington of the President, Stettinius
was the only person available on the spot. He, too, was about to leave
for New York, and was unwilling to act. There was next a suggestion
that Badoglio should be taken to Malta. Of course joint Allied action
would be the best, and there was still a hope that the State Department would agree that this was a matter in which the Supreme
Commander could reasonably interfere on military grounds. But if
they continued to 'waffle', I suggested that the Marshal should be
entertained as a guest in the Villa Rivalta, which belonged to
SACMED. He would then be under the care of an Allied Commander,
responsible to the Combined Chiefs of Staff.

Eventually both Sforza and Bonomi gave Badoglio most categorical
guarantees: the first, that he would not urge the prosecution of the
Marshal, and the second, that he would protect him. Bonomi repeated
his assurance both to Charles and to Ambassador Kirk. Not unnaturally, the State Department were not anxious to help us over this affair
because of the recent dispute over the Italian governmental crisis.
Nevertheless, both we and they were in honour bound to protect the
man who had negotiated with us the title deeds of our authority.

Alexander and I made it clear that in the event of any renewed
threat against Badoglio's liberty, British security services should ar-

range to fly him immediately to Malta. In the event, the matter faded out. The Marshal was allowed to live on peacefully until the end of the war. At a later stage, he was removed from the Senate, but he was not subjected to any greater persecution.

My work in London was now completed. The Cabinet had approved my formal paper for implementing the details of the New Deal, political and economic. I was ready to leave for America on 9 December. All had been arranged with the Prime Minister and the President; I had my marching orders and my documents. But the Acting President of the Allied Commission for Italy was destined to go not west but east; not to Washington, but to Athens; not to obtain American support for a scheme of peaceful reform for which we were to share the responsibility, but to help to fight a revolution from the burdens and dangers of which our American allies were to stand aside.

CHAPTER TWENTY-ONE

The Liberation of Greece

AT the beginning of 1944, there was a vague understanding that Greek affairs would in due course come under General Wilson and therefore within the field of my responsibility. In point of fact, partly for practical reasons and partly because of the desire to keep control in British hands, as late as the middle of the year the Foreign Office was definitely insisting that Bulgaria, Roumania and Greece should remain under Lord Moyne and General Paget in the Middle East. When the Prime Minister was in Italy in August, Greek affairs were discussed with General Wilson and all his staff and advisers. Lord Moyne and General Paget were summoned to attend. Murphy had, much to my regret, left to rejoin Eisenhower. But his successor, Kirk, was either present or kept informed.

Two events now settled my future. The aeroplane bringing Lord Moyne and General Paget broke down, and they were therefore not present at the initial discussions. George Papandreou, the Greek Prime Minister, after seeing Churchill alone, accepted his proposal that the Greek Government should move at once to Italy.

Papandreou accepted enthusiastically, the more so as he wants to keep the five EAM Ministers (who have at last agreed to join) away from the poisonous atmosphere of intrigue which reigns at Cairo.

All previous Greek Governments in exile have been broken in the bar of Shepheard's Hotel.[1]

It was decided to accommodate them at Salerno, south of Naples.

The H.Q. of [Military Liaison] Balkans will come to Naples together with as much of General Hughes's relief organisation and of U.N.R.R.A. as is necessary.

One airborne brigade will be ready to move from Bari to Athens and two

[1] 21 August 1944.

other brigades (either from M.E. or from Italy) according to the *general* state of the war when the Germans in Greece surrender or retire.

General Scobie (an excellent choice) will act as . . . force commander. . . .[2]

Here at least was a plan.

General Paget is naturally rather sore but the P.M. is seeing him this morning. He is a fine fellow and I am sure will appreciate the strong arguments for the transfer.

Roger [Makins] attended a meeting of generals, etc. (with Leeper), to work out details.

12 noon. Meeting at Embassy with Moyne, Steel, Leeper and Roger on Greece. Moyne . . . charming as ever. But rather a strained atmosphere![3]

When Churchill left Italy after a long visit, he was somewhat in the position of Balaam. Instructed by the Foreign Office to ease me out of my somewhat equivocal role, he had blessed me with a number of new and important jobs. He was pressing me to become Chief Commissioner of the Allied Control Commission for Italy, as well as taking over Balkan affairs generally (Roumania was on the point of collapse), and particularly to be responsible for Greece. I could not help being amused at Roumania declaring herself at this time to be a 'cobelligerent'. 'I never thought that when I suggested the phrase "cobelligerent" to Eisenhower in Tunis last September that it would become so famous an expression!'[4] The Italians were, of course, infuriated. Owing to hesitations in London, however, we were not able to launch our mission to Roumania and Bulgaria.

At this time began my association with Rex Leeper, our Ambassador to the Greek Government.[5] It was a happy chance for me to find myself working closely with this attractive and sympathetic man. Not only was he a brilliant classical scholar with a wide knowledge of art and letters, but he had a remarkably quick and accurate grasp of the changing kaleidoscope of Greek politics. He understood the Greeks, and they understood him. He had infinite patience as well as great personal charm. But in spite of his blandness and kindness he was not easily taken in. If he believed in mankind, he had a healthy distrust for most men, and all politicians. Not only was he utterly

2 Ibid.
3 22 August 1944.
4 23 August 1944.
5 Afterwards Sir Reginald Leeper.

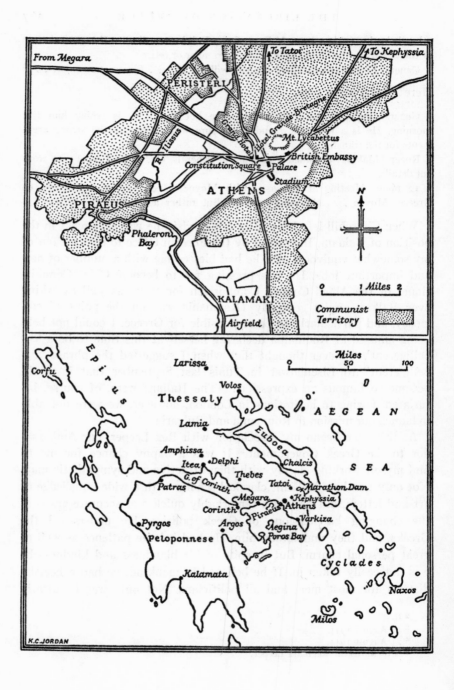

From Megara

To Tatoi   To Kephyssia

PERISTERI

Cross Hotel
Hotel Grande Bretagne
Mt. Lycabettus

R. Ilissus

British Embassy

Constitution Square   Palace

ATHENS   Stadium

PIRAEUS

N

Phaleron
Bay

0   1 Miles 2

KALAMAKI

Airfield

Communist
Territory

Corfu

EPIRUS

Larissa

Miles
0   50   100

Volos

Thessaly

AEGEAN

Lamia

Euboea

Amphissa

Chalcis

Itea   Delphi

Thebes

SEA

G. of Corinth

Tatoi   Marathon Dam

Patras

Megara   Kephyssia

Corinth   Piraeus   Athens

Pyrgos   Argos   Aegina   Varkiza
Poros Bay

Peloponnese

Cyclades

Kalamata

Naxos

Milos

K.C. JORDAN

devoid of jealousy, but he had the supreme gift of being able to work in a team.

In the course of this last year of the war, I found myself as a political Minister with four Ambassadors more or less responsible to me: Noel Charles for Italy; Ralph Stevenson for Yugoslavia; Duff Cooper for France; and now Rex Leeper for Greece. There were later to be John Le Rougetel for Roumania and William Houston-Boswall for Bulgaria. Naturally our work together varied according to the state of the campaign and the developments in the countries to which they were accredited. Nevertheless, these relations were bound to be delicate and could easily have degenerated into disputes and wrangles. In fact, I was most fortunate with those with whom I worked. All these diplomats owed their primary allegiance to the Foreign Secretary and the Foreign Office; yet they found themselves acting more or less under my control, as adviser to the Supreme Allied Commander. If they accepted the situation so readily, it was because they were wise enough to see that the life and strength of their clients depended upon the attitude of the high military command. Everyone relied upon what A.F.H.Q. would give them (from troops to victuals). I was supposed to have by this time considerable influence with the various military, air and naval authorities. Moreover, since in war everyone is broadly on the same side, there were strong influences for co-operation. In Greece, the greatest test was to come.

Modern, like ancient, Greece is a country with rapid and sometimes spectacular changes in personal and public fortunes. The First World War was followed by the fatal incursion into Asia Minor and the tragic loss, material and moral, that followed. In the first reaction had come harsh vengeance upon those who had advised this ambitious expedition. Then, at the end of 1923, King George II had been deposed and had left the country. Subsequently, for four relatively prosperous years, there were stable republican Governments under Venizelos. But Greece, like every other country, was swept up in the economic crisis of 1929-31. Strikes and rising prices ensued. Election followed election at almost annual intervals. An attempted Venizelist *coup d'état* failed in March 1935, and was followed by a general election in the same year at which Venizelists abstained. In the autumn of

1935 there was a plebiscite on the return of the monarchy. The conduct of the voting was generally regarded as an open scandal. But it resulted in King George II's return. He did his best, with commendable impartiality, to reconcile the royalists or so-called Populist Party with the republicans or Venizelists. In the general election in January 1936, the two parties were almost equal, with fifteen Communists holding the balance. The usual manœuvring followed, with the politicians of the two great parties differing in nothing essential except the question of the monarchy. The conduct of affairs was made almost impossible by their equal but impotent rivalries. The Army then stepped in. It declared that it could not remain passive if either of the two bourgeois parties fell to the tempting bait of the fifteen Communists and accepted office with their support. Its leader, General Metaxas, became first Minister of War and subsequently Prime Minister. The parties, unwilling to make any concession to each other, voted in his support, and Parliament adjourned until the autumn of 1936. But it did not meet again. In August of that year, Metaxas suspended the Constitution and instituted a dictatorship. He certainly had considerable qualities and like many dictators made a substantial improvement in roads, transport and even education. But he died a few months after the Italian attack on Greece in the autumn of 1940, and was succeeded by Ioannis Tsouderos.

On 1 March 1941, a bold and noble decision was taken by the British Government. At the expense of our commitments in the desert war, but in loyal accordance with our traditional friendship, Churchill and his Cabinet decided to go to the aid of Greece. Within six weeks the Germans took over the incompetently managed Italian campaign. The Greeks were forced to capitulate on 24 April, and British and Greek troops were driven to Crete. Crete fell to one of the most violent assaults in the history of war. The Germans, who had entered Athens at the end of April, were able, not unexpectedly, to form a series of Quisling Governments, chiefly composed of former royalists. The King and Tsouderos were forced to leave Crete with our troops, first for Egypt and later for London. By the middle of the summer the German control of Greek territory was complete, and was to remain so for over three years.

With a disloyal puppet Government, a foreign military occupation, a mountainous country with bad communications, and a long tradition of banditry, a partisan or patriotic movement soon came into being. The National Liberation Front—or EAM—was quickly formed, but in fact it was under the control of the Greek Communist Party (KKE). In the spring of 1942, EAM announced the formation of the ELAS, that is bands of partisans under their authority, by some praised as patriots, by others denounced as mere Communists. In the early summer other guerrilla bands began to appear in the mountains. Of these, the most important was EDES, which owed loyalty to the republican political leadership. A body called EKKA, of moderate Left-wing tendencies, soon followed.

Information regarding all these activities began to reach Middle East Headquarters, and in the autumn of 1942 British officers and emissaries were sent to Greece. Their original purpose was to destroy the German communications, and their intentions were to return to Egypt. But they were ordered to remain as a British Military Mission, and their task was to organise and support the guerrilla movements, regardless of their political affiliations, with the object of continuing to impede German communications and of harrying them in every possible way. Thus the guerrilla war in the Balkans developed with the active help of British authority, in Greece as in Yugoslavia.

On the wisdom of such a step, opinions differ. The Duke of Wellington, in conversation with Lord Mahon, once expressed a typically penetrating view: 'I have always had a horror of revolutionising any country for a political object. I have always said—if they rise of themselves well and good, but do not stir them up; it is a fearful responsibility.' The British Government might claim that in all the work they did in the various occupied countries, they were acting within the strict limits of the Duke's dictum. The guerrillas had started on their own. Our objects were not political; they were military. At a time of our great weakness, the various bodies of partisans gave us substantial military assistance. Nevertheless, our responsibility was great, and in some cases a heavy price had in the end to be paid.

In Greece, once the decision was taken, a steady flow of officers, military material, supplies, and above all, golden sovereigns began to descend. I was soon to learn the particular characteristic of partisans.

Nothing would suit them but specie. In Europe they must be wooed, like Danae, with gold sovereigns. In other parts of the world they are usually content with Maria Theresa silver dollars.

During the spring of 1943, the guerrillas were active all over the mainland under the guidance and inspiration of Brigadier Myers and the officers of the British Mission. But the same sinister developments as in Yugoslavia and afterwards in Italy showed themselves in Greece. ELAS began to attack and if possible eliminate all other rival guerrilla bands. In addition to the sufferings imposed by the German occupation, the Greek population was now threatened with civil war.

In February 1943 there was trouble in the regular forces evacuated to the Middle East, stimulated no doubt by Communist agents. Accordingly, the King and the Tsouderos Government, which had been living in exile in London, decided, with the full support of the British Government, to go to Cairo. There was a Cabinet reshuffle, and a number of republicans were brought in. In Greece itself, as the result of the efforts of the British Mission, an attempt was made to negotiate a 'National Bands Agreement'. (Throughout all this period we had some hold on ELAS, because they depended on us for arms, money and, to some extent, food. Without the bold and courageous work of British soldiers and airmen, the guerrilla movement would have collapsed.) The Agreement was finally signed in July, and a joint committee was formed with three ELAS representatives, one from EDES and one from EKKA. At the same time, the politicians remaining in Athens requested the King to declare officially that the future of Greece and its constitution, whether monarchist or republican, should be settled after the war by free elections. To this the King acceded and on 4 July broadcast his intentions accordingly. In August 1943 six resistance leaders, four ELAS, one EDES and one EKKA, were brought to Cairo. Although they represented radically different opinions, political and economic, they were all republicans. They now required that the King should not return to Greece until after a plebiscite, and their demand was backed by the republican Ministers in the Cabinet. They also asked that the Ministries of War, Justice and Interior should be given to the leaders of the various guerrilla bands and should function in Greece itself. As might be expected, all this led to a great dissension between Roosevelt and Churchill, and in the last weeks of August and the early days of September 1943 the two statesmen finally agreed that the King should return to Greece only after the Germans had left or been driven out, and that the plebiscite should be held after his return.

It is difficult for those accustomed to the more orthodox methods of electioneering among Anglo-Saxon nations to realise the tremendous power of any Government on the spot in most other countries to win a plebiscite. Dictators always win them by overwhelming majorities, as Napoleon III and others have proved. The argument, therefore, about whether the King should be in Greece when the vital decision was taken was not an academic one; it was of vital importance.

The Italian surrender in September 1943 naturally raised the hopes of the patriots in every Mediterranean country. When, therefore, the resistance delegates returned from Egypt in the middle of September with nothing but the King's refusal, the winter was spent in a bitter warfare between ELAS and EDES. The attack was begun by ELAS, and it was only in February 1944, partly from exhaustion and partly from British moral and material pressure, that it was brought at least to a temporary truce by the Plaka Agreement. The various bodies thereby promised to abandon this internecine struggle and turn their attention to the Germans. They also undertook to use all their efforts to facilitate the return of Allied troops to Greece when the time came.

In the beginning of 1944, although the formal transfer of responsibility had not taken place, I began to interest myself in Greek affairs and found out what I could. It was clear that whether Cairo or Algiers was to be in the lead, material aid would have to come largely from our Anglo-American resources. A meeting was held in Cairo towards the end of March, attended by both General Wilson and General Paget, the new Commander in the Middle East, and all the 'top brass', and including Rex Leeper, as well as Moyne and myself. After discussion of a number of matters, chiefly concerned with rationalisation of the machinery for dealing with the Balkan partisans of different kinds, Leeper gave us his opinion as to the contemporary Greek scene. The discussions which had ended in the Plaka Agreement still left open two problems: the first was that 'of a Greek Commander-in-Chief', which he felt could be quietly dropped because no one could agree on any particular nominee. The second was the question of the 'Political Committee'.

EAM had, after an interval of silence, announced the establishment of a purely EAM committee under the chairmanship of Bakirdzis, an ex-EKKA representative, who had transferred to EAM and was now disowned by EKKA. They had sent messages to M. Tsouderos and to G.H.Q. M.E. informing them in high-sounding terms of the formation and aims of this committee. M. Tsouderos had replied to EAM informing them that he still adhered to the policy of forming a Government of National Unity and that they should join in the discussions with the other parties in Athens.

But EAM did not respond to this appeal. The Political Committee, established in the Greek mountains, became more and more a Communist front organisation and a potential rival Government. Some officers in the Greek forces in Egypt demanded the reconstruction of the legitimate Government on similar lines. To meet part of their demands, Tsouderos tried to strengthen himself with messages from Athens, both from Archbishop Damaskinos and from some of the remaining politicians, in favour of the King's withdrawal. Leeper strongly recommended that the King should accept a regency. But all this depended on his self-effacement, which was not forthcoming, although he later agreed not to return to Greece without the consent of his Government.

Unhappily, the bitter conflict about the King gave an opportunity for the malcontents in the regular Army. A Greek brigade, which Alexander was hoping to bring into Italy, where any reinforcements were greatly needed, mutinied and was thus put out of action. The troubles now spread to the Greek Navy; the sailors, and some of the officers, declared in favour of a republic and demanded the resignation of the existing Government. In the painful task of dealing with the mutinous troops, Churchill had to take a very strong line. It was an unpleasant duty, requiring the use of armed force. The ring-leaders had to be arrested and although in fact there were few casualties and the Greek infantry brigade was finally starved into surrender, the incident was a sad one and left the situation hopelessly confused. Churchill had to explain and defend his policy both to Roosevelt and Stalin.

Sophocles Venizelos, the son of Greece's greatest leader in modern times, now accepted office as Prime Minister. But he was unable to hold the position. It was at last agreed, after a great meeting held in the Lebanon, attended by representatives of all the conflicting bodies, that a new Greek Government should be formed on a comprehensive basis under the leadership of Papandreou. This certainly, in Churchill's words, 'held promise for the future'; but, since the position of the King was not really faced, it also held the seeds of fresh disorders. About this time I had a talk with M. Politis, the Greek member of the Advisory Council for Italy. He described the ELAS partisans as partly Communists and partly bandits. He did not regard them as so well organised as Tito's followers, but he was insistent that a much more comprehensive Government must be formed and that the royal question must be settled. The truth was that the Communists cleverly used the question of the King to cause disorder and confusion.

Leeper carried through the Lebanon Conference with consummate skill, and on 24 May a Government of National Unity was in fact formed. The Americans and even the Russians seemed to accept the position that Greece was a special British interest.

Next, the Greek Army had to be reorganised. Papandreou wished to disband the irregulars, but General Wilson shared my view that this was quite impracticable for a Government in exile. To give an order to disband the guerrillas would merely result in losing any influence over them. General Wilson was now more or less in control of affairs and, whether *de jure* or not, *de facto* I had taken over from Lord Moyne. Early in June we were having many discussions on this problem:

At 3 p.m. Brigadier Benfield (from Cairo) who explained to me M. Papandreou's scheme. He wishes to form a Greek National Army by *normal* means—viz., calling up men and appointing regular officers. This involves asking the Greek partisans and irregulars to dissolve themselves. I do not believe they will agree to this.

I discussed [this] later with [General Wilson], who shares my views. He thinks the irregulars should be made the basis of the national Army, and gradually weaned from extremism by infiltration of moderate elements. EAM is more likely to agree. Will Papandreou? We decided to draft telegrams on the matter to Cairo and London respectively.[6]

I was now exchanging frequent messages with Leeper, who was still in Egypt. I was doubtful about any agreement reached on a personal basis between Papandreou and the King. ELAS and EAM had a good deal of support in what were called progressive circles in Bloomsbury, Fleet Street and Westminster. Our only hope of aligning the moderate

[6] 8 June 1944.

and centre influence in Greece seemed to be to rid ourselves of too close an association with the royal cause. In any case, it was a difficult choice.

Meanwhile, the Americans, while agreeing to participate in relief and rehabilitation, made it clear in a formal telegram in July from General Marshall that they would take no other responsibility.

The Communists soon began to make unacceptable demands before agreeing to take positions in the Government according to the Lebanon understanding. They wanted ELAS to continue as a separate body until the liberation. They demanded that the supreme commander of the resistance forces should be chosen from ELAS. They required seven vital Ministries to go to members of the Political Committee, and a branch of the Government to be set up in Greece in the mountains. It was sometimes difficult to remember that during all these disputes the Germans were in occupation of Greece and controlled cities, harbours and communications. Yet such is the rugged nature of the country and so strong the tradition of banditry, that when lawlessness had become patriotism, it was almost impossible for the Germans to exercise authority over the country as a whole.

The situation was almost equally worrying for us. 'Greece is going sour on Ambassador Leeper, I am afraid,' I wrote, and added at the same time another prophecy:

I should not wonder if Yugoslavia does the same on us. The P.M. is trying to go too fast and not leaving enough to the Ban (Subašić) and Tito themselves. I learned with the Giraud–de Gaulle affair *not* to interfere *too* much and not to appear *too* interested in the result.[7]

At A.F.H.Q. we seriously discussed whether we ought to make any agreement with the Greek Government before entering Greece or whether it would be better to leave our hands untied. Churchill and Eden were publicly attacking EAM for obstructing Greek unity. Leeper informed us that Papandreou himself took the view that if civil war was to be avoided, British troops must enter Athens within forty-eight hours of a German withdrawal. However, at the beginning of August, EAM, whether under Russian instructions or not we could not tell, suddenly changed their mood. All sweetness and light, they agreed to take up their ministerial posts. When Churchill was in Cairo at the

[7] 6 July 1944.

end of August on one of his journeys, he saw Papandreou and began to make plans for the movement of troops into Greece as the Germans withdrew. The task given for such a force was

to install the Greek Government, who should fly in as soon as an airfield is in our hands; to accept or effect the surrender of any German troops who capitulate on the spot; and to open the way for relief.

All this was clearly to be under General Wilson's command. The forces were to consist of

a Parachute Brigade from Italy followed by the 23rd Armoured Brigade from the Middle East and certain other units, amounting in all to about a division, which General Wilson can find without affecting General Alexander's operations.

The channels of the Piraeus would be swept, which would take a week, but for which Admiral Cunningham would like a month's notice. All this, of course, depended upon American acquiescence. Their Chiefs of Staff were not willing for their own aeroplanes to be used in such an operation; we should have to send some of our own planes from General Eisenhower's command in France. While Churchill explained to Papandreou that he could not accept any definite obligations for the dispatch of British armed help, he made it fairly clear that we would do our best.

Meanwhile, the Greek Government was to move from the contagion of the Middle East into the new and, as it was hoped, healthier atmosphere of Salerno. Roosevelt agreed to this plan and also to the use of American planes. Towards the end of August, Churchill was back in Naples.

The whole circus back in great form. The P.M. was very pleased with the President's reply about Greece, agreeing to all his proposals, including the use of American aeroplanes to carry British troops to Athens and to the immediate move of the Greek Government from Cairo to Naples.[8]

By the end of the first week of September, all the arrangements for British troops to go to Greece in the event of a German withdrawal were gradually sorted out.

There are all kinds of problems about proclamations, political warfare directions, legal position of the British forces, money for the troops (the

[8] 27 August 1944.

present Greek currency is in a condition of run-away inflation and a loaf of bread costs 60 million drachmas!), about which my office is appealed to by A.F.H.Q. for advice.

The Americans (especially Colonel Spofford of G.5) are being very reasonable and helpful, as I knew they would be when the operation was transferred from the control of Cairo to that of Caserta.[9]

The vital moment was now approaching. Events in Bulgaria and Roumania were not helping us as regards the Greek Communists.

The Bulgarian situation is *very* unsatisfactory, even alarming. I fear the F.O. have 'missed the bus' again. If they had allowed us to handle it, instead of Cairo, I believe we could have got the armistice signed *before* the Russian intervention. Had the Bulgarian delegates come here, I would have treated them as we did the Italians in Sicily. After all, we have the strategic air force in our hands. . . .

While a pedantic argument about terms and clauses was going on between London and Washington, the Russians seized the initiative. I fear our prestige in the Balkans will suffer correspondingly. Already the Greeks are restive and the Communist members of the Papandreou Government may easily resign. They are arguing that Greece should be looking to the rising sun of the Kremlin, not the setting orb of Downing Street.[10]

The Germans were now definitely beginning to move out. Even with my limited knowledge, the position seemed to be dangerous.

So far as I can see there is little chance of getting to Athens (for the operation is not really 'on' if the approaches are defended). At the same time, the Russians are approaching Sofia and may advance into Thrace. The Germans are leaving the islands and the Peloponnese, and if there is a gap, unfilled by a legitimate Greek Government, EAM/ELAS will undoubtedly seize the authority and another Communist (or brigand) Government will be installed in the Balkans.[11]

During the next weeks all kinds of alarming news reached us. ELAS were massacring civilians as well as soldiers throughout the northern Peloponnese. The outrages at Pyrgos might be a foretaste of what would happen in the rest of the Peloponnese and later in Athens. The Bulgarians reported that rival Greek guerrillas—ELAS and EDES— were quarrelling with them about the administration in Thrace. The

[9] 3 September 1944.
[10] 11 September 1944.
[11] 12 September 1944.

inevitable delays in getting a British operation into being were resulting

in a grave danger of EAM seizing the power wherever the Germans are leaving. Moreover, we fear that the Soviets will encourage the Bulgarians (who are to leave northern Greece) to hand over to EAM. However, our plans are making a little progress. We have seized Cythera and the Greek Commission are on their way to the evacuated islands.[12]

Leeper and I were now working closely together and having almost daily meetings. The Greek Government were naturally getting very restive sitting at Salerno and watching events develop rapidly in Greece as the Germans were gradually withdrawn. The important thing seemed to be to get the Generals, Zervas of EDES and Saraphis of ELAS/EAM, to meet us, and agree upon a concerted plan.

We organised a full conference at Caserta on 25 September at which Papandreou and four of his Ministers met with the two Generals, Zervas and Saraphis. During the morning, military conversations were held between our General Scobie and the guerrilla leaders. This was followed by a meeting between the guerrilla leaders and the Greek Cabinet Ministers. The soldiers, including the guerrillas, went to lunch with General Wilson, and the politicians came to me. Although the atmosphere was not too good on the first day, things gradually improved.

Papandreou had a talk alone with me in the garden. He seemed very anxious and was most keen that we should send the Government into Greece *at once*, even if it could not go to Athens. Any further delay would weaken its prestige, and make it impossible for the ELAS/EAM members of his Government (even if they wished to) to play the game. The gap after the departure of the Germans would be filled. If the Government and the British troops were not there, the Communists would step in and build themselves too strong a position to allow of their subsequent ejection.[13]

The next day, the Caserta Agreement was signed. Leeper told me that the Greeks, after their traditional tug-of-war, had behaved very well. I urged upon him that we must have a plenary session and a document signed by all parties, embodying the political and military agreements. This was accordingly done.

[12] 18 September 1944.
[13] 25 September 1944.

In effect, this agreement placed all guerrilla forces under the Greek Government and General Scobie, who was to command the British expedition. I immediately sent copies to Ambassador Kirk, as well as Mr. Offie, his chief assistant, and General Rookes, the American Deputy Chief of Staff, an officer of great charm and distinction. One of the great advantages of moving the control of the Greek problem from Cairo to Caserta was that we could at least keep our own Americans informed. Whatever might be the subsequent difficulties between London and Washington on Greek politics, there was nothing but the greatest sympathy and co-operation from the American officers and civilians who were our comrades.

After further discussion, I suggested that we should put the Greek Government into Patras on the Gulf of Corinth as soon as possible. If a gap was allowed to continue, I could not see how a Government could be returned with any authority. Something must be done to secure the position.

Although I had obtained approval from London and General Wilson's full authority for this move, the Greek Government suddenly lost its nerve. They now did not want to go to Patras or, indeed, to anywhere in the Peloponnese. They could not afford a failure; there were not enough British troops; there were no Greek troops; the relief supplies would be disappointingly small; and so forth and so on. After some discussion, I persuaded Leeper that it would be unwise to report this. We should appear

foolish and vacillating in the eyes of the P.M. if one day we telegraph *urgently* for permission to send an expedition and introduce the Government into Patras; and the next day say that we have thought better of it and that we and the Greek Government are now taking counsel of our fears.[14]

But if the Greek Government did not want to go to Greece, the Crown Prince, who unexpectedly arrived on the next day, certainly did.

The Crown Prince, or Diadoch, called to see General Wilson on the morning of 30 September. Leeper and I were also present.

I felt sorry for the Prince. He was obviously sincere and anxious to do his best for his brother and the dynasty. But I fear he suffers under the usual illusions of royalty. He believes that he has only to show himself in Greece for a 'landslide' to take place.[15]

[14] 30 September 1944.
[15] Ibid.

We tried to explain to him that if he were to go now to Greece, the carefully constructed Government of Papandreou would fall to pieces. The only beneficiaries would be EAM/ELAS, who would take over the country.

A long and rather painful discussion followed. It was clear that the King does not regard himself as bound by his declaration that he would not go back to Greece without the consent of his Government. There was always something equivocal about this situation. It has even been maintained that the King's letter was so couched as to have an ambiguous meaning in Greek, although the English version seemed clear . . . and satisfactory enough. Of one thing I am certain, that even Winston's popularity will not enable him to force a king upon Greece by British arms.

In spite of his disappointment at our attitude, the Crown Prince behaved with exquisite courtesy, and the luncheon that followed went off well.

During the next week I had to retire to hospital with an infection of the throat and lung, but I soon recovered and was able to take up the thread of Greek affairs. Our chief problem was that of supply. The Middle East could no longer help us, since General Paget had given up his authority to General Wilson. I began to make some inquiries of a discreet (and indiscreet) nature into the state of preparation.

Food fortunately is all right—but only because it is to be drawn from general Army stocks and therefore even the Cairo planners could not help it being there. Drugs and medicines are the same—and I suspect for the same reason.

But when I ask about blankets, clothing, transport, nails and small tools for house repair, soap, fertilisers, seeds, etc., everything is 'on order' and 'expected in December'. (What would happen if the Germans left Greece too soon, the planners don't seem to have thought of.)

But 'on order' means that the order has been registered with the vast machinery of Washington (which I remember so well from Ministry of Supply and Colonial Office days) and 'expected in December' means that if there were any ships and the ships were allocated to the job and did leave America in October they would probably reach Alexandria in December.[16]

I at once turned to the Americans, and Colonel (now General) Spofford of G.5, who was a really brilliant officer, promised to help.

One of the many absurdities is the position about clothing. The American Red Cross have 600,000 garments which they want to *give* to the Greeks.

[16] 4 October 1944.

UNRRA says goods must be *sold*, not *given*. So the American Red Cross are threatening to *give* them to the French, who (being sensible people) have contracted out of UNRRA altogether.

Later, I was to change my view on this question, at least to urge that the Greek Government might be allowed to sell such gifts in order to mop up currency and produce some revenue.

The first British units went ashore at Patras on 4 October, but only under great pressure could we persuade any member of the Greek Government to go there. Finally, Papandreou agreed to fly to Patras on 11 October and install there a High Commissioner for the Peloponnese, probably Panayotis Kanellopoulos. This plan, however, in fact broke down, much to my regret, for the whole Greek Government preferred to wait until they could go into Greece as a body. More trouble was reported from the north, where the Bulgarians stated that they had entered the country at the request of the Soviet Government. Since Churchill was now back in Italy on his way to Moscow, I was able to report the situation to him. The port of Patras would be rapidly cleared, and supplies would soon begin to move in. Colonel Jellicoe, who commanded the leading British troops, proved to be an officer of great quality and managed to establish some relations with the ELAS leader, Aris.

Churchill and Eden held a great conference at Caserta on 8 October with almost everybody one could think of present, including Brooke, Ismay and Alexander. Eden had a talk with Papandreou, and afterwards the Prime Minister came out and subjected him to a monologue which was chiefly confined to the merits of monarchy.

M. Papandreou looked very uncomfortable—but not more so than the rest of us.

When the homily was over, the party left for the airfield.[17]

I confess that I was not sorry to see them go.

In driving back with Anthony, I was able to discover that the [object of the Moscow] visit was:
  (a) To try to find out the Russian military plans.
  (b) To try to settle the Polish question.
  (c) To try to unravel some of the Balkan tangles—especially the armistice with Bulgaria and the position in Thrace.

Anthony seemed very distressed at the obvious ill effect on Papandreou of Winston's royalist sermon. He asked me to do what I could to smooth things over.

[17] 8 October 1944.

I called on Papandreou and found him, as usual, both voluble and interesting. Greece and Britain must always be linked together. We shared common interests. Greece should be a fortress guarding the Imperial route. At present, Roumania was almost entirely under the control of the Soviet Union—a puppet State. Bulgaria, owing to traditional patriotism, was not yet wholly under Soviet control, yet it was bound to fall more and more under Russian influence.

M. Papandreou went on to say that we could not disguise from ourselves the fact that British prestige had fallen, in spite of our great victories in the West and in Italy, while that of Russia had risen in the Balkans generally. Moreover, in our desire to attack the Germans we had roused and armed most dangerous Communist forces in Greece itself. He did not regard Communism as a political party in the ordinary sense. He regarded it as a revolutionary movement. For the moment, because this suited Moscow, EAM were serving [in] the Government, but he knew that the moment that it was thought more advantageous, the order would be given to leave the Government and make as much trouble as possible. The same policy, he observed, was being followed by the Communist movement in Italy.

With regard to Italy, he thought our policy had been wise, generous and far-seeing. He finally turned to the needs of Greece. First, Bulgaria must be made to evacuate Greek territory. If it were really true that Bulgarian troops were necessary to act as a flank guard for the Russian Army, this should be regulated with a proper agreement with the Greek Government. Secondly, as large a force of British troops as possible must land in Greece to preserve order. As long as the Germans were occupying Salonika and other important points there was some justification for this. Thirdly, a Greek National Army must immediately be formed. It must play its part, however modest, for as long as the war with Germany continued. If it was only possible to have the equipment for infantry battalions, that would do. The artillery could be British. Finally, an immense effort must be made for relief.

I was impressed by Papandreou's earnestness; but of course, he exaggerated the resources at our command. There was, after all, still a bitter campaign to be fought in Italy. After I had asked some questions, he brought up the matter of the King.

He said that compared with the great historic issues which we had been discussing, the question of monarchy was really less important. The great divisions were not as between republican and monarchist, but as between revolutionary and evolutionary. It would therefore be tragic to divide the moderate forces on what was really an obsolete debate. At the same time, the situation was very delicate. He had listened with considerable concern to Mr. Churchill's observations. He was still more worried by the fact that this was the only Greek question on which Mr. Churchill had spoken to him.

I naturally replied that all the other questions had already been discussed with the Foreign Secretary and that Mr. Churchill felt that he was discharging a moral obligation. In reply, Papandreou said that he regarded Churchill as the greatest of all living statesmen—one of the really great men in the world. He appreciated his sense of personal loyalty and tradition. Nevertheless, the practical difficulty remained.

When the Government got to Athens certain changes of Ministers would have to be confirmed; certain decrees would have to be signed. How was this to be done if the King was in England? At the same time, if the King were to come to Greece the Government would immediately collapse and EAM would seize power by revolution.

A Regency Commission of three or four old and revered statesmen, if possible including personal friends of the King, could be appointed in a position of trustees. Once the Greek Government was back in Athens, this matter could be brought to a conclusion. It was indeed urgent.

Our news from Greece was harrowing. On 12 October the Germans were withdrawing on a very large scale, but destroying all communications as they went. Had they acted on that day by a common effort throughout the country, the Communists might perhaps have seized power. Fortunately for us, they waited another six weeks before the attempt was launched. 'Operation Manna'—the return to Athens—had been fixed for 15 October. In the evening of Friday 13 October, I went on board H.M.S. *Orion*, Admiral Mansfield's flagship. General Scobie and some of his staff came at the same time. We did not, of course, sail until one minute after midnight on Saturday the 14th. Thus I was embarked willy-nilly and almost by chance upon the culminating stages of a new adventure.

The situation was not altogether without hope. We had at least the Caserta Agreement on which to base ourselves, and there was every chance that if we could arrive quickly the Greek Government might be able to assert its authority. Yet even if we avoided actual revolution, the task of restoring any kind of civilised life in Greece after her many years of suffering and dislocation would indeed be baffling and dangerous.

In the early hours of Sunday 15 October we reached our rendezvous outside Poros Bay. That part of our expedition which had sailed from Alexandria duly joined us. We had brought with us, in addition to *Orion*, only *Sirius* and one or two other destroyers. We were now joined by the cruisers *Aurora*, *Ajax* and *Black Prince*, as well as a number of destroyers, landing ships and minesweepers. A further convoy of landing craft, merchantmen, 'gantry-ships', together with the Greek battleship *Averoff*, were behind us. In the battleship were the Greek Government, accompanied by Leeper. Altogether, there were forty ships in the first group, some seventy or eighty in the second. We proceeded at a slow rate, the minesweepers leading. Behind the minesweepers were the cruisers, *Orion* leading and *Aurora* immediately behind us. General Scobie and I were allowed up on the bridge throughout the day. There was a heavy overcast sky, with occasional rainstorms, but the sea was calm.

About 9 or 9.30 the first serious hitch. We had seen a number of mines going up in front of us as the sweepers touched them off. Then a sweeper is blown up (a British ship). We can see her through our glasses—she is all over to the starboard, but still afloat. A great scurrying of motor launches and craft of various kinds to help her. There are a number of casualties—but we are not told how many.[18]

An hour later, a Greek minesweeper struck a mine and sank, and another British minesweeper was damaged. We had now reached a position opposite the northern point of Aegina.

It is incidentally rather lucky for us that the commandos had managed to clear the German gunners out of Aegina a day or two ago. There were some very strong coastal batteries (at the southern and northern ends of the island) which would have caused us terrible damage as we passed by—or halted—embroiled in the problems of the minefield.

In view of the difficulties of the minesweepers and the formidable character of the minefield, the Admiral took a wise decision:

We reversed and returned a few miles to a point opposite Poros harbour. Here we waited until the sweepers could get ahead and widen the channel.

[18] 15 October 1944.

The half-sinking sweeper, which was first hit, passed us—towed by M.L.s—and I think got safely into Poros harbour. Another also got to safe anchorage. But a small water-ship . . . struck a mine very near to us—just off our starboard bow—and went down like a stone. Twelve men were saved, the other ten or fifteen were drowned.

Meanwhile, a number of mines which had been cut from their moorings began to float down the line and became the target for a great variety of weapons.

It was rather like trying to shoot rabbits in thick bracken. The mine is hard to see and hard to hit. Sometimes they are penetrated and thus flooded. Sometimes they are exploded. One was successfully exploded very near to us by a 'pom-pom'—an excellent shot, which was received with appropriate applause.

In the early afternoon, the Admiral decided to resume our progress. A few more mines were cut adrift or exploded, and the claimed bag for the day amounted to between forty-five and fifty. Finally, the leading section of the flotilla was brought successfully to anchorage before nightfall in Phaleron Bay, a few miles from the shore. The second part was halted for the night in Poros Bay.

Altogether it was a thrilling experience—it really gave one an idea of the problems confronting a navy today, and the skill of all concerned. Fortunately we were not troubled with enemy aircraft. Only one approached us (a Ju. 88) and was promptly shot down by Spitfires who had got themselves into Megara airfield yesterday.

After we had anchored we decided, in spite of telegraphed protests from one of the Greek Ministers in the *Averoff*, to make no attempt to land that night. The news seemed fairly satisfactory. One battalion of the Airborne Brigade was well established in Athens, another would arrive at Megara the next day and march in from there. British troops had been rapturously received by the mass of the population. The next day, Monday, reports began to come in as to the state of the harbours and the town.

In the inner harbour of the Piraeus the German demolitions are very severe. In other places, they are not so bad. The power station was saved by ELAS troops, who beat off the German attack upon it. So there is light and power. The Marathon dam is not destroyed. Explosive charges are known to have been put in, but are said to have been removed, by a mixture of courage and bribery thoroughly worthy of Odysseus. If there is no delayed-action explosion, that means that the water supply is safe.[19]

A number of Swedish relief ships had arrived and were working wonders, for supplies of all kinds, especially food, were the great need. But already difficulties were developing between ELAS and the port authorities and the Greek Royal Government. It seemed to us that the only course was to stick to the letter and spirit of the Caserta Agreement. Every difficulty should be reported to the superior officers of the various organisations. Nevertheless, these first reports were a little disturbing. We heard from Papandreou and his Government that they wished to make a formal entry on Wednesday. Naturally Leeper and I would keep out of all this; it must be purely a military party with the Greek Government in the centre of the stage. I did not understand until later why the Greek Government would not land on Tuesday. The explanation was simple and moving. It was on a Tuesday that in 1453 Constantinople was captured by the Turks. This day has never been forgotten. Its consequences in Greece and indeed throughout the Balkans have been overwhelming. Although the Greek Government had been exiled from their country since the German occupation and had for months and years been passionately looking forward to their return, so powerful was this memory that they preferred to remain idle on their battleship, rather than risk the ill-fortune that would follow an important decision on so fatal a day. This made a great impression upon me at the time. When, some twelve years later, I was faced with the problem of Cyprus, I remembered this incident as an example of the undying feelings of the Greeks, oppressed for more than four hundred years by the Turkish domination.

On Wednesday 18 October I left the *Orion* at 7 a.m.

I picked up Leeper (from the *Prince David*—ex-Channel steamer, plying in happy days of peace between Dover and Calais or Newhaven and Dieppe).[20]

We went first to the Grand Hotel, where a suite of rooms had been prepared for us overlooking Constitution Square, and from there to the British Embassy. (I did not realise at the time how many weeks I was to spend in this building and in what exciting conditions.)

[19] 16 October 1944.
[20] 18 October 1944.

We found the Swiss Chargé d'Affaires who was in process of handing over the property for which he had been responsible since 1940 to one of Leeper's staff. The old Greek Chancery servant appeared and in a very emotional scene greeted me as the British Ambassador, shook me warmly by the hand, and burst into tears! When it was explained about Leeper, he repeated the process. It was really rather moving and the old chap's devotion and loyalty were really genuine.

The British Embassy was built by Venizelos for his personal use and subsequently acquired by us. It was a fine house, admirable for entertainment and not altogether unsuited to a siege.

We then returned to the hotel, and from the balcony we watched a remarkable scene. A vast crowd had collected during the morning, partly unorganised spectators and partly an organised procession.

The latter were entirely EAM (or KKE Communist) with representatives of ELAS (the Communist guerrillas) who were allowed to take part in small numbers. These processions had quantities of banners and other symbols, and were obviously well organised, under a single control. They were quite orderly and very cheerful. The banners commonly bracketed the names of Stalin, Roosevelt and Churchill. The whole crowd, whether Communist or bourgeois, seemed very pro-Ally and particularly pro-British.

At last, after a considerable interval taken up by good-humoured singing, cheering and counter-cheering, at about noon the Prime Minister, Papandreou, appeared on the balcony of a house on the side of the square immediately facing the Palace. On either side of him, looking rather uncomfortable, were General Scobie and Admiral Mansfield. The earlier part of the morning had been taken up with a drive through the town and attendance at a Te Deum in the Cathedral.

The Greek Prime Minister was well received and made a long and impassioned speech. The organised EAM bands (which together made up about half the crowd) interrupted, but not offensively, from time to time by chanting their choruses: E—A—M—we—want—no—King—etc. These did not seem to disturb M. Papandreou unduly, but clearly caused some annoyance to the quiet part of the assembly.

Papandreou obviously tried to raise general enthusiasm, overriding internal political issues, by continual reference to the Dodecanese, Northern Epirus and other territorial claims. Although the situation was clearly dangerous, I felt that the immediate crisis was over.

Had there been any longer delay between the departure of the Germans and the arrival of the Greek Government; or had the Government arrived without the disembarkation of substantial numbers of British troops and Air Force at the same time, I think EAM would have seized power. This *coup d'état* would perhaps have not been bloody, but it would have been successful.

But, of course, we did not know whether any orders had come from Moscow and, if so, of what kind.

Later in the day, various staff officers arrived from Caserta, and under General Scobie's presidency a conference took place.

My only contribution . . . was:

(a) Unless Papandreou deals *at once* with the *currency* situation, there will be a most serious crisis and a collapse of the Government.

(b) Unless some way can be found to disarm ELAS forces (and all other guerrilla forces) in the territories evacuated by the Germans and to start a Greek National Army into which the better guerrilla elements should be incorporated, there will be a most dangerous situation leading inevitably to civil war.

(c) Unless relief supplies can be rapidly landed and backed up by a better delivery programme than we have any assurance of to date, we shall cause a great disappointment to the population which will react *against* the legitimate Government.[21]

All these proposals were agreed, but how were we going to get any real action to carry them out? Washington was suspicious and hostile, London was deeply concerned with many other problems. On the currency question, we had received no advice, either from the War Office or from the Treasury.

In the course of the evening of the same day, between 6 and 7 p.m., I made two royal calls. The first was on Princess Nicholas of Greece, the mother of the Duchess of Kent. I thought it a proper courtesy in case she might be in difficulties or wished to send a message to her daughter. She seemed, however, to be well provided, inhabiting a large and comfortable palace, and I was given an excellent tea. The Princess, a lady of fine presence and great beauty, reminded me of the great Edwardian figures of the past. While commenting on the faults and low behaviour of the Germans, she was deeply concerned with the dangers of revolution and Communism. She had heard that an attempt by the Communists to seize power in Greece would not be long delayed; she proved to be right.

[21] Ibid.

Princess Andrew of Greece, whom I next saw, was living in humble, not to say somewhat squalid, conditions. Her brother, Lord Louis Mountbatten, had been sending urgent telegrams to General Wilson asking for news. Princess Andrew had stayed in Greece throughout the occupation, obviously working hard and devotedly upon relief, especially for children, in co-operation with the Swedish Relief Scheme and Swiss Red Cross.

She made very little complaint, but when I pressed her to know if there was anything we could do for her, she admitted that she and her companion (an old lady-in-waiting who must, I think, have been the governess) needed food. They had enough bread; but they had no 'stores' of any kind—sugar, tea, coffee, rice, or any tinned foods. (These are now going to be given to her by the Army—and the officer whom I sent to call on her yesterday had been very good and some stores have arrived today.)[22]

She went on to speak of her son.

Apparently the boy is in our Navy—a Lieutenant or Sub-Lieutenant—and is doing very well. The Princess was hoping he might be in the Mediterranean; but he has gone to the Far East.

This was Prince Philip, now Duke of Edinburgh.

The next day I left Athens for Caserta. I went at once to General Wilson's conference and reported as best I could on the situation. We decided to take uniforms for the Greek Army from British stocks and hope for replacements. As I expected, the Greek currency crisis was now reaching its peak.

The final stage of inflation has been reached, when the value of the drachma has practically—indeed completely—disappeared. This means that all the shops put up their shutters, and buying and selling stops, with consequent hardship, misery and despair.

The suggestion comes from Athens to send 200,000 gold sovereigns. But of course these will just go down the drain in a few days.[23]

With the help of some of our advisers, we prepared a scheme and sent Commander Southard, an active and intelligent officer, back to London to try to get agreement from the War Office, the Treasury and the Bank of England. We wanted to issue B.M.A. (British Military Administration) notes as a new currency, like the temporary Rentenmark, until a fresh Greek currency could be introduced.

[22] Ibid.
[23] 21 October 1944.

On 21 October I had to go out to meet Churchill and the Moscow party on their way home. Eden had stayed in Cairo and was to come later to meet us in Athens. At dinner at General Wilson's, Churchill

gave us a most interesting account of the Moscow visit and was obviously pleased with the reception which had been given him. The Russians were more forthcoming than they had ever been before. The fact that Stalin dined at the British Embassy (which is absolutely without precedent) made a great impression. He also came to the airfield to see them off.

According to him, the military discussions had gone well and the Russians had disclosed more of their plans than usual. Molotov, the Foreign Minister, was a very hard bargainer and both he and Vyshinsky pedantic and legalistic. Some progress had been made with Polish problems and Churchill had told the Poles that they must accept the Curzon Line and then get what other concessions they could.

On *Yugoslavia,* the talks resulted in a really useful declaration and there now seems a good chance that Tito and Subašić will come to terms. (But the F.O. and Winston *must* abandon the King.) On the Control Commissions for Bulgaria, Roumania and Hungary there was a lot of very stiff argument and we got the worst of it. Greece was satisfactory. Altogether, the results were *well* worth the visit and the P.M. seemed more hopeful about the future than I have ever known him.[24]

It was on this occasion that Churchill had made, as he thought, satisfactory arrangements as regards the Russian and Western influence in the different countries. In Roumania, Russia was to have 90 per cent predominance. Yugoslavia and Hungary were to be 50-50. In Bulgaria, Russia was to have 75 per cent. But in Greece, in accord with the United States, Britain was to have 90 per cent influence and Russia only 10 per cent.[25] When he told me all this, I wondered what would come out of that 10 per cent.

On 26 October I got a message from Eden to go to Athens as soon as possible. I was glad to return to Greece and lucky to get a lift in Air Marshal Slessor's plane, a Mitchell B.25. Kit Steel came with me, and soon after arrival we drove to the Embassy where we found Ambassador and Mrs. Leeper, Eden, Bob Dixon, as well as Lord Moyne. We were now to embark upon two or three rather hectic days.

Outwardly the situation was calm, though we all knew that it was perilous. All the classical conditions for a revolutionary situation

[24] Ibid.
[25] Churchill, *Triumph and Tragedy,* p. 198.

existed. The Government was weak and returning from a long exile without authority of prestige. The futile and seemingly irrelevant struggles between the old parties, Venizelist and Populist, had greatly injured the reputation of the democratic politicians to the advantage of the Communists, a situation which they had not failed to exploit. The problem of the King's position still remained unsettled. The German occupation, which had been brutal and destructive, had led to a complete breakdown of the social fabric. 'Numbers of the former middle class stood in the same queue with the poor, patiently waiting for a bowl of soup. Destitution, like a gigantic bulldozer, had levelled the social distinctions of the past.'[26] As we well knew from the information given us by the members of the British military mission working under the brilliant leadership first of Brigadier Myers and then of Colonel Woodhouse, the Communist Party, which had been almost crushed out of existence during the four years of the Metaxas dictatorship, was now the most active and the most effective organised body in Greece. In fact it controlled EAM and under the guise of the National Liberation Movement was all ready to seize power. It had entered on a bitter campaign to liquidate as far as possible the rival partisan groups. It had driven and contained EDES to the mountains of Epirus. The number of British troops were small and had entered more as a token force than as a truly military expedition. Since the Italian surrender in the autumn of 1943, the British control of the partisans had been much weakened by the fact that ELAS had succeeded in seizing practically the whole armament of the Italian Pinerolo Division in Thessaly.

Yet everything on the surface appeared quiet. We could only suppose that the Russians had honoured the agreement they had made at Moscow with Churchill and that stern orders had gone out to the Communist partisans.

In these circumstances, though the danger remained, we concentrated upon the immediate needs of the Greek people. The financial position was desperate, and Allied supplies were quite inadequate. Eden's presence helped us to do what was possible by way of improvisation. The meetings at the Embassy were almost continuous. During 27 October,

[26] D. George Kousoulas, *Revolution and Defeat* (London, 1965), p. 151.

We dispatched an enormous number of telegrams calling for cruisers, coffee, gold sovereigns, oil seeds, aeroplanes and various other commodities which were believed to be useful in a monetary crisis. We had interminable discussions about the state of the port and different estimates from a large number of Army and Navy officers of the tonnage which would be cleared. We broke into the late Ambassador's (Sir Michael Palairet) cellar and refreshed ourselves with his champagne. Finally, about 2 a.m., we retired to our fevered couches, conscious of our splendid efforts and each other's shortcomings.[27]

In order to get all this into working order, I prepared a plan for a committee of economic and political advisers to be set up to help General Scobie, and this was agreed. It was to consist of Steel, as my representative; a financial expert, E.H.M. Lloyd, to be assisted by Sir David Waley, who was being sent specially from the Treasury; and Commander Jackson, who was being lent from the Middle East Supply Centre. Harold Caccia would later replace Steel, and his position on the Italian Commission could be filled by Henry Hopkinson. We did our best to inform the Americans of what was happening, but their Ambassador took rather a detached interest.

All the next day, Sunday, we waited for Waley.

At last he arrived (about 8 p.m.), landing with the help of flares specially arranged.

Waley's coming was rather like that of Sir Omicron Pie. All these provincial practitioners are all very well. At last the great London specialist had come—a guinea a mile and a big fee as well. He is a splendid little man, obviously a strong character, and a charming, even boyish, smile and sense of fun. He listened patiently (at a consultation which took place after dinner), approved the remedies so far applied, thought an operation urgent, thought the patient would probably die but nevertheless there would be no trouble about the death certificate—and sent us all to bed a little deflated but much impressed.[28]

I had to go back for urgent Italian affairs on the 30th. But I got back to Greece on the afternoon of 1 November and found all our advisers hard at work. Waley left us with a splendid memorandum— which I called the 'Child's Guide to Stabilisation'—which everybody accepted *en principe,* and finally this was put before Papandreou on the afternoon of 3 November. Papandreou was accompanied by an Under-Secretary of Finance and the Acting Governor of the Bank,

[27] 27 October 1944.
[28] 29 October 1944.

Zelotas. Svolos, who was of some importance as an EAM representative, was also present. The Greeks asked for an increase in supply and a loan.

I opened the discussion in reply to Svolos and dealt only with supply. But I began (rather firmly) by saying I would not ask H.M.G. to give any further assistance unless it was quite clear that they would carry out all the things necessary, not only to make the stabilisation but to preserve it. The most important of these were, naturally, the alteration of the system of calculating wages and a real attempt to achieve budgetary equilibrium by other than purely inflationary means. That is, they must cut down expenditure on salaries, etc., they must tax, and they must—as soon as possible—start saving and internal loans.

All this was accepted, and Papandreou was clearly grateful that I pressed Svolos (his Communist or EAM Finance Minister) so hard.[29]

Waley dealt with the question of the loan and went over the budget figures, and sounded his warnings solemnly but in a singularly attractive way; it was a masterly performance. We finally agreed to recommend to the British Government that the new drachma and the B.M.A. notes should be interchangeable, thus giving confidence in the new drachma. Notes up to three millions would be made available at once, although this must be an agreement between Governments and not revealed to the public. Nor would we allow the B.M.A. notes to be exportable or convertible into English sterling.

I had to return to Caserta on 4 November and found General Wilson somewhat concerned.

A terrible 'how-de-do' has been started among the Americans by our performances in Greece. It is of course a delicate matter. The Americans participate for relief and rehabilitation but *not* for politics or military operations. Naturally, it is not too easy to draw the line, and they are equally offended by being asked in or left out.

Unfortunately, Bob Dixon wrote a record of all the extraordinary performances on the nights of 26 and 27 October and gave it to SAC. He gave it to CAO (General G. Clark) who gave it to General Spofford (G.5 American). *Hinc illae lacrimae!* The Americans were up in arms. Not only had we held meetings at the British Embassy with Secretary of State, Lord Moyne, General Wilson, Admiral Cunningham and myself. But we also gave (or thought we had given) orders contrary to the C.C.S. directive which governs the *prices* at

[29] 3 November 1944.

which relief stores are to be sold. In our effort to get some revenue for the Greek Government, we had broken the laws of the Medes and Persians.[30]

We managed to laugh this off somehow. Fortunately, I was able to say that an American expert had been sitting, at least informally, on Scobie's committee. But this little incident was a warning.

I flew back to Athens on 7 November and found that things had slipped a little. Waley had agreed to stay with us and was handling the Greeks with consummate skill, but

the usual Greek confusion reigns. No one stays 'put' for long. Waley gets them to agree to a scheme at the end of a long day's talk. But during the night they have lots of new and bright ideas, and so by the next morning he is back where he started.[31]

Meanwhile, no progress was being made on the side of public order. The Greek Mountain Brigade was to be brought from Italy to help the Government, but otherwise they had nothing but the remains of the gendarmerie. The great armed forces were in the hands of ELAS.

A new National Guard is to spring into being on 20 November (like Athena from the head of Zeus). No one has ordered uniform or equipment for these 10,000–20,000 men (I suppose they expect it to appear in the same way from General Wilson's tummy.)[32]

One of the major difficulties of the Greek Government was that it had no revenue. Such supply as we could obtain we wanted to give to them to *sell*. But the Swedish distributors of Red Cross supplies regarded themselves merely as agents for various international bodies and insisted that relief must be given free to the people. At a meeting with Papandreou, the Swedes finally agreed to our plan, and this led on clause by clause to the memorandum which Waley had prepared. There must be a new wage level; there must be some attempt to raise revenue; there must be taxes. Finally the last special touches were put to the necessary decrees and proclamations for the stabilisation, which was announced on 9 November. The rate was to be one new drachma for 50,000,000,000 old and 600 new drachma to the £ sterling, convertible into B.M.A. notes.

[30] 5 November 1944.
[31] 7 November 1944.
[32] Ibid.

Let us hope it will restore confidence! At present everyone sells gold in the morning and [the] drachmas in the evening! The loss may perhaps be outweighed in the public mind by a sense of relief and the hope of stability in the future. But this depends, we know, on the Government obtaining a revenue by sales of supplies, taxation and/or borrowing internally. Under present conditions, the last two are very difficult. If they are driven to print notes every week to pay their employees and fail to draw in equivalent notes by one of these methods, a fresh inflation will occur in a few months' time, leading to a fresh collapse.[33]

The same morning I saw Papandreou, whom I found in good heart, and this was followed by a procession of the three battalions of the so-called 'Mountain Brigade' marching through the streets. They had left Greece in 1941; they had fought at Alamein; they had been in the Eighth Army in Italy; they had captured Rimini only a few weeks ago. Although they had been concerned in the mutiny in Egypt earlier in the year, they were now regarded as fine and reliable troops. The crowd was enthusiastic, but it seemed more bourgeois and less working-class than that which I had seen in earlier demonstrations. Still, the arrival of this brigade certainly increased confidence.

11 November was the actual day for stabilisation, as well as being Armistice Day, and again this was celebrated by a parade. A service took place at the Unknown Warrior's tomb, but none of the ELAS troops arrived. Archbishop Damaskinos officiated.

This splendid figure—well over six foot—in black robes, with a black hood draped over his Orthodox hat, and a long black ebony cane with a silver top, intoned a blessing in a fine musical baritone, with appropriate hierarchical gestures, dignified, traditional, and immensely impressive.[34]

The money reform was followed by an enormous luncheon party given by the Greek Government to 'Sir Waley', 'Sir Leeper' and myself. It must have gone a long way to unstabilising the currency, for it was obviously based on black-market food.

On leaving for Naples on the 13th I felt that we had done our best. There were immense problems ahead for the Government and people of Greece. But if only the Moscow agreement held, there was a good chance of getting through. I had now to take up Italian affairs, which would involve me in a visit to London. All that I could do before

[33] 9 November 1944.
[34] 11 November 1944.

leaving was to urge General Wilson to prepare some plan in case the agreement broke down and ELAS tried to make trouble.

One last decision was taken before I left. General Wilson, as Supreme Commander, against the advice of the experts, accepted General Scobie's proposal that we should guarantee some extra rations to the Greeks. The amounts were negligible, but the principle seemed to be contrary to the rules, especially the Washington rules. Nevertheless, it seemed to me that a Supreme Commander must break rules in order to remain supreme.

This was the end of the first act in my connection with Greek affairs. I was to return unexpectedly a few weeks later to find a dark and tragic sequel.

CHAPTER TWENTY-TWO

The Greek Rebellion:
1. The Battle for Athens

THE first telegrams reaching London on Greek affairs were encouraging. Everything depended upon the success of Papandreou's negotiations with the Communist leaders for the demobilisation of the guerrillas. He therefore asked the leading EAM Ministers in his Government, Svolos, Tsirimokos and Zevgos, to draft a decree themselves for the approval of the whole Cabinet. Under its terms, the forces both of EDES and ELAS, as well as the Greek military units in the Middle East, were to be demobilised on 10 December. A National Army was to be organised of which the Mountain Brigade, the so-called 'Sacred' Battalion, an EDES unit, and an ELAS brigade were to be the core. The ELAS brigade, in effect Communist guerrillas, were to be approximately equal in numbers and armament to the combined forces of the rest.

Since much misunderstanding as well as misrepresentation were to follow the breakdown of this agreement, its terms are important. The so-called Mountain Brigade was naturally considered by the Communists (and later by their sympathisers or dupes) as 'reactionary', for it was created out of the loyal remnants of the Greek armed forces after the mutiny in the Middle East. It was now commonly known as the Rimini Brigade, because of its exploits as part of the Allied forces in Italy, culminating in the capture of that town. The Sacred Battalion was composed of Army officers and its sympathies were no doubt 'bourgeois'. But with the ELAS brigade, the balance could be regarded as fair. In any event, the significance of the agreement lay in the acceptance by the Communists of the immediate demobilisation of all the guerrillas throughout Greece and the equality between Left and

Right in the forces which were to be the foundation of the new National Army.[1]

This compact was indeed a triumph of Papandreou's diplomacy. On 28 November, he announced to the Press the terms of the draft and expressed his confidence that the formal document would be signed that very day. On the same afternoon, the Communist leaders repudiated their word. They sent proposals which were quite unacceptable. They now demanded the demobilisation of both the Mountain Brigade and the Sacred Battalion, and although in the course of frantic discussions Papandreou did his best, it was clear that the decision had been taken by the Communist leaders to make a direct bid for power. The six Ministers belonging to EAM resigned from the Government. The EAM police refused to hand over their arms, as had been agreed. Notice of a general strike was proclaimed. At this point Churchill promised full support to both General Scobie and Papandreou. It was clear from the statement which Scobie issued on 1 December that the constitutional Government would be maintained until a Greek State could be established with legal armed forces, and free elections could be held.

On Sunday 3 December the civil war began. Much argument subsequently developed as to precisely how the demonstrations in Constitution Square on that Sunday led to a clash between the crowd and the police. Some of the more naïve of the foreign commentators placed all the blame upon the police for having fired a machine gun into the civilian crowd, causing a number of casualties. But it should be remembered that among the so-called civilian crowd were many fully-armed ELAS guerrillas. Moreover, the police had been ordered to use blank cartridges to disperse the mob. There was strong reason to believe that the fatal shots were in fact fired by a Communist *agent provocateur*. Wherever the truth may lie, it is certain that the events of Sunday 3 December, although perhaps a convenient date for historians to mark the beginning of the December Revolution, were not its cause. The Communist rebellion was not provoked by an unfortunate clash during a political demonstration. It was the result of a definite decision taken by the Communist leaders, Siantos and Ioan-

[1] Kousoulas, *Revolution and Defeat*, p. 199.

nides, at least five days before.[2] Unfortunately, what we have now learned from the careful and well-documented revelations of many historians was at that time obscure. All we knew was that a bloody incident had taken place in full view of rows of foreign correspondents situated in the Hotel Grande-Bretagne on one side of the square. They had, as it were, a ringside seat, at what was soon to be denounced as a deliberate action by the 'Fascist police' of Athens, firing upon a harmless crowd. The diplomatic victory was certainly won by EAM that day.[3] Nor did this sowing of falsehood fall on infertile ground.

The British people had now endured more than five years of war. The hopes of a rapid end to the war in Western Europe were fading. Internal pressures in a somewhat unnatural coalition, created in the moment of danger under the leadership of one man of supreme genius, were beginning to develop. Since the outcome of the war was no longer in doubt, the minds of ambitious politicians were turning more and more towards the opportunities of peace. There were elements in the Press and outside ready to show special hostility to Churchill. Many had accepted his Premiership as a regrettable necessity in the stress of crisis. But they did not like his domination and hoped, whether consciously or unconsciously, to restore as rapidly as possible the régime of mediocrity. Many sections of the Press, therefore, especially *The Times* and the *Daily Chronicle*, as well as the *Manchester Guardian*, were dangerous opponents throughout the Greek crisis. Others, both in the Press and Parliament, were genuinely concerned but gradually willing to learn and accept the facts. Yet from the very beginning, two men never hesitated. From 3 December, Churchill took direct control of the situation and from the first anxious days till the end of the rebellion gave full support, first to Scobie and Leeper, and then to Alexander and myself. Equally, Ernest Bevin, both at this time and until the end of the rebellion, stood with rock-like loyalty against the wave of sentimentalist emotion which at one time seemed to threaten both the stability of the Government and the strength of Anglo-American friendship.

During these first days I was in London on my Italian mission. I saw Eden and Churchill from time to time and read all the telegrams as they came in from Athens. On 5 December, Churchill announced these

[2] Ibid., p. 207.
[3] Sir Reginald Leeper, *When Greek Meets Greek* (London, 1950), p. 101.

sad events in Parliament and was roughly handled, especially by Aneurin Bevan and others from the Left. Nor were there critics lacking in other parts of the House.

Stettinius, the American Secretary of State, issued a statement on the very day that British troops were brought into action, severely criticising British policy. The principle of 'allowing liberated countries to work out their problems of government without influence from out-side' was perhaps sound; but it was in practice inapplicable to the actual military and political conditions in Athens. In Greece, as elsewhere, the resistance movements had been presented by our propaganda as bodies of romantic idealists fighting with Byronic devotion for the freedom of their country. In fact, with all their genuine patriotism, they had become the instrument of Communist ambitions. If an important section of the British Press accepted the popular view, it was not altogether a matter of surprise that Stettinius fell for the sensational accounts that had come from many of the American correspondents. The result was certainly unfortunate; for British troops had to fight the campaign of liberation without American help and, indeed, subjected to the exaggerated and sometimes offensive demonstrations of American neutrality. We could not then know that the Americans would soon learn their lesson, and three years later would carry the burden of repelling another and equally dangerous Communist assault upon the liberties of the Greek people.

On 8 December, a full debate took place in the House of Commons, about not only recent events in Greece, but also in Holland, Belgium and Italy. It thus covered the whole field of so-called 'interventions in liberated countries', which were an inevitable part of the concluding stages of the war.

I went to the House of Commons and heard Winston. His speech was a superb parliamentary performance and its courage magnificent. . . . Anthony's brilliant 'wind-up' was complementary to the P.M.'s introduction and filled in many points of detail—especially about Greece. The framers of the amendment made a great tactical error in making it so wide. If they had narrowed it to Greece, the P.M. would not have been able to develop the general argument, and here Belgium, Holland . . . , etc., were of great assistance to him in expounding his theme. The British Press is bad so far, the American worse.[4]

4 8 December 1944.

There were some noble Churchillian passages. He repelled with indignation the new fashion of equating democracy with mob law. There was one splendid phrase of more than ephemeral value: 'Democracy is no harlot to be picked up in the street by a man with a tommy gun.'[5]

Although the victory in the House was overwhelming—only thirty Members, and those of no great weight, voted against the Government—I was conscious that there was genuine anxiety in many quarters. Later, the true facts came to be known. The horrible atrocities of which the Communists were guilty were demonstrated to visiting trade union representatives. Above all, the British soldier, not only the best ambassador but the best political critic in the world, was able to judge the true character of the ELAS revolution. Then the voice of criticism began to be hushed. But while the argument lasted, it was sharp and distasteful. In a sense, much of the Press, in their refusal to face facts, reminded me of the pre-war days. Then criticisms of Hitler and Fascists were in many quarters thought bad form. Now it was apparently ill-mannered to show any lack of confidence in Communists.

Nevertheless, the origin of the Greek Revolution of December 1944 is still obscure. There had been a series of arrangements, culminating in the Caserta Agreement, by which all the guerrilla forces were to be put under British command. Even up to the very last moment it seemed as if the vital question of their demobilisation would be agreed in the form proposed by the EAM members themselves. The agreement made at Moscow as to the allocation of interest in various Balkan countries seemed to hold fast. Why, then, was there this sudden change? What happened at the end of November 1944 to induce the Communist leadership in Greece to plunge the country into civil war? Historians are not yet agreed. Some believe that a decision was taken at a purely local level, without reference to the Communist hierarchy. Others maintain, and indeed can adduce some supporting evidence, that it was decided upon by the highest Soviet authority.[6] Perhaps the simplest explanation is right. In spite of Churchill's direct orders to Scobie, which were shown by Papandreou

[5] *Hansard*, 8 December 1944.

[6] F. A. Voigt, *The Greek Sedition* (London, 1949), pp. 210–12 and 254, reprints a letter, purportedly from the Communist General Markos, which refers to 'Comrade Stalin's historic message of December 1944, which induced us to launch the popular uprising.'

to his Communist colleagues, and in spite of the clear interest of the British Government in regulating Greek affairs on normal lines, the Communist leaders may at the last moment have been moved to take advantage of two favourable situations: first, the weakness of General Scobie's forces and military dispositions; second, the growing fissure between the British and American Governments on the handling of liberated nations. Thus Stalin may not have stimulated or even approved the revolution. Indeed, he may have been disturbed by its developments. The Moscow Press certainly did not join in the denunciations of Churchill that were common in Britain and America. Not one word of reproach came from *Pravda* or *Izvestia*.[7] Stalin may have decided to let the affair take its own course, at any rate in the initial stages. If the British Government, alarmed at the coldness of its American allies, or intimidated by its critics at home, had decided to let the matter slide and allow revolution or civil war to develop in Greece without any British intervention, then there would have been no loss so far as the conduct of the war against Hitler was concerned. Under any other leadership but that of Churchill this might well have happened. But the old bulldog had got a firm hold of events, and nothing could make him release his grip. Even the diversion of large forces from Alexander's already attenuated armies did not deter him. So, largely by the steadiness of Churchill, supported by Bevin, whose spirited defence of the Government's policies to the T.U.C. was of decisive effect, Greece, which first gave liberty to the world, was not destined, as were so many other countries in Central and Eastern Europe, to be sucked into the maelstrom of totalitarian enslavement.

On the evening of the debate Churchill sent for me. I found him alone in the 'Annexe', very exhausted and in rather a petulant mood. After some general talk, he made a sudden attack on me for 'deserting my post'. He almost hinted that my absence from Rome and Athens was really 'poltroonery'. I told him firmly that I had come to England on his orders; that I was now President of the Allied Commission in Italy; that I had received a few hours earlier the approval of the meeting of Ministers for my Italian proposals. Finally, I reminded him that he had already sent a message to the President, telling him that I would be in Washington in a day or two to discuss all these questions and, in addition, the supply problems of the Mediterranean and of liberated Europe.

[7] Churchill, *Triumph and Tragedy*, p. 255.

He admitted all this, but still said that he felt instinctively that I should go back and help Alexander. I said that nothing would give me greater pleasure and I would set out immediately. He must clear things with the President and send some other Minister to Washington.

He rambled on in rather a sad and depressed way. The debate had obviously tired him very much and I think he realised the dangers inherent in the Greek policy on which we are now embarked. He has won the debate but not the Battle of Athens.[8]

The next morning I received a note from him, written after I had left him, in which he said:

This morning the Foreign Secretary informed me that he thought you ought to go east and, as you gathered last night, that also is my view. I am sure it is important that you should be with Alexander and available to advise on the political questions which are so plentiful now both in Rome and in Athens. This seems to me to be a field of action incomparably superior to what was mapped out for you in Washington. I am sure you will not fail to grasp the opportunity presented, remembering always that our maxim is 'no peace without Victory'.

Meanwhile, John Wyndham rang up very early to say that Field-Marshal Alexander's plane had been delayed. I could therefore go back with him the next day if it was so agreed. I spent an extraordinary morning in the Private Secretary's room in the Foreign Office, with a great deal of cross-telephoning between Eden, Churchill and myself, Eden being in the country and Churchill still in London. The Prime Minister had changed his mind and now thought that I should go to Washington. But Eden believed that it would be better for me to go to Athens. 'Then I said I wanted to go to Athens but still more wanted some orders.'[9] In the afternoon I got a firm decision. It was for Athens and Alexander. Naturally I was delighted.

The supply problem in Washington is certainly insoluble. The political problem in Athens is probably insoluble also. But the second is human and exciting, and in a field where I feel what talents I have will be more useful.[10]

Anticipating this decision, I had arranged a meeting for 3 o'clock between Foreign Office and War Office officials so that all the necessary arrangements could be made to carry on my Italian and supply plans.

[8] 8 December 1944.
[9] 9 December 1944.
[10] Ibid.

All the telegrams were finished and sent off by 7 o'clock. Richard Law undertook my task. Roger Makins was now in Washington, and with his help and that of Lord Halifax all the matters on which I had been working were eventually settled.

Alexander and I left at 6 o'clock the next morning with our small staffs and arrived at Caserta in the early afternoon. Wilson, now a field-marshal, had not yet left for Washington, and we were able to discuss all the latest news from Greece with him and General Gammell. We left Italy at 9.30 the following morning, 11 December. Our party consisted of Alexander, Brigadier Mainwaring (his B.G.S.), Rupert Clarke (his A.D.C.), John Wyndham and myself.

We arrived at Kalamaki aerodrome about 1.30. . . . After about an hour's delay, owing to the road between the airfield and the centre of the town being under shell fire from the insurgents. we left for General Scobie's H.Q. Alex. was in one tank, I in another. (The room provided for a middle-aged politician is not great.) It was quite an interesting progress and I could see through the periscope what was going on. Actually, things were fairly quiet, and there seemed not more than a certain amount of sniping.[11]

When we reached Headquarters, General Scobie explained the situation. I watched with interest how quickly the Field-Marshal made himself aware of the rather disagreeable facts. Actually, the position could hardly have been worse. We had been taken by surprise, hoping up to the last that things would be settled, and we had underestimated the military skill, determination and power of the insurgents.

At present, the British forces (and the Embassy) are besieged and beleaguered in the small central area of Athens. We hold about 5–10 out of 50 square miles of built-up area (Athens and Piraeus). The airfield at Tatoi is lost, and nearly 800 Air Force H.Q. and ground staff cut off in that suburb. Our airfield at Kalamaki is very insecure and the communications between it and the main body in Athens all under fire. We do *not* hold a port at all. We have lost the Piraeus, Port Heracles, etc. We are defending on the beaches at Phaleron Bay, but we have no real communication between the airfield and the beaches or between Athens and the beaches. In other words, we have no secure base anywhere from which to operate.[12]

From the General's headquarters we went to the Embassy where we were received by Leeper. The Ambassador asked about the military situation, to which the Field-Marshal replied in these words:

[11] 11 December 1944.
[12] Ibid.

You are in a grave situation. Your seaport is cut off, your airport can only be reached by tank or armoured car, you are outnumbered, your dumps are surrounded and you have three days' ammunition. I can put that right in time, but it may take a fortnight. It will need two fighting divisions to come from Italy. The heavy stuff will have to be landed on the open beaches of Phaleron and December is not the best month for that.[13]

We then discussed the political situation, and Leeper had no difficulty in persuading us that the King should be asked to agree to the Archbishop being appointed Regent. The reasons for this were simple but convincing. Although ELAS commanded a large support from the guerrilla or 'patriot' forces, our information led us to the conclusion that many of those who were enrolled among the rebels were not really Communists in the true sense of the word. They were definitely afraid that the King's Government would be Right-wing and reactionary. They feared that too much latitude would be given to the collaborators. They had been persuaded by their leaders that the original plan for demobilisation, although accepted by the Communist command, was unfair. But above all, they connected the King with the Metaxas dictatorship and they genuinely believed that the King's return would be the signal for widespread action against the popular forces. Moreover, although the old Liberal and Venizelist politicians were violently anti-Communist, indeed almost more so than the Conservatives, they had a long tradition of opposition to the Crown. Thus, what might be called the moderate and bourgeois elements in the country were divided over a largely obsolete argument, while the nation was faced with a Communist revolution which, if once successful, would never be reversed. The regency would in our view bring these forces together in the only practicable way. The monarchists would be satisfied by the preservation of the régime; the republicans would be encouraged by the absence of the King.

Alexander and I then adopted a procedure which we followed on many subsequent occasions; we dispatched a joint telegram to the Prime Minister. This method was not very welcome either to the Foreign Office or to the Chiefs of Staff. But it had the great advantage from our point of view that all our recommendations from now on were joint, and that no wedge inserted in London could divide us in the field of operations. The first part of the telegram set out the military position in its stark reality, and the orders which the Field-

[13] Leeper, pp. 114–15.

Marshal was giving for reinforcements. He did not disguise the difficulties and dangers; the besieged forces might well be starved out before help could arrive. Everything would depend on the weather and the possibility of landing craft being able to use the beaches in Phaleron Bay until the Piraeus could be cleared and held. On the political side, we recommended immediate action for the appointment of the Archbishop as Regent. Only he could take the necessary steps to appoint, if he thought fit, a successor to Papandreou. He was one of the few notabilities who had remained in Athens throughout the German occupation, and held a high reputation for his stern resistance to their demands. He alone could as Regent initiate negotiations with the rebels when the time was ripe. Thus 'we might get the effect of conciliation without ourselves being the promoters of it'. This was the best answer to the accusation of violent intervention. The Field-Marshal followed this up with a personal telegram to the Prime Minister, asking permission for himself and me to see the Archbishop, in order to leave him in no doubt about our political and military intentions. But it was no use doing so until we could get the regency question settled. How soon could we get the King to act?

The next day brought an offer from Porphyrogenis, one of the representatives of the insurgents, to General Scobie. Alexander and I, with Leeper's help, settled the terms of the reply.

[They] are very moderate and reasonable (and correspond to our weak military position!). We ask them to withdraw from Attica (so far as the regular irregulars are concerned). Those in Athens to lay down their arms— and then steps for a settlement.[14]

The Prime Minister's answer reached us late in the afternoon and gave us some encouragement. All the military measures were agreed; but as regards the regency the King was obdurate. He proposed the appointment of the Archbishop as Prime Minister, which would not, of course, do at all. We therefore sent off a strong reply, urging the Government at home to bring more pressure upon the King.

Alexander now returned to Caserta, and at his request and with Leeper's full approval I remained in the Embassy. My position had of course a certain delicacy, but I did my best to reduce any danger of divided authority. I was happy to read many years later the Ambassador's generous account of our co-operation.[15]

[14] 12 December 1944.
[15] Leeper, p. 115.

Life in the Embassy was indeed strange. There were about fifty people, including servants and guards, sleeping and living in the house. Except for a little exercise in a small part of the garden, which had a wall round it, no one was allowed out at all except on duty. Even to get to this garden you had to risk a sniper's bullet. All the front rooms were evacuated and the beds put in the passages. The dormitories of secretaries and typists were admirably arranged by Mrs. Leeper, who presided with grace and dignity over the many weeks of the siege.

Mrs. Leeper is a really splendid woman. She keeps all the Embassy staff, male and female, in a good temper, and with the slender resources available, she and the cook produce really remarkable results.

The rebels are about 200–300 yards away and hold all the territory immediately over the Ilissus river. To go from the Embassy to H.Q., one should go in an armoured car or tank, or else drive as fast as possible in a 'thin-skinned' car through some back streets.

All meals are in common—in the hall or lounge of the house. 24–26 sit down. Rations are Army rations on rather a reduced scale.

There is no heat (for there is no electric power to drive the oil-heating apparatus). There is no water (for the rebels have drained Hadrian's reservoir, on which we depended). There is no light (for the rebels have the power station).

We have fortunately filled all the baths; we have a lily pond in the garden; and today we have found a disused well, which will probably give us at least water fit for cooking and some washing.[16]

On this day, 13 December, there was a great addition to our staff— Osbert Lancaster arrived as Press Attaché, a tower of strength, common sense and fun.

Until reinforcements arrived, the few troops at General Scobie's command could only carry out tactical defensive movements. There was a good deal of sniping and shelling. In the Ambassador's study the bullets came through the window, but there was a corner in which one could sit without undue risk. We expected an attack from a large formation in the Stadium area, but this was broken up by the Air Force. Mount Lycabettus, the hill behind the Embassy, was held by our troops, but the lower slopes, curiously enough, were very difficult, partly because many of the insurgents were in civilian clothes. We had very little heavy artillery—a few 25-pounders and some tanks. Nor did

[16] 13 December 1944.

we wish to be responsible for the destruction of a great part of the city.

A very heavy attack was made on us last night. The rebels rushed the H.Q. of one of our armoured brigades and got in. The fighting is still going on there now. It is about 300 yards from the Embassy.[17]

On 14 December, Papandreou came to see the Ambassador and me. We strongly urged him to allow us to telegraph to the King, recommending the regency, and we felt we had convinced him. But there were some hesitations, for naturally he and his Government were afraid the Archbishop would make drastic alterations. The same morning, the Archbishop came to see us. It was my first meeting with him. Since, unlike most Greeks, he spoke neither French nor English, we had to rely on interpreters.

I was impressed by the wide grasp of European politics, the good sense, humour, and courage of this ecclesiastic. He is willing to accept the regency, but realises the difficulties. He shares our view that there must be no reprisals and no counter-revolution.[18]

Later in the evening I went to see Papandreou at his office, which was in the defended area. I had hoped to obtain a copy of a telegram to the King, recommending the appointment of the Archbishop, but I was disappointed.

He had executed an absolute *volte-face*. He said that *all* the leaders of the parties were against a regency. That it would be regarded as a sign of weakness; that Communism must be absolutely crushed, etc. He produced two colleagues (Populists or royalists) who took the same line. I returned very discouraged.

The day's fighting had not gone well. The rebels were eventually thrown out of the armoured brigade headquarters, but they took a hundred prisoners, which was very bad.

We expect another heavy attack tonight. The rebels are forming up both behind our house (on Lycabettus) and in front (in the area across the Ilissus). In the latter area, the R.A.F. are trying to disperse them with machine-gun fire.[19]

London bombarded us with telegrams, among them one informing us that Papandreou had advised the King against the regency, or so

[17] Ibid.
[18] 14 December 1944.
[19] Ibid.

the King had stated. The Field-Marshal telegraphed us on 15 December to say that he was appointing General Hawksworth, the commander of X Corps in Italy, to take charge of the operations in Athens and the Piraeus. This would free Scobie for the general problems and give us a first-class and experienced field commander. We had talked over this plan before Alexander left, and I was glad to see how quickly it had been implemented.

The news from home was still disturbing. Although our arrival in Athens had been well received and hopes were widely expressed that Alexander and I would be able to negotiate a settlement, there was still no real understanding of the difficulties and dangers with which we were faced. Churchill's somewhat truculent speech had won admiration from some of his American friends, such as Harry Hopkins. But Hopkins no longer had the same position with Roosevelt as in the past, and the State Department continued to be obstructive. The American Press was also highly critical and eagerly absorbed the superficial picture presented by the correspondents who were shut up with the Greek Government in the Hotel Grande-Bretagne. Nor was the military prospect encouraging. We could only hope to complete a rescue operation by clearing Athens and Attica and perhaps in due course parts of the Peloponnese. We could not embark upon a military campaign in central and northern Greece. In Salonika there was an uneasy truce between the rebels and the legitimate Government which owed much to the skill of the British representative on the spot. Since the winter had halted the Italian campaign, it was possible for Alexander to withdraw two or even, if necessary, three divisions to clean up the situation in Greece. But they would soon be wanted for the spring offensive in Italy. It was therefore greatly to our interest, after having first proved our power, to negotiate a settlement if this could include a general handing-in of arms and if possible a return of prisoners. But although we could hardly hope to reach a complete pacification, even partial measures would help to calm the country as a whole. We needed therefore no exhortations from the British and American commentators. It was in the Field-Marshal's interest, with his wider commitments, to conclude the operations in Greece with the greatest possible speed.

Meanwhile, we anxiously awaited our fate. Whether we should suffer that of Gordon in Khartoum, or whether reinforcements could be landed in time across the beaches of Phaleron Bay, would depend on the chance of a few weeks of fine weather and calm seas.

The next days were chiefly employed in trying to persuade all the Greek politicians to recommend the regency to the King. On 15 December, Scobie, Leeper and I called on Papandreou and urged him strongly to adopt this course.

We gave three grounds—

First. That Greece must have a 'Head of State' at this crisis. They had at present neither the advantage of a monarchy nor of a republic. We all knew the King could not come to Greece. And there was not a President. Therefore we argued for a regency in principle. Again, when a truce had been arranged or the rebels in the immediate vicinity of Athens captured or driven back, there would have to be negotiations for a peace settlement. These ought to be conducted under the presidency or chairmanship of a Greek, not a British Minister or general.

Secondly. The Archiepiscopal appointment would do much to satisfy American opinion.

Thirdly. It would help the position of H.M.G. Mr. Churchill had carried the day by his prestige. But there was great and growing criticism at home and this move would help H.M.G. enormously.[20]

Papandreou, apparently moved by our arguments, was now in favour of a regency, but one of three persons. He suggested the Archbishop General Plastiras (now returned to Athens from exile) and M. Dragumis, a much respected friend of the King. He believed this solution would have the support of Sophoulis. Leeper and I then saw Sophoulis, the old respected liberal leader, the heir of the Venizelist tradition. He had been against a regency, but he and his friends would now accept it. He preferred one regent—the Archbishop. All this was duly reported by us to London. Late in the evening we received Papandreou's message and also one from Sophoulis, to be sent to the King by our channels. Papandreou was still for three regents; Sophoulis for one. Plastiras next called to see us.

He has been in exile for about twelve years. He is a keen republican. He was a dictator, but resigned voluntarily (this makes him a 'good' dictator) and held elections, after which he left Greece. He was very much against the rebels, but otherwise did not disclose his hand.[21]

But the day was destined to end with the usual confusion.

[20] 15 December 1944.
[21] Ibid.

After dinner an emissary came from the Archbishop to say that everything had now been agreed between himself, Papandreou and Sophoulis. Papandreou and Sophoulis would recommend to the King one Regent (the Archbishop), Plastiras would become Prime Minister, Papandreou and Sophoulis joint deputy Prime Ministers.

About midnight came the emissary again. M. Sophoulis has now ratted on this arrangement. The Archiepiscopal emissary said 'C'est dégoûtant'!

Early the next morning, 16 December, Kanellopoulos called to see me. He had now become Minister of Finance in the beleaguered Government, in the place of Svolos who was representative of EAM. He was for the Archbishop as sole regent.

10.30. Went to H.Q. Got through without a bullet. Saw Scobie and told him the present situation. The military situation should begin to improve, as Hawksworth and the 4th Division are arriving.[22]

At noon I called on the Archbishop, taking with me David Balfour of the Embassy, an admirable interpreter.

A very good interview. My opinion of His Beatitude is confirmed each time I see him. About the rebels, he wishes to be quite firm; but he wants no counter-revolution. I said that there was a proper distinction between the condonation of sin and its forgiveness. This pleased him.[23]

The rebels replied the same day to Scobie's final offer to terms. Although they accepted one of his conditions, they refused the other. They continued to demand the demobilisation of the Rimini Brigade. After considerable discussion a reply was agreed. The flow of visits to and from the politicians continued and Leeper handled them with patience and skill. We continued to hope for the best.

On Sunday 17 December, fresh telegrams began to pour in from London.

The politicians . . . have told the King that they are opposed to the regency from the Greek point of view. But they feel they must accept it if it is true, as Macmillan and Leeper (especially Macmillan) tell them, that H.M.G. and Churchill will fall unless it is agreed. They have totally misrepresented my arguments; even the one which I used about public opinion at home, they have exaggerated out of all knowledge. Thus they have enabled the King to say to the P.M. and Anthony that his Greek advisers are against the regency and to make trouble between me and London. . . . Winston and Anthony

[22] 16 December 1944.
[23] Ibid.

. . . are naturally slightly puzzled. Anyway, on present form the King holds out. I have, of course, immediately telegraphed [my account] to London Later in the day, a very nice telegram came personally from Winston to me.[24]

Before lunch the Archbishop came to the Embassy at his own request. He told us that the politicians were now trying to impose a kind of political declaration upon him.

The object of this was (a) to make the Archbishop give a testimonial of the most fulsome kind in favour of the Government, (b) to tie the Archbishop's hand as to a future settlement. For instance, it made him say that no EAM supporter (whether he had taken part in the rebellion or not) should ever be employed either in the Army or civil service! His Beatitude wished to have our advice. I told him that the Government seemed to regard him not merely as a prelate of the Church, but as St. Peter himself. He replied, 'No it is not Heaven that they want, it is the earth.' Finally, we strongly advised him to insist on writing his own declaration in his own way.[25]

In the late afternoon Major Mathews, who was serving as interpreter and liaison officer with the Archbishop, came to say that the whole idea of a declaration had now been abandoned. The Greek Ministers would not accept the statement in its new form. This was the first sign to me of an attitude natural enough among the Greek politicians, but dangerous so far as our immediate needs were concerned. Encouraged by Churchill's determined attitude and the arrival of reinforcements, they began to hope that we should not only be able to rescue the Government in Athens and its vicinity, but achieve a complete victory over the Communists throughout the whole length and breadth of Greece. This explained their continued hesitations about firm advice to the King concerning the regency. It was not merely that they feared for their own appointments, but many of them were genuinely concerned about the moderate and central position which the Archbishop was determined to maintain. I thought that this mood had to be dealt with firmly. After hearing this report I went to see General Scobie, for whom the Greek Government had a deep respect.

I asked him (and he agreed) to go to Papandreou and tell him quite plainly that we were *not* (repeat *not*) prepared to become the tool of a Right-wing reaction throughout Greece. We wished a settlement of conciliation and

[24] 17 December 1944.
[25] Ibid.

we would not allow ourselves to be dragged into a long war from one end of Greece to the other to exterminate the Communist Party.[26]

During the next two days arguments continued about the telegram to the King, and as the siege still continued, the tempers of all those in the Embassy began to get a little frayed. The officials were not allowed out, and this told especially on the girls. I made a point of walking to Military Headquarters once or twice a day to gain a little relief. On the 18th, John Wyndham, whom I had sent to Caserta a few days before, returned with thirty-six eggs and twelve bottles of whisky! This certainly helped to brighten us, as spam and biscuits began to pall.

Meanwhile Alexander from his headquarters in Caserta was supporting us loyally in demanding a political, as well as a military, solution. On 15 December he told the Prime Minister that the best chance was through the Archbishop. If we could not get this he feared that he would have to send further large reinforcements from the Italian front in order to make sure of clearing the whole of the Piraeus and Athens. Churchill did not altogether like this and was still hesitating to bring pressure upon the King, especially in view of the ambivalent attitudes of the Ministers. We could only wait.

There is no heating in the house and the cold is very tiresome—so are the draughts. I sit mostly in the Chancery (half-basement) where John also sleeps. A bullet came through the window a day or two ago. We call this room 'Pratt's Club', and now that we have gin and whisky, there is a little party there every evening before dinner, with some of the girls, which helps to cheer things up.[27]

There was also an alluring but pernicious drink known as 'ouzo'.

On 19 December, after visiting Army Headquarters, I learned that

the position militarily is improving, except for the Air Force H.Q. at Kephyssia, who have been surrounded and cut off for over a fortnight and may have to surrender—to the tune of some 700—which will be very unfortunate. A tank rescue party is trying to get through to them, but it will not be easy.[28]

In the evening I had a long talk with the Greek Prime Minister and found him, as usual, agreeable and forthcoming, but I felt that he was

[26] Ibid.
[27] 18 December 1944.
[28] 19 December 1944.

in a mood, from our point of view at least, of dangerous optimism. He would not hear of compromise or conciliation, and talked of nothing but a complete victory over the Communists.

He may be right from his point of view and perhaps from the long-term view of Europe. But I don't think he has any idea of our military difficulties or of the dangers on his northern frontier. We do not wish to start the Third World War against Russia until we have finished the Second World War against Germany—and certainly not to please M. Papandreou.

An angry telegram had reached me that evening from Churchill.

He is annoyed with me for having pressed the regency with arguments about the political position at home and Anglo-American relations instead of confining myself to purely Greek considerations.[29]

The Greek Ministers had naturally exaggerated my argument of the political needs of the British Government in order to protect themselves. Churchill complained that I had taken his name in vain and that this was wrong even in a good cause. However, I felt he would soon forgive me, as indeed he did.

As the British military pressure in Greece increased, vague communications kept coming across the line, through Porphyrogenis and others. Scobie maintained his terms, which were after all very modest: the rebels must retire from Attica and lay down their arms in Athens and Piraeus. Then negotiations could start for a general reconciliation. These conditions, if accepted, would have left them a formed army in the north of Greece and a definite frontier line. They not only failed to accept these favourable conditions while they were still available, but tried to add many more of their own, all of which would have been impossible for us to accept.

After talking matters over with Leeper on the evening of the 19th, I decided to go to Caserta the next day. I felt that I must see Alexander and discuss the whole position with him. I therefore left early on the 20th, taking with me Harold Caccia and Edward Warner, one of Leeper's staff. After luncheon with Alexander at the hunting lodge in Caserta Palace, there was a full conference. In addition to the Field-Marshal, there were present Air Marshal Slessor, General Harding and General Theron (representing Field-Marshal Smuts). I had Harold Caccia with me.

[29] Ibid.

It was finally decided:

(a) That General Harding shall draft a telegram setting out the military situation for Alex. to send to Winston. That the telegram should be ready for
me to see tomorrow morning before leaving for Greece.

(b) General Theron would telegraph to Smuts setting out the military situation
broadly and the political in greater detail and strongly urging Smuts to advise the King of Greece *in favour* of the regency. (Smuts has been appealed to by the King of Greece, who has telegraphed to him saying that
Winston is putting great pressure on him to appoint the regent. I was glad
to hear this!) Smuts has a great influence with the King. . . .

(c) I should continue to press the regency on H.M.G. and on all Greek politicians whom I could influence locally.

We would have an early meeting in Athens, when present military operations
had progressed a bit further.[30]

There was much Italian work to be got through, and I feared that
my plans, on which I had lavished so much effort, were now going
forward in only a rather desultory way. But it was impossible for me to
do much more than send off some encouraging telegrams to Washington. It was agreeable, if perhaps rather unfair, to enjoy a comfortable
dinner that night in my home in Naples, with all the prior luxury of a
hot bath.

Early the next morning, after we had gone through the text together, Alexander's personal telegram to Churchill was duly dispatched.

It will do a lot of good, and should put the situation in a more realistic
perspective. Poor Winston! What with Greece, Poland, and the German
breakthrough on the Western Front, this is going to be a grim Christmas.[31]

This message certainly made a great impression upon the Prime
Minister. It ran as follows:

In answer to your signal of 19 December, I am most concerned that you
should know exactly what true situation is and what we can do and cannot
do. This is my duty. You would know the strength of British forces in Greece,
and what additions I can send from Italian front if forced by circumstances to
do so.

Assuming that ELAS continue to fight, I estimate that it will be possible to
clear the Athens–Piraeus area and therefore to hold it securely, but this will
not defeat ELAS and force them to surrender. We are not strong enough to

[30] 20 December 1944.
[31] 21 December 1944.

go beyond this and undertake operations on the Greek mainland. During the German occupation they maintained between six and seven divisions on the mainland, in addition to the equivalent of four in the Greek islands. Even so they were unable to keep their communications open all the time, and I doubt if we will meet less strength and determination than they encountered.

The German intentions on the Italian front require careful watching. Recent events in the West and the disappearance and silence of the 16th S.S. Division opposite Fifth U.S. Army indicates some surprise move which we must guard against. I mention these factors to make the military situation clear to you, and to emphasise that it is my opinion that the Greek problem cannot be solved by military measures. The answer must be found in the political field.

Finally, I think you know that you can always rely on me to do everything in my power to carry out your wishes, but I earnestly hope that you will be able to find a political solution to the Greek problem, as I am convinced that further military action after we have cleared the Athens–Piraeus area is beyond our present strength.[32]

At the same time I thought it wise to send a personal letter to Eden which I did by the hand of an officer returning that day.

I am afraid you and Winston may have thought that we were getting a little rattled at Athens, but that is not the case. It is true that we have been through a very peculiar experience and have narrowly escaped a first-class disaster. Since the dispositions originally made were suitable to a jamboree and not to a battle, we only just avoided a large-scale massacre of soldiers and diplomats.

We have, however, now moved into a new phase. We are gradually obtaining a military ascendancy in Athens and the Piraeus, but even this will be in my view a little longer and more difficult than some people seem to think. . . .

Both Alex. and I agree that there is no (repeat no) military solution of the Greek problem. It can only be solved by a political agreement. That is why we have battled so long and by so many means for the Archiepiscopal regency. I know the Prime Minister thought that I was over-anxious for this, but I assure you that Rex Leeper and I felt, and still feel, that it was the only way to get the thing loosened up at all. The King is obstinate and I gather now falls back on constitutional niceties. All I can say is, 'Constitution my foot'. He did not care two hoots about the Constitution when he made Metaxas dictator. As for the politicians . . . they beat anything I have yet seen in the Mediterranean. . . .

Anyway, if we cannot get the Regent, we shall have to think of some other method. . . . In the end we shall have to call the conference ourselves.

[32] Reproduced in Churchill, *Triumph and Tragedy*, p. 269.

. . . Moreover, I think it is very easy to jump to false conclusions about Greek opinion. I am not quite certain that there is so much opposition to EAM/ELAS as many suppose. It is always difficult to tell political opinion, even in one's own country. For instance, can you tell me whether the Conservatives or Labour will get in at the next election? I am certain that there is a large amount of sympathy with EAM in Greece, that a moderate, reasonable, progressive policy could detach the vague, radical element from the hard, Communist core. The policy [which some] would like to follow will have the result of solidifying, not liquefying, EAM/ELAS forces.

General Theron nobly carried out his undertaking and sent a strong message to Smuts in which he stated Alexander's unwillingness to weaken his Italian front any further and the need for a political solution once Athens and the Piraeus were cleared. He went on to urge that the King would gain whichever way things turned out. If the civil war continued, all the moderates would be alienated, and the people would turn eventually to the King for leadership. If, on the other hand, his action was successful he certainly would not fail to get full credit. A copy of this welcome telegram reached me on Christmas Eve.

On the 21st I returned to Athens to find that further messages were passing through intermediaries across the lines. We made it clear in reply that we could guarantee that there would be no reprisals, and a political amnesty for all who were not guilty of criminal acts, and we would in addition undertake to get a conference under way if the truce conditions were accepted.

The military situation is improving, but progress is necessarily slow. I [put forward] the idea that the Field-Marshal on arrival should reply by asking the ELAS Committee to come and see him. This seemed rather revolutionary to all at first sight (Leeper approves) and may still be a little premature. General Scobie was more receptive than I supposed likely.[33]

We were now looking forward to Alexander's arrival in Athens, but unfortunately a message arrived that the weather was too bad for flying. He was therefore to come by destroyer and hoped to arrive late on the night of the 24th—Christmas Eve. I still felt concerned at the attitude of some of the Greeks, who in their determination to eliminate the Communists, and forgetful of Britain's difficulties and commitments, would fight to the last British soldier to achieve this end.

[33] 23 December 1944.

Nevertheless, I recognised their fear that, without a final and crushing victory, there might be another round after the end of the war. And so it was to prove. Luckily for Greece, the Americans, who were now demonstrating their neutrality by driving about in cars and jeeps draped with the American flag, would take up the torch from our hands.

Christmas Eve was another day of waiting.

The sniper who shoots down our *street* is being active, but he seems to be letting us alone in the *garden*.[34]

In the late afternoon the Archbishop came. His visits were always welcome.

I am much impressed with his shrewdness and moderation. What his knowledge of theology may be, I do not know; but he has a very complete knowledge of politics and a much wider point of view than the Greek politicians whom I have hitherto met. We went through with him the text of his Christmas allocution. He tells the insurgents that they must lay down their arms; at the same time he indicates that there must be a peace of reconciliation, not a truce followed by reprisals.[35]

Just after dinner we got a mysterious telegram from the Prime Minister asking us to see a message which he had sent to Alexander. Unfortunately his destroyer had been still further delayed owing to the terrible weather, and he was not expected till Christmas Day. We were thus left perplexed and speculating.

11.30 p.m. We had a nice little service in the drawing-room of the beleaguered Embassy; nearly all the staff and the soldiers not on duty attended. Mrs. Leeper had made some sweet little Christmas trees—out of nothing—and Mr. Osbert Lancaster had cut out some silhouettes (St. Joseph, the Virgin, the Holy Child in the Manger, the Kings and Shepherds) which, with a light behind them, made a charming decoration.

We had some carols at appropriate points in the Communion Service, which was over about 12.15 a.m. Thus began Christmas Day 1944.

The guns are firing briskly—there is a night attack on a part of the town behind Lycabettus.[36]

One piece of news was brought to us by our Intelligence officers. The atrocities were growing worse, and our troops, some of whom had

[34] 24 December 1944.
[35] Ibid.
[36] 25 December 1944.

started rather doubtful about the rights and wrongs of the British Government's action, were now getting angry.

The letter censorship shows that this is almost universal—even among the Glasgow Communists who are said to be well represented in the Paratroop Brigade.

Alexander turned up at 11 a.m. after a trying journey. He revealed to us the clue to the mystery by producing the telegram, which ran as follows: 'Two friends of yours, of which I am one, are coming out to join you.' This of course could only mean the Prime Minister and the Foreign Secretary. Leeper and I discussed with Alexander our proposal to summon a conference 'generally representative of Greek political opinion', including ELAS delegates. The Archbishop would take the chair. Although we were convinced that this was the best plan, it was clear that we must now await the new arrivals.

In the afternoon of Christmas Day Alexander, Leeper and I went to the airfield. It was bitterly cold, with a biting wind from the mountains. We therefore persuaded the Prime Minister to stay in the plane for our talk.

I had expected rather a difficult time—but Winston was in a most mellow, not to say chastened, mood. After two hours (in which Alex. was most helpful and Anthony also) the whole strategic, tactical and political problems were reviewed and general agreement reached.[37]

We decided to proceed with our plan for a conference. A draft communiqué had already been prepared, and all that we had to do was to substitute Churchill as the convener of the conference, and to warn both the Archbishop and Papandreou. Churchill, Eden and their part went off in an armoured vehicle to the Piraeus (most of which we had by now recaptured) and from thence to the *Ajax*, to which Admiral Mansfield had now transferred his flag.

We managed to get both Papandreou and the Archbishop to the ship by about 7 p.m., of course in a 'hard' vehicle. Churchill decided to see Papandreou first, since he was the actual Prime Minister, and Leeper was present at this interview. Both were therefore spared the embarrassing scene in which the Archbishop, waiting on the deck, somehow got mixed up with the crew's fancy-dress festivities. Not unnaturally, he was mistaken for a comical figure and was himself somewhat surprised that one of His Majesty's ships seemed to have

[37] Ibid.

been momentarily taken over by a gang of men with blackened faces and playing various unusual instruments. However, it was all put right, and Churchill, who had been for several weeks teasing me about my admiration for this 'pestilent priest, a survival from the Middle Ages', seemed to like the Archbishop.

By 8 p.m. everything was decided. The conference would be called the next day at 4 p.m. It would be small but fully representative, and three or four delegates from ELAS would be invited. The Archbishop and the Greek Prime Minister withdrew, and the Ambassador went off also, to give the formal invitations and to see that General Scobie sent the necessary guarantee to the ELAS Central Committee that passes would be provided should they wish to attend. I was induced to stay on the *Ajax* for dinner and

was made to explain, argue, discuss *and* listen! It was exhausting but quite amusing . . . Eden was very friendly—he has evidently had a rough time. The King of the Hellenes has been very obstinate and Winston unwilling to press him unduly.[38]

The next day the Archbishop came to the Embassy in the morning and we went over the names of the delegates, the draft of his opening speech and the drill to be followed. We also arranged what to do in the event of ELAS accepting or refusing the invitation. There was an enormous amount of confabulation and argument as to who should attend. Sophoulis at first refused, partly because he did not wish to meet ELAS, partly because he did not agree on the limitation of numbers. The royalist branch of the Populist or Conservative Party would not accept Maximos as their leader but wanted separate representation. Papandreou, who began to see the possible developments, was not much attracted by the plan, but he also tried to get more of his friends invited.

Finally, the Ambassador sent *written* invitations to the selected delegates and we made it clear by various means that they must either accept without further argument or take the responsibility of publicly refusing Mr. Churchill's invitation.[39]

We had persuaded Churchill and Eden to stay on the *Ajax*, partly for security and partly for comfort, but they turned up at the Embassy after lunch. I was very concerned at the cold and feared that Churchill

[38] Ibid.
[39] 26 December 1944.

would get a dangerous chill. But we were able to borrow a few stoves from the Army during the Prime Minister's visit.

At 3.30 a message came [from ELAS] asking for an hour's delay; to this we agreed. The Greek politicians are gathered at the Grande-Bretagne; the ELAS delegates will be taken to H.Q.; we wait at the Embassy. The meeting is to be at the Greek Ministry of Foreign Affairs, but this is being kept as dark as possible on security grounds. We are already a little shaken by the discovery this morning of large quantities of dynamite under the Grande-Bretagne. The communiqué [about the conference] was duly published last night on the B.B.C. It should have a good effect [at home].[40]

We had arranged to bring the Greek politicians from the Grande-Bretagne to the place of meeting. The Archbishop came to the Embassy and we all started off in two armoured vehicles just before 5 p.m. Lincoln MacVeagh (the American Ambassador), Colonel Popov (the Soviet representative), and the French Minister were invited as observers, and all accepted. This we considered rather a *coup* for us.

Since there was no electric light, the conference room was lit by hurricane lamps on a large oval table. The Archbishop took his seat in the middle. On his right was Churchill in the uniform of an Air Commodore, and next to him Eden. On his left were Alexander, Leeper and I. The Greeks sat opposite. At one end of the table were the three observers and at the other end places were left for the ELAS representatives. It was very cold to start with, but it soon warmed up with the heat of the lamps and the people. The ELAS representatives had not appeared, nor had any message reached us, although their lines were near. The noise of guns, machine-guns and rifle fire could be heard as we waited. Finally, it was decided to start the conference without them, rather than admit complete failure. Accordingly, the Archbishop opened with a short speech of welcome to Churchill, very dignified and very well expressed. He then called upon him to speak.

The P.M. had been speaking for about five minutes, when there was a loud knock on the door. The ELAS delegates had arrived!

We all stood up. Three men in English battledress came in. They bowed and we bowed. We took our seats and the conference began again. The Archbishop repeated his speech. It was again translated. Then the P.M. began and spoke for about twenty to twenty-five minutes—of course it took longer with the interpreting. His speech was very good—clear, firm and persuasive.

[40] Ibid.

He left no doubt in the minds of the ELAS on the one hand of our military power. On the other hand, he made it clear to the politicians that he did not mean us to be used for a reactionary policy. He wanted peace, amnesty, and a continuation of the work of relief and economic rehabilitation.[41]

Churchill went on to state categorically that Stalin was supporting our intervention. He went a long way to suggest that Roosevelt had also agreed, as indeed he had in August.[42] If we could have published his telegram to Churchill at that time it would have had a great effect. But 'the President has let us down badly and Winston is very hurt about it'.[43] Eden then said a few words, useful, conciliatory and short. Alexander made a similar speech in excellent style and taste: 'Instead of . . . putting my brigades into Greece, I should like to see Greek brigades coming to help me in Italy in the war against our common enemy.'[44]

The Archbishop then asked for questions. After a pause, Maximos made a short speech and Papandreou followed. Then one of the ELAS representatives, Partsalides, rose.

He is the secretary of EAM—a professor, of extreme and fanatical Communist opinions. A nice-looking fellow, with a pleasant smile and beautiful white teeth, he spoke in a quiet and soothing voice as if butter would not melt in his mouth. The other two delegates are Siantos, a nasty rat-faced man, the secretary of the Communist Party, and General Mantakas—a big burly Cretan—nice-looking, rather English in appearance.[45]

Partsalides was courteous and smooth. He welcomed Churchill's actions, claimed to represent the mass of the Greek people and hoped for peace between Britain and Greece.

I thought it all very disingenuous, especially remembering the frightful atrocities these men are committing both on our troops and harmless fellow-countrymen throughout Greece. Winston was much moved, however.

Sophoulis then raised the question of representation, and Eden explained that we had merely convened on an unofficial basis a number of people as a start. We thought it better to keep the conference small, but they could of course settle this themselves and co-opt anybody they

41 Ibid.
42 Churchill, *Triumph and Tragedy,* pp. 99–100.
43 26 December 1944.
44 Ibid.
45 Ibid.

wished. Churchill then got up and thanked the delegates for what they had said.

The conference would now—having been initiated by us—pass entirely to Greek hands. 'We have begun the work. You must finish it!' We all then went out, the P.M. leading. We shook hands with all the delegates, including ELAS, as we went round the table to the door. The foreign observers came out with us. The P.M. went straight to the ship. It was about 6.30 when we left.[46]

As I walked back to the Embassy with Harold Caccia, the guns were firing in a battle near the Stadium, and rifles were cracking away.

I did not feel that the conference would produce an immediate result, but hoped that it would lay the foundations for something. The main thing was to get the regency, for the regency would lead to a change of Government and give general confidence throughout the country.

Alexander and I went to the ship for dinner for another long evening. There were a lot of telegrams from Montgomery about the battle in Belgium, and these and other subjects relieved the tension. But most of our talk was on the Greek affairs. 'Fortunately Winston has fallen for the Archbishop.' We got back to the Embassy about 2 a.m.

The Archbishop came to see us at 10 o'clock the following morning, 27 December, and reported on the proceedings after we left. They had apparently been pretty rowdy. They had gone on until 10 p.m. and then had adjourned until the next day.

Our own sources (listening outside!) had already given us this information. At one point General Plastiras was heard to shout at one of the Communists: 'Sit down, butcher!'[47]

Churchill arrived from the ship about 1.15 and we all lunched at the Embassy.

He was in good form and had been taken by Alex. to an 'observation post' from which he could see the whole city and get an idea of the fighting. Of course this affair is a sort of 'super Sidney Street' and he quite enjoyed having the whole problem explained to him by a master of the military art.

[46] Ibid.
[47] 27 December 1944.

After luncheon MacVeagh, the American Ambassador, came for an interview with Churchill at which I was not present, but from his appearance when he left it was clear that he had learned some home truths. There was then a Press conference, partly 'off' and partly 'on' the record, at which both Churchill and Eden were very impressive. After this the Archbishop came again and told us the situation. The conference had adjourned at 4 p.m. Meanwhile, the ELAS delegates asked to see Churchill privately, to which, on the Archbishop's strong recommendation, he replied by letter, courteously declining.

Winston was very inclined to see them, but I persuaded him (and Anthony agreed) that if we were going to put our money on the Archbishop, we must let him play the hand as he thought best. Winston partly wanted to see them as a good journalist, and partly because he has an innocence which is very charming, and sometimes dangerous. He believed he could win them over. But I felt he would much more probably be deceived and betrayed.[48]

When Churchill and the Archbishop met together that afternoon, we tried to induce them to use the basement or the back of the house which were safe. But Churchill was adamant. I can see them now: the Archbishop, with his great head-dress and robes, and Churchill in his uniform, reclining on the sofa, pushed back against the far wall of the Ambassador's study, which was believed to be out of the line of fire. Nevertheless, he delighted in the broken and patched windows and the marks of the bullets on the far wall.

Little progress was being made because the ELAS demands were intolerably high. Accordingly, the Archbishop had adjourned the meeting for the present. It was clear that until the question of the regency was decided, there could be no advance. Churchill, having seen things for himself, now agreed with our estimate of this problem. Leeper and I therefore saw Papandreou, and urged him to send a message to the King on behalf of the whole Government, to report the unanimity of the conference in favour of the establishment of the regency and to make a formal recommendation accordingly. After some discussion, Papandreou agreed. But it was not an easy task.

We got in touch with the Archbishop—of course to find that he had already issued a communiqué covering these three points—and a fourth, viz., that Papandreou had this morning tendered his resignation. There are certainly no flies on the Regent-elect!

[48] Ibid.

I returned to the ship about 11.30 p.m. to report.

Winston is more and more delighted with the Archbishop but is still worrying about his refusal to grant a private interview to the ELAS delegates.[49]

On the next day, we had arranged to leave the airfield at 1 p.m. to return to Naples. But Alexander, Leeper and I were summoned to the cruiser in the morning. We found Churchill still fussing about the ELAS delegates. He thought he would stay another day and summon a further meeting of the conference. He did not like the idea of going home without a peace or a truce obtained. I argued in favour of his immediate return to secure the regency. This would be a service to Greece which could only be performed in London. Finally, to clinch the matter, it was decided to issue a communiqué which would publicly commit the British Government to the regency. At last we got away, reaching Naples in the late afternoon.

So ended in a dramatic way the first phase of the Greek rebellion. The danger for Athens was ending. The next step would be a truce and then perhaps a peace. Towards all this, this indomitable old man, at grave personal risk to his health and even his life, had made an incomparable contribution. He was to return six weeks later to receive the greatest ovation that any foreigner has ever received in the ancient city of Athens.

[49] Ibid.

CHAPTER TWENTY-THREE

The Greek Rebellion
2. Peacemaking

I WAS now back in Rome, in the Villa Parisi, a house which John had obtained for me in the Via Nomentana outside the Porta Pia. The house was large, warm, with excellent bathrooms, but ugly beyond imagination, being built in a kind of pseudo-French style, with gilt and mirrors everywhere. But it served us very well. Here we spent the last day of the year 1944. It was just two years since I had started on this strange enterprise in the Mediterranean.

The news had reached us on 30 December that the King of the Hellenes had at last agreed to appoint the Archbishop as Regent. It was true that in order to induce the King to take this step Churchill and Eden had given him a number of assurances which he either misconstrued or exploited. Among these was the expectation that the Regent should keep closely in touch with the King 'and lend a willing ear to his directives'. It soon began to be clear that some mischief would ensue, especially with regard to the alleged undertaking that no EAM representatives would be included in any new Government.

But I felt that the regency was a real gain:

In the first place, it is a move; and when a political situation has got into a 'jam', the great thing is to bring about some kind of movement. I hope very much that the new Government which the Archbishop will appoint will be able to break into the EAM position and detach the more moderate from the more extreme elements . . . It is now up to us to steer the Archbishop.[1]

Although I had a great deal of work ahead of me in Italy, in the next stages it was necessary to make frequent journeys to Athens. We had to ensure that the Commander-in-Chief, the Ambassador and I

[1] 31 December 1944.

always took the same line, and if we had any differences, that we settled them amongst ourselves and did not disclose them to London. There were some awkward moments, but this major purpose was achieved.

After the appointment of the Regent, the first thing was to get a Government. As the result of a good deal of negotiation General Plastiras accepted the post of Prime Minister on 4 January. Plastiras had been at first unwilling; then, like all generals, had overestimated the needs of the new National Army and also the ability of the British to give it the equipment which he wanted. He began by demanding an Army of 200,000 to be wholly equipped by us. However, under the wise but effective pressure of the Regent, Plastiras abandoned this condition, and a new Government was formed on a comprehensive basis. Finance, an almost hopeless task, was in the hands of George Sideris, a Venizelist of considerable experience; Foreign Affairs, including the management of the Press, were entrusted to one of the ablest and subtlest of the personalities available—Ioannis Sophia-nopoulos.

ELAS were now beginning to press General Scobie to bring the fighting to an end, and their delegation under Zevgos even declared that they had accepted the General's terms. But, as usual, they raised many other points, such as the future of the Mountain Brigade and the gendarmerie, all of which Scobie very properly declared to be a matter for a Greek Government to decide. The Regent refused to meet the deputation but sent a message expressing his pleasure 'in their readiness to discuss the cessation of hostilities'. Meanwhile, Philip Broad rang up from Caserta with a message from Alexander, saying that Scobie and Leeper wanted to withdraw the truce terms and give ELAS an ultimatum.

I am against this. We should leave things as they are and let the situation develop a little. Broad rang me back later to say that the F.M. agreed with my view.[2]

Instructions were sent to Athens accordingly.

After some talk with Alexander, it seemed best for me to go to Greece. I reached the Embassy in the late afternoon of 4 January. I found the Ambassador looking rather worn but very pleased to see me.

[2] 2 January 1945.

Just as we were going to bed General Scobie rang up to express his concern over the deteriorating position in the Peloponnese, especially at Patras. Admiral Mansfield, who was lying off that port in the *Orion*, and Brigadier Hunt, the commander of the brigade there, sent discouraging reports. I finally agreed to send a message to Alexander. It was clear that we must either evacuate Patras, removing our troops and loyal partisans, or else reinforce it.

The next day the Field-Marshal arrived.

He was very understanding and seemed quite glad to have come at this stage. On Patras he had accepted my view, and ordered a brigade from Italy and an armoured regiment. But they can hardly arrive until the 11th and there will be an awkward interval.[3]

He also brought with him Brigadier Mainwaring, a most intelligent and experienced officer, to replace Scobie's present Chief of Staff. Mainwaring proved a paragon of skill and strength throughout the rest of the troubles. In addition, Alexander extended General Hawksworth's functions to cover not merely Athens but all operations in Greece, for we were beginning to be worried about Salonika.

On 6 January the morning was spent in preparing plans for the next phase, since the military position was improving rapidly. I was anxious that the Greek Government

should deal with *all* the questions which have been the subject of controversy (Mountain Brigade, Sacred Battalion, gendarmerie, police, purge of Quislings, amnesty, etc.) and thereby isolate the Communists altogether from the general body of EAM supporters.[4]

Although this must to some extent depend on the reorganisation of the Greek Army, it was a useful exercise. After luncheon, Alexander, Leeper and I went for a walk.

The whole atmosphere of Athens is changed to an unbelievable degree. *All* the population are walking and sunning themselves in areas in which it was dangerous even to be seen a few days ago. We walked down to the Stadium and through all the areas across the Ilissus, which was strongly held by the insurgents last week and from which they used to 'snipe' us in the Embassy.

The Field-Marshal was very generally recognised. The soldiers of course saluted and the civilians bowed—by taking off their hats or

[3] 5 January 1945.
[4] 6 January 1945.

waving to him. It was quite extraordinary to see the delight of the people in what had now come to be called 'the Second Liberation'.

I now began to feel that General Scobie's original truce terms were largely obsolete, and we would look very foolish if ELAS suddenly accepted them. They were only asked to withdraw from Athens to the borders of Attica and to lay down their arms in Athens. But they had now been driven from Athens and would soon be expelled from Attica. Moreover, there was still the question of prisoners and hostages. I therefore drafted a communiqué withdrawing the terms. I naturally consulted with Alexander and the Ambassador. Osbert Lancaster, as the Press expert, titivated it up with a view to the British and American Press, and General Scobie readily agreed. The next day we had a conference of the British Press at which I tried to explain our reasons for withdrawing the present truce conditions.

I hope they will not be too hostile. It is evident that most of them are ignorant of the true situation. Even if they send sensible reports home, most of the editors do not print them.[5]

The announcement made in Scobie's name stressed the changes in the situation since the original terms were offered. There was now a Regent and a new Government. There was no fear of a royalist *coup*. Although prisoners had been taken on both sides, ELAS had refused the Red Cross permission to visit their prison camps. There was also the question of civilian hostages, taken contrary to the rules of civilised warfare. The two conditions which General Scobie had hitherto offered for the truce must now be considered to be withdrawn. But he would always be ready to discuss terms.

We then began to consider what should be the proper terms of a truce to supersede the old ones if Scobie were asked. Rather half-hearted attempts by ELAS to get in touch with us were continually being made.

A man arrived on a tricycle at the American Embassy this afternoon, but his credentials seemed rather shadowy.[6]

So there was no time to be lost. We agreed that a new truce must demand

5 7 January 1945.
6 Ibid.

a line further forward, and will also require the disarming of ELAS forces east and south of this line—i.e. Boeotia, Attica and all the Peloponnese—also the Cyclades islands. This will allow us to strengthen our position in Salonika.

When we had got everything agreed, the Field-Marshal and I returned to Naples. The last stages of the battle for Athens and Attica were now about to be reached.

Churchill seemed rather annoyed that we had withdrawn General Scobie's truce terms without consultation with London. But the 'tricyclist' episode satisfied us that we were only just in time. After some discussion, Alexander and I decided not to answer Churchill's telegram, for we felt sure that things would soon begin to move. Indeed, by 10 January a number of rather excited messages were arriving, both from Leeper and Scobie. A properly constituted delegation from ELAS had now turned up with Zevgos and others. The General and the Ambassador asked for authority to present the truce terms which we had left with them. Since they telegraphed both to London and Caserta, things became rather confused. Moreover, although during the day they seemed quite happy with these terms, by midnight they wanted to step them up. They wished to do so

by putting back the line to include Lamia and Volos and also to include a withdrawal at Salonika. After talking it over, Alex. and I decided to accept Salonika but *not* the advance northwards . . . to Volos and Lamia, and telegraphed accordingly to London and Athens.[7]

Finally, early on 12 January, a message arrived that the truce had at last been signed. There was only one omission. Although prisoners of war were to be exchanged, the Communists absolutely refused to surrender the civilian hostages they had taken. Leeper and Scobie, after much thought, decided not to insist. ELAS were absolutely determined to break off the negotiations rather than to agree. In my view, our representatives reached the right decision, although it was a bitter blow. Certainly a continuation of the hostilities could have inflicted greater damage upon ELAS, but we would not have got back the civilian hostages. They would either have been murdered, as indeed thousands already had been, or taken further and further away and probably perished from hardship. The best hope was to conclude

[7] 10 January 1945.

the truce at once and put forward this question of the return of the hostages as one of the first items in the peace negotiations which would soon follow. Plastiras was angry and the Regent deeply hurt. In a public statement the Archbishop declared how profoundly shocked he had been to learn of the Communist refusal to release innocent men and women. But he did not recede from the agreed offer of conciliation. So the truce was reached at last.

The battle for Athens, which had raged for five weeks and had been fought by our soldiers, street by street, was now ended. Public opinion at home, which at first had been confused and easily misled, had begun gradually to realise the issues at stake. Nothing did more to confirm their growing dislike of the forces which had hitherto been regarded as patriots than this matter of the hostages. Between 15,000 and 20,000 unhappy people of all ages had been dragged miles from their homes and subjected to unspeakable brutalities. In addition, in the next few days the atrocities committed in Athens and the suburbs during the course of the ELAS occupation were revealed. In Peristeri alone, some 1,500 people had been murdered in cold blood. The T.U.C. delegation, which came out under Sir Walter Citrine, saw at least 250 bodies taken out of the trenches into which they had been flung, and laid out for identification. As they stated in their report, these people had been the victims of organised murder, executed at close quarters in an area in which no fighting was taking place. Many were shot with their hands tied behind their backs. This report from such a distinguished body of trade union leaders did much to inform and shock the British people.

At the time I recorded some general reflections:

11 January. On thinking over events in Greece, I . . . feel that—in addition . . . to the Communist plotters of KKE—the King of the Hellenes is the real villain of the piece. Far back at Cairo in the winter of 1943 he twisted and turned. Had he written a clear letter (and not an equivocal one) at that time, saying that he would not return until called by a vote of the people, this powerful weapon of anti-monarchical propaganda would not have been available to the extremists. It must be remembered that Greece has always been about evenly divided between monarchists and republicans. The King has been head of a party . . . not of the State. The Venizelist tradition is similarly republican—and pro-British.

But the tragic side of this division is that it disunites the bourgeois parties instead of letting them come together in opposition to Marxism and revolution. . . . The issue of the second half of the twentieth century will not be monarchism *v*. republicanism, but a liberal and democratic way of life versus the 'proletariat dictatorship of the Left' and the police State.

Again, if the King had given a frank pledge after the Lebanon Conference, Papandreou's position—instead of being obscure and open to misrepresentation—would have been solid. . . .

Even after Alex. and I got to Athens on 11 December, had the King immediately accepted our joint recommendation, instead of wasting three precious [weeks] in futile bargaining and intriguing . . ., I think the Archbishop might have stopped the fighting at that early stage. At least he would have, by his mere existence as Regent, prevented so large a rally of EAM/ELAS supporters to the extreme leadership of Siantos and the Communist Party.[8]

Even after the truce there was still a long way to go, but we had passed an important—indeed a vital—milestone in our journey.

General Scobie could not but regret that he had not been given another few weeks or even days to destroy the ELAS forces. He feared, and with reason, that they would lie low and make another effort. The truce was to take effect from 1 a.m. on 15 January, and in the last day or two some further advance was made. The Greek Government had made a formal request to General Scobie for the necessary military dispositions to restore law and order throughout Greece. But by now we were approaching the opening of the last phases of the campaign in Italy. It was therefore of vital importance to limit our efforts in Greece. Whatever military equipment we could give them, we would be willing to provide. Unhappily, we had no help even in this field from the Americans. But before anything else I felt it was now necessary to concentrate upon the peacemaking, and to turn the truce into something more precise and more lasting.

Accordingly, on 16 January, Alexander and I left again for Athens. There was a full discussion between Leeper, Caccia, Scobie, the Field-Marshal and myself. The Ambassador seemed rather pessimistic about the chances of getting the Greek Government to accept our programme. In accordance with our practice, Alexander drafted the military and I the political contribution to a joint telegram to Churchill. It was all done and dispatched in the early hours of 17 January.[9] Its main purpose was to urge immediate negotiations and to

---

[8] 11 January 1945.
[9] This telegram is reproduced as Appendix 2.

set out a broad and generous basis upon which peace might be restored. The release of the hostages and disarmament of all the Greek forces were the most important points for the Government to demand. In return, the question of the amnesty must be faced. The much disputed Mountain Brigade and Sacred Battalion could be broken up and used as cadres in the National Army. The question of the elections and the issue of the monarchy could be held over till the end of the war. We proposed that we should ask for delegates to be appointed to a peace conference as rapidly as possible. If negotiations failed, the truce would be denounced. But the kind of terms that we proposed were generous—perhaps over-generous—and therefore those who rejected peace would be exposed and discredited. While it was quite wrong to undertake any large-scale operations throughout the whole of Greece, something could be done with the forces at our command. In effect, the proposals which we made were the basis on which the Peace of Varkiza was to be signed three weeks later.

On the 17th, after spending the day visiting troops, Alexander and I called upon the Archbishop. Our object was to enlist his support for our plan.

The F.M. began by giving a rather defeatist account of the military future.[10]

The purpose of this was to deflate the Greek attitude a little. But the Archbishop did not react very favourably. I then developed my political thesis and here also had rather a frigid reception,

especially regarding the 'amnesty'. Eventually, we found a formula on this, to *include* all those merely charged with taking up arms against the Government, but to *exclude* men charged with offences—murder, rape, looting and the like—which are punished in any respectable Army by court-martial.[11]

On the other points, especially on the question of the conference, or offer of a conference, we made progress. Nevertheless, the taking of hostages among civilians and the refusal to surrender them as part of the truce had roused very strong feelings.

He would not find it easy to persuade his Government to meet the ELAS people at all, without making the surrender of the hostages a prerequisite or *condition préalable* to the meeting.[12]

[10] 17 January 1945.
[11] Ibid.
[12] Ibid.

However, we went through all the questions that would have to be settled if the conference did take place—date, place, composition, chairmanship, etc. The Archbishop agreed that Plastiras should not lead the Government team but rather Sophianopoulos—a more flexible negotiator. Altogether, it was not a bad interview, and I felt satisfied.

Sophianopoulos proved very helpful during the next few days, and everything seemed to be moving towards the opening of the conference. A number of problems arose about its composition, particularly by the arrival of some representatives of a group called ELD, Socialists, who, late in the day, had broken with KKE, the purely Communist party which dominated EAM. These people were represented by a gentleman called Tsirimokos, who appeared to rouse even greater animosity with our Government friends than the Communists themselves.

The preliminary negotiations for the conference were tedious and exhausting. They were prolonged over a long period and, as I was anxious to return to Italy as soon as possible, I became somewhat impatient. The only relaxation was to be found in my many conversations with the various Greek personalities:

. . . Sophianopoulos, Pericles Rallis and Makropoulos, who are to be the three Government delegates. S. is the clever one—the others rather mute. We went over the whole ground and made much progress on the *content* of the Government programme. But on the tactics the Greeks are very insistent to know how far we will back them if the conference fails and force is the only way out. If they feel they have enough backing, they will take rather a tough line at the conference—which they believe is the only hope of success. I promised to think this over and let them know.[13]

I finally informed them that in my opinion the British

should now make a *public* announcement that if the conference fails, we shall support the Greek Government with all our military power. We should add that the Government will put forward most conciliatory and generous proposals, to be framed in consultation with us. I think this method is the *only possible way* to give us any chance of converting the truce into a peace. Any weakness will merely make ELAS more intransigent.[14]

I got back to Naples on the 21st but, unhappily, on 25 January fresh troubles began. No agreement could yet be reached about the dele-

[13] 19 January 1945.
[14] 20 January 1945.

gates, and Caccia warned me that the conference was unlikely to meet without great delay, if at all. Accordingly, I once more set off for Athens. I was afraid that the Government would overplay their hand.

Moreover, I fear that, H.M.G. having acceded to my request to promise the Greek Government full support, [the Greeks will] try to squeeze us unduly.[15]

When I arrived, the Ambassador explained to me the general position. There was still a rather dreary argument as to whether ELAS would send principals or stooges. However, in the event, by most skilful diplomacy, the Archbishop got his way, and the Communists included in their delegation at least two of their leading men. But the preliminary negotiations were prolonged and tedious. The only advantage was that I was able to deal with some other matters. There were useful talks on supply and finance, as well as some advance in a return to more orderly conditions. General Plastiras, although unwilling to abolish the *état de siège,* or martial law, had in fact got rid of one of its effects by agreeing that examining magistrates should have some real power, and by a gradual emptying of the prisons.

While awaiting the next stages, I thought it would be useful to see something of other parts of Greece. On 27 January, therefore, I flew to Crete. The night before we sent off a signal to the commander of the small British force there, hoping that we might be met by a car or a jeep and enjoy a picnic lunch. Actually, we had a reception of unprecedented splendour and enthusiasm. It was a glorious and almost cloudless day, and flying fairly low we had a splendid view of the islands. We swung away east a little to avoid Milos, still in German hands.

We left behind us Naxos—and thought of poor abandoned Ariadne—and then, high in the sky, above a light thin bank of vapoury cloud, the snow-capped and magnificent peaks of Mount Ida came into view.[16]

We landed on a small strip near Heraklion and to my surprise I saw a large number of people and vehicles waiting. I was greeted by vociferous applause and the sound of sharp military orders; then I realised that this visit to Crete would indeed be memorable. First, the civil governor of half the island, M. Pappaioannis, came to meet me.

[15] 25 January 1945.
[16] 27 January 1945.

P. is the father of his people—a Cretan figure on heroic lines—with white head, and three years in the mountains, and a great Cretan chieftain, who has fought alongside and led his clansmen. He wears the black Cretan cap (a sort of glengarry), not, indeed, with those queer fringes hanging down over the forehead (like a Victorian aunt) but the bandage type, with one end tucked up to look like a Phrygian cap.[17]

The position in Crete was indeed strange. On the eastern end of the island were cooped up 10,000 Germans in a sort of voluntary imprisonment. I had been warned by the military staff at Caserta against encouraging them to surrender. For we should then, under the rules of war, be obliged to support them, and there were no means of doing this under existing conditions. Pappaioannis was anxious that the Germans should either be left to starve or be liquidated by himself and his friends. It seemed an awkward dilemma.

I was then introduced to the military governor; to the head of the new National Guard, being formed that very day; to the Mayor; to the head of EOK, the loyal guerrillas; to the Greek naval officer in charge; and, last of all, to Major Smith-Hughes, the British liaison officer who had been working in Crete for nearly three years. A procession was then formed to the town. It was very impressive. There were men and women of every age and type. I drove in an open car, lent by the local Archbishop, flying a handsome yellow flag with a cross and other ecclesiastical symbols.

On arrival in the main square of Heraklion, we were taken into a sort of town hall or municipal offices. The streets were packed. The entire population seemed to be turned out. At different places on the road were stationed guards of honour—splendid-looking bandits, with beards, and black Cretan caps and a most formidable appearance. Sometimes the newly-formed National Guard, in more orthodox British uniforms; we stopped and inspected these. On getting into the town hall, through the cheering crowds and the flowers and kisses, I was duly presented to further leading citizens and officials, both laymen and clerics.[18]

The Archbishop was, as usual, a notable figure, almost as impressive as the Archbishop of Athens. A number of toasts were drunk in excellent brandy. I was next pushed out on the balcony to address the crowd, which was growing in size every moment.

[17] Ibid.
[18] 27 January 1945.

It was all rather ridiculous, because although they naturally could not understand a word, I thought it polite to shout as loud as possible. The interpreter had not a very good voice. It would have been better the other way round. However, everyone was in a merry mood, and I [produced] a few Greek sentences for the end.[19]

After the speech, which was followed by an eloquent address by M. Pappaioannis, we came out of the town hall and drove through a fresh storm of plaudits and flowers to Knossos. The last time I had been at Knossos was in 1930 on a 'Hellenic cruise' with the usual complement of British scholars and Greek guides. Now there was a splendid cortège of Cretans, mostly armed with tommy-guns and bandoliers. We returned to Heraklion for lunch. M. Pappaioannis apologised profusely for the meagre fare, since the programme had only been laid on at such short notice.

However, we had hors d'œuvres—macaroni—lamb cutlets and vegetables—pork and potatoes—caramel pudding—coffee, so we did not do too badly. We also had large quantities of excellent Cretan wine—rather like luncheon port—and of course 'ouzo' (a sort of vodka) with black olives and biscuits, before the luncheon began. Not bad for a starving island, one part of which is still occupied by the Germans!

More processions and visits followed the lunch. At the airport there were further speeches and, in spite of my protests, they insisted upon packing into the aeroplane casks of wine, baskets of olives and other delicacies.

When I got back, the arguments about the membership of the conference were still proceeding. To my mind nothing mattered except that Siantos himself should be present, and I was able to persuade the Archbishop to work upon this basis.

On the 30th, since there was still no news from the rebel headquarters, I decided to go to Salonika. Harold Caccia came with me. The Mitchell was out of action, so I borrowed a Wellington from the A.O.C., which seemed serviceable enough. Here I was met by Brigadier Lovett and Consul-General Rapp. Both of these had done remarkably well through a very difficult period. We had only small forces against the formidable and well-equipped armies of ELAS. Fortunately the ELAS general, Birkadjis, a buccaneer and an adventurer, was a man with whom reasonable relations could be made and preserved. He had been a regular Army officer, holding a D.S.O. won

[19] Ibid.

in the First World War. By a mixture of firmness and suavity, a crisis was avoided. Even during the worst period of the Battle of Athens, ELAS troops in Salonika remained quiet, although threatening, insolent and insufferably provocative.

But the Brigadier knew his [own] weakness and the Consul knew his man. Interminable discussions, with long historical digressions, filled the day—and as each day went by without an actual attack, the British situation in Athens began to improve, with corresponding effects in Salonika.[20]

We had some useful talks on the next stages.

The economic situation at Salonika is, of course, desperate. The perimeter which we hold has a radius of some twenty miles. The city of 400,000 people lives entirely on charity. The greater part of the rich plain and of Macedonia as a whole (on which alone Salonika can live) is in enemy hands.[21]

I told the pilot that we must start by 3.30 p.m. to get back, if possible, by daylight. When we got to the airfield, neither pilot nor crew had turned up. Nor had they taken any precautions to keep the engines warm, and the icy wind and cold had done their work.

For two hours, with every effort and coaxing, with new batteries and the like, the engine both of the port and starboard side refused to move. (There was no supplementary self-starter available.) At last, when we had quite given up hope, both engines started and we finally took off about 5.45. By this time, a large number of people, mostly brigadiers, had mounted the plane. We finally left with about ten passengers.

The trip back alarmed even our military travellers. Darkness came on rather rapidly. Our pilot, although a somewhat casual young man, was a most skilful 'night flyer'. He brought us successfully through clouds and storms, and after much buffeting we saw to our relief the lights of Athens. There was no system of electric lighting on the Kalamaki airfield, only flares. In the gale, these blew out as soon as they were lit. The pilot flew round and round,

seeking a moment when his opportunity for landing coincided with at least a reasonable path of light showing him the runway. At last he succeeded, and we landed successfully about 8 p.m.

A reply had now come in from ELAS. It was not altogether satisfactory, and there was some argument as to whether it should be accepted. We heard the next day, 31 January, that the ELAS delega-

[20] 30 January 1945.
[21] Ibid.

tion, led by Siantos and including Partsalides, Tsirimokos, and General Saraphis, was on its way with three other individuals. We therefore persuaded the Regent and the Ministers to accept the situation, and all except the disputed figure of Tsirimokos would be taken to the house which had been prepared for their reception. The position of Tsirimokos was really ludicrous. The best way out seemed to be either that he should declare himself to be a Communist, or that the conference should be reduced to two a side; or, as another possibility, that a man called Theos, a declared Communist, should be elected in place of Tsirimokos. All this caused me concern, for I was sure that

if we do not handle the membership of Tsirimokos with great circumspection, the conference will not meet. S. and P. will go home, rather than accept a humiliating rebuff on this affair. It would of course be an act of real folly to allow the conference to break down—or not to meet—on this piffling issue.[22]

But it took much tedious negotiation before the matter could be settled. I had to warn the Regent that he was the convener of the conference and it was essential for his prestige, as well as the Government's, that it should at least meet. It was also necessary for me to say quite firmly that the continued support of H.M.G. must depend upon the Greek Government being able to take our advice to bring the conference into being.

Eventually, with poor Sophianopoulos almost in tears, Tsirimokos was accepted, and proved, indeed, quite useful. It was a storm in a teacup, but in the somewhat Oriental atmosphere with which we seemed now to be surrounded it wasted time and energy, and so far as the British were concerned, exacerbated tempers. However, the Greeks seemed to enjoy it all very much.

At 5.30 on the evening of 2 February, a message came for me from the Regent to say that everything at last had been agreed and the conference would start at 9 o'clock.

At 7 p.m. Sophianopoulos appeared at the Embassy, very spick and span and highly delighted with himself. You would have thought that no hitch of any kind, or argument, had occurred. . . . We went through his speech and wrote a summary of the Government proposals for him. One of the advantages of the row about personalities attending the conference is that everyone seems to have lost interest in the substance. S. accepted all our proposals without a murmur, although many of them covered points which

[22] 1 February 1945.

have been the subject of bitter dispute for weeks (e.g. the disbandment of the Sacred [Battalion] and the Mountain Brigade).[23]

After dinner we heard the conference was actually meeting in a fine villa some miles from Athens at a small resort called Varkiza and that Sophianopoulos's opening speech had been duly delivered. At the early stages of the conference the British were not present. Brigadier Mainwaring was called in to assist in the military details—the arms which ELAS were to hand over and the line behind which they were to retreat. The final figures agreed were 41,500 rifles, 15 machine-guns, 163 mortars and 32 field-guns of all types. But the military terms were not the most difficult to arrange.

Siantos absolutely refused to accept the Government's formula for the amnesty. He demanded its extension to all crimes—even murder, rape, looting or arson. This, of course, is because he fears the break-up of the sort of Communist OGPU or terror gangs, who dominate the towns and villages and on whose continuance his power depends. He would face the disarmament and disbandment of his regular forces, who are of a better type. He cannot tolerate the loss of the core of his revolutionary organisation.[24]

The following day I prepared telegrams for the Prime Minister and asked for authority in the last resort to threaten Siantos with all our military resources if he did not yield. At 12.30 p.m. I called upon the Archbishop at his request. He was very grateful for my offer of obtaining further promise of support from Churchill, but he thought it not yet necessary. The discussions would not be called off. Like all arguments in Greece they would continue for a long time.

So matters dragged on. On 5 February we learned that Siantos was likely to accept a compromise formula about the amnesty, at least in principle. The conference had been adjourned for several days; he now wished it to resume to discuss the details.

So the conference is still alive! It is very interesting to see the line the Communists are taking. Probably they have decided not to break off on any point, at least till the Three-Power [Yalta] Conference is over. They seem persuaded that Stalin will do something to help them. For my part, I feel sure that he will try to bargain Greece against Poland.[25]

[23] 2 February 1945.
[24] 3 February 1945.
[25] 5 February 1945.

There was now likely to be a lull, since it was clear that nobody wished the conference to collapse, at least immediately. I was urgently needed in Italy in connection with my new post and I therefore decided to go back for a few days.

On 10 February—my fiftieth birthday—I set out again with John Wyndham and the faithful Miss Campbell to return to Athens.

I found the Embassy in good heart. The conference has practically foundered once or twice, but has scraped through. The question (a) of disarmament, (b) formation of National Army, produced a deadlock among the Greeks. It was eventually solved (after about nine hours of argument) by the invaluable Brigadier Mainwaring. If peace is eventually concluded and these clauses are effectively carried out, there ought to be a very good level of actual disarmament. ELAS declared (a) the position of their various divisions, (b) their armament. Of course they understated (b). But the fact that they were prepared to talk with even this degree of frankness makes me hopeful.[26]

At about 8 p.m. on Sunday 11 February, a message came from the Regent's private secretary, M. Georgiakis, to say that the situation was desperate. After four hours of discussion no agreement could be reached. He suggested that the Ambassador and I should come to Varkiza to try to settle the final point. We reached the house about 9.45 p.m. and found the delegates gathered in the large lounge-sitting-room of a newly-built villa. After ten days' use it was in a somewhat squalid condition.

The conference consisted of three Government delegates, MM. Sophiano-poulos, Pericles Rallis, and Makropoulos on one side of the table; Siantos, Partsalides and the now famous or infamous Tsirimokos on the other. Two secretaries and two shorthand clerks on one end; the Ambassador and I took our seats at the other (looking and feeling rather like the Kings in The Gondoliers).[27]

The Ambassador explained in a few words the reason for our arrival and asked each side to state their position. Encouraged by this, Sophianopoulos made a long but masterly speech covering the whole course of the discussions. He was very conciliatory. He explained that after days of labour with the assistance on various technical points of the British officers, notably Brigadier Mainwaring, agreement had been reached on the difficult questions of

the amnesty; disarmament of irregular forces; formation of new National Army; the future of the gendarmerie or police; the political liberation of the

[26] 10 February 1945.
[27] 11 February 1945.

citizens, including the right of association in trade unions and of public meetings; the purging of collaborators from the public service and their punishment in suitable cases; the return of hostages and prisoners.[28]

One final question remained—the extent to which military or martial law under the *état de siège* should be lifted. This speech lasted for an hour. Then Siantos rose.

[He] is a set-faced, sly, shifty-looking man—of middle height, in battledress, rather bald (with an irritating kind of tousled hair on the back of his head). He looked tired and exhausted—but I think this was partly affectation. He spoke as if all the weight of the world's cares were upon his shoulders—the weary Titan. He began very quietly—almost inaudibly—gradually working up to his various points of climax. His injured-innocence method was subtle and effective. You felt almost convinced by the end that there had been no civil war, no insurrection, no disorders even—except in a Pickwickian sense. There had been a certain confusion, due to misunderstanding. There had been no crimes—perhaps, and naturally enough in the circumstances, some regrettable incidents on both sides.

He went on to thank the British—his friends and allies. He was grateful for our presence there that night. He and his friends had only one object—the constitutional liberties of the Greek people.

As regards disarmament, complete agreement had been reached and the agreement would be carried out sincerely and honestly. (I had that morning received from most secret sources the orders for trying to evade the terms—make secret dumps of the best weapons, hand over only inferior ones and so forth—which [the] ELAS command had already sent out to the various divisions and formations! So much for sincerity!)

On the question of constitutional liberties, he and his friends felt very strongly. One might almost have thought he was a Liberal professor of the nineteenth century. Any form of martial law—even the modified system proposed by the Government—or any suspension of the normal processes of civil law could not be reconciled with liberty.

He gravely feared that the clause in the amnesty allowing common-law crime to be punishable would be abused—more particularly if men were to be arrested without warrant. It would be the instrument of a proscription under the guise of law. And in any event, he did not believe in anything except a few crimes, on both sides, in the heat of battle. (I thought of the mutilated bodies of men and women, of all ages, found at Peristeri and elsewhere.) S. is going back to the mountains—to persuade his forces to accept the peace and

[28] Ibid.

disarm, and the refugees who have come away from Athens to return to their homes. How can he do this, if they are to be in terror of illegal arrest, under a system of martial law, without the constitutional guarantees provided by the processes of civil law?

(This was a very important point and there was something in it. I myself had been working hard to prevent these widespread arrests.) Siantos could not therefore agree even for a short period the right of arrest without warrant. He could not sign a peace with such a clause. If he did so he would be repudiated.

These splendid constitutional sentiments brought us nearly to midnight. I then asked for clarification. Was I right in thinking that on the question of freedom from arrest without warrant

the Government proposed to continue the suspension till *after the completion of disarmament;* EAM proposed that the normal system should be restored immediately *after the signature of the* peace.[29]

Both sides agreed that this was the point at issue. I then asked how long the disarmament was likely to take. I suggested perhaps fifteen days in principle; twenty days in practice. Was that so? Both sides agreed. Then there were fifteen to twenty days about which it was proposed to endanger all the work of the conference and plunge Greece into civil war? Nobody seemed to be able or willing to deny this; so the Ambassador and I felt we might break off the formal meeting for an interval of reflection. We went into another room hoping to be able to consult together alone, but of course first the Government delegates and then the ELAS delegates insisted upon joining us.

It soon became clear from our talk with the Government side that the twenty days had considerable importance. For they hoped during this period to make a large number of arrests of suspicious characters. When we saw Siantos it was clear that they were equally thinking of their supporters in Athens and the Piraeus.

S. knows very well that lots of these people have committed atrocious crimes. But he knows also that lots more will be arrested 'on suspicion' and by this means kept safely under lock and key for a long time. But these are the very people whom he relies on to rebuild the Communist cells in the great cities.[30]

[29] Ibid.
[30] 12 February 1945.

It was now about 2 a.m. We next conferred with Georgiakis, the Regent's trusted secretary. A possible compromise was put forward; that the normal civil method of arrest by magistrate's warrant should be restored in Athens and the Piraeus *immediately* after the signature of the Peace. Over the rest of Greece it should come into force after the effective carrying-out of a disarmament.

The argument for this would be that the Government had been in . . . occupation of Athens and Piraeus for several weeks and had had time to organise normal methods, whereas in the other parts of Greece there were no magistrates, no prefects or mayors—in fact none of the apparatus of civil government.

Georgiakis went back to see both sides in separate rooms to tell them this was our decision.

After some little time, he came back to tell us that it would 'do the trick'.

At about 2 a.m., therefore, the full conference resumed. I explained the compromise plan as a suitable and reasonable settlement. Both sides showed proper surprise and delight at so novel, unexpected, and reasonable a proposal. After a good deal of talk on various details of its application, it was finally agreed.

It was then about 3 a.m. and Siantos thought it was about time to go to bed. But I felt that it would be a fatal mistake to break off without some agreement signed. Surely, I said, M. Pericles Rallis and M. Tsirimokos, both eminent lawyers, could rapidly draft a text. But there was only one typist and he very inexpert—a one-finger performer.

After some talk, work was begun, but by about 4 a.m. it was clear, first, that no proper draft had really been made covering the agreements reached during the ten days of the conference and secondly, that the task was too great to be accomplished tonight; thirdly, that Siantos refused absolutely to sign the document until he had proper time to go through it.

But I was still determined not to leave, even at 4 a.m., without a signature.

It was therefore decided to prepare a summary of the points agreed; a statement that full agreement of all points at issue had been reached by the conference; that a Greek text was being prepared but that owing to the late hour this could not be ready till later in the day; that it would be formally signed at 2 p.m. today; that the short document was signed in the presence of myself and the Ambassador.[31]

The typing of this document by the only means available took another hour, but at last it was ready, including the communiqué to be issued. At about 5 a.m. the full conference met again. After the formal signatures Sophianopoulos made a short speech, Siantos also, and I added a few words of congratulations and good wishes. We left at 5.30 a.m. on 12 February.

The document, of course, was not ready at 2 p.m. There was much argument about wording, but it was signed at 7 p.m.

We were just in time, for the Yalta Conference was now ending, and we had every hope that Churchill and Eden would stop at Athens on the way back. Their first messages, while congratulating us on our result, had not realised our hopes. Churchill could not come himself.

The Regent . . . was very disappointed. So both Leeper and I telegraphed separately to Winston, urging him to come, if only for a few hours. We were correspondingly delighted to get a telegram, early this morning, announcing the arrival of the whole party at 4.30 p.m. today.[32]

It was a beautiful evening, a cloudless sky, the sea, mountains and city lit by the wonderful Greek light which has a quality all its own. After various presentations at the airfield we set off for Athens for the Regent's house, which was between the British Embassy and the old Palace in Constitution Square.

After a few minutes of formalities, the procession reformed. This time the Regent and the P.M. rode together in an open car, which drove at a snail's pace through a wildly enthusiastic mass of people.

The Greek soldiers lining the streets could not control the vast crowds, and I was anxious about the danger of some disaster. However, we got through at a footpace and entered the palace by the side door. When we came out on to the terrace overlooking Constitution Square, there was an extraordinary scene.

Here was an upturned sea of faces and a crowd of a size and character beyond anything I have seen. The estimates range from 20,000 to 70,000. I believe 40,000 would be about right. The whole square (except for a space left empty in front of the 'Tomb of the Unknown Warrior') . . . was packed.

[31] Ibid.
[32] 14 February 1945.

All the houses, windows and roofs, were black. The Grande-Bretagne alone must have held hundreds. And the old Palace behind us was full at every window and roof. The reception was remarkable not only for its enthusiasm, but for its orderliness.

There was little of the organised chanting to which we had become so accustomed, 'E—A—M', 'E—D—E—S'. Even the royalists made no separate demonstration. It was a democratic crowd, applauding the Archbishop and Churchill as democratic leaders; totalitarian techniques were out of place.

Having seen the crowd on the day of Papandreou's entry on 14 October, I was struck with the difference. In that crowd there were two bitterly hostile sections; there was a sense of challenge all through and a sense of tension. In this crowd, there was a sense of relief, as well as of triumph; a feeling of gratitude and pride, of a people who had been through a hard and gruelling test and gladly acknowledged and honoured those who they knew had brought them through—the Archbishop-Regent, representing Greek effort, and the British Prime Minister, representing in his person all that they admire in their ally—courage, fairness, and determination.[33]

The Archbishop spoke a few dignified words. Churchill's reply was extempore but admirably phrased. Perhaps the time taken to translate each sentence helped him. The last words were memorable:

Let none fail in his duty to his country. Let none fail to rise to the occasion of these splendid days. Let the Greek nation stand first in every heart, first in the thoughts of every man and woman. Let the future of Greece shine in their eyes. From the bottom of my heart I wish you prosperity. From the bottom of my heart I hope that Greece will take her proper part in the ranks of the nations that have suffered so terribly in this war. Let right prevail. Let party hatreds die. Let there be unity. Let there be resolute comradeship. Greece for ever! Greece for all![34]

There were a few suitable ceremonies, followed by short speeches from General Plastiras and Eden. There was much music and wild cheering. After meeting the leading Ministers in the Cabinet Room of the palace, a gathering which lasted nearly three-quarters of an hour, we left, the Regent now alone in his car, Churchill and Eden together, the Ambassador and I behind. From the palace to the Embassy there were vast crowds and much cheering. A huge dinner at the Embassy fol-

[33] Ibid.
[34] Leeper, p. 154.

lowed with thirty-six people. I sat on Churchill's right and he was in excellent form, having enjoyed what was his personal triumph. At 10.30 the Regent came round for a talk at which only Churchill, Eden, Leeper and I were present. The discussion was partly light and gay and partly serious, and Churchill and the Archbishop seemed to get on if possible even better than before. At midnight Churchill and his party left. But Eden and his officials remained, and the next day we had a long conference on Greek, Italian and Yugoslav affairs.

Since the Field-Marshal had never seen Marathon, I thought we had better spend the afternoon in taking him there. When that battle was fought, the Persians were twenty-six miles from Athens; when Alexander took over the Middle East Command the Germans were seventy miles from Cairo.

That night there was a return dinner given by the Greek Government. Somehow or other large quantities of food and drink were produced, and there was a great deal of speech-making. The evening ended with a discussion with the Greek Ministers on economic and financial affairs. Eden gave them a good lecture, urging them not to lean entirely on us but to do more themselves. This went well enough until Sideris, the Finance Minister, replied with a long, dreary and whining peroration. When I took Eden to say goodbye to the Regent, he told him what had happened, and the Regent seemed delighted at the plain speaking.

The next day we all left Athens.

The British Press received the Peace of Varkiza with much praise and some shamefacedness. Nor did they grudge the Prime Minister his triumph, the accounts being full and enthusiastic. I was given a generous share of the credit. Much emphasis was put, and rightly so, upon the moderate character of the terms and the generosity shown. Nevertheless, neither then nor perhaps until much later were the true lessons learned.

It was assumed all through that the EAM, with its instrument ELAS, was a genuine resistance movement, composed of patriots of all kinds. This was not so. While many of the guerrillas were no doubt attracted from high motives of national pride, the guiding forces were Communists of the most rabid kind. I believed that we might, with moderation and fairness, win back a large number of their supporters and at any rate lay the foundations for more liberal policies in the future. Greece had too often oscillated between dictatorship and political confusion. Moreover, while long and almost fantastic political crises were common and accepted in Greek affairs, there was a sharp revulsion amongst the mass of the people from the criminal actions and the dreadful atrocities of the ELAS forces. Nevertheless, Yalta must have had its effect. Stalin had perhaps connived at the breach of the Moscow arrangements and allowed the Communists to try to seize Greece if they could get away with it. But when the British Government reacted so firmly, and when Churchill's resolution was so clearly demonstrated, Stalin no doubt thought that it would be best to call off this attempt and wait for a better occasion. Even from Bulgaria or Albania or Yugoslavia partisan forces could not be collected in sufficient strength to withstand the formed armies which Churchill had put into Greece. On reflection, it was clear to me that Siantos had received orders to reach an agreement. He fought hard and skilfully for his own people and, above all, to preserve the essential elements of the Communist movement. Colonel Popov was on the spot and in touch with Stalin. Siantos was no doubt told that it would be better now to *reculer pour mieux sauter*.

Many of my Greek friends reproached us then and later that we had not forced the issue and carried on the campaign in Greece to a point at which revolutionary Communism could be totally suppressed. Many of our British friends believed that Communism was only a form of Leftism, which could be softened by kindness or cajolery. In the essentials our Greek critics were right. Had we possessed the power; had we not had to face the hostility of Washington and the American Government; had we not been committed to a hard and difficult spring campaign in Italy, with insufficient forces; had British public opinion been fully seized of the truth; then indeed we might have completed the task.

Although the ending of the rebellion relieved me of major anxieties about Greek affairs, I was still responsible for helping and advising SACMED, all the more because of the heavy commitment of British forces. A continuous flow of information continued, therefore, between the Embassy at Athens and my office at Caserta. On 28 February I had received a message from Leeper as follows:

I want your help badly together with that of the Field-Marshal. The Greeks need a call to proper action and we must all come together and do it both on the political and the military side. Could you and the Field-Marshal possibly come over here by the weekend? I am sorry to be such a nuisance, but I doubt whether I can do this successfully by myself.

When I consulted Alexander, he seemed rather annoyed that the Ambassador should not be able to handle all this himself. It was obviously difficult for him to spare the time when planning the spring offensive, and dealing with urgent questions in northern Italy and Yugoslavia. The trouble was chiefly caused by Plastiras's appointments, political and military.

It appears that the Plastiras Government is behaving rather stupidly. The forcing of Pericles Rallis out of office was a dangerous sign of a 'Right-wing' reaction. All kinds of military appointments are being made, mostly of elderly Venizelist generals who were friends of Plastiras in 1922 and are unsuitable either politically or professionally.[35]

Moreover, there was a new proposal facing Alexander. On the day after the message from Athens, he gave me some disturbing news.

. . . he had now definite instructions to go as 'deputy' to General Eisenhower. He will be leaving shortly. It is really rather hard on him to be a 'Deputy Commander' and it will be a most difficult task. It will require all his firmness, as well as his tact, if he is to achieve anything. Of course, he ought (on professional grounds) to have the command. But the disproportion between British and American troops makes this impossible. It is a great blow to me, for my association with Alex. has always been so delightful.[36]

It also seemed to me that this change was quite unnecessary now that the dangerous German counter-attack in the Ardennes had been dealt with successfully. In the event, this plan fell to the ground. We agreed, meanwhile, that I should go to Athens, since the Ambassador was clearly feeling in need of support.

I armed myself with a directive from Alexander, demanding that the selection of officers both of General and Field rank be made on professional grounds only. He made it clear that he could not justify the heavy drain on his resources at this critical moment unless he could be satisfied that efficiency would take the place of nepotism. As usual, I fell back upon the Regent. He was anxious to keep Plastiras for the present, and indeed he hoped to keep him up to the elections. But he believed that he could get him to accept our terms of co-operation.

[35] 1 March 1945.
[36] 2 March 1945.

When I called to see General Plastiras, I found him still more the *grand chef*. The Greek Army was making splendid progress; there was no disorder throughout the country; all the people had absolute faith in him personally; there was no need in his view for British troops to remain, except perhaps in Salonika. Considering that a great part of Greece was still in ELAS hands, in spite of the effective collection of arms, this seemed rather unrealistic. I then began to press him a little about the formation of the National Army in accordance with the Varkiza Agreement. As regards the precise terms, the General did not think these important; but he was making a real effort to get some of the junior ELAS officers and N.C.O.'s into the Army under selection boards.

Earlier in the morning, General Scobie had been to see me. . . . General Scobie thinks General Plastiras stupid. General P. regards General S. as bone-headed.[37]

The same day I received a visit from Siantos, Partsalides and Tsiri-mokos; they had a number of detailed complaints against the Government regarding the carrying-out of the Agreement. I did not think, however, that they made a very strong case. One of their grievances struck me as somewhat naïve.

They said that although they were free to print their newspapers, the newsboys who sold them were set on by the people![38]

The next evening the Ambassador and I called on the Regent again, and he seemed relieved at our view that no immediate change should be made in the Government. It would be wise to postpone this as long as possible.

The Chiefs of Staff were now beginning to press for the removal of all our troops from Greece, to which Plastiras would no doubt have agreed in return for equipment. Both Scobie and the Ambassador were much concerned, and after long arguments it was finally decided in the middle of April to leave not merely one but two divisions for the present. This was satisfactory, since I did not want to get again into a position where we had only one division, enough to get committed but not enough in the event of trouble to keep order effectively. Moreover, the rapid progress of the war in Germany seemed to justify this course.

[37] 13 March 1945.
[38] 14 March 1945.

The final offensive in Italy was about to be launched, and it was tempting, of course, to take out another division to support it. But with his usual broad-mindedness, Alexander accepted our conclusions. We must either get out of Greece or be sure of our strength.

I returned to Italy on 17 March, and only one further visit to Greece became necessary before the collapse of Germany. I arrived in Athens on 10 April to find that a change from Plastiras to Voulgaris had taken place. Admiral Voulgaris, an agreeable and attractive figure, with a great deal of common sense, made it quite clear that his Ministry's sole purpose was to make the necessary reconstruction in the life of the country to allow the elections and the plebiscite about the monarchy to take place as soon as possible. It would be a 'service' Government. But now, unexpectedly, the Americans began to take a hand in the affair. Having, officially at any rate, shown an unfriendly neutrality at the time of danger, they now changed their position.

There is an additional complication due to the Americans having rather 'taken up' Plastiras. They have been showing him a lot of attention lately and sending over all kinds of people from the U.S. on various excuses. Kind people say that the Americans liked Plastiras because he was a republican. More suspicious folk say that they were trying to get concessions for post-war trade. This latter view is supported by the fact that they practically got Plastiras to sign a most favourable aviation agreement, which would have given Pan American Airways a powerful and predominant position. Fortunately, we heard of this and stopped it in time. But this would explain the American attitude and especially Stettinius's observation at a Press conference that the American Ambassador had not been consulted by the Regent on the change of Government.[39]

The next day marked the culmination of our talks in February, when Eden and the Yalta party visited us. Our proposals had now been approved by the Cabinet, and the new system was to come into immediate effect. All British missions and advisers were to be co-ordinated under the Ambassador. General Scobie would be relieved by a corps commander whose work would be confined to commanding British troops. General Smallwood had come as head of the Military Mission, and Admiral Turner and Air Commodore Turtle were already here. Sir Quintin Hill had already arrived as Financial Adviser. We duly held a conference at 11.30, and I explained the new

[39] 9 April 1945.

system. I ended with a suitable tribute to General Scobie, who had shown really remarkable courage and devotion throughout.

> The only mistake I made was to give my notes afterwards to the secretary to help him with the minutes, but to forget that at this point my notes ran 'Flowers for General Scobie'![40]

The last day was one of farewells. In the evening there was a small family dinner made more agreeable by Sir Michael Palairet's champagne. I had laid down a principle, which was not repudiated by the Foreign Office, that in the presence of the Foreign Secretary it was legitimate to break into the former Ambassador's cellar. We felt that this principle might be extended on matters of national importance. Since Admiral Voulgaris was our guest, after some discussion this seemed justifiable. After dinner a more serious conference began in the Ambassador's room.

> Only the Admiral, the Ambassador, Harold Caccia and I. Except that we got terribly sleepy (both Leeper and I actually fell asleep at different times), it was a success. The Admiral is really a very attractive personality and very human. He is humorous, sly, cynical—and understands what suits him. Compared to Plastiras, he is a paragon. P. was stupid, vain, pig-headed, romantic, living in the past. Voulgaris is clever, sensible, pliant, sceptical—and lives in and is determined to enjoy the present. . . . He wants the elections as soon as possible, but recognises that practical difficulties will make it impossible till the autumn. For that reason, he rather favours the National Council. He wants a Centre, even a Left-Centre, policy. He adheres to Varkiza. But he was frank about the extent of the anti-KKE reaction and the violence of the feelings roused by the barbarities of the civil war. 'A revolution or a rebellion anyone can understand. But why unspeakable atrocities, more suitable to barbarians than to Greeks?'[41]

The last sentence summed up in a single phrase the feelings of nearly all Greek people. The memory of those fearful accounts of violence and cruelty had not yet faded.

Although in the last few weeks there were a certain number of problems, including Churchill's demand that the plebiscite should take place within four months, in spite of the clear impossibility on practical grounds, there was no further need for me to assist the Ambassador in person. This, therefore, turned out to be my last visit.

[40] 10 April 1945.
[41] 11 April 1945.

My relations with Leeper had been happy throughout the whole of our work together. I had for him a high regard which I have retained, and his continued friendship has been precious and firm.

I have one other pleasant incident to record. The Archbishop retired in the autumn of 1946. I had seen him in London when he came to visit the new Foreign Secretary, Ernest Bevin. But, alas, I was not to see him again, for he died in 1948. But on the eve of his retirement I received the following letter:

Athens, 17 September 1946

My very dear friend,

At the moment when I relinquish my duties as Regent, I cannot but recall those days when I first undertook my difficult task, and which will always remain in my memory linked with your beloved person. Your penetrating intelligence, your qualities of leadership, your unfailing tact, your devotion to my country, and the friendship you have shown to me since then, have been of invaluable assistance in the difficult path I have had to follow.

With feelings of love and gratitude I send my warmest greetings to my dear Mr. Macmillan, whose admirer and devoted friend I shall always remain, and I pray that the Grace of God may always rest upon him and that he may be blessed with happiness in his great country.

Damaskinos

CHAPTER TWENTY-FOUR

The End of the Campaign

THE long-drawn-out struggle in Italy, with the hard-fought battles throughout the peninsula, had led to much suffering as well as disillusionment. In spite of our efforts to revive the economic life of the country and to ensure the more generous distribution of food, conditions were still distressing. Whatever the United States might now wish to do for political or other reasons to assist Italy, the United Kingdom could not add to its commitments without sacrificing other and even more compelling claims, partly in Europe and partly in the devastated colonies of the Far East. In the political field, in spite of a number of difficulties which came to a head while I was in London in December 1944, the Bonomi Government had survived and even strengthened its position. But there were dangerous pitfalls ahead.

On 30 December 1944 I was at Naples, and we had a long discussion at the Commander-in-Chief's Political Committee. There had been a lot of trouble over an agreement between the C.L.N.A.I. (Committee of National Liberation), representing the partisan movements in northern Italy, and A.F.H.Q. and the Italian Government. Alexander was firm and I thought right in his decisions. The lesson of Greece was that we had to get control over these movements right from the start. Assuming that the campaign might end in the early summer, now was the time to have a clear understanding and to infiltrate the partisans with British officers and reliable Italians. It was at this time that I first came into touch with Signor Parri, the joint commander of the military command of the resistance movement, and the banker Pizzoni, both admirable and courageous patriots. A bipartite agreement was eventually made between Alexander and the C.L.N.A.I. for cooperation and financial support. This was supplemented by an agreement with the Italian Government. The actual negotiation of all this was a somewhat difficult matter, for delicate phrasing had to be adopted, especially in relation to the terms of the armistice and the powers of the Allied Military Government, in order to satisfy the somewhat pedantic attitude of the Foreign Office and the State Department. Many of the legal difficulties seemed to me to be largely illusory; the main thing was to get a firm grip of the resistance groups before they became, as in Greece, mere instruments of Communism.

I was in Rome on the last day of the year and on New Year's Day went to the Commission's office where, although it was a general holiday, a number of leading officials were at work. There were plenty of problems.

On the Italian side, there are a large number of questions still to be settled. The food ration, the Italian forces, the housing situation, the prisoners of war in Italy, and the use and misuse of the 'Purge'. In addition, industrial reconstruction, local elections, the transport problem, and the partisan movement in northern Italy are pressing matters. . . . As far as I can see, the team here is pretty good on the administrative but very weak on the economic side. They have been hampered by A.F.H.Q. and still more by C.C.S. and C.C.A.C. [Combined Chiefs of Staff and Combined Civil Affairs Committee] at Washington.[1]

In taking over the Acting Presidency of the Commission, I accepted, for the first time in two years, an executive post.

All I can do . . . is to go into a number of specific problems and ask for information. . . . There is in the A.C. a large and rather unco-ordinated organisation, very nervous about criticism and rather uncreative. I must try to stimulate without unduly alarming it.[2]

Fortunately, I had in Rear-Admiral Stone and Brigadier Lush two admirable men, loyal and energetic.

During January and February a large number of telegrams flowed backwards and forwards about the precise wording of my directive. First, Washington wanted to extend the new policy to cover financial as well as political and supply questions. Then, in a moment of pettiness, Washington accused the British of ill-will towards Italy, in a series of astonishing telegrams for which Stettinius, the successor to Cordell Hull, made himself responsible. I continued to urge that at least my directive on the practical application of the New Deal should be implemented. Negotiations proceeded at an Oriental pace. At any

[1] 1 January 1945.
[2] 2 January 1945.

rate, I could not be accused of wasting my time in Greece. The delay was due to the behaviour of the State Department, now apparently without any firm direction, and cherishing fantastic conceptions. 'The Americans wanted to "liquidate" as soon as possible the whole situation arising from the war in Europe.'[3] Vain ambition! Illusory hope!

A number of distinguished American correspondents joined in the fray. They even accused us of wishing to annex Sicily, as well as the Italian colonies! This type of troublemaker had been active, at different periods, even since 'Torch'. But now, as war was drawing to an end, tempers were getting more than usually frayed. A sense of impatience began to grow which particularly affected those far away from the battle fronts. Yet, even when accusations against the British 'domination' of the Commission began to be repeated in high quarters in Washington, the morale of those actually working in the Commission remained unaffected. The splendid standard of Allied co-operation, which had been set by General Eisenhower at the beginning of the Mediterranean campaign, was maintained at A.F.H.Q. until the end.

Apart from an interminable discussion on the actual wording of my directive, the Americans now began once more to press the Foreign Office about a proposed peace treaty. This did not seem to Eden a good plan, and I now agreed with him. Any peace treaty would have to include severe conditions, as well as concessions. It might be as much of a shock as an encouragement to the Italian people. We proposed, therefore, that as soon as the war with Germany was over, we would make a peace with Italy before any question arose of a peace with Germany. Churchill agreed with this suggestion and it was accordingly put forward by Lord Halifax, our Ambassador in Washington, on 17 January. The State Department, however, went dumb; no reply was ever forthcoming.

While I was waiting for the formal instructions to reach me, some dangerous issues emerged. The question of the purging of Fascists had always been a difficulty since we first landed on Italian soil. The dismissal of all those tainted with Fascism had been demanded in the original armistice terms. But it was extremely difficult to define or apply this doctrine. Moreover, the process was slow. While the sword of 'epurazione' was dangling over the necks of every civil servant,

[3] Woodward, *British Foreign Policy in the Second World War*, pp. 406–7.

great and small, the efficiency of the public service was naturally much impaired. In addition, there had been occasions when some particular individual, although of Fascist antecedents, possessed most valuable technical knowledge and skill. Such, for instance, was a high official in the communication system throughout southern Italy, who had shown a good deal of courage in helping us to operate in the early days— while Rome was still held by the Germans—by giving us all the charts of the submarine cables at Anzio and Naples. Attacked by the Allied Commission and the Italian Government, he was saved by A.F.H.Q. at the request of the Chief Signal Officer. This was only one instance of many. The threat to Badoglio, in December 1944, was another. Yet it was on Badoglio's signature that the whole armistice depended.

Early in 1945, a similar problem arose concerning General Roatta. He had been assistant chief of the General Staff at the time of the fall of Mussolini and was deeply implicated in the plot that removed him. I first heard of his arrest on 10 January, when I was in Greece, and on my return to Italy discussed the situation with the Marchese Lucifero, Minister of the Household to Prince Umberto, the Lieutenant-General.

General Roatta is to be tried in a week, and the trial [will] perhaps reveal a lot of details surrounding the signing of the armistice in September 1943, as well as Secret Service papers covering 1934–39, probably very damaging to the U.S. and British Governments.[4]

I felt worried about all this but decided not to allow Alexander to take any action unless we had the clear support of the American Government. They had backed out on the Badoglio trial, and I was anxious to avoid any repetition of this strain on Allied relations. Since the charge against Roatta was that he had used the Intelligence division of the General Staff as an instrument of terrorism in the interests of Fascism, there was no real reason why the armistice negotiations should be brought into the trial. Nor could anyone say whether evidence of his activities in September 1943 would be beneficial to him or not. However, I was anxious to be on the safe side and I therefore arranged that Stone should

ask Bonomi to arrange that no evidence shall be admitted, either by prosecution or defence, which involves (a) Allied operations, (b) documents belong-

[4] 12 January 1945.

ing or alleged to belong to any Allied Government. *But* he is not to *demand* this, without further authority from me or the F.M. Meanwhile, Broad will telegraph on my behalf to the F.O. for a ruling as to whether we should insist on this; Offie will telegraph on Kirk's behalf in similar terms to the State Department. By this means, if we decide to act, I will get the Americans committed. I refuse to act unilaterally, although Kirk and Offie would like me to do so. But would they share the responsibility when the row comes, and Mr. Drew Pearson attacks us for interfering with Italian justice?[5]

Neither the Foreign Office nor the State Department answered our question directly, but sometimes even in the confusion of Italian politics we had a lucky break. Before any final steps to bring him to trial, the General disappeared.

Roatta, owing to real or feigned illness, had been transferred from the Regina Coeli prison to the Virgilio military hospital.

On the night of 4 March 1945 he succeeded—how, was never discovered—in making his escape, and in spite of all the efforts of the Government to trace his whereabouts—including the offer of a reward of a million lire—he succeeded in remaining hidden, until some time after the Allied military régime in Italy was finished.[6]

Not unnaturally, there was a lot of criticism. The Left saw in this incident a reactionary Fascist plot. The Carabinieri had shown either inefficiency or complicity, perhaps both. The Government was shaken. But by now events were moving rapidly, and the Communists, who were at that time the only people who could have injured Bonomi's Government, preferred to wait. Their hopes were centred on the north.

At last, on 31 January, the formal directive covering the New Deal was dispatched by the Combined Chiefs of Staff. The terms were hardly changed from those which I had submitted early in December.

Fortunately, the text of the public statement is not yet settled, and there must be forty-eight hours' delay in order to inform the members of the Advisory Council ahead of the publication. So I may *just* do it, if the Greek conference does not last too long! It will be a 'damned close-run thing'.[7]

But I underestimated the power of procrastination of our rulers. Stettinius now decided against any public statement.

[5] Ibid.
[6] Harris, *Allied Military Administration of Italy, 1943–1945*, p. 224.
[7] 3 February 1945.

His reason is that the concessions fall so far short of what the U.S. Government would like for Italy that any statement will cause nothing but disappointment.[8]

We now proposed that I should make an oral statement to the Italian Government and to the Advisory Council, based upon the directive. The Italians, who were quick to see that something was wrong, appealed directly to the Yalta Conference, asking for Allied status, and for greater economic and financial help. But of course there were other countries with greater claims—France and, above all, Belgium. The British Government quite naturally felt that the liberated Allies had at least as good a claim as the Italians. The discussions at Yalta were perfunctory. Naturally, I wanted to do everything possible for the Italians in my charge. Indeed, when we talked in Athens, on his return from Yalta on 14 February, I urged Eden

not to let his natural irritation with American exaggerations affect his judgement. Italy is a British interest, in the sense that we do not want to see an important Mediterranean power in dissolution or in a state of permanent revolution. We do not want to see Italy break up and/or 'go Communist'.[9]

But the question of Allied status would take weeks, if not months, to settle. There were more practical questions ahead. Finally, disregarding all the welter of telegrams, I came to my own decision. I had the full support of Rear-Admiral Stone and Brigadier Lush. Our plan was simple.

There will be a meeting of the Advisory Council for Italy at 10.30. Stone will attend then and explain the main points of the new directive. At 4 p.m. he and I will call on Bonomi (P.M.) and De Gasperi (Foreign Affairs) and go through the points with them. At 5.30 I will have a Press conference. We went through the various papers and settled a few outstanding points.[10]

This programme was duly carried out, and Stone and I called upon Bonomi and De Gasperi at 4 p.m. on 24 February. I went through in detail the *aide-mémoire* containing all the changes proposed.[11] Italy had obtained a new international position and greater and in some cases full freedom of action. In the transferred territory the Allied Commission would now be charged only with the function of consulta-

[8] 9 February 1945.
[9] 15 February 1945.
[10] 23 February 1945.
[11] This document is reproduced as Appendix 3.

THE END OF THE CAMPAIGN

tion and advice. Naturally, so long as the campaign lasted, overriding military needs had to be protected, but the rights of the Allied Government would be held in reserve and not affect day-to-day administration. The Italian Government could now freely and directly conduct their relations with other Governments. They need no longer operate through the Political Section of the Allied Commission, which would be abolished. They would have a free right to appoint and receive ambassadors to and from Allied countries. They would be granted the advantages of secret communication through diplomatic bags. As regards internal affairs, decrees and laws passed by the Government need no longer be submitted for approval. Nor need assent be given by the Allies to administrative appointments, from the highest to the lowest. The only exception concerned the appointments for such offices as the Chief of Staff and Defence Ministries, which would still require the agreement of SACMED. The Allied officers working in the areas under Italian jurisdiction would be withdrawn. Liaison officers and technical experts would remain only if invited to do so. Cultural relations between the Allies and Italy were to be re-established by the means of an exchange of books and visits of eminent professional men, scholars and artists. The rest of the document set out the plan of economic reconstruction in which the Allies were ready to assist the Italian Government.

After we had been through the document in detail, a few points were raised. For instance, could the Italians have ciphers as well as diplomatic pouches, to which the answer had to be no, since their ciphers were known to be insecure. Both Bonomi and De Gasperi

seemed gratified (if a trifle alarmed) by the concessions. Like all people who cry out for freedom, they are a bit taken aback if it is given to them. However, in general, they appeared fairly satisfied. Like most Latin races, they are interested in the theoretical and juridical aspect; we eschew [these], and go for the practical.[12]

They still hankered after the status of 'ally', but apart from any question of British resentment at the events of 1940, it could hardly be expected that the French should be ready to accept this concept in principle, although they were ready enough to operate something like it in practice. The Italian Ministers were also

[12] 24 February 1945.

very anxious about the withdrawal of our local officials, from 'Italian Government Italy'. They fear the disimprovement in administration standards which will surely follow.

I reported to the Foreign Office the Italian Government's reactions, which naturally had in them an element of Oliver Twist. Noel Charles felt that the events of the last few days had done much to re-establish British prestige, and to counteract the innuendoes of the less respectable American Press correspondents who had so long tried to undermine our position in the Mediterranean.

The next task, disregarding all the troubles and foolish accusations still being levelled at the Commission in Washington, was to tighten up and improve the structure at H.Q.; to make and achieve the best possible co-operation with Italian industry; to increase the pace of 'civilianisation'; and to expedite supplies of all kinds. These matters occupied the next few weeks.

In the lull before the resumption of the offensive, we had one major anxiety—the problem of coping with the partisan forces in northern Italy. In the early spring, the view was widely held that the German withdrawal in northern Italy would not be rapid owing to communication and transportation difficulties. The fanatical Fascists and the various neo-Fascist organisations would stick to the Germans, although mass desertion might be expected at the end. The important thing was first for the Army and then the A.M.G. officers to push forward and take control. Some of the patriot bands were to be incorporated as reconnaissance units in the Italian combat groups; others should be immediately enlisted as individuals. Every attempt was to be made, as the Germans retired, to treat the partisans as Allies and to award them decorations and honours. At the same time we felt that immediately the Germans began to crack, there would be an indiscriminate demand to join the resistance movement. Every man who had sat upon the fence would leap hastily down upon the winning side. All the thousands of Vicars of Bray would attune their doctrine to the one now dominant. Our best hope was to confine supplies to food and clothing; to regulate the quantities; to see that the British and American task forces moved as rapidly as possible to the important centres; and to collect the partisans at central points, partly to arrange with them any share they or their nominees should have in local administration, and partly to organise the ceremonial handing over of arms.

At this stage it was important neither to underrate nor to exaggerate the strength of the partisans. We must not try to play them up into a separate Government; nor should we discourage them unduly. Many people believed that the Communists were the strongest party in Italy, and that when elections came this would be proved. How far they would be content with playing a constitutional role was obscure. Some observers believed that Italy would break up under two rival Governments, one in the north and one in the centre and south. Meanwhile certain other steps were taken to help escaping patriots to be dealt with at reception centres and to be given pay and food while waiting absorption into the Army or civilian work. This had the valuable effect of draining off a number of men. Nevertheless, I was rather concerned to find towards the end of March that arms and ammunition were still being put into the hands of the resistance groups in considerable quantities. On taking this up with A.F.H.Q. I was assured that precautions were now being taken only to drop these close behind the German line where they were intended for use in the offensive which was now about to be launched. On 26 March, I had a conversation with Bonomi on the plans for northern Italy when it fell into our hands. Although it would be under Allied Military Government in the initial stages, I was anxious to strengthen the hands of the Italian Government and increase their prestige in every possible way. It was vital to neglect no method which could help to prevent violent action by the Communists.

I proposed that a Government statement should be broadcast; that although in A.M.G. territory, victory meetings should be held in Milan, Genoa, Turin, Venice, etc., at which the Government members of all parties should speak. Then there was a question of re-forming the Government—to include [the] Socialists and Action Party—and to get some new figures from the North. I am also keen that the new Italian 'gruppi' (or combat brigades) should lead the march in; and of course if they go in, there is no reason why the Prince should not visit them—and at the same time his subjects in the north of Italy.[13]

This last suggestion I put forward to Alexander who treated it with sympathy, and arrangements were made accordingly. Bonomi too seemed grateful.

On 16 April Pizzoni, the non-party chairman of the C.L.N.A.I. in

[13] 26 March 1945.

Milan, came to see me. (He was known to the Resistance by the name of Longhi.) He was a banker, genial, good-tempered, educated at London University, sensible and patriotic. He did not conceal his anxieties. Some of the Communists wanted to get rid of him, but I encouraged him to continue to hold firmly to his position and try to moderate the extremists.

He had some useful bits of advice as to how we might succeed in dealing with the . . . 'Patriots' after liberation. The chief problem—as usual—will be disarmament. Longhi will *not* go on with politics, but go back to business. It seems a pity and I told him so.[14]

Although there was bound to be some confusion when liberation came, the arrangements which we had made proved broadly successful, at least as far as Italian territory was concerned. We were of course much aided by the rapidity of the last offensive, launched on 9 April and concluded by the end of the month. But delicate problems remained. In the last days of the war, the Italian Government wanted to send their representatives to the north and approached Rear-Admiral Stone, the Deputy Commissioner. I did not think this was a good idea and minuted as follows:

1. I have discussed with the Field-Marshal the suggestion that three or four of the leading Italian Ministers should go to northern Italy.
2. We both feel that this is not advisable. It should certainly not be even considered until after the C.L.N.A.I. representatives have accepted the invitation to Rome and we know the outcome of their discussions.
3. The precedent of Canossa is still remembered in Italy.
4. If you wish to use this as a directive in your discussions with Bonomi, please do so.

The next step was to stop paying the large subsidies to the partisan groups. If we could deprive them of money and arms, the prospects of peaceful reconstruction would become more favourable.

Credit for the comparatively peaceful transition is due partly to Pizzoni himself; partly to Parri who, a few months later, became Prime Minister in succession to Bonomi and thus symbolised full association of the north with the centre and south of Italy; and partly to the quiet, persistent and devoted work of many British and American officers in every field. These men had been dropped by parachute and risked their lives as liaison officers with the resistance groups over a

[14] 16 April 1945.

long period. They were reinforced by the forward officers of the Army and of A.M.G. who handled difficult situations with a combination of tact and firmness. Italy owes a great deal to the moral, as well as material, aid which we gave her tortured people when the great day came. The proof of our success is to be found in the subsequent political history of the country. It was the last great achievement in this field of Anglo-American organisation. I was proud indeed to preside over one of its important elements—the Allied Commission.

During the summer and autumn months of 1944, many plans had been made for providing relief to Balkan countries. General Hughes's organisation had for this purpose been moved from Cairo to Caserta. But all through we were short of ships, as well as of supplies, particularly clothing. As early as October 1944 we had put in our demands.

Statisticians have worked out that if the citizens of the U.S.A. would accept a standard of clothing for themselves 3½ times as good as that enjoyed by the British, the present capacity of America could in one year produce sufficient to re-clothe the whole of Europe. But the slogan naturally is 'no rationing in a Presidential [election] year'.[15]

In Roumania, by the last months of the campaign, the position had disintegrated. King Michael's *coup d'état* in August 1943 had resulted in the disarming of the German forces. Bulgaria had equally made an attempt to declare war on Germany. But in both cases the Russians had seized the initiative, and by the time that Le Rougetel got to Roumania and Houston-Boswall to Bulgaria there was little to be done except to secure some kind of British presence in the Armistice Commission. The Moscow Agreement as to the percentage of influence in various Balkan countries really settled the matter. I was provided from time to time with admirable summaries of the situation. But I could not help drawing the conclusion that in these two countries at any rate, as well as in Hungary, the game was up. In January, Le Rougetel stayed with us at Caserta on his way home and gave me an interesting report of the Russian management of the Control Commission in Roumania.

They seem determined to get everything they can out of the country. They have taken away a large part of the machinery of the oil wells (which incidentally belongs to British and American shareholders) and they are now

[15] 12 October 1944.

deporting a large part of the population. They take men and women (children are left behind) to work in Russian coalmines, etc. But as they put them into open cattle trucks (with no heating) in the bitter winter weather, their action seems not only brutally cruel but very stupid—since few of them will ever arrive.[16]

With a kind of cynical logic, the people whom they condemned for this purpose were drawn from the 600,000 Roumanian citizens of German descent who had been settled in Roumania for many generations, even centuries.

In Albania, where our officers had organised a strong and loyal resistance movement with pro-Allied views and anti-Communist sentiments, the situation steadily worsened. General Hoxha was gaining control, and although the British and American Governments very properly refused him recognition, we were instructed to send in relief. In the end, Albania fell completely into the Communists' hands and our friends were in danger of 'liquidation'. I remember well Colonel Bill McLean and Julian Amery pleading for me to make arrangements to take out Abas Kupi and other members of his organisation. This I did without any authority and have never regretted doing so. The small country of Albania, with a peasant and clan tradition, not only went Communist at this time but has remained the pillar of traditional Marxism. Indeed, the struggle of this tiny orthodox David challenging the Russian revisionist Goliath has a somewhat ludicrous aspect. Meanwhile, Albania had to be written off by us during the last months of the war even more completely than Roumania or Bulgaria.

With Austria, we were not directly concerned, although the news came to us of the difficulties of arranging an agreement on the zones of occupation. Strangely enough, this was the one country—in addition to Germany—in which Russia agreed to a division of authority, although they were not ill placed to impose their will. At the time, I watched what was happening in the last days of April with detached interest. More than ten years later I was to sign a treaty by which Austria was finally freed from Allied occupation—Russian, French, British and American.

Further apprehension was caused by the French operations on the Italian frontier. Eden was anxious that French troops should be

[16] 15 January 1945.

withdrawn from Italian areas as soon as operational conditions permitted. On the other hand, General Mark Clark felt that the French threat to the Val d'Aosta in north-west Italy was a valuable factor in pinning down a number of German divisions. By 20 April it was thought that the Germans would move these troops eastwards to assist in the desperate position which was beginning to threaten them south of the Po. At this point, in spite of the political implications, I pressed Eden to support Alexander and Clark's desire to put these tactical and strategic considerations ahead of all others. I felt justified in urging this for two reasons. After the many frustrations from which Alexander's campaign had suffered through the continued weakening of his forces, it seemed right not to impose at this stage a fresh obstacle to final success. Secondly, I believed that the further the French intruded the less was the ultimate danger. If they were to go into territory beyond the Val d'Aosta to which they could advance no possible claim, the military character of the campaign would be emphasised. With this view Churchill agreed, and telegraphed accordingly both to Eisenhower and to me.

In the event, the French were ordered to withdraw on 30 April, their tactical function having been performed. But the general in command flatly refused to accept these instructions without the agreement of his Government. The sequel was one of the many painful problems that confronted us after the defeat of Germany.

After the irritation caused by the minor infiltration into north-west Italy, the danger of major occupation of the north-east provinces by Tito's Yugoslav partisans proved far more serious. The provinces of Venezia Tridentina and Venezia Giulia, with their substantial majorities of Austrians, Slovenes and Croats, particularly in the rural areas, were especially vulnerable. It was decided at an early stage that Military Government must be set up as soon as possible throughout the area. In August 1944 General Wilson gave a warning to Marshal Tito about the attitude which the Allies would take up. Both the State Department and the Foreign Office felt that the Allies should control both provinces, pending a post-war settlement. Early in 1945, when it became clear that it would be difficult, in view of operations in Austria, to occupy the whole of Venezia Giulia, Alexander took the line that what was absolutely necessary was the control of Allied lines of communication from Trieste and the port of Pola. Hence a military division of Venezia Giulia by a fixed boundary would meet his needs. However, this was not a very advantageous solution politically. It was likely to involve the ultimate recognition of Yugoslav sovereignty in an area east of the line. Alexander and I thought it might be better to arrange a tripartite occupation, with Yugoslavia as one of the partners, on the analogy of the agreements made for Austria.

Since time was pressing, Alexander decided to see Tito himself. The State Department were insistent that we ought to put A.M.G.

in *all* Venezia Giulia. If Tito is there first, this will in fact be impossible, and I think it is much more realistic to admit it.[17]

But Alexander still wished to negotiate a purely military arrangement, which was certainly realistic. By securing to us Trieste, this would meet our immediate needs.

The Americans strongly objected. As 'trustees' for Italy (they said) we should insist on occupying all Venezia Giulia and setting up Military Government in accordance with the Italian armistice terms. This is all very well in theory; in practice, it is difficult to see how we are going to eject Tito.[18]

However, in view of the American objections, I had to advise Alexander to ask for instructions from the Combined Chiefs of Staff. This meant that he could only 'sound' Tito at this meeting and make some recommendation on his return, in the light of his talk.

Of course, this matter (which may easily become urgent) ought to have been dealt with at the [Yalta] Conference. But they either overlooked it or shirked it.[19]

At the meeting, which took place at Belgrade on 21 February, Tito agreed with regard to the lines of communication to Trieste and that Allied Military Government should operate within the zone of our communications. But he asked for his civil administration, already installed, to be retained, although he agreed that these authorities should be responsible to A.M.G. He did not wish Alexander to occupy the Istrian peninsula, but offered an additional line of communication to Austria through Ljubljana.

It soon became clear that Tito intended to extend his authority over as large a part of Italy as possible. East of the Isonzo, the Yugoslav

[17] 17 February 1945.
[18] 20 February 1945.
[19] Ibid.

Partisans were in complete control except where the Germans still remained. They were making every effort to extend their authority to the whole province of Udine. Nor did they despise any methods, including the subversion of Italian brigades where the Communists were the majority.

On the Field-Marshal's return we had a most difficult report to make. Alexander, who saw great military difficulties in imposing our government over the head of strong Partisan forces, put forward two possible courses. First, to divide Venezia Giulia into two sections, leaving the eastern one to Tito; the second, to establish Military Government over the whole region but to allow the Yugoslavs to play a part in it. The State Department fought both these proposals with the greatest vigour as a matter of principle. But nobody was prepared to answer Alexander's vital question. If the Yugoslavs opposed his occupation of the whole of Venezia Giulia, was he to use force? To this no answer was forthcoming except to authorise bringing up the United States II Corps to strengthen the military position.

On the morning of 26 April, the Field-Marshal held his usual political meeting. The end of the campaign was approaching; the German surrender was only a few days off. But this serious question remained unsettled.

Venezia Giulia was the most important item in a long agenda. We still have no instructions. After a long discussion, the draft prepared by Deputy C. of S. (Lemnitzer), suggesting occupation of all Venezia Giulia in default of instructions, was turned down. I carried my proposal that the F.M. (if not instructed to do something more for *political* reasons) would content himself with trying to get Trieste and the Robertson (or Wilson) line. This can be defended against Tito and/or Stalin as a *military* necessity to secure Allied communications into Austria.[20]

Alexander reported to the C.C.S. the plan which he intended to follow unless otherwise instructed. He would seize those parts of Venezia Giulia which were essential to his operations, including Trieste and the communications leading to it and from it into Austria. He would occupy Pola. In this area he would set up his Allied Military Government. This would operate through suitable local groups, whether Italian or Yugoslav. At the same time, he would inform Marshal Tito of his intention and tell him that any of his forces in this area must

[20] 26 April 1945.

come under his own command. But the Chiefs of Staff were not satisfied, and sent peremptory orders that the whole of Venezia Giulia, including Fiume and the Quarnarolo Islands, should be taken over by Allied troops. The Russians were being asked to bring pressure upon Tito to withdraw his forces. Yet the C.C.S., obviously alarmed at the consequences of their instructions, added that 'before any actual conflict, he should communicate with the Combined Chiefs'. This seemed to us a strangely unrealistic view of the situation.

In fact, events moved too fast for Washington and London. Our main task was to reach Trieste before the Yugoslavs, and this was achieved by the New Zealand Division on 2 May, without serious conflict with the Yugoslav Army. The German garrison was still in the town and had to be dealt with. but General Freyberg, with his usual aplomb, succeeded in his double purpose and also entered Gorizia, which had been partially occupied by Tito's troops.

There followed consolidation by both sides. But many difficulties lay before us, and there were anxious moments before an accommodation could be reached. The war with the Germans was soon to end; but the new conflicts and rivalries in Europe were about to begin.

Another country which caused us increasing concern was Poland. Its future was no affair of ours, except as it affected the morale of the Polish Corps under Alexander's command. As each month went by, the bright hopes by which General Anders and his gallant troops had been sustained began to fade. The Teheran Conference was discouraging, but not yet fatal. If Poland was to lose the territory east of the Curzon Line, she was to be compensated by the Oder-Neisse frontier. But at the beginning of 1944 General Anders and his leading officers began to express deep anxiety. A People's Council of Poland was set up in Warsaw. The Russian armies began to cross into the old pre-1939 Poland and on 11 January 1944 definitely announced the annexation to Russia of all territory east of the Curzon Line.

After my visit to General Anders in April 1944, I kept in touch with him through the military liaison department. In May of that year, when the delegates from the People's Council were sent to meet representatives of the Union of Polish Patriots, there was created a nucleus of what later became the Lublin Committee. Neither its composition nor its character were attractive to the Polish armies in the field. All through the summer the Russian troops were driving into Poland, and after the capture or liberation of Lublin on 23 July 1944, a manifesto announced the formation of a Polish Committee of National Liberation to which Russia undertook to give the administrative responsibility. This was in fact a mere façade. The key positions were held by Communists, and the few non-Communists were later eliminated. The tragic uprising of Warsaw followed, one of the poignant and terrible episodes of the war. On 29 July the Polish Communists broadcast from Moscow, inciting the resistance movement in Warsaw to rise in revolt against the Germans. On 1 August the great movement began. But the Russians turned the main drive of their army south through Roumania and made no real attempt to rescue Warsaw. The British and American Governments tried in vain to persuade the Russians to allow them to use their air bases for our relieving planes to land and refuel. But the usual cruel negative was maintained, Oriental and impassive, until on 2 October the fearful news came that the Warsaw revolt had collapsed. Thus the greater part of those who might prove dangerous to Communist domination had been successfully removed by the Germans. In all this tragic story, followed by the Moscow Conference, we in Italy could take no part. Yet the flower of Polish manhood was enrolled in those splendid armies that had marched out of Russia nearly two years before and were now fighting loyally and bravely at our side.

On 15 September 1944 I had a long talk with General Anders at Alexander's mess.

He was very sensible, recognising the necessity of first defeating the German enemy. But he is naturally very bitter about the Russians and the tragedy of Warsaw.[21]

At the same time, I felt that he would be ready to co-operate in any reasonable settlement, and I was glad that we had arranged to send him home to confer with the Polish Government in London.

The whole sad story continued, in which the intransigence of the Polish parties in London may have played its part. Nevertheless, the Lublin Committee was merely an instrument in Russian hands, and when the Yalta decisions were announced, accepting this body as a Provisional Government, they were naturally a grievous blow to our

[21] 15 September 1944.

Polish friends. The formula about the inclusion of democratic representatives from Poles abroad was regarded as a sham. The reaffirmation of a common desire of Russia, Britain and America 'to see established a strong, free, independent and democratic Poland'[22] was received with bitter contempt. These decisions were made known on 12 February 1945, and General Anders's immediate reaction was to ask the Field-Marshal to take the Polish troops out of the line. On the 16th he sent his famous telegram to London, in which he stated that II Corps (Anders's army) refused to recognise the Yalta decision, but regarded the Polish Government in London as the sole representative 'of the majesty of a sovereign Poland'.

It was in these painful circumstances that I met General Anders on 17 February. The Field-Marshal had asked him to dinner, together with his A.D.C., Prince Lubomirski. Alexander wisely encouraged the General to speak frankly, without interruption. He was naturally in a mood of cruel disillusionment, almost despair.

A rather painful discussion—or rather monologue—in which General A. said that Poland was finished, betrayed by her allies. It was now merely a question of time before all Europe would succumb to Bolshevism.[23]

There was little we could say; but we were deeply distressed. It was a terrible evening.

Perhaps the greatest loss which the Poles had suffered had been the death of General Sikorski, the first Prime Minister of their exiled Government. I felt sure that had he been alive,

the Polish Government in London would never have been allowed to drift into the futile and fatuous position it now occupies.

General Anders was about to leave for London for discussions. I knew that his soldierly loyalty would remain unaffected, but it was clear that his troops must be disturbed.

At the worst, they will disintegrate into a rabble of refugees. At the best, they will be kept enough together to hold a sector of line, without attacks or counter-attacks. I do not think they could now be used offensively.[24]

This judgement was proved wrong. I had underestimated the marvellous dignity and devotion of Anders and his comrades. They fought

[22] Yalta Declaration, 11 February 1945.
[23] 17 February 1945.
[24] Ibid.

with distinction in the front of the attack in the last battles of April. They had lost their country, but they kept their honour.

On 13 April the news came to us of President Roosevelt's death. I had of course heard of his deterioration in health, which everyone noticed at Yalta.

Moreover, the publication of a photograph showing the President with Churchill and Stalin had caused a great impression, since the President appeared so weak and thin.[25]

Nevertheless, his death was a great shock. He had ruled for so long an America which was first a friendly neutral and then a loyal ally that it seemed the end of an era. A memorial service for the President was held in Rome.

The church was full and the service impressive. The whole Italian Cabinet attended, also the Lieutenant-General (Prince Umberto). The service was rather too long, but well done.[26]

The final offensive in Italy had been launched on 9 April.

The F.M. has just begun his battle in Italy. It has made a good start; but of course our forces are very weak and the Germans have some of their best divisions.[27]

Little news now reached us of this battle, and we had no clear picture of its likely development.

The real difficulty of the north is the number of uncertain factors. If we know whether the Germans will fight back every inch of the ground or ultimately surrender *en masse,* it would be much easier to make our plans. I think that we may very likely see something between the two—that is, the Germans and Italian Fascist forces might be split into two or more groups and gradually forced to a position where the inner core would remain for a time and ultimately give in.

But all this was doubtful. Indeed, if the Germans decided to fight it out, it might prove impossible to bring the matter to a conclusion without sending more troops to Alexander.

He is trying now to fight a final battle without sufficient forces. By good tactical use of his overwhelming air strength, and by his superiority in gun

[25] 14 April 1945.
[26] 15 April 1945.
[27] 12 April 1945.

power and ammunition, he may be able to bring it off. But it will be a very remarkable achievement and we must be prepared for delay.[28]

I was now determined to see something of this battle, for I knew it would be the last and it seemed a pity to miss it. Also, I wanted to see something of the Military Government officers in action. For many months the line had been static. Now it would become highly mobile, and I could see what really happened when A.M.G. had to follow close behind the armies.

I left Rome on 20 April for Florence. General Mark Clark sent a car to meet me and an officer to give me the news, which was encouraging. We left Florence again at 5.30, arriving at Forli in an hour. Here we were met by Air Commodore Con Benson, an old friend, the Chief A.M.G. officer of the Eighth Army, and some of his staff. After a short talk with him and his officers, I went to dine with the Army Commander, General Dick McCreery, who was formerly Alexander's Chief of Staff in Tunisia. He had taken over the Eighth Army when General Leese went to Burma.

After dinner the General took me to his caravan and explained to me the course of the battle up to date. He was really hopeful now of a big result—the Poles and the New Zealanders had opened very well on the Eighth Army front.

The former claim to have killed 2,000 Germans. The latter have inflicted big losses also. And they have both been dealing with first-rate German divisions—paratroops and Panzers.[29]

Con Benson had laid on an excellent programme of A.M.G. activities for the next day.

We started from Forli (in the modern Municipio of which I had spent the night in Fascist luxury) and our trip covered Faenza, Imola (just captured—to the neighbourhood of which Eighth Army was moving today), Lugo, Ravenna, Classe, Cesena, Rimini, Riccione, and Pesaro. Our tour covered meeting the provincial officers and discussing various problems with them (Colonel Bowman, the U.S. Regional Commissioner, was our guide), seeing a repaired pumping station and the need of further repairs to control the drainage system of the valley; visiting an Italian mine-clearance squad at work; seeing institutions for the reception and care of civilian refugees; and a

[28] Ibid.
[29] 20 April 1945.

hundred and one other activities, great and small, carried out under Allied supervision and assistance.[30]

All these officers were 'teed up' to go forward and take over in the northerly provinces of the region.

In addition to these professional activities, which were the excuse or reason for the trip, I was able, under the guidance of Major Newton of the Eighth Army, an expert archaeologist, to see something of Ravenna and Rimini.

Rimini has been pretty badly destroyed—unfortunately the lovely so-called Temple of Malatesta has been much battered.[31]

Ravenna had been more fortunate. San Vitale, the mausoleum of Galla Placidia, the Baptistery of the Orthodox, Sant' Apollinare Nuovo, the Baptistery of the Arians and Sant' Apollinare in Classe— all these were more or less intact and their magnificent series of mosaics preserved. A dinner was then given in my honour at Riccione, with sixty or seventy officers present. Colonel Bowman presided, and toasts were drunk with great enthusiasm, all the greater because they had learned that it was my Silver Wedding day.

From Riccione I motored back to Imola where I slept in a comfortable caravan at the Field-Marshal's 'Caledon Camp' near Eighth Army Headquarters. The next morning I started off by jeep with General McCreery. The battle was in full swing and going well. We visited the 56th Division under General Arbuthnot and then the 24th Guards Brigade under Brigadier Erskine.

They were about 1,000 yards from the most forward positions. The Scots Guards and the Coldstream were held up by a bridge (which the Buffs had tried to rush before it was destroyed). The engineers would take six hours, and then the advance would continue. It was clear that everyone was in good heart, in spite of some heavy fighting.[32]

We lunched at Eighth Army advanced headquarters, where I found my old friend John Harding who had now, much to his delight, been given command of XIII Corps. The afternoon and evening we spent with the New Zealand Division and the Poles.

[30] 21 April 1945.
[31] Ibid.
[32] 22 April 1945.

The Poles have fought splendidly and were in crashing form. Not a word about politics or the future of Poland; nothing but triumphant exposition of their operations. I hardly recognised General Anders, whom I had last seen in very gloomy mood at Caserta. 'Une très jolie petite bataille; nous avons tué plus que deux mille Boches; on les sent partout.'[33]

The next day, 23 April, was indeed a red-letter day. The Eighth Army had lent me a car and a military policeman, and I drove into Bologna with Stewart Brown, an American, the Commission's Public Relations Officer, and my A.D.C., Lieutenant Atkinson. At Bologna, which the Poles and the Americans had entered the day before, we found considerable excitement, but no confusion. Brigadier Hume, who commanded the A.M.G. of the Fifth Army, had arrived and installed himself in the splendid and undamaged Municipio. The Fascist Black Brigade just before leaving had shot two well-known Liberal leaders. They were now lying in state in the Municipio and a large but orderly crowd was streaming by with flowers and tears.

One of the murdered men, known as Mario, was old, white hair, fine well-cut face—obviously a man of character. The coffins were open so that friends and admirers could see the faces of their leaders for the last time. They had been shot against the wall of the Municipio—the bloodstains were clear. Above the place where they had stood were already flowers and—pathetically—photographs of men and women of all ages who had been put to death during recent months by the Fascist Black Brigade.[34]

The Prefect—a Fascist—had failed to make his escape in time. He had been shot by the partisans next to his last victim. You could see the brains spattered against the brick and the blood on the ground.

We spent the morning discussing affairs with various A.M.G. officers and some Italians.

The Committee of National Liberation came to see us and appeared fairly calm and reasonable. Provisional appointments to the posts of Prefect and Mayor have already been agreed and the town was in pretty good shape. Water—and a limited supply of electricity—are available. There seems a fair amount of food. The population is swollen by an influx of villagers from the battle area. It is probably now 600,000, instead of a normal 400,000–500,000.

We lunched at a restaurant which the Military Government had already taken over and where Italian cooks now served American

[33] 22 April 1945.
[34] 23 April 1945.

rations to Allied officers instead of Italian food to German officers; there was a moral in this.

General Hume, Brown, Atkinson and I then started off in two jeeps for Modena. The situation in this town, about twenty miles north-west of Bologna, was not known. We had tried to get in the day before but had been turned back by heavy firing. But it was said that American tanks had been through it that morning.

The drive was quite amusing, and even exciting. There was some traffic going forward and at each village the people turned out with flowers, etc. About five miles from the town we passed an American infantry battalion, advancing in rather a gingerly fashion. We asked them what they were doing, and they said they were going to attack and occupy Modena in due course.

We drove on into the town, hoping to anticipate them.

There was a little desultory sniping but not much more.

Our arrival at the Municipio (or Town Hall) caused some excitement. There was a lot of shouting and embracing. The leader of the partisans kissed me on both cheeks on being told that I was the famous Haroldo Macmillano—said by the B.B.C. to be the ruler and father of the Italian people. I was presented with an armlet and taken into the Town Hall to be formally enrolled.

Either because this caused rather a crowd, or because the hour of siesta was over, or because a procession of Fascists was being taken off to prison camps, things suddenly began to hot up.

A two-hour duel began between the partisans (who were quite well armed) and a number of Germans and Fascists who had taken up some pretty good positions in various windows, etc.

Our partisans behaved well and began to shoot up the Germans in a remarkably professional way.

They got a machine-gun on to one particularly tiresome group of snipers (who commanded the main street) and did quite well with hand grenades.

Since there were no British or American troops, and I was in civilian clothes, although now decorated with a partisan armlet, I and my companions tried to take as little part in all these operations as honour would allow.

But naturally one had to pretend to do something. It was really quite an exciting little action while it lasted and quite spirited. Of course a lot of partisans fired off their pieces quite aimlessly and threw grenades just for fun. Indeed, these gentlemen and their curious assortment of rifles, grenades, tommy-guns, etc., caused me more alarm than our opponents.

Finally, the fighting died down and we felt it decent to leave. We had got our jeeps into position under a portico near the main street.

After a lot of hand-shaking and cheering, we got in and made a dash down the street. All went well—scarcely a shot fired—till we came to the barrier which we had passed without incident on entering. Some chap *outside* this barrier had been stirred into activity by the noise (or perhaps awakened from his afternoon sleep). Anyway, he covered the exit fairly effectively. We jumped hastily from our jeeps, and got as near to the walls on each side— rather inglorious but wise. Some of our friends turned up, and eventually they got him from the window of a neighbouring house. We then left . . . without further incident. A very interesting episode.

Brown and I naturally claimed that we had 'liberated' Modena!

We returned to Bologna where my car and military police escort had prudently remained. The crowds were gay but not violent. A few alleged Fascist girls had been shaved, and our A.M.G. officers had rightly protested. But the partisans attributed this incident to the rivalries of foolish boys and not to political motives.

We are going to try to disband and disarm the 3,500 partisans in Bologna on Wednesday (the 25th). They are all to be paraded, and marched past General Clark. They will hand in their rifles and get a sort of certificate from Field-Marshal Alexander. (This has already worked in some places further south and I am told that in the black market these certificates command a good price—which is encouraging.) They are given a choice of joining the Italian Army (if of the right age) or going into special centers where we shall try to feed them and look after them until they can be employed by the Allies or returned to normal civilian employment.[35]

Atkinson and I returned to Caledon Camp, where the Field-Marshal arrived for dinner, a very cheerful occasion, everyone in tremendous heart about the battle, which continued to go well.

When I got back to Rome I found that Vittorio Orlando, Prime Minister of Italy at the end of the First War, had been brought to luncheon.

I enjoyed the old man. He is eighty-four and reminds me a good deal of Lloyd George. He is a Sicilian (as Ll.G. [was] a Welshman) and thus a little

[35] Ibid.

outside the ordinary Italian type and cast of thought. He has a great deal of humour and seemed very much alive. . . . We talked till 3.30. Orlando was pessimistic about the immediate future, but confident of the ultimate recovery of Italy. He does not think Communism will last in its Marxist form, but will have to adapt itself to the Italian genius or fail to maintain itself in the long run.[36]

By now the battle was moving fast, and I knew that the end was near. The Germans were completely defeated, and nearly 70,000 prisoners had already been taken. Having finished all the necessary tasks, both in my own duties and in assisting Alexander in the delicate problem which lay before him—the expected German surrender—I slipped away to Assisi. Young Robert Cecil, who had been wounded and had joined my staff as an additional A.D.C., came with me.

Robert and I started in real English April weather at 10 a.m. for a walk to the little monastery (Eremo delle Carceri), where St. Francis lived, on the slopes of Mount Subasio. It took about three hours (there and back) and although rather fatigued, it did me good. It was really wonderful to have a peaceful day in such lovely surroundings. We got very hot in the sunny intervals and cooled off by the rain showers.[37]

We spent the afternoon in the great churches—the upper and lower churches of San Francesco, Santa Chiara, and San Rufino. In the evening we heard the news that the partisans at Milan had seized and hanged Mussolini and other Fascists. Luckily we did not learn the horrible details till later.

At nightfall, a message came from Alexander to say that the German delegates had signed the military surrender on the terms agreed. We had settled all this, and I wanted to be out of the way, for it was a military and not a political affair. My absence would help to prevent any suspicion on the part of the Russians that there was a political aspect.

I am delighted, especially for Alex's sake, that his triumphant battle (there are now 100,000 prisoners) has been followed by the surrender of the armies opposed to him. It is a complete vindication of his strategical and tactical dispositions.

Now, except for the final stages in Germany and elsewhere, the war was virtually at an end. After listening to the wireless, we walked in

[36] 24 April 1945.
[37] 29 April 1945.

the square outside the great church and pondered in the night on the mutability of human affairs.

. . . I never expected to be at Assisi to hear the news of the end of the Mediterranean campaign and the last stages of the European war. It seems sometimes six weeks, six years, or six decades since the war began. And it is hard to 'take in' its end—or approaching end. . . .

Hitler has lasted [twelve] years—with all his power of evil, his strength, his boasting. St. Francis did not seem to have much power, but here in this lovely [place] one realises the immense strength and permanence of goodness—a rather comforting thought.[38]

I was glad to have been quietly at Assisi at this tremendous moment in history.

[38] Ibid.

CHAPTER TWENTY-FIVE

The German Surrender

T HE first indications that some of Kesselring's officers wished to treat for terms had reached us on 8 March. This news came through the American O.S.S. According to this information, representatives both of the S.S. and the O.K.W. commanders were expected to arrive at Lugano in Switzerland and would be ready to discuss the capitulation of German forces in northern Italy.

Alexander sent for me immediately and told me what had happened. Remembering all the complicated preliminaries to the Italian armistice, I advised him first to send a personal message to the Prime Minister and the C.I.G.S., setting out clearly the course he was proposing to pursue; secondly, after hearing from London, to report the news and the plan of operation officially to the Combined Chiefs.

If German officers want to do business, they must go into Switzerland; they must have a signed letter of authority from Marshal Kesselring; they must agree to come to A.F.H.Q.; and the discussions must be for a military surrender only—there can be nothing on the political or governmental level.[1]

We composed a message together, which was dispatched on 9 March. The substance ran as follows:

1. O.S.S. in this theatre on 8 March made information available that Waffen-S.S. General Karl Wolff, top S.S. officer North Italy, together with O.K.W. representative, presumably from Kesselring's staff, plus Dollmann and Simmer, were expected to arrive at Lugano, Switzerland, prepared to discuss capitulation German forces in North Italy. Subsequent information 9 March confirms that Wolff has in fact arrived and has indicated willingness to try to develop programme to take North Italy out of conflict. He considers mere military surrender difficult and prefers that capitulation be preceded by statement to German people from German leaders North Italy that struggle is hopeless and is merely causing needless German bloodshed. He states Kesselring not yet won over and his adherence is considered essential to plan.

[1] 9 March 1945.

Wolff, however, states that Rahn, who is German Ambassador to Fascist Italian Government, is in accord with him. Wolff claims Himmler unaware of his activities. Wolff is proceeding immediately to Kesselring to endeavour to sell plan to him and will keep in touch with O.S.S. representatives.

2. Prior to meeting in Switzerland, Dollmann promised to produce recently captured C.L.N.A.I. leader Parri as evidence of their good faith and ability to act. Information now received that Parri was in fact delivered unconditionally in Switzerland 9 March and is in good health.

3. Further discussions being held by O.S.S. with Wolff but results not yet available here. In view of these discussions O.S.S. suggest representatives my Headquarters be prepared to go to Switzerland to deal with situation in case of favourable developments.

4. If further negotiations between O.S.S. and Wolff develop to extent that German representatives appear genuine and have specific proposals to discuss, I propose to act on following lines:

(a) The German *parlementaires* must come to Berne with signed authority from Marshal Kesselring that they have authority to treat.

(b) O.S.S. to arrange a meeting place either at American or British Embassies at night. If Embassies too difficult, another meeting place can be considered.

(c) I will send Major-General Lyman L. Lemnitzer, my American Deputy Chief of Staff, and Major-General T. S. Airey, my British Chief Intelligence Officer, to Berne.

(d) They will be instructed to tell the Germans:

(1) that they must come to A.F.H.Q. for detailed military discussions;

(2) that they must arrange a method of communication with Kesselring;

(3) that the discussions will only deal with the method of surrender on a purely military and not a governmental or political basis.

5. Please note that two of the leading figures are S.S. and Himmler men, which makes me very suspicious. Nevertheless it is as well to be prepared.

6. Request your agreement with above proposed procedure. I shall not send representatives to Berne as proposed in para. 4 (c) above until I receive your authorisation. You will be kept fully informed of future developments.

At the time I did not attach too great an importance to this contact. We had already received similarly optimistic reports from the American O.S.S., which had come to nothing. Besides, the Germans named were mainly S.S. men, and I thought it more likely that we should be approached by the old regular Army rather than by the Hitler–Himmler crowd.

On 11 March (Sunday) Alexander told me that he

had heard from London and reported officially to C.C.S. his proposed action on the German approach. He seems to think we may really be able to do business—but not probably immediately. He was also pleased at a message from the P.M. The plan of sending him as Deputy Commander to Eisenhower is dropped. Alex. is much relieved; it would have been a most difficult and awkward position.[2]

For the next week I was in Athens ; but a day or two after my return Alexander told me that there was little progress with the German negotiations. Kesselring appeared now to have left the Italian front, and this would necessarily slow things up. On 29 March, at SACMED's political meeting, we had a long discussion on the terms for a possible military surrender. We had received no guidance from home, which was on the whole an advantage. We were still worried about the 16,000 enemy troops in Crete, the greater part of whom were Germans. General Robertson now felt that it might be safe to accept their surrender because he would be able to give them some food and ship them off to the Middle East where they could be cared for. This, of course, was a small matter ; but it made us begin to wonder how we should deal with the whole German Army if it surrendered to us in northern Italy.

In these and subsequent discussions, Alexander was able to clarify his mind as to the terms and the methods of procedure. But nothing happened for three weeks. On 24 April, while Alexander's armies were giving the Germans a terrific hammering, Wolff suddenly reappeared in Switzerland. He now claimed to have full powers from General von Vietinghoff, the successor to Kesselring. In accordance with the plan that we had arranged, two German officers, Lieutenant-Colonel von Schweinitz, representing the German Commander-in-Chief, and Major Wenner, representing S.S. General Wolff, were brought to our headquarters at Caserta. The first claimed to have full authority from von Vietinghoff, Commander of Army Group 'C', Commander-in-Chief South-West, and Commander of the Wehrmacht in Italy. His credentials were dated 22 April 1945. Major Wenner produced similar documents dated 25 April 1945 and signed by Wolff. At this meeting the Chief of Staff, General Morgan (British), and the Deputy Chief of Staff, General Lemnitzer (American), represented the Commander-in-Chief. General Airey (Chief Intelligence Officer) was also present.

[2] 11 March 1945.

Alexander kept me fully informed. The third and decisive meeting took place at 2 o'clock on 29 April, and it was this thrilling news that Alexander telephoned to me in Assisi. The last page of the typewritten report, of which I have a faded copy, has a certain dramatic interest.

Lt.-General Morgan: I understand that you, Lieutenant-Colonel von Schweinitz, are prepared to sign terms of surrender on behalf of General von Vietinghoff, Commander-in-Chief South-West. Is this correct?

Lt.-Col. von Schweinitz: Yes.

Lt.-General Morgan: And that you, Major Wenner, are prepared to sign on behalf of S.S.-General Wolff, Supreme Commander of S.S. and Police and plenipotentiary General of the German Wehrmacht in Italy. Is this correct?

Major Wenner: Yes.

Lt.-General Morgan: I have been empowered by Field-Marshal Alexander, Supreme Allied Commander, to sign on his behalf. The terms of the Instrument of Surrender will take effect from 12 noon Greenwich Mean Time on 2 May 1945. Is this correct?

Lt.-Col. von Schweinitz: Yes.

Lt.-General Morgan: I now ask you to sign the documents and I will sign them after you.

Lt.-Col. von Schweinitz: I wish to make a statement which repeats which I said at the previous meetings. I have received powers from General von Vietinghoff, which have certain limits. I am taking it on my own responsibility to exceed these limits set by General von Vietinghoff. I assume that my Commander-in-Chief will approve my action but I cannot give an absolute assurance to this effect.

Lt.-General Morgan: We accept that.

The German attitude was correct, and we now had to await the return of the delegates.

I motored back to Rome in a happy mood. A luncheon party had been arranged at my villa to which were invited, in addition to the leading officials of the Commission, Bonomi, the Prime Minister, De Gasperi, Minister of Foreign Affairs, Togliatti, the Communist leader, and one or two others. Although it was possible that the German signatures to the surrender agreement might be repudiated, it seemed most unlikely. But the secret had not yet leaked.

The Italians were quite cheerful, but of course apprehensive of each other. De Gasperi talked a lot about Trieste. I could give him no news for certain. Togliatti is torn between loyalty to Moscow and to Italy. The former will prove the stronger. . . .[3]

[3] 30 April 1945.

I had a long discussion with Bonomi.

> He improves on acquaintance. . . . He has considerable political flair. Whether he has the 'guts' to go through a difficult and semi-revolutionary period, I do not know. Perhaps after twenty-five years, his nerve has improved! Whenever I see him, I preach strength and determination. . . . After all, he has a wonderful position—no Parliament and no election. Nothing, except his own weakness, can lead to his fall.[4]

After lunch I left by car for Caserta, where I found Alexander and his principal officers in an expectant mood but calm and restrained. The German delegates had got back to their H.Q. at Bolzano, but no sure news of the acceptance had yet come through. There was one weak point. In spite of the negotiators being duly accredited, they had very properly made it clear that higher authority must confirm their actions. We had therefore to wait.

The next two days, 1 and 2 May, passed in a hectic atmosphere.

> Apart from all that is happening outside our Mediterranean theatre (such as Hitler's death!), every hour has brought a change of news.[5]

We were in permanent consultation. General McNarney (U.S.) joined our talks and Offie, in Kirk's absence, represented the American Ambassador.

> We had, on 1 May, communication with Wolff in Bolzano, but no exact messages. We could not tell whether or not the agreement signed on Sunday would be honoured.

In the course of 1 May, we heard that von Vietinghoff had been dismissed. Then it was reported that Wolff and his friends were under arrest. Later the news came that Kesselring had taken over once more but wanted forty-eight hours before making up his mind. Next, we were asked to arrange an air rescue for Wolff. Then this request was cancelled.

Finally, early in the morning of 2 May, we got a message that Kesselring and Wolff, after four hours' telephoning to each other, had reached an agreement and that the terms of the surrender would be carried out.

> But Kesselring still wanted twenty-four hours' delay before publication. To all these messages we always returned the same reply—that the signed agree-

[4] Ibid.
[5] 1 and 2 May 1945.

ment must be kept. Finally, in the course of the afternoon of the 2nd, we picked up radio messages *en clair* from German H.Q. at Bolzano, giving the necessary orders to the various units for the surrender. On this we sent a final message to Wolff (and through him to Kesselring) that since three messages were being sent *en clair*, we should make the public announcement at 6.30 p.m. We decided this at a meeting at 5 p.m. on the 2nd and the announcement was duly made. At 7.30 the P.M. spoke in the House of Commons.

All through these days we had to keep making appropriate replies to the Germans; inform Combined Chiefs of Staff through Alexander's official telegrams; keep London informed through my channels—quite a job. And I was determined to get an announcement at a time when Winston could speak in the House!

In these surrender negotiations we had followed much the same technique as with Italy.

We finished the day by listening to Churchill's House of Commons speech, most of which was on the 9 p.m. news.

I am so delighted with his tribute to Alex. and the army of Italy. We have won after all—by a short head! Now for bed—after two very wearing days.[6]

On the next day we heard that Berlin had fallen. Still, we were the first, and Alexander had a right to be proud. In spite of our anxieties, the actual carrying-out of the surrender proceeded in an orderly way. But this was still only a military surrender.

The German plan is now becoming pretty clear. It is to obtain *de facto* what they failed to obtain *de jure*, viz., a surrender to the British and Americans instead of to the Russians. They are now making and will go on making these piecemeal surrenders—holding the Eastern line with rearguards and trying to save their men, not their territory.[7]

Naturally the Germans knew that if their people became prisoners of war to us or the Americans, they would be looked after, fed, cared for and ultimately returned to Germany. But if they fell into Russian hands, they would probably never be seen or heard of again.

Kesselring (through Wolff) has sent Alex. a message asking to be put in touch with Eisenhower—a very interesting development.[8]

Although from the German point of view this was their best chance, the British and Americans stood resolutely by the alliance and in spite

[6] Ibid.
[7] 4 May 1945.
[8] Ibid.

of all Stalin's suspicions, Churchill and Truman kept both the letter and the spirit of their undertakings.

On 7 May, the following message was circulated on behalf of the Field-Marshal to Fifteenth Army Group and repeated to the many organisations, missions, rear headquarters, delegations and bases under his command.

At 0241 hours 7 May, a representative of the German High Command signed the unconditional surrender of all German land, sea and air forces in Europe to the Allied Expeditionary Force and simultaneously to the Soviet High Command.

All forces under German control are to cease active operations at 0001B hours 9 May.

It seemed, therefore, that 8 May was now to be V.E. Day.

We organised at short notice a little party at noon in my room in Caserta Palace. We invited all our staff, including servants from Naples, drivers, batmen, orderlies, etc., and all Kirk's staff. It seems almost impossible to imagine that it is all really over.[9]

On the next day a short and impressive religious service was held with a large number of commanders and troops, representing all the forces under Alexander's command. Other similar ceremonies were held throughout the whole of Italy. It was at one of these that a chaplain was said to have begun his bidding prayer with the following words: 'Almighty God, forasmuch as it is partly by Thy efforts that we have won this great victory. . . .' Whether this was sound theology or not, it seemed only fair, for we had done quite a lot ourselves.

So ended six years of the most terrible war in our history. We had surmounted many perils by air and land and sea. We had been buffeted by fierce tempests, but were now moving into calmer waters. Yet who could tell what fortune might await our Empire and our people after the storm?

[9] 8 May 1945.

Appendixes

Appendix One

Record of Conversation on H.M.S. Nelson *at Malta,*
29 September 1943

1. Marshal Badoglio opened the conversation with a statement on several points which he said he had in mind:
   (*a*) His desire to see the formation of a Government on a broad, liberal basis.
   (*b*) A declaration of war by the Italian Government against Germany on the return of the Government to Rome.
   (*c*) In the interval, he emphasised, the Italians are in a *de facto* state of war and fighting against the Germans in Corsica, Dalmatia, etc.
   (*d*) He stated that as soon as it would be possible to move Italian troops from Sardinia, he would be able to put eight Italian divisions at the disposal of the Allies.
   (*e*) He expressed the fear that Italian prisoners taken by the Germans might be liable to treatment as *francs-tireurs* and, as such, to summary execution.

2. General Eisenhower stated that in his opinion the efforts which the Italians are at present making is ample proof of their intention to co-operate, but that in view of (*e*) above, it would appear necessary that Marshal Badoglio's Government, which, after all, is the only legal Italian Government, declare war immediately.

3. Marshal Badoglio replied that he had already considered that point of view, but that the power of the Government at the moment extended over only a small part of Italy, which rendered a declaration of war in these circumstances extremely difficult.

4. General Eisenhower, however, pointed out that to the contrary the other exiled Governments, occupying not an inch of their national territory, have declared war against Germany. He expressed a desire to have the Badoglio administration undertake the administration of Sicily and other liberated areas, but it was not clear to him how such an arrangement can be made unless a declaration of war is undertaken.

5. Marshal Badoglio promised to refer this question to the King who, he said, in any event must decide. Under Italian law only the King can declare

war. Badoglio therefore stated that he would reserve his answer until he could consult with the King.

6. General Eisenhower stated that everything Marshal Badoglio does to wage war actively against Germany will raise his Government by that much in the esteem of the United Nations. He pointed out that for three long years Italy has been an enemy of the United Nations and there has been built up a mass psychology which is not as willing to accept the Italians as soldiers in the field as it might be. Therefore, General Eisenhower stated, it is Marshal Badoglio's duty today to do so just as quickly as possible. He enquired if Marshal Badoglio would so advise the King.

7. Marshal Badoglio replied that he understood General Eisenhower's point of view and would present it exactly to the King as stated because his point of view corresponds to that of General Eisenhower.

8. General Eisenhower enquired whether it is Marshal Badoglio's purpose to seek anti-Fascists and invite them to participate in his Government.

9. Marshal Badoglio replied that the choice of members of the Government will be made by the King—he himself is only a soldier, he stated, knowing very little of politics.

10. General Eisenhower expressed his sympathy as a soldier but stated that the Italian Government must assume an anti-Fascist complexion if it is to fight with the Allies.

11. In the letter [see below] which he will give him, General Eisenhower will so state, but Fascism is one of those things we are fighting which we regard with deadly enmity.

12. Marshal Badoglio indicated that he understood all of this.

13. General Eisenhower reiterated that the extent he would be permitted by his Governments to co-operate with the Italians will depend upon this point.

14. Marshal Badoglio said that the fight will be (a) against Fascism, (b) against Germany, in that order.

15. Marshal Badoglio read a letter from the King asking for the participation of Count Dino Grandi, stating in effect that Grandi made the initial attack against Mussolini and really is responsible for Mussolini's downfall. Grandi's presence in the Government would ruin the status of the Republican Fascist Government.

16. General Eisenhower said he would refer this question to his Governments. In his personal opinion, however, Grandi had been so closely associated for so long a period of time in the minds of our public opinion with Fascism that now for him to be included in the Italian Government would be subject to adverse misinterpretation.

17. Marshal Badoglio said that Fascism fell with the dissolution of the Grand Council. The leader of the attack was Grandi. If Grandi should today fall into the hands of the Fascists, he would be torn to pieces by them.

18. General Mason-MacFarlane at this moment pointed out that it would

be necessary to make use of some men who in the past have been associated with Fascism, owing to the twenty years that have passed.

19. Marshal Badoglio then read another portion of the King's letter to the effect that Grandi would be able to create a schism among the Fascists and his presence in the Italian Government as Minister of Foreign Affairs would be a factor of tremendous importance in the war against Fascism and in injuring the Republican Fascist Government.

20. General Eisenhower replied that as soldier to soldier he fully understood all of this, but he could not overlook the fact that public opinion in Allied countries had crystallised on this subject and, as he had stated before, on a matter of this importance it would be necessary for him to consult his Governments.

21. Marshal Badoglio then said that the King's idea is to invite the chiefs of the different parties—that is, the political parties—in Italy as they are now constituted, with especial reference to the most influential people. In his opinion the King has today the best knowledge of available men in Italy. The King would name these men, Marshal Badoglio said, because while the Marshal is competent to choose generals, he is not able to choose politicians. He assured General Eisenhower that he would give a liberal character to the Government. If he discovers that any one of the Ministers does not follow the policy line laid down, he will be obliged to leave.

22. General Eisenhower said that he would refer the matter to his Governments. The President and the Prime Minister have indicated an outline of things which are necessary for collaboration. He said that it would be advisable that if the King takes additional people into his Government, he submit their names a priori informally through General Mason-MacFarlane's mission, and that this kind of co-operation would facilitate matters.

23. General Eisenhower then explained that he had no desire to interfere in internal Italian affairs, but that he could not overlook our Allied public opinion.

24. Marshal Badoglio said that he had every intention to avoid any possible friction between the Italian Government and the Allies and he is certain that he will come to a general accord.

25. General Eisenhower said that he could count on our understanding.

26. At this point General Eisenhower informed Marshal Badoglio of the message from Washington regarding the American desire to have Count Sforza visit Brindisi in the near future.

27. Marshal Badoglio said that he knew Count Sforza well and recalled having been with him at the signing of the Treaty of Rapallo. He said, however, that the King does not regard Sforza with sympathy because of a declaration against the Monarchy made by Sforza some time ago. Marshal Badoglio recognised, he said, that Sforza is doing useful work in the United States and he fully appreciates it. Marshal Badoglio stated that he would

make a further effort to persuade the King of the advisability of permitting Sforza to visit Brindisi.

28. General Eisenhower stressed that our Governments attached great importance to Sforza's return to Italy and that it would have an excellent effect in our taking Italy into the Allied fold.

29. Marshal Badoglio stated that he hopes that by now General Eisenhower considers him a complete collaborator and that he would be grateful if General Eisenhower would tell him something about the Italian campaign and what the Allied goal might be—just an idea of the plan of the campaign.

30. General Eisenhower replied that we are building up to drive the Germans out of Italy. The first move is to drive the Germans out of southern Italy—then out of Rome. He said that he had not as yet consulted General Alexander regarding certain details of the plan, but that personally he considered that German departure from Rome is something of the not too distant future.

31. Marshal Badoglio suggested that if Italian troops are necessary, there are troops in Sardinia (two divisions of infantry and one paratroop division). Marshal Badoglio hopes that some Italian troops would be allowed to participate in the entrance into Rome. General Alexander said that complete plans of the Italian campaign had been prepared but that participation of the Italian troops would depend upon an Italian declaration of war.

32. General Eisenhower offered the suggestion that if Italy declares war and co-operates with the Allies, he personally would promise that a token participation of Italian troops would be approved for entry into Rome.

33. Marshal Badoglio said that he understood perfectly that when military plans are made it is difficult to change them. In connection with his suggestion regarding the entry of Italian troops into Rome, he has in mind: (a) the effect it would have on the Republican Fascist Government in the north; and (b) he is certain that the Germans will do in Rome what they have done in Naples, that is, rob, loot and kill. He pointed out that Rome is not only the capital of Italy, but that there was a distinct obligation resting on the Italian Government to defend the Vatican. For that reason Badoglio asked that Italian troops participate. They would come from Sardinia to Fiumicino and would be in Rome in one day—the Nimbo paratroop division.

34. General Eisenhower said that General Alexander would consider the use of the Italian paratroop division in every way. He said that we have heard lots of good about that division. There is no difficulty about that point.

35. Marshal Badoglio said that German resistance at Salerno is due to Kesselring, who stands for resistance all along the line. In his opinion, he said, and you must excuse me, the Allies always give the impression of helping Kesselring's plans. He offered a suggestion that the Spezia-Rimini line has one weak spot, which is near Rimini. Marshal Badoglio spoke of his knowledge of Italy which justified his assurance in offering strategic sugges-

tions and apologised with a smile for the characteristic love of old men to offer advice to younger men.

36. General Eisenhower made the suggestion that speaking as a soldier it is apparent that Italian troops have been through three years of a discouraging war. He suggested that as we go along and have Italian troops participate with us, it is regarded as of the highest importance that Marshal Badoglio select the very best Italian divisions and concentrate the equipment of others if necessary so that these divisions will be well equipped and well supplied when the battle starts. He further suggested that Marshal Badoglio take other troops of lesser value and use them on lines of communication, labour battalions, work on the docks, etc. He added that as the United Nations' armies expand he could not promise to undertake to equip all Italian divisions. We shall help, of course, he added, with the enormous amount of Italian equipment now in our hands as the result of the Tunisian and Sicilian campaigns.

37. Marshal Badoglio replied that he agreed and, in fact, was already in the process of taking the action recommended.

38. General Eisenhower requested that General Mason-MacFarlane be kept advised of whatever progress might be made along these lines so that at the proper time the necessary inspection could be made.

39. Marshal Badoglio pointed out that at the present moment he is the head of the Italian Government and that these matters would be ironed out by the respective staffs. Marshal Badoglio would be grateful, he said, if we could pass on to him whatever enemy intelligence might be available and keep him informed of the Allied build-up.

40. General Eisenhower informed Marshal Badoglio that General Alexander's headquarters will shortly be moved to Italy (Bari) during the first week of October, and would provide liaison with Marshal Badoglio's staff.

41. Marshal Badoglio said that he would be very happy to provide General Alexander with any facilities necessary.

42. General Alexander promised to provide Marshal Badoglio with such enemy intelligence as might be available and said he would be able to give him a vast amount of detailed information regarding the position of enemy units now in Italy.

43. General Eisenhower said that he would direct his staff to the effect that the only publicity regarding today's meeting would be that limited to discussion of details of military operations against Germany and that no reference would be made to the signing of any document. General Eisenhower requested that Marshal Badoglio adopt a similar policy.

44. Marshal Badoglio agreed.

45. General Eisenhower added the request that Marshal Badoglio endeavour to galvanise the Italian military action against Germany and to expedite as much as lay in his power a declaration of war against Germany.

46. Marshal Badoglio pointed out that one of his chief difficulties lies in the field of propaganda. Only the Bari radio station is available to him.

47. General Eisenhower requested Marshal Badoglio to present him with an estimate of his needs in this respect and said that the Allies would do their best to co-operate with the Marshal, using the experts available in the theatre.

48. Marshal Badoglio asked he be permitted to contact Marshal Messe, now a prisoner of war in England. Messe was formerly Aide to the King and in Marshal Badoglio's opinion could effectively go on the air at the B.B.C. in England. Marshal Badoglio suggested the use of outside radios as being most listened to and respected by the Italian population.

49. General Eisenhower asked Marshal Badoglio to send whatever material he desired to Marshal Messe for broadcasts and promised to send the suggestions to London through the proper channels.

50. General Eisenhower expressed his thanks to Marshal Badoglio and said that he hoped that great good would come from the meeting. Marshal Badoglio in reciprocating referred to the situation prevailing in 1918 when the Italians, he said, gave the decisive blow to the Germans. He also said that at that time there were with the Italian Army three British divisions and one American regiment, all of whom co-operated closely in the German defeat.

51. The meeting was adjourned at about 12.15 P.M.

Copy of Letter from General Eisenhower to Marshal Badoglio, dated 29 September 1943

29 September 1943

My dear Marshal Badoglio,

The terms of the armistice to which we have just appended our signatures are supplementary to the short military armistice signed by your respresentative and mine on 3 September 1943. They are based upon the situation obtaining prior to the cessation of hostilities. Developments since that time have altered considerably the status of Italy, which has become in effect a co-operator with the United Nations.

It is fully recognised by the Governments on whose behalf I am acting that these terms are in some respects superseded by subsequent events and that several of the clauses have become obsolescent or have already been put into execution. We also recognise that it is not at this time in the power of the Italian Government to carry out certain of the terms. Failure to do so because of existing conditions will not be regarded as a breach of good faith on the part of Italy. However, this document represents the requirements with which the Italian Government can be expected to comply when in a position to do so.

It is to be understood that the terms both of this document and of the short military armistice of 3 September may be modified from time to time if military necessity or the extent of co-operation by the Italian Government indicates this as desirable.

Sincerely,
Dwight D. Eisenhower,
General, United States Army,
Commander-in-Chief, Allied Forces.

the Italian Government can be expected to comply, when in a position to do so.

It is to be understood that the terms both of this document and of the short military armistice of September may be modified from time to time if military necessity or the extent of co-operation by the Italian Government indicates this as desirable.

Sincerely,

Dwight D. Eisenhower,

General, United States Army,

Commander-in-Chief, Allied Forces

Appendix Two

Message to Prime Minister and Foreign Secretary from Field-Marshal Alexander and Resident Minister Macmillan, dated 17 January 1945

1. The Greek operation has passed through two phases and has entered upon the third. Phase 1 was the siege of Athens. The necessary military action was by reinforcements with sound tactical dispositions; the only political action possible was the appointment of the Archbishop as sole Regent. Both these actions were taken. Phase 2 covered the final cleaning-up of the city and the pursuit of the insurgents into open country. Meanwhile a Government was formed commanding more general confidence than that of M. Papandreou. This phase ended with the truce on 11 January, which became effective at 1 a.m. on 15 January. Phase 3 now begins.

2. Militarily, our purpose must be to reduce our commitments to the minimum necessary to carry out the obligations which we have incurred and to fulfil our political purposes. Politically, we must secure a settlement of Greek affairs generally acceptable to the Greek people and likely to be lasting. At the same time, this settlement must take fully into account public opinion in Great Britain.

3. The object of a truce is to lead to a peace.

   (*a*) Negotiations should be begun at once. Delay will give the insurgents a breathing-space, and may effect division of Greece into two semi-states:
   (i) ELAS in north relying on Slav support; (ii) the Government in the south relying on us.

   (*b*) Negotiations should be between the Greek Government and representatives of what remains of EAM/ELAS. This is what Regent proposed in his message to ELAS Central Committee immediately after signing of the Truce. We may find practicable to have representatives of the secessionists at the meeting.

   (*c*) In our view the Archbishop should be urged to preside. If General Plastiras presides, the meeting may break up in disorder.

   (*d*) The military situation has been restored by U.K. and Empire troops.

H.M. Government has therefore the right to insist upon the Greek Government putting forward terms agreeable to them. We should like discretion to arrange for British observers at any conference if we find it desirable.

4. The Greek Government should ask only for two things:

(*a*) the release of hostages;

(*b*) the disarmament of all irregular forces, ELAS and any others.

(In any territory still subject to German occupation such as Crete, special arrangements will have to be made.)

5. The Government terms in return should include those set out . . . and already broadly accepted. . . . But greater precision will have to be given to three points:

(*a*) The break-up of the Mountain Brigade and the Sacred Regiment which we suggest shall be used as cadres for the new National Army.

(*b*) The terms of the amnesty.

(*c*) Elections.

6. If all irregular forces are satisfactorily disarmed, there is no reason why the Mountain Brigade and the Sacred Regiment should not be broken up at once, as suggested in 5 (*a*).

7. There may be trouble over the amnesty. The Government will naturally wish to punish the insurgent leaders and criminals. This of course is the reason why ELAS very providently retained the hostages. We were glad to see . . . that you are in favour of a general amnesty with the exception of persons 'individually guilty of acts which are either contrary to the rules of war or amenable to the ordinary criminal codes of civilised countries'. We fear that the last phrase may be misinterpreted. In most civilised countries to take up arms against the King or the established Government is a criminal act. We assume you to mean something quite different, and this must be clarified.

8. Since this civil war is all about one single question, power, and since under present conditions whoever holds arms and equipment in Greece holds power, we should recommend granting a general amnesty on as wide a basis as possible. It would of course become effective only after general surrender of arms. After all, any amnesty arising from a peace will cover the leaders, Siantos, and so on. The really dangerous men will thus escape. There is only moral satisfaction and little practical advantage in executing a few low-class criminals. If no peace can be reached, and the irregulars have to be disarmed by other means, an amnesty certificate might well be given to individual insurgents voluntarily surrendering their arms.

9. As regards elections, these should be held as early as possible and General Plastiras's statement about Allied observers reaffirmed.

10. We propose, therefore, to pursue the problem of obtaining an early peace on the general basis set out above. It will be very difficult for the Greek

Government to agree to paragraph 8. We propose to talk it over frankly with the Regent and let him prepare the ground, so that we may obtain as generous a formula as possible. The single purpose of effecting disarmament should be held firmly in view and nothing else be allowed to obscure it.

11. In addition, we shall suggest to the Regent and Plastiras to include at the appropriate moment one or more representatives of the secessionists from EAM in the Government. . . . This would prove particularly valuable if no peace can be concluded.

12. If the peace negotiations break down, the truce will of course automatically come to an end. We shall naturally keep the negotiations alive while we are getting military advantage from the ELAS retirement. The rebellion may therefore continue but under the following political conditions:

(a) The monarchical question will have been removed from the field of controversy in Greece and elsewhere.

(b) A Regent and a strong Government will have been appointed, commanding wide confidence in Greece.

(c) The EAM coalition will have been broken.

(d) The terms offered and rejected will appear generous, perhaps overgenerous, to world opinion, and British and American publics correspondingly reassured.

(e) Those who reject the peace will be exposed and discredited.

13. The military situation today is as follows:

We are in control of practically the whole of Attica, Boeotia and part of Thessaly up to the general line inclusive Volos–Lamia–Amphissa–Itea. In the Peloponnese we have a secure base at Patras–Araxos and are in process of gaining control of the country south as far as the general line Argos–Pyrgos. We control land communications between Athens and Patras via Corinth. We are firmly established at Salonika. It is confidently expected that ELAS regular forces will have retired behind and beyond the line as agreed to in the truce by 24 January. From the military point of view, we have successfully completed all of and more than the operations [proposed] . . . and we have secured a truce.

14. One of the principal objects of the proposed peace terms will be to secure the disbandment and disarmament of all Greek irregular forces. If we fail, we shall be faced with a situation where ELAS forces are still in the field. In this case, it is not proposed to undertake extensive operations with British forces to eliminate ELAS, as this will be a major and may be a limitless commitment.

15. Nevertheless, with the strength of the British forces in Greece at our disposal and having regard to the key points now held by us, it should be possible to clear all country east and south of the northern line demarcated in the truce. This would include the whole of the Peloponnese. Behind this line, it will be for the Greek Government to recruit, equip and train sufficient

forces to undertake operations to eliminate all irregular forces in the remainder of Greece, or if this proves impossible, then eventually to take over the area occupied by the British forces, so as to allow us to withdraw from the country. This of course will have the disadvantage of leaving a Greece divided into two parts: southern Greece controlled by the Greek Government, with outposts at Salonika and Corfu, and northern Greece still in the hands of ELAS. This is the worst case and will mean that three British divisions must be detained in Greece until Government troops are strong enough to take over. This will be a matter of some months, depending to a large extent on the speed with which arms and equipment can be provided for the Greek Army. If on the other hand ELAS agree to disband and disarm, our military commitment will progressively decrease corresponding to the rate at which ELAS complies with these terms. This may be a matter of some weeks. But in view of the dangers of a fresh insurrection, it will not be possible to withdraw all British military support until the Greek Government has sufficient armed force to meet it. In this case, our commitment will be in the nature of one division. We have not referred to the commitments which may involve the Royal Navy and Royal Air Force. But an appreciation affecting these two Services can be sent if required.

16. . . . H.M. Ambassador . . . agrees.

Appendix Three

Aide-Mémoire for Communication to the Italian Government by the Acting President of the Contents of the New Directive on the Functions of the Allied Commission

1. In accordance with the declaration of the President of the United States of America and the Prime Minister of the United Kingdom of Great Britain, the Allied Governments propose to relax the control of the Italian Government under the Armistice in the matter of day-to-day administration and only to exercise such control when Allied military interests require.

2. The Political Section of the Allied Commission is being abolished as of 1 March 1945. The Italian Ministry of Foreign Affairs will deal with the Chief Commissioner on matters of major policy, and on matters of minor policy and routine business it will address itself to whatever Section (Economic or Civil Affairs) of the Commission may be appropriate to the subject involved. Matters involving the travel of diplomatic and other public officials will hereafter be dealt with on behalf of the Commission by the Office of the Executive Commissioner.

3. The Italian Government will continue, as at present, to have direct relations with foreign diplomatic representatives accredited to the Quirinal. The Allied Commission should be kept generally informed by the Italian Government of any negotiations in which they engage with other Governments. Facilities for the use of secret bags will be granted to the Italian Government for use in correspondence with their diplomatic representatives abroad. Undeposited cipher facilities cannot be allowed for the present.

In so far as these negotiations have to do with economic and financial matters, the Economic Section and its Finance Sub-commission should be kept informed of their progress.

It would be convenient if the Italian Government would furnish a periodic summary of all negotiations completed or pending with other Governments.

4. The Allied Commission will limit its dealings with respect to territory under the jurisdiction of the Italian Government to consultation with and advice to the Ministers of the Italian Government.

5. The advisory functions of the Sub-commissions of Education, Monuments and Fine Arts, Local Government, Legal and Labour in territory under the jurisdiction of the Italian Government will be performed only when requested by the Italian Government.

6. It will no longer be necessary for the Italian Government to obtain the approval of the Allied Commission for decrees and other legislation enacted by the Italian Government in the territory under the jurisdiction of the Italian Government.

Nevertheless, the Allied Commission should be informed of proposed decrees some time before their enactment, in order to enable the Chief Commissioner to consult with the Italian Government as to their application to territory under the jurisdiction of Allied Military Government (A.M.G.), and to lay plans for their effective implementation in such territory when appropriate.

7. It will no longer be necessary for the Italian Government to obtain approval of the Allied Commission for Italian appointments, whether to national or local offices, in territory under the jurisdiction of the Italian Government except with regard to the attached list (Note 'A') of positions having military significance. The Italian Government will have the right to alter appointments made previously by A.M.G. authorities.

8. The Allied Commission officers stationed in the field in the territory under the jurisdiction of the Italian Government will be withdrawn. As a first step, it is intended to abolish by 1 April 1945 the Regional Offices of the Allied Commission for Sicily, Sardinia, and the Southern and Lazio–Umbria Regions. Representatives of the Allied Commission will, however, be sent into territory under the jurisdiction of the Italian Government when necessary and certain specialist officers with economic functions will remain in such territory for a limited period.

9. It is the desire of the Allies to encourage free trade in knowledge and learning with the Italian people. Arrangements will be facilitated for the flow between Italy and the United Nations of books and other publications of a scientific, political, philosophical and artistic nature, and for the movement of scholars, artists and professional men between Italy and the United Nations.

10. The Allies welcome the decision to hold local elections in territory under the jurisdiction of the Italian Government as soon as may be.

11. The Allied Nations desire to make concessions with regard to Italian prisoners of war now or hereafter held in Italy, other than those captured since the Armistice was signed. Provided that arrangements can be made for the services of such persons to continue to be made available on terms satisfactory to the Supreme Allied Commander, their status as prisoners of war will be terminated.

12. It is essential that the Italian Government formulate and implement appropriate economic controls and take all other steps possible, both in order

to ensure that maximum production and effective and equitable distribution and control of consumption of local resources possible under existing conditions be secured, and as a prerequisite to increased economic assistance.

13. In the joint programme of essential Italian imports, now being prepared by the Inter-Ministerial Committee for Reconstruction and the Economic Section of this Commission, there will be some supplies for which the combined United States–United Kingdom military authorities will assume responsibility for procurement (Category 'A') and other supplies for which they will not assume responsibility (Category 'B'). A definition of the supplies which fall into Category 'A' follows:

(a) Those quantities of agreed essential supplies necessary to prevent disease and unrest prejudicial to military operations, such as food, fuel, clothing, medical and sanitary supplies.

(b) Those supplies, the importation of which will reduce military requirements for the import of essential civilian supplies for the purposes referred to in this paragraph, such as fertiliser, raw materials, machinery and equipment.

(c) Those materials essential for the rehabilitation of such of the Italian communication facilities, power systems and transportation facilities as will directly further the Allied military effort.

14. The programme for which the military authorities assume responsibility will be maintained for the duration of combined (United States— United Kingdom) operations in Italy. For this period, and within the limits defined in paragraph 13, Italy will be treated as a whole. The date of the termination of military responsibility will be fixed by the Allied Nations.

15. In addition to the programme of supplies for which the military assume responsibility for procurement (Category 'A'), the Allied Commission will assist the Italian Government in the preparation of programmes of supplies designed to rehabilitate Italian industry. Such programmes, referred to as Category 'B', will be handled under procedures already notified. The purchasing of supplies in Category 'B' programmes will be undertaken immediately, without reference to the present difficult shipping position, in order that the supplies so purchased may be called forward as and when shipping space becomes available.

16. The Allies desire that industrial rehabilitation in Italy be carried out by the Italian Government to the fullest extent permitted by Italian resources and such supplies as it may be possible to import under the terms of paragraphs 13, 14 and 15 above, and subject to the limitation in paragraph 19 below. The sole exception to this principle is to be made in the case of industries involving the production or repair of munitions or other implements of war, which will be rehabilitated only to the extent required by the Supreme Allied Commander in the discharge of his military mission, and to the extent necessary to further the Allied military effort in other theatres. The priority order in which Italian industry will be rehabilitated (after the

rehabilitation of industries essential for Allied military purposes) will be determined by the Italian Government, with the assistance and advice of the Allied Commission.

17. The prime responsibility for the control of inflation in Italy, including the imposition and administration of the appropriate financial controls and economic controls and appropriate utilisation of supplies, rests with the Italian Government. In this connection, as in others, the Allied Commission stands ready to advise and assist.

18. The extent to which exports are to be stimulated and the development of machinery to handle export trade are for determination by the Italian Government. For the time being, the Italian export programme will necessarily be limited by certain shipping, military, financial and supply factors. The applicability of these factors to individual programmes will be worked out between the Italian Government and the Economic Section of the Allied Commission along the lines already discussed by the Economic Section with the Inter-Ministerial Committee for Reconstruction.

19. Nothing contained in the above should be taken as constituting a commitment by the Allied Nations with respect to shipping. Any supplies to be imported into Italy must be transported within such shipping as may be allocated from time to time by the Allied Nations.

Harold Macmillan

24th February, 1945

NOTE 'A'

List of Italian Government appointments requiring prior approval by the Allied Commission

Minister of War
Minister of Marine
Minister of Air
Any other Minister of Armed Forces who may be created
Under-Secretary for Telecommunications
Director of Railroads
Director-General of Public Security
Commanding General, CC.RR
Chief of Staff, CC.RR
Commanding General, GG.FF
Appointments in the Army, Navy and Air Force in accordance with current practice

Index

Muscatelli, M., 248
Muselier, Admiral, 250, 270–1
Mussolini, Benito, declares war, 66, 149; invades Greece, 67; arrives in North Africa with white charger, 67; calls Mediterranean 'Mare Nostrum', 285; fall of, 305–6, 318, 336; resentment against, 336; rump Government of, 379; Victor Emmanuel's support of, 388; death of, 579
Myers, Brigadier, 472, 492

Nahas Pasha, 224
Namsos, 51
Naples, 381, 393–4, 395–6, 397, 432, 477, 516, 531, 535, 555; battle for, 323, 326; health and economic situation in, 381, 410; King George VI in, 434; Tito and Churchill meet in, 440
Naples, Prince of, 384
Narvik, 21, 25, 37, 38, 49–51
National Fire Service, 70
National Service Bill (1941), 95, 104
Neapolitan Committee of National Liberation, 397
Nelson, Donald, 106
Nelson, H.M.S., 335, 591–96
Nenni, Pietro, 413
Neutrality Act (U.S.A.), 76
'New Deal' (For France), 243–5, 248, 249
Newton, Major, 575
Nicholas of Greece, Princess, 489
Niukkanen, Juho, 26
Noguès, General, 151, 186, 189, 197–201, 225, 232, 237, 244, 266, 268, 363. *Also see illustrations*
North African Economic Board (N.A.E.B.), 224–5, 234, 302, 431
Norway, 21, 22, 26, 35, 40, 51–52. *See also* Narvik

O'Brien, Tom, 454
Occupied Enemy Territory Administration (O.E.T.A.), 377
O'Dwyer, Brigadier-General, 451–2
Offie, Secretary, 480, 559
Oran, 161
Orion, H.M.S., 484–5, 487, 529
Orlando, General, 410, 461
Orlando, Vittorio, 578–9
Orvieto, 421
Osborne, Sir D'Arcy, 312, 322, 434, 459
Oslo, 35, 40

'Overlord', Operation, 143, 212, 300, 372, 404, 415–17, 432

Paget, General, 425, 466–7, 473, 481
Palairet, Sir Michael, 553
Palewski, Gaston, 265
Palmer, Sir William, 72–73
Papaioannis, M., 536–8
Papandreou, George, 466, 475–84, 488, 493–6, 499, 502, 509–15, 520–3, 525, 533
Paris, Comte de, 180–1
Parri, Ferruccio, 582
Partsalides, Dimitrios, 523, 540, 542
Patras, 480–2, 529
Patton, General George S., 201. *Also see illustrations*
Pazzi, Signor, 383
'Peace offensives', 10
Peake, Charles, 131
Pearl Harbour, 67, 104, 106, 109, 116, 118
Pearson, Drew, 559
Pechkoff, Colonel, 249
Percival, General, 125
Pétain, Marshal, 151, 156, 162, 164, 165, 166, 167, 168, 185, 214, 216, 229, 277. *See also* Vichy
Peter, King of Yugoslavia, 436–45
Peter the Great, 15, 16
Peyrouton, Marcel, as Governor for Algeria, 174, 225, 237; hated by Gaullists, 174; doubtful record of, 174; Giraud's attitude to, 200, 253; not consulted over 'New Deal', 244; de Gaulle demands dismissal of, 266, 268; resignation of, 270–3, 286; prosecution of, 364, 367. *Also see illustrations*
Philip, André, 265, 268, 275. *Also see illustrations*
Phillimore, Lord, 20
'Phoney War', 9
Piedmont, Prince of, 385, 409, 453
Pius XII, Pope, 453, 459–60
Pizzoni, Signor, 563–4
Plaka Agreement (Greece), 473
Plastiras, General, 511–2, 524, 528, 532, 535, 536, 547, 550–2
Pleven, René, 131, 347, 356
Poland, 3, 4, 7–8, 110, 114, 411, 491, 570–3, 576
Poletti, Colonel, 392–3
Politis, M., 475
Popov, Colonel, 522, 549

DATE DUE

AUG 12 '69			
MAY 5 '70			
MAY 3 '72			
AP 11 '79			
MY 4'83			
APR 19 '84			